CONSTITUTIONAL DESIGN FOR DIVIDED SOCIETIES: INTEGRATION OR ACCOMMODATION?

Edited by

SUJIT CHOUDHRY

Constitutional Design for Divided Societies: Integration or Accommodation?

Edited by
SUJIT CHOUDHRY

OXFORD
UNIVERSITY PRESS

*This book has been printed digitally and produced in a standard specification
in order to ensure its continuing availability*

OXFORD
UNIVERSITY PRESS

Great Clarendon Street, Oxford OX2 6DP

Oxford University Press is a department of the University of Oxford.
It furthers the University's objective of excellence in research, scholarship,
and education by publishing worldwide in

Oxford New York

Auckland   Cape Town Dar es Salaam   Hong Kong   Karachi
Kuala Lumpur Madrid Melbourne Mexico City   Nairobi
New Delhi Shanghai   Taipei Toronto
With offices in
Argentina Austria Brazil Chile Czech Republic France Greece
Guatemala Hungary Italy Japan South Korea Poland Portugal
Singapore Switzerland Thailand Turkey Ukraine Vietnam

Oxford is a registered trade mark of Oxford University Press
in the UK and in certain other countries

Published in the United States
by Oxford University Press Inc., New York

ISBN 978-0-19-953541-5

Summary Contents

Detailed Contents

Acknowledgements

The majority of the papers appearing herein were originally presented at a workshop in Toronto in October 2006, under the auspices of the Ethnicity and Democratic Governance Major Collaborative Research Initiative (MCRI), a five-year, interdisciplinary project funded by the Social Sciences and Humanities Research Council of Canada.

That conference generated two interrelated publication projects. A selection of the conference papers appeared in a special issue of the *International Journal of Constitutional Law* (I•CON) which was published in Fall 2007 (volume 5, number 4). This volume is much more expansive in scope, and is structured differently. It contains the papers which appeared in I•CON, and a large number of additional chapters which include an introduction and an overview chapter outlining the integration-accommodation debate which provides the intellectual framework for the entire volume.

Editing these two collections of essays simultaneously, on a very tight set of deadlines, has been a complicated and challenging task. Along the way, I have accumulated a large number of debts.

First and foremost, I thank the authors for their patience and perseverance. I am particularly grateful to authors from outside the legal academy, who were subjected to the idiosyncrasies of legal citation.

Norman Dorsen and Michel Rosenfeld generously invited me to guest edit a symposium issue of I•CON, and suggested the possibility of publishing an expanded set of essays as an edited volume. Richard Simeon and John McGarry, who coordinate a team of scholars under the Ethnicity and Democratic Governance MCRI who examine the strategies and policies available to states for developing democracy in multi-ethnic societies, graciously allowed me to use our first workshop as the vehicle for these publications. Along with Luc Turgeon, they also organized the workshop. Finally, in a model of collegiality, Simeon and McGarry jointly shaped the overall structure and content of this volume with me, while permitting me to lead the publication project. Bruce Berman and Jennifer Clark of the Ethnicity and Democratic Governance MCRI have been supportive of this project as well.

At OUP, I am grateful to John Louth for initially considering our volume proposal, especially given the reluctance of most academic presses to publish edited collections. My editor, Alex Flach, has worked closely with me over the last several months. He has been wonderfully supportive, while at the same time ensuring that we kept on track. Hayley Buckley has skilfully managed the production process.

Karen Barrett, the Managing Editor of I•CON, deserves enormous credit for the vast amount of work she did in editing the papers which ultimately appeared in the journal. Moreover, she helped to define and manage the relationship between the two editorial processes, and I am very grateful to her for her advice. Tiffany Tsun, my student research assistant, has been exemplary. She has tirelessly worked to copyedit, reference, and format the various chapters for publication, and coordinate communications with the contributors. Without her superb work, these publications would not have been possible. I also thank our copyeditor, Alarik Skarstrom.

I acknowledge the financial support of the Social Sciences and Humanities Research Council of Canada, through its funding of the Ethnicity and Democratic Governance MCRI.

Toronto
October 2007

Table of Cases

Bosnia and Herzegovina

- Case No. U-44/01, Decision (Sept. 22, 2004)
- Case No. U-4/04, Partial Decisions I–II (Mar. 31, Nov. 18, 2006)
- Case No. U-5/98, Partial Decisions I–IV (Jan. 29, Feb. 18, July 1, Aug. 18, 2000)
- Case No. U-05/98, Request for Evaluation of the Constitutionality of Certain Provisions of the Constitution of Republika Srpska and the Constitution of the Federation of Bosnia and Herzegovina, Partial Decision pt. 3

Canada

- A.G. Quebec v. Blaikie, [1979] 2 S.C.R. 1016
- Attorney General of Quebec v. Quebec Protestant School Boards, [1984] 2 S.C.R. 66
- R. v. Beaulac, [1999] 1 S.C.R. 768
- Ford v. Quebec (A.G.), [1988] 2 S.C.R. 712.
- MacDonald v. City of Montreal, [1986] 1 S.C.R. 449
- R v. Oakes [1986] 1 S.C.R. 103
- Reference re Amendment of Canadian Constitution, [1982] 2.S.C.R. 793
- Solski (Tutor of) v. Quebec (Attorney General), [2005] 1 S.C.R. 201, 2005 SCC 14

Fiji

- Chandrika Prasad v. Republic of the Fiji Islands, [2001] 2 L.R.C. 743
- In re the Constitution, Reference by HE the President [2002] F.J.S.C. 1, Misc. 001.2001S (Mar. 15 2002)
- In re the President's Reference, Qarase v. Chaudhry, [2004] F.J.S.C. 1, Misc. 001.2003 (July 9, 2004)
- President of Fiji Islands v. Kubuabola, [1999] F.J.S.C. 8, Misc. Case No. 1 of 1999 (Sept. 3, 1999)
- Qarase v. Chaudhry, [2003] F.J.S.C. 1, CBV0004.2002S (July 18, 2003)

South Africa

- Ex parte Chairperson of the Constitutional Assembly: In re Certification of the Constitution of the Republic of SA, 1996 (4) SA 744 (CC); 1996 (10) BCLR 1253 (CC)
- Governing Body, Mikro Primary School, and Another v. Minister of Education, Western Cape, and Others 2005 (3) SA 504 (C)
- Matatiele Municipality v. President of the Republic of South Africa, 2007 (1) BCLR 47 (CC)
- Seodin Primary School and Others v. MEC of Education, Northern Cape and Others [2006] 1 All SA 154 (NC)

United Kingdom

- Att Gen's Ref. (No.2 of 2001), [2001] 1 W.L.R. 1860, [2003] UKHL 68
- H.M.A. v. R. [2004] 1 A.C. 462, (2003) S.C. (PC) 21
- MacCormick v. Lord Advocate, [1953] S.C. 396

United States

- Georgia v. Ashcroft, 539 U.S. 461 (2003)
- Holder v. Hall, 512 U.S. 74 (1994)
- Meyer v. Nebraska, 262 U.S. 390 (1923)
- Shaw v. Reno, 509 U.S. 630 (1993)

PART I

INTRODUCTION AND OVERVIEW

1

Bridging comparative politics and comparative constitutional law: Constitutional design in divided societies

*Sujit Choudhry**

1. Introduction: Comparative constitutional law missing in action

The Human Development Report (HDR), published annually by the United Nations Development Programme, is an unlikely stimulus for reflection upon the state of the field of comparative constitutional law. Although the Human Development Reports take a broad understanding of development, constitutional law has never occupied center stage. However, the HDR 2004 is different. Entitled *Cultural Liberty in Today's Diverse World*, the HDR 2004 opens up by stating that "[m]anaging cultural diversity is one of the central challenges of our time".[1] The report supports this contention by drawing on a wide range of examples, from disputes over official languages in Afghanistan and Sri Lanka, to the political representation of ethnic and religious minorities in Iraq and Fiji, to demands for asymmetric regimes of regional autonomy in Quebec and Catalonia, to the competing nationalisms of Northern Ireland, Bosnia-Herzegovina and Cyprus. The report goes further, and offers a particular diagnosis of, and set of solutions for, this phenomenon. In its view, these conflicts flow from a denial of "cultural liberty".[2] As the report states, "[p]eople want the freedom to practice their religion openly, to speak their language, to celebrate their ethnic or religious heritage without fear of ridicule or punishment or diminished opportunity".[3] Among the solutions it proposes to counteract the denial of cultural liberty, constitutional

* Scholl Chair, Faculty of Law and Department of Political Science, University of Toronto. Email: sujit.choudhry@utoronto.ca
[1] UNITED NATIONS DEV. PROGRAMME (UNDP), HUM. DEV. REPORT 2004: CULTURAL LIBERTY IN TODAY'S DIVERSE WORLD 1 (2004).
[2] *Id.*
[3] *Id.*

law takes center stage. Although it approves of the standard liberal constitutional instrument to protect cultural liberty, a constitutional bill of rights backed by judicial review, it also proposes the adoption of "policies that explicitly recognize cultural differences"[4] and which reject assimilation, such as federalism, consociation, and legal pluralism.

There is much to question in both the HDR 2004's understanding of the causes of linguistic, ethnic, religious, and cultural conflict—which we can loosely term ethnic or ethnocultural conflict—and the coherence of its particular combination of policy prescriptions. But the report is surely correct in highlighting that how societies should respond to the opportunities and challenges raised by ethnocultural divisions—and in so doing promote democracy, social justice, peace, and stability—is one of the most difficult and important questions of contemporary politics. Even the most casual review of the popular media drives the point home. In a wide range of cases, spanning several continents, in both the developed and developing world, it is arguably the central issue of political life. Consider the following examples, which are live issues as this introduction goes to press. Belgium has been unable, for nearly four months, to craft a coalition government that includes both Flemish and French speakers in compliance with the Belgian Constitution, which mandates a linguistically balanced cabinet. Nepal continues to grapple with the unanticipated rise of minority nationalism among Hindi-speakers in the southeast of the country, who have demanded the abandonment of Nepal's unitary constitution and the restructuring of the country along federal lines. Turkey is engaged in renewed, armed conflict with Kurdish rebels who have long sought regional autonomy, official language status for Kurdish, and constitutional acknowledgement of the multinational character of Turkey. Finally, in the dénouement to the Yugoslavia civil war, the final status of Kosovo remains unclear, with Serbia offering regional autonomy, and Kosovo demanding independence and threatening to issue a unilateral declaration of independence. These examples could be supplemented by numerous others.

In this volume, we term these political communities "divided societies". It is important to define precisely what a divided society is, by clarifying what it is not. In *Democracy in Plural Societies*, Arend Lijphart famously drew a contrast between two kinds of political community—culturally homogeneous political communities—which were not beset by political division—and plural societies, which were.[5] But as Jürg Steiner pointed out soon thereafter, Lijphart had seemingly (and likely inadvertently) erred in conflating diversity with political division.[6] As a category of political and constitutional analysis, a divided society is

---

[4] *Id.* at 2.

[5] AREND LIJPHART, DEMOCRACY IN PLURAL SOCIETIES: A COMPARATIVE EXPLORATION 71–74 (Yale Univ. Press 1977).

[6] Jürg Steiner, *The Consociational Theory and Beyond*, 13 COMP. POL. 339 (1981) (book review). Arend Lijphart quickly corrected this error, which he did not consistently make in DEMOCRACY IN

not merely a society which is ethnically, linguistically, religiously, or culturally diverse. Indeed, whether through conquest, colonization, slavery or immigration, it is hard to imagine a state today that is not diverse in one or more of these dimensions. The age of the ethnoculturally homogeneous state, if there ever was one, is long over. Rather, what marks a divided society is that these differences are politically salient—that is, they are persistent markers of political identity and bases for political mobilization. Ethnocultural diversity translates into political fragmentation. In a divided society, political claims are refracted through the lens of ethnic identity, and political conflict is synonymous with conflict among ethnocultural groups.

A lot is at stake in how divided societies respond to the challenges raised by the equation of ethnocultural identity and political interest. The extreme consequences of the failure to address these challenges adequately are well known: discrimination and exclusion, forced assimilation, civil war, ethnic cleansing, and even genocide. But even in the absence of violence, in states where the rule of law and respect for fundamental human rights prevail—consider Spain, Belgium, and Canada—failing to respond to these challenges appropriately can have a corrosive effect on ordinary politics. In the absence of trust and expectations of reciprocity across members of different ethnocultural groups, it may become impossible to reach political decisions on important questions of public policy such as the environment, health care, and the economy, especially if the burdens and benefits of those policies are—or are perceived to be—distributed unevenly along ethnic lines. If political decisions are made, they may be condemned as discriminatory. In other cases, political debates on routine policy issues can escalate quickly into political dramas of respect and recognition that are removed far from the actual interests at play, and that are out of proportion to the significance of the issue at hand. Every political issue is assessed through the lens of ethnocultural identity.

How divided societies respond to these challenges is of the highest practical importance. But it is conceptually challenging as well. As the HDR 2004 reminds us, constitutional design in divided societies bears a particularly heavy burden, because it plays multiple roles. It is useful to distinguish between two accounts of the function of a constitution in a divided society—the *regulative* conception and the *constitutive* conception. On the regulative conception, as Stephen Holmes has argued, constitutions both enable and disable political decision making.[7] Constitutions enable decision making by creating the institutions government, by allocating powers to them, by setting out rules of procedure to enable these institutions to make decisions, and by defining how these institutions interact.

PLURAL SOCIETIES: A COMPARATIVE EXPLORATION, *id. See* Arend Lijphart, *Consociational Theory: Problems and Prospects*, 13 COMP. POL. 355 (1981).

[7] STEPHEN HOLMES, PASSIONS AND CONSTRAINT: ON THE THEORY OF LIBERAL DEMOCRACY (Univ. Chicago Press 1995).

Constitutions also disable decision making, by enacting procedural roadblocks to decision making (such as supermajority rules) and by setting substantive limits on political decision making (such as bills of rights). In a divided society—as in any society—a constitution must fill this regulatory role.

Yet in a divided society, a constitution must go further and constitute the very *demos* which governs itself under and through the constitutional regime. In divided societies, because of a history of conflict or a lack of a shared existence, the constitution is often the principal vehicle for the forging of a common political identity, which is, in turn, necessary to make that constitutional regime work. To some extent, the constitution can foster the development of a common political identity by creating the institutional spaces for shared decision making among members of different ethnocultural groups. Concrete experiences of shared decision making within a framework of the rule of law, and without recourse to force or fraud, can serve as the germ of a nascent sense of political community. For the same reason, against the backdrop of division and a lack of trust, the process of debating and negotiating a constitution can also help to create the political community on whose existence the constitutional order which results from that process depends.

But a constitution can also constitute a demos by encoding and projecting a certain vision of political community with the view of altering the very self-understanding of citizens. For example, a bill of rights can embody a conception of the polity as consisting of rights-bearing citizens of equal status irrespective of differences in race, religion, or ethnicity. This is the idea of civic citizenship, most famously presented by Ernest Renan, which can be characterized in the following way.[8] A constitutional order must meet two constraints, the *legitimacy* constraint and the *stability* constraint. The legitimacy constraint is normative, while the stability constraint is sociological. The ambition of liberal constitutionalism is that a constitutional order must both be legitimate and must enjoy the allegiance of a sufficient number of its citizens to work. On the liberal conception, the conditions for the legitimate exercise of public power are the rights and institutions of representative government that one finds in a typical liberal democratic constitution. These rights and institutions are generated by a process of what Frank Michelman has termed a "contractarian constitutional justification", from the starting point of citizens assumed free and equal.[9] The ambition of the civic conception of citizenship is that these same conditions also supply the necessary motivational element for those institutions to work. Additionally, the connection between legitimacy (normative) and stability (sociological) is not contingent. Rather, it is conceptual—in other words, it is the ambition of the

---

[8] Ernest Renan, Qu'est-ce qu'une nation (Mille et une nuits 1997) (1882); Sujit Choudhry, *Citizenship and Federations: Some Preliminary Reflections, in* The Federal Vision: Legitimacy and Levels of Governance in the United States and the European Union 377 (Kalypso Nicolaidis & Robert Howse eds., Oxford Univ. Press 2001).

[9] Frank I. Michelman, *Constitutional Legitimation for Political Acts*, 66 Mod. L. Rev. 1 (2003).

civic conception of citizenship that citizens view themselves as part of the same constitutional-legal order, *precisely because* that order is legitimate.

Given the multiple and critical roles that constitutions must play in divided societies, it is not surprising that constitutional design would figure centrally in the HDR 2004's policy recommendations. Moreover, these recommendations are deeply informed by comparative experience, and draw upon actual examples of constitutional provisions and practices from divided societies which appear to have responded successfully to the challenges of political mobilization on the basis of ethnocultural difference with a measure of success. The report cites examples from countries as diverse as India, Spain, Switzerland, and South Africa. In taking a comparative constitutional approach, the report tracks domestic constitutional politics in many divided societies, where comparative constitutional experience is frequently looked to as a source of lessons learned, of mistakes and dangers to be avoided, and models to be adapted and followed.

So constitutions matter, and matter centrally in the response to the challenge of divided societies. But while comparative constitutional law occupies center stage, it is striking that comparative constitutional law as a scholarly discipline has largely been missing in action. To be sure, there are exceptions. Two contributors to this volume, Yash Ghai and Stephen Tierney, have squarely addressed the question of constitutional design for divided societies in important contributions.[10] Donald Horowitz, a political scientist and a legal scholar, has been a major figure in academic debates for over two decades.[11] However, viewed as a whole, the field has been largely silent on the role of constitutional design in divided societies.

Proof can be found in the HDR 2004 itself. Constitutional design figures centrally in the report. Yet, of the twenty-two scholars who prepared background studies and papers for the report, not one is a legal academic. The extensive bibliography is almost entirely bereft of references to the legal literature, because there is relatively little material to cite. Instead, the experts consulted by the UNDP are prominent political theorists, political philosophers, and scholars of comparative politics. The literature cited by the report is likewise drawn from these fields. The choice made by the UNDP regarding who to consult and which materials to reference reflects the fact that the academic center of gravity for the study of divided societies lies in political science and, for the most part, outside the mainstream of legal scholarship.

Scholars of comparative constitutional law may find this claim surprising, especially because the field has never been more vibrant, and the literature is increasingly sophisticated. To understand exactly how the field is disconnected from the academic and scholarly debates surrounding constitutional design for

[10] *See, e.g.,* AUTONOMY AND ETHNICITY: NEGOTIATING COMPETING CLAIMS IN MULTI-ETHNIC STATES (Yash Ghai ed., Cambridge Univ. Press 2000); STEPHEN TIERNEY, CONSTITUTIONAL LAW AND NATIONAL PLURALISM (Oxford Univ. Press 2004).
[11] DONALD L. HOROWITZ, ETHNIC GROUPS IN CONFLICT (Univ. Cal. Press 2000).

divided societies requires a brief explanation.[12] For nearly two decades, the focus of comparative constitutional law has been on comparative approaches to the protection of universal human rights within a liberal democratic constitutional order—what Michael Ignatieff has usefully termed the "rights revolution".[13] To a considerable extent, the scholarly agenda for the field has been set by, and has closely tracked, constitutional practice. The resurgence of comparative constitutional law as an academic discipline accompanied the transition to democracy in many of the former communist countries of Eastern and Central Europe, the former military dictatorships of South America, and South Africa.[14] The transition to democracy was usually accompanied by the adoption of rights-based constitutionalism. Moreover, well-established democracies, such as Canada, New Zealand, and the United Kingdom, also adopted judicial review and bills of rights in roughly the same time period. The shift to rights-based constitutionalism often occurred through political processes which were comparatively informed. So the field has tended to focus on those jurisdictions which have turned to rights-based constitutionalism relatively recently, as well as more established constitutional systems which have served as benchmarks for comparison. The result is a literature oriented around a standard and relatively limited set of cases: South Africa, Israel, Germany, Canada, the United Kingdom, New Zealand, the United States, and to a lesser extent, India.

In connection with these jurisdictions, the field is largely concerned with a set of closely interrelated questions:

- Should constitutions contain a justiciable bill of rights, or does a bill of rights transfer too much power to the judiciary and judicialize politics?[15] Should a bill of rights be an ordinary statute, a special statute that presumptively prevails over inconsistent laws, or an entrenched part of a constitution that asserts its supremacy over ordinary law?[16]

- What should the institutional arrangements surrounding the enforcement of a bill of rights be? Should countries adopt judicial supremacy or combine judicial review with legislative supremacy?[17] Should rights review be the exclusive responsibility of the courts, or the joint responsibility of the executive,

---

[12] I will develop these arguments more fully in RETHINKING COMPARATIVE CONSTITUTIONAL LAW (work-in-progress).

[13] MICHAEL IGNATIEFF, THE RIGHTS REVOLUTION (Anasi 2000).

[14] RAN HIRSCHL, TOWARDS JURISTOCRACY: THE ORIGINS AND CONSEQUENCES OF THE NEW CONSTITUTIONALISM (Harvard Univ. Press 2004).

[15] *Id*; Jeremy Waldron, *The Core of the Case Against Judicial Review*, 115 YALE L.J. 1346 (2006); MARK V. TUSHNET, TAKING THE CONSTITUTION AWAY FROM THE COURTS (Princeton Univ. Press 2001).

[16] Janet L. Hiebert, *Parliamentary Bills of Rights: An Alternative Model?*, 69 MOD. L. REV. 7 (2006).

[17] Mark Tushnet, *Judicial Activism or Restraint in a Section 33 World*, 53 U. TORONTO L.J. 89 (2003) (reviewing ROACH, *infra* note 19); Stephen Gardbaum, *The New Commonwealth Model of Constitutionalism*, 49 AM. J. COMP. LAW 707 (2001).

legislative and judicial branches?[18] Does dispersed responsibility for rights review create an interinstitutional dialogue over matters of rights protection?[19]

- What rights should a bill of rights contain? In addition to traditional civil and political rights, should it also entrench socioeconomic rights?[20] Should it protect rights to private property, and if so, to what extent?[21]

- What should the scope of application of a bill of rights be? Should a bill of rights only have vertical effect to govern relations between citizens and the state, or should it also apply horizontally to private relationships?[22]

- How should a bill of rights be interpreted?[23] Should courts have recourse to comparative and international law in constitutional interpretation, and if so, how?[24]

The question of how constitutional design should respond to challenges created by divided societies has not motivated this intellectual agenda. This may be a function of the fact that the terms of the scholarly debate were framed by, and in response to, the vast literature on the American constitutional experience. To be sure, some of the most important justifications of the American practice of judicial review proceed from the assumption that some groups will systematically be unable to protect their interests in the political process—so-called "discrete and insular minorities".[25] In particular, race has undoubtedly been, and remains, a central category in American constitutional politics. But the United States is not a divided society in the specific sense defined above. While the United States is religiously, racially, and ethnically diverse, that diversity has not served as a widespread and pervasive basis for political mobilization, as it has in other societies. The unarticulated assumption embedded in

---

[18] Janet L. Hiebert, *Interpreting a Bill of Rights: The Importance of Legislative Rights Review*, 35 BRIT. J. POL. SCI. 235 (2005); Janet L. Hiebert, *Parliament and the Human Rights Act: Can the JCHR Help Facilitate a Culture of Rights?*, 4 INT'L J. CONST. L. 1 (I•CON) (2006).

[19] KENT ROACH, THE SUPREME COURT ON TRIAL: JUDICIAL ACTIVISM OR DEMOCRATIC DIALOGUE? (Irwin Law 2001).

[20] Craig Scott & Patrick Macklem, *Constitutional Ropes of Sand or Justiciable Guarantees? Social Rights in a New South African Constitution*, 141 U. PA. L. REV. 1 (1989).

[21] TOM ALLEN, THE RIGHT TO PROPERTY IN COMMONWEALTH CONSTITUTIONS (Cambridge Univ. Press 2000).

[22] Aharon Barak, *Constitutional Human Rights and Private Law Justice*, 3 REV. CONST. STUD. 318 (1996); Stephen Gardbaum, *The "Horizontal Effect" of Constitutional Rights*, 102 MICH. L. REV. 388 (2003).

[23] INTERPRETING CONSTITUTIONS: A COMPARATIVE STUDY (Jeffrey Denys Goldsworthy ed., Oxford Univ. Press 2006).

[24] Sujit Choudhry, *Migration as a New Metaphor in Comparative Constitutional Law*, in THE MIGRATION OF CONSTITUTIONAL IDEAS (Sujit Choudhry ed., Cambridge Univ. Press 2006); Sujit Choudhry, *Globalization in Search of Justification: Toward a Theory of Comparative Constitutional Interpretation*, 74 IND. L.J. 819 (1999); Sujit Choudhry, *The Lochner Era and Comparative Constitutionalism*, 2 INT'L J. CONST. L. (I•CON) 1 (2004).

[25] For the seminal statement of this view, see JOHN HART ELY, DEMOCRACY AND DISTRUST: A THEORY OF JUDICIAL REVIEW (Harvard Univ. Press 1980).

the study of rights-based constitutionalism in the United States is that the bill
of rights should not be viewed as a response to the fact of ethnocultural division. Comparative constitutional law has taken its cues from the American
literature, and framed its questions around it.

This conception of the field's academic agenda is oddly disconnected from
constitutional practice. In many divided societies, racial, ethnic, religious, or linguistic status was the basis for the unjust distribution of primary social goods in
the Rawlsian sense—liberty and opportunity, income and wealth, and the bases
of self-respect. In some cases, the oppression occurred at the hand of majorities,
as in Northern Ireland. In other cases, empowered minorities were the perpetrators of injustice, as in South Africa. Yet in other cases, both majorities and
minorities had a hand in injustice, as occurred in the republics of the former
Yugoslavia. Bills of rights are meant to serve as hard checks on political power
to ensure that such abuses will not occur again and to provide groups with the
political incentive to acquiesce and participate in the new constitutional-legal
order. But as mentioned above, bills of rights have been also looked to as constitutive documents to transform the political self-understanding of citizens. A bill
of rights calls upon citizens to abstract away from race, religion, ethnicity, and
language, which have previously served as the grounds of political identity and
political division, and instead to view themselves as citizens who are equal bearers
of constitutional rights.

So reframing the study of comparative approaches to rights protection to link
it to the actual constitutional agendas motivating the adoption of bills of rights
is a matter of some urgency.[26] But just as serious a mistake as the failure of the
field to comprehend what functions bills of rights play in divided societies is the
assumption that bills of rights are the only aspect of constitutional design worthy
of comparative study. As discussed in detail below, bills of rights are but one of
the tools available to constitutional designers for divided societies, and with good
reason. Rights depend on the independence and impartiality of judicial institutions for their enforcement. In divided societies, the manipulation of judicial
appointments can operate to undermine the ability of a bill of rights to safeguard
human rights and to prevent the abuses that may give rise to ethnocultural conflict. In Sri Lanka, for example, the Sinhala-dominated Supreme Court has been
viewed as being partial to Sinhalese nationalism of the Sri Lankan government.[27]
A related point is that the efficacy of bills of rights presupposes a culture of fidelity

[26] For an attempt, see Sujit Choudhry, *Bills of Rights as Instruments of Nation-Building in
Multinational States: The Canadian Charter and Quebec Nationalism* (U. Toronto, Legal Studies
Research Paper No. 1006905, Aug. 2007), <http://ssrn.com/abstract=1006905> (last visited Oct.
20, 2007).
[27] Jeyaratnam A. Wilson, The Break-up of Sri Lanka: The Sinhalese-Tamil Conflict
(Univ. Hawaii Press 1988).

to law—especially on the part of the executive—which may have been a casualty of ethnocultural strife. Disregard and disrespect for the orders of a court may render a bill of rights of little practical value.

But even if these concerns could be addressed, there are limitations that inhere in bills of rights that point to the limitations of rights-based constitutionalism as the principal response to ethnocultural conflict. First, bills of rights are a form of ex post control which can be enforced only after delay and financial cost, and through remedies that may not adequately redress the violation of the right, long after the damage is done. Second, bills of rights raise questions of under-enforcement, arising from the gap between general, abstract constitutional textual provisions and the doctrinal tests developed by the courts to implement and enforce those guarantees.[28] These gaps are a widespread feature of constitutional interpretation, and are deliberately created by courts for reasons of democratic legitimacy and institutional competence. The consequence is that constitutional adjudication can rarely discipline all forms of unequal or unfair treatment. For example, the unequal distribution of the costs and benefits of legislation that is facially neutral on ethnocultural lines may escape constitutional scrutiny.

Finally, and perhaps most fundamentally, bills of rights are based on the liberal precept of neutrality as the appropriate strategy to prevent ethnocultural cleavages from translating into political division. The idea was to privatize religious belief, through protecting the right to engage in private religious practice and by rendering the state impartial among conflicting religious doctrines. However, while it may be possible for the state to be neutral on questions of race and ethnicity, it is not possible for the state to be neutral on every type of ascriptive identity. Consider language. The state must designate a language—or a limited set of languages—as the working language of the legislature and the courts, the internal working language of government, the language in which the state communicates with its citizens, and the language of education. Neutrality is simply not an option. Not surprisingly, conflict over official languages is a major political issue in linguistically diverse societies. Bills of rights have little to say about how these difficult but unavoidable choices should be made.

Bills of rights accordingly should be viewed as one, but far from the only element of constitutional design in divided societies. Although the protection of human rights is an important issue for constitutional politics in divided societies, it is certainly not the only one on the table. Indeed, it is difficult to fully comprehend the constitutional politics of rights-protection in divided

---

[28] *See, e.g.,* RICHARD H. FALLON, JR., IMPLEMENTING THE CONSTITUTION (Harvard Univ. Press 2001); Lawrence Gene Sager, *Fair Measure: The Legal Status of Underenforced Constitutional Norms*, 91 HARV. L. REV. 1212 (1978); Richard H. Fallon, Jr., *Judicially Manageable Standards and Constitutional Meaning*, 119 HARV. L. REV. 1274 (2006).

societies without reference to other features of constitutional design with which it may be in deep tension. Consider the following example from Bosnia and Herzegovina. The Dayton Peace Accords—which are the constitution of Bosnia and Herzegovina—incorporate the *European Convention on Human Rights* and its protocols into domestic law. But the Dayton Accord brought peace to Bosnia and Herzegovina, in part, through the creation of a confederation between the Federation of Bosnia-Herzegovina and Republika Srpska, and presupposes that each unit is the principal home of its "constituent peoples"—Serbs for the former and Croats and Bosniaks for the latter. Bosnia and Herzegovina has structured its electoral practices to reflect the ethnic character of its confederal arrangements. For example, the Dayton Accords create a three-person presidency, consisting of a Serb, a Croat, and a Bosniak. Under electoral legislation, the Bosniak and Croat members of the presidency may be elected only by voters in the Federation of Bosnia-Herzegovina, and the Serb member only by voters in Republika Srpska. The European Commission for Democracy through Law (the Venice Commission) has recently criticized these provisions for being incompatible with Article 1 of Protocol No. 12 to the *European Convention*, which guarantees the right to equal enjoyment of any right protected by law, including the right to elect a President, for two reasons. First, they conflate territorial and ethnic representation, and "assume that only members of a particular ethnicity can be regarded as fully loyal citizens of the Entity capable of defending its interests".[29] Second, they exclude from membership in the Presidency entirely persons who are not Bosniaks, Croats, or Serbs. More generally, according to the Venice Commission, the *European Convention* and its protocols embody and encode a vision of political community "based on the civic principle" and "representation of citizens", as opposed to "ethnic representation".[30] On their face, these concerns are unobjectionable. But the response to the Venice Commission is that these power-sharing arrangements, structured on the basis of ethnicity, are what made peace possible and ensure its stability. Thus, there may be an ineluctable tradeoff between peace and justice. Indeed, the European Court of Human Rights has taken pains not to disturb electoral arrangements which do not operate on an ethnically neutral basis in divided societies.[31] So situating rights-based constitutionalism within the context of other constitutional provisions and practices sharpens our understanding of how they operate as standards for internal constitutional critique, as drivers of constitutional reform, and the sources of resistance to rights-based constitutionalism.

---

[29] European Commission for Democracy through Law, *Opinion on the Constitutional Situation in Bosnia and Herzegovina and the Powers of the High Representative*, para. 69, CDL-AD (2005) 004 (Mar. 11, 2005).

[30] *Id.* at para. 44.

[31] Mathieu-Mohin and Cherfayt v. Belgium, 113 Eur. Ct. H.R. (Ser. A) (1987).

Because comparative constitutional law has principally focused on bills of rights, largely to the exclusion of other aspects of institutional design, it needs to turn elsewhere for guidance. Fortunately, the question of how constitutional design should respond to the problem of political mobilization around ethnocultural identities has been hotly debated in comparative politics for over two decades. The leading figures in this debate have been Arend Lijphart and Donald Horowitz. This debate is reviewed below, as Lijphart and Horowitz in many ways have defined the parameters of scholarly discussion of these issues.

What is worth noting at the outset is that in stark contrast to comparative constitutional law, bills of rights hardly figure into this debate at all. The Lijphart-Horowitz debate has instead focused on a wide range of issues, including electoral systems, the choice between parliamentary and presidential systems for structuring the relationship between the executive and legislature, as well as different forms of federal government. The debates surrounding these issues in comparative constitutional perspective have attracted minimal attention from legal scholars. The premise of this volume is that comparative constitutional law must expand its intellectual agenda to encompass issues that have hitherto been the exclusive domain of comparative politics in order to be of relevance to the most pressing problems of modern constitutionalism. In other words, there is a need to bridge comparative politics and comparative constitutional law through a genuinely interdisciplinary conversation.

The structure of the volume takes the need for interdisciplinarity seriously. The keystone of the volume is an overview chapter by three scholars of comparative politics who have written extensively on constitutional design in divided societies—John McGarry, Brendan O'Leary, and Richard Simeon ("Integration or accommodation? The enduring debate in conflict regulation"). In their chapter, McGarry, O'Leary, and Simeon describe two different families of constitutional strategies for managing ethnocultural diversity. They term these two sets of responses integration and accommodation. After describing and illustrating each set of strategies with concrete examples—and the different variations within each set—they offer a preliminary assessment of the success of each in promoting justice, stability, and democracy.

The volume as a whole is structured as a series of responses to the overview chapter. One set of responses is theoretical in nature, and addresses the questions of whether the dichotomy between integration and accommodation is the correct way to understand the choice in constitutional design for divided societies, and if so, whether one or the other strategy is the preferable one. In addition, these contributions also turn their mind to the practice of the migration of constitutional models for managing ethnocultural diversity, and ask what implications this practice has for our understanding of the debate over constitutional design for divided societies. To foster an interdisciplinary conversation, the contributors to this section come from outside comparative politics. Alan Patten ("Beyond the dichotomy of universalism and difference: Four responses to cultural diversity") and Will Kymlicka ("The internationalization of minority rights") are political theorists; Sujit Choudhry ("Does the world need more Canada? The politics of the Canadian model in constitutional politics and political theory") and Richard Pildes ("Ethnic identity and democratic institutions: A dynamic perspective") are constitutional theorists.

The second set of chapters explores the integration-accommodation debate through a series of case studies. The use of concrete examples serves important functions. It helps to clarify and sharpen our understanding of the sometimes abstract debate between integrationists and accommodationists. In addition, by exploring how these competing constitutional strategies play out in practice, it is possible to get a handle on the costs and benefits associated with each one. Finally, sustained and theoretically informed reflection on constitutional practice may force us to reconsider the cogency of the theories themselves. As some of the chapters suggest, the dichotomy between accommodation and integration may be insufficiently nuanced to accurately describe the function of numerous constitutional provisions in divided societies.

The chapters containing case-studies have been prepared by contributors who work in comparative politics and comparative constitutional law. In comparative constitutional law, there are chapters from Anver Emon ("The limits of constitutionalism in the Muslim world: History and identity in Islamic law"), Yash Ghai and Jill Cottrell ("A tale of three constitutions: Ethnicity and politics in Fiji") and Stephen Tierney ("Giving with one hand: Scottish devolution within a unitary state"). In comparative politics, there are chapters from Jacques Bertrand ("Indonesia's quasi-federalist approach: Accommodation amid strong integrationist tendencies"), Boye Ejobowah ("Integrationist and accommodationist measures in Nigeria's constitutional engineering: Successes and failures"), Michael Keating ("Rival nationalisms in a plurinational state: Spain, Catalonia and the Basque Country"), and two chapters from John McGarry and Brendan O'Leary ("Iraq's Constitution of 2005: Liberal consociation as political prescription" and "Consociation and its critics: Northern Ireland after the Belfast Agreement"). Finally, Richard Simeon (comparative politics) and Christina Murray (comparative constitutional law) co-author a chapter on South Africa ("Recognition without empowerment: Minorities in a democratic South Africa").

The next three sections of this introduction address the following issues: the debate between Arend Lijphart and Donald Horowitz which has defined the approach of comparative politics to constitutional design for divided societies (section 2); the relationship between the overview chapter by McGarry, O'Leary, and Simeon and that debate (section 3); and the contributions of the remaining chapters to the choice between integration and accommodation set up by the overview chapter (section 4).

2. The Lijphart-Horowitz debate

Since a central goal of this volume is to bridge the divide between the hitherto disconnected literatures in comparative politics and comparative constitutional law on constitutional design for divided societies, it is important to get a handle on the state of the debate in comparative politics. The leading figures are Arend Lijphart and Donald Horowitz. Their debate, which has consisted of numerous published exchanges over more than two decades, continues to define the field.[32]

---

[32] For Lijphart's contributions, see generally LIJPHART, *supra* note 5; AREND LIJPHART, POWER-SHARING IN SOUTH AFRICA (Univ. Cal. Berkeley Inst. Int'l Stud. 1985); Arend Lijphart, *Consociation: The Model and its Applications in Divided Societies, in* POLITICAL CO-OPERATION IN DIVIDED SOCIETIES 166 (Desmond Rea ed., Gill and Macmillan 1983) [hereinafter Lijphart, *Consociation*]; Arend Lijphart, *Self-Determination versus Pre-Determination of Ethnic Minorities in Power-Sharing Systems, in* LANGUAGE AND THE STATE: THE LAW AND POLITICS OF IDENTITY 153 (David Schneiderman ed., Les Éditions Yvon Blais 1991), *reprinted in* THE RIGHTS OF MINORITY CULTURES 275 (Will Kymlicka ed., Oxford Univ. Press 1995) [hereinafter Lijphart, *Self-Determination*]; Lijphart, *supra* note 6; Arend Lijphart, *Power-Sharing, Ethnic Agnosticism, and Political Pragmatism*, 21 TRANSFORMATION 94 (1993) [hereinafter Lijphart, *Power-Sharing*]; Arend Lijphart, *The Alternative Vote: A Realistic Alternative for South Africa?*, 18 POLITIKON 91 (1991) [hereinafter Lijphart, *The Alternative Vote*]; Arend Lijphart, *The Framework Document on Northern Ireland and the Theory of Power-Sharing*, 31 GOV'T & OPPOSITION 267 (1996) [hereinafter Lijphart, *The Framework Document*]; Arend Lijphart, *Constitutional Choices for New Democracies*, 2 J. DEMOCRACY 72 (1991) [hereinafter Lijphart, *Constitutional Choices*]; Arend Lijphart, *The Puzzle of Indian Democracy: A Consociational Interpretation*, 90 AM. POL. SCI. REV. 258 (1996) [hereinafter Lijphart, *The Puzzle of Indian Democracy*]; Arend Lijphart, *Constitutional Design for Divided Societies*, 15 J. DEMOCRACY 96 (2004) [hereinafter Lijphart, *Constitutional Design for Divided Societies*]; Arend Lijphart, *Consociational Democracy*, 21 WORLD POL. 207, 213 (1969) [hereinafter Lijphart, *Consociational Democracy*]; Arend Lijphart, *Democratization and Constitutional Choices in Czecho-Slovakia, Hungary and Poland 1989–91*, 4 J. THEORETICAL POL. 207 (1992); Arend Lijphart, *The Evolution of Consociational Theory and Consociational Practices, 1965–2000*, 37 ACTA POLITICA 11 (2002); Arend Lijphart, *Non-Majoritarian Democracy: A Comparison of Federal and Consociational Theories*, 15 PUBLIUS: J. FEDERALISM 3 (1985) [hereinafter Lijphart, *Non-Majoritarian Democracy*]; Arend Lijphart, *Consociation and Federation: Conceptual and Empirical Links*, 12 CAN. J. POL. SCI. 499 (1979) [hereinafter Lijphart, *Consociation and Federation*]; Arend Lijphart, *Review Article: The Northern Ireland Problem; Cases, Theories, and Solutions*, 5 BRIT. J. POL. SCI. 83, 94 (1975) [hereinafter Lijphart, *Review Article*]; Arend Lijphart, *Majority Rule Versus Democracy in Deeply Divided Societies*, 4 POLITIKON 113 (1977) [hereinafter Lijphart, *Majority Rule*]; Arend Lijphart, *The Wave of Power-Sharing Democracy, in* THE ARCHITECTURE OF DEMOCRACY: CONSTITUTIONAL DESIGN, CONFLICT MANAGEMENT AND DEMOCRACY 37 (Andrew Reynolds ed., Oxford Univ. Press 2002) [hereinafter Lijphart, *The Wave of Power-Sharing Democracy*]; Arend Lijphart, *Time Politics of Accommodation: Reflections—Fifteen Years Later*, 19 ACTA POLITICA 9 (1984); Arend Lijphart, *Comparative Perspectives on Fair Representation: The Plurality-Majority Rule, Geographical Districting, and Alternative Electoral Arrangements*, 9 POL'Y STUD. J. 899 (1980).

Both Lijphart and Horowitz write against the backdrop of pluralist accounts of democratic politics put forward by American scholars such as Seymour Lipset.[33] Democracies, such as the United States, are characterized by sharp disagreements over the direction of public policy. The question posed by Lipset is why political actors who lose within democratic institutions do not respond to those losses by turning on the system itself and attempting to undermine it. The pluralist response is the theory of crosscutting cleavages, such as the phenomenon that "individuals belong to a number of different interests and outlooks".[34] Crosscutting cleavages have two moderating effects. First, as a consequence of membership in multiple social groups, individuals will come into contact with a multiplicity of perspectives, and will possess a complex set of interests, which will tend to moderate their political attitudes. Second, in the absence of sharp partisan division among individuals, political elites will likewise be subject to the pressure to moderate their political positions. Through these two mechanisms, crosscutting cleavages promote political moderation and blunt partisan division.

For Horowitz's contributions, see generally DONALD L. HOROWITZ, A DEMOCRATIC SOUTH AFRICA: CONSTITUTIONAL ENGINEERING IN A DIVIDED SOCIETY? (Univ. Cal. Press 1991) [hereinafter HOROWITZ, A DEMOCRATIC SOUTH AFRICA]; HOROWITZ, *supra* note 11; Donald L. Horowitz, *Constitutional Design: Proposals Versus Processes, in* THE ARCHITECTURE OF DEMOCRACY: CONSTITUTIONAL DESIGN, CONFLICT MANAGEMENT, AND DEMOCRACY, *supra* note 29, at 15 [hereinafter Horowitz, *Constitutional Design*]; Donald L. Horowitz, *Ethnic Conflict Management for Policymakers, in* CONFLICT AND PEACEMAKING IN MULTIETHNIC SOCIETIES 115 (Joseph V. Montville ed., Lexington Books 1990) [hereinafter Horowitz, *Ethnic Conflict Management*]; Donald L. Horowitz, *Ethnic and Nationalist Conflicts, in* WORLD SECURITY: TRENDS AND CHALLENGES AT CENTURY'S END 225 (Michael T. Klare & Daniel C. Thomas eds., St. Martin's Press 1991); Donald L. Horowitz, *Encouraging Electoral Accommodation in Divided Societies, in* ELECTORAL SYSTEMS IN DIVIDED SOCIETIES: THE FIJI CONSTITUTION REVIEW 21 (Brij V. Lal & Peter Larmour eds., Nat'l Ctr. Dev. Stud. 1997); Donald L. Horowitz, *Constitutional Design: An Oxymoron?, in* DESIGNING DEMOCRATIC INSTITUTIONS (Ian Shapiro & Stephen Macedo eds., Nomo Series No. 42, NYU Press 2000) [hereinafter Horowitz, *Constitutional Design: An Oxymoron?*]; Donald L. Horowitz, *A Splitting Headache*, 34 THE NEW REPUBLIC 33 (Feb. 23, 1987) (book reviews); Donald L. Horowitz, *Democracy in Divided Societies*, 4 J. DEMOCRACY 18 (1993) [hereinafter Horowitz, *Democracy in Divided Societies*]; Donald L. Horowitz, *The Alternative Vote and Interethnic Moderation: A Reply to Fraenkel and Grofman*, 121 PUB. CHOICE 507 (2004) [hereinafter Horowitz, *The Alternative Vote*]; Donald L. Horowitz, *Strategy Takes a Holiday: Fraenkel and Grofman on the Alternative Vote*, 39 COMP. POL. STUD. 652 (2006) [hereinafter Horowitz, *Strategy Takes a Holiday*]; Donald L. Horowitz, *Incentives and Behaviour in the Ethnic Politics of Sri Lanka and Malaysia*, 11 THIRD WORLD Q. 18 (1989); Donald L. Horowitz, *A Harvest of Hostility: Ethnic Conflict and Self-Determination after the Cold War*, 1 DEFENSE INTELLIGENCE J. 137 (1992); Donald L. Horowitz, *Irredentas and Secessions: Adjacent Phenomena, Neglected Connections, in* IRREDENTISM AND INTERNATIONAL POLITICS 9 (Naomi Chazan ed., Lynne Rienner 1991); Donald L. Horowitz, *How to Begin Thinking Comparatively about Soviet Ethnic Problems, in* THINKING THEORETICALLY ABOUT SOVIET NATIONALITIES 9 (Alexander J. Motyl ed., Columbia Univ. Press 1992); Donald L. Horowitz, *Structure and Strategy in Ethnic Conflict; A Few Steps toward Synthesis, in* ANNUAL WORLD BANK CONFERENCE ON DEVELOPMENT ECONOMICS 1998, at 345 (Boris Pleskovic & Joseph E. Stiglitz eds., World Bank 1999); Donald L. Horowitz, *Explaining the Northern Ireland Agreement; The Sources of an Unlikely Constitutional Consensus*, 32 BRIT. J. POL. STUD. 193 (2002).

[33] SEYMOUR MARTIN LIPSET, POLITICAL MAN: THE SOCIAL BASES OF POLITICS (Doubleday 1960).

[34] LIJPHART, *supra* note 5, at 10.

This account of the nature of political cleavages is closely tied
competitive model of democratic politics. On the pluralist view
acterized by shifting coalitions and majorities, which change fi
Political parties compete for the median voters at the center of
trum, and electoral competition creates pressures toward mod
tional terms, the paradigm assumed by Lijphart and Horowi
democracy modeled on the Westminster system, with elections on the ba..
single member plurality voting (first past the post, or FPTP), and with the governing party commanding the confidence of the majority of the legislature and
an official opposition, and with a unitary constitution in which there are no alternative centers of political power. Cabinets are formed on a winner-take-all basis,
with the opposition party focusing on providing parliamentary opposition from
outside the government.[35] The assumption is that parties will cycle in and out of
government, as they assemble shifting coalitions of voters in their competition
for the political center. Since there is no permanent exclusion of any segment of
society from political power, the losers under a regime of competitive politics
accept this loss in the hope that they will win another day. Political competition
does not threaten political stability.

The competitive paradigm of democratic politics depends on two assumptions—that opposition parties will eventually share power and that, because of
the shifting nature of majority coalitions, governing parties will not abuse their
power. But as Lijphart famously argued in *Democracy in Plural Societies*, these
assumptions do not hold in deeply divided societies. In divided societies, cleavages are mutually reinforcing, not crosscutting. The result is a system of "segmental cleavages", where political divisions map onto "lines of objective social
differentiation", such as race, language, culture and ethnicity.[36] If crosscutting
cleavages produce moderation, segmental cleavages produce immoderation.
Political mobilization occurs on the basis of segmental identities, and political
parties respond by organizing themselves on this basis.

The existence of segmental cleavages challenges the assumptions of competitive politics. Under these conditions, democracy would not actually lead to
competition for median voters. Rather, the dominant characteristic of divided
societies is the ethnic political party, with individuals casting votes for parties
of their own ethnicity. As Horowitz writes, "[t]his is not an election at all, but a
census".[37] There is no political competition across ethnic divides. The political
consequences of the institutions of majoritarian democracy in divided societies
will depend on the precise demography of the policy in question. If there is a clear
ethnic majority, the result is not a temporary minority which will eventually
cycle into power, but a persistent minority which will permanently be in opposition and excluded from political office. The twin assumptions of competitive

[35] Lijphart, *Majority Rule, supra* note 32.
[36] LIJPHART, *supra* note 5, at 3.
[37] Horowitz, *Ethnic Conflict Management, supra* note 32, at 116.

olitics—that minorities will eventually cycle into power, and a majority will not abuse its power—do not hold. The danger is a "majority dictatorship",[38] with no political restraints on the potential, inherent in Westminster democracy, for the winning party to discriminate in public expenditure and the distribution of public offices in favor of its supporters. As Horowitz argues, "the results could be brought about under conditions perfectly consistent with the procedural assumptions of democracy. The results are an artifact of the interaction of demography with the rules of the game".[39] In other cases, where there is no clear majority, coalitions of minorities can produce the same effect. Minorities that are persistent losers with no prospect of wielding power lack the incentive to compromise or negotiate, because there is no reward for doing so. They may eventually step outside of politics and turn to violence. If the minority is a minority nation, it may attempt to secede. In any case, the result will be political fragmentation.

Thus, both Lijphart and Horowitz trade on an image of political pathology. A democracy in which crosscutting cleavages interact with the institutions of competitive politics to moderate political behaviour is a centripetal democracy; a democracy in which the institutions of competitive politics interact with segmental cleavages is a centrifugal democracy that will literally fly apart. They also proceed from a shared assumption that "[p]urely procedural conceptions of democracy are thus inadequate for ethnically divided polities, for the procedure can be impeccable and the exclusion complete".[40] Nonetheless, they propose radically different solutions to this problem.

Lijphart's proposal is consociational democracy. While "[t]he essence of the Westminster model is the concentration of political power in the hands of the majority", Lijphart argues that the basic impulse behind the consociational model "is to *share, diffuse, separate, divide, decentralize*, and *limit* power".[41] Lijphart has set out two iterations of the institutional details of the consociational model. In its original formulation, it consisted of four elements: A grand coalition cabinet encompassing representatives of the major ethnic segments; proportionality in legislative representation, representation in cabinets, civil service, police, military, and public expenditure; mutual vetoes on vital interests, since notwithstanding participation in grand coalition cabinets, the representatives of ethnic groups may nonetheless be outvoted; and segmental autonomy, either consisting of federalism (where territorial boundaries follow ethnic boundaries) or nonterritorial federalism with respect to policy areas closely linked to ethnic identity (such as schools).[42] More recently, Lijphart has simplified the model.[43] The two

---

[38] Lijphart, *Review Article, supra* note 32.
[39] Horowitz, *Democracy in Divided Societies, supra* note 32.
[40] *Id.*
[41] Lijphart, *Consociation, supra* note 32, at 168.
[42] For these details, see Lɪᴊᴘʜᴀʀᴛ, *supra* note 5; Lijphart, *Consociation and Federation, supra* note 32; Lijphart, *Non-Majoritarian Democracy, supra* note 32.
[43] Arend Lijphart, *Constitutional Design for Divided Societies, supra* note 29; Arend Lijphart, *The Wave of Power-Sharing Democracy, supra* note 32.

primary elements are: Power sharing, consisting of the participation of major ethnic groups in political decision making, especially the executive; and group autonomy, especially over education and culture. Proportionality and the minority veto are now secondary characteristics that reinforce the first two.

Consociational democracy is designed to work differently than a majoritarian democracy in a divided society. The fragmentation of political representation through proportional representation allows for legislative representation of territorially dispersed minorities who may be outvoted under FPTP in single member districts. The fragmented nature of the legislature creates incentives for political leaders to cooperate across ethnic lines. Leaders of ethnic minorities can leverage their legislative power to secure executive power sharing, through the formation of a grand coalition cabinet. The possibility of sharing power gives all parties a stake in the survival of the constitutional system, in contrast to a situation where minorities are perpetual outsiders. Similarly, mutual vetoes and segmental autonomy provide additional incentives for leaders of ethnic leaders to participate within politics, because they can rest secure that their fundamental interests will be protected.

The consociational model has generated an enormous literature.[44] An important issue is how rigid Lijphart's institutional criteria are. Lijphart has stated that each of the institutional requirements can be implemented in different ways, tailored to the specific circumstances of each society.[45] Thus, a consociational framework can be spelled out in a formal legal text or be found in unwritten rules of political practice. Minorities can be overrepresented or on a proportional basis. The scope of segmental autonomy and the veto will vary by context. Likewise, whether segmental autonomy takes the form of territorial or nonterritorial autonomy (or both) will depend on the geographic distribution of ethnic communities. An important choice to be made is between executive power sharing which is expressly stated to be on an ethnic basis, and whether power sharing should be framed on the basis of ethnically neutral criteria, such as passing a threshold of popular support in legislative elections. Lijphart describes the former as predetermination, and the latter as self-determination.[46] The advantage of the latter is that it allows individuals to voluntarily associate with ethnic parties or with non-ethnic parties, and can self-adjust for changes in relative population. The benefit of the latter is that it ensures the inclusion of ethnic minorities in government.[47]

In subsequent work, Lijphart has also expanded the repertoire of consociational devices. Thus, he has included bicameralism and legal pluralism as

---

[44] For reviews see, see Ian S. Lustick, *Lijphart, Lakatos, and Consociationalism*, 50 WORLD POL. 88 (1997); Rudy B. Andeweg, *Consicational Democracy*, 3 ANN. REV. POL. SCI. 509 (2000); Matthijs Bogaards, *The Uneasy Relationship between Empirical and Normative Types in Consociational Theory*, 12 J. THEORETICAL POL. 395 (2000).

[45] Lijphart, *Consociation, supra* note 32.

[46] Lijphart, *Self-Determination, supra* note 32.

[47] Lijphart, *The Wave of Power-Sharing Democracy, supra* note 32.

additional forms of power sharing and segmental autonomy, respectively.[48] Provincial consent to constitutional amendments can be a mechanism to protect both power sharing and segmental autonomy.[49] In addition, although a grand coalition cabinet assumes a parliamentary system, he also included presidential and semi-presidential systems within the family of consociational democracies.[50] As a consequence, there are two ways to read Lijphart. On one reading, the consociational model is less of a specific constitutional package than a set of general principles of institutional design which are consistent with a broad set of constitutional packages.[51] This is the best explanation for his controversial categorization of India as a consociational democracy although it lacks minority vetoes, on the basis that the Congress Party was a grand coalition.[52] On a second reading, Lijphart is still committed to specific constitutional choices. Thus, he has a clear preference for parliamentary government over presidential government, because the former is more likely to be ethnically inclusive than the latter, since a president will be drawn from a single ethnic group and presidential elections are majoritarian in nature.[53]

Horowitz has been highly critical of the consociational model, and his own proposals grow out of these criticisms.[54] The major shortcoming of the consociational model, according to Horowitz, is that it is "motivationally inadequate" because it does not offer a coherent account of why leaders of ethnic groups would have an incentive to cooperate and enter into a power-sharing arrangement in the first place.[55] While the incentives for minority leaders are clear, the incentives for majority leaders are much less so, if sharing power is not necessary to control the state. As a consequence, consociation is more likely where there is no clear majority. And even there, the likely outcome is not a grand coalition in the specific sense in which Lijphart defines it, a coalition of all major ethnic groups. Depending on how the rules governing coalitions are structured, and the underlying demographic facts, what may occur is a coalition that includes some ethnic groups while excluding others as long as it commands a majority of the legislature.[56]

Legislative elections held under proportional representation (PR) would only compound the problem. Lijphart supports PR because it would enable the

---

[48] For bicameralism, see Lijphart, *Consociation and Federation, supra* note 32, at 506. For legal pluralism, see Lijphart, *The Puzzle of Indian Democracy, supra* note 32.

[49] Lijphart, *Consociation and Federation, supra* note 32.

[50] Lijphart, *Consociational Democracy, supra* note 32.

[51] *Id.* This is how one can read Lijphart's first statement of the consociational model in his 1969 article in *World Politics*.

[52] Lijphart, *The Puzzle of Indian Democracy, supra* note 32.

[53] Lijphart, *Constitutional Choices, supra* note 32.

[54] For a recent summary of these criticisms, see Horowitz, *Constitutional Design, supra* note 32, at 15.

[55] *Id.* at 20.

[56] To be fair, Lijphart agreed from outset that incentives to form a consociation were weak in this kind of situation. *See* Lijphart, *Consociational Democracy, supra* note 32, at 217–218.

election of representatives from ethnic parties who would otherwise not secure seats in the legislature. But PR would also facilitate intraethnic competition, reducing the probability of dominant parties within each ethnic segment. This has a number of consequences. The most serious is that ethnic parties which attempt to adopt moderate policies to bridge ethnic divides come under attack from extremist parties in a process of ethnic outbidding. Instead of competition for the moderate center for median voters (in a majoritarian system with cross-cutting cleavages), there is competition on the extremes.

Ethnic parties will respond to the extremes, because there is no possibility of being rewarded for moderate policies by members of other ethnic groups. As a consequence, there are electoral penalties on, as opposed to incentives for, moderate political behaviour and cooperation across ethnic lines, which undermines the stability of interethnic coalitions. Given these electoral dynamics, Horowitz suggests that successful consociations are the result of crosscutting cleavages or resolved ethnic conflict, as opposed to successful solutions to ethnic strife.

Horowitz's criticisms proceed from the assumption that if there is a clash between statesmanship and electoral self-interest, the latter will always prevail. Similarly, even if consociational arrangements are constitutionally entrenched to render them less vulnerable to electoral calculations, Horowitz's view is that those arrangements are unstable because they will not be supported by ongoing motivations of self-interest. As a consequence, he proposes a set of electoral arrangements that creates the political incentive toward ethnic moderation that Lijphart's allegedly lacks.[57] The key is to "make moderation pay"[58] by rewarding ethnic parties electorally who appeal across ethnic lines to members of ethnic groups outside their own. The basic calculation is that the possibility of crossethnic support should offset electoral losses from intraethnic competition on the extremes. But crossethnic support will only be forthcoming if ethnic parties moderate their platforms and moderate their conduct while in office.

Thus, ethnic moderation depends on vote transfers across ethnic lines—or what Horowitz refers to as "vote pooling". The key mechanism is the alternative vote (AV). Alternative voting electoral systems require winning candidates to secure a majority of the votes cast. Voters rank candidates in order of preference. If no candidate is successful after first preferences have been counted, the bottom candidate is dropped from the ballot and votes cast for that candidate distributed according to the second preferences. The theory behind the alternative vote is that it creates the incentive for parties representing a majority ethnic group to appeal across ethnic boundaries in order to secure an absolute majority through second preferences. The possibility of interethnic vote transfers creates

[57] The clearest account is set out in Horowitz, *Constitutional Design: An Oxymoron?, supra* note 32.
[58] Donald L. Horowitz, *Making Moderation Pay: The Comparative Politics of Ethnic Conflict Management, in* CONFLICT AND PEACEMAKING IN MULTIETHNIC SOCIETIES, *supra* note 32, at 451.

the incentives for moderation by protecting the moderate middle from electoral competition on the extremes.

This difference in electoral system—proportional representation for Lijphart, alternative vote for Horowitz—would have important implications for the respective roles of political elites and voters. Lijphart advocates the pooling of seats in post-electoral coalitions, through negotiations among political elites. Ethnic parties still only communicate with, and appeal to, members of their own ethnic group. By contrast, Horowitz envisions direct appeals by ethnic parties to voters of other ethnic groups during election campaigns, who must decide to provide their electoral support. The net effect is to shift power away from ethnic elites toward voters, who would make their decisions on the basis of party platforms during elections. However, ethnic parties still play an important role. Horowitz envisions pre-electoral, interethnic coalitions of parties who would enter into reciprocal arrangements to exchange the votes of supporters in different constituencies. Indeed, there could conceivably be competing interethnic coalitions. Yet voters themselves would play a much more important role in moderating ethnic conflict than they would under consociation, where party leaders are the most important actors. The net result is to create a second best for pluralist politics in divided societies, by designing electoral incentives to encourage crossethnic political appeals that are a substitute for crosscutting cleavages.

Horowitz supports the use of AV for legislative elections. Because of the potential of AV to foster interethnic cooperation, contrary to Lijphart, he also advocates a presidential form of government. A presidential election would provide another opportunity for vote pooling across ethnic divides, if the electoral system were designed correctly—for example, through the use of AV, or a requirement of obtaining a minimum level of support in different regions of the country as a proxy for support from different ethnic groups. Indeed, because the country as a whole is more heterogeneous than individual legislative districts, the prospects for vote pooling are greater.[59] A single president, although from one ethnic group, could legitimately lay claim to support from more than one ethnic group, and could rise above ethnic politics. By contrast, a power-sharing cabinet does not possess the capacity to transcend ethnicity. Horowitz terms his approach the "incentives" approach.

Although their arguments are at times framed at a high level of abstraction, for Lijphart and Horowitz, theirs has never been a strictly academic debate. Rather, they have set out competing proposals for constitutional design for divided societies with a view toward contemporary, real-time application. Both Lijphart and Horowitz wrote against the backdrop of the "third wave" of democratization, which began with the transition to civilian rule in Portugal in 1974. Lijphart

---

[59] Horowitz also supports federalism as a device for reducing ethnic conflict. *See* HOROWITZ, *supra* note 11, at 601–628. However, since the focus of the Lijphart-Horowitz debate has been on AV and presidentialism, I will not discuss it here.

argues that the third wave was largely successful until the early 1990s, when democratization spread to the ethnically divided societies of Eastern and Central Europe.[60] Democratization foundered because constitutional design had not properly accounted for ethnic division. Horowitz shares the same view, arguing that "[i]n many countries... a major reason for the failure of democratization is ethnic conflict".[61]

Given the ultimately practical motivation underlying the literature, it is not surprising that the debate between Lijphart and Horowitz revolved around case studies. Both scholars traded in examples. Thus, they offered competing dissections of past constitutional experiments. According to Horowitz, the first Nigerian constitution (discussed by Ejobowah in this volume) failed because it granted the largest ethnic group, the Hausa, a single province—a form of segmental autonomy under consociational theory—from which they dominated the country.[62] By contrast, Lijphart claims that the constitution failed because it was not consociational enough.[63]

Likewise, they disagree on the legacy of the failed experiment in consociational power sharing in Northern Ireland between 1973 and 1974. Horowitz argues the lesson is that Northern Ireland should have opted for AV instead of the single transferable vote, which had operated to polarize the electorate and not reward ethnic moderation.[64] Lijphart was originally skeptical regarding the prospects of consociation working in Northern Ireland, in particular because of the lack of a clear balance of power.[65] The fact of a seemingly permanent Protestant majority and Catholic minority, where the former could dominate the latter, made consociation unstable. Partition, Lijphart argued, was a better alternative. But now Lijphart holds that there is no alternative to power sharing, since majoritarian rule of any kind in Northern Ireland has always been a Protestant dictatorship. The adoption of a consociational arrangement in the Good Friday Agreement (also known as the Belfast Agreement, discussed in this volume by McGarry and O'Leary) is proof of the inevitability of consociation.[66]

Lijpjart and Horowitz also offer differing assessments of the adoption of the AV in Fiji in 1997 (discussed in this volume by Ghai and Cottrell). Lijphart states that Fiji is the only divided society to have adopted the AV as a method of resolving ethnic conflict, and that the collapse of this constitutional regime in 2000 pointed to the inability of the AV to moderate ethnic politics.[67] Horowitz counters that the 1997 electoral system consisted of a mix of open seats elected by AV,

---

[60] Lijphart, *The Wave of Power-Sharing Democracy, supra* note 32.
[61] Horowitz, *Democracy in Divided Societies, supra* note 32.
[62] HOROWITZ, *supra* note 11.   [63] LIJPHART, *supra* note 5, at 163.
[64] Donald L. Horowitz, *The Clear Consociational, and Risky, in* NORTHERN IRELAND AND THE DIVIDED WORLD: THE NORTHERN IRELAND CONFLICT AND THE GOOD FRIDAY AGREEMENT IN COMPARATIVE PERSPECTIVE 89, 99–100 (John McGarry ed., Oxford Univ. Press 2001).
[65] Lijphart, *Review Article, supra* note 32.
[66] Lijphart, *The Framework Document, supra* note 32.
[67] Lijphart, *The Wave of Power-Sharing Democracy, supra* note 32.

and a larger number reserved seats allocated on an ethnic basis, which undercut the ability of AV to create incentives for moderation.[68] Thus, the problem was not with AV, but rather, that Fiji did not go far enough in adopting AV.[69]

Without a doubt, the most famous debate between Lijphart and Horowitz occurred with respect to South Africa (as discussed in this volume by Simeon and Murray). Several years before the negotiated transition to democracy, Lijphart set out a specific set of proposals for a consociational constitution for post-apartheid South Africa.[70] The key proposals were elections based on proportional representation at the municipal, provincial and national level, executive power sharing at the both the national and provincial level (with a rotating chair at the national level), proportionality in the civil service, armed forces, policy and judiciary, a mixture of territorial federalism (with units as ethnically homogeneous as possible) and nonterritorial federalism (for culture and education), and a mixture of absolute and suspensive vetoes. Given the use of racial classifications as a tool of racial discrimination, Lipjhart argued for self-determination over predetermination of segments. Horowitz responded by proposing the AV and a strong executive president also elected by AV, as well as a federalism based on heterogeneous units.[71] Not surprisingly, Lijphart was deeply critical of Horowitz.[72]

The debate between the two scholars over their competing proposals for South Africa, as well as their subsequent exchanges, highlights a series of critical issues, some of which have yet to be resolved. The relative costs and benefits of intraethnic competition and interethnic political cooperation is at the heart of the Horowitz-Lijphart debate. A major issue is the vote pooling potential of the AV. The question in each case will be the balance between the votes lost from intraethnic competition and the votes gained from interethnic cooperation. As Benjamin Reilly has shown, this is dependent on the existence of ethnically heterogeneous constituencies.[73] The larger the number of ethnic groups and the greater the degree to which ethnic groups are dispersed, the greater the potential for vote pooling. For this reason, Reilly argues that vote pooling has much greater potential in Asia than in Africa, including South Africa, because

---

[68] Horowitz, *Constitutional Design: An Oxymoron?, supra* note 32, at 265–268.

[69] For the ongoing debate over alternative voting (AV) and the lessons to be drawn from Fiji, see Jon Fraenkel & Bernard Grofman, *A Neo-Downsian Model of the Alternative Vote as a Mechanism for Mitigating Ethnic Conflict in Plural Societies*, 121 PUB. CHOICE 487 (2004); Jon Fraenkel & Bernard Grofman, *Does the Alternative Vote Foster Moderation in Ethnically Divided Societies?: The Case of Fiji*, 39 COMP. POL. STUD. 663 (2006); Horowitz, *The Alternative Vote, supra* note 32; Horowitz, *Strategy Takes a Holiday, supra* note 32.

[70] LIJPHART, *supra* note 32.

[71] HOROWITZ, A DEMOCRATIC SOUTH AFRICA, *supra* note 32.

[72] Lijphart, *The Alternative Vote, supra* note 29; *see also* Lijphart, *Power-Sharing, supra* note 32; Arend Lijphart, *Book Reviews: Comparative Politics,* 86 AM. POL. SCI. REV. 560 (1992) (reviewing LEWIS H. GANN & PANN DUIGNAN, HOPE FOR SOUTH AFRICA? (1991) and DONALD L. HOROWITZ, A DEMOCRATIC SOUTH AFRICA? CONSTITUTIONAL ENGINEERING IN A DIVIDED SOCIETY (1991)).

[73] BENJAMIN REILLY, DEMOCRACY IN DIVIDED SOCIETIES: ELECTORAL ENGINEERING FOR CONFLICT MANAGEMENT (Cambridge Univ. Press 2001).

of "the demographic legacy of apartheid which deliberately segregated different races".[74] And even if the demographic preconditions for the success of AV may be present, particular histories of interethnic conflict may prevent its success. The introduction of the AV for presidential elections in Sri Lanka was followed by the commencement of the civil war and the withdrawal from electoral politics of significant elements in the Tamil community, which has blunted the moderating potential of AV. In contexts where the demography is lacking, or the political culture unsupportive, AV may be unable to yield ethnic moderation, and proportional representation may be the better alternative.

Another issue in the Horowitz-Lijphart debate is a fundamental normative disagreement over the mechanisms of interethnic cooperation. Put simply, the choice for ethnic minorities is between two theories of representation. Under the consociational model, minorities protect their interests through holding important offices. Power sharing guarantees that ethnic minorities will sit in the legislature and the executive, in proportion to their share of the population. As well, proportionality will ensure minority representation in the civil service, police, military, and judiciary. Representation is conceived of as representation by members of the same ethnic group—such as descriptive representation. Under the incentives approach, representation is conceived of in terms of electoral influence. Vote pooling is designed to foster the election of members of the ethnic majority with the votes of the ethnic minority within a constituency. This means that members of one ethnicity will be represented by members of another ethnicity, which will, at the very least, come at the cost of minority representation in the legislature and executive. If ethnic moderation is more likely under vote pooling, then it comes at the cost of descriptive representation. There is an unavoidable trade-off between the two.

This leads us to the final issue—the practical question of whether the incentives approach or the consociational model is more likely to be adopted. Lijphart argues that it is naïve to expect ethnic minorities to sacrifice office holding for influence, especially as part of a post-conflict constitutional agreement.[75] The incentives approach asks ethnic minorities to put their trust in members of a majority. But that same majority may have abused its power under the previous regime, which in turn may have led to ethnic conflict and violence. After interethnic conflict has occurred, the trust necessary for vote pooling may simply be absent. Lijphart suggests that a minority will instead seek credible commitments of security and protection from abuse. By way of illustration, Lijphart suggests that vote pooling in Iraq would produce a government dominated by the Shia but supported by Sunni and Kurds , and that "it is...hard to imagine that Kurdish and Sunni members of a broadly representative constituent assembly would ever agree to a constitution that would set up such a system". [76] On this point, Horowitz appears

---

[74] *Id.* at 192.   [75] Lijphart, *Constitutional Design for Divided Societies, supra* note 32.
[76] *Id.* at 98.

to agree with Lijphart. Moreover, in response to Horowitz's point that majorities have no incentive to enter into consociation with minorities, Lijphart suggests that the threat of future violence may be sufficient.

By contrast, it is much harder to tell a story of how the incentives approach would get off the ground. Even Horowitz, who clearly favors the incentives approach, argues that it will be unattractive to both political leaders from ethnic majorities and minorities, since it opens up their respective electorates to interethnic competition, from which they are insulated under the consociational model. Since Horowitz is of the view that, once up and running, the incentives approach produces more stable politics because there is a greater likelihood of ethnic moderation, there is a disjoint between which constitutional arrangement is likely to be adopted and which arrangement, in his view, is likely to be stable.[77]

3. Integration versus accommodation

There are several striking differences between the Lijphart-Horowitz debate, and the integration versus accommodation debate as set out by McGarry, O'Leary, and Simeon ("Integration or accommodation? The enduring debate in conflict regulation").

Lijphart and Horowitz both take the durability of political mobilization on the basis of ethnic identities to be a given and construct their theories of constitutional design around them. Although neither claims that it is inevitable that this should occur—in other words, that difference should translate into political division—they both assume that once no mobilization has occurred on this basis, it is very hard to undo, especially if it eventually leads to, and is in turn fed by, violent conflict and civil war. As a consequence, they both rule out strategies for the resolution of ethnic conflict that involves the elimination of ethnic differences. Not only would such methods be ineffective, they may make ethnic conflict worse. So Lijphart writes:

> Although the replacement of segmental loyalties by a common national allegiance appears to be a logical answer to the problems posed by a plural society, it is extremely dangerous to attempt it. Because of the tenacity of primordial loyalties, any effort to eradicate them not only is quite unlikely to succeed, especially in the short run, but may well be counterproductive and may stimulate segmental cohesion and intersegmental violence rather than national cohesion.[78]

Horowitz similarly dismisses the expectation that ethnic political division, once mobilized will disappear, as naïve. Where they disagree is how to institutionally respond to this basic set of facts about political life.

---

[77] Horowitz, *Constitutional Design: An Oxymoron?, supra* note 32.
[78] LIJPHART, *supra* note 5, at 24.

But as McGarry, O'Leary, and Simeon note, this is a set of assumptions that does not underlie every set of constitutional strategies on how to respond to the facts of a divided society. The overview chapter distinguishes between two general approaches to this issue. Each proceeds from a different set of assumptions about the durability and depth of ethnic political divisions. On the one hand, there are "accommodationists", who "insist that in certain contexts, national, ethnic, religious and linguistic divisions and identities are resilient, durable and hard". Notwithstanding their different policy prescriptions, McGarry, O'Leary, and Simeon place both Lijphart and Horowitz into this camp. But on the other hand, there are "integrationists", who are less willing to accept the equation of ethnic identity and political interest. Integrationists reject the idea that ethnic difference should necessarily translate into political differences. They argue for the possibility of a common public identity, even in the midst of considerable ethnocultural diversity. As McGarry, O'Leary, and Simeon note, they hold to this position even when ethnicity has served as the basis of political mobilization, because "ethnic identities are seldom as longstanding or as deep as supporters of accommodation suggest". Political identities are malleable, and crosscutting cleavages, even if absent, can be fostered.

These fundamentally different assumptions over the durability of politically mobilized ethnocultural identities reframe the debate over constitutional design for divided societies. In particular, it translates into a much broader set of policy options than the Lijphart-Horowitz debate has generated. In general terms, accommodation commends "dual or multiple public identities", and "minimally, requires the recognition of more than one ethnic, linguistic, national or religious community in the state". Integrationists, by contrast, "believe political instability and conflict result from group based partisanship in political institutions", and therefore, "turn[s] a blind eye to difference for public purposes". In this connection, McGarry, O'Leary, and Simeon draw a useful distinction between integrationists and assimilationists, which tracks the public and private divide. Assimilationists argue that the most secure foundation for public, political integration is ethnocultural assimilation, rendering impossible political mobilization around ethnic difference. As a consequence, they argue in favor of a range of public policies that would forcibly eradicate or provide strong incentives for the elimination of ethnocultural differences. Integration, by contrast, supports constitutional strategies that would promote a common public identity without demanding ethnocultural uniformity in private and associational life.

A specific example of how an integrationist and an accommodationist would differ is in their treatment of political parties. Despite important differences between them, Lijphart and Horowitz proceed from the shared starting point that in a divided society, ethnic political parties are inevitable, that attempts to suppress them are futile and easy to circumvent, that broad-based parties which purport to be non-ethnic in nature in fact are controlled by members of the majority ethnic group, and that denying democratic space to ethnic political parties would drive them out of political institutions and into the streets. Integrationists, on the other hand, are vigorously opposed to ethnic parties, and instead favor aggrega-tive political parties which bring together individuals of different ethnicities. As a matter of constitutional design, some integrationists may even argue for bans on parties which are organized on an ethnic or regional basis.

Moreover, there are varieties *within* each school of thought, generating an ever broader scope for constitutional choice than the Lipjhart-Horowitz debate has generated. McGarry, O'Leary, and Simeon distinguish among three schools of integrationists: Republicans, liberals, and socialists. Republicans are champions of the civic nation, and "veer toward integral nationalism", with its emphasis on shared bonds of political identity among the citizenry. Liberals "promote the lib-eral values of choice and freedom", in contrast to "the strong community of repub-licans". Socialists "regard social classes as the key component of social thought and practice, and regard the promotion of distributive justice as the appropriate public priority". These different versions of integrationism generate disagreement on constitutional particulars. For example, McGarry, O'Leary, and Simeon note a difference of opinion between republican and liberal integrationists on federal-ism. Republican integrationists—they use France and Turkey as examples—are opposed to political decentralization, on the basis of the constitutional theory that federalism undermines the sovereignty and indivisibility of the nation. Liberal integrationists support federalism, not in order to accommodate minor-ity nationalism, but in order to protect liberty and expand the opportunities for democratic citizenship.

Similarly, McGarry, O'Leary, and Simeon differentiate among four varieties of accommodation: Centripetalism, multiculturalism, consociation, and ter-ritorial pluralism. However, upon closer examination, it is apparent that these categories overlap to a considerable extent. The clearest contrast is between cen-tripetalism and consociation, with Horowitz and Lijphart offered as the leading examples. Multiculturalism, according to McGarry, O'Leary, and Simeon, calls for "a group's self-government in matters the group defines as important"—such as a nonterritorial version of segmental autonomy, which is a primary feature of consociation. Pluralist federation, defined as a federalism "which respects his-toric nationalities, languages or religions", is a territorial version of segmental autonomy. So within the accommodationist camp, the principal contrast remains between Lijphart and Horowitz, although McGarry, O'Leary, and Simeon rightly emphasize that the consociational package can in fact be disaggregated into its constituent components.

McGarry, O'Leary, and Simeon introduce important elaborations on the consociational model. In particular, McGarry, O'Leary, and Simeon distin-guish between three varieties of executive power sharing—the grand coalition or "complete" consociations (such as Bosnia-Herzegovina's collective presi-dency), "concurrent" consociations in which a representative of the majority of each group is represented, and "plurality" consociations, in which a plurality of each group's representatives participates in the government (for example, like the Northern Ireland power-sharing executive). In addition, McGarry, O'Leary, and Simeon place the various accommodationist responses on a spectrum, with some regarded as stronger forms of accommodation while others are much closer to integration. McGarry, O'Leary, and Simeon rightly place Horowitz on the integrationist end of the accommodationist spectrum. Indeed, at times it is hard to distinguish Horowitz's institutional prescriptions from the ones that an integrationist would propose. For example, republican integrationists support a strong executive president as "a unifying figure capable of standing above group and faction"; Horowitz is also a strong supporter of a presidential system in the hope that it would promote "a trans-ethnic identity". Nonetheless, because of his belief that once differences have been mobilized, they are hard to unwind, Horowitz clearly falls into the accommodationist camp.

McGarry, O'Leary, and Simeon then offer a preliminary assessment of each family of responses along the dimensions of stability, justice and democracy. To a considerable extent, this assessment turns on the prior question of the durability or malleability of ethnic identities. Thus, with respect to stability, integrationists argue that accommodation will fuel instability and deepen divisions, because it empowers elites who have a vested interest in maintaining these divisions. They also point to the failure of consociations (such as Cyprus in 1963, Lebanon in 1975), and pluralist federations (such as the former communist federations of Eastern and Central Europe) as proof that accommodation does not work. Integration is a realistic alternative, precisely because crosscutting identities exist and can be fostered. Accommodationists counter that integrationist policies do not work in divided societies because segmental divisions are real. Promoting integration in this context "creates at best an unstable equilibrium" that leads to assimilation, accommodation, or secession. In conclusion, McGarry, O'Leary, and Simeon believe that the success of integration or accommodation is a product of demography. Integration is more likely to succeed with respect to dispersed ethnic groups, whereas accommodation will be necessary when groups exist "powerful enough to resist assimilation but not strong or united enough to achieve secession".

The integration-accommodation debate, as set out by McGarry, O'Leary, and Simeon, clearly provides a different framework within which to debate the issue of constitutional design for divided societies than the framework provided by the numerous exchanges between Lijphart and Horowitz. But is it a better framework? It is, for at least three reasons.

First, it is more historically informed. Lijphart and Horowitz take the fact that ethnic differences have been politically mobilized as their starting point, and are focused on how constitutional design should respond today. But rarely do Lijphart and Horowitz turn to the historical causes of present-day ethnic conflict. In *Democracy in Plural Societies*, Lijphart rarely describes what ethnic conflict is or has been over. By contrast, Horowitz devotes considerable attention to this issue in *Ethnic Groups in Conflict*. But he rarely deploys this analysis in his contemporary assessment of constitutional options. For both, history figures mostly as a source of historical case-studies of successful and unsuccessful experiments in constitutional design.

By contrast, the various integrationist approaches remind us, as Will Kymlicka argues, that ethnic conflict is very often part and parcel of nation building, which is designed to produce a degree of common national identity across the entire territory of the state, to be shared by all of its citizens.[79] The means employed include policies centered on language, history and culture, and the centralization of legal and political power.[80] Constitutions have played a central role in this process, both in the regulative sense of creating institutions with state-wide authority to permit the creation and enforcement of these policies, and in the constitutive sense of projecting an image of political community meant to be internalized by citizens. The goals of nation building are diverse. David Miller has suggested that one reason for nation building is to provide the necessary motivational element missing from liberal accounts of political legitimacy.[81] A sense of identification with a particular set of liberal democratic institutions and laws moves individuals to make those institutions work, and to accept their demands. Ernest Gellner argued that linguistic homogenization is a tool of economic integration and the enhancement of economic opportunity, since it permits citizens to become members of a mobile and flexible workforce across the entire state.[82] The use of nation building as a tool of political consolidation originated in Western Europe, and spread with the rise of nationalism to Eastern and Central Europe, and with decolonization to Asia and Africa. Ethnic conflict has arisen when ethnic minorities resist nation building efforts. For example, minority nations, whose members formed complete, functioning societies on their territory, with a large degree of self-rule, prior to their incorporation into the larger state resist nation-building efforts, and engage in minority nation building as a defensive response.

The history of nation-building reminds us where ethnic conflict often comes from. But it also reminds us that integrationist policies have historically been important—if not entirely successful—tools for the political consolidation of an ethnically diverse population into the unified citizenry of a single state. This leads us to the second benefit of the integration-accommodation framework to conflict regulation—it sharpens our understanding of the contemporary politics of conflict regulation. In the debate over conflict regulation, proponents of accommodation often claim to have a more realistic understanding of the intractability of ethnically based political divisions, and can lay claim to a more pragmatic set

---

[79] Will Kymlicka, Multicultural Odysseys: Navigating the New International Politics of Diversity (Oxford Univ. Press 2007).

[80] Eugene Weber, Peasants Into Frenchmen: The Modernization of Rural France, 1880–1914 (Stanford Univ. Press 1976).

[81] David Miller, On Nationality (Oxford Univ. Press 1995).

[82] Ernest Gellner, Nations and Nationalism (Cornell Univ. Press 1983).

of responses to those divisions. Integrationists are depicted as naïve and lacking a sense of history. However, integrationists draw on historical antecedents that serve as powerful normative benchmarks for contemporary debates. The integrationist approach to political consolidation exerts a powerful hold over the political imagination. Even if integrationists are overly optimistic, it is important to understand where that optimism comes from.

Third, framing the debate between integrationists and accommodationists as turning on an underlying debate on the durability or malleability of ethnic identities brings to the fore that prior question. Since Horowitz and Lijphart dominate the literature, and share the view that politically mobilized ethnic identities are givens to be accommodated, this issue is not at the heart of comparative politics. However, this premise merits interrogation. As Richard Pildes ("Ethnic identity and democratic institutions: A dynamic perspective") usefully points out, the dominant assumption in the literature may be a function of the fact that ethnic claims appear at "critical political moments," such as the formation of states or the immediate aftermath of armed conflict. Pildes does more than argue that the political salience of ethnic identities is fluid. In addition, he suggests that the structure of political competition can create the incentive for political entrepreneurs and elites to mobilize ethnic identities politically. Pildes supports this point by drawing on examples from India, Africa, and the United States. As a consequence, rather than static conceptions of ethnic identity driving constitutional design, constitutional arrangements should be deployed to create crosscutting cleavages.

But other contributions to the volume are much more sanguine than Pildes about how malleable politically mobilized ethnic identities are. In their chapter on Iraq, McGarry and O'Leary ("Iraq's Constitution of 2005: Liberal consociation as political prescription) begin by noting that proponents of integrationist constitutional arrangements for Iraq "see Iraq's current problems as based on sectarianism and ethnocentrism, usually of recent rather than rooted in established or age-old hatreds". Their defence of Iraq's constitution as an example of liberal consociation proceeds from the assumption that integrationist accounts of the phenomenology of ethnic identities in Iraq are incorrect. Pointing to "the current civil war, and recent election and referendum results", McGarry and O'Leary conclude "that Iraq is deeply divided, with a divided past", and that "these divisions cannot be overcome easily in the near future". Their chapter on Northern Ireland ("Consociation and its critics: Northern Ireland after the Belfast Agreement") likewise treats the static or dynamic nature of politically mobilized ethnic identities as the fundamental issue on which constitutional design depends. They argue that "[f]or over a century, historic Ulster, and the Northern Ireland that was carved from it, had been divided electorally into two rival ethnonational blocs". The strength of this cleavage is reflected in the minimal and declining levels of electoral support received by nonethnic parties, a reality "that will not be easily transformed by changes in the electoral system".

4. Lessons for the integration-accommodation debate

What other lessons do the remaining chapters offer for the integration-accommodation debate?

First, although McGarry and O'Leary do not say so explicitly, it is implicit that each variety of integration and accommodation amounts to a comprehensive and mutually exclusive constitutional strategy. Each perspective favors certain options over others across a number of different dimensions of constitutional design, ranging from symbolic issues (such as the wording of preambles) to the choice of official languages; the existence and character of internal political boundaries; the nature of the electoral system used to elect the legislature; the selection process, composition and powers of the political executive, the bureaucracy, and the judiciary; the rules governing the formation of political parties; and the relationship between religious institutions and the state.

However, as a number of the chapters demonstrate, actual constitutions—including those which are closely identified with one of these two perspectives—contain a mixture of integrationist and accommodationist elements. Tierney ("Giving with one hand: Scottish devolution within a unitary state") explores the system of asymmetric federalism established in Scotland through the Scotland Act 1998. Tierney argues that the devolution settlement is accommodationist in some respects, but "[i]n other ways . . . the settlement embodies strong centralizing or integrative tendencies". So on the one hand, the Scotland Act confers considerable regional autonomy on Scotland of a highly asymmetric nature (given that no such autonomy is conferred on England and much less autonomy on Wales), which is acknowledgment of Scotland's claims to nationhood within the United Kingdom, alongside explicit symbolic recognition of its national status. But on the other, civil servants in Scotland and the entire United Kingdom "operate within one employment and promotion system". The central government retains control over taxation, and central institutions such as the House of Lords and the new Supreme Court do not reflect the United Kingdom's plurinational nature in their composition or manner of appointment.

Choudhry's ("Does the world need more Canada? The politics of the Canadian model in constitutional politics and political theory") discussion of the "Canadian model" of multinational federalism leads to a similar conclusion. Choudhry argues that although the Canadian model has been presented as a paradigmatic instance of accommodation, on careful examination, it consists of a mixture of accommodationist and integrationist strategies that extend far beyond multinational federalism. The Canadian constitution creates a federation in which the boundaries of the province of Quebec were drawn so that francophones constitute a majority and are not outvoted by Canada's anglophone majority. In addition, Quebec has jurisdiction over policy areas to ensure the survival of a French-speaking society, including language and education. But since provinces have limited jurisdiction, important decisions of interest to the citizens of Quebec lie within federal jurisdiction, such as immigration policy, income taxation, foreign policy, and defence. Citizens of Quebec must participate in the institutions of the common state in order to shape important political decisions which directly affect them. In addition, institutions of shared rule at the federal level, although they display some accommodationist elements, are largely integrationist—the House of Commons is directly elected by the citizenry; the federal House of Commons and Senate pass bills by simple majority vote, with no formal role for the Quebec government, or Quebec members of Parliament or Senators in the federal legislative process; and the constitutional conventions of responsible government for a Westminster democracy apply without any modification for the fact that Canada is a multinational state.

Bertrand ("Indonesia's quasi-federalist approach: Accommodation amid strong integrationist tendencies") tells a similar story. From early independence, the Indonesian state emphasized the building of a strong nation with a unitary constitution, and rejected proposals for a federal Indonesia put forth by Dutch colonial authorities. The inspiration was republic integrationism. This integrationist approach worked for the most part; where it did not, as in Aceh and Papua, resistance was harshly repressed. Since 1998, however, Indonesia has adopted a more accommodationist strategy in dealing with ethnonationalist groups. Thus, legislation has been enacted, which on paper, grants Aceh and Papua significant degrees of autonomy. However, the rest of Indonesia is still organized on unitary grounds. Moreover, Bertrand claims that there are "powerful behavioral norms that pull the Indonesian political elite persistently in the direction of supporting strong measures to preserve national unity rather than accommodating diversity". To Bertrand, this constitutional mindset explains why Indonesia's recent institutional experiment in autonomy has not been implemented.

Ejobowah ("Integrationist and accommodationist measures in Nigeria's constitutional engineering: Successes and failures") likewise argues that Nigeria has combined integration with accommodation. The principal institution of accommodation has been federalism, which "has enabled territorially concentrated groups to have their own self-governing units and preserved the country by fragmenting groups and undermining their coherence". The effect of this accommodation has been to quarantine some political conflicts at the state level by multiplying the centers of power subject to political contestation. The principal integrationist elements have been central control over oil revenue, which is largely generated by activity in the Niger Delta, and which is redistributed to the regions; and a presidential system of government with an electoral system which requires widespread support from across the country (a proxy for ethnicity). For Ejobowah, the integrationist elements have been the principal sources of constitutional failure, for two reasons. First, it failed "to free the presidency from the control of the most powerful groups", because politicians from large ethnic groups enjoy a competitive advantage, since they can count on the support of several states. Second, central control over oil revenues "confers great economic importance on executive offices" which distribute oil wealth. This has spawned "a destructive patronage system" in which office holders offer "political clients licences to sell" oil, and has generated often violent conflict.

The fact that actual constitutions contain a mixture of integrationist and accommodationist elements raises the question of why this is the case. Choudhry suggests although multinational federalism has as its goal the preservation of the territorial integrity and political unity of the state, it could instead perversely fuel secession. Integrationist constitutional instruments offset this danger, by binding the federal subunit to the state, for example, by requiring its citizens to participate in shared institutions. Choudhry also notes that integrationist and accommodationist approaches can be combined in different ways. In a multinational federation, one strategy is to limit the scope of accommodation, for example, by forcing certain decisions to be made in common institutions in which a national subunit does not have a veto. Another is to balance an accommodationist strategy in one area of constitutional design against an integrationist strategy in another. He suggests that in Canada, multinational federalism has been counterbalanced by the nation-building aspects of the *Canadian Charter of Rights and Freedoms*.

If the combination of integrationist and accommodationist elements is deliberate, the next question is whether such a combination is in fact stable. Choudhry suggests it is not. He argues that the Canadian constitutional crisis of the mid 1990s—during which Quebec nearly seceded from Canada—was traceable to the competing constitutional logics flowing from the intertwining and mutual reinforcement of constitutional text and constitutional politics. Combining integrationist and accommodationist elements within the same constitutional system fuels further demands and rounds of constitutional politics to perfect the constitutional text. For example, the accommodation of Quebec (reflected in the federal nature of Canada) and the Charter (which embodies a notion of Canada of equal citizens who bear identical constitutional rights irrespective of province of residence) came into conflict over proposals to constitutionally recognize Quebec as a distinct society. If such recognition would allow Quebec to justifiably limit Charter rights to enable it to preserve and promote its linguistic identity, it collides with the idea of the Charter as the spine of equal citizenship.

The Canadian debates over the recognition of Quebec's distinctiveness constitutionally—recently recapitulated in the debate in the fall of 2006 over whether Quebec should be recognized as a nation—suggest that an important topic for comparative study should be the constitutional dynamics created by the inclusion of integrationist and accommodationist elements within the same constitutional document. Canada illustrates the impact of a hybrid constitution on the politics of constitutional amendment. As Pildes recounts in his chapter, Bosnia and Herzegovina furnishes an example of the impact of constitutional adjudication. The Dayton Peace Accords—which are the constitution of Bosnia and

Herzegovina—combine two sets of conflicting elements. On the one hand, it sets up a confederation between the Republika Srpska and the Federation of Bosnia-Herzegovina, and presupposes that each unit is the principal home of its "constituent peoples"—Serbs for the former and Croats and Bosniaks for the latter. But the Dayton Peace Accords also incorporate the *European Convention of Human Rights* into domestic law. As a consequence, a range of policies adopted by each constituent unit to define itself in ethnically specific terms—such as describing the Republika Srpska as "a State of Serb People" and terming "Bosniaks and Croats as constituent peoples" of the Federation of Bosnia-Herzegovina, the renaming of cities to connote that they are exclusively Serbian, and the adoption of ethnically specific official coats of arms—was held by the Constitutional Court of Bosnia-Herzegovina to be an unconstitutional form of discrimination.[83]

Emon ("The limits of constitutionalism in the Muslim world: History and identity in Islamic law") also points to the problem of competing constitutional logics embedded in the same constitutional text. Emon argues that the contemporary constitutions of Islamic states are beset by an internal contradiction on precisely the issue of accommodation versus integration. On the one hand, they take the integrationist line on religious freedom, and the rights of religious minorities in particular. But on the other hand, they are accommodationist with respect to the status of Islamic law. They recognize and institutionalize difference, as opposed to adopting a stance of neutrality with respect to the religious identity of the majority. The problem is that the two sets of constitutional commitments are in deep tension with each other. The challenge for Islamic constitutionalism is how to resolve this tension. Emon argues that "resort to theories of accommodation or integration, by themselves... does not adequately address the roots of the tension or offer constructive modes of resolution". Rather, the answer is to historically situate and contextualize the rules of Islamic law, which were framed centuries ago and today "are applied in settings marked by profound institutional, political, and social alterations".

Second, several chapters argue that the dichotomy between integration and accommodation—even taking into account the variations within each—may require further refinement. Patten ("Beyond the dichotomy of universalism and difference: Four responses to cultural diversity") suggests "the dichotomous way of thinking... is too simple to do justice the problems being considered", and is a "simplification" which "leads to a serious distortion of the possible solutions to the problems raised by diversity, the normative grounds available on behalf of those solutions, and the ways that real-world conflicts should be understood". Instead of two families of responses, there are four: Disestablishment (where the

---

[83] *See* Case No. U-5/98, Partial Decisions I–IV (Jan. 29, Feb. 18, July 1, Aug. 18, 2000) (Bosn. & Herz.); Case No. U-44/01, Decision (Sept. 22, 2004) (Bosn. & Herz.); Case No. U-4/04, Partial Decisions I–II (Mar. 31, Nov. 18, 2006) (Bosn. & Herz.) (decisions available at <http://www.ustavnisud.ba/eng/odluke/>). See also David Feldman, *Renaming Cities in Bosnia and Herzegovina*, 3 Int'l J. Const. L. (I•CON) 649 (2003) for a general discussion.

state gives no recognition to any cultural identity), nation building (where the state promotes one cultural identity for all of its citizens), cultural preservation (where the state promotes the survival of distinct cultures), and equality of status (where the state accords cultures equal public status, but does not guarantee their survival). The first two are different and mutually inconsistent interpretations of integrationism, whereas the last two are different and mutually exclusive interpretations of accommodationism. Patten explores each of these different principles by reference to language policy.

Tierney also challenges the idea that integration and accommodation capture the full range of ways in which states can respond to ethnic political mobilization. He does so in two related ways, both in the context of substate nationalism. First, Tierney challenges the use of the term accommodation to describe the constitutional demands of substate nations. To Tierney, the term accommodation implies a hierarchical relationship with "the entity doing the accommodating...and the entity being accommodated". It is precisely this hierarchical relationship that substate nations challenge. Thus, "substate national societies call for partnership *with* the dominant society rather than accommodation *by* it". This reframing of the demands of substate nations leads Tierney to distinguish between two different ways in which a substate society participates in political decision by the large polity—what he terms "partnership integration" and "assimilationist integration". Whereas the former "provides for the equal engagement of the state's national societies", the latter consists of "the subjection of substate national societies to decisions by the center in...which the substate units have only minimally or inadequately participated". In Tierney's opinion, Scottish devolution is more the latter than the former, which means that the United Kingdom has not yet fully embraced plurinational federalism.

Choudhry likewise seeks to challenge the binary framework established by McGarry, O'Leary, and Simeon, in context of his reflections on the Canadian case. He distinguishes between two ways to accommodate minority nationalism—"accommodation as institutional separateness" and "accommodation designed to facilitate participation in common institutions". In the context of minority nationalism, McGarry, O'Leary, and Simeon, appear to comprehend accommodation as the former, not the latter. The principal example of accommodation as institutional separateness is ethnofederalism—the creation of a federal subunit in which an ethnic minority constitutes a majority, and where the subunit has jurisdiction over matters crucial to the survival of the ethnic minority. But in the Canadian case, an equally important method of accommodation has been to facilitate the participation of francophones in common federal institutions, without being asked to use English. Thus, the constitution declares both English and French to be the official languages of Canada, permits both languages to be used in parliamentary debates, provides that statutes must be enacted in both languages, and gives francophones the right to use French in court proceedings and to communicate with and receive services in French where there is sufficient demand.

Simeon and Murray also seek to supplement the taxonomy established by McGarry, O'Leary, and Simeon by describing a constitutional strategy they term "recognition without empowerment". In their view, this is the best way to make sense of the South African case. The South African constitution gives strong recognition to diversity and difference in "cultural and social life" while seeking to the greatest extent possible to prevent ethnocultural differences from entering the design of the political system. Thus, the constitution grants the right to receive education in the official language of one's choice; there are eleven official languages in total. But the South African constitution rejects any form of executive power sharing, opting instead for a modified Westminster model of government and opposition with competitive party politics. In their view, this strategy has been a success, because it prevented linguistic and ethnic differences among black South Africans from becoming bases of political division by relegating them to the private sphere and removing them as topics of political debate.

Third, the chapters also suggest that accommodation may be deployed as a transitional stage toward integration. Accommodation may be the only practical option at important moments in the lifecycle of a constitutional order, such as the transition to democratic rule. But once the order is operational, and members of ethnic groups develop reciprocal bonds of trust, it may be possible to move to a more integrationist set of political institutions. Simeon and Murray describe the South African constitutional transition in these terms. The apartheid regime and the African National Congress (ANC) negotiated an interim constitution (which came into force in 1993) in which any party winning 20 percent of the seats in the National Assembly (elections are held on the basis of proportional representation) would be entitled to a deputy president, and any party winning at least 5 percent to representation in the cabinet. The result was a government of national unity led by the ANC which included the National Party and the Inkatha Freedom Party. The goal was to ensure the success of the transition by giving major parties a stake in its survival. The 1996 constitution, by contrast, opted for a majoritarian political system on the Westminster model with no executive power sharing.

Fourth, the chapters extend the scope of traditional debates over constitutional design for divided societies, by broadening the spheres with respect to which the choice between integration and accommodation must be made. One way of understanding the South African transition (described by Simeon and Murray) is in the following way: The grand bargain between the apartheid regime and the African National Congress was to agree to a liberal democratic constitutional order with limited and transitional arrangements for power sharing (which were intended and had the effect of including the National Party in a government of national unity) while leaving the pattern of white ownership in the economy largely untouched, at least for an initial period. In other words, integration in the political order was agreed to in exchange for accommodation in the economic order. To focus on the constitution to the exclusion of the economy would arguably miss the actual choices and trade-offs that made the transition to democracy possible in the context of deep racial divisions.

Ghai and Cottrell's analysis of Fiji also makes clear the link between the constitutional and the economic orders in divided societies. The two major ethnic groups in Fiji are indigenous Fijians and Indians. Ghai and Cottrell read Fijian history, in large part, as a conflict between Fijians, who wished to preserve their traditional land holdings, and the demands of the market, which required land for sugar plantations that were heavily dependent on imported Indian labor. The political economy of ethnic conflict in Fiji has shaped constitutional politics and constitutional design, with Indians and Fijians on opposite sides of a debate over the alienability of land, in addition to a debate over the structure of political institutions on racial or nonracial lines. A major goal for Fijians has been to use the constitution to protect their land holdings. As a consequence, there is a constitutional prohibition on the alienation of their land holdings to non-Fijians.

Keating ("Rival nationalisms in a plurinational state: Spain, Catalonia and the Basque Country") appears to suggest that the literature has been too focused on formal constitutional design as a mechanism for accommodating minority nationalism, and has therefore ignored subconstitutional and informal mechanisms of accommodation which may be equally, if not more, important. He makes this point through his discussion of the Spanish case, where political parties and statutes have played an important role in the accommodation of Catalan nationalism. The leading Catalan political party—the Convergència i Unió— has been an important political player at the national level, because it has fielded parliamentary candidates. For most of the time since 1993, Spanish governments from across the political spectrum were dependent on CiU support to maintain power, although the CiU did not join the government. The CiU used its political power to secure considerable autonomy for Catalonia through statute. By contrast, although the constitution provided the framework within which debates over Catalan autonomy took place proclaiming at once "the indissoluble unity of the Spanish nation" as a whole, while recognizing within the Spanish nation and under the constitution the right to autonomy of the nationalities—the relevant provisions of the constitution have remained unaltered since 1978.

McGarry and O'Leary ("Consocation and its critics: Northern Ireland after the Belfast Agreement") bring home the importance of security issues in crafting constitutional arrangements for divided societies. They argue that the focus of consociational theory has been "on the design of and need for agreement on *political* institutions", but that minimal attention "has been paid to a number of crucial sectors in violently divided places, such as the design of the police and security forces", and policies toward paramilitary forces (including their integration into the police and security forces), disarmament, and so on. They argue that disagreement on security issues was much greater than disagreement on the design of the political system. The fact that the Belfast Agreement was silent on these issues, in their view, undermined the effectiveness of the consociational arrangements which it set up. They conclude that "[h]ad the security issues been better managed from the start, it was not inevitable that the institutions would have been unstable".

Finally, the chapters highlight the growing international role in crafting constitutional structures for divided societies. Kymlicka notes the growing role of the international community in "endorsing some models of integration and accommodation while discouraging others", and the use of economic, technical and military incentives to back up those recommendations. Kymlicka challenges the view set out in the overview chapters that integration is promoted by the international community. Instead, Kymlicka argues that within the Untied Nations, there appears to be a division between the treatment accorded to "indigenous peoples" and "minorities". Indigenous peoples are entitled to self-government, whereas minorities are only entitled to the traditional liberal freedoms and the right to non-discrimination. Kymlicka also examines the attempt within the Council of Europe to develop a distinct set of norms for "national minorities", which would have encompassed a right to regional autonomy. However, this effort failed, raising serious questions about the potential of international law to advance the claims of national minorities. At most, there is "a political practice of case-specific interventions" supportive of autonomy, which appears to be "rewarding belligerence".

Choudhry argues that Kymlicka has played a major role in encouraging the adoption of multinational federalism as a constitutional device to accommodate the claims of national minorities for over a decade. Moreover, although in recent work he has become more skeptical regarding the possible transplantation of this model outside North America and Western Europe, he is still arguing that it has been successful in those regions. Choudhry argues that Kymlicka's model of multinational federalism is largely based on Canada's constitutional arrangements, and so is, in fact, the Canadian model. He then seeks to contextualize the rise of the Canadian model in political theory, by observing that it coincided with a severe constitutional crisis within Canada that nearly led to the breakup of the country. Choudhry argues that the rise of the Canadian model and its promotion internationally was also an intervention in domestic constitutional politics, designed to shore up support for the Canadian model at home. He further argues that the true lesson of the model is the limited ability of rules governing constitutional amendment to regulate existential moments of constitutional politics in multinational polities, such as secession.

O'Leary and McGarry also discuss the central role of international involvement in facilitating the consociational arrangements in place in Northern Ireland. A critical factor, in their view, was the decision of the United Kingdom to directly involve the Irish government in the resolution of the Northern Ireland conflict. Another factor was the role played by the United States to encourage a political settlement. O'Leary and McGarry generalize from the Northern Ireland experience to paint a different picture of international involvement than Kymlicka. In their view, there has been extensive "[b]enign exogenous action" which has "facilitated power-sharing settlements elsewhere, not just in Northern Ireland" but also "in Bosnia and Herzegovina, Macedonia, Iraq, and Afghanistan". In their view, far from being an unprincipled and ad hoc practice, international involvement "can play positive roles and can tip the balance in favor of negotiated or induced agreements".

2

Integration or accommodation?
The enduring debate in conflict regulation

John McGarry*, Brendan O'Leary**, and Richard Simeon***

Two prevalent sets of public policies are available to democratic states willing or obliged to manage national, ethnic, and communal diversity. The orthodox wisdom drives under the banner of integration while the other flies under the flag of accommodation. Integration promotes a single public identity coterminous with the state's territory. It commends a common and functional single public house, a Le Corbusier-style tower block with uniform apartments. It makes no formal commendation on how private apartments should be maintained or decorated. Integrationists primarily seek the equality of individual citizens before the law and within public institutions. With the sole exception of the state's citizenship they are against the public institutional recognition of group identities, but they accept collective diversity in private realms. They see integration as the key to a progressive politics, political stability, public unity, and the transcendence of group-based chauvinism.

Accommodation, by contrast, commends a legally flexible condominium complex, one that respects historic hybrids, add-ons, multiple architects, and contrarian interior designers, and makes no effort to achieve uniformity in the mansion ensemble. Accommodation promotes dual or multiple public identities, and its proponents advocate equality with institutional respect for differences. They believe that is what is required for the stable management of deep diversity. To confuse matters, some integrationists insist they are accommodationists because they are not assimilationists, whereas some accommodationists insist they are integrationists because they are not advocates of the breakup of sovereign states.

* Professor of Political Studies; Canada Research Chair in Nationalism and Democracy, Queen's University, Kingston, Ontario. McGarry would like to thank the Carnegie Corporation of New York and the Social Science and Humanities Research Council of Canada for research funding. Email: mcgarryj@post.queensu.ca

** Lauder Professor of Political Science; director of the Penn Program in Ethnic Conflict, University of Pennsylvania. O'Leary would like to thank the Lauder endowment and the Social Sciences and Humanities Research Council of Canada for aiding his research. Email: boleary@sas.upenn.edu

*** Professor of Political Science and Law, University of Toronto; MacKenzie King Visiting Professor, Department of Government, Harvard University; Email: rsimeon@wcfia.harvard.edu

Integration and accommodation constitute two major repertoires in the feasible set of strategic responses to group diversity. But they do not cover the full range of state responses. Elsewhere, we have divided this set into those that eliminate and those that manage differences.[1] Genocide, expulsion, assimilation, and territorial downsizing are used to eliminate differences. Integration, while respecting differences in the private domain, involves the elimination of differences in the public sphere. It aims at public homogenization through common citizenship. By contrast, arbitration, control, centripetalism, consociation, credible multiculturalism, and territorial pluralism are the major proposals for managing difference. Accommodation encompasses the last four of these proposed strategies. It allows for the public and institutional expression of differences in the public sphere. While integration responds to diversity through institutions that transcend, crosscut, and minimize differences, accommodationist strategies seek to ensure that each group has the public space necessary for it to express its identity, to protect itself against tyranny by the majority, and to make its own decisions in domains of critical importance.

1. Distinguishing integration and accommodation from assimilation

Integration and accommodation as public policies need to be distinguished from assimilation, with which the former especially is often confused. The confusion arises because some integrationists favor assimilation as an end goal, or less vigorously, they see it as a welcome byproduct of the success of their endeavors.

Assimilationists seek the erosion of private cultural and other sorts of difference among citizens as well as the creation of a common public identity, through either fusion or acculturation. Fusion involves two or more communities mixing to form something new (A+B=C). Acculturation involves one community adopting the culture of another and being absorbed into it (A+B=A). Assimilation, therefore, erodes both the public and private differences between and among groups. Assimilation may occur without the help of public policy, or as a direct or indirect result of it. Neither integration nor accommodation, by contrast, requires cultural conformity across the public and private dimensions of life. Integration promotes a common public space but the maintenance of private cultural differences or, more strictly, indifference towards such differences. Accommodation promotes both the public and private maintenance of cultural difference.

---

[1] John McGarry & Brendan O'Leary, *Introduction: The Macro-Political Regulation of Ethnic Conflict, in* THE POLITICS OF ETHNIC CONFLICT REGULATION: CASE STUDIES OF PROTRACTED ETHNIC CONFLICTS 1 (John McGarry & Brendan O'Leary eds., Routledge 1993); Brendan O'Leary, *The Elements of Right-Sizing and Right-Peopling the State, in* RIGHT-SIZING THE STATE: THE POLITICS OF MOVING BORDERS 15 (Brendan O'Leary, Ian S. Lustick & Thomas M. Callaghy eds., Oxford Univ. Press 2001).

Integrationists and accommodationists converge in rejecting coercive assimilation. They condemn ethnocide, the killing of cultures, linguicide, the killing of languages, and theocide, the deliberate killing of particular religious cultures. Linguicide may take the form of homogenizing and standardizing mutually intelligible languages, which are stigmatized as dialects, socializing children in schools into the standard language, in some cases into what is known as received pronunciation (RP). Other languages may be declared illegal. Until the early part of the twenty-first century, Turkey practiced coercive linguistic assimilation. The Kurds, for example, were coded as "mountain Turks" who had lost their language through some mysterious conjunction of amnesia and life at higher contours.[2] A typical symptom of this assimilationist enterprise is the official refusal to provide public education in minority languages, especially in the tertiary sector. Coercive religious assimilation involves standardization, monopolization, and socialization under a state church, and illegalizing rivals. In Ireland, under various English and British rulers, and indeed throughout the United Kingdom, Roman Catholicism was declared illegal, and Acts of Uniformity were passed. The law was famously understood as not recognizing that such a person as a Roman Catholic existed.[3] "Historical standardization" also indicates assimilationist policies. People on small islands thousands of miles from metropolitan France during the Third Republic were taught in their textbooks about "Our Ancestors, the Gauls". Whatever else the Gauls may have been distinguished for in the storybooks of Asterix or the texts of Julius Caesar, they were not the ancestors of the said children. Schools in assimilationist programs standardize mythologies, to persuade children that they share a common ancestry, whether fact or fiction.[4] The curriculum emphasizes homogeneity and equates acculturation with civilizing the acculturated. Coercively assimilationist states ensure that the units of territorial governance do not respect nationality, ethnicity, language, or religious identity. Instead, public administration is usually formally organized on formal, rationalist and hierarchical principles related to size, economy of scale, or other efficiency criteria. Functional professionalism matters more than the recognition of historic, cultural, ethnic or sacred ties. The same goes for the organization of public housing, when it exists, and the organization of public schools. The institutions are uniform everywhere—with the same patterns, styles, numbers of people required to be in the vicinity, and, of course, curricula. The most overt marker of a coercively assimilationist state is the illegalization of minority nationalist, ethnic and communal parties.

---

[2] HASSAN ARFA, THE KURDS: AN HISTORICAL AND POLITICAL STUDY (Oxford Univ. Press 1966); U.S. HELSINKI WATCH COMM., DESTROYING ETHNIC IDENTITY, THE KURDS OF TURKEY (1988).
  [3] Maureen Wall, *The Penal Laws 1691–1760, in* CATHOLIC IRELAND IN THE EIGHTEENTH CENTURY: COLLECTED ESSAYS OF MAUREEN WALL 1 (Gerard O'Brien ed., Geography Publ'n 1989).
  [4] EUGEN WEBER, PEASANTS INTO FRENCHMEN: THE MODERNIZATION OF RURAL FRANCE, 1870–1914 (Chatto & Windus 1979).

Assimilation's advocates proclaim that it promotes nation building, with benefits for social solidarity, stability, and territorial integrity, and civilizational uplift. John Stuart Mill famously remarked that it was much better to become part of the British or French culture than to be a Highlander or some wild Breton sitting on a rock.[5] His disciple, Lord Durham, argued that assimilation into British culture and institutions would civilize the French Canadians. Many on the left believe assimilation to be of great benefit to rocksitting communities, described by Friedrich Engels as "unhistoric peoples".[6] Assimilationists are often benevolent paternalists, believing that assimilation is the best way to help native or indigenous peoples.[7] The same mentality may be displayed toward purportedly "strange" immigrants, or those from poverty-ridden cultures. The cosmopolitan argues that assimilation breaks parochial, bigoted, small-scale and constraining cultures.[8] Interculturality, movement across cultural boundaries, and the transformations of cultural boundaries, as a result of fusion, are beneficial. Assimilation here is additive: A and B fuse to become C, but the new C benefits from the cultures of both A and B. Libertarians believe assimilation reflects people's choices, albeit socialized choices, over the long run and maintain that governments should not artificially preserve dying cultures and languages. This is the equivalent of protecting industries that would not survive in free private markets.[9]

Both integrationists and accommodationists formally oppose coercive assimilation, and the preceding apologias, but there is a subtle parting of the ways. Integrationists tend to favor voluntary assimilation, because of some of assimilation's presumptive benefits, and especially because it makes blindness to difference easier to achieve in the public domain. They are predisposed toward voluntary inducements to fuse, such as policies that mix people in schools, workplaces and neighborhoods. They are more interested in what Robert Putnam calls building "bridging capital" than "bonding capital".[10] Accommodationists are usually open-minded about voluntary assimilation, but by contrast are much less concerned to promote it, less likely to think it will happen, and more likely to believe it will be destabilizing because it will create fear of extinction in at least one community.

[5] JOHN STUART MILL, UTILITARIANISM, ON LIBERTY AND CONSIDERATIONS ON REPRESENTATIVE GOVERNMENT 391–398 (Harry Burrows Acton ed., J.M. Dent & Sons 1988) (1863).

[6] HORACE BANCROFT DAVIS, NATIONALISM AND SOCIALISM: MARXIST AND LABOUR THEORIES OF NATIONALISM TO 1917 (Monthly Rev. Press 1967).

[7] For a conservative expression of this view, see THOMAS FLANAGAN, FIRST NATIONS? SECOND THOUGHTS (McGill-Queen's Univ. Press 2000).

[8] Jeremy Waldron, *Minority Cultures and the Cosmopolitan Alternative*, 25 U. MICH. J.L. REFORM 751 (1992).

[9] *See* Chandran Kukathas, *Are There Any Cultural Rights?*, 20 POL. THEORY 105 (1992).

[10] ROBERT PUTNAM, BOWLING ALONE: THE COLLAPSE AND REVIVAL OF AMERICAN COMMUNITY (Simon & Schuster 2000).

2. Integration

Webster's 2003 dictionary instructs us that the verb to integrate and its noun have the following meanings:

> **integrate** 1: to form, coordinate, or blend into a functioning and united whole: UNITE 2: to find the integral of... 3a: to unite with something else b to incorporate into a larger unit 4a *to end the segregation of and bring into equal membership in society or an organization* b DESEGREGATE (school districts) v.i. to become integrated.

> **integration** 1: The act or process or an instance of integrating as a: incorporation as equals into society or an organization of individuals of different groups (as races) b coordination of mental processes into a normal effective personality or with the individual's environment 2a: the operation of finding a function whose differential is known b: the operation of solving a differential equation.[11]

The conventional political understandings of integration are apparent here. Meaning 3a of the verb, "to unite with something else", is unproblematic. Meaning 1 "to form, coordinate, or blend into a functioning and united whole" suggests an overlap with assimilation, which aims to make people culturally similar. However, here we draw attention to meaning 1a of the noun, namely the "incorporation as equals into society or an organization of individuals of different groups (as races)". Integration aims at equal citizenship. Its theme is to turn a blind eye to difference for public purposes. Brian Barry, a strong advocate of integration, accurately captures the liberal philosophy of integration, as the privatization of national, ethnic, and cultural differences.[12] In common political institutions some level of public homogeneity, such as a shared language, is thought to be necessary for deliberation and for building trust. Other differences, however, should be privatized. The analogy is explicitly conceived as identical to the political strategy developed to manage religious differences in post-medieval Europe. Christians had slaughtered one another to impose their brand of truth through state power. The outcome was either the victory of one side and the establishment of a state church to which others had to conform or a bloody draw that led to the confinement of religious differences to private choices. Integrationists think the same strategy is appropriate for collective cultural differences in modern democratic states.[13]

Integrationists believe political instability and conflict result from group-based partisanship in political institutions. A state that serves the interests of one (or some) nationality, religion, ethnicity or language will promote the countermobilization of the excluded communities, and hence conflict. To avoid the ethnically partisan state, integrationists counsel against the ethnicization of political parties

[11] MERRIAM WEBSTER'S COLLEGIATE DICTIONARY 650 (11th ed. 2003) (italics added).
[12] BRIAN BARRY, CULTURE AND EQUALITY: AN EGALITARIAN CRITIQUE OF MULTICULTURALISM 25 (Harvard Univ. Press 2001).
[13] *Id.*

or civic associations. They prefer parties which stand formally for nonethnic agendas, such as the Republicans and Democrats in the United States (US), or Labour, Conservatives and Liberal Democrats in Great Britain, because they crosscut religious and ethnic alignments.[14] Integrationists favor electoral systems that discourage the mobilization of parties around cultural differences, preferring systems that require winners to achieve broad-based support. Integrationists back executive systems that favor candidates who rise above religious, linguistic and ethnic faction. They frown on the delegation of public policy functions to minority nationalities, or ethnic or religious groups. They oppose publicly funded religious school systems, and any form of autonomy, territorial or nonterritorial, based on groups.[15]

At least three types of integrationist can be identified: republicans, liberals, and socialists. Republicans support the civic "nation-state". Liberals champion the nation-state and international liberal institutions, preferably as preludes to the construction of a cosmopolitan political order. Socialists have been divided with regard to the nation-state. Some see it as a barrier to the creation of a global socialist civilization; others see it as a bastion against the global capitalist order.

Republicans derive inspiration from a range of political thinkers who considered the conditions under which city state or agrarian republics would flourish, notably Niccolò Machiavelli, James Harrington, Jean-Jacques Rousseau, Thomas Jefferson, and Immanuel Kant. They all thought citizens needed sufficient property and sufficient equality to be sturdy and independent of the state and oppressive social organizations.[16] Civic virtue among citizens was best promoted through a common and deliberative public culture. Shared citizenship, education, language, religion, and military service for the republic all serve to integrate the polity.[17] In modern times such republicans veer toward integral nationalism.[18] They oppose group-based remedies to address disadvantage.[19] They champion a nation of individuals, and promote integration as a prelude to assimilation. The clearest examples of such republicanism are found in contemporary France and Turkey: Jacobinism and Kemalism are assimilationism's bedfellows.[20]

The antecedents of liberal integrationism are found in both utilitarian and rights-based defenses of the value of liberty.[21] The key premise of liberal

[14] SEYMOUR MARTIN LIPSET, POLITICAL MAN: THE SOCIAL BASES OF POLITICS 12–13 (Expanded ed. Heinemann 1983).
[15] See BARRY, *supra* note 12, *passim*, for criticisms of delegating public authority to minorities.
[16] CRAWFORD BROUGH MACPHERSON, THE LIFE AND TIMES OF LIBERAL DEMOCRACY (Oxford Univ. Press 1977).
[17] JEAN-JACQUES ROUSSEAU, THE SOCIAL CONTRACT (Penguin Books 1968); JEAN-JACQUES ROUSSEAU, THE GOVERNMENT OF POLAND (Willmore Kendall trans., Hackett 1985).
[18] PETER ALTER, NATIONALISM (Edward Arnold 1989).
[19] Cynthia Ward, *The Limits of "Liberal Republicanism": Why Group-based Remedies and Republican Citizenship Don't Mix*, 91 COLUM. L. REV. 581 (1991).
[20] Ümit Cizre, *Turkey's Kurdish Problem: Borders, Identity and Hegemony, in* RIGHT-SIZING THE STATE: THE POLITICS OF MOVING BORDERS, *supra* note 1, at 222.
[21] Herbert Lionel Adolphus Hart, *Between Rights and Utility, in* THE IDEA OF FREEDOM: ESSAYS IN HONOUR OF ISAIAH BERLIN 77 (Alan Ryan ed., Clarendon Press 1979).

integrationism is the notion of the individual. Liberal integrationists promote the conditions enabling strong individuals, not the strong community of republicans. They promote the liberal values of choice and freedom. They would free all from the potentially negative stereotyping and prejudicial characteristics of their culture of origin. They challenge the coerced solidarity associated with assimilation. They promote equality among individuals because they are wholly opposed to discrimination based on culture of origin, though not on ability or morals. Liberals advocate the idea of careers open to talents, the free market, and political competition to facilitate flourishing individualism. Conflict in socially diverse polities is blamed on partisan discrimination by state authorities, and on manipulative demagogues who pursue group mobilization strategies for their own narrow, self-interested purposes.[22] Liberal integrationism is particularly strong in the United States.

Socialist integrationists regard social classes as the key component of social thought and practice, and regard the promotion of distributive justice as the appropriate public priority, and social democrats regard substantive social citizenship as the best means to its realization.[23] Politics based on nationality, religion, ethnicity or language use are seen as inhibiting "correct" working class politics.[24] In the classical socialist perspective, the primary source of conflict is attributed to the capitalist mode of production, and those who profit from it are responsible, jointly and severally, for promoting divisions among nationalities, ethnicities, religious and linguistic groups, and for obscuring the fact that members of such communities have objectively similar class interests. Conflict among such communities tends to be attributed to material causes. Socialist integrationism is popular with the European left and Marxists everywhere, including in the South African Communist Party.[25]

Republican integrationists have a more expansive view of what should be publicly homogenized than their liberal counterparts. French and Turkish republicans, for example, maintain a sharp secularism (laicism) in which religious symbols and dress are banned from schools, because that creates rigorous equidistance of the public domain from religion.[26] Liberals are more open to a soft "multiculturalism" of lifestyles, which allow for a more diverse public sphere. Republican integrationism therefore veers in an assimilationist direction, and

---

[22] Laura Silber & Allan Little, The Death of Yugoslavia (Penguin 1996).

[23] Thomas Humphrey Marshall, Citizenship and Social Class (Thomas Humphrey Marshall & Tom Bottomore eds., Pluto Press 1992).

[24] Frank Parkin, Marxism and Class Theory: A Bourgeois Critique (Columbia Univ. Press 1979).

[25] *See, e.g.* Bogdan Denitch, Ethnic Nationalism: The Tragic Death of Yugoslavia (Univ. Minn. Press 1994).

[26] Alfred Stepan, *The World's Religious Systems and Democracy: Crafting the "Twin Tolerations"*, *in* Arguing Comparative Politics 213 (Oxford Univ. Press 2001); Marc Howard Ross, *Dressed to Express: Islamic Headscarves in French Schools, in* Cultural Contestation in Ethnic Conflict 191 (Cambridge Univ. Press 2007); Ernest Gellner, *Kemalism, in* Encounters with Nationalism 81 (Basil Blackwell 1994).

French and Turkish intellectuals and policy makers have difficulty in distinguishing integration from assimilation. Republicans favor a unitary state, majoritarian or winner-takes-all political institution, and a monistic conception of sovereignty possessed by the nation. Republicans generally champion centralization, and favor administrative "deconcentration" rather than political decentralization. The constitutions drafted by republicans frequently proclaim the state as a nation-state, "one and indivisible", and prohibit federalism because it would splinter the sovereignty of the national people.[27] Republicans oppose restrictions on the will of the sovereign people—such as a court with the power to strike down statutes, though some republican constitutions have tried to put some changes such as altering the state's territory beyond the popular will.[28] Additionally, republicans champion a nation-building executive: either a president, directly elected by the nation, a unifying figure capable of standing above group and faction, and of acting decisively, or a prime minister with the same traits backed by a legislature chosen through a majoritarian voting procedure. They favor national and state-wide political parties over regional, ethnic or linguistic parties, and may even execute laws that require a party to be organized on a statewide basis if it is to contest elections, as in Vladimir Putin's Russia.[29]

Liberal integrationists value political competition, such as the electoral struggle to hold executive and legislative office in representative democracies.[30] Competitive elections allow office holders to be held accountable and inhibit abuses of power by incumbents who may fear electoral retribution. But elsewhere in the public domain, liberal integrationists champion the values of public impartiality, professionalism, and meritocratic career structures, including in the army and the police. Liberals, especially those who found their arguments on human rights, do not share the republican faith in the unrestrained sovereign people or place their trust in responsible conduct by elected office holders. They generally favor restricting legislative action with a bill of individual rights, enforced by an independent judiciary able to strike down statutes. The liberal tradition, particularly in the United States, is influenced by the interpretations of Charles-Louis

[27] 1958 Fr. Const. art. 1: "France shall be an indivisible, secular, democratic and social Republic"; Turk. Const. art. 3: "The Turkish state, with its territory and nation, is an indivisible entity"; Ukr. Const. art. 2: "Ukraine is a unitary state. The territory of Ukraine within its present borders is indivisible and inviolable".

[28] Turk. Const. art. 4: "The provision of Article 1 of the Constitution establishing the form of the state as a Republic, the provisions in Article 2 on the characteristics of the Republic, and the provision of Article 3 shall not be amended, nor shall their amendment be proposed"; Ukr. Const. art. 157: "The Constitution of Ukraine shall not be amended, if the amendments foresee the abolition or restriction of human and citizens' rights and freedoms, or if they are oriented toward the liquidation of the independence or violation of the territorial indivisibility of Ukraine".

[29] See О политических партиях—Федеральный Закон N. 95—ФЗ, от 11.07.2001 (Окончательная версия) [Russian Federal Law on Political Parties No. 95, July 11, 2001, (Final Version)], art. 3.2.

[30] Brendan O'Leary, *The Logics of Power-sharing, Consociation and Pluralist Federations, in* Settling Self-determination Disputes: Complex Power-sharing in Theory and Practice 47–48 (Marc Weller and Barbara Metzger eds., Martinus Nijhoff forthcoming 2008).

de Secondat, baron de Montesquieu and of John Locke made authoritative in *The Federalist Papers*.[31] That tradition aims to check tyranny by dividing, separating, and checking power.[32] American liberals champion federation over unitary states in territorial governance because they think liberty is better protected through a division of powers. They argue that the demos-constraining features of the American federation protect individuals from populist majorities.[33] An analogous argument is that a federation may inhibit tyrannies by ethnic or religious majorities, provided functions are appropriately separated.[34]

American liberals emphatically reject what, pejoratively, they call "ethnofederalism", such as the drawing of political boundaries to enable ethnic minorities to become local majorities within some federative units.[35] They maintain that ethnofederalism leads to local tyrannies of the majority and encourages secession. Instead they support national federations, such as federations that aim at mono nationbuilding, turning many states into one integrationist federation in accordance with the latin motto adopted by the United States government, *e pluribus unum,* meaning "one from many".[36] Such thinking, influenced by American political scientists, led integrationists to commend national federations for South Africa and Iraq.[37]

Actual national federations come in two empirical configurations. In the American paradigm, no (minority) nationality, religious or linguistic community controls a federal unit. In the second, where demography or geography renders such design impossible, each significant minority is divided across several federative units rather than concentrated in a single larger unit. National federations usually are described by their exponents as "territorial", because they share power among regionally defined communities rather than national or

[31] James Madison, Alexander Hamilton & John Jay, The Federalist Papers (Isaac Kramnick ed., Penguin 1987) (1788).
[32] Louis Hartz, The Liberal Tradition in America (Harcourt, Bruce & World 1955).
[33] William H. Riker, Federalism: Origin, Operation, Significance (Little, Brown 1982); William H. Riker, Liberalism Against Populism (W.H. Freeman 1982).
[34] Donald Rothchild & Philip G. Roeder, *Power Sharing as an Impediment to Peace and Democracy, in* Sustainable Peace: Power and Democracy after Civil Wars 29 (Philip G. Roeder & Donald Rothchild eds., Cornell Univ. Press 2005).
[35] Jack Snyder, From Voting to Violence: Democratization and Nationalist Conflict (W.W. Norton 2000); Philip Roeder, *Soviet Federalism and Ethnic Mobilisation,* 43 World Pol. 196 (1992); Carol Leff, *Democratization and Disintegration in Multinational States: The Breakup of the Communist Federations,* 51 World Pol. 205 (1999); Valerie Bunce, Subversive Institutions: The Design and the Destruction of Socialism and the State (Cambridge Univ. Press 1999); Rogers Brubaker, Nationalism Reframed: Nationhood and the National Question in the New Europe (Cambridge Univ. Press 1996).
[36] Brendan O'Leary, *An Iron Law of Nationalism and Federation? A (neo-Diceyian) Theory of the Necessity of a Federal Staatsvolk, and of Consociational Rescue,* 7 Nations & Nationalism 273 (2001); John McGarry & Brendan O'Leary, *Federation as a Method of Ethnic Conflict Regulation, in* From Power-sharing to Democracy: Post-conflict Institutions in Ethnically Divided Societies 263, 268–296 (Sid J.R. Noel ed., McGill-Queen's Univ. Press 2005).
[37] Andreas Wimmer, *Democracy and Ethno-religious Conflict in Iraq,* 45 Survival 111 (2003); Kanan Makiya, *A Model for Post-Saddam Iraq,* 14 J. Democracy 5 (2003).

ethnic communities. But a territorial federation is both a pleonasm and an ideological construct. All federations are necessarily territorial, and the ideological label obscures the fact that such a federation builds one nation at the expense of other possible collective identifications, including other nations. A national federation disorganizes actual or potential national minorities in favor of the dominant nationality or in favor of building a wider civic allegiance. The federation is treated as the outcome of a collective unitary national and sovereign subject rather than as a compact of sovereign states or peoples.[38]

Socialist integrationists advocate a strong welfare state, with redistribution and public investment in deprived areas to deal with the presumed "material basis" of ethnic and other collective identities. They are much less likely than republicans to champion the nation as the key unit of social solidarity. Indeed, some socialists prefer to speak of "constitutional patriotism" rather than nationalism, even when the nationalism is "civic".[39] Socialists are more likely than liberal integrationists to be critical of procedural or difference-blind approaches to inequalities between communities, and may support temporary affirmative action policies to create equality. For instance, in post-apartheid South Africa, the integrationist African National Congress (ANC) dominated government has championed affirmative action policies, pending full integration. Socialists who do not like affirmative action insist on social policies that are universal and do not target particular economic, racial, ethnic or religious categories. Integrationists of the left are sometimes distrustful of elites in general and place their faith in "bottom-up" or mass-based collective action as the solvent for national, ethnic, religious or linguistic conflicts. They call for ethnic, linguistic and religious elites to be challenged by civil society, particularly trade unions, civic associations, and political parties that crosscut ethnic or religious communities.[40] Socialist integrationists, by definition favor social integration, such as the mixing of communities, as do all integrationists. They stand out against segregated schools, workplaces or residential communities and believe that social mixing promotes social solidarity and a commonality of interests.

Integration is arguably the dominant goal and embodies the received wisdom regarding conflict regulation and conflict resolution in the longer established democracies. The political class of the European Union advocates integration

---

[38] SAMUEL H. BEER, TO MAKE A NATION: THE REDISCOVERY OF AMERICAN FEDERALISM (Belknap Press Harvard Univ. 1993).

[39] Jürgen Habermas, *Citizenship and National Identity*, 12 PRAXIS INT'L 1 (1992); Jürgen Habermas, *The European Nation-State: Its Achievements and its Limits: on the Past and Future of Sovereignty and Citizenship*, 9 RATIO JURIS 125 (1996); JÜRGEN HABERMAS, BETWEEN FACTS AND NORMS: CONTRIBUTIONS TO A DISCOURSE THEORY OF LAW AND DEMOCRACY (William Rehg trans., MIT Press 1996); JÜRGEN HABERMAS, THE POSTNATIONAL CONSTELLATION: POLITICAL ESSAYS (Max Pensky trans., 1st ed. Polity Press 2000).

[40] Rupert Taylor, *Northern Ireland: Consociation or Social Transformation?*, in NORTHERN IRELAND AND THE DIVIDED WORLD: POST-AGREEMENT NORTHERN IRELAND IN COMPARATIVE PERSPECTIVE 36, 47 (John McGarry ed., Oxford Univ. Press 2001).

to manage Europe's immigrants. The United Nations, the World Bank, the International Monetary Fund (IMF), and the OSCE's High Commissioner on National Minorities generally advocate integration.[41] So do numerous peace academies, peace research institutes, and academic conflict resolution centers.[42] But within particular states integration is more likely to be supported by some groups than by others. The political sociology of integration, on quick inspection, suggests that it is nearly always associated with large majorities, such as dominant communities like the Arabs of Iraq, or rather small minorities such as immigrant communities or middlemen minorities that have left their ancestral territory for a new homeland, like the Turkomen of Iraq, or indigenous members of communities living on their ancestral homeland but interspersed among the majority population like the Christians of Iraq.[43] In the United States, integration, by contrast, is associated with many African Americans who are not a majority, voluntary immigrants, resident on their long-term ancestral territory, or sufficiently concentrated territorially. This makes their political preferences comparatively unusual but explicable because of their previous status as slaves and their current status as a dispersed minority historically subject to racist maltreatment. They have not been able to organize a successful territorial nationalist movement.

Normally and conspicuously absent from the list of groups that support integration are large minorities, especially those communities that are territorially concentrated and nationally mobilized. This gives us a clue as to the context in which integration is most likely to work, a subject to which we shall return.

3. Accommodation

The dictionary consulted previously tells us about the contemporary usages of the verb to accommodate and its noun, accommodation, namely:

> **accommodate.** transitive verb 1: to make fit, suitable, or congruous. 2: to bring into agreement or concord: RECONCILE. 3: to provide with something desired, needed, or suited (as a helpful service, a loan, or lodgings). 4a: to make room for b: to hold without crowding or inconvenience. 5: to give consideration to: allow for accommodate the special interests of various groups.
> intransitive verb: to adapt oneself; also: to undergo visual accommodation.
>
> **accommodation.** 1: something supplied for convenience or to satisfy a need: as *a*: lodging, food, and services or traveling space and related services usually used in plural

---

[41] WILL KYMLICKA, MULTICULTURAL ODYSSEYS: NAVIGATING THE NEW INTERNATIONAL POLITICS OF DIVERSITY (Oxford Univ. Press 2007).

[42] See HUGH MIALL, OLIVER RAMSBOTHAM & TOM WOODHOUSE, CONTEMPORARY CONFLICT RESOLUTION 54–55 (Polity 1999), for a list of conflict-resolution centers and peace institutes, many of which are associated with integrationist perspectives.

[43] John McGarry & Brendan O'Leary, *Iraq's Constitution of 2005: Liberal Consociation as Political Prescription* (in this volume).

tourist accommodations on the boat overnight accommodations b: a public convey-
ance (as a train) that stops at all or nearly all points *c:* LOAN. *2: the act of accommo-*
dating: the state of being accommodated: as a: the providing of what is needed or desired
for convenience b: ADAPTATION, ADJUSTMENT c: a reconciliation of differences:
SETTLEMENT d: the automatic adjustment of the eye for seeing at different distances
effected chiefly by changes in the convexity of the crystalline lens; also: the range over
which such adjustment is possible.[44]

The etymology is suggestive. The words are from the Latin *ad* (to or toward)
combined with *commodare* (to make fit), which in turn is derived from *commodus*
(suitable). We have italicized the dictionary definitions presently used in politics and in the conflict-regulation debate. "Reconciliation", "adaptation", and
"adjustment to the special interests and needs of groups" convey what is involved.
It was not an accident that the doyen of consociational theory, Arend Lijphart,
chose *The Politics of Accommodation* as the title of his first book.[45]

Accommodation, minimally, requires the recognition of more than one ethnic, linguistic, national, or religious community in the state. It aims to secure
the coexistence of different communities within the same state, though supporters of accommodation may support secession or partition if accommodation is
impossible. Accommodationists see themselves as responsible realists, though
some offer arguments about the value of diversity following in the much analyzed
footsteps of the German Romantic Johann Herder.[46]

Contrary to some allegations, the academic supporters of accommodation
are not usually primordialists—who allegedly think that national, ethnic, religious, and linguistic groups have existed since time immemorial and will remain
a permanent fixture of politics.[47] But accommodationists do insist that in certain

[44] MERRIAM WEBSTER'S COLLEGIATE DICTIONARY, *supra* note 11, at 8 (italics added).
[45] AREND LIJPHART, THE POLITICS OF ACCOMMODATION: PLURALISM AND DEMOCRACY IN
THE NETHERLANDS (Univ. Cal. Press 1968).
[46] Frederick M. Barnard, *National Culture and Political Legitimacy: Herder and Rousseau*, 44 J.
HIST. IDEAS 231 (1983); FREDERICK M. BARNARD, SELF-DIRECTION AND POLITICAL LEGITIMACY:
ROUSSEAU AND HERDER (Clarendon Press 1988); ISAIAH BERLIN, VICO AND HERDER: TWO
STUDIES IN THE HISTORY OF IDEAS (Hogarth Press 1976); Louis Dumont, *Interaction between
Cultures: Herder's Volk and Fichte's Nation, in* ETHNICITY, IDENTITY AND HISTORY: ESSAYS IN
MEMORY OF WERNER J. CAHNMAN 13 (Joseph B. Maier & Chaim Waxman eds., Transaction
Publishers 1983); Louis Dumont, *German Identity: Herder's Volk and Fichte's Nation, in* ESSAYS
ON INDIVIDUALISM: MODERN IDEOLOGY IN ANTHROPOLOGICAL PERSPECTIVE 113 (Chicago
Univ. Press 1986); Carlton J.H. Hayes, *Contribution of Herder to the Doctrine of Nationalism*, 32
AM. HIST. REV. 719 (1927); JOHANN G. HERDER, REFLECTIONS ON THE PHILOSOPHY OF THE
HISTORY OF MANKIND (Frank E. Manuel ed., Univ. Chi. Press 1968); Vicki Spencer, *Herder and
Nationalism: Reclaiming the Principle of Cultural Respect*, 43 AUSTL. J. POL. & HIST. 1 (1997); Isaiah
Berlin, *Herder and the Enlightenment, in* ISAIAH BERLIN, THE PROPER STUDY OF MANKIND: AN
ANTHOLOGY OF ESSAYS 359 (Henry Hardy & Roger Hausheer eds., Pimlico 1998).
[47] There are some lucid, recent discussions of ill-considered academic antiprimordialism. *See*
Francisco J. Gil-White, *How Thick is Blood? The Plot Thickens . . . : If Ethnic Actors are Primordialists,*
What Remains of the Circumstantialist/Primordialist Controversy?, 22 ETHNIC & RACIAL STUD.
789 (1999); Francisco J. Gil-White, *Are Ethnic Groups Biological "Species" to the Human Brain?*
Essentialism in our Cognition of Some Social Categories, 42 CURRENT ANTHROPOLOGY 515 (2001);

contexts, national, ethnic, religious, and linguistic divisions and identities are resilient, durable, and hard, rather than malleable, fluid, soft, or transformable. Political prudence and morality requires adaptation, adjustment, and consideration of the special interests, needs, and fears of groups so that they may regard the state in question as fit for them. Accommodationists believe the existence of such identities (and cleavages) is empirically testable, at least in democracies. We can examine for which parties people vote, and in what type of civic associations they participate, and for how long such patterns have existed.[48] The strength of territorial identities, and differences in the values, preferences, and attitudes of various groups, and their perceptions of political or economic inequality may also be measured. Where divisions are enduring and deeply divisive accommodationists think attempting integration is likely to be unfair, and likely to fail, especially because it usually means a political choice in favor of one, and usually the largest, community. The main forms of accommodation are now known as centripetalism, multiculturalism, consociation, and territorial pluralism—as found, especially, in pluralist federations—and we shall treat them in order.

Centripetalism

Centripetalism involves a set of institutional prescriptions associated with the American political scientist and lawyer, Donald Horowitz, and his supporters.[49] The notion emphasizes "convergence", "centrism", or "bringing together" and is usually juxtaposed by its academic proponents with consociation, which is (contentiously) seen as generating centrifugal (or fissiparous) politics.

Centripetalists claim the tyrannical properties of majority-rule institutions may be tempered through votepooling electoral systems, which facilitate or mandate the election of moderate ethnic politicians, that is, those who are capable of reaching out to other ethnic communities.[50] Centripetalists counsel against electoral systems which they assert favor ethnic partisans, so they often condemn proportional representation, and particularly party-list proportional representation with low thresholds, or the single transferable vote (STV) in multi-member constituencies with a significant number of seats. Votepooling electoral systems, according to their proponents, should require at least winning candidates to pool

---

Donald L. Horowitz, *The Primordialists, in* Ethnonationalism in the Contemporary World: Walker Connor and the Study of Nationalism 72 (Daniele Conversi ed., Routledge 2002).

[48] Brendan O'Leary, *Debating Consociational Politics: Normative and Explanatory Arguments, in* From Power-Sharing to Democracy, *supra* note 36, at 3, 49–50.

[49] Donald L. Horowitz, A Democratic South Africa? Constitutional Engineering in a Divided Society 180–190 (Univ. Cal. Press 1991) [hereinafter Horowitz, A Democratic South Africa?]; Donald L. Horowitz, Ethnic Groups in Conflict (Univ. Cal. Press 1985) [hereinafter Horowitz, Ethnic Groups in Conflict].

[50] Benjamin Reilly, Democracy in Divided Societies: Electoral Engineering for Conflict Management (Cambridge Univ. Press 2001); Benjamin Reilly & Andrew Reynolds, Electoral Systems and Conflict in Divided Societies: Papers on International Conflict 2 (Nat'l Acad. Press 1999).

votes from among different ethnic voters,[51] and encourage campaigns focused on centrist moderate voters in heterogeneous constituencies (hence the expression "centripetal"). Such systems should appeal to the rationality of politicians, by "making moderation pay".[52]

Two particular electoral systems are advocated by centripetalists. The first relies on territorial distributive requirements and is considered especially useful for presidential elections. A presidential electoral college is one example of a distributive requirement. A majority of the electoral college votes need not be the same as a majority of the popular vote, and may obligate successful candidates to focus their campaigns across a range of member states. Horowitz's favorite example of a territorial distribution rule is that applied for presidential elections in Nigeria after 1979.[53] The then new constitution stipulated that a winning presidential candidate needed at least a plurality of the popular vote, and at least a quarter of the vote in at least two-thirds of the nineteen states.[54] The rule tacitly required any competitive presidential and vice presidential team to appeal across the north and south of Nigeria and, minimally, to two of its three largest ethnic communities. The second frequently advocated votepooling system is the "alternative vote", a preferential voting system used both for legislative and presidential elections. In a single member district the winning candidate must win an absolute majority of first preference votes or a majority of votes after the transfer of lower order preferences from eliminated candidates.[55] The alternative vote (AV) was implemented by the Organization for Security and Cooperation in Europe (OSCE) for presidential elections in Republika Srspka in 2000.[56] Though this federative entity has a large Serb majority, the OSCE believed that the alternative vote would facilitate the election of a moderate Serb by increasing the pivotality of the non-Serb minority.[57]

Centripetalists also support the "conciliatory potential of federalism".[58] Federations may allow statewide minorities to become regional majorities, and may make possible asymmetrical autonomy arrangements for regions with special problems or distinctive identities. Such concessions may undercut support for secessionists. Federations are also supported because they disperse power away from the center, thus inhibiting authoritarianism; quarantine conflict at

---

[51] HOROWITZ, A DEMOCRATIC SOUTH AFRICA?, *supra* note 49, at 163–195.

[52] Donald L. Horowitz, *Making Moderation Pay: The Comparative Politics of Ethnic Conflict Management, in* CONFLICT AND PEACEMAKING IN MULTIETHNIC SOCIETIES 451 (Joseph V. Montville ed., Mass. Heath 1989).

[53] HOROWITZ, A DEMOCRATIC SOUTH AFRICA?, *supra* note 49, at 207.

[54] NIG. CONST. 1979, arts. 126(1)(b) & (2)(b).

[55] Clive Bean, *Australia's Experience with the Alternative Vote,* 34 REPRESENTATION 103 (1997); Peter Hain, *The Case for the Alternative Vote,* 34 REPRESENTATION 121 (1997); Arend Lijphart, *The Alternative Vote: A Realistic Alternative for South Africa?,* 18 POLITIKON 91 (1990).

[56] SUMANTRA BOSE, BOSNIA AFTER DAYTON: NATIONALIST PARTITION AND INTERNATIONAL INTERVENTION 232–233 (Oxford Univ. Press 2002).

[57] *Id.*

[58] HOROWITZ, A DEMOCRATIC SOUTH AFRICA?, *supra* note 49, at 214.

the local level (such as the Muslim-Christian disputes over Sharia law in northern Nigeria); provide a training ground for local politicians to engage in ethnic bargaining at the local level; and promote crosscuttting politics both through facilitating inter- and transethnic alliances based on common regional interests, and facilitating intragroup divisions and group proliferation within regions.[59]

Consider Table 1 on page 68, which lays out a continuum of state policy responses towards difference. The section which concerns this chapter runs from integration through accommodation. Centripetalism belongs toward the integrationist end of accommodationist approaches. Indeed, if the line between these categories is seen as blurred, centripetalism arguably straddles it. Horowitz's ideas on votepooling promote a transethnic identity, as politicians who focus exclusively on their own communities should be disadvantaged. He explicitly favors politicians who "can find ways of transcending their own ethnic affiliations".[60] A single-person presidential executive seems particularly pointed in this direction, as it is difficult to see how such a person can fully represent distinct communities as opposed to representing what they share in common. On federations, his ideas are close to those of the "national federalists" already discussed. Horowitz favors strong federations, in other words, centralized federations, and has recommended these for South Africa and Iraq. He has supported the partition of federal units belonging to large ethnic communities even against their will, as a technique for preventing regional majoritarianism, and as a technique for stabilizing and unifying the state.

Thus Horowitz commends Nigeria as an example of centripetalism.[61] Initially, the Nigerian First Republic was made up of three regions, dominated by the Yoruba, Ibo, and Hausa-Fulani, respectively. This design was widely blamed for exacerbating divisive ethnic politics, and hastening the brutal war over Biafra's failed secession.[62] Nigeria's military dictators subsequently restructured the federation into nineteen states (now thirty six), some of which are dominated by the three large communities, some by other smaller minorities, and some by no single community.[63] In the case of contemporary Iraq, followers of Horowitz

---

[59] Donald L. Horowitz, *The Many Uses of Federalism*, 55 DRAKE L. REV. 101 (2007).

[60] HOROWITZ, A DEMOCRATIC SOUTH AFRICA?, *supra* note 49, at 207.

[61] *Id.* at 217–220.

[62] James O'Connell, *Conflict and Conciliation: A Comparative Approach Related to Three Case Studies—Belgium, Northern Ireland and Nigeria, in* CONSENSUS IN IRELAND: APPROACHES AND RECESSIONS 157 (Charles Townshend ed., Clarendon Press 1988); Kaye Whiteman, *Enugu: The Psychology of Secession, 20 July 1966 to 30 May 1967, in* NIGERIAN POLITICS AND MILITARY RULE: PRELUDE TO THE CIVIL WAR 111 (Keith Panter-Brick ed., Athlone 1970); Martin Dent, *Federalism in Africa, with Special Reference to Nigeria, in* FEDERALISM AND NATIONALISM 169 (Murray Forsyth ed., Leicester Univ. Press 1989); ROTIMI T. SUBERU, FEDERALISM AND ETHNIC CONFLICT IN NIGERIA (U.S. Inst. Peace Press 2001); LARRY DIAMOND, CLASS, ETHNICITY AND DEMOCRACY IN NIGERIA: THE FAILURE OF THE FIRST REPUBLIC (Macmillan 1988).

[63] HOROWITZ, A DEMOCRATIC SOUTH AFRICA?, *supra* note 49, at 217–220; *see* John Boye Ejobowah, *Integrationist and Accommodationist Measures in Nigeria's Constitutional Engineering: Successes and Failures* (in this volume).

recommended a "national federation" based on the eighteen governorates established under Saddam's regime, and hoped that it would be imposed by the American-led Coalition Provisional Authority. The alleged virtue of such a design was the belief that it would divide the Kurds, Sunni Arabs and Shi'a Arabs among several different governorates respectively, and thereby promote intercommunity and crossprovincial alliances, and an inclusive Iraqi national identity.[64]

However, Horowitz is clearly not an integrationist as we have defined the term. He does not favor engineering social mixing or the privatization of culture, and has argued for bi- and multilingualism, and other forms of public support for minority cultures, in different contexts. He is not a critic of what Snyder and others have criticized as "ethno-federalism", and favors at least some self-government for minorities, particularly small ones that do not threaten the state; and his votepooling measures, particularly those designed for elections to legislatures in parliamentary systems, are aimed at promoting interethnic power sharing albeit through a coalition of moderate ethnic parties. Unlike integrationists but like other accommodationists, Horowitz is what we deem a realist, who has clearly stressed the durability of ethnic divisions, and who denies that catch-all parties or civic associations can easily supplant their ethnic counterparts.[65] Finally, we treat him here as an accommodationist and not as an integrationist because this is how he identifies himself, including in correspondence with us.

Multiculturalism

Taken literally, multiculturalism implies accommodation as we have defined it, that is, the protection and maintenance of multiple communities both in public and private realms. But in most of North America and Europe, so-called multiculturalism is not practiced literally. To do so would mandate the promotion of public schools for cultural minorities, including immigrant minorities, and programs designed deliberately to allow them to retain their language of origin, or other forms of cultural autonomy such as those advocated by the Austro-Marxists, Karl Renner and Otto Bauer, and promoted today in a limited way in places like Hungary, Estonia, and Russia.[66] Self-styled Western multiculturalism has avoided such policies. Instead, it has been aimed, generally, at the promotion of a single mainstream public culture, albeit one that is less one-sided, assimilationist or conformist than was once the case in the quite recent past. The idea is

---

[64] Wimmer, *supra* note 37; Adeed Dawisha & Karen Dawisha, *How to Build a Democratic Iraq*, 82 FOREIGN AFF. 36 (2003); Makiya, *supra* note 37.

[65] HOROWITZ, ETHNIC GROUPS IN CONFLICT, *supra* note 49, at 334–342; and HOROWITZ, A DEMOCRATIC SOUTH AFRICA?, *supra* note 49, at 28–30.

[66] OTTO BAUER, THE QUESTION OF NATIONALITIES AND SOCIAL DEMOCRACY (Ephraim Nimni ed., Joe O'Donnell trans., Univ. Minn. Press, 2000); Karl Renner, *State and Nation, in* NATIONAL CULTURAL AUTONOMY AND ITS CONTEMPORARY CRITICS 15 (Ephraim Nimni ed., Routledge 2005).

not to support immigrants retaining publicly their own separate instit
politics, but simply to tolerate such differences in private domains, while a
promoting integration and mixing in common public institutions through
example, English as a second language programs, and the provision of hospit
and other public services in the minority language. The object is to assist minorities in adapting to the dominant society. This is how we should understand decisions to allow Muslim schoolgirls to wear headscarves in public schools in the
United Kingdom, to change the common public school curricula to reflect the
citizen's multicultural origins in the United States, or to permit Sikhs to join the
mainstream police while retaining turbans in Canada. This type of self-styled
"multiculturalism" does not advocate public support for cultural communities
to remain viable and separate for the long term, such as funding mosques for
Muslim immigrants in Europe, or Polish language schools for Polish migrants
in Ireland.

An accommodationist "multicultural" policy in Europe and North America
would accommodate both non-Western and perhaps even some illiberal practices. Western multiculturalism, however, is heavily liberal, and more unicultural
than it may pretend. It involves an emphasis on voluntary and fluid group membership. One is not obliged to be a group member; not automatically coded as a
member of a group; and group membership does not necessarily involve exclusionary rights for the group. The American brand of multiculturalism, involving
a cosmopolitan absorption of all that is seen as good in the cultures of the world,
has been satirized by Stanley Fish, one of the *enfants terribles* of U.S. academe, as
"boutique multiculturalism".[67] A boutique multiculturalist, in Fish's view, resists
the force of the culture that he or she allegedly appreciates at precisely the point
at which it matters the most to its strongly committed members. So Western
multiculturalists tolerate other cultures, but only up until the point at which
these cultures challenge liberal principles. They will not accept child marriage,
the inferior status of women in public or marriage laws, or clitoridectomy. Many
Western multiculturalists display a rather shallow tolerance of the cultures of
non-Western immigrants, while typically juxtaposing their liberal nationalism
with (Eastern European or Balkan) ethnic nationalism—which is deemed exclusivist, based on endogamous marital practices, hostile to group interaction, and
segregationist. Such multiculturalism is, in our view, "pseudo multiculturalism".
It is liberal integration in disguise.

Credible accommodationist multiculturalism involves, by contrast, one of the
three following arrangements. The first entails some respect for a group's self-
government in matters the group defines as important and some broad appreciation of the principle of proportional representation of all groups in key public
institutions—not necessarily through quotas but certainly through public targets

[67] Stanley Fish, *Boutique Multiculturalism*, in THE TROUBLE WITH PRINCIPLE 56 (Harvard
Univ. Press 1999).

·esentation of groups, such as in the military, in elite edu-
the judiciary. The second offers groups a share of public
ional arrangements—which involves cross-community
autonomy and proportionality, and sometimes, mutual
And the third provides for territorially based commu-
r through pluralist federation or a pluralist union state
ionalities, languages or religions (such as the United
and Northern Ireland, the Kingdom of Spain and
... three approaches require some minimum public support,
...ough legislation or expenditures, for different communities. All are consistent
with some support for non-Western cultures of immigrants in Europe and North
America, though many consociationalists and pluralist federalists, including the
authors of this article, are liberals.

Consociation

Consociation is rightly associated with the innovative work of Arend Lijphart.[68]
It is different from multiculturalism because consociations address deep antagonisms with executive power sharing and minority vetoes in addition to the
credible multiculturalist repertoire of autonomy and proportionality. The first
and key conflict regulating mechanism in a consociation is a cross-community
power-sharing executive, in which representative elites from different communities jointly prevent conflict. Although Lijphart originally identified a grand
coalition in which all communities are represented as the key indicator for consociation, what matters is some element of jointness in executive government across
the most significant communities.[69] Consociation does not require every community to be represented in the government, nor does it require everybody within
a particular community to support all of its representatives in the government.
We may distinguish between "complete" consociations such as Lijphart's grand
coalition, "concurrent" consociations in which representatives of the majority
within each of the main groups is in government, and "plurality" consociations

---

[68] Lijphart's major essays of the last 30 years are collected in AREND LIJPHART, THINKING
ABOUT DEMOCRACY: POWER SHARING AND MAJORITY RULE IN THEORY AND PRACTICE
(Routledge 2007). See also LIJPHART, *supra* note 45; Arend Lijphart, *Typologies of Democratic
Systems*, 1 COMPARATIVE POL. STUD. 3 (1968); Arend Lijphart, *Consociational Democracy*, 21
WORLD POL. 207 (1969); AREND LIJPHART, DEMOCRACY IN PLURAL SOCIETIES: A COMPARATIVE
EXPLORATION (Yale Univ. Press 1977); AREND LIJPHART, *Consociation and Federation: Conceptual
and Empirical Links*, 12 CAN. J. POL. SCI. 499 (1979); AREND LIJPHART, POWER-SHARING IN
SOUTH AFRICA 83 (Univ. Cal. Press 1985); Arend Lijphart, *The Evolution of Consociational Theory
and Constitutional Practices, 1965–2000,* 37 ACTA POLITICA 11 (2002); Arend Lijphart, *The Wave
of Power-Sharing Democracy, in* THE ARCHITECTURE OF DEMOCRACY: CONSTITUTIONAL DESIGN,
CONFLICT MANAGEMENT AND DEMOCRACY 37 (Andrew Reynolds ed., Oxford Univ. Press 2002)
[hereinafter Lijphart, *The Wave of Power-Sharing Democracy*]; *see generally* INSTITUTIONAL DESIGN
IN NEW DEMOCRACIES: EASTERN EUROPE AND LATIN AMERICA (Arend Lijphart & Carlos H.
Waisman eds., Westview Press 1996).

[69] O'Leary, *supra* note 48, at 3–43.

in which at least a plurality of each significant group's representatives are in government.[70] Bosnia and Herzegovina mandates a grand coalition in its presidency (complete consociation in the executive).[71] Northern Ireland's legislature requires a concurrent majority of Assembly members registered as unionists and nationalists respectively to elect its two First Ministers (concurrent consociation in the executive). Furthermore, Northern Ireland's executive may function, such as by staying in office and promoting legislation, without absolute majority support from one community (plurality consociation).[72]

Second, consociation mandates the principle of proportionality. Proportionality is commended throughout the critical components of the public sector, not just the executive, but also the legislature, the judiciary, and the elite levels of the bureaucracy—including the police service and army.[73] Consociationalists emphasize the need for group representativeness in both elected and unelected political institutions. Professionalism and impartiality occur, and are legitimate only, once the demand for representativeness has been met. They prefer proportional representation electoral systems—or, where that is not possible, systems which achieve the same outcomes, such as through what Americans typically call set-asides. However, accommodationists may differ over the merits of particular proportional electoral systems. Lijphart favors list-based proportional representation (list-PR) because he believes it facilitates discipline and control by party leaders, and thus eases the making and maintenance of consociational settlements.[74] One danger of list-PR, is that if it is used with a low threshold, hardliners may be able to wreck consociational deals, because they can form their own party and win support without reducing the vote and seat share of their ethnic bloc. Other accommodationists prefer the single transferable vote (STV) version of proportional representation, because it has a higher effective threshold than most forms of list-based proportional representation, because it retains the principle of proportionality, and may facilitate transfers in favor of candidates and

---

[70] *Id.* Brendan O'Leary, *Consociation, in* THE ROUTLEDGE ENCYCLOPAEDIA OF THE SOCIAL SCIENCES 3 (Adam Kuper & Jessica Kuper eds., Routledge 2005).

[71] BOSN. & HERZ. CONST. 1995, art. V. The Constitution of Bosnia and Herzegovina is Annex No. 4 of the General Framework Agreement for Peace in Bosnia and Herzegovina: *see* the Dayton Peace Accords on Bosnia (1995), *available at* http://www.state.gov/www/regions/eur/bosnia/bosagree.html.

[72] Agreement Reached in the Multi-party Negotiations, Ir.-N. Ir.-Brit., Apr. 10, 1998, Cm. 3883, strand 1, para. 5(d)(i), *available at* http://www.nio.gov.uk/agreement.pdf [hereinafter Belfast Agreement].

[73] For the provision for a proportional executive in the Northern Ireland's agreement see Belfast Agreement, strand 2, paras. 15–16; for its provision on the legislature, see Belfast Agreement, strand 2, para. 2; for legislative committees (both chairs and membership), see Belfast Agreement, strand 2, paras. 5(a) & 8. The Belfast Agreement calls for "the development of a police service representative in terms of the make-up of the community as a whole" (Belfast Agreement, Policing and Justice, para. 1) and establishes a new Human Rights Commission, with a membership "reflecting the community balance" (Belfast Agreement, Rights, Safeguards and Equality of Opportunity, para. 5).

[74] Lijphart, *The Wave of Power-Sharing Democracy, supra* note 68, at 37, 53.

parties prepared to maintain power sharing.[75] STV, however, is only appropriate for highly literate and numerate electorates.

The third consociational principle is autonomy or community self-government. This is the system that Lijphart described in the Netherlands. It bears a superficial resemblance to the system of religious management that operated in the Ottoman empire in which "people of the book", Muslims, Jews, and Christians, and sometimes Zoroastrians, were permitted to administer their own marital, property, and inheritance laws.[76] But unlike the millet system which privileged Muslims over the *dhimmi* (the subordinated monotheists who refused to convert to Islam) consociation recognizes parallel societies, equal but different, and rejects the hierarchical ranking of groups. Community self-government may display a kind of functional autonomy that allows for separate personal laws on marriage and inheritance, separate schooling and university systems, and separate publicly funded media. But community self-government may also take a territorial form—though that is distinctly characteristic of formally pluralist territorial governance in federations or union states, which we shall shortly examine. Community self-government in consociations mandates public support for the maintenance of diverse communities both now and into the future. It should, therefore, be distinguished from what we have labeled Western or pseudo multiculturalism.

Lastly, rigid consociations, constructed amid high historic mistrust or antagonisms, may endow each partner to the consociation with veto rights, enabling them to prevent legislative or constitutional changes that threaten their fundamental interests. Iraq's constitution requires constitutional changes to be approved by a simple majority of citizens and not be opposed by two-thirds of those voting in three historic governorates, which tacitly gives veto rights to Kurds, Sunni Arabs (if they are strongly unified,) and Shi'a Arabs.[77] Sometimes executive power sharing and proportionality rules grant every major community *de facto* veto powers. Where they do not, however, minorities usually seek formal veto rights. Likewise autonomy sometimes accomplishes *de facto* veto provisions within a community's jurisdiction. But we may usefully distinguish opt-out provisions that do not block others from pursuing a certain policy and that result in institutional and policy asymmetries from veto rights that prevent majorities from pursuing their preferred course of action even within their own jurisdictions.

Consociation can be undemocratic or democratic, formal or informal, liberal or corporate. In an undemocratic consociation, such as the communist Yugoslavia, a

[75] Brendan O'Leary, *The Nature of the Agreement*, 22 FORDHAM INT'L J.L. 1628 (1999); JOHN MCGARRY & BRENDAN O'LEARY, THE NORTHERN IRELAND CONFLICT: CONSOCIATIONAL ENGAGEMENTS 13 (Oxford Univ. Press 2004).

[76] BAT YE'OR, THE DHIMMI: JEWS AND CHRISTIANS UNDER ISLAM (David Maisel, Paul Fenton & David Littman trans., Fairleigh Dickinson Univ. Press 1985); *see generally* 2 CHRISTIANS AND JEWS IN THE OTTOMAN EMPIRE: THE FUNCTIONING OF A PLURAL SOCIETY: THE ARABIC-SPEAKING LANDS (Benjamin Braude & Bernard Lewis eds., Holmes & Meier 1982).

[77] IRAQ CONST. art. 137.

communist elite from each group controlled the federal government but was not democratically representative of the nationality in question.[78] A democratic consociation has open elections among competing elites, but elites from each sizable community are represented in the executive along complete, concurrent or plurality patterns. A formal consociation is entrenched by way of constitutional or statutory law. Power-sharing executives in Bosnia-Herzegovina[79] and Belgium[80] are constitutionally entrenched, as was Cyprus's consociation between 1960 and 1963,[81] and South Africa's interim consociation between 1994 and 1996.[82] In Northern Ireland formal consociational provisions are entrenched by way of a U.K. parliamentary statute, an interparty agreement, and an international agreement between the British and Irish governments, but not in a codified constitution because the U.K. does not have one.[83] The quality of its entrenchment is a source of considerable controversy. The U.K. government, in our view, breached the interparty and international agreement by unilaterally suspending the agreed institutions on a number of occasions since 2000. But consociation may be an informal matter of convention. The Swiss' "magic formula", by which the seats on the collective presidency of the federal executive are assigned on a roughly proportional basis to the main linguistic, religious and party constituencies, is an informal consociational practice.[84] Formally each member of the Swiss executive council is elected in turn by a majority vote of the two chambers of the Swiss federation.[85] Canada's federal executive is established, formally, as a result of the winner-take-all rules of the Westminster model of government, but francophones are represented proportionately in cabinet by convention.[86] On the other hand, there are formal statutory provisions that ensure that at least three of the Canadian Supreme Court's nine justices must be from Quebec.[87]

A corporate consociation accommodates groups according to ascriptive criteria, such as ethnicity or religion or mother tongue, and tacitly assumes that

---

[78] SUSAN L. WOODWARD, BALKAN TRAGEDY: CHAOS AND DISSOLUTION AFTER THE COLD WAR 38 (Brookings Inst. 1995).

[79] BOSN. & HERZ. CONST. 1995, art. V.

[80] BELG. CONST. art. 99(2).

[81] CYPRUS CONST. 1960, app. D, arts. 1 & 46.

[82] S. AFR. (Interim) CONST. 1993, §§ 84(1) & 88(2).

[83] The Northern Ireland Act, 1998, c. 47, pt. III, § 16(3) & §§ 18(2)–(4); Belfast Agreement, *supra* note 72, strand 2, paras. 15–16; Agreement between the Government of the United Kingdom of Great Britain and Northern Ireland and the Government of Ireland, Ir.-N. Ir.-Brit., Apr. 10, 1998, Cm. 4292 [hereinafter British-Irish Agreement].

[84] Jürg Steiner, *Switzerland: "Magic Formula" Coalitions, in* GOVERNMENT COALITIONS IN WESTERN DEMOCRACIES 315 (Eric C. Browne & John Dreijmanis eds., Longman 1970).

[85] *Id.*

[86] Sid J.R. Noel, *Canadian Responses to Ethnic Conflict: Consociationalism, Federalism and Control, in* THE POLITICS OF ETHNIC CONFLICT REGULATION: CASE STUDIES OF PROTRACTED ETHNIC CONFLICTS 49 (John McGarry & Brendan O'Leary, eds., Routledge 1993).

[87] Supreme Court Act, R.S.C., 1985, ch. S 26, § 6 (Can.). There is a constitutional convention that three judges must come from Ontario, two from the Western provinces, and one from the Atlantic provinces.

group identities are fixed, and that groups are both internally homogeneous and externally bounded.[88] Lebanon once allocated parliamentary seats between Christians and Muslims in a fixed ratio of six to five, now changed to a ratio of one to one.[89] Bosnia-Herzegovina's constitution stipulated a three-person presidency consisting of one Bosniak and one Croat, each directly elected from the territory of the Federation of Bosnia-Herzegovina, and one Serb directly elected from the territory of the Republika Srpska.[90] Belgium's constitution provides that the cabinet be equally divided among French and Dutch speakers with the "possible exception" of the prime minister[91] while Cyprus's Constitution of 1960 provided for a Greek president and a Turkish vice president, and a Council of Ministers composed of seven Greek ministers and three Turkish ministers.[92] Since corporate consociations privilege ascriptive identities, politicians, and voters with transgroup identities cannot easily thrive.

A liberal consociation, by contrast, allows groups to self-determine their organization and representation. It rewards whatever salient political identities emerge in democratic elections, whether these are ethnic, religious, linguistic, or other criteria based on programmatic appeals.[93] South Africa's transitional power-sharing arrangements (1994–1996) allocated deputy presidencies and cabinet seats on the basis of party strengths and not ascriptive characteristics.[94] The interim constitution stipulated that any party holding at least eighty seats (20 percent of the total) was entitled to designate a deputy president and that if no party or only one party passed this threshold, the two largest parties were entitled to so designate. Any party winning at least twenty seats (5 percent) was entitled to at least one cabinet position. A party's total number of cabinet positions was proportional to the number of seats it held in the National Assembly relative to the number of seats held by other parties prepared to participate in government.[95] While Canada requires that at least three of its nine Supreme Court justices come from Quebec, it does not require that they be from any particular community within the province.[96] Northern Ireland's Belfast Agreement combines both corporate and liberal elements. Its first and deputy first minister are elected

---

[88] For a standard integrationist criticism of this approach, see ROGERS BRUBAKER, ETHNICITY WITHOUT GROUPS (Harvard Univ. Press 2004).

[89] The Ta'if Accord, 1989, pt. II Political Reforms, § (A)(6) (Leb.).

[90] BOSN. & HERZ. CONST. 1995, art. V

[91] BEL. CONST. art. 99(2).

[92] CYPRUS CONST. 1960, app. D, arts. 1 & 46.

[93] Arend Lijphart, *Self-Determination versus Pre-Determination of Ethnic Minorities in Power-Sharing Systems, in* THE RIGHTS OF MINORITY CULTURES 257 (Will Kymlicka ed., Oxford Univ. Press 1995); MCGARRY & O'LEARY, *supra* note 75, at 32; Brendan O'Leary, *supra* note 48, at 3–43; John McGarry, *Liberal Consociation and Conflict Management, in* IRAQ: PREVENTING A NEW GENERATION OF CONFLICT 169 (Ben Roswell, David Malone & Markus Bouillon eds., Lynne Rienner Press 2007).

[94] S. AFR. (Interim) CONST. 1993, §§ 84(1)–(2) & 88(2).

[95] *Id.*

[96] Supreme Court Act, R.S.C., 1985, ch. S 26, § 6 (Can.).

as a team by a majority of the legislative assembly, plus a concurrent majority of nationalist and unionist members.[97] In effect these two positions are corporate and guaranteed to one nationalist and one unionist. The other ten ministers, by contrast, win office through an allocation algorithm, the d'Hondt method, that is liberal or "difference-blind". It operates according to the strength of representation won by parties in the Assembly, not their national identity.[98] While Cyprus's 1960 Constitution was based squarely on corporate consociational principles, the recent United Nations plan for Cyprus (the Annan plan) envisaged a move towards liberal principles. While the Senate was to be comprised of equal numbers of Greek and Turkish Cypriots, elected by the two communities voting separately, the presidency and vice presidency were no longer to be assigned to particular communities but were to be rotated between the representatives of the island's two territorial units. The latter formulation opened the possibility, at least in principle, of someone achieving one of these offices who is identified just as a Cypriot rather than as a Greek Cypriot or Turkish-Cypriot.[99]

Consociationalists generally commend formal executive power sharing, proportionality and autonomy arrangements over conventional arrangements, especially when there are deep divisions and security preoccupations. Leading academic consociationalists usually are supporters of democratic and liberal consociations, though they are often (unfairly) accused by integrationists of being undemocratic and illiberal, and of being primordialists.

Territorial pluralism

Communities that are territorially concentrated and ethnically or nationally mobilized may be managed through territorial pluralism, either in a pluralist federation or in a pluralist union state.[100] A pluralist as opposed to a national federation has internal boundaries that respect nationality, ethnicity, language or religion. Where the federation-wide majority is a majority in every federal unit, we have an unambiguous national federation, as in the United States, Germany, Australia, or the Latin American federations. Where all, or virtually all, of a minority within a federation is converted into a self-governing majority within its own single federal unit, as in Belgium, we have an unambiguously pluralist federation. Between these two polar types, there exists an ambiguous type of

---

[97] Belfast Agreement, *supra* note 72, at strand 1, para. 5(d)(i).
[98] Brendan O'Leary, Bernard Grofman & Jorgen Elklit, *Divisor Methods for Sequential Portfolio Allocation in Multi-Party Executive Bodies: Evidence from Northern Ireland and Denmark,* 49 Am. J. Pol. Sci. 198 (2005).
[99] The Comprehensive Settlement of the Cyprus Problem, arts. 3(2), 5(1) & 5(2)(a), *available at* http://www.un.org/Depts/dpa/annanplan/annanplan.pdf (2004) (known as the "Annan Plan", final version presented by the Secretary-General of the United Nations to the Parties on Mar. 31, 2004).
[100] For a useful treatment of institutions based on territorial pluralism, see Autonomy, Self Governance and Conflict Resolution: Innovative Approaches to Institutional Design in Divided Societies (Marc Weller & Stefan Wolff eds., Routledge 2005).

federation, consisting of ethnic, linguistic or national minorities divided across several federal units, in each of which they may be majorities. Where such federations originate from the partition of minority nations without their consent, as occurred in Nigeria in the late 1960s, we think they should be categorized as national federations. Where, by contrast, such a pattern develops organically, as in the case of Switzerland's linguistic minorities, two of which are divided across several cantons, we have a federation which is plurilingual but not plurinational in form.

Pluralist federations can be more or less pluralist. Full pluralist federations entail three complementary arrangements. First, they involve significant and constitutionally entrenched autonomy for federative entities, both in the constitutional division of powers and in the allocation of fiscal resources. The powers of the federative entities cannot be rescinded unilaterally by the federal government. It is for this reason that we do not regard India as a formal federation. The Indian Constitution permits the Union parliament to make laws with respect to any matter under the jurisdiction of the states[101] and the Union government to take over the government of a state.[102] In other respects, however, India is more pluralistic, notably in the move toward more linguistically homogeneous states. Second, a pluralist federation may have consensual, indeed consociational, rather than majoritarian decision making rules within the federal government. A consensual federation has inclusive executive power sharing and representative arrangements in the federal government, and institutionalizes proportional principles of representation and allocation of public posts and resources.[103] Consensual federations create strong second chambers representing the constituent regions and have strong regional judiciaries and a regional role in the selection of federal judges. They do not create strong single-person presidencies, or senates that are mirror images of the house of representatives. Third, full pluralist federations are plurinational. They recognize a pluralist rather than monist conception of sovereignty. The plurinational character of the federation is recognized in the state's constitution, or through its flag and symbols, or through official bilingualism or multilingualism which treats the federation as a multi-homeland, a partnership between or among distinct peoples. Iraq's 2005 Constitution stipulates in article 3 that it is a "country of many nationalities".[104] Article 4 makes Arabic and Kurdish the country's two official languages, while article 12 stipulates that "the flag, national anthem, and emblem of Iraq shall be fixed by law in a way that represents the components of the Iraqi people".[105] A plurinational federation

[101] INDIA CONST., arts. 249–250.
[102] *Id.* art. 356.
[103] Brendan O'Leary, *Power-Sharing, Pluralist Federation, and Federacy, in* THE FUTURE OF KURDISTAN IN IRAQ 47 (Brendan O'Leary, John McGarry & Khaled Salih eds., Univ. Penn. Press 2005).
[104] IRAQ CONST. art. 3.
[105] *Id.* arts. 4, 12.

involves collective territorial autonomy for the partner nations. Nations, by definition, seek to be collectively self-determining, and a plurinational federation is incompatible with the partition of a national community's territory across several federative units, as happened in Nigeria, and as some integrationists wanted for Iraq. A plurinational federation may permit asymmetric institutional arrangements.

There are few examples of federal constitutions that are fully pluralist in design. Iraq is an incomplete example and its future is uncertain. Any viable federation of the European Union will have to be fully pluralist. Pluralist federation enjoys some advocacy among contemporary academics. The French-speaking politicians who designed the Canadian federation were pluralist federalists, though its principal English-speaking founder, Sir John A. MacDonald, was not. The Austro-Marxists who wanted to reform the Austro-Hungarian empire were pluralist federalists, and so were the Marxist-Leninists who came to power in the Soviet Union, at least on paper.

Pluralist territorial accommodation extends beyond federation. There is a class of union states—usually inappropriately classified as unitary states—that recognize historic nationalities and their boundaries. We believe that this is the apt way to characterize the United Kingdom of Great Britain and Northern Ireland, the Kingdom of Spain and the Kingdom of Denmark. In each case, jurists and constitutional tradition privilege a centralized sovereignty, and treat autonomy as a rescindable gift of the central political institutions. However, the state is a composite that respects historically incorporated territories and grants them extensive autonomy and indeed national recognition. India similarly calls itself a union state rather than a federation and refuses to recognize national minorities. It has, however, reorganized itself to respect historic linguistic communities.[106]

In federations, institutions of self-government exist across the whole state. In union states, they are more likely to exist across only part of the state. This asymmetry may be the result of majorities being happy with government from the state's central authorities while minorities insist on self-government.[107] Thus, Zanzibar has home rule within Tanzania but there is no analogue to Zanzibar's institutions in Tanganyika—the Union parliament is its parliament.[108] The United Kingdom has home rule parliaments in Northern Ireland and Scotland, but the Westminster parliament is the sole parliament for England and the sole parliament entitled to pass primary statutes for Wales, which has a National Assembly with executive and administrative autonomy and limited powers to

---

[106] Katharine Adeney, *Constitutional Centring: Nation Formation and Consociational Federalism in India and Pakistan*, 40 J. COMMONWEALTH & COMP. POL. 8 (Nov. 2002); BALVEER ARORA & DOUGLAS V. VERNEY, MULTIPLE IDENTITIES IN A SINGLE STATE: INDIAN FEDERALISM IN COMPARATIVE PERSPECTIVE (Konark 1995).

[107] John McGarry, *Asymmetry in Federations, Federacies and Unitary States*, 6 ETHNOPOLITICS 105 (2007).

[108] B.P. SRIVASTAVA, THE CONSTITUTION OF THE UNITED REPUBLIC OF TANZANIA 1977: SOME SALIENT FEATURES, SOME RIDDLES, ch. 304 (Dar es Salaam Univ. Press 1983).

amend Westminster statutes.[109] The Kingdom of Denmark grants home rule to Greenland, and the Faeroe Islands, but the common parliament is also Denmark's parliament.[110]

When autonomous and asymmetric institutions are entrenched, by way of the constitution or by an international treaty, there exists a federacy, namely a unit of government that enjoys a distinctive federal relationship with the state (the core of which may be a federation, a union state or a unitary state).[111] The relationship is federal because neither party can unilaterally alter the other's competences. Normally the pattern involves a trade off, such as full domestic autonomy for the federacy in return for the federacy's having less involvement in the core or common institutions than its resources or size might otherwise permit. Federacies exist to accommodate the Aland Islands and Greenland.[112] One of us has argued that the complete and full implementation of the Belfast Agreement would make Northern Ireland a federacy.[113]

Accommodationists typically seek to accommodate minorities within the state. But some academics and minority leaders have argued that this approach is too state-centered or integrationist. Standard territorial pluralism cannot adequately meet the needs of mobilized national communities that spill over state borders, such as the Azeris, Basques, Irish, Kurds, Magyars, and the Serbs. Such communities will not be satisfied with either consociational or pluralist territorial accommodation. They will invariably seek to establish or reestablish linkages across state borders. In other words, they will insist on crossborder institutions, ranging from functional cooperation to confederal institutions. Irish nationalists in Northern Ireland insisted, during the negotiations that produced the Belfast Agreement, on crossborder political institutions linking Northern Ireland with the Irish republic, as well as autonomy within the U.K. and consociation within Northern Ireland.[114] Magyar minorities in Hungary and Slovakia, the Turkish minority in Cyprus, Serbian minorities in Bosnia-Herzegovina, and Austrian minorities in Italy (South Tyrol) seek crossborder links with their "kin-state" as well as autonomy and perhaps consociation, within their host states. Comprehensive accommodation encompasses interstate institutions as well as intrastate institutions.

Accommodation is less popular among advocates of a strong central government than is integration. Nevertheless, many democratic states practice accommodation. Within the past forty years, Spain, Belgium, the United Kingdom,

[109] *See* Northern Ireland Act, 1998, c. 47; Government of Wales Act, 1998, c. 38; Scotland Act, 1998, c. 46.
[110] DEN. CONST. 1953, pt. IV, § 28.
[111] DANIEL JUDAH ELAZAR, EXPLORING FEDERALISM (Univ. Ala. Press 1987).
[112] The Greenland Home Rule Act, Act No. 577 of Nov. 29, 1978 (Den.); Act on the Autonomy of the Aland Islands, 1993 (Fin.).
[113] Brendan O'Leary, *The Belfast Agreement and the British-Irish Agreement: Consociation, Confederal Institutions, A Federacy, and a Peace Process, in* THE ARCHITECTURE OF DEMOCRACY, *supra* note 68, at 293.
[114] MCGARRY & O'LEARY, *supra* note 75.

Italy, and even France, have moved toward systems that accommodate minorities through autonomy, whether through pluralist federations, devolution within union states or federacies. States, and international organizations like NATO, the UN and OSCE also have been prepared to back, or even impose, consociation, pluralist federations, and federacies in situations of conflict and ethnic polarization, including in Northern Ireland, Bosnia-Herzegovina, Iraq, Burundi, and, abortively, in Cyprus. On occasion, international organizations, including the Council of Europe and European Union have moved beyond an integrationist defense of individual rights towards a more accommodationist perspective. Their reluctance to go further is not difficult to explain. Formally the international system is a club of states while accommodation is most likely to be sought by sizable minorities that do not control their states.

4. Engagements between integrationists and accommodationists

We summarize the range of integrationist and accommodationist approaches in Table 1 on page 68, and the institutional inventories associated with them in Table 2 on pages 70–71. The approaches range from integration to disintegration. The endpoints of assimilation and disintegration lie beyond the scope of this chapter. The distinction between integration and accommodation, while definitionally unambiguous, does not sufficiently demarcate individual authors, who may cut across the distinctions.

Republicans are placed towards the assimilationist end of the integration category because their promotion of the common good and of deliberation towards this end appears hostile to any form of group accommodation.

Socialists are next because of the dominant socialist view that ethnic or cultural identities are not real or are not objective forms of difference, as epitomized by the socialist concept of "false consciousness". Some socialists have a teleological philosophy of history, in which the planet will eventually be unified under cosmopolitan socialism. They are not accommodationists. But, for tactical reasons, Leninists have been prepared to accommodate nationalities en route to a global socialist order.[115] There is an honorable branch of the socialist tradition, represented by the Austro-Marxist tradition, which is accommodationist. We deal with them later.

We have placed liberals next. They are the most likely to define themselves as integrationists, given the centrality in liberal thought of the public-private distinction, and the importance of state neutrality among rival conceptions of the good. While the essential liberal category is the individual, liberals are more

---

[115] WALKER CONNOR, THE NATIONAL QUESTION IN MARXIST-LENINIST THEORY AND STRATEGY (Princeton Univ. Press 1984).

Table 1. State response to ethnic and national diversity: From integration/non-accommodation to accommodation/disintegration

Assimilation	Integration				Accommodation			Secession/Partition
	Republicans	Socialists	Liberals	Centripetalists	Multiculturalists	Consociationalists	Territorial pluralists	
	Promotion of the common good	Promotion of class consciousness	Promotion of individualism	Group-recognition; Incentivize inter-group coalitions of moderates; Decentralization to (a) appease groups to avoid secession (b) divide potential nationalities	Group recognition; Proportionality; Cultural autonomy	Group recognition; Cross-community executive power-sharing; Proportionality; Autonomy; Veto Rights	Group recognition; Territorial self-government; Cross-border institutional linkages	

accommodative than republicans because they tend to tolerate moral pluralism, which dovetails with cultural pluralism. They are more accommodative than many socialists because of their focus on autonomy and equality, and the corollary that the cultural values of individuals need to be taken seriously.

The accommodationist family of approaches, by contrast, represents a significant shift. The chief difference with integrationists, which unites all accommodationists, is the public and private recognition of substate ethnic, linguistic, religious, or national group categories. Accommodationists stress the need to address the needs and aspirations of such communities rather than primarily the needs and aspirations of the nation (with the nation coterminous with the state), class, or individual. We have placed centripetalists in the accommodation category because of their support for ethnic self-government, public provisions for minorities and interethnic power sharing. They are positioned towards the integrative end of this category because of their restricted focus on accommodating ethnic moderates rather than radicals, their preparedness to partition territorial units belonging to large minorities, and their support for politicians who "transcend" their ethnic origins by reaching out to other groups. Credible multiculturalists are next because they strongly value cultural pluralism per se rather than promoting accommodation only as a prudent strategy for achieving political stability. Consociation is more accommodationist than centripetalism because it is inclusive towards radicals and not just moderates, and because it may incentivize politicians whose appeal is restricted to their distinct community and not just those who appeal beyond their ethnic base. It is considered more accommodative than multiculturalism because it combines the multicultural institutions of autonomy and proportionality with the additional devices of executive power sharing and minority vetoes. Finally, there is territorial pluralism. It is at the most accommodative end of the integration/accommodation spectrum because it converts minorities at the state-wide level into majorities within regions. Particularly radical are forms of territorial pluralism that encompass not just self-government but linkages between minority regions and other states.

Just as republican integration is the most likely of the integrationist strategies to develop into assimilation, territorial pluralism, which converts a minority into a majority with a geographic base of its own, is the most likely of the accommodationist strategies to lead to state break-up or disintegration. The placement of the accommodation approaches to the left of the category of disintegration reminds us, however, that all accommodationist approaches are "integrationist", in the basic sense that they are aimed at holding states together. It is only if accommodation fails that disintegration occurs.

Vigorous debates have been waged not just between supporters of the two major rival approaches, but also between supporters of different integrationist and accommodationist options, and, in particular between centripetalists and consociationalists. The debate has focused on which approach best contributes to

Table 2: The Institutional Repertoires of Integrationists and Accommodationists

Institution	Integration	Accommodation
Constitutional preamble	Nation-state, one people	Plurinational state, several peoples or nationalities or faiths
State languages	One official (public) language	More than one official (public) language
Bill of rights	Statewide bill of rights; Exclusive emphasis on individual rights	State and regional bills of rights; Emphasis on both individual and group rights
Territorial division of powers	Centralized	Decentralized
Internal political boundaries	A unitary state with no significant internal boundaries, or a federation with no boundaries that create territorial units in which national, ethnic, religious, or linguistic minorities are regional majorities	Internal boundaries organized to allow minorities to be self-governing; support for pluralist federations, pluralist union states, and federacies; centripetalists accept partition of large minority regions
Separation of powers within central or federal government	May favor a division of powers as a way to prevent abuses of power	Unlikely to regard separation of powers as sufficiently protective of minorities
Legislatures	Representative of individuals and (nonethnicized) regions	Quotas for corporate consociationalists; proportionality achieved through a proportional representation electoral system for liberal consociationalists
Judiciary, Bureaucracy	Emphasis on difference-blind compositional rules; impartiality; professionalism; meritocracy (although some may support temporary provisions for affirmative action)	Stress on descriptive representation of communities in key public posts
Executive	Single-person presidency; parliamentary system based on majoritarian (impartial) principles;	Power-sharing (interethnic) coalition either through a collective or rotating presidency, or a parliamentary executive. Consociationalists favor inclusive power-sharing coalitions. Centripetalists favor majoritarian (and sometimes minimum-winning) interethnic coalition based on moderates

Table 2: (*Cont.*)

Institution	Integration	Accommodation
Electoral system	Single-member plurality; alternative vote; majority runoff	Proportional representation (party list and single transferable vote) for consociationalists; alternative vote and regional distribution rules in presidential elections (e.g. U.S. electoral college; Nigeria, post-1979) for centripetalists
Political parties	Favors state-wide and "programmatic" parties; sometimes favor rules that require parties to have statewide organization	Acceptance of party system that is based on sub-state national, ethnic or religious communities
Civic associations	Favors "bridging" associations, i.e. those that transcend national, ethnic linguistic and religious groups	Acceptance of "bonding", i.e. group-based associations
Church-state relations	Separation of church and state: public funding of secular mixed schools	Public support for different religions; public funding for religious schools
Ties between minority communities and kin in neighboring states	Hostile to cross-border public institutional linkages	Supportive of cross-border public institutional linkages

three fundamental sets of values, stability, justice, and democracy. We examine each in order.

Stability

What is most likely to promote stability, peace, and the avoidance of violence? Integrationists regularly charge that accommodation is perverse as it will increase instability and maintain, or even deepen, divisions. The criticism presumes that rational and self-interested political elites have an interest in maintaining divisions between communities, and that accommodating them gives them resources to consolidate their position at the expense of those who stress crosscutting issues.[116] Institutionalizing and privileging particular identities reinforces allegiance to such elites. It may also promote resentment among those who are not

---

[116] Paul R. Brass, *Ethnic Conflict in Multiethnic Societies: The Consociational Solution and Its Critics, in* ETHNICITY AND NATIONALISM: THEORY AND COMPARISON 333 (Sage 1991); PIERRE

privileged and can fuel conflict. The Lebanese civil war of 1975–89 is usually explained from this perspective because of the privileges which Christians and Sunni Muslims enjoyed over Shi'a, Druze and others.[117] They were particularly resented by the Shi'a, whose share of the population was thought to be growing, and who wanted a greater share of the spoils. In the Soviet Union, Yugoslavia, and Czechoslovakia, pluralist or ethnofederal institutions are alleged to have created identities and divisions where none had existed previously, and to have done so needlessly. Rogers Brubaker maintains that the Soviet regime went to "remarkable lengths, long before glasnost and perestroika, to institutionalize both territorial nationhood and ethnocultural nationality as basic cognitive and social categories".[118] Once the political space began to expand under Mikhail Gorbachev, these categories quickly came to "structure political perception, inform political rhetoric, and organize political action".[119] According to Jack Snyder, the Soviet Union created political organizations and markets centered on ethnic differences. This is regarded as perverse because it is seen as unnecessary. The decision to adopt ethnofederalism was "arguably . . . a strategy of rule chosen by its Communist founders, not a necessity forced upon them by the irresistible demands of ethnic groups".[120]

Integrationist critics of consociation and centripetalism maintain that it is implausible to argue that ethnocentric elites will reach deals or make them work. If it does work, it will be on only a temporary basis, as the underlying divisions remain intact. The critics argue that consociations have either broken down (in Cyprus in 1963 and in Northern Ireland in 1974) failed to become properly consolidated (Northern Ireland since 1998), or are held together by international force (Bosnia-Herzegovina).[121] It is also argued that alleged examples of successful consociations, such as Switzerland, the Netherlands, Austria, and Belgium, were either only partly consociational or not consociational at all.[122] Integrationist critics of pluralist federations, which some of them term "ethnofederations", observe that they have had a "terrible track record".[123] Such federations,

ELLIOTT TRUDEAU, THE ESSENTIAL TRUDEAU (McClelland & Stewart 1998); DAVID D. LAITIN, NATIONS, STATES, AND VIOLENCE (Oxford Univ. Press 2007).

[117] See SAMIR KHALAF, CIVIL AND UNCIVIL VIOLENCE IN LEBANON: A HISTORY OF THE INTERNATIONALIZATION OF COMMUNAL CONFLICT (Columbia Univ. Press 2002), for a subtle account of the interplay between Lebanon's internal conflicts and pressures that encourage external interventions.

[118] BRUBAKER, *supra* note 35, at 9.

[119] *Id.* at 9.

[120] SNYDER, *supra* note 35.

[121] Philip G, Roeder, *Power Dividing as an Alternative to Ethnic Power Sharing, in* SUSTAINABLE PEACE: POWER AND DEMOCRACY AFTER CIVIL WARS 51, 60 (Philip G. Roeder & Donald Rothchild eds., Cornell Univ. Press 2005); Anthony Oberschall and L. Kendall Palmer, *The Failure of Moderate Politics: The Case of Northern Ireland, in* POWER SHARING: NEW CHALLENGES FOR DIVIDED SOCIETIES 77 (Ian O'Flynn & David Russell eds., Pluto Press 2005).

[122] Brass, *supra* note 116, at 335–336; Brian Barry, *Review Article: Political Accommodation and Consociational Democracy,* 5 BRIT. J. POL. SCI. 477 (1975).

[123] SNYDER, *supra* note 35.

it is argued, have failed to remain democratic, or have fallen apart, throughout the Caribbean (West Indies); all parts of Africa (Nigeria, Mali, Ethiopia, Cameroons); and throughout Asia (Pakistan; Union of Malaya; Burma).[124] Of all the states in post-communist eastern Europe, integrationist critics of pluralist federalism point out that it was only pluralist federations that broke up and that all of them did.[125]

Such critics maintain that integration is a more realistic response to ethnic division than accommodation. Some argue that integration is more feasible because ethnic identities are seldom as longstanding or as deep as supporters of accommodation suggest.[126] Accommodationists are often accused of believing in "ancient hatreds", of exaggerating the internal homogeneity of ethnic groups (or of believing that intragroup divisions can only aid ethnocentrism), and ignoring the existence of crosscutting identities or the capacity of people to develop them. They are seen as primordial pessimists who take the existence of ethnicity as an "objective fact", when, in reality, it is a choice made by people. Accommodationists are said to uncritically accept "the primacy and permanency of ethnicity", and to ignore the power of human agency, the point, "central to both liberalism and Marxism, that human freedom is a power, a Promethean force".[127] This belief in the superficiality and malleability of ethnic identity leads integrationists to maintain that it is both realistic and sensible to support progressive, integrative, or "bridging" social forces against divisive elites, and to support parties that have crosscutting appeals over those with ethnic appeals.

Accommodationists respond that promoting integration amid deep diversity creates at best an unstable equilibrium: either assimilation will occur or communities will demand special consideration, such as accommodation or, if that is unavailable, secession.[128] Without public support, weaker cultures or communities either acculturate or react with a backlash, seeking public redress, subsidies, the institutionalization of their culture in the curriculum, political autonomy, or power sharing. In some circumstances, the backlash may come from the majority community, as with the American Christian right, or the traditional Hindu right in India, which sees secular integration as damaging to their majority status.[129]

Supporters of accommodation are skeptical of the typical integrationist view that ethnic identities are universally malleable or superficial, or of recent vintage.

[124] O'Leary, *supra* note 36.

[125] BRUBAKER, *supra* note 35; BUNCE, *supra* note 35; Leff, *supra* note 35; Roeder, *supra* note 35; Snyder, *supra* note 35.

[126] For a critical treatment of such integrationist arguments in contemporary Iraq, see McGarry and O'Leary, *supra* note 43.

[127] Taylor, *supra* note 40, at 40; Brass, *supra* note 116, at 338; BRUBAKER, *supra* note 88.

[128] *See generally* McGarry & O'Leary, *supra* note 1.

[129] KEVIN PHILLIPS, AMERICAN THEOCRACY: THE PERILS AND POLITICS OF RADICAL RELIGION, OIL AND BORROWED MONEY IN THE 21ST CENTURY (Penguin Books 2006); PETER VAN DEN VEER, RELIGIOUS NATIONALISM: HINDUS AND MUSLIMS IN INDIA (Univ. Cal. Press 1994); AINSLIE T. EMBREE, UTOPIAS IN CONFLICT: RELIGION AND NATIONALISM IN MODERN INDIA (Univ. Cal. Press 1990).

Accommodationists accept that such an account may be true in some contexts, but insist that the presence of deep divisions should be subject to empirical verification and judgment. Voters in deeply divided places are unlikely to be willing to be satisfied with standard integrationist protections, such as a bill of rights. They are most unlikely to put their trust in presidents from other groups or to believe in the impartiality of a professional judiciary. They will be reluctant to place their faith in crosscutting political parties even if the electoral system makes it difficult for minority parties to win office. Accommodationists think it is unrealistic, in such settings, to place much faith in the ability of civil society organizations to counter elite ethnocentrism because civil society organizations are likely to be ethnic in their composition and ethnocentric in their appeal—"bonding" rather than "bridging" in character.[130] Their relations may be neither civil nor societal. Deeply divided places render the integrationist goal of social mixing problematic, so it has to be coercively and persistently imposed. Segregated schools and segregated neighborhoods exist in divided polities because they are, however regrettably, popular partly because they are considered safe by parents and residents. Accommodationists argue that engineering mixing and integration are either unrealistic in any reasonable time horizon, or are only likely to occur in the context of accommodationist institutions which may generate confidence in the survival of one's own community and build trust after successful coexistence with others.

Accommodation's supporters claim that the track record of their institutions are much better than integrationists allege, but there are some notable and heated internal divisions on which accommodationist institutions work best.[131] Those who emphasize territorial pluralism maintain that it is not a panacea, but that its success depends on a number of specified conditions being met. Failures are not evidence of an inherent flaw. Indeed, such failures are often exaggerated and their long periods of success in staunching flows of blood overlooked. Failures may flow from a range of factors, including design flaws, external interference, extraneous issues connected with managing the transition from war to peace, the coercive origins of a federation or union, or from authoritarian rather than accommodative practices. It is a major error, territorial pluralists believe, to hold up the example of the former communist federations as evidence that pluralist federations are bound to fail. These countries were not authentic, democratic pluralist federations, but rather, communist party dictatorships and, as such, were systems of ideological integration. They collapsed after attempts to recentralize the polity (for example, after the communist coup against Mikhail Gorbachev, after Slobodan Milosevic's bid to impose Serb hegemony, after Václav Klaus' attempt to impose centralist neoliberalism on the Slovaks, and after the Dergue ran an

---

[130] John McGarry, *Introduction: The Comparable Northern Ireland, in* NORTHERN IRELAND AND THE DIVIDED WORLD, *supra* note 40, at 1, 23.
[131] WILL KYMLICKA, POLITICS IN THE VERNACULAR: NATIONALISM, MULTICULTURALISM, AND CITIZENSHIP 116–117 (Oxford Univ. Press 2001).

Amhar dominated regime in Ethiopia).[132] Accommodationists believe that those Euro-federalists who seek to strip the European Union of its pluralist institutional characteristics will doom their project to ignominious failure: the EU can only work if it combines territorial pluralism and the accommodation of its constituencies within its central institutions.[133]

Henry Hale has argued, in thinking that is superficially similar to Horowitz's, that the failure of Nigeria's first republic, and the disintegration of the Soviet Union, did not flow from ethnofederalism per se, but from the existence of a "dual power structure", such as where a single "core ethnic region" dominates the federation, with a core region defined as one that possesses at least 50 percent of the state's population, or that is 20 percent larger than the next largest region.[134] What is distinctive to Hale is his recommendation that institutional designers focus on dividing the largest group; he finds no evidence against granting minority groups control over their own regions.

There is also an intra-accommodationist debate between centripetalists and consociationalists—over which is most conducive to stability—that is at least as intense as the debate between integrationists and accommodationists. Horowitz endorses the integrationist criticism of consociation that it is unlikely that ethnic group leaders will agree to compromise sufficiently both to achieve and maintain consociational power-sharing institutions. He maintains that because consociation is necessarily based on the idea of a "grand coalition"—for example, on a broad intercommunal executive containing both moderates and radicals from previously warring ethnic segments—it cannot work. Successful consociations are "as rare as the Arctic rose".[135] Consociations are only likely to work where they are unnecessary, that is, where there are only mild divisions. Consociations "are more likely the products of resolved struggles or of relatively moderate cleavages than they are measures to resolve struggles and to moderate cleavages".[136]

Horowitz also argues that the emphasis by consociationalists on proportional electoral systems is likely to exacerbate matters in divided societies because these facilitate sectional appeals by politicians and favor radicals over moderates. They facilitate political fragmentation within ethnic communities, and promote "outbidding".[137] This emphasis on intrabloc divisions points to a difference between accommodationist and integrationist thinking: it is not true that the former consider ethnic groups to be monoliths, as is frequently alleged by

[132] McGarry & O'Leary, *supra* note 36.
[133] O'Leary, *supra* note 75.
[134] Henry E. Hale, *Divided We Stand: Institutional Sources of Ethnofederal State Survival and Collapse*, 56 WORLD POL. 165 (2004).
[135] Donald L. Horowitz, *Explaining the Northern Ireland Agreement: The Sources of an Unlikely Constitutional Consensus*, 32 BRIT. J. POL. SCI. 193, 197 (2002).
[136] Donald L. Horowitz, *Constitutional Design: An Oxymoron?, in* DESIGNING DEMOCRATIC INSTITUTIONS 253, 256 (Ian Shapiro & Stephen Macedo eds., NYU Press 2000).
[137] ALVIN RABUSHKA & KENNETH A. SHEPSLE, POLITICS IN PLURAL SOCIETIES: A THEORY OF DEMOCRATIC INSTABILITY (Merrill 1972).

integrationists. Rather, accommodationists think that in divided polities, the most salient intrabloc divisions are likely to be those between ethnic moderates and radicals and to believe, unlike integrationists, that the existence of intrabloc divisions does not necessarily point toward conflict reduction. Rather than generally endorsing proportional representation, Horowitz argues for a majoritarian electoral system based on votepooling (also known as the alternative vote). Votepooling allegedly produces, in either parliamentary or presidential elections, a moderate interethnic coalition likely to cooperate against the extremes on their own sides, and it therefore allegedly creates strong electoral incentives against ethnic outbidding.

Horowitz understands that his centripetal approach faces an "implementation problem", that is, that warring elites may be as unlikely to accept institutions that favor moderate politicians as they will be to compromise over consociation. He and his supporters believe that their catch-22 can be overcome with the assistance of outside or "other" forces.[138] In 2000, Horowitz suggested that the way out of the dilemma created by the failure of ethnic elites to accept centripetal institutions was for internal parties to put "constitutional decision-making in other hands", including outside governments and international organizations.[139] Recently, he called for a "strong American push" in a centripetalist direction for Iraq and noted that "departing colonial powers left their imprints on new constitutions all over Asia and Africa, and many of these proved durable" and that "[i]t is time for the U.S. to do the same".[140] In 2003, Andreas Wimmer, a supporter of centripetalism, called for a "strong dose of outside interference" to establish centripetal institutions in Iraq.[141] Horowitz and other centripetalists maintain that their implementation problem is no greater than that of consociationalists because both centripetalism and consociation are likely to require intervention. The difference, they argue, is that centripetal institutions, once implemented, are self-sustaining and require minimal intervention, whereas consociation is likely to need ongoing intervention, as they think that the example of Bosnia-Herzegovina suggests.[142]

Supporters of consociation regard centripetalism's emphasis on votepooling as generally unrealistic, both at the elite and societal levels, and as most unlikely to accomplish political stability. They have demonstrated that Horowitz's claims for the accommodative properties of the alternative vote are theoretically and empirically unwarranted.[143] Consociationalists claim that existing leaders in polarized polities are more likely to be willing to agree with consociational than

[138] Horowitz, *supra* note 136, at 260; Wimmer, *supra* note 37, at 127.
[139] Horowitz, *supra* note 136, at 277.
[140] Donald L. Horowitz, *The Sunni Moment*, WALL STREET JOURNAL, Dec. 14, 2005, at A20.
[141] Wimmer, *supra* note 37, at 127.
[142] Horowitz, *supra* note 136 , at 255, 260; *id.* at 122–123.
[143] Jon Frankel & Bernard Grofman, *The Merits of Neo-Downsian Modeling of the Alternative Vote: A Reply to Horowitz*, 133 PUB. CHOICE 1 (2007).

centripetal deals. After all, consociations guarantee them a share in power. Such leaders are more likely to agree on proportional than centripetal electoral systems, because they can win votes and seats on their own preferred platforms, for example, as leaders of national, ethnic, religious, or linguistic communities. This is particularly true of radical elites that are the most ready to resist integrationist impositions. Proportionality norms, embedded in consociations, enhance stability because they better match the rival parties' respective bargaining strengths and their conceptions of distributive justice. As a result, consociationalists think that there will be less need for external actors to play a coercive role in maintaining accommodation. And as proportionality norms pose fewer barriers to entry for the political success of new political forces than plurality and majority-based alternatives, they may even contribute to long-term stability by allowing integrationist forces to emerge without artificial support. The consociational emphasis on proportionality explains why consociationalists, unlike Horowitz, reject single-person presidencies. Consociationalists would point to the polarizing effects of the presidential institution in Sri Lanka. Such executive systems cannot proportionately represent different communities, even if they are, as Horowitz maintains is possible, supported by a multiethnic coalition of political parties.

Consociationalists argue that it is not true that centripetal coalitions based on moderates are more stable than consociational coalitions.[144] Centripetal coalitions may be faced with outbidding and destabilizing opposition from excluded radicals, and such outbidding may make it difficult for moderates to cooperate. Inclusion in power-sharing coalitions, on the other hand, may make radicals less extreme, because it provides them with opportunities to have their concerns addressed, and gives them a stake in the system.[145] Inclusion in consociational settlements may strengthen the position of moderates within radical factions, a possibility centripetalists omit or ignore.

It is just not the case, consociationalists argue, that rival ethnic elites have little incentive to form and maintain consociational coalitions.[146] They may do so because the alternative is civil war, and because consociation or pluralist territorialism opens access to what is said to motivate all politicians—political power. Consociationalists argue that it is not true that consociations have failed everywhere. They point to the success of consociation in maintaining peace in Bosnia-Herzegovina since 1995, and in Lebanon for much of the period since 1943. Consociationalists observe the success of Northern Ireland's consociational deal in bringing peace to the region. They argue that the failure before 2007 to consolidate the 1998 Belfast Agreement's power-sharing institutions can be traced

---

[144] McGARRY & O'LEARY, *supra* note 75.

[145] *Id*; Paul Mitchell, Geoffrey Evans & Brendan O'Leary, *Extremist Outbidding In Ethnic Party Systems Is Not Inevitable: Tribune Parties in Northern Ireland* (Pol. Sci. & Pol. Econ. (PSPE) Working Paper No. 6, 2006), *available at* http://www.lse.ac.uk/collections/government/PSPE/WorkingPapers.htm.

[146] LIJPHART, *supra* note 45, *passim*; McGARRY & O'LEARY, *supra* note 75, ch. 1.

to the pace and content of policing reform, demilitarization, and paramilitary decommissioning rather than to the dilemmas of power-sharing per se.[147]

While centripetalists and consociationalists disagree on much, they acknowledge that virtually all democratic states in which groups are politically mobilized into parties and civic associations along national or ethnic lines have eventually adopted significant elements of power sharing (whether consociational or centripetal) in the central government and territorial pluralism. They reason, therefore, that accommodation is preferable to integration, and a workable and normatively acceptable alternative to partition or breakup.

Distributive justice

Integrationists and accommodationists dispute the social justice of their respective recommendations. Integrationists claim that recognition and public power for a group may lead it to repress its own members, as happens with those religious communities that discriminate against women.[148] They argue such arrangements privilege the identity of some groups' members over those of other groups—either other ethnic groups or bridging groups that stress class or gender—or over those who belong to no group. Integrationist critics of consociation point to the consociational arrangements in which certain communities are privileged, that is, to corporate consociations. Thus, under the 1995 Dayton Accords, only Bosniaks and Croats from the Federation of Bosnia-Herzegovina and Serbs from Republika Srpska, could aspire to the country's three-person presidency, or to its indirectly elected upper chamber.[149] Bosniaks and Croats from Republika Srspka, and Serbs from the Federation could not, and nor could anyone who does not identify with one of the three main ethnic communities. In Northern Ireland, voting arrangements for "key measures", and for the election of first and deputy first ministers, privilege those who identify as nationalist or unionists over those who do not.[150] In Lebanon, the allocation of seats in the legislature has favored Christians over non-Christians, while the informal allocation of the presidency, premiership and speakership, creates a hierarchy among Christians, Sunni Muslims and Shi'a Muslims, while leaving everyone else out.[151] Such privilege causes instability because such arrangements are unfair and create a hierarchy of citizenship.

Integrationist critics of pluralist territorial arrangements argue that they lead to unfair treatment of regional minorities. Americans are particularly likely to make such arguments, reflecting their experience of how Southern whites used "states rights" to maintain slavery and later the "Jim Crow" segregationist regime.[152]

---

[147] McGARRY & O'LEARY, *supra* note 75.   [148] Wimmer, *supra* note 37, at 123.
[149] BOSN. & HERZ. CONST. 1995, art. V.
[150] Belfast Agreement, *supra* note 72, strand 1, paras. 5(d)(i) & (ii).
[151] The Ta'if Accord, pt. II Political Reforms, § (A)(6) (Leb.).
[152] Charles D. Tarlton, *Symmetry and Asymmetry as Elements of Federalism: A Theoretical Speculation,* 27 J. POL. 861 (1965).

American critics of the communist federations argue that these privileged "titular" nationalities over the others. British integrationists point to the discrimination against Catholics by Northern Ireland's Protestant majority through the Stormont Parliament between 1921 and 1972.[153] Eric Nordlinger supported consociation to regulate conflicts but rejected pluralist federations because they would allow the region's "dominant segment to ignore or negate the demands of the minority segment".[154] Recently, Andreas Wimmer worried that "ethnically-based" autonomy in Iraq "may heighten, rather than reduce the risks of gross human rights violations, especially for members of ethnic minorities living under the rule of the majority government in a federal unit".[155] Since group rights promote privilege, integrationists argue that individual rights are what are needed in a diverse place and that they provide sufficient protection to all.[156] Pluralist federation is also seen as unfair to state-wide majorities, and to other minorities, if it interferes with the fair allocation of the state's common wealth and resources. One criticism of Iraq's 2005 Constitution popular among integrationists is that it allegedly discriminates against territories allegedly without oil, such as places dominated by Sunni Arabs.[157]

Accommodationists respond that integrationist rhetoric frequently hides dominant interests beneath its veneer of neutrality or impartiality.[158] It is no accident that dominant communities generally champion integration while minorities generally prefer accommodation to integration. Privatizing culture, accommodationists argue, is inherently biased against weaker cultures.[159] A single official language and single national identity will usually favor the language and identity of the state's dominant community. The same holds for integrationist state structures, executive design and public sector composition. Unitary states and national federations will favor dominant communities, as will majoritarian

---

[153] *See* Hugh Roberts, *Sound Stupidity: The British Party System and the Northern Ireland Question, in* THE POLITICS OF ANTAGONISM: UNDERSTANDING NORTHERN IRELAND 100–136 (Brendan O'Leary & John McGarry eds., 2d ed., Athlone 1996).

[154] ERIC NORDLINGER, CONFLICT REGULATION IN DIVIDED SOCIETIES: OCCASIONAL PAPERS IN INTERNATIONAL AFFAIRS 21 (Harvard Univ. Ctr. for Int'l Aff. 1972).

[155] Wimmer, *supra* note 37, at 123.

[156] BARRY, *supra* note 12; CHANDRAN KUKATHAS, THE LIBERAL ARCHIPELAGO: A THEORY OF DIVERSITY AND FREEDOM 4–5 (Oxford Univ. Press 2003).

[157] Kanan Makiya, *Present at the Disintegration*, N.Y. TIMES, Dec. 11, 2005 at 13; Yahia Said, *Federal Choices Needed*, AL-AHRAM WEEKLY, Mar. 2–8, 2006, *available at* <http://weekly.ahram.org.eg/print/2006/784/sc6.htm>; Middle East Report No. 52, Int'l Crisis Group, *The Next Iraqi War? Sectarianism and Civil Conflict* (Feb. 27, 2006), *available at* <http://www.crisisgroup.org/home/index.cfm?id=3980&l=1>, at ii (require free registration); Horowitz, *supra* note 140.

[158] Jeff McMahan, *The Limits of National Partiality, in* THE MORALITY OF NATIONALISM 107 (Robert McKim & Jeff McMahan eds., Oxford Univ. Press 1997); MARGARET MOORE, THE ETHICS OF NATIONALISM (Oxford Univ. Press 2001) (especially at pages 102–103).

[159] Such reasoning is easiest to see in the case of linguistic cultures—established languages, lingua francas, merely through resolving co-ordination difficulties, are likely to drive out less widely used languages unless there is public regulation. For a subtle theory of "ethnic capital formation and conflict", see Ronald Wintrobe, *Some Economics of Ethnic Capital Formation and Conflict, in* NATIONALISM AND RATIONALITY 43 (Albert Breton *et al.* eds., Cambridge Univ. Press 1995).

single-person executives and public sectors with difference-blind composition rules. Integration is often merely assimilation with good manners. Some multiculturalists insist integrationism is a form of Western colonialism which imposes its conception of liberal culture.[160]

Liberal accommodationists argue that properly constructed systems of territorial pluralism or consociations do not require corporate privileges, and even centripetalists acknowledge that this criticism of consociation is unfair. Pluralist territorialists argue that many minority communities, contrary to the conventional integrationist wisdom, have civic rather than exclusivist ethnic national identities,[161] and are more likely to develop the former when in secure possession of their own territorial units of government. Quebec, Catalonia, Scotland, and Kurdistan are all no more likely, and in some cases far less likely, to repress or control minorities than the broader states of which they are member regions. What is essential, pluralist territorialists argue, is not to deny territorial autonomy to stateless nations but rather to ensure that these nations implement accommodationist arrangements for their own regional minorities.[162]

Liberal consociationalists (and centripetalists) grant that the privileging of particular communities occurs in corporate consociations, but insist that consociational institutions may also be liberal in nature: for example, they may reward any party with electoral support rather than specified groups.[163] As we have already discussed, the rules for constituting South Africa's executive between 1994 and 1999 and Northern Ireland's executive (apart from its first and deputy first ministers) since 1998, are based on liberal consociational principles. This fact has not stopped one critic from asserting that d'Hondt, the rule used for executive composition in Northern Ireland, privileges certain identities. Peter Emerson, the director of the de Borda Institute, advocates the replacement of the d'Hondt rule for electing the executive and its replacement with PR-STV, so that "all assembly members could participate on an equal basis without using any sectarian labels". The fact that d'Hondt treats all members equally and does not require them to use any labels, sectarian or otherwise, seems to have escaped him.[164] These liberal consociational mechanisms are fair to all groups, including nonethnic groups and are fairer to small groups than either integrationist electoral and executive institutions. Most consociationalists eschew corporate devices and prefer liberal rules that equally protect whatever groups emerge in free elections. They prefer "self-determination to pre-determination".[165] They understand that parties

[160] James Tully, Strange Multiplicity: Constitutionalism in an Age of Diversity (Cambridge Univ. Press 1995).
[161] Michael Keating, Plurinational Democracy: Stateless Nations in a Post-sovereignty Era 57 (Oxford Univ. Press 2001).
[162] *Id.* at 165.
[163] Lijphart, *supra* note 93; O'Leary, *supra* note 48; McGarry, *supra* note 93.
[164] Peter Emerson, *Reforming the Belfast Agreement: Just What's at Stake?*, Belfast Telegraph, Sept. 23, 2003.
[165] Lijphart, *supra* note 93.

to consociational pacts may make entrenchment deals, such as settlements that institutionally represent (and privilege) certain identities, and that they may do so both for self-interested reasons because they have genuine existential anxieties about the security of the communities they represent. But liberals think that it is usually desirable and possible to protect groups without corporatist principles. For example, two of us argued in 2004 that under the review provided for within Northern Ireland's Belfast Agreement, the parties should make changes that would remove as many corporate principles as possible. We commended the use of the d'Hondt formula for the appointment of the first and deputy first ministers, with a built-in safeguard to ensure that neither nationalists nor unionists could assume both positions.[166] These changes have been taken up in the St. Andrew's Agreement of 13 October, 2006.

While Horowitz has acknowledged that liberal consociations are fair among different ethnic communities, consociationalists have criticized centripetal vote-pooling institutions for unfairly privileging the majority or largest group over others groups. This is because politicians from such groups have to pool fewer votes to win office than politicians from smaller groups. Such groups have to pool fewer votes.

On the question of resource distribution, territorial pluralists generally reject the idea that distributive justice requires centralized control of resources, or a central government with a monopoly of, or even the preponderant share of, fiscal resources whether from royalty payments or income taxes. That after all is to presume integration. Central control of resources and fiscal instruments may be appropriate where citizens share a common national identity or are willing to regard themselves as part of a common insurance pool. But where no such unified nation or demos exists, the promotion of fiscal or resource centralization may be deeply divisive. It may also encourage coercively assimilationist fantasies in the capital city. However, territorial pluralism may be impossible unless there is some distribution of resources across the state. But equally, it may be impossible for some minorities to exercise meaningful autonomy, and minorities which see themselves as penalized by unfair distributive mechanisms may seek to secede or destabilize the state. Accommodationists, therefore, support a complex balancing act, involving adequate distribution to make territorial pluralism feasible but without excessive centralization that would make territorial pluralism meaningless. There may be disputes among accommodationists on whether or not a particular settlement reflects this balance.[167] Accommodationists are prepared to support a progressive income tax, uniformly applied throughout the state, the proceeds of which are redistributed through equalization formulae. They may be willing to agree to provisions for the per capita allocation of revenues from

---

[166] McGARRY & O'LEARY, *supra* note 75, app. A.

[167] For example, see the rival views on the natural resource provisions of Iraq's 2005 constitution in McGarry & O'Leary, *supra* note 43 and Horowitz, *supra* note 140.

natural resources, but some will not want such a procedure to enhance the powers of the federal treasury. In some pluralist federations where the center has been a source of despotic abuse, regions are unwilling to grant the federal government any significant fiscal powers until it has earned trust.[168]

Democracy

Can either integration or accommodation make a stronger claim to be consistent with democratic values? As readers will have anticipated, integrationists and accommodationists regard their preferred strategies of political design as more democratic than those of their respective rival. Integrationists believe that accommodationists undermine democracy.[169] Republicans think that all types of federation, national or pluralist, are "demos-constraining". They interfere with the general will. They regard consociations as the surrender of public power to interest groups. Some integrationist critics, particularly on the left, focus on the consociational practice of negotiations and accommodation among *elites*.[170] They see such summit diplomacy as inconsistent with the development of a modern participatory democracy, which does not restrict civic responsibility to voting in elections or even membership in political parties, but encourages active and ongoing political engagement through a wide range of voluntary associations. Some have even argued that consociation requires public deference towards leaders.[171] Liberals generally share republicans support for majoritarian forms of democracy, providing there are protections for individuals through a bill of rights. They focus on what they condemn as the anticompetitive nature of consociational politics and cite Lijphart's one-off and unfortunate description of consociation as government by elite "cartel". If everyone is in government, integrationists charge, how can governing parties be held to account at election time? Consociation's inclusive dispositions are said to render opposition politics impossible. Thus, Brass claims that the price of consociation is "abandoning a viable opposition politics".[172] Without opposition, there is no one to hold the government accountable, even between elections, and no one to pose as an alternate government. This last set of concerns about consociation are shared by centripetalists, reflecting their links with the American liberal tradition.[173] Centripetalists argue that their votepooling coalition, unlike a consociational "grand coalition", can be based on minimum-winning rules and therefore is quite consistent with opposition and competitive politics.

---

[168] O'Leary, *supra* note 36.
[169] Courtney Jung & Ian Shapiro, *South Africa's Negotiated Transition: Democracy, Opposition and the New Constitutional Order*, 23 POL. & SOC'Y 269, 273–274 (1995); Horowitz, *supra* note 136, at 256–257.
[170] Taylor, *supra* note 40.
[171] Brass, *supra* note 116, at 339; Paul Dixon, *Why the Good Friday Agreement in Northern Ireland is Not Consociational*, 76 POL. Q. 357, 359 (2005).
[172] Brass, *supra* note 116, at 334, 339.
[173] HOROWITZ, A DEMOCRATIC SOUTH AFRICA?, *supra* note 49, at 256–257.

Accommodationists, whether supporters of consociation, centripetalism, multiculturalism, or territorial pluralism, share the basic position that majority rule in divided places is likely to be partisan rule, and to be seen as such, even when it is padded with integrationist safety mechanisms.[174] Consociationalists have argued that the electoral systems that are favored by integrationists usually do not even produce majority rule, but rather minority or plurality rule.[175] The single member plurality system that is favored by some integrationists frequently results in politicians being elected with plurality rather than majority support. When it is combined with the minimum-winning rule for forming executives and party whipping, the result can be government by a faction (a slim majority of a minority).[176] Consociationalists also point out that the alternative vote in single member districts, which is favored by centripetalists, eliminates small parties (likely to be supported by minorities) and artificially boosts the legislative majority of the winning party which may facilitate the abuse of power. They argue that an advantage of proportional representation, by contrast, is that it makes it more likely that there will be a genuine legislative majority supported by a majority of voters.[177] Consociationalists also point out that the majoritarian Westminster model which is often positively contrasted with consociation does not necessarily provide strong oppositions. Plurality rule can convert electoral minorities (in first preference votes) into unassailable legislative majorities, and sometimes can reduce the opposition to an ineffective rump, one that excludes important minorities. This outcome happens frequently in Caribbean democracies. An extreme case occurred in the Canadian province of New Brunswick in 1987 when the Liberals won every seat in the legislature with 60.4 percent of the vote.[178]

In any case, the accusation that consociational executives lack democratic opposition is only (partially) accurate when leveled at grand or complete consociational executives, such as coalitions in which all parties from all segments are represented.[179] In fact, in most alleged cases of grand coalition small parties may be in opposition. Between 1999 and 2002, the four major parties in Northern Ireland sat in government, with 89 of the Assembly's 108 seats.[180] Five parties and nineteen members of legislative assembly (MLAs) were still left in

[174] W. ARTHUR LEWIS, POLITICS IN WEST AFRICA (Oxford Univ. Press 1965) (especially Lecture III, The Plural Society).

[175] Arend Lijphart, *The Alternative Vote: A Realistic Alternative for South Africa?*, 18 POLITIKON 91 (1991).

[176] Jack H. Nagel, *Expanding the Spectrum of Democracies: Reflections on Proportional Representation in New Zealand*, in DEMOCRACY AND INSTITUTIONS: THE LIFE AND WORK OF AREND LIJPHART 113 (Markus Crepaz, Thomas Koelbe & David Wilford eds., Univ. Michigan Press 2000).

[177] *Id.* at 176.

[178] Stewart Hyson, *A One Party Legislature: Where's 'Her Majesty's Loyal Opposition' in the Loyalist Province?*, 11 CAN. PARLIAMENTARY REV. 22 (1998).

[179] O'Leary, *supra* note 48.

[180] O'Leary, *supra* note 75, at 1665, tbl. 2.

opposition. But consociational executives may also be concurrent (restricted to parties commanding majority but not total support within their respective segments) or weak (if at least one of the segmental parties in office commands only plurality support within its group). They also may be based on some but not all segments. In such cases, significant parties will exist outside the government to criticize its policies. In any case, mechanisms can be deployed to render the government more accountable—through empowering backbenchers to hold the ministers of other parties to account through interpellation and enhancing the powers of auditors, ombudsmen and courts.

Consociational institutions can also foster a competitive politics. If seats in the executive are based proportionately on seats in the legislature, then there are incentives for all political parties to compete, within or across ethnic groups, to increase their share of legislative and executive positions. Consociation's supporters happily concede that their preferred system depends on the capacity of leaders to make compromises and persuade their followers to accept such compromises, but insist that effective settlements require leaders who are authentic representatives of their communities.[181]

Consociationalists tend to be skeptical rather than sanguine about the merits of participatory democracy. They observe that active participation from civil society may simply lay bare deep divisions and make it difficult to achieve agreement, as happened in Canada between 1987 and 1992.[182] But that said, the shaping of consociational settlements, their ratification, and their aftermaths need not be the exclusive property of political elites. In Northern Ireland, the policing reform that followed the Belfast Agreement resulted from a widespread consultation process that involved 2,500 written submissions and public meetings in every district council area (attended by 10,000 people and at which 1000 spoke).[183] The agreement itself was ratified by simultaneous referenda in both parts of Ireland. It was, therefore, a democratic advance on its predecessor, the Sunningdale Agreement of 1973, which was an elite deal arrived at during a private British government retreat and not ratified by referendum.[184] If the Belfast Agreement is renewed and survives, it will owe no small part of its durability to its original popular endorsement. Lastly, it is likely that the benefits of deliberative democracy depend greatly on the participants sharing a common language and frame of reference. Therefore, it may be more attainable within linguistically homogeneous substate communities than in diverse country-wide settings.

---

[181] LIJPHART, *supra* note 45, at 53.

[182] PETER H. RUSSELL, CONSTITUTIONAL ODYSSEY: CAN CANADIANS BECOME A SOVEREIGN PEOPLE? (3d ed., Univ. Toronto Press 2004).

[183] THE REPORT OF THE INDEPENDENT COMMISSION ON POLICING FOR NORTHERN IRELAND (HMSO 1999) (known as The Patten Report).

[184] Stefan Wolff, *Context and Content: Sunningdale and Belfast Compared, in* ASPECTS OF THE BELFAST AGREEMENT 11 (Rick Wilford ed, Oxford Univ. Press 2001).

5. When is integration or accommodation appropriate?

Today, democratic states, if they decide not to break up or downsize territorially, are limited normatively and practically to variants of integration and accommodation when responding to diversity. Within the past half century or so, these two methods have displaced normatively and at the level of lip-service rival strategies based on assimilation, control, partition, and even ethnic expulsions. There is still a predilection for integration among Western states, citizens in some communities, and indeed among western academics. But there is considerable support for accommodation, and some evidence of growth in such support. This paper has endeavored to be fair toward the two broad sets of strategies. Indeed, it is our view that each has some empirical and normative merit in particular demographic and historic contexts. To conclude, we shall briefly describe the contexts in which each method is most appropriate, focusing on their relative merits. A more comprehensive analysis is beyond the scope of this paper.

Integration

Integration into a single public identity is facilitated when social cleavages within a state are crosscutting rather than reinforcing, assuming that each cleavage is of roughly equal potential salience. Integration has been helped in places like India and Switzerland where linguistic and religious divisions (and in the latter case, tribal and caste) divisions have overlapped and crosscut each other. In other words, integration is more likely when societies are not deeply polarized along national, ethnic, religious, or linguistic lines, when ethnicity, class, and other social cleavages are incongruent, or when there is already extensive heterogeneity, hybridity and mixing.

Integration may also be successful with minorities that are small in number and interspersed among others and well disposed to the strategy. A small and dispersed minority usually cannot aspire, realistically, to public recognition through either territorial autonomy or consociation, and it is difficult to build coalitions out of such minorities. Territorially dispersed groups find it difficult to mobilize to defend their culture, even if the technological and media revolutions make this easier than it once was. Integration is particularly workable when the minorities involved are not "homeland peoples", or those who are living on their ancestral territory. In such cases they are less likely to see themselves as national communities, entitled to some form of autonomy.

However, not all immigrants have the same potential to integrate. Those for whom their religion mandates bringing the sacred into the public domain find it more difficult to integrate than those who do not, especially if the public domain is already explicitly or tacitly defined by the public agenda of another religion or if it is already secular. Likewise those who see themselves as diasporas and who maintain contact with their homelands and entertain a return of the exiles may be less likely to integrate. There is some evidence that the integration of many European immigrants into the United States, Argentina, Australia, Canada, and New Zealand in the nineteenth and early twentieth centuries was facilitated by the fact that they lacked what anthropologists call a "high culture". In other words they were often not extensively educated or fully literate.[185] Many contemporary immigrants in the wealthy democracies, by contrast, are professionals with training from foreign universities who may find it easier to maintain their culture of origin.

Fully successful integration depends on the willingness of the state and its dominant community to accept the partial privatization of their culture, and to accept new members into its political community. Even large territorially concentrated minorities may be integrated if the offer of equal citizenship, with public laws that are equal and non-discriminatory, is made early enough. Once a minority has become nationally mobilized in reaction to blocked integration, however, it is likely to be too late for it to be won back into acceptance of integration. Lastly, integration may be facilitated if the state lacks a dominant community, and if, as a consequence, its single public identity is genuinely composite. Countries that are very diverse, and have no staatsvolk, such as Tanzania, may therefore find it easier to promote integration than those with two or three major communities.

Accommodation

Territorial accommodation works best for and is most sought by the middle-sized battalions that are concentrated in their own national space. Territorially concentrated groups living on their own homelands will likely reject integration as a (not so subtle) way of letting their culture die. The demand for autonomy is likely to come not just from large territorially concentrated groups. Many Corsicans have called for autonomy from France. Native communities in Canada have demanded autonomy since the late 1960s when the Canadian government, influenced by the American civil rights movement, tried to integrate them into a common Canadian citizenship. The South Tyrolese, helped by the neighboring state of Austria, have helped secure increasingly extensive autonomy within Italy.[186] Large, nationally mobilized minorities are likely to insist, not just on

---

[185] On the distinction between high and low cultures, see ERNEST GELLNER, NATIONS AND NATIONALISM 56 (2d ed., Blackwell 2006); on immigration and transformations of ethnic communities in the U.S., see *inter alia,* THOMAS SOWELL, ETHNIC AMERICA: A HISTORY (Basic Books 1981); LAWRENCE H. FUCHS, THE AMERICAN KALEIDOSCOPE: RACE, ETHNICITY, AND THE CIVIC CULTURE (Wesleyan Univ. Press 1990); ROGERS M. SMITH, CIVIC IDEALS: CONFLICTING VISIONS OF CITIZENSHIP IN U.S. HISTORY (Yale Univ. Press 1997).

[186] *See* Farimah Daftary, *The Matignon Process and Insular Autonomy as a Response to Self-Determination Claims in Corsica, in* EUROPEAN YEARBOOK OF MINORITY ISSUES 1 2001/2002, at 299 (Kluwer Law Int'l 2003); HAROLD CARDINAL, THE UNJUST SOCIETY (Douglas & McIntyre 1999); Stefan Wolff, *Settling an Ethnic Conflict through Power-Sharing: South Tyrol, in* MANAGING AND SETTLING ETHNIC CONFLICTS: PERSPECTIVES ON SUCCESSES AND FAILURES IN EUROPE, AFRICA AND ASIA 57 (Ulrich Schneckener & Stefan Wolff eds., Palgrave Macmillan 2004).

autonomy, but on power sharing within the federal government. The situation of the Quebecois, the Turkish Cypriots, and the Kurds of Iraq, is quite different in this respect from that of the Corsicans, Moldova's Gagauz, or the South Tyrolese. Their choice is not between integration and accommodation, but between accommodation and secession.

Consociation is demanded by territorially dispersed and interspersed minorities, including small ones, where politics has been deeply polarized and where the relevant minority has sufficient bargaining power. Burundi's Tutsi community, with its fears of retribution by the sizable Hutu majority, and its strength in the armed forces, will not be satisfied with a majoritarian government based on equal citizenship.[187] In deeply divided places, we are skeptical that Horowitz's centripetal approach will result from free negotiations between the parties.

In some cases, where nations spill over state borders, neither consociation nor pluralist federation may be sufficient to achieve a functioning accommodation of the major groups. Northern Ireland's peace agreement required institutions that linked the British and Irish governments, and Northern Ireland with the Irish Republic.[188] In most contexts, such transstate settlements are difficult to imagine, but they may become more feasible when the relevant states participate within an overarching institutional framework, such as the European Union.

The fact that integration and accommodation are both more politically feasible in some contexts rather than others helps to explain why both these strategies are adopted by democratic states, acting singularly or jointly, and indeed why states may combine one approach to one group with another approach to another group. States are more pragmatic than academics, though they are not equally pragmatic. Many states follow integrationist policies for immigrants and accommodationist policies toward nationally mobilized communities. The international community, which usually preaches integration, has been prepared to back accommodation where that has been demanded, if only, and unfortunately, after rebellion has threatened order.[189]

6. Conclusion

Nation-states are, by disposition, integrationist or assimilationist. They are the role models in world politics. The impetus for accommodation comes not from generous nation-states, but from those whose boundaries, placements, and numbers make them unlikely to fit within the existing configurations of nation-states.

---

[187] RENE LEMARCHAND, THE DYNAMICS OF VIOLENCE IN CENTRAL AFRICA (book manuscript in press, Univ. Pa. Press).
[188] Belfast Agreement, *supra* note 72, strands 2 & 3.
[189] Will Kymlicka, *The Evolving Basis of European Norms of Minority Rights, in* EUROPEAN INTEGRATION AND THE NATIONALITIES QUESTION 35, 51–55 (John McGarry & Michael Keating eds., Routledge 2005).

Estimations of power usually decide whether a government will pursue integration or accommodation toward a particular community. The mobilization capacity of a community partly shapes its orientation toward either integration or accommodation. In general, integration is the politics of the historically weak or the newly arrived, whereas accommodation shapes the politics of those powerful enough to resist assimilation but not strong or united enough to achieve secession.

Nation-state regimes will choose integrationist strategies that will achieve assimilation as a long-run byproduct, but such strategies will only work easily with the weak (especially the dispersed) or the grateful (the voluntary immigrant). Such regimes become accommodationist by necessity rather than from Herderian generosity. They recognize multinationality, multiethnicity or multilingualism as brute facts which cannot be altered except at unacceptable costs. They adopt accommodation to forestall or stop violent politics or secession.

Minorities may underestimate or overestimate their bargaining power and pursue integration when they could achieve accommodation, or pursue accommodation when the regime is only likely to offer them integration. Their success will depend on their correctly appraising the nature of the state that contains them, and exploiting such opportunities for changes that come their way.

More empirical testing is required to evaluate these assumptions. This paper will have served its purpose if it has succeeded in showing the main contours of the normative and constitutional debate. We make no suggestion that the debate is resolved.

PART II
THEORETICAL PERSPECTIVES

3

Beyond the dichotomy of universalism and difference: Four responses to cultural diversity

*Alan Patten**

When political theorists discuss cultural diversity, they often operate with a basic dichotomy. They argue that institutional responses to diversity can be either "integrationist" or "accommodationist" in character: that institutional responses can be based on either a model of "universal" citizenship or one of "differentiated" citizenship.

With its organizing distinction between a "politics of universalism" and a "politics of difference", Charles Taylor's widely read essay "The Politics of Recognition" is, perhaps, the most conspicuous example of a reliance on this dichotomy.[1] But similar dichotomies can be found throughout the literature. For instance, Iris Marion Young's engagement with problems raised by culture and identity is built around an opposition between ideals of "assimilation" and "difference".[2] In the same vein, Will Kymlicka's influential work on cultural diversity has been shaped by a binary opposition between "group-differentiated" or "minority" rights and the "common rights of citizenship".[3] Furthermore, Brian Barry accepts these binary definitions of the range of possibilities, when he sets out to defend "unitary republican citizenship" against the "multiculturalism" advocated by Taylor, Young, Kymlicka, and others.[4]

All of these different, yet related, dichotomies represent alternative approaches that a state might adopt toward the various identities and cultural attachments

* Associate Professor of Politics, Princeton University. Email: apatten@princeton.edu
[1] CHARLES TAYLOR, *The Politics of Recognition, in* MULTICULTURALISM AND "THE POLITICS OF RECOGNITION": AN ESSAY 25 (Amy Gutmann ed., Princeton Univ. Press 1992).
[2] IRIS MARION YOUNG, JUSTICE AND THE POLITICS OF DIFFERENCE ch. 6 (Princeton Univ. Press 1990).
[3] WILL KYMLICKA, MULTICULTURAL CITIZENSHIP: A LIBERAL THEORY OF MINORITY RIGHTS (OXFORD POLITICAL THEORY) (Oxford Univ. Press 1996).
[4] BRIAN BARRY, CULTURE AND EQUALITY: AN EGALITARIAN CRITIQUE OF MULTICULTURALISM (Harvard Univ. Press 2002).

of its citizens. To be more precise, they refer to alternative principles of constitutional and institutional design that a state might follow in responding to diversity. By a "principle", I have in mind a general guideline that helps to organize judgments about particulars by articulating an objective that is worth pursuing or a standard that is worth following. To count as a principle, a guideline must be sufficiently general and abstract to be helpful for a range of different kinds of cases and situations. It should also help to clarify the rationale for the particular policies and designs it recommends. In this sense, the principles in question are intermediate principles: they serve to connect particular policies and designs with values and objectives.

Understood in this way, the principles of institutional design are natural focal points for normative reflection on possible constitutional and institutional responses to diversity. They offer guidelines on how the state should respond to diversity, and, although they may not refer explicitly to values, they leave political theorists and others in a position to reflect on the objectives and values that underlie different state policies. Although my focus in this chapter will mainly be on these normative issues, it is worth noting that principles of this kind are also useful for empirical work. They help to organize observed policies under different headings in a way that facilitates empirical analysis of the relationship between approaches to diversity and other variables and outcomes. Empirical researchers can ask: What social and political outcomes are observed when the state follows one principle or another? Indeed, one reason why principles like these can be useful for empirical work is that they organize particular observations in ways that reflect the underlying issues that researchers, and citizens more generally, do or ought to care about.

The main contention of my paper is that the dichotomous way of thinking about the principles under discussion is too simple to do justice to the problems being considered. Of course, theoretical simplification is a part of abstraction and, as such, is sometimes an important tool of analysis. However, for people interested in the problems of constitutional and institutional design, the simplification to be discussed here leads to a serious distortion of the possible solutions to the problems raised by diversity, the normative grounds available on behalf of those solutions, and the ways that real-world conflicts should be understood. Although the dichotomy may be sufficient for some kinds of comparative analysis, when analysts interested in public policy rely on it they are likely to find themselves muddled about the basic rationale and objectives of the policy options they are considering and confused about whether specific policies are "working" or not.

We do better if we distinguish four distinct principles of institutional and constitutional design, which I label "disestablishment", "nation building", "equality of status", and "cultural preservation". As I will argue, this fourfold distinction does a better job of capturing the normative logic of the various approaches to diversity than do the standard dichotomies. As a result, it provides a superior empirical organization of the different sorts of actions that states may take in response to diversity, as well as a better insight into the underlying value conflicts and choices.

In addition to clarifying the differences among the four principles, I will also make some points about the strengths and weaknesses of each. It will not be my aim to single out any one of the principles for a full-scale defense (or criticism), but I do want to assert enough about each to motivate their inclusion in the repertoire of options from which constitutional and institutional designers may choose. Equality of status is often overlooked by political theorists, even though it is an obvious way of understanding actual practice, in certain cases. Consequently, I will pay special attention to laying out its normative appeal and to distinguishing it from cultural preservation. When equality-of-status policies are viewed through the distorting lens of the cultural-preservation principle, they open themselves up to a number of difficult and avoidable objections. Again, though, I should emphasize that my aim is not to defend equality of status against all the alternatives, but to secure for it a place in the repertoire of policy options alongside the others. Each of the principles, in my view, is appropriate in certain contexts and inappropriate in others.

I shall develop these points mainly with reference to the case of linguistic diversity, though I will not hesitate to draw on other examples where they are helpful; additionally, I think that the framework I develop may be generalized beyond the linguistic case. Language policy is important and controversial in its own right, and it is also one of the leading examples referred to in the general literature on culture and multiculturalism. Debates about language policy involve a basic conflict between the advantages to everyone of having a common language and the special importance that most people attach to their own language. For this reason, perhaps more so than for other forms of cultural attachment and belonging, linguistic debates give rise to the dichotomous approaches mentioned at the outset. Despite this temptation to dichotomize, I shall argue that we are better off thinking about institutional responses to linguistic diversity using the fuller fourfold range of principles.

1. Disestablishment

When Taylor writes of the "politics of universalism", he has in mind a principle with two distinguishable parts.[5] First, it extends to all citizens a full set of basic liberal rights and entitlements, including rights to freedom of conscience, speech, and association, and entitlements to various protections of the welfare state. Second, it calls upon the state otherwise to adopt a stance of difference-blindness with regard to the diverse cultures and identities of its citizens. Taylor associates

---

[5] TAYLOR, *supra* note 1, at 37–44.

the principle with the Kantian idea that what commands respect for persons is their status as rational agents who are capable of directing their own lives. The principle takes individuals as individuals and extends to each an identical basket of entitlements useful for pursuing their own lives.

It is fairly clear what the first aspect of universalism involves and how it forms part of a possible response to difference and diversity. With their package of rights and entitlements, individuals enjoy the freedom to form, express, and revise cultural and other identities in the spheres of private life and civil society. It is less clear, on the other hand, how the second aspect of universalism should be understood. What does it mean for the state to adopt a stance of difference-blindness?

In answering this question, the main point to emphasize about the universalism principle is that it is actually two different principles. This is because there are two quite distinct ways that a state might achieve difference-blindness. A state might consider itself difference-blind because it gives no recognition or assistance to *any* cultural identity to which its citizens are attached (I shall call this the "disestablishment" principle). Or it might consider itself difference-blind because it picks out *one* cultural identity and systematically promotes it for all citizens (the "nation building" principle). On both of these views, the state makes no attempt to acknowledge, accommodate, or assist the variety of different cultures and identities to which citizens are attached in a diverse society.

The first of these forms of difference-blindness models itself on a standard liberal approach to religion, which is grounded in the value of neutrality.[6] The state is neutral with respect to religion when it refuses to regard the success or failure of any particular religion followed by its citizens as an appropriate reason for it to act. Instead, the appropriate response to religious diversity is for the state to establish a framework of rules that is fair to all individuals, and then to permit individuals to develop their own religious convictions and to choose their own religious affiliations within the space left to them by these rules. Depending on the choices and convictions of individuals, some religions will flourish and others may decline or even disappear. The key marker of the state's neutrality, here, is its intentions: a state is neutral on matters of religion when it does not intentionally set out to promote or maintain any particular religion. Instead, it directs its attention to establishing fair background conditions under which different religious forms of life can strive for success.[7]

As I shall emphasize later, neutrality does not necessarily imply difference-blindness. To take this final step, it is important to say something more concrete about how the state establishes fair background conditions. It does imply

---

    [6] *Id.* at 56–61.
    [7] See JOHN RAWLS, POLITICAL LIBERALISM 190–200 (Columbia Univ. Press 1993) for a formulation of the liberal idea of neutrality that incorporates the notion of fair background conditions. I discuss this formulation in more detail in Alan Patten, *Liberal Neutrality and Language Policy*, 31 PHIL. & PUB. AFF. 356 (2003). For a related formulation, see BARRY, *supra* note 4, at 27–29.

difference-blindness if one assumes that the best way for the state to establish a fair or level playing field is by refusing to extend recognition to anyone. On this view, which is sometimes referred to as disestablishment or the "separation of church and state", the state refuses to acknowledge, accommodate, or assist any particular religion.

These reflections on religion suggest a possible interpretation of the politics of universalism. We might think of universalism as the attempt to generalize the neutrality-based idea of disestablishment from religion to broader questions of cultural recognition. As we will see in a moment, there can be problems with this generalization from religion to culture. On some issues the state can hardly help but take a stand on certain matters of culture and identity. I will discuss and develop this point in a moment by first considering why universalism understood this way seems a powerful position.

One reason is that there are many instances in which it does, in fact, seem possible for the state to avoid taking a stand on questions of culture. A person's culture is connected with his tastes and preferences, and with a range of decisions about how to live. It is connected, that is, with his decisions about food, dress, music, celebrations, patterns of domesticity, forms of discourse, sexuality, and so on. There may occasionally be good reasons for the state to seek to influence these decisions (such as when there is a danger of harm to others), but it is hardly unavoidable that the state would take a stand on them. In these areas, a stance of neutrality that parallels religious disestablishment does at least seem possible. More than that, it seems plausible to think that the state ought to adopt such a stance on many of these questions. For the state to seek to manage and manipulate the choices of its citizens in these areas would offend precisely those Kantian ideals of autonomy and agency that Taylor associates with universalism.

To be sure, many legitimate state decisions will impact individual decision making about what forms of life to adopt. For example, changes in the tax code or a decision to provide publicly subsidized day care might influence patterns of domesticity, which, in turn, will be entangled with beliefs that would commonly be thought of as "cultural". But if these state policies do not set out to encourage or discourage a particular form of culture—if they were justified, for example, by a concern for gender equality— then they do not violate the principle of neutrality at the level at which it is being applied here. A "disestablishmentarian" response to cultural diversity would not rule out policies of this kind, but it would condemn policies that consciously set out to encourage or discourage particular forms of cultural life.

It might be responded that belief in gender equality (or any goal the state might adopt) is itself culturally inflected, and thus the tax or day-care policy is encouraging and discouraging particular forms of culture after all. While this is true, it is less damaging to the approach under consideration than is sometimes supposed. It is perfectly open to the proponent of neutrality to argue that the principle of neutrality should be applied on some kinds of questions and not on others.[8] Presumably the neutralist favors neutrality because she believes in certain values and principles that appear to demand it in a range of different areas. It would be incoherent for her to be neutral about those values and principles. In the example at hand, it would be perfectly coherent for someone to believe in values like autonomy, equal respect, gender equality, and so on, but, at the same time, be in favor of state neutrality with regard to the particular choices people make, and the identities they express, within a framework defined by those values. It is analogous to thinking that a university should impose a degree of structure on its curriculum and, at the same time, that it should leave students free from pushing and prodding to make their own choices within the spaces left by the structure.

So one way in which we might make sense of the idea of difference-blindness associated with universalism is by saying that the state should not establish any particular culture or identity. It should treat fairly the different identities and cultural attachments that citizens will have and should not set out intentionally to encourage or discourage any of them. I call this claim the disestablishment principle and regard it as a plausible reading of what Taylor, Kymlicka, Barry, and others have in mind when they talk about universalism. It is also, I have tried to suggest, a plausible view in itself, one that is connectable with the assumption that there is value and dignity in individuals charting their own courses in life, without being pushed or prodded in one direction or another on the basis of collective judgments about valuable cultures and identities.

Although I have suggested that the disestablishment principle is a reasonably plausible view for at least some of the decisions about culture a state could face, it might seem as though this is not true in the area of language policy. Language looks like one of those areas of social life in which the state can hardly help but take a stand for or against certain identities and cultural attachments. The state cannot help but use some language or other(s) in conducting its own internal business, in offering services to its citizens, in organizing the public school system, and so on.

This is a genuine limit on the disestablishment principle, which will be important later when I consider the equality-of-status principle. But for now it is worth observing that the disestablishment principle is not entirely inapplicable in the area of language policy. Certainly, the state does not need to legislate the private language choices of its citizens. It can leave citizens free from coercion and inducement to determine how to communicate with one another in the domains of family life, religious association, civil society, and the economy.

A state that follows the disestablishment principle in this area would not prohibit people from using particular languages in private situations. Thus, the

---

[8] GEORGE SHER, BEYOND NEUTRALITY: PERFECTIONISM AND POLITICS 13–14 (Cambridge Univ. Press 1997); Jeremy Waldron, *Legislation and Moral Neutrality, in* LIBERAL NEUTRALITY 61 (Robert E. Goodin & Andrew Reeve eds., Routledge 1989).

long-standing restrictions by the Turkish government on publications in the Kurdish language represent a violation of the disestablishment principle.[9] (They also violate the first "basic rights" principle of Taylor's universalism.) On the other hand, the famous U.S. Supreme Court case *Meyer v. Nebraska*, which established the right of parents to send their children to a school offering instruction in a language other than English, worked within the framework of the disestablishment principle.[10] The Court did not dispute the possibility that a restriction in this area might serve some recognizable goal of public policy, but it insisted that, even if this were the case, parents should have some space that is free from interference by the state to make choices for their children.

The disestablishment principle is also at issue in cases where, rather than prohibiting the use of particular languages in certain situations, the state is requiring their use. Many countries have linguistic regulations relating to the packaging of consumer goods, and some (such as France) mandate the use of a national language at conferences, on web sites, and in other areas of language use by private actors in the economy and civil society. These policies conflict with the disestablishment principle, though, as we shall see, they may well be supported by one of the other principles in the policy maker's repertoire, such as the nation-building or cultural-preservation principle.

2. Nation building

The second model of universalism adopts a very different approach to culture. It stresses the values that may be realized when citizens share certain forms of culture and identity, typically including a shared language, a common national identity, and a democratic political culture. Instead of prohibiting the state from promoting any particular cultural identity, the claim here is the opposite: the state should encourage its citizens to converge on certain forms of culture and identity. I call this view "nation building", since it is often the position of people who believe that fostering a strong and inclusive nation is instrumental to the realization of various kinds of values. The nation-building principle is "blind to difference", since it seeks convergence by all citizens on a single national identity and culture, but it is obviously difference-blind in a very different way than the disestablishment principle.

---

[9] A report by *Human Rights Watch* suggests that restrictions on Kurdish language expression have been eased somewhat in recent years. Kurdish-language publications and broadcasts are now permitted, however publications are still routinely confiscated and broadcasts are given very brief airtime and are restricted in content. *See* HUM. RTS. WATCH, TURKEY: VIOLATIONS OF FREE EXPRESSION IN TURKEY, pt. IX Restrictions on the Use of the Kurdish Language (1999), *available at* <http://www.hrw.org/reports/1999/turkey/>.

[10] *Meyer v. Nebraska*, 262 U.S. 390 (1923).

Young seems to have had something like the nation-building principle in mind when she opposed her ideal of difference with the ideal of assimilation.[11] Insofar as she assumes that the ideal of assimilation is the only alternative to that of difference—so that arguments against the former, in effect, count as arguments in favor of the latter—her reasoning is undermined by the possibility of more than one interpretation of the liberal attachment to universalism. This, I take it, is Brian Barry's basic point when he insists against Young that liberals do not endorse any "ideal of assimilation" and, instead, associates liberalism with neutrality regarding particular forms of cultural expression and attachment.[12]

Still, it is clear that liberals (and others) do sometimes adopt a nation-building response to diversity, and their reasons for doing so are not always bad ones. The classic example of nation building, perhaps, is the French state following the 1789 Revolution.[13] The Jacobins and their nineteenth-century successors regarded nation building as an essential instrument in the struggle to consolidate and extend the gains of the Revolution. All inhabitants of France had to be made into French citizens, who spoke French and identified patriotically with French republican values. A common language and framework of belonging would secure for all citizens the conditions of political and social equality. It would also orient citizens toward the republic and its values and, thus, weaken the forces of reaction and counterrevolution. To achieve these objectives, the French state insisted on the use of French in all public business (something it continues to do today), and it consciously used the public school system, and other instruments of public policy, to diffuse the French language among all citizens and to forge a French national identity.

The French model, of course, has been emulated by many states since the nineteenth century. In the area of language policy, for instance, the advantages of having all citizens converge on the use of a single national language have struck many state builders as compelling.[14] A convergence of all citizens on such a language could:

1. enhance social mobility, by ensuring that all citizens are able to use the language in which much of the economy and civil society operate;

---

[11] It is worth noting, though, that "convergence" need not mean "assimilation". "Convergence" (or "integration", as it is sometimes put) implies that all citizens would come to share some common language and identity. By contrast, "assimilation" conjures up the idea that differences beyond this common language and identity would be eliminated, or, in other words, that citizens would not continue to use their "mother" tongue in certain non-public contexts, or would not think of their national identity in "hyphenated" terms (Italian-American, Irish-Canadian, etc.). Although it is certainly true that many actual nation-building projects have aimed for assimilation rather than convergence, this is not strictly called for by the normative arguments considered in the text. As such, I will generally assume the weaker, convergence-oriented version.

[12] BARRY, *supra* note 4, at 69–71.

[13] EUGEN WEBER, PEASANTS INTO FRENCHMEN: THE MODERNIZATION OF RURAL FRANCE, 1870–1914 (Stanford Univ. Press 1976).

[14] Alan Patten, *Political Theory and Language Policy*, 29 POL. THEORY 691 (2001); Alan Patten & Will Kymlicka, *Introduction: Language Rights and Political Theory: Context, Issues, and Approaches, in* LANGUAGE RIGHTS AND POLITICAL THEORY 1, 37–42 (Will Kymlicka & Alan Patten eds., Oxford Univ. Press 2003).

2. foster economic development, by placing at the disposal of employers a linguistically uniform workforce, capable of working together and of mastering new tasks and technologies with the help of manuals and training materials written in a standard language;

3. facilitate democratic deliberation, by establishing a single language in which citizens can communicate with each other in formal and informal contexts;

4. promote social solidarity, by helping to solidify a shared sense of national identity;

5. improve the efficiency of public institutions, by saving money on language training, translations, interpreters, and so on.

Very similar arguments are often made in favor of policies that encourage new immigrants to acquire, as swiftly as possible, the national language and identity of their adopted country. It is argued both that, unless immigrants learn the national language, they will face exclusion from the economic, political, and cultural life of their new home, and that ongoing linguistic diversity will push downward the general level of trust and social solidarity. Like the arguments made in the state-building context, all of these arguments are recognizably universalist in form. They explicitly call for the promotion of a particular language and culture; however, they do so for the sake of universal values, such as liberty, equality, and democracy.

Articulating a sense shared by many critics, Taylor suggests that universalism is ultimately a confused and hypocritical position. It seems both to claim neutrality and to advocate the active promotion of a particular culture and identity. Taylor complains, for instance, that universalism's "supposedly neutral set of difference-blind principles is in fact a reflection of one hegemonic culture" and says that, with the politics of universalism, the "particular [is] masquerading as the universal".[15]

This criticism of universalism depends, however, on conflating the two variants of universalism that I have sought to distinguish. If one regards the two views as a single politics of universalism, then universalism is bound to seem hypocritical and confused. If, instead, one recognizes that they have distinctive logics and rely on different sorts of values and normative considerations, then this charge is harder to make. Unlike the principle of disestablishment, the nation-building principle need not claim neutrality. Its guiding principle is that the state cannot afford to be neutral about national culture and identity if various substantive values (social mobility, democracy, and so forth) are to be advanced. It is, thus, no great objection to universalism of this stripe to point out its incompatibility with neutrality or its connection with a particular culture; the non-neutral promotion of a particular culture is the whole point.[16]

---

[15] TAYLOR, *supra* note 1, at 43–44.

[16] It should be conceded that, on one interpretation of neutrality, this overstates the point somewhat. According to this interpretation, a policy is neutral whenever it can be supported by

As we have seen, the idea of disestablishment is committed to neutrality as its guiding principle. However, it is much harder to make the argument that there is confusion or hypocrisy. To be sure, the call for neutrality itself rests on a commitment to certain substantive values, and it would be incoherent to call for neutrality about those values. Neutrality, as I have presented it, rests on a certain Kantian view of respect for autonomous agency. In this weak sense, universalism reflects and promotes a particular culture. But, as I argued earlier, this is just to say that we are neutral on some sets of questions *because of* a commitment to some particular values (for example, because of a commitment to autonomous agency, we are neutral about *what* choices agents make). This is only problematic if one understands the neutralist to be making the incoherent claim that neutrality itself rests on neutral grounds—something that no thoughtful defender of neutrality or the disestablishment principle would ever want to say.[17]

The view that Taylor may have in mind in his critical remarks about universalism is a *composite* of the disestablishment and nation-building principles. On this view, the state responds to certain forms of diversity with a policy of disestablishment and to other forms of diversity with a policy of nation building. A genuine composite need not be confused or hypocritical. In a genuine composite, care is taken not to confuse the logic and normative basis of one component with the logic and bases of the other. Additionally, some principled reason is provided for treating a given issue or situation according to the logic of one component rather than the other; this is not decided in an ad hoc or morally arbitrary way.

This sort of composite universalism strikes me as a plausible, even powerful recipe for how the state might respond to diversity. As I suggested earlier, on some issues the state cannot help but promote a particular culture or identity, or it can, but if it tried to do so, significant values would be jeopardized. In these cases, nation building seems plausible and appealing. As we have seen, nation builders argue that a common national culture and identity are key conditions for the realization of substantive values such as social mobility and democracy. In many other cases, however, it seems perfectly possible for the state to refuse

reasonably weighty and plausible public reasons, where a public reason is roughly a reason that could be accepted by people who are otherwise committed to a plurality of different conceptions of the good. If nation-building policies are done for good public reasons (such as to promote equality of opportunity), rather than out of any assumption about the intrinsic superiority of the national culture, then on this view there need be no departure from neutrality. This concession does not, however, diminish the important difference between the disestablishment and nation-building principles. For the proponent of the former principle, the assumption is that the relevant public reasons recommend the equal treatment of each culture and, in particular, the equal refusal to extend any positive benefit to any one of them. For the proponent of nation building, by contrast, the assumption is that these reasons require the privileging of a particular culture and language— that of the nation. These are very different interpretations of the public reasons that are in play, and it is important not to conflate them.

[17] Jeremy Waldron, *supra* note 8, at 61; BARRY, *supra* note 4, at 27; SHER, *supra* note 8, at 13–14.

to promote any culture or identity, and no great value would be lost if it did. In these cases, disestablishment shows equal respect for all and thus should be given great priority.

3. Cultural preservation

So far I have distinguished two distinct principles that might guide the state's response to diversity. Both can be considered universalist, and it is possible to combine the two into a composite view. However, the point to emphasize is that each has its own logic and policy implications. When critics fail to disentangle the two variants of universalism, it becomes all too easy for them to dismiss universalism as incoherent and hypocritical.

Just as Taylor's "politics of universalism" admits two distinct interpretations and, thus, is really two principles, the same is true of what he terms the "politics of difference". According to Taylor's original formulation, a politics of difference extends to all citizens a basic package of standard liberal rights, plus a set of difference-sensitive policies designed to reach out to members of cultural minorities and provide acknowledgement, accommodation, and assistance to their ways of life.[18] The difference model does not abandon the idea of individuals as autonomous seekers of their own conceptions of the good, but it adds to this view of individuals the idea that they are also bearers of a cultural identity that they do not share with all other citizens.

Once again, the second aspect of this model gives rise to two distinct interpretations, suggesting that it is possible to distill from the politics of difference two rather different principles. In certain key passages of Taylor's essay, the requirement of assistance and accommodation to diverse identities is equated with giving bearers of those identities the resources they need for their groups, in fact, to survive as distinct entities.[19] Thus, the second aspect of the politics of difference is expressed through a set of policies designed to secure the cultural preservation of minorities—groups whose distinctness would otherwise be jeopardized by the homogenizing pressures of the majority culture. I shall say that policies having this objective follow the principle of cultural preservation.

A second possible interpretation of the politics of difference, by contrast, does not make the aim of cultural preservation the measure of assistance or accommodation to various identity groups. Instead, the guiding principle is what I shall call equality of status. On this view, the state should seek to extend to minority cultures the *same* recognition—the *same* forms of acknowledgement, accommodation, and assistance—that it extends to the majority. If, for instance, the state decides to designate as holidays the days associated with the majority religious

---

[18] TAYLOR, *supra* note 1, at 37–44, 58–61.
[19] *Id.* at 58 & 61.

faith (such as Sundays, Christmas, and so forth), then it should also give the same designation to days associated with minority religious faiths or make some comparable accommodation. Or, if the state offers public services, and conducts public business, in the majority language, then it should also be prepared to do so in various minority languages spoken by its citizens.

This version of the politics of difference is distinct from the first version, insofar as equality of status is no guarantee of cultural preservation. A group whose culture enjoys equal public status with that of the majority's may still have difficulty flourishing, or even surviving, because of the personal choices made by group members. As we shall see in a moment, the two principles of difference also rest on quite distinct normative foundations.

Taylor's main example of a government that is guided by the cultural preservation principle is Quebec and its Charter of the French Language.[20] Although it is possible to view Quebec's language policies through the lens of the nation-building principle, Taylor is right to suggest that the survival of the French language in North America has always been a preoccupation of politicians and policy makers in the province. To preserve and promote the French language in Quebec, the charter makes it impossible for most residents of the province to send their children to publicly funded schools that operate in a language other than French. It also requires all medium and large businesses to operate in French, and it insists (in its current version) that French be the most prominent language on all commercial signs.[21]

Taylor argues that liberals ought to be open to Quebec's policies and to the cultural preservation principle more generally. In part, this is because he does not seem to notice the equality-of-status alternative. Taylor's dichotomous conceptualization of the horizon of possibilities encourages an argument by process of elimination. He is skeptical about universalism, because he thinks it has internal problems of coherence and believes that cultural preservation is the only other alternative. Against this argument, I have defended universalism from the charge of internal incoherence and introduced a second possible version of the politics of difference. Even if Taylor were right to reject universalism, it would not follow that cultural preservation was the only alternative.

Taylor also adds a more positive argument in defense of the cultural preservation principle. To have a particular cultural identity, he assumes, is not just to have a set of present-oriented needs and preferences. It is also to have a future-oriented desire that subsequent generations should carry on one's cultural identity. "After all", he asks rhetorically, "if we're concerned with identity, then what is more legitimate than one's aspiration that it never be lost?"[22] To show due recognition for a person whose cultural identity takes this form, it is necessary, Taylor

---

[20] TAYLOR, *supra* note 1, at 52–61; *see also* Charter of the French Language, R.S.Q. ch. C-11 (2007) (Can.).

[21] Charter of the French Language, § 58.

[22] TAYLOR, *supra* note 1, at 40.

believes, for the state to adopt policies that actively seek to assist cultural groups to survive. This is exactly what the politics of universalism cannot do. As Taylor puts it, such a model is "inhospitable to difference because it can't accommodate what the members of distinct societies really aspire to, which is survival".[23]

Liberals have often opposed Quebec's language policies, sometimes because they believe that the specific instruments used to promote French go too far in restricting the use of other languages, and sometimes because they think that the preservation of a culture or language is not, in any case, an appropriate goal for a state to pursue.[24] This latter objection obviously hooks up with the idea of state neutrality introduced earlier in connection with the disestablishment principle.

The strongest formulations of the liberal challenge combine these two forms of objection.[25] For the sake of argument, suppose that all citizens of some community enjoy a full set of liberal rights and that income and wealth are fairly distributed. Suppose, also, that the disestablishment principle is guiding the state's linguistic policies, and that there are no historical injustices that have not been remedied in an appropriate way. Under these idealized circumstances, it is still possible that a minority language may fare poorly and that it may even face a threat to its future survival. There may be some more economically and culturally dominant language spoken in the same environs that exerts a strong gravitational pull on the speakers of the minority language. The cultural preservation principle would direct the state to intervene in this situation to enhance the status of the vulnerable language and lower the status of the more dominant one. For many liberals, however, it is hard to justify this intervention. Given the strong assumptions made about the background circumstances, it seems plausible to say that the anticipated decline of the vulnerable language reflects the choices and preferences of its speakers and prospective speakers. On the whole, liberals want to create an environment in which individuals may follow their own choices and preferences, and they oppose structures that allow some subset of citizens to impose their choices and preferences on everyone.

In my view, this is a fairly fundamental challenge to the cultural preservation principle. If the only interpretation of the politics of difference were the one offered by Taylor, then it would be tempting to conclude that some form or other of the politics of universalism (perhaps the composite described earlier) is the most defensible position. This conclusion would leave little room for minority cultural or linguistic rights beyond the standard set of liberal rights (some of which protect private cultural and linguistic practice).

---

[23] *Id.* at 61.

[24] *See* BARRY, *supra* note 4, at 65–68; Anthony K. Appiah, *Identity, Authenticity, Survival: Multicultural Societies and Social Reproduction, in* MULTICULTURALISM: EXAMINING THE POLITICS OF RECOGNITION 149, 163 (Amy Gutman & Charles Taylor eds., Princeton Univ. Press 1994).

[25] *See, e.g.,* BARRY, *supra* note 4, at 63–68; Michael Blake, *Language Death and Liberal Politics, in* LANGUAGE RIGHTS AND POLITICAL THEORY, *supra* note 14, at 210, 218–220; Patten, *supra* note 14, at 705–709.

In the next section, I will show that this conclusion would be mistaken, since there is an alternative interpretation of the politics of difference that is not vulnerable to the liberal challenge sketched above. Before turning to this alternative, however, it is worth noting that the liberal challenge does not rule out all applications of the cultural preservation principle, and thus this principle should remain in the repertoire of the institutional and constitutional designer, to be followed in the appropriate situations. One reason for this is that the liberal challenge rests on several very strong assumptions, which will often not be satisfied in real-world cases. Wealth and income are not typically distributed fairly, and, more to the point, their unfair distribution often does coincide, to some extent, with cultural or linguistic differences. In certain specific circumstances, policies designed to support vulnerable languages or cultures may be an effective way of rectifying unfair economic disadvantage. If a language policy can encourage more economic activity to take place in the language generally spoken by disadvantaged people, then this may narrow the disparity with the more advantaged. Another strong assumption is that all historical injustice has been remedied. Again, it is conceivable that cultural preservation policies could be part of an appropriate remedy for an injustice against a cultural or linguistic community that has not been remedied.

In the debate during the 1970s over language policy in Quebec, one of the principal arguments in favor of policies to defend French appealed to considerations of equal opportunity.[26] This form of argument on behalf of the cultural preservation principle should also not be neglected. One can imagine situations (and Quebec in the 1970s was plausibly one of them) in which the decline of a language would leave significant numbers of speakers with seriously diminished opportunities. Suppose that the decline of the language expressed itself, in part, in the use of some other stronger language in various high-status domains of communication, such as white-collar employment. Then anyone who had not, and could not, achieve a minimal degree of competence in the stronger language would face a curtailed range of options. The same would be true for people who did achieve competence in the stronger language but who were excluded, nevertheless, because of discrimination based on mother tongue.

I take it that this is the sort of scenario that Kymlicka has in mind when he argues that minority cultural rights may be necessary to secure a context of choice for members of vulnerable societal cultures.[27] It should be said, though, that the empirical circumstances needed for an argument of this form to prove viable are rather demanding. It must be the case: (*a*) that the culture to be defended is offering a more-or-less adequate range of options and opportunities to its members (it

---

[26] The gap between the economic opportunities of English and French speakers in Quebec is most fully detailed in REPORT OF THE CANADA ROYAL COMMISSION ON BILINGUALISM AND BICULTURALISM—THE WORK WORLD (Queen's Printer 1969). For a good overview, see MARC V. LEVINE, THE RECONQUEST OF MONTREAL: LANGUAGE POLICY AND SOCIAL CHANGE IN A BILINGUAL CITY ch. 2 (Temple Univ. Press 1990).

[27] KYMLICKA, *supra* note 3, ch. 5.

is a "societal culture") but that it risks not being able to do so in the near future because too many of its members are defecting, as it were, to another culture; (*b*) that the decline of the culture would strand some significant number of people who are unable to integrate into the more powerful majority culture and now would face a loss of opportunities within their own; and (*c*) that the policies of cultural preservation would make just the difference in preventing the culture from going into decline and thus preserving the opportunities of all of its members. As I have said, these demanding conditions may well have been satisfied in Quebec in the 1970s, though it is unlikely they would be satisfied in many cases in which minority cultures demand rights. Thus, this hardly seems like a promising general strategy for defending minority cultural rights.

Cultural preservation, then, is a distinct, third principle that may guide the state's response to diversity. The state is not evenhandedly refusing to help any particular identity or culture to survive or flourish; nor is it singling out one national identity and language and seeking to integrate all citizens into that framework. Instead, it is propping up vulnerable cultures and identities by giving them the resources they need to survive. This third form of state response to diversity is subject to an important liberal challenge and, for this reason, does not seem a reliable, general way of defending minority rights. Nonetheless, there are specific empirical situations in which it would be appropriate for institutional or constitutional designers to follow this principle. Consequently, it belongs in the repertoire of possible responses to diversity.

4. Equality of status

The equality-of-status principle rests on very different normative considerations than that of cultural preservation. To see this, let us return to an unresolved problem from the earlier discussion of universalism. I introduced the idea of neutrality and said that the disestablishment principle was one way of expressing a commitment to this idea. The guiding idea of neutrality is that the state should not set out to encourage or discourage the success of any particular form of life but, instead, should seek to establish fair background conditions under which different forms of life can each strive for success. Neutrality is connected with disestablishment via the thought that one obvious way in which the state could establish fair background conditions is by refusing to help or hinder any particular form of life.

I also noted that disestablishment is a response to cultural diversity that is not available for every kind of case. In some areas of policy (such as language), the state cannot help but become involved in promoting particular cultures and identities or could only avoid it at the cost of other important values. I did not explore further this limitation of the neutrality/disestablishment approach but, instead, moved on to a distinct form of universalism, which carries no pretence of neutrality, namely nation building.

Is neutrality possible in situations where disestablishment is impossible? Neutrality and disestablishment are often conflated in the literature, and so the answer to this question is typically assumed to be "no". However, I think that equality of status is also a way of realizing neutrality. Consider the case of religion and public education. One way in which the state can observe neutrality on religion is by keeping all forms of religion out of the schools. This is neutrality as disestablishment. But another way for the state to observe neutrality would be through an *even-handed* recognition of various religions in the schools (a model that Britain has experimented with).[28] This approach would allow religion into the schools and could even allow sectarian schooling, but it would insist that all religions be afforded some roughly comparable time or space in the curriculum or school system. Although the two approaches have quite different institutional implications, both are forms of neutrality. Neither aims for a specific religious outcome, such as convergence on a common national religion or the maintenance of vulnerable religions. Instead, the idea shared by each is to specify certain conditions that treat the members of different religions equally and, in this respect, are fair.

In contexts where disestablishment is possible it will often be a superior form of neutrality to evenhandedness, mainly because the evenhanded approach will always have to face difficult decisions about which groups to include and which to exclude. But as we have seen, for example, with the case of language, disestablishment is not always possible. Where this is true, neutrality is only possible through evenhandedness.

What could evenhandedness mean as a response by the state to cultural diversity? One could imagine a range of different answers to this question, but all of them, I think, would be variations on the idea of equality of status. The most straightforward way for the state to establish fair background conditions for the culture of the majority and for that of minorities is by extending the same public treatment to each. This means cultural rights for minorities as well as for the majority.

I have already illustrated this idea of neutrality through equal status with the case of religious schooling. For language policy, the implications are equally striking. Unlike someone committed to the principles of nation building or cultural preservation, the maker of language policy who is committed to the idea of neutrality does not set out to promote some particular linguistic outcome. Instead, the aim of language policy is to establish fair background conditions under which speakers of different languages can each strive for the success and

[28] *See* Education Act of 1944, c. 31 (amended by Education Reform Act, 1988, c. 40 and consolidated into Education Act, 1996, c. 56) (establishing the Tripartite System or the grammar school system); *see also* MICHAEL MEREDITH SWANN (LORD SWANN), EDUCATION FOR ALL: REPORT OF THE COMMITTEE OF INQUIRY INTO THE EDUCATION OF CHILDREN FROM ETHNIC MINORITY GROUPS (HMSO 1985); Meira Levinson, *Liberalism Versus Democracy? Schooling Private Citizens in the Public Sphere,* 27 BRIT. J. POL. SCI. 333, 337 (1997).

survival of the language communities with which they identify. Since fair background conditions cannot mean disestablishment (the state must use some language[s] or other), the only way to realize such conditions is by offering some roughly equivalent form of assistance (perhaps prorated according to demand) to each of the various languages spoken by citizens. In this way, a kind of equality of treatment can be achieved without the evident absurdity of linguistic disestablishment. I take it that something like this idea of equal treatment lies behind Canada's official bilingualism and the European Union's official languages policy, both of which seek to establish an equality of status among several recognized languages.[29]

The idea of neutrality is often associated with an attitude of indifference or benign neglect toward minority rights. On the view of neutrality I am proposing, this is not at all the case. Indeed, this view offers a way of defending minority rights that has largely been ignored by theorists. Unless certain minority rights are acknowledged, members of minority communities could reasonably complain that they do not have a fair opportunity to realize their culture-related aspirations. This argument, as I have stressed, does not characterize the state as following the cultural preservation principle. Instead, it calls upon the state to be truly neutral on questions of culture, by treating fairly the different sorts of cultural aspirations that its citizens may have.

The same points can be seen by reconsidering what I earlier termed the "liberal challenge" to the cultural preservation principle. Even if we grant all of the assumptions of the liberal challenge, it still would not follow that any linguistic outcomes could be regarded as simply the product of individual choices and preferences. If only the majority language receives public recognition and assistance, and minority languages enjoy no comparable status, then any tendency for native minority-language speakers to use the majority language, rather than their own mother tongue, would have to be explained, not just in terms of individual choices and preferences but also with reference to the state's decision to favor the majority language. Individuals make their choices, and adapt their preferences, in the context of this state preference. For the liberal challenge to have bite, it would need to add one more assumption. It needs to assume that the different languages enjoy the same public status.[30] With this assumption in place,

---

[29] *See generally* Patten, *supra* note 7, at 370–373. For the EU's policies on official languages, see generally A Language Policy for the European Community: Prospects and Quandaries (Florian Coulmas ed., Walter de Gruyter 1991); The Language Question in Europe and Diverse Societies: Political, Legal, and Social Perspectives (Dario Castiglione & Chris Longman eds., Hart Publ'g 2007). For Canada's official bilingualism, see Official Languages Act, R.S.C., ch. 31 (4th Supp. 1985) (Can.); The Canadian Charter of Rights and Freedoms, part I (§§ 1–34) of the Constitution Act, 1982, Schedule B to the Canada Act 1982, ch. 11, § 16 (U.K.) (declaring English and French to be the official languages of Canada).

[30] In fact, Barry makes just such an assumption in his critique of Taylor and cultural preservation: Barry, *supra* note 4, at 66. But when he summarizes his conclusions about language rights, later in the book, this assumption drops out of the picture: Barry, *supra* note 4, at 103–109.

linguistic outcomes can plausibly be regarded as simply a working out of individual choices and preferences. This is just to say that the liberal challenger has to recognize certain minority-language rights.

Although the equality-of-status principle is seldom developed explicitly by political theorists interested in minority cultural rights, it is arguably implicit in some of the theories that they propose. In Kymlicka's work, for instance, one finds the argument I mentioned earlier that minority cultural rights may be necessary to secure a context of choice for members of vulnerable societal cultures. But alongside this claim one also finds a point about fairness. It is wrong, according to Kymlicka, to think of the state as, in general, neutral between the different cultures of its citizens. In its choices about official languages, school curricula, internal boundaries, state symbols, and so on, the state tends to favor some groups and disfavor others. These inequalities seem unfair and should either be justified or rectified by offsetting policies offering recognition to nondominant cultures.[31]

While Kymlicka tends to write as if these two points are separate steps of a single argument, I think it makes sense to see them as two separate arguments, each with their own logic, policy implications, and domains of applicability. Neither of the considerations adduced by Kymlicka depends in any way on the other to generate its conclusions about the normative desirability or urgency of cultural protections, rights, and so forth. If specific cultural protections are needed to stem a cultural disintegration that would otherwise produce a loss of context of choice, then it would not seem necessary to demonstrate, additionally, that the threatened culture is disfavored by the design of major institutions of the state. The threats to autonomy and equality of opportunity seem reason enough for concern. Conversely, if the state is favoring some cultures and not others, then this strikes me as a form of inequality that should be redressed (or excused in some way), regardless of whether or not the members of the disfavored culture also face a loss of their context of choice.

By running together these distinct ways of thinking about state responses to cultural diversity, Kymlicka makes it hard for his readers to tell when minority rights are called for, what kinds of policies they would find expression in, and what criteria to apply in judging whether or not they are a success. To the extent that he is arguing within the logic of the cultural preservation principle, the aim of minority rights is to protect cultures that are doing a reasonable job of providing opportunities to their members ("societal cultures") but are vulnerable to disintegration because of the assimilative attraction of the majority culture. The policies needed to protect the culture may require some inequality of status between majority and minority—it would only be a special case in which they enjoy equal status—and the measure of success of those policies is whether the vulnerable culture is actually protected or not. By contrast, the arguments he

[31] KYMLICKA, *supra* note 3, at 108–115.

makes within the equality-of-status paradigm apply more generally to all minority cultures (whether or not they are vulnerable societal cultures); they call for equal status as a matter of course; and their success is not measured by looking at outcomes (which depend, in part, on the choices people make within the framework of equal status) but is solely dependent on the degree to which institutions manage to achieve truly equal status.

Brian Barry is another writer who runs into trouble by failing to distinguish the different possible state responses to diversity. When he is discussing neutrality and religion, he is careful to note that neutrality could take either a disestablishment form or an equal-status form; both strategies, he insists, leave religious outcomes up to people's private choices.[32] But when he turns to the question of cultural and linguistic rights and is engaging in his polemics against Taylor, Young, and others he tends to forget about the equal-status alternative and simply assumes that they have in mind cultural preservation. This may be an accurate reading of Taylor, but it is not at all obvious in the case of Young. Aside from what these writers or others may have written, it simply is not engaging with the case for minority rights stated in its strongest possible form. More importantly, Barry's own conclusions about the justification of minority cultural rights do not reflect an adequate engagement with the equality-of-status principle.[33]

5. Conclusion

I have been arguing in favor of a more nuanced understanding of state responses to cultural diversity than is common in recent theoretical discussions. Instead of a crude dichotomy between the politics of universalism and the politics of difference, we should distinguish at least four approaches. I have called these: disestablishment, nation building, cultural preservation, and equality of status. Let me conclude with a few remarks about why it is important to make these more nuanced distinctions.

One reason is that, without them, we risk misunderstanding the real-world conflicts in which recognition is an issue. Consider, for instance, Taylor's main example in his essay, the debate over language rights in Canada and Quebec. Once we have mapped out the field of possibilities in the way that I am proposing, it becomes apparent that Taylor's characterization of what is at stake in this conflict is seriously misleading. Taylor suggests that the Canadian debate about language rights is best illuminated as a clash between the politics of universalism and the politics of difference. But in my view, it is much more plausible to see that

[32] BARRY, *supra* note 4, at 29.
[33] *See supra* note 30. Samuel Scheffler is another prominent liberal writer who resists the discourse of cultural rights and multiculturalism largely on the basis of an evaluation of the cultural preservation principle. Samuel Scheffler, *Immigration and the Significance of Culture,* 35 PHIL. & PUB. AFF. 93 (2007).

debate as a conflict between the two different forms of the politics of difference I have identified. It pits the view that Canada's two national languages should each enjoy equal status through a policy of official bilingualism against the view that French should receive special protections to ensure its survival in Quebec through policies such as Quebec's *Charte de la langue française*.[34]

The dichotomous view is also likely to be unhelpful in thinking about conflicts over recognition in the United States or France. In these cases, the main debate will often oppose a universalist and a difference-oriented position. Nevertheless, it is important to be clear about which variants of these views we are talking about. The terminology might encourage one to associate the universalist side of such debates with the ideal of neutrality and assume that the difference view would be aiming for cultural preservation. But I doubt that this is the debate in many cases. It is more likely that the universalist position will be a form of nation building (and thus decidedly non-neutral) and the difference-based view a form of equality of status (and thus based on a view of neutrality).

Moreover, getting these different distinctions right is not just important for understanding the dynamics of these struggles over recognition. It is also important for reaching a better understanding of the normative principles that are at stake. If we take the normative heart of policies of cultural recognition to be cultural preservation, then that view is bound to seem weak and implausible. Unless some of the special empirical conditions mentioned earlier are satisfied, the politics of universalism, in some form or other, will win the argument. If, as I have urged, however, neutrality is taken to be the core concern of cultural recognition, then the aims of such policies will be harder to dismiss. This does not mean that cultural recognition will always be the right view. Sometimes disestablishment and nation-building are compelling positions. However, it does mean that the politics of difference should itself be considered a powerful view that has to be taken seriously.

[34] R.S.Q. ch. C-11 (2007) (Can.).

4

The internationalization of minority rights

*Will Kymlicka**

Debates regarding integration and accommodation are a familiar feature of the political life of many countries and, indeed, are often the most enduring and contentious aspect of domestic politics. But these debates are not solely domestic. The international community plays an increasingly important role in shaping these debates, endorsing some models of integration and accommodation while discouraging others. And this endorsement is not just a matter of exhortation or moral support. Countries that follow the recommendations of the international community may gain access to vital financial, technical, and even military assistance in addressing their ethnic conflicts. In short, international organizations influence both the policy choices that states make regarding diversity and the likelihood that the chosen policies will succeed.

Therefore, any comprehensive examination of the integration/accommodation debate must look closely at the attitudes of the international community. When does the international community favor integration, and when does it favor accommodation? McGarry, O'Leary, and Simeon state that integration is the dominant strategy for regulating diversity, favored by Western states and by the officials of intergovernmental organizations such as the United Nations and the Bretton Woods institutions.[1] This is more or less correct as a generalization, but it obscures a much more interesting and complicated story. Various international organizations have struggled with this issue for the past fifteen years without any clear resolution and their current policies and practices remain full of ambiguities and inconsistencies. This chapter aims to bring out some of these complexities and to highlight some of the challenges they raise for those involved in debates concerning integration and accommodation.

I will begin by examining the norms that have been formulated within the United Nations, that divide nondominant ethnocultural groups into two broad categories—"indigenous peoples" and "minorities". According to the UN,

* Canada Research Chair in Political Philosophy, Queen's University, Kingston, Ontario. Email: kymlicka@post.queensu.ca

[1] *See* John McGarry, Brendan O'Leary & Richard Simeon, *Integration or Accommodation? The Enduring Debate in Conflict Regulation* (in this volume).

indigenous peoples have much stronger claims to self-government than minorities. I will argue that, while it is indeed important to distinguish different categories of ethnocultural groups, this particular categorization is inadequate to address
the actual patterns of ethnic political mobilization and conflict around the world.
I will then consider recent attempts by the Council of Europe to develop norms
relating to the category of "national minorities", which potentially can take us
beyond the "indigenous vs. minority" dichotomy. However, I will argue, these
attempts too have proven inadequate, in ways that raise deep questions about the
capacity of international law to articulate and protect minority rights.

1. The basic international framework

What is the view of the international community toward integration and accommodation? This is, of course, a hopelessly vague question, since the "international
community" is not a single monolithic actor with a single set of beliefs or attitudes. Even if we restrict our attention solely to such treaty-based intergovernmental organizations as the United Nations and its agencies or the World Bank
and the Council of Europe, there is no one consensus position. Each has its own
distinct mandate or function that gives it a unique interest in, and perspective on,
issues of ethnic diversity. There are profound differences among, as well as within,
these organizations in their approaches to the governance of that diversity.

Let us look first at the United Nations. The UN is a key actor in this debate,
not only because it claims to represent and speak for all the peoples of the world
but also because it has addressed the question of integration and accommodation explicitly and has developed formal statements of its position. Moreover, its
official position is surprisingly simple; namely, that "indigenous peoples" have a
right to accommodation, whereas "minorities" have a right to integration.

This basic distinction between indigenous peoples and minorities is reiterated
throughout the UN's activities, be it in the field of environmental protection,
economic development, or human rights. However, it is articulated most clearly
in two key texts—the 1992 Declaration on the Rights of Persons Belonging
to National or Ethnic, Religious and Linguistic Minorities[2] and the draft
Declaration on the Rights of Indigenous Peoples, which remains a draft despite
thirteen years of intensive debate.[3] The former adopts an integrationist approach

---

[2] Adopted by the General Assembly in Resolution 47/135. *See* U.N. Doc. A/RES/47/135/Annex
(Dec. 18, 1993).
[3] First introduced in the Working Group on Minorities in 1993, the draft declaration was
approved by the Human Rights Council in 2006. *See* Human Rights Council Res. 1/2, Annex,
U.N. Doc. A/HRC/RES/1/2/Annex (June 29, 2006). The Council approved it by a vote of 30
in favor to 2 against (Canada and Russian Federation), with 12 abstentions and forwarded to the
General Assembly for consideration; as of this writing, action is still pending. However, despite its
lack of legal force, its core ideas have been picked up by various organizations and agencies within

for minorities, focusing on nondiscrimination and civil rights; the latter adopts an accommodationist approach for indigenous peoples, focusing on self-government and institutional pluralism.[4]

This basic approach has been reaffirmed by the two UN working groups that have developed and interpreted these key texts. In 2000, Asbjorn Eide and Erica-Irene Daes, the then chairpersons, respectively, of the UN's Working Group on Minorities and Working Group on Indigenous Populations explained their understanding of the differing rationales underlying the two documents.[5] Their statements point to three basic differences between minorities and indigenous peoples: (*a*) minorities seek institutional integration while indigenous peoples seek to preserve a degree of institutional separateness; (*b*) minorities seek to exercise individual rights while indigenous peoples seek to exercise collective rights; (*c*) minorities seek nondiscrimination while indigenous peoples seek self-government. These statements by important UN figures confirm the fundamentally integrationist approach of the minority rights declaration, and the fundamentally accommodationist approach of the indigenous rights declaration.

Daes gives a particularly clear statement of the distinction:

> Bearing the conceptual problem [of distinguishing indigenous peoples from minorities] in mind, I should like to suggest that the ideal type of an "indigenous people" is a group that is aboriginal (autochthonous) to the territory where it resides today and chooses to perpetuate a distinct cultural identity and distinct collective social and political organization within the territory. The ideal type of a "minority" is a group that has experienced exclusion or discrimination by the State or its citizens because of its ethnic, national, racial, religious or linguistic characteristics or ancestry.
>
> ... From a purposive perspective, then, the ideal type of [a] "minority" focuses on the group's experience of discrimination because the intent of existing international standards has been to combat discrimination, against the group as a whole as well as its individual members, and to provide for them the opportunity to integrate themselves freely into national life to the degree they choose. Likewise, the ideal type of "indigenous peoples" focuses on aboriginality, territoriality, and the desire to remain

the UN system, and similar ideas have been articulated by the International Labour Organization and in the draft declaration on indigenous rights of the Organization of American States (OAS).

[4] I will use the accommodation/integration terminology adopted by McGarry, O'Leary, and Simeon, *supra* note 1, although it is potentially misleading. What they call integrationist models often involves some degree of accommodation of cultural diversity within common institutions. For example, a "duty to accommodate" is part of the immigrant multiculturalism policy in Canada, even though this clearly qualifies as an integrationist policy in their typology. Conversely, what they call accommodationist models can often be seen as a way of ensuring that self-governing groups are, nonetheless, connected to (and in that sense integrated into) a larger state. Provincial autonomy for Quebec accommodates an aspiration for autonomy, but it also integrates a potentially secessionist group into a larger federal political order. The terms "integration" and "accommodation" should be understood with these provisos in mind.

[5] Comm'n on Hum. Rts. Sub-Comm. on Promotion & Prot. of Hum. Rts., *Working Paper on the Relationship and Distinction between the Rights of Persons Belonging to Minorities and those of Indigenous Peoples*, U.N. Doc. E/CN.4/Sub.2/2000/10 (July 19, 2000) (prepared by Asbjorn Eide & Erica-Irene Daes) [hereinafter Eide & Daes, *Working Paper*].

collectively distinct, all elements which are tied logically to the exercise of the right to internal self-determination, self-government, or autonomy.[6]

The parallels between Daes's two "ideal types" and the ideal types of integration and accommodation developed by McGarry, O'Leary, and Simeon are both clear and direct.

It is worth noting here that although Eide and Daes are primarily concerned with explaining the different entitlements of the two kinds of groups, as envisaged under the relevant UN declarations, they are not simply talking about legal distinctions. They are also making claims about the *aspirations* of the two groups. If international norms accord different rights to minorities than to indigenous peoples, this is because the two groups are presumed to want different kinds of rights. According to Daes, "The facts remain that indigenous peoples and minorities organize themselves separately and tend to assert different objectives, even in those countries where they appear to differ very little in 'objective' characteristics".[7] Steven Wheatley makes a similar claim: "There is no objective distinction that can be made between groups recognized as minorities, national minorities, indigenous peoples and peoples. What distinguishes these groups is the nature of their political demands: simply put, minorities and national minorities demand cultural security; peoples demand recognition of their right to self-determination, or self-government".[8]

This, then, is the UN's basic theoretical framework for addressing these issues, although the organization's actual practices are more complicated than its formal declarations would suggest. The UN endorses integration and nondiscrimination for national, ethnic, religious, and linguistic minorities, even as it endorses accommodation and autonomy for indigenous peoples. We can see echoes of this approach in other major intergovernmental organizations, such as the World Bank or International Labour Organization, which have adopted similar formal policies espousing autonomy for indigenous peoples while endorsing nondiscrimination and integration for minorities.[9]

2. Limitations of the international framework

The UN approach has the virtue of simplicity; however, it is arguably inadequate to the real-world challenges of ethnic diversity. With regard to indigenous peoples, its approach is widely and rightly seen as beneficial, helping to empower historically subordinated groups and to disseminate best practices for the effective

---

[6] *Id.* at paras. 48–49.

[7] *Id.* at para. 41.

[8] Steven Wheatley, Democracy, Minorities and International Law 124 (Cambridge Univ. Press 2005).

[9] *See* Will Kymlicka, Multicultural Odysseys: Navigating the New International Politics of Diversity (Oxford Univ. Press 2007) (chs. 6–7).

participation and self-government of indigenous peoples. The UN Working Group on Indigenous Populations has served as the nerve center for a vibrant transnational network of community activists, nongovernmental organizations (NGOs), academics, philanthropic foundations, and policy makers; with considerable success, this network has diffused the ideas and standards contained in the draft declaration on indigenous rights. It has been particularly effective in encouraging and legitimizing the mobilization of indigenous peoples in Latin America.[10]

The UN's approach to minorities, by contrast, has been less successful. Its Working Group on Minorities has not become the locus of a global network in defense of minority rights. And even though the UN's declaration on minority rights has a clearer normative status than the draft declaration on indigenous rights—since it has been adopted unanimously by the General Assembly—the former has not had nearly the same public impact and is rarely invoked by minorities around the world.

There are several difficulties confronting the UN approach to minorities; the central problem, however, is the underlying assumption that "ethnic, national, racial, religious or linguistic" minorities can all be lumped together, and that they all seek integration rather than accommodation. This is, at best, a drastic overgeneralization, and at worst a serious misinterpretation of the issues. As others discuss in depth,[11] there are many cases worldwide where minorities seek accommodation rather than integration. Some of the most well known and protracted struggles for autonomy around the world involve groups that are considered minorities rather than indigenous peoples by the UN—groups such as the Scots, Catalans, Chechens, Kosovar Albanians, Kurds, Kashmiris, and Tamils. Indeed, in the early 1990s, it was precisely the upsurge of ethnic conflicts involving autonomy-seeking substate nationalist minorities that led the UN to take an active interest in formulating standards regarding minorities.[12] And yet, remarkably, the text that resulted—the 1992 declaration on minority rights—far from providing guidance for dealing with such minority claims for autonomy, actually renders them invisible by presupposing that minorities, by definition, are only interested in integration.

The problem is not simply that a model based on a stark dichotomy between autonomy-seeking indigenous peoples and integration-seeking minorities is inadequate to deal with a number of important real-world cases. The deeper problem is that this very way of dividing up the ethnocultural landscape may obscure the actual issues involved in the choice between accommodation and integration.

In order to understand the problem, we need to step back and examine the broader patterns of ethnic politics in contemporary democracies. Relations

---

[10] *See* ALISON BRYSK, FROM TRIBAL VILLAGE TO GLOBAL VILLAGE: INDIAN RIGHTS AND INTERNATIONAL RELATIONS IN LATIN AMERICA (Stanford Univ. Press 2000).

[11] *See generally* other chapters in this volume.

[12] *See* KYMLICKA, *supra* note 9, at ch. 2, on the impetus given to the UN's standard-setting activities by these ethnonationalist conflicts.

between the state and minorities in the Western democracies are highly differentiated by group. Certain generic civil and cultural rights are guaranteed to the members of all ethnocultural groups; however, there are also a number of "targeted" rights that apply only to particular categories of groups. The precise categories vary from country to country, but they typically fall into the same basic pattern. The most common distinction is between "old" minorities, which were settled on their territory prior to its becoming part of a larger, independent country, and "new" minorities, which were admitted to a country as immigrants after it achieved legal independence. The old minorities are often called "homeland" minorities, since they have been historically settled within a particular part of a country for a long period of time and, as a result of that historic settlement, have come to see that part of the country as their historic homeland. The minority's homeland is incorporated within a larger state or, perhaps, divided between two or more countries; nonetheless, the minority still has a strong sense of attachment to this homeland and often nurtures memories of an earlier time, prior to the origin of the modern state, when it had self-government over this territory.

There is a nearly universal tendency within the Western democracies to distinguish the rights of old homeland minorities from those of new immigrant minorities. As Perry Keller notes, this distinction is "found in the laws and policies of almost every European State".[13] The same is true in North America.[14]

Of course, these broad categories of old and new minorities are themselves quite heterogeneous. Within the category of new minorities, for example, many countries accord a different legal status to different subcategories, such as asylum seekers, temporary guest workers, illegal immigrants, and permanent immigrants. These may be crucially important legal distinctions but, insofar as any of these new minorities are accorded minority rights, they fall on the integration side of the ledger. In many countries, some of these new minorities are not granted any minority rights and are subject to policies of either assimilation or exclusion. But even in those countries that grant minority rights to some new minorities, often under the aegis of "multiculturalism", these are based on ideas of integration, not accommodation, and do not entail territorial self-government, official language status, or legal pluralism.

Similarly, there are important distinctions to draw within the category of old minorities. The most important distinction is between indigenous peoples and other historically settled homeland minorities, often called national minorities.

---

[13] Perry Keller, *Rethinking Ethnic and Cultural Rights in Europe*, 18 Oxford J. Leg. Stud. 43 (1998). For a helpful overview of these distinctions as drawn in the Nordic countries, see Lauri Hannikainen, *The Status of Minorities, Indigenous Peoples and Immigrant and Refugee Groups in Four Nordic Countries*, 65 Nordic J. Int'l. L. 1 (1996)

[14] For details of the Canadian case, see Will Kymlicka, *Ethnocultural Diversity in a Liberal State: Making Sense of the Canadian Model(s), in* Belonging? Diversity, Recognition and Shared Citizenship in Canada 39–86 (Keith Banting, Thomas Courchene & Leslie Seidle eds., Inst. Res. Pub. Pol'y 2007). For the American case, see the (dated) overview in Sharon O'Brien, *Cultural Rights in the United States: A Conflict of Values*, 5 L. & Inequality J. 267 (1987).

The former include the Indians and Inuit in Canada, the Aboriginal peoples of Australia, the Maori of New Zealand, the Sami of Scandinavia, the Inuit of Greenland, and Native American tribes in the United States; the latter include the Québécois in Canada, the Scots and Welsh in Britain, the Catalans and Basques in Spain, the Flemish in Belgium, the German-speaking minority in South Tyrol in Italy, the French- and Italian-speaking minorities in Switzerland, and Puerto Ricans in the United States.[15] Here, again, this is an important distinction for many legal purposes but, in relation to issues of minority rights, both types of old minorities fall on the accommodation side of the ledger. They both seek and, increasingly, are accorded various rights to self-government over their traditional territory, as well as the right to use their language and express their culture in its public spaces.

To understand the UN's approach, and its limitations, we need to examine this distinction between indigenous peoples and national minorities in more depth. To oversimplify, the term "indigenous peoples" arose primarily in the context of New World settler states and refers to the descendants of the original non-European inhabitants of lands colonized and settled by European powers. Most of the early work on indigenous issues at the UN, for example, focused on the so-called Indian populations in Latin America. "National minorities", by contrast, is a term invented in Europe to refer to the European groups that lost out in the tumultuous process of European state formation over the past five centuries, and whose homelands were incorporated (in whole or in part) into larger states dominated by a neighboring European people. National minorities were active players in the process by which the early modern welter of empires, kingdoms, and principalities in Europe was turned into the modern system of nation-states. However, they either ended up without a state of their own (as in the case of the Catalans) or found themselves on the wrong side of the border, cut off from their coethnics in a neighboring kin-state (as occurred with ethnic Germans in Denmark and Italy).

These are the core cases for the two categories. A preliminary and crude way of distinguishing them is to say that national minorities have been incorporated into a larger state dominated by a neighboring European people, whereas indigenous peoples have been colonized and settled by a distant colonial European power. But there are other ways of marking the distinction between the two types of groups that supervene on this basic historical difference. It is widely accepted, for example, that the subjugation and incorporation of indigenous peoples by European colonizers was a more brutal and disruptive process than the subjugation and incorporation of national minorities by neighboring societies, and that this has left indigenous peoples weaker and more vulnerable. It is also often

---

[15] The Flemish form a numerical majority in Belgium, but were historically subordinated to the French-speaking elite. They are often considered a "minority" according to definitions that emphasize nondominant status rather than numbers per se, and as a case of "minority nationalism", in the sense of contesting the earlier French-dominated state nationalism.

assumed that there is a supposed "civilizational" difference between indigenous peoples and national minorities. Whereas national minorities typically share the same modern (urbanized, industrialized) economic and sociopolitical structures as their neighboring European peoples, indigenous peoples are often assumed to have retained premodern modes of economic production, engaged primarily in subsistence agriculture or a hunter-gatherer lifestyle. And, as a result of large-scale colonizing settlement, it is assumed further that indigenous peoples, unlike national minorities, have been relegated, typically, to isolated and remote areas.

Thus, both in their core cases and in everyday usage the two terms refer to quite different types of groups, each rooted in fundamentally different historical processes and differing in their contemporary characteristics, including degrees of vulnerability, modes of production, and habitats. Both, however, are old minorities, having a historic presence on their traditional territory that predates the formation of the current state. As such, they are both homeland minorities, living on or near historic homelands that has been incorporated into a larger state dominated by another national group. In recognition of this fact, there has been a widespread tendency within Western democracies to adopt an accommodationist approach toward both types of groups. This typically involves some form of territorial autonomy, combined with official language rights (in the case of national minorities) and land claims and customary law (in the case of indigenous peoples). Both groups are distinguished from new minorities—those formed through immigration or refugee flows after the establishment of the state—whose cultural claims are typically addressed through a more integrationist approach, based on nondiscrimination, civil rights, and the reform of common institutions to make them more accessible to, and respectful of, the new minorities.

We now see how the UN approach to the accommodation/integration issue differs from the established practice of Western democracies. In two key contexts, UN norms and Western practices converge: both endorse a norm of accommodation for indigenous peoples, and both endorse a norm of integration for new minorities. They diverge, however, with regard to the central case of national minorities or, more generally, on the case of homeland minorities that do not qualify as indigenous peoples, whether it is the Scots in Britain, the Kurds in Turkey, or the Tibetans in China. In the practice of Western democracies, such national minorities are typically accorded accommodation, although, under the UN norms, they would be presumed to come under the integration approach. In the practice of Western democracies, national minorities belong with indigenous peoples on the accommodation side of the ledger; according to UN norms, they would belong, with the new minorities, on the integration side.

Why have UN norms diverged from Western practices in this way? I will return to this question below; however, part of the answer lies in the special vulnerability of indigenous peoples and, hence, in their more urgent need for accommodation. As noted earlier, the subjugation of indigenous peoples by European colonizers was typically a more brutal and disruptive process than the subjugation of national minorities by neighboring European societies, and this has left indigenous peoples more vulnerable and, hence, in greater need of international protection. As a result, there was a plausible moral argument for giving priority to indigenous peoples over national minorities in the development of rights to self-government in international law.

However, what began as a difference in the relative priority and urgency of the claims of indigenous peoples and national minorities has paved the way for an almost total rupture between the two at the level of international law. If we take the stance of international organizations as our reference point—rather than the practice of Western democracies—it would appear that rights of self-government are claimed legitimately only by indigenous peoples, rather than by homeland minorities more generally. Across a wide range of international documents and declarations, indigenous peoples have been distinguished from other homeland minorities, and claims to territory and self-government have been restricted to the former. Under the current UN framework, national minorities are lumped in the same category as new minorities, ignoring their distinctive needs and aspirations in relation to historic settlements and territorial concentration. As a result, the distinction between indigenous peoples and other homeland minorities has acquired a significance and a rigidity in the international community that is entirely missing in the theory and practice of Western liberal democracy.

The attempt to draw a sharp distinction between indigenous peoples and national minorities, and to put national minorities in the same legal category as new minorities, raises a number of difficult questions. It creates (*a*) moral inconsistencies, (*b*) conceptual confusion, and (*c*) unstable political dynamics.

The sharp distinction in rights between the two types of groups is morally inconsistent, because whatever arguments exist for recognizing the rights of indigenous peoples to self-government also apply to the claims for self-government by other vulnerable and historically disadvantaged homeland groups. Miriam Aukerman compared the claims of indigenous peoples with those of national minorities in postcommunist countries and noted the strong similarities in their underlying goals and justifications. As she puts it, "Indigenous peoples and Central-East European [national] minorities share the goal of preserving their distinctive cultures, and justify their claims to group-differentiated rights with similar appeals to self-determination, equality, cultural diversity, history and vulnerability".[16]

Indeed, this inconsistency becomes clear from the explanations and justifications offered for the proposed indigenous rights norms by the experts chairing the two UN working groups in 2000. As noted earlier, they accord targeted rights to indigenous peoples beyond those available to all other minorities because of three key differences: the former seek institutional integration, individual rights, and

[16] Miriam Aukerman, *Definitions and Justifications: Minority and Indigenous Rights in a Central/East European Context*, 22 Hum. Rts. Q. 1011, 1045 (2000).

nondiscrimination, whereas the latter seek institutional separateness, collectively exercised rights, and self-government. These are all pertinent differences between indigenous peoples and new minorities, such as immigrants, but they do not distinguish indigenous peoples from national minorities. On all three points, national minorities typically fall on the same side of the equation as indigenous peoples.

In an earlier document prepared for the Working Group on Indigenous Populations, Daes offers a somewhat different account.[17] She states that the crucial feature of indigenous peoples, which distinguishes them from minorities in general, is their strong attachment to a traditional territory that they view as their historic homeland:

> [A]ttachment to a homeland is ... definitive of the identity and integrity of the [indigenous] group, socially and culturally. This may suggest a very narrow but precise definition of "indigenous," sufficient to be applied to any situation where the problem is one of distinguishing an indigenous people [from] the larger class of minorities.[18]

But this criterion—"attachment to a homeland"—obviously differentiates homeland minorities (including national minorities), in general, not indigenous peoples, in particular. Elsewhere, Daes claims that it is "possible to identify at least two factors [in the case of indigenous peoples] which have never been associated with the concept of 'minorities': priority in time and attachment to a particular territory".[19] But here again, these factors apply to old homeland minorities generally, not just to indigenous peoples.

In short, because virtually all of the moral principles and arguments invoked at the UN to defend indigenous rights also apply to national minorities, an attempt to draw a sharp distinction in legal status between national minorities and indigenous peoples is morally problematic. It is also conceptually unstable. The problem is not merely how to justify the sharp difference in their legal rights but how to identify the two types of groups in the first place. The very distinction between indigenous peoples and other homeland minorities is difficult to draw outside the original core cases of Europe and European settler states.

In the West, there is a relatively clear distinction to be drawn between European "national minorities" and New World "indigenous peoples". Both are homeland groups, although the former have been incorporated into a larger state dominated by a neighboring people, whereas the latter have been colonized by a remote colonial power. It is far less clear how we can draw this distinction in Africa, Asia, or the Middle East, or whether the categories even make sense there. Depending on

---

[17] Comm'n on Hum. Rts., Sub-Comm. on Prevention of Discrimination & Prot. of Minorities, Working Group on Indigenous Populations, *Working Paper on the Concept of "Indigenous People"*, U.N. Doc. E/CN.4/Sub.2/AC.4/1996/2 (July 6, 1996) (prepared by Erica-Irene Daes) [hereinafter Daes, *Working Paper 1996*].

[18] *Id.* at para. 39.

[19] *Id.* at para. 60.

how we define the terms, we could say that none of the homeland groups in these regions are "indigenous", or that all of them are.

In one familiar sense, no groups in Africa, Asia, or the Middle East fit the traditional profile of indigenous peoples. All the homeland minorities in these regions were incorporated into larger states dominated by neighboring groups rather than into settler states dominated by European settlers.[20] In that sense, they are all closer to the profile of European national minorities than to New World indigenous peoples. For this reason, several Asian and African countries insist that none of their minorities should be designated as indigenous peoples. In another sense, however, we could say that, in these regions, all homeland groups (including the dominant majority group) are indigenous. During the era of colonial rule, all homeland groups, majority and minority alike, were designated as "natives" or "indigenous" in relation to the colonial rulers. Thus, from that perspective, all homeland groups in postcolonial states (including the dominant group) are equally "indigenous". And, indeed, the governments of several Asian and African countries declare that *all* their historic groups, majority and minority, should be considered indigenous.[21]

These two approaches yield diametrically opposed results but the upshot in both cases is to undermine the possibility of distinguishing the category of indigenous peoples from that of national minorities. Whether we say that all homeland groups are indigenous or that none are, we end up in either instance without a basis for identifying a subset of minorities as indigenous peoples, distinct from national minorities or other homeland minorities.

For this reason, some commentators have argued that the legal category of "indigenous people" should apply only to European settler states in the New World and not to Africa and Asia.[22] If the UN adopted this approach, it would mean, in effect, that all minorities in Asia or Africa, both old and new, fall under

---

[20] *Cf.* Amal Jamal, *On the Morality of Arab Collective Rights in Israel*, ADALAH NEWSLETTER, Apr. 2005, at 12 (arguing that Israel should be included as a European settler state, and, hence, that the Palestinians fit the traditional definition of an indigenous people).

[21] *E.g.*, Zambia's report to the UN, which states, "Zambia does not have the classifications of indigenous populations and minority communities as defined by the United Nations Organization. Zambia has ethnic groups that are all indigenous". U.N. Doc. CRC/C/11/Add.25 (Nov. 19, 2002), para. 470. Lennox describes this as "representative of the commonly held view" among African states. *See* Corinne Lennox, *The Changing International Protection Regimes for Minorities and Indigenous Peoples: Experiences from Latin America and Africa* (paper presented to Annual Conference of International Studies Association, San Diego, Mar. 2006) (on file with author). As Mamdani notes, however, there is often an important exception to this claim that all ethnic groups are considered indigenous; in many African countries, groups brought to the country during the period of colonial rule often are still considered immigrants or foreigners, such as the indentured laborers from India whom the British moved throughout the British Empire. See MAHMOOD MAMDANI, CITIZEN AND SUBJECT (Princeton Univ. Press 1996) for a discussion of the ways these colonial-era migrant groups are (mis)treated by many postcolonial citizenship regimes in Africa. It remains true, however, that all precolonial groups are often called indigenous, including the dominant group.

[22] *See, e.g.*, André Béteille, *The Idea of Indigenous People*, 39 CURRENT ANTHROPOLOGY 187 (1998).

the integration framework of the UN's minorities declaration, not the accommodation framework of the indigenous declaration.

The UN, however, has not taken this approach. Instead, it has made the
assumption that some homeland minorities in Africa and Asia are as deserving
of—and as much in need of—autonomy and accommodation as indigenous
peoples in the Americas. In order to protect such groups, therefore, the UN has
attempted to reconceptualize the category of indigenous peoples so that it covers
at least some homeland minorities in postcolonial states. From this perspective,
we should not focus on whether homeland minorities are dominated by settlers
from a distant colonial power or by neighboring peoples. What matters, simply, is
the fact of their domination by others and their vulnerability, and, thus, the need
to find appropriate means to remedy these conditions.[23] If homeland groups are
dominated and vulnerable, we should use the international norms of indigenous rights to protect them, even if their oppressors are their historic neighbors
and not colonizing settlers from afar. Hence, the UN approach has encouraged
groups in Africa and Asia to identify themselves as indigenous peoples in order to
gain greater international visibility and protection.

The difficult question this raises, however, is how to identify which homeland
groups in Africa or Asia should be designated as indigenous peoples for the purposes of international law and practice, and on what basis? Once we start down
the road of extending the category of indigenous peoples beyond the core case of
New World settler states, there is no obvious stopping point. Indeed, there are
significant disagreements within various international agencies about how widely
to apply the category to homeland minorities in postcolonial states. Some would
limit it to those peoples who were especially isolated geographically, such as the
hill tribes or forest peoples in southeast Asia or pastoralists in Africa.[24] Others
would limit it to groups that fall outside the market economy—that is, to groups
living as hunter-gatherers or subsistence cultivators but not involved in trade or
the labor market. (This seems to be one of the World Bank's criteria, invoked to
deny indigenous status to the Berbers in Algeria.)[25]

---

[23] According to Daes, attempts to distinguish long-distance colonizing settlement from incorporation into states dominated by neighboring societies rest on an "unjustified distinction". Daes,
Working Paper 1996, supra note 17, at para. 63. Similarly, the Working Group on Indigenous
Populations/Communities in Africa, established by the African Commission on Human and
People's Rights (created by the Organization of African Unity [OAU]), has stated that "[d]omi-
nation and colonisation has [*sic*] not exclusively been practised by white settlers and colonial-
ists. In Africa, dominant groups have also after independence suppressed marginalized groups,
and it is this sort of present-day internal suppression within African states that the contemporary African indigenous movement seeks to address...". Comm'n on Hum. Rts., Sub-Comm. on
the Promotion and Prot. of Hum. Rts., Working Group of Experts on Indigenous Populations/
Communities, *Report of the African Commission on Human and Peoples' Rights,* U.N. Doc. E/CN.4/
Sub.2/AC.5/2005/WP.3 (Apr. 22, 2005), at 6.

[24] WORLD BANK, IMPLEMENTATION OF OPERATIONAL DIRECTIVE 4.20 ON INDIGENOUS
PEOPLES: AN INDEPENDENT DESK REVIEW, para 1.4 (Operations Evaluation Department, World
Bank, Report No. 25332).

[25] *Id.* Box 3.1.

These narrow definitions of indigenous people are clearly inconsistent with the way the term is used in the New World. In Latin America, for example, the term applies not only to isolated forest peoples in the Amazon, such as the Yanomami, but also to peasants in the highlands who have been in intensive contact and trade with the larger settler society for five hundred years, such as the Maya, Aymaras, or Quechuas. Similarly many indigenous peoples in North America, such as the Mohawks, have been involved in either settled agriculture and/or the labor market for generations. To limit the category to groups that are geographically isolated or not involved in trade or the labor market would be to exclude some of the largest and most politically influential indigenous groups in the New World.

Accordingly, other commentators would extend the category of indigenous peoples in postcolonial states much more widely in order to encompass all historically subordinated homeland minorities that suffer from some combination of political exclusion, poverty, or cultural vulnerability. (This seems to be the recent approach of the International Labour Organization [ILO], at least in southeast Asia).[26] On this view, the label "indigenous peoples" would become virtually synonymous with "homeland minority"; it would cease to be a subcategory of homeland minority. The difference between the narrower and broader conceptions of indigenous peoples is potentially enormous—estimates of the number of people who would qualify as "indigenous peoples" in Indonesia range from 2 percent to 60 percent of the population, depending on whether a narrower or broader definition is used.[27] There is, then, an enormous literature on this question of how to apply the category of "indigenous peoples" in Africa and Asia, and on the relative merits of broader and narrow definitions.[28] This is a matter of ongoing debate within various intergovernmental organizations, each of which has adopted different definitions, to the consternation of commentators who wish that a single definition would be adopted across the international community.[29]

From my perspective, however, the fact that different definitions are being used by different intergovernmental organizations is not the only, or even the primary, problem. The more serious problem is that all of these proposed approaches, whether narrow or broad, invoke criteria that are clearly a matter of degree. Homeland minorities in postcolonial states form a continuum in terms of their cultural vulnerability, geographical isolation, level of integration into the market, and political exclusion. We can, if we like, set a threshold somewhere along this

[26] *See e.g.*, Manuela Tomei, Indigenous and Tribal Peoples: An Ethnic Audit of Selected Poverty Reduction Strategy Papers (Int'l Labour Org. 2005).
[27] Pieter Evers, *Preliminary Policy and Legal Questions about Recognizing Traditional Land in Indonesia*, 3 Ekonesia 1 (1995).
[28] *See* Benedict Kingsbury, *"Indigenous Peoples" in International Law: A Constructivist Approach to the Controversy*, 92 Am. J. Int'l L. 414 (1998).
[29] For an overview of these variations, and the calls for greater consistency, see World Bank Legal Dep't, *Legal Note on Indigenous Peoples* (Apr. 8, 2005), *available at* <http://siteresources.worldbank.org/INTINDPEOPLE/Publications/20571167/Legal%20Note.pdf> and World Bank, *supra* note 24.

continuum in order to determine which of these groups are called "indigenous peoples" and which are "national minorities"; however, any such threshold is likely to appear arbitrary and incapable of bearing the weight that international law currently places upon it. International law treats the distinction between indigenous peoples and national minorities as a categorical one, with enormous implications for the legal rights each type of group may claim. In the postcolonial world, however, any attempt to distinguish indigenous peoples from national minorities on the basis of their relative levels of vulnerability or exclusion can only track differences of degree, not the difference in kind implied by international law.[30]

The attempt to preserve such a sharp distinction is not only morally dubious and conceptually unstable, it is also, I suspect, politically unsustainable. The problem here is not simply that the category of indigenous peoples has gray areas and vague boundaries, with the potential for being over- or under-inclusive. That is true of all targeted categories, and there are well-established techniques of democratic deliberation and legal interpretation for dealing with such boundary disputes. The problem, rather, is that too much depends on which side of the line the various groups fall, and, as a result, there is intense political pressure to change where the line is drawn. Consequently, whatever the choices made and however arrived at, the result is probably unsustainable politically.

As should be clear by now, the current UN framework provides no incentive for any homeland minority to identify itself as a national minority, since this category provides no rights that are not available to any other ethnocultural group, including new minorities. Instead, all homeland minorities have an overwhelming incentive to define, or redefine, themselves as indigenous peoples. If they present themselves to the international community as a national minority, they get nothing other than generic minority rights premised on the integration model; if they come, instead, as an indigenous people, they have the promise of rights to land, control over natural resources, political self-government, language rights, and legal pluralism.

The increasing tendency for homeland groups in Africa, Asia, and the Middle East to adopt the label of indigenous peoples is thus not surprising. An interesting case is the Arab-speaking minority in the Ahwaz region of Iran, whose homeland has been subjected repeatedly to state policies of Persianization, including the suppression of Arab language rights, the renaming of towns and villages to erase evidence of their Arab history, and settlement policies that attempt to swamp the Ahwaz with Persian settlers. In the past, Ahwaz leaders have complained to the UN Working Group on Minorities that their rights as a national minority were

---

[30] See this frank admission of the chairman, Asbjorn Eide of the UN Working Group on Minorities: "The usefulness of a clearcut distinction between minorities and indigenous peoples is debatable. The Sub-Commission, including the two authors of this paper, have played a major role in separating the two tracks. The time may have come for the Sub-Commission to review the issue again.... The distinction is probably much less useful for standard setting concerning group accommodation in Asia and Africa." Eide & Daes, *Working Paper, supra* note 5, at para. 25.

not respected.[31] But since the UN does not recognize national minorities as having distinctive rights, the Ahwaz have run into a dead end. Thus, they have relabeled themselves as an indigenous people and begun participating in the work of the Working Group on Indigenous Populations. Similarly, various homeland minorities in Africa, which once sent representatives to the Working Group on Minorities, have now started rebranding themselves as indigenous peoples and participating in that working group, primarily in order to gain protection for their land rights.[32]

This is just the tip of the iceberg. Any number of minorities are now debating whether to adopt the label of indigenous peoples, including the Crimean Tatars, the Roma, or Afro-Latin Americans. Even the Kurds—the textbook example of a stateless national minority—are debating whether to redefine themselves as an indigenous people, so as to gain international protection. So, too, with the Palestinians in Israel, the Abkhaz in Georgia or Chechens in Russia, and the Tibetans in China.[33]

In all of these cases, minorities are responding to the fact that generic minority rights are "regarded as fatally weak"[34] and as "completely inadequate... to their needs",[35] since generic rights are premised on integration and do not protect any claims based on historic settlement or territorial attachments. Given international norms as currently conceived, recognition as an indigenous people is the only avenue for pursuing protection for these interests. Perhaps, in time, the Scots and Basques will also claim this status. After all, what homeland minority would not want the same rights—as currently formulated—that are accorded indigenous peoples?

While the tendency for national minorities to adopt the label of indigenous peoples is not surprising, it is also not sustainable. The net effect of such shifts in self-identification would be the total collapse of the international system of indigenous

[31] For the Ahwaz Education and Human Rights Foundation's presentation to the Working Group on Minorities, see <http://www.ohchr.org/english/issues/minorities/group/11session.htm>. For the presentation to the Permanent Forum on Indigenous Issues, see <http://www.ahwazstudies.org/main/index.php?option=com_content&task=view&id=2048&Itemid=47&lang=EN>.

[32] For list of African organizations attending meetings of the Working Group on Minorities, see <http://www.ohchr.org/english/issues/minorities/main.htm>. For the (overlapping) list of African organizations attending the Working Group on Indigenous Populations, see U.N. Doc. A/HRC/Sub.1/58/22*. For a discussion of how groups move from one to the other, see Lennox, *supra* note 21.

[33] For examples and discussion, see Ursula Dorowszewska, *Rethinking the State, Minorities and National Security, in* CAN LIBERAL PLURALISM BE EXPORTED? 126–134 (Will Kymlicka & Magda Opalski eds., Oxford Univ. Press 2001) (on the Crimean Tatars); Edo Banach, *The Roma and the Native Americans: Encapsulated Communities within Larger Constitutional Regime,* 14 FLORIDA J. INT'L L. 353 (2002); Ilona Klimova-Alexander, *Transnational Romani and Indigenous Non-Territorial Self-Determination Claims,* 6 ETHNOPOLITICS 395 (2007) (on the Roma); Jamal, *supra* note 20; Hassan Jabareen, *Collective Rights and Recognition in the Constitutional Process,* 12 ADALAH NEWSLETTER (Apr. 2005) (on the Palestinians); Lennox, *supra* note 21 (on Afro-Latinos); and Aukerman, *supra* note 16 (on various Eastern European cases).

[34] Russel Lawrence Barsh, *Indigenous Peoples in the 1990s: From Object to Subject of International Law?,* 7 HARV. HUM. RTS. J. 33, 81 (1994).

[35] Aukerman, *supra* note 16, at 1030.

rights. Many states supported the UN draft declaration on indigenous rights only because it was seen as exceptional, relevant to a very specific and relatively small and peripheral set of groups, and not as a precedent that could be invoked by other, larger homeland groups, such as national minorities. As we will see below, various intergovernmental organizations have repeatedly and explicitly rejected attempts to codify rights of self-government for powerful substate national groups, in part, because of geopolitical security implications. They are not going to allow such groups to gain rights of self-government through the back door simply by redefining themselves as indigenous peoples. Yet there is very little within the current UN indigenous rights machinery that prevents such a shift from taking place.

If more and more homeland groups adopt the indigenous label, the likely result is that the international community will retreat from its current commitment to robust accommodation rights for indigenous peoples. Indeed, the first signs of such a retreat are already visible. There are a number of ways this retreat could take place. The most obvious is that member states may bring negotiations on the UN and Organization of American States (OAS) draft declarations to a halt.[36] Or they may gut these declarations of their substantive content—for example, by excising rights to land or self-government, and by moving toward a more integrationist approach. Or they may attempt to limit sharply the scope of application of these declarations—perhaps by limiting them to "remote" groups that do not participate in the wage economy, such as forest dwellers. Whatever the technique, the result of such a retreat would be to undermine the major progress that has occurred to date on behalf of indigenous people.

This suggests that the long-term future of the targeted track for the indigenous at the UN and other intergovernmental organizations is not yet clear. This track is often cited as the clearest success in the development of international minority rights, but this judgment may be premature. Indeed, it has been a success, but it is in danger of becoming a victim of its own success. Achievements in the New World, particularly in empowering indigenous peoples in Latin America, are encouraging intergovernmental organizations to redefine and extend the category in ways that are morally inconsistent, conceptually unstable, and politically unsustainable.

3. Rethinking the approach

The UN is not unaware of these difficulties with its current approach to minority rights. Many key actors within the UN realize that the simple distinction between

[36] The Draft Declaration finally came up for adoption by the General Assembly in November 2006, and was widely expected to pass, but instead it was deferred, largely due to concerns by African countries about the definition of indigenous peoples. For the African Group's objections, see its Draft Aide Memoire (Nov. 9, 2006), *available at* <http://www.iwgia.org/graphics/Synkron-Library/Documents/InternationalProcesses/DraftDeclaration/AfricanGroupAideMemoireOnDeclaration.pdf>.

autonomy-seeking indigenous peoples and integration-seeking minorities does not capture the reality of ethnic relations around the world, and that many different types of homeland minorities—not just indigenous peoples—seek autonomy. Indeed, the UN has direct hands-on experience with these claims for autonomy, since such claims are at the root of some of the most difficult and violent ethnic conflicts around the world, which it is often called upon to help resolve. In many cases, the UN has intervened actively to support the autonomy aspirations of national minorities, as in Cyprus (for the Turkish minority), Sudan (for the Southern peoples), Iraq (for the Kurds), Indonesia (for Aceh and Papua), Sri Lanka (for the Tamils), and Burma (for the Karens and others). Indeed, in Cyprus, the UN essentially drafted a new constitution (the "Annan Plan") proposing federalization and consociational power sharing as a means to overcome the long-standing conflict between the Greek majority and Turkish national minority.

Analogous situations have arisen in postcommunist Europe, although in this context it has been European organizations (such as the European Union, the Organization for Security and Cooperation in Europe [OSCE], and NATO) that usually have taken the lead role in conflict resolution. In several cases of conflict between states and homeland minorities in postcommunist Europe, intergovernmental organizations have pushed for the adoption of some form of federal or quasifederal territorial autonomy—for example in Serbia (for Albanians), Bosnia (for Serbs), Macedonia (for Albanians), Ukraine (for Russians in Crimea), Moldova (for Slavs in Trans-Dniestria), Georgia (for Abkhazia), and Azerbaijan (for Armenians).

Thus, in a wide range of cases, the UN and other intergovernmental organizations have endorsed an accommodationist rather than integrationist approach toward national minorities. Moreover, they have justified this preference for a more accommodationist approach by citing "best practices" from the Western democracies. The Annan Plan for Cyprus, for example, explicitly drew on strategies used in Switzerland and Belgium to accommodate their substate national groups. Similarly, the EU's proposals for the former Yugoslavia were based on the model of autonomy for the German national minority in Italy. These Western examples are presented as successful models of how a liberal-democratic state should deal with its national minorities; they were not understood as regrettable deviations from an ideal of integration. In these and other ways, the UN has been actively involved in diffusing the theory and practice of autonomy regimes for national minorities to policy makers, journalists, community leaders, and academics around the world.[37]

In short, the UN exhibits a degree of inconsistency regarding the appropriate treatment of national minorities. In terms of norms, the UN presupposes that national minorities seek only integration (and are entitled only to integration) and belong in the same legal category as new minorities. In the actual practice of case-specific conflict resolution, however, the UN has set aside this presupposition,

---

[37] *See* KYMLICKA, *supra* note 9, for more on the role of international organizations in diffusing discourses and models of minority rights.

acknowledged the necessity of considering accommodationist alternatives to integration, and helped to diffuse models and best practices of accommodation.

In my view, this willingness to consider accommodationist alternatives is essential if the UN is to play a constructive role in resolving conflicts between states and national minorities. There was (and is) no plausible alternative to autonomy in such countries as Sudan, Iraq, Indonesia, and Sri Lanka. However, the fact that the UN's recommendations for accommodation in specific cases deviate from the norms and expectations of its own minorities declaration does create some obvious problems. For one thing, its recommendations appear ad hoc: Why is the UN supporting autonomy for national minorities in Indonesia and not, say, in Pakistan? Why is the UN supporting autonomy for the Kurds in Iraq but not for the Kurds in Iran? Why are intergovernmental organizations supporting autonomy for Albanians in Macedonia but not for Hungarians in Slovakia? At best, these recommendations seem arbitrary, and, at worst, they appear to be rewarding belligerence. An obvious explanation for why the UN is supporting autonomy for some national minorities and not others is simply that the former took up arms and engaged in violent struggles. In virtually all of the cases where the UN has endorsed autonomy for national minorities, it is after the minorities resorted to violence. By contrast, where national minorities have peacefully and democratically mobilized for autonomy, they typically receive no support from the international community and, instead, are told that international norms on the rights of minorities do not recognize a right to autonomy.[38]

The perverse effect is to increase the incentive for autonomy-seeking national minorities to take up arms, as this is the only way they can obtain any international support. At the same time, this state of affairs may delegitimize the very idea of autonomy, since it easily could be perceived as a payoff to bellicose minorities, rather than as a principled approach to the management of ethnocultural diversity.

Obviously, it would be preferable if the UN or other intergovernmental organizations could find a more principled basis on which to evaluate national minority claims to autonomy. To pretend that national minorities do not seek autonomy, as the UN declaration does, is to bury one's head in the sand. To support autonomy only in cases of violent conflict, as the UN practice of case-specific intervention does, may unintentionally encourage aggression. Developing a more consistent and principled approach to national minorities would not only enable more effective international intervention but also would help to stabilize the current framework for indigenous rights since, as we have seen, the absence of any

[38] The ethnic Hungarians in Slovakia and Romania have repeatedly complained that their peaceful mobilization for autonomy has received no support from international organizations and indeed has often been discouraged. *See* Margit Bessenyey-Williams, *European Integration and Minority Rights: The Case of Hungary and its Neighbours, in* NORMS AND NANNIES: THE IMPACT OF INTERNATIONAL ORGANIZATIONS ON THE CENTRAL AND EAST EUROPEAN STATES 227–258 (Ron Linden ed., Rowman & Littlefield 2002).

recognition of national minority rights puts unsustainable pressure on the policy track regarding indigenous peoples.

Unfortunately, the prospects for the development of new international norms regarding the rights of national minorities are not good. There has only been one attempt at the UN to develop such norms, and that was stillborn. In 1994, Liechtenstein circulated in the General Assembly's Social, Cultural and Humanitarian Affairs Committee a draft Convention on Self-Determination through Self-Administration, which recognized a right of internal autonomy for all "peoples", where peoples were explicitly defined to include not only indigenous peoples but also homeland national minorities.[39] However, this draft was never debated seriously and quickly disappeared from view.

A more sustained effort to develop new norms for national minorities has occurred at the regional level within Europe. I will describe these European initiatives in some depth, because I believe they shed light on the prospects for reform at the global level. Recent European efforts to codify new minority rights norms have run into difficulties that would also surface, perhaps even in stronger form, at a global level.

When the Berlin Wall fell and communism collapsed in 1989–90, a number of violent ethnic conflicts involving national minorities emerged in the postcommunist countries, undermining the transition to liberal democracy. As a result, several European organizations attempted to formulate norms and standards for the treatment of national minorities that could guide these countries in dealing with such issues. This initiated a period of intense debate within Europe about the appropriate treatment of national minorities, and about whether autonomy, as a right or norm, should figure in that treatment.

This debate was particularly intense between 1990 and 1993. After the collapse of communism, the very first statement by a European organization on minority rights—the 1990 Copenhagen declaration of the Conference on Security and Co-operation in Europe (CSCE)[40]—explicitly endorsed territorial autonomy as a best practice. Article 35 of the declaration states:

> The participating States note the efforts undertaken to protect and create conditions for the promotion of the ethnic, cultural, linguistic and religious identity of certain national minorities by establishing, as one of the possible means to achieve these aims, appropriate local or autonomous administrations corresponding to the specific historical and territorial circumstances of such minorities and in accordance with the policies of the State concerned.[41]

[39] *See* U.N. Doc. A/C.3/48/L.17 (Nov. 1993). *See also* THE SELF-DETERMINATION OF PEOPLES: COMMUNITY, NATION, AND STATE IN AN INTERDEPENDENT WORLD (Wolfgang Danspeckgruber ed., Lynne Rienner 2002), where the draft convention is reprinted together with legal commentaries.
[40] The precursor to the OSCE.
[41] Conference on Sec. & Coop. in Eur. [CSCE], *Document of the Copenhagen Meeting of the Conference on the Human Dimension of the CSCE*, June 29, 1990, 29 I.L.M. 1306–1309 (1990), at para. 36.

An even stronger endorsement of territorial autonomy came in 1993, in Recommendation 1201 of the Council of Europe Parliamentary Assembly. It provides that

> [i]n the regions where they are a majority the persons belonging to a national minority shall have the right to have at their disposal appropriate local or autonomous authorities or to have a special status, matching this specific historical and territorial situation and in accordance with the domestic legislation of the state.[42]

Unlike the 1990 CSCE declaration, this recommendation recognizes territorial autonomy as a right, not merely as a best practice. It was widely hoped and assumed that this text's provisions would play a central role in the Council of Europe's Framework Convention for the Protection of National Minorities, which was being drafted at the same time.

In short, there was much talk of an emerging right to autonomy in Europe in the early 1990s. A concrete expression of this idea was the decision of the European Commission in 1991 to require Yugoslav republics seeking independence to establish a "special status" for regions where national minorities form a local majority, modeled, in part, on the example of South Tyrol.[43]

However, as it turns out, the Parliamentary Assembly's Recommendation 1201 reflects the high-water mark of support for territorial autonomy within European organizations. Since then, there has been a marked movement away from it. The framework convention, adopted just two years after Recommendation 1201, decisively rejected the Parliamentary Assembly's advice and avoided any reference to territorial autonomy. Not only is territorial autonomy not recognized as a "right", it is not even mentioned as a recommended practice. Nor does territorial autonomy appear in any subsequent declaration or recommendation by European organizations, such as the series of Hague, Oslo, and Lund recommendations adopted by the OSCE from 1996 to 1999,[44] or the new draft constitution of the European Union.[45] Moreover, the Venice

---

[42] EUR. PARL. ASS., RECOMMENDATION 1201 ON AN ADDITIONAL PROTOCOL ON THE RIGHTS OF NATIONAL MINORITIES TO THE EUROPEAN CONVENTION ON HUMAN RIGHTS, 44TH SESS., REC. 1201, art. 11 (Feb. 1993).

[43] RICHARD CAPLAN, EUROPE AND THE RECOGNITION OF NEW STATES IN YUGOSLAVIA 30–33 (Cambridge Univ. Press 2005).

[44] Org. for Sec. & Coop. in Eur. [OSCE], *The Hague Recommendations Regarding the Education Rights of National Minorities* (Jan. 1996), *available at* <http://194.8.63.155/documents/hcnm/1996/10/2700_en.pdf>; OSCE, *The Oslo Recommendations Regarding the Linguistic Rights of National Minorities* (Feb. 1998), *available at* <http://osce.org/documents/hcnm/1998/02/2699_en.pdf>; OSCE, *The Lund Recommendations on the Effective Participation of National Minorities in Public Life* (Sept. 1999), *available at* <http://www.osce.org/documents/hcnm/1999/09/2698_en.pdf>.

[45] The European Free Alliance, a coalition of minority nationalist parties from various regions of Western Europe (e.g., Catalonia, Scotland, Flanders, South Tyrol), proposed that the EU constitutional treaty contain a clause that recognized "the right of self-government of all those territorial entities in the Union whose citizens have a strong and shared sense of national, linguistic or regional identity". The proposal was never seriously debated. Eur. Convention, Secretariat, *Democracy at Many Levels: Constitutional Reform*, CONV 298/02 (Sept. 24, 2002), at para. 3 (prepared by Neil

Commission[46] has ruled that national minorities do not have rights of self-determination, even in the form of internal self-determination.[47] For all intents and purposes, ideas of autonomy have disappeared from the debate about "European standards" on minority rights.

There are a number of reasons for this. For example, there was strong opposition to the idea of entrenching a right to territorial autonomy for national minorities in the West and to the notion that there might be international monitoring of how Western states treated their minorities. France, Greece, and Turkey have traditionally opposed the very idea of self-government rights for national minorities, and, indeed, they deny the very existence of national minorities. Even those Western countries that accord autonomy to their substate national groups do not necessarily want their own laws and policies regarding national minorities subject to international monitoring. The treatment of national minorities in various Western countries remains a politically sensitive topic, and many countries do not want their existing majority-minority settlements, often the result of long and painful negotiation processes, reopened by international monitoring agencies. In short, while they were willing, at first, to insist that postcommunist states be monitored for their treatment of minorities, Western democracies had no wish to have their own treatment of national minorities examined.

This resistance from within the West might have been sufficient to scuttle any attempt to formulate a right to self-government for national minorities. But the more immediate difficulty was the growing recognition by European organizations that it was unrealistic to apply or expect to impose such a norm of self-government in the postcommunist region. Any idea of minority self-government was bitterly opposed by postcommunist countries as a threat to their very existence.

Why was there such resistance to autonomy for national minorities in postcommunist countries? To answer this question, we need to step back and consider why Western democracies, over time, have become more comfortable with the idea of autonomy for their own national minorities. I would argue that there have been two key preconditions in the West that have lowered the risk to states and the dominant national groups in accepting national minority claims: (*a*) the existence of reliable human rights protections, and (*b*) the "desecuritization" of ethnic relations, such that the treatment of minorities is seen as an issue of

MacCormick). See Neil MacCormick, *The European Constitutional Convention and the Stateless Nations,* 18 INT'L AFF. 331 (2004), for the failed efforts to strengthen the recognition of "stateless nations" in the European constitution.

[46] The European Commission for Democracy through Law, the Council of Europe's advisory body on constitutional matters.

[47] VENICE COMM'N, OPINION OF THE EUROPEAN COMMISSION FOR DEMOCRACY THROUGH LAW ON THE INTERPRETATION OF ARTICLE 11 OF THE DRAFT PROTOCOL TO THE EUROPEAN CONVENTION ON HUMAN RIGHTS ANNEXED TO RECOMMENDATION 1201 OF THE PARLIAMENTARY ASSEMBLY, §3 (Feb. 21, 1996), *available at* <http://www.venice.coe.int/docs/1996/CDL-MIN(1996)004-e.asp>.

domestic politics rather than regional geopolitics. Neither was present in post-communist Europe in the early 1990s.

For majorities in the West, the consolidation of robust legal mechanisms for protecting human rights and the development of a human rights culture, generally, have provided guarantees that the accommodation of minority claims to self-government would not result in islands of tyranny in which the basic security or rights of citizens would be in jeopardy. These guarantees dramatically lowered the stakes involved in debates about minority rights. In postcommunist Europe in the early 1990s, however, these guarantees were absent. Dominant groups lacked the confidence that they would be treated fairly within self-governing minority regions. Indeed, in those cases where minorities seized territory and established their own autonomous governments, the results—if not outright ethnic cleansing—were often various forms of discrimination and harassment against anyone who did not belong to the minority. Ethnic Georgians were pushed out of the Abkhazia region of Georgia when it declared autonomy and/or sovereignty; ethnic Croats were expelled from the Serbian-dominated region of Slavonia when it declared autonomy; and ethnic Serbs were forced from Albanian-dominated Kosovo when it achieved autonomy—and so on. Neither side could rely on effective legal institutions and an impartial police to ensure that human rights were respected.

These fears for individual security were compounded by geopolitical fears regarding the security of the state. A crucial precondition for the adoption of multination federalism in the West has been the desecuritization of state-minority relations. With respect to both national minorities and indigenous peoples in the West, there is no longer any anxiety that they will collaborate with enemies of the state, and this allows claims for self-government to be treated as part of normal democratic politics. In postcommunist Europe, however, the perception of homeland minorities as potential fifth columns likely to collaborate with neighboring enemies remains pervasive, and so ethnic relations remain highly securitized.

In order to understand this perception, we need to recall the history of the region. The current configuration of states in Central and Eastern Europe is the result of the breakdown of three empires after World War I—the Russian Romanov empire, the Austro-Hungarian Habsburg empire, and the Turkish Ottoman empire—and the more recent collapse of the Soviet empire in 1989. Each of these empires encompassed the homelands of several national groups, many of which became independent states emerging from the ashes of the former empires (for example, Poles, Romanians, Czechs and Slovaks, Bulgarians, Serbs, Latvians, and so forth).

This process of state formation in the aftermath of imperial breakdown created several distinctive security problems relating to homeland minorities. First, the boundaries of these newly independent states typically (and inevitably) left some members of the national group on the wrong side of a new international border. When the border between Germany and Poland was drawn, there were many ethnic Germans on the Polish side of the border. Similarly, there were large numbers of ethnic Hungarians on the Romanian side of the border with Hungary; ethnic Russians on the Latvian side of the border with Russia; ethnic Turks on the Bulgarian side of the border with Turkey; and ethnic Albanians on the Macedonian side of the border. Often, these kin-state minorities are thought to have a higher loyalty to their kin-state than to the states in which they live. As a result, there is anxiety that such minorities are irredentist—that is, that they wish to redraw international boundaries so as to unite (or reunite) the territory where they live with their adjacent kin-state. Indeed, it is often assumed that they would collaborate willingly with their kin-state if it militarily invaded the country in order to claim this territory, as, indeed, some have done at various times in the twentieth century. No state is likely to accord self-governing powers voluntarily to a minority under these circumstances.

Where homeland minorities take the form of irredentist kin-state minor-ities, there is a much greater likelihood that ethnic relations will be perceived as a threat.[48] But this is not inevitable. There are factors that can either allevi-ate or exacerbate the problem. If, for example, the neighboring states are close allies, integrated into larger regional economic and security organizations, such that the kin-state has no interest in destabilizing its neighbor, this will alleviate the problem. This, of course, is precisely what has defused the problem of kin-state minorities in Western Europe. In the past, Belgium, Denmark, and Italy resisted according strong rights to their ethnic German minorities because they were perceived as kin-state minorities with a primary loyalty to Germany. But once Germany became a close ally rather than a potential enemy, as a result of the EU and NATO, the transborder affiliations of ethnic German minorities became unimportant (and came to be viewed, for that matter, as a potential asset in ongoing processes of regional integration).[49] In the postcommunist countries in the 1990s, however, there was no equivalent of the EU and NATO to turn potential enemies into allies. In the absence of regional security arrangements, postcommunist countries were in an almost Hobbesian state of nature, distrust-ful of all their neighbors. And in this context, the presumed disloyalty of kin-state minorities was quickly perceived as a security threat.

Another key factor in these considerations is the balance of power between a state, its minorities, and the neighboring kin-state. The perceived threat to state security obviously is reduced if the state feels itself to be a strong state confronting weak enemies, whether these are internal irredentist minorities or their kin-states across the border. Unfortunately, in the postcommunist world, the balance

---

[48] By contrast, many of the paradigmatic examples of national minorities in the West do not have a kin-state (e.g., Catalans and Basques; Scots and Welsh; Québécois; Puerto Ricans).

[49] The same applies to other potential kin-state minorities in the West that are linked by ethni-city to a neighboring state. The French in Switzerland or Belgium are not seen as a fifth column for France; neither are the Flemish for the Netherlands nor the Swedes in Finland. This is testament to the success of the EU and NATO in desecuritizing national minority politics in Western Europe.

of power has tended to exacerbate rather than alleviate the problem. In many cases, the national groups that acquired independence after imperial collapse view themselves as historically weak, confronted with minorities and kin-states that have been historically dominant. The result is the phenomenon known as "minoritized majorities"—majorities that continue to think and act as if they are weak and victimized minorities and, therefore, continue to live in existential fear for their survival.

This phenomenon is pervasive in the postcommunist world, as well as in much of the developing world, but is virtually unknown in the West (at least in a geo-political sense), and so needs some explaining. If one simply looks at the numbers and ignores the historical background, it may appear that kin-state minorities in most postcommunist countries are fairly small and weak. Ethnic Hungarians in Slovakia, for example, represent about 15 percent of the population and, hence, are relatively powerless in relation to the overwhelming ethnic Slovak major-ity in the country. Historically, however, the Hungarians were members of the privileged and dominant group within the larger Habsburg empire and were active collaborators in Habsburg policies to create Hungarian hegemony in the region. The ethnic Slovaks, by contrast, were subordinated, subject to coercive Magyarization campaigns. Since independence, this hierarchy has, of course, been reversed; Slovaks are now the dominant group, and Hungarians are the threatened minority subject to Slovak nation-building policies. But the memory remains. Slovaks view ethnic Hungarians not merely as a potentially irredentist group loyal to their kin-state but as a historically powerful and privileged group that had collaborated with a hegemonic imperial power to oppress the Slovak language and culture. In the absence of effective regional security arrangements, the fear persists that this could happen again—that is to say, that the Hungarian minority could collaborate with the Hungarian kin-state to subordinate Slovaks once again and crush their national independence.

We see the same phenomenon in Poland regarding the German minority or in Romania and Serbia vis-à-vis the Hungarian minority. The same state of affairs may be found in the Baltics, Ukraine, and Moldova regarding the Russian minor-ity; in Croatia and Bosnia with reference to the Serbs; and in Bulgaria regarding the Turkish minority, to name but a few. In all these cases, minorities are seen (rightly or wrongly) as allies or collaborators with external powers that have his-torically oppressed the majority group, and the majority group, in turn, reacts as a "minoritized" majority.

In short, several factors were at work exacerbating the securitization of ethnic relations in postcommunist Europe. The phenomenon of homeland minorities seeking self-government can raise difficulties at the best of times, since it chal-lenges the state's claim to represent a single people and to derive its legitimacy from an undivided popular sovereignty. However, this challenge becomes that much greater in a state where (a) the homeland minorities are potentially irre-dentist minorities with loyalty to a neighboring kin-state; (b) the national groups forming the majority in the state were historically subordinated by the neighboring kin-state in its former capacity as an imperial power; and (*c*) there are no regional security arrangements to guarantee nonaggression. Where these factors are present, as they were and are in much of postcommunist Europe, the likely result is a pervasive securitization of ethnic relations.

This securitization is reflected in three assumptions that dominate public debate on minorities in the region. The first is that minorities are disloyal, not just in the sense that they lack loyalty to the state (that is equally true of secessionists in Quebec or Scotland) but in the stronger sense that they have collaborated with former oppressors and will continue to collaborate with current enemies or potential enemies. The second assumption follows from the first: that a strong and stable state requires weak and disempowered minorities. Put another way, ethnic relations are seen as a zero-sum game; anything that benefits the minority is seen as a threat to the majority. Therefore—the third assumption—the treatment of minorities is above all a question of national security.

Thus, the two main factors that enabled dominant groups in the West to accept accommodation policies—namely, human rights guarantees and desecuritization—were absent, or only weakly present, in postcommunist Europe in the early 1990s. Given this fact, it is hardly surprising that attempts to promote autonomy were strongly resisted in postcommunist Europe.[50] The homeland minorities seeking self-government were often perceived as geopolitical threats to the security of the state, as well as threats to the individual human rights of people living in the potentially self-governing territory. Under these circumstances, it would have been surprising indeed if there had been much genuine interest in Western models of accommodating national minorities. Instead, most postcommunist states clung firmly to an integrationist agenda, maintaining the goal of turning themselves into centralized, unitary, and monolingual nation-states, premised on a singular and undifferentiated conception of popular sovereignty.

The distinctive history of imperialism and minority collaboration in the region also creates another important obstacle to the adoption or tolerance of autonomy—namely, perceptions of historic injustice. In many postcommunist countries, there is a strong sense that historical wrongs have not yet been acknowledged or remedied. Some say that this focus on historical rights and wrongs is unique to Eastern Europe, and that Western democracies have managed to get beyond this backward-looking obsession with history and to focus, instead, on forward-looking coexistence.[51] It is certainly true that feelings about historic injustice run

---

[50] These are not the only reasons for opposition to territorial autonomy in postcommunist Europe. For a discussion of a range of other such issues, see KYMLICKA, *supra* note 9, at ch. 6.

[51] This is a familiar trope of the extensive literature that distinguishes a "forward-looking" civic nationalism in the West from a "backward looking" ethnic nationalism in the East. *See, e.g.,* MICHAEL IGNATIEFF, BLOOD AND BELONGING (Farrar Straus & Giroux 1993), and the discussion in WILL KYMLICKA, POLITICS IN THE VERNACULAR ch. 12 (Oxford Univ. Press 2001).

deep in many postcommunist countries. But the same is true in many Western countries, as well. Appeals to historical injustice are increasingly common in the West. Consider the recent explosion of writing on the issue of reparations to African-Americans for the historic wrongs of slavery and segregation. Claims for the rectification of historic injustice are also a vital part of contemporary mobilization by indigenous peoples in New Zealand, Australia, and Canada, and even of some immigrant groups—such as, for example, Japanese-Americans seeking compensation for their detention in World War II.

As we have just seen, however, there is an important difference in the nature of the historic hierarchies in the West and in postcommunist Europe. In the West, it is almost always a *minority* that is seeking apology and compensation from the state that has historically mistreated it. Hence the argument from historic injustice operates to strengthen minority rights claims, and to buttress the argument for greater equality between majority and minority. It is invoked to pressure the majority to say, in effect, that never again will we try to expel, subordinate, or oppress you.

In postcommunist countries, however, it is typically the *majority* that feels it has been the victim of oppression, often at the hands of minorities acting in collaboration with foreign enemies. Hence the majority wants the minority to express guilt, and to offer an apology, as a way of saying that never again will the minority be disloyal to the state. We see this in the Czech Republic regarding the German minority; in Slovakia with reference to the Hungarian minority; and in the Baltics, vis-à-vis the Russian minority. In short, the sort of historic injustice that is central to postcommunist debates, unlike that in the West, is the historical oppression of the majority group by its minorities in collaboration with a kin-state or foreign power. This truly distinguishes Eastern Europe from the Western experience, although there are, to be sure, comparable examples from Africa and Asia.[52]

In this context, arguments about historic injustice work *against* minority rights claims. In the West, homeland minorities typically would have been stronger had it not been for historic injustices perpetrated by the larger state— for example, there would have been more people speaking the minority's language and practicing its culture, over a wider area. Minority rights can be seen, in part, as a way of acknowledging and remedying that harm. In postcommunist countries, however, historic injustice is often understood as having expanded the scope and prestige of the minority's language and culture at the expense of the majority. Indeed, taken to their logical conclusion, arguments of historic

---

[52] For example, members of the Sinhalese majority in Sri Lanka often express this sense of historic injustice. It is widely believed that the minority Tamils collaborated with, and were unfairly privileged by, the British colonizers, and remain willing to collaborate with neighboring India against the Sri Lankan state in order to defend those privileges. *See* SANKARAN KRISHNA, POSTCOLONIAL INSECURITIES: INDIA, SRI LANKA AND THE QUESTION OF NATIONHOOD (Univ. Minn. Press 1999).

injustice may suggest that minorities have no right at all to exist on the territory of the state, if their very presence is related to such an historic injustice. Were it not for unjust Russian and Soviet imperialism, there would be few Russians in the Baltics. But for unjust Ottoman imperialism, there would not be all that many Turks in Bulgaria. If the goal is to remedy the wrongs created by these historic injustices, why not try to undo the Russification of the Baltics, either by expelling the Russians or by insisting that they assimilate to Estonian and Latvian culture? Why not try to reverse the Turkification of Bulgaria under the Ottomans, whether by expelling the Turks or by insisting they assimilate to Bulgarian culture?[53]

These profound differences between East and West in human rights protection, geopolitical security, and in the nature of historic injustices create, therefore, obvious grounds for opposition within postcommunist countries to the adoption of autonomy for national minorities.[54] Given these obstacles, it is not surprising that efforts to codify a right to autonomy for national minorities have failed. While the international community has shown some willingness to consider this idea in the case of indigenous peoples, internal self-determination has proven too controversial in the case of European national minorities. As then OSCE High Commissioner on National Minorities Max van der Stoel observed in 1995, claims to territorial autonomy meet "maximal resistance" in the states of the postcommunist region, and so it was more "pragmatic" to focus on modest forms of minority rights.[55] As a result, European organizations have not only backed away from formulating territorial autonomy, as a legal norm, they have also, in many cases, stopped recommending it as a best practice. The OSCE high commissioner, in particular, has said that territorial autonomy should be viewed not as a best practice but as a last resort and has discouraged various minorities from putting forth autonomy demands on the grounds that such demands are destabilizing under existing conditions of geopolitical insecurity.[56] Far from imposing provisions for minority self-government on postcommunist Europe, some European organizations are now actively discouraging it.

[53] This is precisely what Bulgaria, for example, tried to do in the 1980s, by forcing all the Turks to adopt ethnic Bulgarian names. The communist Bulgarian government argued that the coerced assimilation of the Turks was simply reversing the unjust pressure that the Ottomans had put on Slavs to convert to Islam and to assimilate to Turkish culture.

[54] In all of these cases, it is important to distinguish objective facts about security threats and historic wrongs from the way these facts are perceived and discussed. Political actors make choices about whether or when to highlight (or exaggerate) these factors in public debate. The perception of kin-state minorities as a security threat and as collaborators in historic injustices against the majority is something that is deliberately inculcated and reproduced by certain political elites for reasons of self-interest.

[55] MAX VAN DER STOEL, PEACE AND STABILITY THROUGH HUMAN AND MINORITY RIGHTS: SPEECHES BY THE OSCE HIGH COMMISSIONER ON NATIONAL MINORITIES 111 (Nomos Verlagsgesellschaft 1999).

[56] *Id.* at 111.

Predictably, then, when the European standards for national minority rights were finally codified, all references to self-government or autonomy were dropped, and a much weaker set of norms were proposed. Indeed, the Council of Europe's framework convention and the OSCE's recommendations are essentially updated versions of the UN's minorities declaration, founded on a clear integrationist approach.

However—as with the UN—this integrationist legal framework coexists alongside a political practice of case-specific interventions more supportive of autonomy. We have already seen how European organizations have intervened in several cases to support the autonomy aspirations of national minorities, in Serbia, Bosnia, Macedonia, Ukraine, Moldova, Georgia, and Azerbaijan. Unfortunately, as was also the case with the UN, these case-specific interventions appear arbitrary, at best, and, at worst, as rewarding belligerence. In short, the European experiment in national minority rights reproduces many of the limitations of the UN approach.

4. Conclusion

If the analysis in this chapter is correct, the international community's approach to minority rights is at an impasse. Intergovernmental organizations are operating with a legal framework that draws a sharp dichotomy between an accommodationist approach to indigenous peoples and an integrationist approach to minorities. This legal framework is wholly inadequate to deal with the actual patterns of ethnic relations around the world and, in particular, is unable to deal with the aspirations to autonomy by homeland national minorities. Yet these aspirations lie at the root of many of the most pressing ethnic conflicts in the world today. In order to manage these real-world conflicts, intergovernmental organizations supplement their legal norms with case-specific interventions that are more accommodationist. However, these case-specific interventions in support of autonomy are often arbitrary and ad hoc.

This combination of unrealistic legal norms and arbitrary case-specific interventions has a number of perverse results, including encouraging and rewarding the resort to violence. Yet it is difficult to see what would be a feasible alternative. Ideally, we might hope to develop a more adequate legal framework, one that moves beyond the simplistic indigenous minorities distinction, in order to address the distinctive needs and claims of various groups, such as homeland national minorities, which do not fit into the current dichotomy. Such a new framework would recognize that, just as indigenous peoples have legitimate claims relating to history and territory that are not addressed by generic integrationist minority rights provisions, so, too, do other homeland minorities. Indeed, we might imagine this as the first step toward a new multitargeted system of international minority rights, with separate legal provisions not only for indigenous peoples and national minorities but also for other distinctive types of minorities, such as the Roma in Eastern Europe or Afro-Latin Americans. These groups also have needs and interests that are not sufficiently protected by the current framework based on the indigenous-minority dichotomy. Various proposals for such a multi-targeted system of minority rights have been made.[57]

Unfortunately, the prospects for reform of the framework of international norms are poor. There is no support at the UN for revisiting the issue of the rights of minorities.[58] Furthermore, the one serious attempt that has been made at a regional level to address the distinctive issues raised by national minorities—namely, the European norms developed by the OSCE and Council of Europe—has retreated to a more cautious defense of generic integrationist minority rights. Some commentators have expressed the hope that other regional inter-governmental organizations—such as the African Union, ASEAN, or the Arab League—might take up the task of formulating their own regional standards of minority rights. It is unlikely this will happen, but, if it did, it is almost certain that they, too, would shy away from endorsing any right to autonomy for national minorities. They might be willing to endorse a norm of autonomy for small and isolated indigenous peoples but not for powerful substate national minorities.

Nor is this simply a matter of a lack of good faith or political will. The reality is that the conditions that have enabled a consensus to emerge within various Western democracies in support of autonomy for national minorities simply do not exist in many parts of the world. Indeed, all of the obstacles that have pre-vented European organizations from codifying a right to autonomy for national minorities apply just as powerfully in other regions of the world. The problems we have seen in postcommunist Europe—such as the securitization of state-minority relations; the fear of human rights violations; and the nature of his-toric hierarchies—are pervasive in Africa, Asia, and the Middle East, as well. If anything, the willingness to consider autonomy for national minorities is even weaker in these postcolonial states than in the postcommunist countries of Eastern Europe.

[57] For example, several NGOs have proposed a "Charter of Romani Rights", to develop targeted rights for the Roma in Europe; and the Parliamentary Assembly of the Council of Europe called for a specific legal instrument regarding the rights of immigrant citizens (Recommendation 1492). For these and other proposals for new targeted rights, see KYMLICKA, *supra* note 9, at ch. 6 and 8.

[58] For example, longstanding calls to turn the 1992 UN Declaration on minority rights into a binding convention have essentially disappeared from the debate. Even Minority Rights Group, the main international advocacy group in the field, has stopped pushing this idea. *See* Minority Rights Group, *Possible New United Nations Mechanisms for the Protection and Promotion of the Rights of Minorities* (Working Paper submitted to UN Working Group on Minorities, 9th Session), U.N. Doc. E/CN.4/sub.2/AC.5/2002/WP3 (May 5, 2003). Other proposals to strengthen the codification and monitoring of international norms have also fallen by the wayside. *See* KYMLICKA, *supra* note 9, at ch. 6.

Under these circumstances, the prospects for gaining an international consensus on a new and more accommodationist framework for addressing the claims of national minorities is virtually nil. For the foreseeable future, we are left with the status quo. As McGarry, O'Leary, and Simeon correctly explain, the status quo is predominantly integrationist. However, as I hope I have shown, the commitment of the international community to an integrationist approach is neither uniform nor stable, and there are multiple if unpredictable avenues open for accommodationist approaches to find international support.

5

Does the world need more Canada? The politics of the Canadian model in constitutional politics and political theory

*Sujit Choudhry**

1. Introduction: Brian Barry versus Will Kymlicka

In the past two decades, numerous political theorists have taken up the question of how constitutional design should respond to ethnic, national, and linguistic division. Just as important as that question is the way in which these theorists have responded to it. Some, rather than deriving constitutional strategies and models from abstract principles of political morality, have turned to real-life examples to buttress their proposed solutions. This is hardly surprising, since political theorists write about urgent problems to which they hope to offer principled solutions that actually work. However, in the subsidiary literature concerned with the accommodation of minority nationalism, the models on offer are often much more complex, consisting of a large number of constitutional instruments meant to operate as a whole. It is precisely in this context—and as just such a model—that Canada has attained considerable prominence.

Given this disproportionate prominence, what is striking about Brian Barry's critique of multiculturalism—in *Culture and Equality*—is his attack on Canadian political theorists and on Canada itself.[1] Although Barry draws on examples from a wide range of jurisdictions and on the work of political theorists of many nationalities, only Canadians and Canada are singled out for opprobrium. For example, the first section of chapter 1 ("Losing Our Way") is a sarcastic rejoinder to Will Kymlicka's *Finding Our Way*, a major study of the accommodation

* Scholl Chair, Faculty of Law and Department of Political Science, University of Toronto. My thanks to Avigail Eisenberg, Jean-François Gaudreault-DesBiens, Patrick Macklem, Ira Parghi, Michel Rosenfeld, Richard Simeon, and Michel Venne for helpful comments. Email: sujit. choudhry@utoronto.ca

[1] BRIAN BARRY, CULTURE AND EQUALITY: AN EGALITARIAN CRITIQUE OF MULTICULTURALISM (Harvard Univ. Press 2001).

of cultural diversity in Canada.[2] On one level, Barry's attack is methodological. He highlights and challenges Kymlicka's heavy reliance on Canada as the basis for the latter's account of the phenomenonology of minority nationalism—that is to say, Kymlicka's position that a culture is synonymous with a nation or people, and that the claims of minority nationalism are, therefore, claims for cultural preservation in the face of assimilative pressures from the majority.[3]

For Barry, Kymlicka universalizes the particular claims of Quebec; hence, his discussion of nationalism "has been skewed" by his understanding of the Canadian case.[4] But Barry's attack extends to the very success and viability of Canada itself. This goes far beyond concerns regarding particular programs. Rather, he argues that since the theoretical defenses for a wide range of Canadian public policies responding to ethnocultural diversity are so deeply deficient and since these defenses are so widely accepted by Canada's political elites, "[i]t may reasonably be asked how it is that Canada does as well as it does".[5] While *Culture and Equality* is a work of political theory, not political economy, Barry nonetheless offers up the notion that Canada succeeds because "'there is a lot of ruin in a nation [as Adam Smith famously remarked]', especially one whose land and coastal waters contain some of the richest natural resources in the world and whose history has been one of permanent peace with the only country with which it shares a land border".[6]

The prominence of Canada is twofold. On the one hand, Canadian political theorists—Joseph Carens, Will Kymlicka, Margaret Moore, Wayne Norman, Allen Patten, Charles Taylor, James Tully, Daniel Weinstock, and others—have set the agenda for normative reflection on the various problems generated by minority nationalism. Indeed, these authors are so prominent it is widely recognized they have come to represent a Canadian "school", one which has profoundly shaped our understanding of these issues. Yet the importance of Canada is more than just a by-product of national academic excellence. The real story is the considerable attention devoted to Canada itself. Not only are Canadians are in the forefront of normative reflection on the problems of minority nationalism but, in the work of these scholars, the Canadian case plays a pivotal role.

This is especially true for Will Kymlicka. *Finding Our Way* celebrates the "Canadian model" of ethnocultural relations.[7] According to Kymlicka, Canada has attracted international attention and is a "world leader...[that]...is now seen as a model by many other countries" because it appears to have coped, successfully, with the diversity arising from immigration, indigenous peoples, and

[2] WILL KYMLICKA, FINDING OUR WAY: RETHINKING ETHNOCULTURAL RELATIONS IN CANADA (Oxford Univ. Press 1998).
    [3] *See, e.g.,* WILL KYMLICKA, MULTICULTURAL CITIZENSHIP: A LIBERAL THEORY OF MINORITY RIGHTS (Oxford Univ. Press 1995).
    [4] BARRY, *supra* note 1, at 309.
    [5] *Id.* at 313.
    [6] *Id.*
    [7] KYMLICKA, *supra* note 2, at 3.

minority nationalism "simultaneously[,] while still managing to live together in peace and civility".[8] There is a particular interest in the Canadian approach to dealing with minority nationalism, according to Kymlicka, because Canada was the first country to use "federalism to accommodate the existence of a regionally concentrated national minority ... by creating a political unit within which a lin- guistically distinct national minority would form a majority and govern itself".[9] Not only does Canada have the longest "experience concerning the relationship between federalism and minority nationalism"[10] but that experience has proved a positive one, since Canadians "have learned to live with a vigorous minor- ity nationalism that in many countries would lead to anarchy or civil war".[11] Because of its evident success, Canada has served and continues to serve as a model for countries that must cope with the pressures of minority nationalism, a trend Kymlicka wholeheartedly endorses. "Canada has relevant experience and expertise to offer the world", he writes, given the lessons Canadians have learned through the lived experience of responding to minority nationalism "over the years—lessons that many other countries want and need to learn if they too are to survive and prosper" and to "avoid unnecessary conflicts and injustices".[12] Since Kymlicka puts the Canadian model into play, Barry's question—how well has this model worked in practice—is entirely fair.

The purpose of this chapter is to complicate and contextualize the discussion of the Canadian model in political theory. For, contemporaneously with the rise of the Canadian model, Canada went through a period of profound constitutional introspection. Since the 1960s, the country has struggled with the constitutional accommodation of Quebec nationalism. During the early 1990s, these debates reached a crisis point that nearly occasioned the breakup of the country. Because the Canadian example draws on Canada's own national experience, I want to revisit this model, viewing it against the backdrop of the constitutional politics of the last few decades. Not only did the emergence of the Canadian model coincide with Canada's worst constitutional crisis but, as it turned out, promoting Canada's success abroad also was an important intervention in domestic constitutional politics, in an attempt to shore up support for the Canadian model at home. The question is whether this model has worked as well as Kymlicka claims. Quebec nationalist scholar Guy LaForest has suggested that, indeed, Canada's "political system does not measure up to our country's reputation abroad" because it fails to acknowledge, both symbolically and institutionally, Quebec's distinctiveness.[13] The focus here will be different. I will argue that Canada provides a cautionary

[8] *Id.* at 2–3.
[9] *Id.* at 2.
[10] *Id.*
[11] *Id.* at 3.
[12] *Id.* at 3–4.
[13] Guy LaForest, *The True Nature of Sovereignty: Reply to My Critics Concerning Trudeau and the End of a Canadian Dream, in* CANADIAN POLITICAL PHILOSOPHY: CONTEMPORARY REFLECTIONS 308 (Ronald Beiner & Wayne Norman eds., Oxford Univ. Press 2001).

tale on the limits of constitutional design and its ability to cope with the threat of extralegal secession by minority nations.

2. The Canadian model: Accommodation and integration

When Kymlicka and Barry evoke the Canadian model, they are referring to how constitutional design can and should respond to the relation between constitutionalism and nationalism. The context in which this issue arises is the multinational state. There is a familiar story here.[14] The constitutional problems of multinational states arise because modern states necessarily engage in a process of nation building, which is designed to produce a degree of common identity, shared by all its citizens, across the entire territory of the state. The means to this end include policies centered on language, history, and culture, and on the centralization of legal and political power. The goals of nation building are diverse. David Miller has suggested that one reason for the nation-building process is to provide the necessary motivational element missing from liberal accounts of political legitimacy.[15] A sense of identification with a particular set of liberal democratic institutions and laws induces individuals to make those institutions work and to accept their demands. Ernest Gellner has argued that linguistic homogenization is, in fact, a tool for economic integration and the enhancement of economic opportunity, since it permits citizens to become members of a mobile and flexible workforce throughout the whole of a country.[16]

But many states also contain national minorities whose members once formed complete, functioning societies on their territory, endowed with a considerable degree of self-rule, prior to their incorporation into the larger state. Multinational states are often the legacy of conquest and empire or of voluntary federation or union. Consequently, many national minorities will resist nation-building efforts and engage in minority nation building as a defensive response. In some cases, minority nationalism is a response to the centralization of political and legal power that often has shifted power away from minorities. In other cases, it is a response to linguistic nation building, which can impair the ability of linguistic minorities to participate fully in economic and political life. Minorities respond to majority nation building by conceiving of themselves as nations and making constitutional claims designed both to protect themselves from the majority's nation-building project and to enable them to engage in a parallel process of nation building focused on the territory where they constitute a majority.

---

[14] *See, e.g.*, WILL KYMLICKA, CULTURALLY RESPONSIVE POLICIES (United Nations Development Programme 2004) (background paper to UNDP Human Development Report 2004).

[15] DAVID MILLER, ON NATIONALITY (Oxford Univ. Press 1995).

[16] ERNEST GELLNER, NATIONS AND NATIONALISM (Cornell Univ. Press 1983).

There are many multinational states in the world—Canada, the United Kingdom, Belgium, Spain, Russia, Sudan, Sri Lanka, Iraq, Malaysia, and India, to name just a few. In these states, constitutional design matters a great deal, since constitutions were and are the principal sites for the majority nation building as well as for the national minorities' resistance to the overarching process of nation-state consolidation. In other words, the political sociology of multinational states cannot be fully understood without careful attention to the politics of constitutional design and interpretation. The Canadian model is a conspicuous example of how constitutional design can accommodate these competing nation-building agendas within a single state. Put simply, the Canadian exemplar responds by challenging the equation of nation and state that underlies not only majority nation building but also the defensive response of minority nations, for which the logical response is to resist incorporation into the majority nation and demand states of their own.

Thus, the interesting question is what, precisely, are the constitutional and nonconstitutional instruments Canada employs to realize the ideal implied when nation and state are not treated as synonymous. Surprisingly, and despite widespread comparative interest, the juridical details of the Canadian model have never been set out in comprehensive fashion by constitutional scholars.[17] Nor have political theorists risen to the challenge. This is true even of Kymlicka. Although he extols the virtues of the Canadian model in *Finding Our Way*, he presents it, for the most part, in outline or simply presupposes it in discussions that are not institutional in their focus—discussions, for example, regarding the political sociology of competing claims of nationhood.

Nonetheless, a useful starting point is what Kymlicka does have to say about the Canadian model in *Finding Our Way*:

> [F]ederalism seems the ideal mechanism for accommodating territorially defined national minorities within a multinational state. Where such a minority is regionally concentrated, the boundaries of federal subunits can be drawn so that it forms a majority in one of the subunits.... Quebec is the paradigmatic example. Under the federal division of powers, the province of Quebec has control over issues that are crucial to the survival of the francophone society, including education, language and culture, as well as significant input into immigration policy.[18]

Kymlicka notes that Quebec has jurisdiction over language, including the language of education and public and private sector employment. Finally, he notes that provincial boundaries and provincial powers are constitutionally entrenched; otherwise, Canada's English majority could evade unilaterally the protection offered to Quebec by federalism.

---

[17] Stephen Tierney's work is a notable exception. *See, e.g.,* STEPHEN TIERNEY, CONSTITUTIONAL LAW AND NATIONAL PLURALISM (Oxford Univ. Press 2005).

[18] KYMLICKA, *supra* note 2, at 135.

Thus, for Kymlicka, Canada's constitutional order comes down clearly on the side of accommodation in the well-known accommodationist–integrationist debate, in comparative politics, about how to manage ethnic, linguistic, religious, and cultural diversity through constitutional design. On the one hand, some scholars have argued for the need to recognize, institutionalize, and empower differences. There is a range of constitutional instruments available to achieve this goal, such as multinational federalism, legal pluralism (for example, religious personal law), other forms of nonterritorial minority rights (minority language and religious education rights), consociationalism, affirmative action, and legislative quotas. But others have countered that such practices may entrench, perpetuate, and exacerbate the very divisions they are designed to manage. These latter scholars propose a range of alternative strategies, falling under the rubric of "integrationism", that blur or transcend differences. Examples of such strategies include: bills of rights, enshrining universal human rights enforced by judicial review; policies of disestablishment (religious and ethnocultural); federalism; and electoral systems designed specifically to include members of different groups within the same political unit and to disperse members of the same group across different units.

For Kymlicka, Canada adopts an accommodationist stance vis-à-vis minority nationalism through multinational federalism. However, on careful examination, it is apparent that the Canadian model consists of a mixture of accommodationist and integrationist strategies that extends far beyond multinational federalism. Moreover, close scrutiny of the concrete legal and institutional details of the Canadian order pays intellectual dividends, since it adds both conceptual clarity and texture to the debate over the relative merits of integration and accommodation as constitutional techniques for the management of minority nationalism. Such scrutiny is important, and its value extends beyond the Canadian case to other multinational polities. There are four main points:

(1) The terms accommodation and integration, although helpful, are potentially misleading because they may encourage us to forget that both integration and accommodation are directed toward the same goal—maintaining the territorial integrity and political unity of the state. This is true, certainly, of multinational federalism in Canada, which was designed to keep Canada together by removing Quebec's motive to secede. Thus, integrationist and accommodationist constitutional strategies as alternative means to the same end are not necessarily in opposition.

(2) Although accommodation and integration are alternatives, they are not mutually exclusive. Indeed, in multinational federations, it makes sense to employ both simultaneously. Multinational federalism carries the risk that—perversely enough—it can fuel secession, rather than enhancing the territorial integrity and political unity of the state. Constitutions thus can use integrationist instruments to offset this danger. The requirement that

Quebecers participate in federal institutions is perhaps the best example in the Canadian context.

(3) The combination of integrationist and accommodationist strategies can be achieved in different ways. One device is to set limits on the scope of accommodation—for example, by forcing certain decisions to be made in common institutions in which a national subunit does not have a veto. This is illustrated by the broad but limited scope accorded to provincial jurisdiction and, on the other hand, by the constitutional entrenchment of provincial participation in common national institutions. Another method is to balance an accommodationist strategy in one area of constitutional design against an integrationist strategy in another; for example, the balancing of multinational federalism against the nation-building aspects of the Canadian Charter of Rights and Freedoms.[19]

(4) Constitutional strategies that appear to be accommodationist may in reality be integrationist. More specifically, it is important to differentiate accommodation as institutional separateness (for example, multinational federalism) from accommodation designed to facilitate participation in common institutions (federal language policy, for example).

In what follows, I will illustrate these points by reference to various aspects of the Canadian constitutional order.

Canadian federalism, of course, is the best known of these features. Both levels of government—federal and provincial—derive their authority from the Constitution. Federalism is constitutionally entrenched against unilateral modification by either level of government, and the limits on the authority of both the federal and the provincial governments are judicially enforceable.[20] Canada is a multinational federation because the boundaries of the province of Quebec were drawn so that francophones would constitute a majority therein and could not be outvoted by the anglophone majority in Canada as a whole. This remains true today—indeed, the territorialization of linguistic communities is greater now than at the time Quebec was created. Moreover, Quebec has been granted a mix of concurrent and exclusive jurisdiction over a wide range of policy areas that gives it the tools to ensure the survival of a francophone society. These areas of jurisdiction include language and control of primary, secondary, and postsecondary education. Inasmuch as language is the driving force behind Quebec's claims for political autonomy, the Canadian model blunts its force by placing language under provincial jurisdiction.

The adoption of federalism and the creation of Quebec was a direct response to the failed viability of the United Province of Canada, a British colony that

---

[19] The Canadian Charter of Rights and Freedoms, part I (§§ 1–34) of the Constitution Act, 1982, Schedule B to the Canada Act 1982, ch. 11 (U.K.) [hereinafter *Charter*].

[20] *See generally* Constitution Act, 1867, 30 & 31 Vict. Ch. 3. (U.K.), *as reprinted in* R.S.C., No. 5 (Appendix 1985).

resulted from the merger of the previous colonies of Lower Canada (later Quebec) and Upper Canada (later Ontario), existing between 1840 and 1867. The history here is complex.[21] In brief, citizens of both Lower and Upper Canada elected equal numbers of representatives to a legislative assembly, although the largely francophone citizens of the former outnumbered the largely anglophone citizens of the latter.[22] The language of government was meant to be English.[23] The goal behind the merger and departure from representation by population was to facilitate the assimilation of francophones—that is, to engage in English-language nation building even before anglophones were a majority. As time went on, Upper Canada became more populous and demanded greater representation in the joint legislature, which was resisted by francophones who feared they would be outvoted on matters important to their identity. The result was political paralysis. Federalism was the solution—providing for representation by population at the federal level while simultaneously creating a Quebec with jurisdiction over those matters crucial to the survival of the francophone society in that province. Had Quebec not been created, it is likely that the French-speaking areas of Canada eventually would have seceded.

It is important to emphasize that federalism is a mechanism for both accommodation and integration, and, because of this, the provinces have extensive but limited jurisdiction and cannot invade the powers of the federal government. The result is that many important decisions of interest to the citizens of Quebec lie within federal jurisdiction—such as criminal law, immigration policy, international trade, macroeconomic policy (including taxation), foreign policy (including the negotiation of international treaties), and defense.[24] The citizens of the subunit must participate in the institutions of the common state in order to shape important political decisions directly affecting them. The juridical equality of the provinces strengthens these incentives, because provincial equality has the important corollary that federal legislative power applies equally across the country. By contrast, were federal legislative power to apply asymmetrically vis-à-vis Quebec, the incentives for Quebecers to participate in national political life would be diminished.

How are the institutions of shared rule at the federal level structured? Although federal institutions demonstrate a mixture of integrationist and accommodationist elements, they are predominantly integrationist. On the integrationist side, the federal government operates independently from the provinces. The federal House of Commons is directly elected by the citizenry, as opposed to

---

[21] KENNETH MCROBERTS, MISCONCEIVING CANADA: THE STRUGGLE FOR NATIONAL UNITY (Oxford Univ. Press 1997).

[22] An Act to Reunite the Provinces of Upper and Lower Canada, and for the Government of Canada, 3 & 4 Vict. ch. 35, § XII (U.K.).

[23] *Id.* § XLI.

[24] For powers of the parliament or federal powers, see Constitution Act, 1867, § 91 (Can.); for exclusive areas of provincial jurisdiction, see Constitution Act, 1867, §§ 92–93 (Can.).

being appointed by provincial governments.[25] The federal Senate is a federally appointed body.[26] Both houses pass bills by simple majority vote; there is no formal role for the Quebec government or even for Quebec MPs or senators in the federal legislative process.[27] Moreover, the constitutional conventions that define a responsible government in a Westminster democracy apply to the House of Commons, with no account taken of Canada's status as a multinational state. In particular, there are no conventions that there be Quebec MPs in the cabinet, that certain portfolios be reserved to Quebec MPs, or that the position of prime minister be held from time to time by a Quebecer.

The lack of any special role for Quebec MPs in the federal House of Commons is in marked contrast to the political practice that had developed in the United Province of Canada. Although the goal of the merger of Upper and Lower Canada was to assimilate its francophone population, what resulted was a form of linguistic dualism within the institutions of the new government. Thus, a practice developed of appointing dual prime ministers—French speaking from Lower Canada and English speaking from Upper Canada. Similarly, cabinets were drawn from both halves of the province. Within the legislature, although English had been enacted as the only official language, French was soon added. Moreover, on occasion, the legislature followed a double-majority rule, in effect, giving the francophone MPs a collective veto. In sum, the United Province of Canada bore some of the characteristics of power sharing we would associate today with consociational democracies such as Northern Ireland and Bosnia-Herzegovina.[28] Thus, the decision to opt for multinational federalism in Canada was not just a decision to accommodate minority nationalism. It was also a decision to reject a consociational method for doing so—with which Canada had had concrete experience—because of the strain created by the demand for representation by population in national institutions. This is an additional lesson to be drawn from the Canadian model.

Nonetheless, there remain elements of accommodation in the design of the Supreme Court and in the range of federal policies on the language of federal institutions. The Supreme Court's membership is capped at nine justices, three of whom must come from Quebec (although it would be entitled to only two on the

---

[25] Constitution Act, 1867, § 37 (Can.).

[26] Members of the Senate are appointed by the Governor-General, on the advice of the Prime Minister; *id.* § 24.

[27] *Id.* §§ 36 (Senate) & 49 (House of Commons).

[28] For the power-sharing arrangement in Northern Ireland, see the section of the Good Friday Agreement that establishes a North/South Ministerial Council including those with executive responsibilities in Northern Ireland and the Irish Government: THE AGREEMENT: AGREEMENT REACHED IN THE MULTI-PARTY NEGOTIATIONS, N. IRELAND – BRITAIN, Apr. 10, 1998, *available at* <http://www.nio.gov.uk/agreement.pdf>; the power-sharing arrangement in Bosnia-Herzegovina is set forth in The Dayton Peace Accords on Bosnia (1995), *available at* <http://www.state.gov/www/regions/eur/bosnia/bosagree.html>. The Dayton Peace Accords divided Bosnia-Herzegovina into two federal units, the Federation of Bosnia-Herzegovina and Republika Srpska, respectively; however, the former is divided into Croat- and Bosniak-controlled cantons.

basis of population).[29] Quebec's representation on the Supreme Court is expressly laid out in statute and may be constitutionally entrenched.[30] Quebec has fought particularly hard to protect its level of representation since the Court is the final arbiter of the federal division of powers, and it is the final court of appeal for matters of provincial law, including Quebec's civil code.[31]

But it is the question of language that is truly central to making sense of the Canadian constitutional project. In large part, this is a function of history. The goal in creating the United Provinces of Canada was linguistic assimilation, based on the assumption that linguistic homogeneity was necessary to the creation of a unified nation-state capable of democratic self-government—anticipating the views set forth by John Stuart Mill in *Considerations on Representative Government*.[32] This aborted attempt at linguistic nation building on behalf of Canada's anglophone majority, in turn, fueled demands for a province with a French-speaking majority in which the institutions of public, social, and economic life would operate in French. But even without this history, language would be a source of conflict, because the state cannot be neutral in linguistic matters, as it can be, say, with respect to religion. A choice must be made as to which language or languages are to be used by the state. In Canada, where linguistic communities had operated with distinct political, economic, and social institutions prior to creation of the federal state, linguistic conflict was inevitable because the stakes were so high. The users of the chosen language would enjoy immediate advantages in the economic and political sphere.

For the federal government, the background assumption is that English will be the dominant language of government because anglophones constitute an overwhelming majority. The Constitution and the Official Languages Act attempt to ensure that French enjoys some degree of official status alongside English in federal institutions, with the underlying goal of facilitating participation by the francophone minority in common national institutions.[33] Thus, the Constitution declares English and French to be the official languages of Canada.[34] Both languages may be used in debates in the federal Parliament, and statutes must be

---

[29] Seats on Canada's Supreme Court are allocated on a regional basis. Currently, three judges come from Ontario, one from the Maritime provinces, two from the Western provinces, and three from Quebec. This allotment of seats is merely a practice or tradition that became a convention (with the exception of Quebec; *see infra* note 30); *see* PETER W. HOGG, CONSTITUTIONAL LAW OF CANADA ch. 8.3 (5th ed., Thomson Carswell 2007).

[30] Supreme Court Act, R.S.C., ch. S 26, §§ 4 (1985) (requiring nine judges) & 6 (requiring three judges from Quebec) (Can.); Constitution Act, 1982, being Schedule B to the Canada Act 1982, ch. 11, § 41(d) (U.K.) (requiring any changes to the composition of the Supreme Court to have unanimous federal and provincial consent).

[31] Civil Code of Quebec, S.Q., ch. 64 (1991) (Can.).

[32] JOHN STUART MILL, CONSIDERATIONS ON REPRESENTATIVE GOVERNMENT ch. 16 (Prometheus Books 1991) (1860).

[33] Official Languages Act, R.S.C., ch. 31 (4th Supp. 1985) (Can.).

[34] *Charter*, § 16.

enacted in both.[35] The Constitution also gives francophones the right to interact with federal institutions in French. Individuals may use either English or French in proceedings before federal courts or tribunals.[36] The Charter of Rights and Freedoms also grants the public the right to communicate with and receive services from the federal government in both English and French, wherever there is sufficient demand and it is reasonable to provide services in both languages.[37] However, federal policies on the internal language of government are rather different. Despite the attempt to create bilingual workplaces, English predominates in some areas.[38]

Within Quebec, the Constitution permits the use of both English and French in the Quebec National Assembly and requires statutes to be enacted in both languages. Similarly, English may be used in any court or tribunal in Quebec. But Quebec attempted legislatively to make French "the language of the Government and the law, as well as the normal and everyday language of work, instruction, communication, commerce and business" through the enactment the Charter of the French Language in 1977, shortly after the victory of the Parti Québécois.[39] The Charter of the French Language declares French the official language of Quebec—not merely of the public sector. The goal is to engage in minority nation building by establishing French as the shared language of all Quebecers. To this end, the Charter of the French Language attempted to make French the exclusive language of the National Assembly and the courts; these measures were struck down as unconstitutional.[40] However, two major portions of the Charter of the French Language have withstood constitutional scrutiny. The first concerns the place of French in the public sector, where it is established as the exclusive language of work within the civil service.[41] The second concerns the promotion of French in the private sector, in order to increase the economic opportunities available to francophones. This policy is both in reaction to Quebec's history, which saw economic power concentrated in the hands of anglophones, and is an instrument of linguistic nation building, whereby French becomes the language not only of politics but economic life as well. The goal is to make French the

---

[35] Constitution Act 1867, § 133; *Charter*, §§ 17(1) & 18(1); Official Languages Act, §§ 4–9.

[36] Constitution Act, 1867, § 133; *Charter*, § 19(1); Official Languages Act, §§ 14–20. Section 133 has been interpreted as giving courts the choice of which language to use in communicating with litigants and in conducting proceedings, not as a language right designed to give choice to the litigants: *MacDonald v. City of Montreal* [1986] 1 S.C.R. 449 (Can.). However, this jurisprudence has been thrown into doubt by *R. v. Beaulac* [1999] 1 S.C.R. 768 (Can.).

[37] *Charter*, § 20; Official Languages Act, §§ 21–24.

[38] Office of the Commissioner of Official Languages, *Making It Real: Promoting Respectful Co-existence of the Two Official Languages at Work* (Apr. 2005) (Can.), *available at* <http://www.ocol-clo.gc.ca/docs/e/language_work.pdf>; Office of the Commissioner of Official Languages, *Walking the Talk: Language of Work in the Federal Public Service* (Mar. 2004) (Can.), *available at* <http://www.ocol-clo.gc.ca/docs/e/work_travail_2004_e.pdf>.

[39] Charter of the French Language, R.S.Q. ch. C 11 (2007).

[40] *Id.* §§ 10–13; A.G. Quebec v. Blaikie, [1979] 2 S.C.R. 1016 (Can.).

[41] *Id.* §§ 14–20.

internal working language of medium- and large-sized businesses in the province. From a constitutional perspective, the prevailing view is that these rules lie within the province's jurisdiction regarding intraprovincial economic activity, notwithstanding their obvious impact on interprovincial and international trade, which fall under federal jurisdiction. This degree of latitude reflects the Court's interpretation of the Canadian Constitution as protecting provincial autonomy, and has created considerable policy space for Quebec.

Where linguistic policy has been most controversial is in the area of education. The responsibility for education lies within provincial jurisdiction and encompasses power over the language of instruction and curriculum.[42] This authority has been crucial for Quebec, because the Constitution has permitted the province to establish and operate a primary and secondary educational system that operates in French and is a prime instance of linguistic nation building. Additionally, this control over education has enabled Quebec to create French-language universities, an indispensable support for the use of French in economic and political life—a power that is the source of considerable controversy in other multinational states. At the same time, this arrangement has denied the federal government the ability to set a standard curriculum in a shared national language, a common instrument of nation building in many countries.

However, in spite of this autonomy in linguistic matters, provincial education policies are still subject to provisions in the Charter of Rights and Freedoms guaranteeing the right to minority-language education. These provisions grant certain categories of citizens the right to have their children receive primary and secondary education in their home language where the numbers warrant. The flashpoint of controversy within Quebec has been the right of anglophones who received their primary school instruction anywhere in Canada in English to have their children educated in English in Quebec.[43] The Charter of the French Language attempted to limit this right to parents who had been educated in English in Quebec; this was struck down as unconstitutional.[44] Another provision of the Charter of Rights and Freedoms, which grants citizens whose children have received their schooling in English anywhere in Canada the right to English-language education in Quebec, also limits Quebec's ability to integrate, linguistically, migrants from other provinces. An attempt to construe this right narrowly was recently found to be unconstitutional.[45] For Quebec, minority-language education rights are very controversial precisely because they limit Quebec's ability to encourage the linguistic integration of those who immigrate there from other parts of Canada, not just that of immigrants from abroad.

---

[42] Constitution Act, 1867, § 93 (Can.).
[43] *Charter*, § 23(1)(b).
[44] *Attorney General of Quebec v. Quebec Protestant School Boards* [1984] 2 S.C.R. 66 (Can.).
[45] *Solski (Tutor of) v. Quebec (Attorney General)* [2005] 1 S.C.R. 201, 2005 SCC 14 (Can.).

The final element of the Canadian model is the Charter of Rights and Freedoms. One of the arguments frequently advanced against the accommodation of minority nationalism through federalism is that it may lead to the creation of local tyrannies. Ethnocultural minorities who constitute a local majority might view the subunit as belonging to them rather than to each one of the subunit's residents. A possible result might be a "sons of the soil" politics encouraging and, perhaps, legitimizing discrimination against internal minorities in the framing of public policy, the delivery of public services, contracting, and public employment. Such discrimination might arise particularly if the internal minorities were members of the national majority. Through its provisions for equality rights and interprovincial mobility rights, the Charter of Rights and Freedoms rules out policies that openly discriminate on the basis of ethnic identity or against recent migrants from other provinces.[46] Not surprisingly, the Charter has generated the most controversy within Quebec in its impact on linguistic nation building. As indicated above, its minority-language rights provisions have limited Quebec's ability to ensure the linguistic integration of migrants' children from other provinces.

On a different front, a portion of the Charter of the French Language that required commercial signage to be in French exclusively was struck down by the Supreme Court as an unjustifiable restriction of freedom of expression.[47] Nonetheless, other aspects of Quebec's language policies—most centrally, the rules governing private sector employment—have remained unscathed.

3. Will Kymlicka and the rise of the Canadian model in political theory

Although the Canadian model continued to evolve well into the 1980s, many of its key features had been in place since the mid-nineteenth century. What, then, explains the sharp rise in academic interest in that model in the mid-1990s? The answer may be found not in Canada but in Eastern and Central Europe. The collapse of the communist dictatorships in the latter region was initially hailed as the "end of history", signifying the near-universal adoption of liberal democracy. Instead, we witnessed the rise of profound ethnic conflict within these democratizing states. Although Kymlicka hardly discussed Eastern and Central Europe in *Multicultural Citizenship*, he made it abundantly clear in his introduction that he was writing against this backdrop:

> [W]e need to supplement traditional human rights principles with a theory of minority rights. The necessity for such a theory has become painfully clear in Eastern Europe and the former Soviet Union. Disputes over local autonomy, the drawing of

[46] *Charter*, §§ 6(2)–(4) & 15.
[47] *Ford v. Quebec (A.G.)* [1988] 2 S.C.R. 712.

boundaries, language rights, and naturalization policy have engulfed much of the region in violent conflict. There is little hope that stable peace will be restored, or that basic human rights will be respected, until these minority rights issues are resolved.[48]

As it turned out, many of these states fulfilled the definition of a multi-national polity. The political sociology of emergent conflict within multinational polities—the competing projects of majority and minority nation building—fit the unfolding pattern of political conflict in these countries. And it followed, in the search for solutions, that multinational federalism was an obvious candidate.

But the advocates of multinational federalism were confronted with a jar-ring state of affairs. Three of the former communist dictatorships of Eastern and Central Europe—Yugoslavia, the Soviet Union, and Czechoslovakia—had already been multinational federations, prior to the transition to democracy, and all three began to disintegrate within a period of eighteen months, between June 1991 and December 1992, shortly after the transition. By contrast, uni-tary states—several with large national minorities (for example, Poland and Hungary)—in which nationalism served as the axis of internal political conflict, did not fall apart. So far from being the solution, a superficial reading of the evi-dence suggested that federalism, at the very least, did little or nothing to prevent state dissolution. If the ambition of multinational federalism is to manage com-peting nation-building projects successfully within a single state, then federalism may, in fact, have been a failure in meeting its most basic objective.

Yet the problem went deeper. One explanation for the rapid disintegration of the multinational federations of Eastern and Central Europe was that federalism simply could not do the work expected of it; the "federal structures inscribed in communist constitutions were hardly fully federal in practice".[49] But since only multinational federations broke up—and all of them did—the suspicion emerged that federalism had fueled secession, whereas unitary state structures had prevented it. Carol Leff's analysis of the three multinational federations sug-gested that, although their breakup had many different causes, federalism did indeed make made things worse for reasons apparently arising from the insti-tutional and political logic of multinational federalism. Following democratiza-tion, the opening up of politics facilitated ethnonational mobilization, which was often based on the airing grievances long suppressed during the communist period. This trend was apparent in both unitary states and multinational fed-erations. However, in multinational states, federal subunits were able to provide an institutional power base for national minorities serving as a springboard to statehood. Because they combined both "territoriality and institutional structure [that is, the institutions of governmental power, public services, and in many cases, a constitutional document]", the federal subunits were "states in embryo"

[48] KYMLICKA, *supra* note 3, at 5.
[49] Carol S. Leff, *Democratization and Disintegration in Multinational States: The Breakup of the Communist Federations,* 51 WORLD POL. 205, 210 (1999).

that were "available for capture and utilization as electorally and constitutionally legitimated platforms for pressing demands and pursuing authoritative negotiation with the center and with other republics".[50] By contrast, in the unitary states "even a territorially concentrated electoral base may do little more than to facilitate minority mobilization and parliamentary representation".[51]

As a result, in Eastern and Central Europe, multinational federalism had the perverse effect of fueling precisely those political forces it was designed to suppress. The region's experience posed a fundamental challenge to multinational federalism as a viable constitutional strategy in that part of the world. The response was despair. As André Liebich wrote, "Federalism has suffered a severe setback in Eastern Europe and all efforts to protect minorities must take account of this fact".[52] The failure of the federations of Eastern and Central Europe also posed a more general challenge to the very idea of multinational federalism, because the accommodation of national minorities was not a problem unique to the region. As Steven Burg suggested, "[t]he disintegration of Yugoslavia has led to a re-evaluation of the idea that a multi-ethnic state is a viable entity".[53]

The best way to respond to the negative examples of Yugoslavia, Czechoslovakia, and the Soviet Union was to identify models where multinational federalism had actually worked—hence the birth of the Canadian model. Canada became one of the central case studies in an ever-broadening comparative discussion. The success or failure of Canada became a critical element in the debate regarding the mere possibility of crafting an accommodation between majority and minority nationalism within a single state.

Among political theorists, Will Kymlicka rose to this challenge with the publication of his landmark *Multicultural Citizenship* in 1995. It is through the evolution of his work that we can best grasp the place of the Canadian model in political theory. At the outset, it is instructive to compare how this multinational exemplar works for Kymlicka with the way in which related models have been dealt with by other scholars of comparative politics. Michael Keating, in his work on "plurinational" states, claims that there are sufficient similarities among enough cases to allow him to refer, plausibly, to this category. However, he carefully observes that "[e]very nationality claim will have a different balance of elements, which may change over time and according to circumstances" because "part of the nationality claim itself is usually based on the supposed uniqueness of the nation".[54] As a consequence, Keating continues, "there is no universal formula for addressing them".[55] By contrast, Kymlicka makes claims in many of

[50] *Id.* at 216.
[51] *Id.*
[52] André Liebich, *Nations, States, Minorities: Why is Eastern Europe Different?*, 42 Dissent 313, 317 (1995).
[53] Steven L. Burg, *Why Yugoslavia Fell Apart*, 92 Current Hist. 357 (1993).
[54] Michael Keating, Plurinational Democracy: Stateless Nations in a Post-Sovereignty Era 6 (Oxford Univ. Press 2001).
[55] *Id.* at 6.

his writings about multinational democracies in general, as compared with the specific multinational democracy of a particular state. Yet he clearly is abstracting from the Canadian experience to make his general claims, although being careful not to tie his work to the actual success of the Canadian case.

Kymlicka does not always acknowledge his debt to the Canadian model. In some instances, Canada is offered as an illustration.[56] For example, Canada is clearly the basis for Kymlicka's account of the institutional design of multinational states in *Multicultural Citizenship*. Thus, he famously states "[w]here national minorities are regionally concentrated, the boundaries of federal subunits can be drawn so that the national minority forms a majority in one of the subunits. Under these circumstances, federalism can provide extensive self-government for a national minority, guaranteeing its ability to make decisions in certain areas without being outvoted by the larger society".[57] The only example he gives is that of Quebec. He goes on to say that multinational federalism also entails special representation rights, which provide for guaranteed representation in central institutions. Again, the only example provided is that of Quebec's representation on the Canadian Supreme Court.[58] So, too, with Kymlicka's discussion of language rights.[59]

Furthermore, Kymlicka uses Canada as the basis for many of his claims regarding the political sociology of multinational federations, even though it is here that one should be most careful, given the variations in the precise character of nation-building projects across jurisdictions. Although the argument, namely, that multinational federalism is the most appropriate response to competing majority and minority nation-building projects took center stage in his subsequent work, Kymlicka briefly alludes to this notion in *Multicultural Citizenship*. The one example he provides is that of the failed attempt to assimilate francophones in the United Province of Canada, and the response it sparked. He guesses that "the same story was repeated a hundred times throughout the British Empire".[60] In later work, Kymlicka turned to the character of politics within multinational federations, and again used Canada as his main or only instance. For example, he first analyzes the problems of mixed federations, which combine both nationality-based and territory-based subunits where the former seek asymmetrical arrangements while the latter resist decentralization and insist that federalism be on a basis of equality. He then offers Canada as the main example, with only

[56] The same tendencies can be found in the work of other Canadian political theorists. *See, e.g.,* Wayne Norman & Jim Tully, *Secession and (Constitutional) Democracy, in* DEMOCRACY AND NATIONAL PLURALISM 84 (Ferran Requejo ed., Routledge 2001); James Tully, *Introduction, in* MULTINATIONAL DEMOCRACIES 1 (James Tully & Alain-G. Gagnon eds., Cambridge Univ. Press 2001); Wayne Norman, *Justice and Stability in Multination States, in* MULTINATIONAL DEMOCRACIES 90 (James Tully & Alain-G. Gagnon eds., Cambridge Univ. Press 2001).

[57] KYMLICKA, *supra* note 3, at 27–28.
[58] *Id.* at 143.
[59] *Id.* at 46.
[60] *Id.* at 55.

a passing reference to Spain.[61] In other cases, Canada figures as the unnamed source of hypotheticals. Thus, when he describes the difficulty of preventing democratic mobilization for secession within multinational federations—up to and including the formation of separatist parties and the holding of referenda on secession—it is clear that Kymlicka is referring to Canada, even though he does not say so.[62]

In *Multicultural Citizenship*, Kymlicka neither acknowledges that his model of multicultural federalism is based on Canada nor does he claim that this model travels. However, in *Finding Our Way* (published in 1998) he refers, openly, to "the Canadian model" for the first time and makes it clear that this was the basis of his earlier account of multinational federalism.[63] In an essay first published in 1996, Kymlicka had previously suggested that successful examples of multi-national federalism could serve as models in responding to the difficulties faced by multination states. While he acknowledges the failure of the multinational federations of Eastern and Central Europe, he argues that "[o]n any reasonable criteria, democratic federations (as opposed to Communist federations) have been surprisingly successful in accommodating minority nationalisms" because they "have not only managed the conflicts arising from their competing national identities in a peaceful and democratic way, but have also secured a high degree of economic prosperity and individual freedom for their citizens".[64] Kymlicka observes that the existing multinational federations have spread through a pro-cess of emulation—that is, that Canada and Switzerland served as models for Yugoslavia, India, Malaysia, and Nigeria.[65] The barely unstated implication is that this process of emulation should continue.

Over the next decade, Kymlicka's work takes up the theme of constitutional transplants. In a series of edited volumes, he explores whether his model, which is both a theoretical account and a defense of the actual practices of Western dem-ocracies, could be useful in understanding and evaluating ethnic conflict in other parts of the world and, beyond that, for devising a response to it.[66] I want to high-light an important shift in Kymlicka's views. Initially, he is highly optimistic and dismissive of any skepticism regarding the migration of the model of multinational federalism. In his first book on Eastern and Central Europe, in 2001, he confronts the concern regarding the potential security threat posed by national minorities

[61] Will Kymlicka, *Minority Nationalism and Multination Federalism, in* POLITICS IN THE VERNACULAR 91, 102–110 (Oxford Univ. Press 2001).

[62] Will Kymlicka, *Reply and Conclusion, in* CAN LIBERAL PLURALISM BE EXPORTED? WESTERN POLITICAL THEORY AND ETHNIC RELATIONS IN EASTERN EUROPE 345, 389–393 (Will Kymlicka & Magda Opalski eds., Oxford Univ. Press 2001).

[63] KYMLICKA, *supra* note 2, at 3.

[64] Kymlicka, *supra* note 61, at 92.

[65] *Id.* at 96.

[66] Kymlicka, *supra* note 62; ETHNICITY AND DEMOCRACY IN AFRICA (Bruce Berman, Dickson Eyoh & Will Kymlicka eds., Ohio Univ. Press 2004); MULTICULTURALISM IN ASIA (Will Kymlicka & Baogang He eds., Oxford Univ. Press 2005).

acting in alliance with kin states, and he argues that this does not justify removing multinational federalism from the domestic political agenda. Kymlicka argues that it is doubly unfair to view the issue of minority rights through the lens of security because such an account is not grounded in justice and creates inconsistencies in the treatment of national minorities in the West, on the one hand, and in Eastern and Central Europe, on the other. His goal is nothing less than the adoption of "a universal code of minority rights that would be monitored and applied in an even-handed way to both Western and ECE countries".[67]

But by the time Kymlicka turns his attention, in 2005, to Asia, his tone and analysis have changed. He identifies a variety of factors that explain why, in the West, majorities were willing to accept minority nationalism. These included the "desecuritization" of minority nationalism arising from collective security arrangements between states containing national minorities and neighboring "kin" states in which members of the majority nation constitute the majority, and the liberal democratic consensus among both minorities and majorities, which reduced the fear that territorial autonomy would lead to the oppression of internal minorities. He then offers a nuanced account of the sources of resistance in Asia to territorial autonomy for minorities, such as the colonial divide-and-rule strategies, which empowered ethnic groups; concerns over geopolitical security; fear of petty tyrannies; and the belief that ethnic mobilization would disappear as a result of modernization and development. Kymlicka's conclusion is not that these sources of resistance are irrational or unfair but, rather, that they make clear that Western models "may not suit the specific historical, cultural, demographic, and geopolitical circumstances of the region".[68] In a new book, Kymlicka has come around to the notion that resistance to the importation of the Canadian model may be reasonable.[69] He openly acknowledges that "liberal multiculturalism has costs, and imposes risks, and these costs vary enormously both within and across societies", and that, in the West, "a fortunate set of circumstances have [sic] lowered the risks of liberal multiculturalism".[70] Thus, a differing set of circumstances could pose high risks. Clearly, Kymlicka's enthusiasm for the transplantation of the Canadian model has dissipated.

The significant transformation of Kymlicka's view of the viability of constitutional transplants is an interesting story in its own right, although I cannot develop it here. I suspect that what drove this change was an underlying shift in the case Kymlicka made for the accommodating minority nationalism—from an account based on a liberal theory of justice to a stability-based account in which liberal principles operate as a constraint on, rather than as the source of,

---

[67] Kymlicka, *supra* note 62, at 388.

[68] Boagang He & Will Kymlicka, *Introduction, in* Multiculturalism in Asia, *supra* note 66, at 1.

[69] Will Kymlicka, Multicultural Odysseys: Navigating the New International Politics of Diversity (Oxford Univ. Press 2007).

[70] *Id.* at 21.

the particular institutional arrangements he advocates. What bears emphasis is a constant in his discourse: that the Western approach to dealing with minority nationalism—that is, the Canadian model—is essentially sound. Kymlicka's initial claim was that the Canadian model was so exceptional it should be adopted by other multinational states, and it would be unjust to not do so. His subsequent skepticism regarding transplants has nothing to do with any perceived deficiencies in the Canadian model. His position is this: if the Canadian model does not travel, it is because the preconditions that allowed it to succeed at home are absent elsewhere. The difficulties in transplanting Canadian constitutional arrangements to other contexts do not detract from their viability at home. The Canadian model is still a success story, contra Barry.

4. The politics of the Canadian model: Canada in constitutional crisis

In order to recontextualize and complicate the picture, as it stands so far, I want to offer an alternative history of the rise of the Canadian model. While it is true that the interest of political theorists in Canada's multinational federalism coincided with the disintegration of the multinational federations of Eastern and Central Europe, this interest also manifested itself during Canada's own constitutional crisis. This alternate history could begin, therefore, in September 1994, with the resurgence of the Parti Québécois (PQ), which won power on a platform that had as its centerpiece the promise to hold a referendum on sovereignty within its first mandate. The PQ proposed a draft bill on sovereignty in the Quebec National Assembly in December 1994 and announced that it would hold a referendum the following year. A referendum took place in October 1995. The results were extremely close, with the proposal failing by 1 percent. Although the referendum question sought a mandate for Quebec to negotiate a new economic and political partnership with Canada, legislation before the Quebec National Assembly (Bill 1) set a one-year time limit on those negotiations, after which Quebec would have issued a unilateral declaration of independence in outright defiance of the Canadian Constitution. Quebec took this prospect seriously and had laid the groundwork to secure international recognition.[71]

The near disintegration of the Canadian federation in the mid-1990s was not completely unexpected. From 1990 onward, the secession of Quebec became a topic of widespread political and academic debate. English book titles from this period bear testimony to the tenor and content of these discussions and, indeed, to the mood in English Canada. A series of books made the case that Canada faced a constitutional crisis that threatened its very existence. Their titles hardly

[71] *See* ROBERT YOUNG, THE STRUGGLE FOR QUEBEC: FROM REFERENDUM TO REFERENDUM? (McGill-Queen's Univ. Press 1999).

conveyed a sense of radiant optimism about the success of the Canadian model in accommodating minority nationalism.[72]

A subliterature appeared that assumed Canada was doomed, and that the country should turn to the difficult question of how secession could occur. Issues such as the debt, borders, citizenship, the rights of aboriginal peoples, the nature of the economic and political relationship between Canada and an independent Quebec, as well as the process of such negotiations (who would participate, how would the public be involved) were debated at countless conferences and workshops. Again, the books that turned to the task of grappling with these hard questions have telling titles, among the most poignant *Can Canada Survive? Under What Terms and Conditions?*[73] In an important respect, English Canada was catching up with Quebec, which had before long turned its mind to the modalities of secession. In the wake of the failure of the Meech Lake Accord,[74] the Quebec government created the Commission on the Political and Constitutional Future of Quebec.[75] One of the commission's principal

---

[72] *See, e.g.,* DAVID J. BERCUSON & BARRY COOPER, DECONFEDERATION: CANADA WITHOUT QUEBEC (Key Porter 1991); THE COLLAPSE OF CANADA? (R. Kent Weaver ed., Brookings Inst. 1992); CONSTITUTIONAL PREDICAMENT: CANADA AFTER THE REFERENDUM OF 1992 (Curtis Cook ed., McGill-Queen's Univ. Press 1994); ROBERT BOTHWELL, CANADA AND QUEBEC: ONE COUNTRY AND TWO HISTORIES (Univ. Brit. Colum. Press 1995); DAVID M. THOMAS, WHISTLING PAST THE GRAVEYARD: CONSTITUTIONAL ABEYANCES, QUEBEC AND THE FUTURE OF CANADA (Oxford Univ. Press 1997); PAUL ROMNEY, GETTING IT WRONG: HOW CANADIANS FORGOT THEIR PAST AND IMPERILLED CONFEDERATION (Univ. Toronto Press 1999); REED SCOWEN, TIME TO SAY GOODBYE: THE CASE FOR GETTING QUEBEC OUT OF CANADA (McLelland & Stewart 1999).

[73] CAN CANADA SURVIVE? UNDER WHAT TERMS AND CONDITIONS? 29 (David M. Hayne ed., Univ. Toronto Press 1997). *See also* YOUNG, *supra* note 71; THE REFERENDUM PAPERS: ESSAYS ON SECESSION AND NATIONAL UNITY (David R. Cameron ed., Univ. Toronto Press 1999); TWO NATIONS, ONE MONEY? (David E.W. Laidler & William B.P. Robson eds., C.D. Howe Inst. 1991); CLOSING THE BOOKS: DIVIDING FEDERAL ASSETS AND DEBT IF CANADA BREAKS UP (Paul M. Boothe ed., C.D. Howe Inst. 1991); GORDON RITCHIE ET AL., BROKEN LINKS: TRADE RELATIONS AFTER A QUEBEC SECESSION (C.D. Howe Inst. 1991); NEGOTIATING WITH A SOVEREIGN QUEBEC (Daniel Drache & Roberto Perrin eds., James Lorimer 1992); STANLEY H. HARTT ET AL., TANGLED WEB: LEGAL ASPECTS OF DECONFEDERATION (John McCallum ed., C.D. Howe Inst. 1992); ALAN FREEMAN & PATRICK GRADY, DIVIDING THE HOUSE: PLANNING FOR A CANADA WITHOUT QUEBEC (Harper Collins 1995); TREVOR MCALPINE, THE PARTITION PRINCIPLE: REMAPPING QUEBEC AFTER SEPARATION (ECW Press 1996); RICHARD JANDA, DUAL INDEPENDENCE: THE BIRTH OF A NEW CANADA AND THE RE-BIRTH OF LOWER CANADA (Varia Press 1998); ECONOMIC DIMENSIONS OF CONSTITUTIONAL CHANGE (Robin W. Boadway, Thomas J. Courchene & Douglas D. Purvis eds., John Deutsch Inst. Stud. Econ. Pol. 1991); MARCEL CÔTÉ, IF QUEBEC GOES … THE REAL COSTS OF SEPARATION (Stoddart 1995); GORDON GIBSON, PLAN B: THE FUTURE OF THE REST OF CANADA (Fraser Inst. 1994); QUÉBEC-CANADA: WHAT IS THE PATH AHEAD? (John E. Trent, Robert Young & Guy Lachapelle eds., Univ. Ottawa Press 1996); This genre of scholarship is not new. For an earlier example, published in the wake of the 1976 election of the Parti Québécois, see MUST CANADA FAIL? (Richard Simeon ed., McGill-Queen's Univ. Press 1977).

[74] The Meech Lake Accord was a package of failed constitutional amendments which included a proposed addition to the Constitution that recognizes Quebec as a "distinct society": 1987 CONSTITUTIONAL ACCORD (Can.), sched. Constitution Amendment, 1987 (Can.).

[75] Act to Establish the Commission on the Political and Constitutional Future of Quebec, S.Q. 1990, ch. 34, & subsequent amendments, S.Q., 1990, ch. 45 (Can.).

contributions to public debate within the province consisted of a large number of original research studies that examined both the substance and process of Quebec secession. Moreover, these studies received widespread media coverage and were debated widely in the national press. In fact, a large reason for the surge of interest in English Canada was precisely because these issues had long since been discussed in Quebec.

Two important questions arise. The first: why was Canada in constitutional crisis for much of the 1990s and, more precisely, what was the exact character of the Canadian constitutional crisis? I turn to this issue below. The second: what was the connection between this debate—in which the future prospects for Canada looked dim indeed—and the rise of the Canadian model? The titles of the books on this subject bear witness to the fact that the discussion concerning Canada's future and the mechanics of taking the country apart was far from marginal.[76] On the contrary, these issues were at the very center of academic and political discourse. In fact, the country seemed able to talk about little else, and no Canadian could ever forget the near dissolution of the federation in 1995. Thus, it is inconceivable that the proponents of the Canadian model could have been unaware of the immediate drama. On the contrary, many proponents of the Canadian model not only recognized the crisis gripping the Canadian constitutional order but viewed the international promotion of the Canadian model as an important element in resolving problems at home.

This link was first made by Pierre Trudeau, in an essay published in 1962, long before the near constitutional collapse of the 1990s.[77] Responding to an argument made by supporters of Quebec independence—that every nation must necessarily have a state—Trudeau asserts that Canadian federalism should be preserved as something precious. For Trudeau, one of the reasons for retaining multinational federalism is not only that it is right for Canada but also that it is right for the world. Canadians should strive to ensure the survival of Canada so it can serve as an international role model, a city on the hill, for countries facing the same linguistic and ethnonational divisions that led to creation of the Canadian model in the first place. He writes:

> It would seem, in fact, a matter of considerable urgency for world peace and the success of the new states that the form of good government known as democratic federalism should be perfected and promoted, in the hope of solving to some extent the world-wide problems of ethnic pluralism. . . . Canada should be called upon to serve as mentor, provided she has sense enough to conceive her own future on a grand scale. . . . Canada could become the envied seat of a form of federalism that belongs to tomorrow's world. . . . Canadian federalism is an experiment of major proportions; it could become a brilliant prototype for the moulding of tomorrow's civilization.[78]

[76] *See supra* notes 72 & 73.
[77] Pierre E. Trudeau, *The New Treason of the Intellectuals, in* Federalism and the French Canadians 151 (Macmillan 1968).
[78] *Id.* at 154, 178, 179.

Clearly, Trudeau is doing much more than simply emphasizing a positive if incidental side effect of the success of the Canadian model. Rather, he is making the stronger claim that Canada's success matters internationally because other countries face problems similar to Canada's, and that Canada's potential influence as an international role model should serve not only as a source of pride to Canadians but also as a reason for them to make its constitutional arrangements work.

These themes were picked up and further developed, nearly thirty years later, by Charles Taylor.[79] In an essay published in 1991, he argues that Canada's constitutional difficulties may be traced to a clash between two different visions of citizenship. In the one, its nature captured and fueled by the Charter, citizens consider themselves the bearers of constitutional rights and as equal members in the Canadian political community, unmediated by membership in any intermediate provincial political communities. In the other, Quebecers view their membership in the Canadian political community as stemming from their membership in a constituent nation of Canada. For Taylor, the solution is to reject a model of uniform citizenship, opting, instead, for "deep diversity" as "the only formula on which a united federal Canada can be rebuilt".[80] However, the case for deep diversity goes well beyond Canada because "in many parts of the world today the degree and nature of the differences resemble those of Canada" and hence "the world needs other models [such as deep diversity] to be legitimated in order to allow for more humane and less constraining modes of political cohabitation".[81] Consequently, Canada "would do our own and some other peoples a favour by exploring the space of deep diversity".[82]

After the failure of the Charlottetown Accord,[83] and the near miss in the 1995 referendum, Taylor continued to press the same themes, albeit with a greater sense of urgency and an acute awareness of the peril that Canada faced.[84] Thus, "the principal threat" to Canada's existence "comes from a problem which is in a sense everyone's in this day and age"—namely, that there are many more nations than states; that it would be impossible for each nation to have its own state; and that there needs to be some way for national groups to exist within the same state.[85] Taylor continues: "Canada's inability to solve this problem, after what seemed like a promising start in favourable conditions, naturally causes consternation, and depressed spirits, abroad."[86] If the Canadian model cannot work in Canada,

---

[79] CHARLES TAYLOR, *Shared and Divergent Values, in* RECONCILING THE SOLITUDES 155 (McGill-Queen's Univ. Press 1993).

[80] *Id.* at 183.

[81] *Id.* (emphasis added).

[82] *Id.*

[83] This is another set of failed constitutional amendments: CONSENSUS REPORT OF THE CONSTITUTION (CAN.), pt. I, § A(1) Canada Clause (1992) (also known as the Charlottetown Accord).

[84] Charles Taylor, *Deep Diversity and the Future of Canada, in* CAN CANADA SURVIVE, *supra* note 73.

[85] *Id.* at 30.

[86] *Id.*

it cannot work in circumstances that are far more difficult. According to Taylor, Canada needs to try to make it work for the sake of the world. This is political theory doubling as constitutional therapy.

Arguing for the success—the necessary success—of the Canadian model was not just an academic endeavor. It was a political intervention in two different but interrelated arenas. It was an intervention in international politics—to offer a practical, viable model dealing with the issue of minority nationalism, which had become a source of political instability in Eastern and Central Europe and beyond. It was also an intervention in domestic constitutional politics—to argue that Canada had hit upon one of the few workable solutions to the accommodation of minority nationalism within a liberal democratic constitutional order. Moreover, there were multiple links between the two agendas. There was the argument, made by Trudeau and Taylor, that Canada should make its constitutional arrangements work to help other countries. Foreign observers have often made this point. American political scientist Charles Doran, writing on why Canadian unity should matter to the United States, asserts that the "failure of the Canadian federal experiment...does not bode well for the ability of other democracies to establish political harmony among their own regional communities", while, conversely, success in Canada "will help to preserve democratic pluralism worldwide".[87] Kofi Annan and Mikhail Gorbachev's public interventions in the Canadian national unity debate demonstrated how important the success of the Canadian model was to the international community struggling with the destructive potential of nationalism.[88]

There are other links between the domestic and international political agendas. The promotion of the Canadian model abroad should be understood, at least in part, as an attempt to reinforce support for the Canadian model at home by instilling national pride. Thus, Canada's politicians have sought to place the Canadian model and example at the heart of its foreign policy by offering it as a pillar of development assistance to deeply divided societies. The previous Liberal government's *International Policy Statement* stated that development assistance should be focused on a few key areas, including the promotion of good governance, with "Canada's commitment...to a federal system that accommodates diversity" as part of that agenda.[89] Liberal MP Michael Ignatieff, in a speech to the Canadian Department of Foreign Affairs and International Trade, in 2004,

---

[87] CHARLES F. DORAN, WHY CANADIAN UNITY MATTERS AND WHY AMERICANS CARE: DEMOCRATIC PLURALISM AT RISK xiv, xv (Univ. Toronto Press 2001).

[88] For Kofi Annan's intervention, see Louise Leduc, *Entrevue avec le secrétaire général de l'ONU [Interview with the Secretary General of the UN]*, LE DEVOIR (Montreal), Oct. 5, 1998, at A4; for Mikhail Gorbachev's intervention, see Miro Cernetig, *Stay United, Bush tells Canada, Gorbachev Cites Fractured USSR*, GLOBE & MAIL, Oct. 10, 1995, at A1.

[89] A ROLE OF PRIDE AND INFLUENCE IN THE WORLD: DEVELOPMENT 12 (Can. Int'l Dev. Agency 2005). For an earlier statement of this position, see Paul Martin, former Prime Minister of Canada, Address on the occasion of his visit to Washington, D.C. (Apr. 29, 2004), *available at* <http://www.uofaweb.ualberta.ca/govrel//pdfs/MartinApril29Washington.pdf>.

stated that Canada has "more institutional memory about the legislative and legal requirements for the accommodation of linguistic and religious diversity than any other mature democracy in the world" and has a "comparative advantage in the politics of managing divided societies"; it should translate its institutional experience into advice for other countries struggling with similar issues.[90] Part of the motivation, no doubt, is to increase Canada's influence abroad. Promoting the Canadian model is an exercise in what Joseph Nye has termed "soft power", whereby a country "may obtain the outcomes it wants in world politics because other countries want to follow it, admiring its values, emulating its example, aspiring to its level of prosperity and openness".[91] Jennifer Welsh has written that simply being a bilingual, federal state should be regarded as a core element of Canadian foreign policy.[92] However, there is a domestic agenda at work here, as well. As the prestige of the Canadian model is enhanced abroad, so, too, is its prestige at home. This convergence of the domestic and the international is best summed up by the marketing phrase used by a leading Canadian bookseller to promote Canadian literature: "The World Needs More Canada". Thus does the international reputation of Canadian authors provide an additional reason for Canadians to value that work.

There is a final link between the international and the domestic. The violent collapse of the multinational federations of Eastern and Central Europe appeared to challenge the viability of multinational federalism not only in that region but in Canada as well. Canadians stared into the constitutional abyss in the 1990s and asked themselves whether the same fate awaited Canada. Philip Resnick, writing in anticipation of the referendum on sovereignty, saw clearly the Canadian crisis in this broader comparative context.[93] For example, in discussing the prospect of violent resistance by aboriginal peoples in northern Quebec to secession, he observed "[w]e do not have to summon up Ossetia, Nagorno-Karabakh or Krajina, but we would be fools not to draw some lessons from what has occurred elsewhere".[94] Moreover, in making the case for transforming Canada from a federation into a confederation, Resnick argued that this was preferable to the alternative of breaking up, as illustrated by the failed multinational federations of Eastern and Central Europe:

> [A] confederal union... would still be preferable to the out and out break-up of Canada. We have the examples of the Soviet Union and Yugoslavia to ponder—multinational

[90] MICHAEL IGNATIEFF, PEACE, ORDER AND GOOD GOVERNMENT: A FOREIGN POLICY AGENDA FOR CANADA 8, 10 (Foreign Aff. & Int'l Trade Can. 2006).
[91] JOSEPH S. NYE JR., THE PARADOX OF AMERICAN POWER: WHY THE WORLD'S ONLY SUPERPOWER CAN'T GO IT ALONE 8 (Oxford Univ. Press 2002).
[92] JENNIFER WELSH, AT HOME IN THE WORLD: CANADA'S GLOBAL VISION FOR THE 21st CENTURY 189 (Harper Collins 2004).
[93] Philip Resnick, *Toward a Multinational Federalism: Asymmetrical and Confederal Alternatives, in* SEEKING A NEW CANADIAN PARTNERSHIP: ASYMMETRICAL AND CONFEDERAL OPTIONS 71 (Leslie Seidle ed., Inst. for Res. on Pub. Pol. 1994).
[94] *Id.* at 85.

federations that have splintered into pieces with major ethnic conflicts and unresolved border disputes carrying over into the post-break-up period. Would the people of ex-Yugoslavia not have been better off for having continued to live in a loose confederation with largely autonomous republics and a shared citizenship rather than in successor republics bought at the price of bitter wars and ethnic cleansing?[95]

So international models—or anti-models—of multinational federalism became part of domestic politics. However, rather than merging the international and the domestic, the response was to deflect these comparisons and keep them out. Here, we return to Will Kymlicka in *Finding Our Way*, which was directed at a domestic audience that, in his view, too quickly compared Canada with developments abroad. Commentators had relied on "apocalyptic scenarios of segregation and violence" that "point ominously to Bosnia or South Africa, as if we were on some slippery slope to civil war or apartheid", he wrote, when in fact those dangers were not genuinely present.[96] *Finding Our Way* was a "reality check" to show that, in fact, the Canadian model was working well.[97] But since he also defended the applicability of the Canadian model abroad, Kymlicka was trying to shut a door that he and others previously had opened.

5. Lessons from the Canadian model in crisis: A procedural and a substantive crisis

A great deal of ink has been spilled over the constitutional difficulties encountered by the Canadian model in the 1990s. Will Kymlicka, Charles Taylor, Alan Cairns, Kenneth McRoberts, and others have traced the origins of the Canadian constitutional crisis to competing constitutional logics, flowing variously from the intertwining and mutual reinforcement of constitutional text and constitutional politics.[98] Put simply, the different parts of the Canadian Constitution are at war with each other; these are, specifically, the accommodation of Quebec, the Charter, and provincial equality. The reason Canada is a federation is because of the existence of a French-speaking population increasingly centered in Quebec. Quebecers refract their nationalist claims through the lens of federalism, assessing the institutions of federalism in terms of their impact on the ability of Quebec to maintain and promote its linguistic distinctiveness. On the other hand, the Charter embodies a notion of Canada as a nation of equal citizens endowed with identical constitutional rights, regardless of which province they inhabit.

---

[95] *Id.*

[96] KYMLICKA, *supra* note 2, at 4.

[97] *Id.* at 5.

[98] *See, e.g.*, KYMLICKA, *supra* note 2; KYMLICKA, *supra* note 3; KYMLICKA, *supra* note 14; Kymlicka, *supra* note 61; KYMLICKA, *supra* note 69; TAYLOR, *supra* note 79; Taylor, *supra* note 84; ALAN CAIRNS, RECONFIGURATIONS: CANADIAN CITIZENSHIP AND CONSTITUTIONAL CHANGE (Douglas E. Williams ed., McLelland and Stewart 1995); McROBERTS, *supra* note 21.

Finally, Quebec notwithstanding, Canada is a mixed federation, combining a nationality-based subunit with territory-based subunits whose members share the same language, and who do not see themselves as members of different nations. Federalism treats every province on a basis of juridical equality, granting each identical powers.

These different constitutional logics have come into conflict over two issues: asymmetrical powers for Quebec and the constitutional recognition of Quebec as a distinct society. The former position is advanced by Quebec as necessary in order to give it the jurisdictional tools to preserve and promote its identity in economic and social circumstances that have changed dramatically since 1867. It is resisted in English Canada, both by those who want to centralize greater power in Ottawa, as part of a nation-building exercise, and by those who believe that special arrangements for any one province are a form of discrimination. Asymmetry, if taken far enough, also creates severe problems of representation at the center, because it poses serious challenges to the conventions of responsible government. As for the second issue, constitutional recognition of Quebec as a distinct society, if designed to augment Quebec's powers alone, raises similar objections. To the extent that such recognition would give greater scope to Quebec to limit Charter rights legitimately—in order to preserve and promote its linguistic identity—so would it come into conflict with the concept of the Charter as the essential foundation of equal citizenship, providing for equal enjoyment of constitutional rights throughout Canada.

There are important comparative lessons here for the debate between integration and accommodation. If the Charter and provincial equality reflect integrationist impulses, and the creation of Quebec represents an accommodationist perspective, combining both elements within the same constitutional system fuels further demands and additional rounds of constitutional politics, all in the name of perfecting the constitutional text. As a consequence, the conventional wisdom is that the Canadian constitutional crisis is *substantive*—that is to say, it is about what the terms of the Constitution should be. However, I want to challenge the conventional wisdom by offering a *procedural* account of the constitutional crisis, in which the near-collapse of the Canadian constitutional system can be traced to the lack of a shared understanding regarding the constitutional procedures within which substantive constitutional politics could occur. Indeed, without such a procedural account, we cannot fully make sense of the Canadian constitutional crisis.

To understand the need for a procedural account, consider the following argument. In politics, we frequently disagree about the substance of public policies. A basic ambition of constitutionalism is to channel disagreements into institutions that reach decisions members of the political community will accept as authoritative. But for institutional decisions to yield political settlements, the decision-making procedures of those institutions must be viewed as constituting and regulating political life without forming part of it—as being indifferent among competing political positions. Were the mechanisms by which political disagreement is managed themselves subject to political contestation in the course of their operation, it would be difficult for institutional settlement to translate into political settlement. The rules for constitutional amendment and their relationship to substantive constitutional politics can be conceptualized in like manner. For example, constitutional drafters probably will agree that constitutions should allow for the possibility of amendment. Thus, in addition to creating the procedural framework for normal politics, constitutions also create the procedural framework for constitutional politics. If the rules of constitutional amendment are to operate effectively, they, too, must be accepted as constituting and regulating constitutional politics—and not forming part of it. They must be seen as operating indifferently among the competing constitutional positions in play.

The problem with this highly simplified picture is that political procedures—both for normal and constitutional politics—are far from substantively neutral themselves. Rather, as Jeremy Waldron has argued, political procedures reflect competing conceptions of the very sorts of values that are the customary fare of both normal and constitutional politics.[99] For example, by determining which individuals and communities can participate in political decision making, and what role those individuals and communities may play, decisional rules reflect substantive judgments about the locus of political sovereignty and, by extension, the very identity of a political community. Thus, the boundary between substantive political disputes and the procedural frameworks within which those disputes are worked out is highly artificial. Liberal democratic constitutionalism depends on the *suspension* of political judgment with regard to institutions and institutional decision-making procedures precisely in order to gain the prospect of political settlements.

The suspension of political judgment with respect to political procedures will become exceedingly difficult to sustain when the substantive dispute challenges the very conception of political community that underlies the decision-making framework within which that debate occurs. With respect to the rules of normal politics, the consequence will be to shift the terrain of disagreement up one level, from normal politics to constitutional politics, which, in turn, is regulated by its own set of procedures, the rules governing constitutional amendment.

The ability of the rules governing constitutional amendment to create and regulate constitutional politics depends on the nature of the issue at hand. We need to distinguish between two varieties of constitutional politics. First, there are rounds of ordinary constitutional politics, which are fairly common in states that are not multinational polities. In these states, the existence of a single national political community is a widely shared assumption that is presupposed by political actors. Accordingly, for liberal democrats the basic question of constitutional design would be how this political community should grapple

---

[99] Jeremy Waldron, *Judicial Review and the Conditions of Democracy*, 6 J. POL. PHIL. 335 (1998).

with the task of democratic self-government, striking the right balance between democratic rule and individual rights. Constitutional politics would focus on the creation and allocation of power to governmental institutions in order to enable democratic decision making. Such politics would also address whether and to what extent the constitution should disable those institutions through the design of decisional rules (such as veto powers, or supermajority requirements), as well as through outright substantive limits on government conduct (for example, constitutional bills of rights).

But for national minorities in multinational polities, the basic questions of constitutional politics are rather different. The issue is not simply how a national political community should structure its decision-making institutions and constrain itself through constitutional mechanisms. Additionally, there is the existential question of whether a multinational polity should exist at all as a unified, national political community comprising the various nations (majority and minority) and, if so, on what terms. Put another way, this means that, in multinational polities, constitutional politics takes place on two levels. On the one hand, there is the sort of constitutional politics that presupposes the existence of a national political community. But in parallel—and simultaneously—multinational polities also engage in constitutive constitutional politics, which concern existential questions that go to the very identity, even existence, of the political community as a multinational political entity. In practice, it is hard to disentangle these two sorts of constitutional politics, because they often touch on similar sorts of issues—the structure of national institutions, federalism, and bills of rights—and often occur at the same time. For example, in Canada, proposals to entrench the Supreme Court of Canada constitutionally—to recognize its unique responsibility as an independent organ of government and final arbiter charged with enforcing the Canadian Charter—were accompanied by demands by Quebec that, given the Court's role as the final judicial arbiter in federal-provincial disputes, three of its seats should be constitutionally guaranteed for judges from that province.

The problem is that it be can be very difficult, if not impossible, to suspend substantive political judgment regarding the procedures for constitutional amendment at moments of constitutive constitutional politics because these procedures might reflect one of the competing constitutional positions at play. And there is no higher level to which the dispute can be shifted. Even if one designed a constitution that created a special set of rules to regulate amendments to the rules for constitutional amendment, the same problem might arise with respect to those rules. It is impossible to continue this strategy ad infinitum. In the absence of agreed-upon procedures for constitutional decision making, institutional settlement cannot yield political settlement. The result may be that the constitutional system itself comes tumbling down.

This, in a nutshell, is what happened in Canada in the mid-1990s. For alongside disagreement on the substantive questions of how Quebec's claims should be accommodated within the Canadian constitutional order and whether Quebec should remain a part of Canada, there was a procedural disagreement over whether the rules governing constitutional amendment should govern the process of secession.[100]

As a strictly legal matter, the Canadian Constitution creates the province of Quebec and defines its territory, erecting its governing institutions and endowing them with limited legal authority over the province. Since unilateral secession clearly does not lie within provincial jurisdiction, provincial legislation purporting to declare independence would be unconstitutional. But the Constitution neither explicitly permits nor prohibits the secession of a province. So a change in Quebec's status from province to independent nation could, in principle, be achieved through constitutional amendment—for example, by terminating the authority of federal institutions over Quebec. Secession through constitutional amendment would necessitate the use of amending procedures that require the consent of the federal government and most of the provinces; unilateral secession would be unconstitutional.

Quebec sovereignists responded by challenging the assumption that Quebec's achievement of sovereignty could be governed by the rules governing constitutional amendment. In one sense, this disagreement has deep roots in Canadian constitutional history and, hence, in reasons specific to Canada. An important theme in Canadian constitutional history has been the search for an amending procedure in which some combination of Canadian political actors would hold the power to amend the Canadian Constitution. This search was driven by the absence of a procedure for constitutional amendment in the Constitution Act, 1867, since the power of amendment, by default, rested with the imperial Parliament. When Canada attained independence, the lack of a domestic amending formula became a constitutional anomaly. Canadian constitutional politics were driven by the search for a domestic amending formula for over fifty years.[101] This proved to be enormously difficult. In order to shift ultimate sovereignty back to Canada, Canadian political actors had to agree on where the locus of sovereignty should lie or, more accurately, on who the constituent actors in a domestic amending procedure should be—the federal government, provincial governments, the national

---

[100] *See generally* Sujit Choudhry, *Referendum? What Referendum?*, 15 Lit. Rev. Canada 7 (2007); Sujit Choudhry, *Ackerman's Higher Lawmaking in Comparative Constitutional Perspective: Constitutional Moments as Constitutional Failures?*, 6 Int'l J. Const. L. (I•CON) (forthcoming 2008); Sujit Choudhry & Jean-François Gaudreault-DesBiens, *Frank Iacobucci as Constitution Maker: From the Quebec Veto Reference, to the Meech Lake Accord and the Quebec Secession Reference*, 57 Univ. Toronto L.J. 165 (2007); Sujit Choudhry, *Popular Revolution or Popular Constitutionalism? Reflections on the Constitutional Politics of Quebec Secession, in* Legislatures and Constitutionalism: The Role of Legislatures in the Constitutional State 480 (Tsvi Kahana & Richard Bauman eds., Cambridge Univ. Press 2006); Sujit Choudhry, *Old Imperial Dilemmas and the New Nation-Building: Constitutive Constitutional Politics in Multinational Polities*, 37 Conn. L. Rev. 933 (2005).

[101] Peter Russell, Constitutional Odyssey: Can Canadians Become a Sovereign People? (2d ed., Univ. Toronto Press 1993) (1992).

population, or various provincial populations. Answering this question, in turn, required the political actors grapple with the basic question of what constituted the terms of political association in Canada—that is, the very nature of the Canadian political community. On that basic question, there was a lack of consensus. The constitutional politics of constitutional amendment, accordingly, took place on two levels. On the one hand, it was intimately concerned with practical questions of constitutional design. On the other, it was a symbolic politics, a struggle over the very meaning of the country.

The inextricable link between the politics of constitutional process and substantive constitutional politics provides the means by which to understand the failure of the procedures for constitutional amendment to regulate the constitutional politics of secession in the mid-1990s. Quebec was a central player in the constitutional politics of constitutional amendment and pushed consistently for a constitutional veto; its position was informed by a vision of the Canadian political community as a multinational federation. But in 1982, the amending procedures now in force were adopted as part of a package of constitutional amendments agreed to by the federal government and the nine provinces over the objections of Quebec. The debate quickly turned to process. Quebec unsuccessfully argued—both in politics and in the courts[102]—that as matter of constitutional convention, it had a right of veto over constitutional amendments affecting its powers, and that this veto applied to the adoption of new amending rules. Quebec's official response to its defeat in this regard was bitter; it viewed the amendments as illegitimate, setting the stage for arguments in the mid-1990s that Quebec was not bound by these rules.

History aside, it was entirely predictable that Quebec would walk away from the amending rules, for the simple reason that those rules beg the question. The rules presuppose that Quebec is a constituent component of the Canadian federation, functioning as a subnational political community with extensive but limited rights of self-government within Canada. Quebec is a constitutionally recognized actor in the process of constitutional amendment with the power to consent, or not, to constitutional amendments; however, its consent is not absolutely required in all circumstances. But it is *precisely* this constitutional vision that the Quebec sovereignty movement challenges, in raising the substantive question of whether Quebec should remain a part of Canada or become an independent state. Not surprisingly the sovereignists rejected the amending rules as a neutral framework within which the question of Quebec's independence could be resolved. To put the point another way, since the sovereignists wished to make a radical break from the Canadian constitutional order, it is hard to imagine they would have subscribed to a process governed by it.

In short, both constitutional history and constitutional theory explain why the procedures for constitutional amendment were perceived by many Quebecers

---

[102] Reference re Amendment of Canadian Constitution [1982] 2 S.C.R. 793.

as far from neutral. As a result, the implicit suspension of political judgment necessary for procedural decisions to be made—under the rules for constitutional amendment and for the sake of achieving political settlement—was no longer possible. Those rules had become part of the constitutional politics and were not thought capable of performing their regulatory function to constrain and channel constitutional politics, since they were perceived as openly favoring one side in constitutional debate. The substantive accounts of the Canadian constitutional crisis may explain how the country arrived at that crisis. But they do not explain why the amending rules were unable to regulate that process.[103]

6. Conclusion: The lesson of the Canadian model for multinational polities

There is, of course, a great deal more to the Canadian story, which cannot be developed here.[104] For the time being, I want to conclude by suggesting that the Canadian problem is a common problem. The constitutional politics of rules for amending are a common point of conflict in multinational polities. These rules are where the most fundamental clashes in nation building occur. By assigning the power of constitutional amendment to certain populations and/or institutions—in various combinations—the rules governing constitutional amendment stipulate the ultimate locus of political sovereignty and are the most basic statement of a community's political identity. The ability to reconfigure the most basic terms of social life must lie with the fundamental agents of political life. By looking to the amending rules, we see who these basic agents are. In multinational polities, assigning roles to national minorities as part of the procedure for constitutional change accordingly acknowledges the fundamental multinational character of the political community. On the other hand, the refusal to acknowledge this translates into a preference for constitutional amending rules that do not recognize and empower the constituent nations of a multinational polity. So it is far from surprising that, recently, in both Iraq and Sri Lanka, a principal arena of constitutional conflict has concerned the design of rules governing constitutional amendment.

The lesson for multinational polities at various stages of constitutional transition may be this. Canada is, indeed, a success story—it is one of the oldest countries in the world, has wrestled with and responded imaginatively to forces that have torn other countries apart, and has achieved a remarkable degree of

---

[103] The flip side to this point may be that the constitutional amending rules reflect the substantive view that the federal government is the national government that represents all parts of Canada, including Quebec. In the event of negotiations regarding secession, the mind-set reflected in, and reinforced by, those rules would make it hard for the federal government to see itself as the representative of the rest of Canada in those negotiations. *See* CAIRNS, *supra* note 98, at 307, 313.

[104] *See supra* note 100.

prosperity and freedom. In large part, the Canadian model operates under law. But, as the Canadian constitutional crisis shows us, a legal approach to the accommodation of minority nationalism has both its strengths and weaknesses. The main problem lies in meeting demands for constitutional change from minority nations. On the one hand, every constitution contains within it a process for constitutional amendment, as does the Canadian Constitution. But rules for constitutional amendment face genuine difficulty in constituting and regulating moments of constitutive constitutional politics, because at those moments, the very concept of political community those rules reflect is placed in contention by the minority nation.

It is, perhaps, at this point in the story that we come up against the limitations inherent in constitutionalism itself, at least with regard to its ability to accommodate minority nationalism.

6

Ethnic identity and democratic institutions: A dynamic perspective

*Richard H. Pildes**

The most urgent problem in the design of democratic institutions today is how best to design such institutions in the midst of seemingly profound internal heterogeneity, conflict, and group differences. In different parts of the world, the relevant differences can be religious, racial, linguistic, tribal, cultural, regional, or perhaps of other forms (as a shorthand, "ethnic differences"). This problem is central, not only to newly forming democracies over the last generation but also to more established democracies, as various groups more assertively press claims for political recognition, representation, and influence. We ought to understand this issue, better than we have thus far, as lying at the intersection of democratic theory and democratic institutional design on the one hand, and questions about the nature of individual rationality and rational choice concerning ethnic group "identities", on the other.

The argument of this chapter is that academic thought and, for the most part, practical institutional design have thus far taken too static an approach to this fundamental problem. In our first phase of confrontation with this issue, theorists and institutional designers have been overwhelmed with the problem as it appears at particularly critical political moments: the moment of state formation; or the moment at which societies emerge from conflict; or the moment at which group demands for inclusion, recognition, and power first become powerfully enough expressed as to require an institutional response. These are the moments at which ethnic identities are likely to seem most fixed, most entrenched, most essential to conceptions of self, and potentially most divisive or explosive. Dominated by the urgency of these tensions at the moment of institutional formation, constitutional framers often respond to the problem as it presents itself at that moment. As

* Sudler Family Professor of Constitutional Law, School of Law, New York University. I am grateful to Laurie Richardson for excellent research assistance with this work. An initial version of this work benefited from the comments of the participants at the Conference on Rationality and Democracy at Hebrew University in Jerusalem, Israel. Sujit Choudhry's editorial comments also improved this work, as did comments from Donald Horowitz. Email: pildesr@juris.law.nyu.edu

a result, the implicit view embodied in the institutions they create is frequently a static one. The institutional perspective takes for granted the nature of these ethnic identities and conflicts as they exist at the moment a state's democratic institutions are forged. In contemporary contexts, the emerging democratic structures often attempt to accommodate these ethnic differences through explicit devices, which can range from guaranteed minority political representation, to minority vetoes, to consociational executive branches, and to other similar structures.

Overwhelmed as theory and practice are by the magnitude of these problems at the moment of institutional formation, however, we neglect to recognize the extent to which ethnic differences can be fluid and capable of changing over time in response to shifting circumstances. In particular, we do not take adequate account of the extent to which the design of democratic institutions both can shape the ways ethnic identities are expressed and the extent to which these institutions, if not well designed, may entrench these identities. The specific design of democratic institutions can make it more difficult for the inherently contingent nature of these identities to be manifested. Moreover, once democratic institutions are constitutionally built along premises that assume particular ethnic identities, those institutions themselves may become impermeable to change, even as changes in social circumstances undermine these original premises.

Thus, the very institutional structures perceived as necessary to address ethnic difference synchronically—that is, at the moment of original democratic institutional formation—often undermine the dynamic possibilities for how these identities might shift and become more muted over time. The United States Senate affords a stark example. It is now the least democratically structured representative institution among Western democracies, as measured by the one-person, one-vote principle. Thirty-four million Californians have the same representation as 500,000 residents of Wyoming (a population disparity of 68:1). When the Senate was originally formed, state-based cultural and political identities were strong, and the original population disparity was only 13:1.[1] If the representative institutions of the United States were being created on a clean slate today, it is difficult to believe that a senate designed as the current one would emerge. State-based identities are thinner today, but even if such state-based differences were to continue to be taken into account to some extent, it is hard to imagine there would be consensus on accommodating these differences to the extent of a 68:1 departure from political equality. Yet the fundamental structure of the Senate is not a subject of discussion in the United States. That it would be changed today is inconceivable. Overwhelmed by the sectional differences at the moment the United States was created, the framers of the Constitution

---

[1] Richard H. Pildes, *The Supreme Court, 2003 Term—Foreword: Constitutionalization of Democratic Politics*, 118 Harv. L. Rev. 29, 85 (2004). Original disparity is calculated from the first official census data. For original population data in 1790, see generally Return of the Whole Number of Persons within the Several Districts of the United States (J. Phillips 1793), *available at* <http://www2.census.gov/prod2/decennial/documents/1790a-02.pdf>.

neglected to build in enough capacity for the basic democratic institutions of the state to be modified over time as the sense of ethnic difference itself changed. Perhaps understandably, the framers of the United States' Constitution missed the essential, but complex logic of this situation—how to address both existing sectional differences while designing a system that did not entrench those differences beyond their "natural" life.[2]

Even if it was understandable that the Constitution's framers, unsure of the sustainability of democratic self-governance, missed this dynamic perspective on the design of democratic institutions, it is less forgivable today. As the overview chapter to this volume attests, the question of how democratic institutions should deal with ethnic difference in various societies is often cast as a debate between integrationists and accommodationists.[3] The former focus primarily on the long-term normative vision of the state; they believe that the risk of long-term entrenchment and solidification of ethnic identities is so great, when political institutions are designed to accommodate group differences, that such accommodations should be avoided. Integrationist approaches often founder at the moment of state formation, however, because of a lack of sufficiently widespread political support at this particularly risk-averse moment. Accommodationists, on the other hand, focus strongly on the immediate, short-term pressures the state faces. Viewing accommodation as a practical necessity to ensure widespread support for and stability of democratic institutions, accommodationists insist that realism requires that an acknowledgment of ethnic differences be built into democratic institutions. If anything, there is growing support today for accommodationist approaches.[4] At the same time, if accommodationist approaches are not designed with great care, they risk precluding the rise of more integrationist politics over time.

Now that we have another generation of experience with these issues, I will argue that the task should not be understood as the need to choose between integration or accommodation writ large. To the extent accommodation is necessary or desirable at the moment of state formation, there is a great deal of difference among the devices and institutional structures through which accommodation is put into effect. The choice of specific structures should be made in a way that builds in the greatest capacity possible for changes in the nature and intensity of ethnic differences over time. If accommodation is necessary, it should be designed, to the extent possible, not to preclude the emergence of more integrationist politics over time. Put in other terms, the task is not to choose between integration and accommodation but to design institutions that enable societies to reach different balances between the two over time.

---

[2] For a superb account of these issues, see MARK A. GRABER, DRED SCOTT AND THE PROBLEM OF CONSTITUTIONAL EVIL (Cambridge Univ. Press 2006).

[3] McGarry, O'Leary & Simeon, *Integration of Accommodation? The Enduring Debate in Conflict-Regulation* (in this volume).

[4] *Id.*

We need a comparative and pragmatic assessment of the different institutional devices democracy has for addressing ethnic difference. That assessment should take a more dynamic perspective on the mutual interaction over time among ethnic identities, ethnic differences, and the design of the institutions and processes through which democratic political competition is channeled. The succeeding sections develop these themes, while many of the chapters in this book provide rich empirical experience from recently created democracies through which we can try to reach general insights about how best to design democratic institutions to manage ethnic difference.

1. Ethnic identity

Let me begin with the issues concerning the nature of ethnic group identity. The general question is how to understand the relationship between democratic institutional design and the formation, mobilization, maintenance, and dynamics of the ways in which individuals come to identify and forge particular group affiliations. These processes of identity formation, expression, mobilization, and the like fuel the group conflicts to which modern democratic institutional design is meant to respond. Without understanding this underlying dynamic, institutional designers will lack a sufficiently deep grasp of the essential problem they are attempting to address.

Academic work has been substantially ahead of practical political action, as well as more journalistic and popular accounts, when it comes to understanding the dynamics of ethnic group conflict in democratic states. I want to stress four points that emerge from this work. I will present them first abstractly, then illuminate with concrete examples.

First, ethnic identities are less a matter of fixed, profound, fundamental psychological and affective attachment than they are fluid and contingent possibilities that become mobilized by specific circumstances. Indeed, in many contexts, citizens do not have a single ethnic identity but, rather, several different potential ethnic identities several of which can become mobilized. In such contexts, the question is not one of ethnic difference, but which of several potential ethnic differences actually become salient. To be sure, background cultural, and historical circumstances determine and limit the range of potential ethnic identities that may be mobilized. Moreover, once certain identities are powerfully mobilized, they can become substantially more hardened and less fluid in the short term. At the moment of acutest group conflict, such as the aftermath of a civil war, the relevant dimensions of group difference are likely to seem most enduring and refractory.

Nonetheless, ethnic identity has been the subject of a great deal of academic work in recent years, both theoretical and empirical, and this work consistently reveals a dynamic process behind the formation, maintenance, and diminishment of these identities.[5] Identities that policymakers take as given instead have been constructed through specific circumstances and processes. In the years since democratization in India, for example, the level of Hindu-Muslim conflict, according to one major study, "has varied so much over time and across locations that an alleged general propensity to ethnic hatred cannot explain much".[6] As a great deal of work documenting similar facts in various societies suggests, these identities are more fluid than is often assumed. This fact can be particularly difficult for Americans to recognize, because the most incendiary group difference in American history—the racial one—appears particularly primordial and enduring. Yet even this "difference" is more fluid and less deterministic, historically, than most Americans recognize, as I will illustrate in a moment.

Second, the most powerful and effective incentives for mobilizing identities along one dimension or another are generated by the competition over political power. Such power is an exceptionally effective vehicle for distributing material resources, whether in the form of patronage, rents, licenses, subsidies, general policies with beneficial distributional effects, or other state-created benefits. Formal political power is also an essential vehicle for distributing the expressive resources Charles Taylor famously denominated "the politics of recognition".[7] Particularly for ethnic groups that perceive themselves to have been exploited previously or excluded from participation under prior regimes, this kind of formal recognition through explicit representation in the institutions of governance can be a fundamental demand.[8]

The third point is a more specific application of the second. There are numerous ways the institutional structures and processes of democratic political competition may be organized, all of them consistent with general principles of democracy. But the particular way in which the structures for democratic competition are designed generates distinct incentives for mobilizing coalitions and identities

---

[5] The analysis in the following pages draws centrally on works such as ROGERS BRUBAKER, ETHNICITY WITHOUT GROUPS (Harvard Univ. Press 2004); DAVID D. LAITIN, IDENTITY IN FORMATION: THE RUSSIAN-SPEAKING POPULATIONS IN THE NEAR ABROAD (Cornell Univ. Press 1998); David D. Laitin, *Marginality: A Microperspective,* 7 RATIONALITY & SOC'Y 31 (1995). *See also* Shaheen Mozaffar *et al., Electoral Institutions, Ethnopolitical Cleavages, and Party Systems in Africa's Emerging Democracies,* 97 AM. POLI. SCI. REV. 379, 379 (2003) (noting "the accumulated findings of over three decades of comparative research on ethnopolitics" attests that "ethnopolitical groups and associated ethnopolitical cleavages are not primordially fixed but constructed in the courts of social, economic, and political interactions ...".).

[6] JACK L. SNYDER, FROM VOTING TO VIOLENCE: DEMOCRATIZATION AND NATIONALIST CONFLICT 289 (W.W. Norton & Co. 2000). This work views "inherent" ethnic conflict to be less significant than the ways in which "the political context has varied in ways that sometimes fan the flames of ethnic rivalries and other times dampen them". *Id.* at 290.

[7] CHARLES TAYLOR, MULTICULTURALISM AND THE POLITICS OF RECOGNITION (Princeton Univ. Press 1992).

[8] Note the following observation regarding democratic politics in India: "But it is no accident that arguably all the potent mobilizations that independent India has seen, in some respects, involve an appeal to self-respect. Most of our politics has been a politics of recognition." PRATAP BHANU MEHTA, THE BURDEN OF DEMOCRACY 49 (Penguin Press 2003).

in one way rather than another. Hence, one of the most powerful forces for constructing and shaping ethnic difference is the structure through which political competition is channeled in a democratic state. That is, democratic institutions cannot be viewed only as responses to pre-existing ethnic differences. They must be designed with an awareness of the extent to which—and to the ways in which—they also construct the very ethnic differences at issue.

Fourth, the design of political institutions can dominate culture in accounting for a society's ethnic differences. This is an intentionally tendentious statement, given that proving dominant causal relationships is no easy task for phenomena as complexly caused as ethnic identity formation and mobilization. I offer it partly based on my own direct study of the American experience, and also because, by putting the point in such strong terms, I aim to call attention to how much more powerful the design of political competition is than often realized in the shaping of ethnic identities. To be sure, background conditions—themselves the outcome of previous modes of "politics" in earlier regimes, including nondemocratic ones—influence the latent identities capable of being mobilized through democratic politics. But formal politics, particularly in democracies, creates one of the most shared and visible public spaces and platforms. Nowhere are more resources devoted to the mobilization of coalitions and group affiliations than in the pursuit of political power. As political elites and entrepreneurs mobilize various identities, including ethnic identities, in efforts to forge winning coalitions, these efforts radiate into other arenas, including more general cultural and social understandings.[9] The structure of political competition both creates incentives to mobilize identities along certain lines rather than others and provides a focal point for the coordination of citizens' strategic choices about how they self-identify. As the political domain mobilizes certain identities and more firmly entrenches them, these identities become culturally more powerful as well. That outbreaks of ethnic violence coincide with the electoral cycle in countries like India, for example, is no accident; political competition in India is

---

[9] A detailed insider's account of these issues in South Africa makes this point regarding ethnic differences there. *See* HEINZ KLUG, CONSTITUTING DEMOCRACY: LAW, GLOBALISM AND SOUTH AFRICA'S POLITICAL RECONSTRUCTION 113 (Cambridge Univ. Press 2000) ("Claims of cultural diversity and difference have come to reflect a complex interaction between real cultural and ethnic identities on the one hand and the claims of political leaders on the other. These leaders' assertions of cultural and ethnic particularities are intertwined with their own attempts either to preserve existing power or to seek future political advantage".). For a similar view about the rise of ethnic parties in Latin America starting in the 1990s, which attributes this rise not to ethnic differences per se, but to changes in legal and other factors that affected the organization of political party competition, see DONNA LEE VAN COOT, FROM MOVEMENTS TO PARTIES IN LATIN AMERICA: THE EVOLUTION OF ETHNIC POLITICS 8 (Cambridge Univ. Press 2005) ("I argue that political institutions and configurations of power within a party system help to determine the likelihood that ethnic parties will form and become successful".). *See also* KANCHAN CHANDRA, WHY ETHNIC PARTIES SUCCEED: PATRONAGE AND ETHNIC HEAD COUNTS IN INDIA 290–294 (Cambridge Univ. Press 2004) (providing an instrumental theory of ethnic voting in "patronage democracies" and observing capacity of political elites successfully to choose whether to mobilize identities around religion, caste, or regional bases).

a principle vehicle for politicizing the latent cultural and ethnic cleavages.[10] Over time, the role of political institutions in shaping these identities can fade into the background and be forgotten. The identities come to be seen as matters of deep attachment and essential cultural difference.

Let me offer a few concrete studies that inform these four general points. One of the best comes from a recent, superb study of ethnic politics in Africa by Daniel Posner, where the country of Zambia, in particular, provides an ideal social-scientific experiment in the relationship between the design of political institutions and the nature of ethnic identity.[11] With respect to ethnic identities, Zambia has four broad, regionally clustered linguistic groups and seventy-two tribal groupings, more locally concentrated. With respect to the institutional design of political competition, Zambia has alternated, since independence, between a multi-party and a one-party system of political competition: multi-party from 1964 to 1972; one-party from 1973 to 1991; and then multi-party again since 1991. The ethnic differences that became politically and hence culturally most salient—linguistic or tribal differences—were profoundly shaped by which one of these institutional systems for political competition was in place.

During the eras of multi-party democratic politics, control of the executive was part of the competitive political process, which also involved competition for representation in the parliament. The effective focus for elections was the national level, because the presidency was the most powerful office. Party labels down the line ensured that parliamentary candidates were representatives of national coalitions; that is, the effect of the competition over the presidency was to ensure that parliamentary elections were also nationalized through party identification. With an electoral design that encouraged the building of nationwide coalitions to gain effective power, political campaigns, candidates, and coalitions became organized around Zambia's linguistic differences. Both the large size of the four groups and their regional distribution created rational incentives for the candidates and parties to calculate that mobilizing potential supporters along linguistic lines would enable effective winning coalitions. On the other hand, the more locally-based tribal differences were not politically mobilized and did not find meaningful expression in these nationally-oriented election campaigns.

The shift to one-party elections involved nothing more than a single change in the Constitution. According to Posner's detailed study, there was no difference in political freedom or in any other dimension associated with the formal, constitutional change to a one-party system. But in the era of one-party elections, effective political competition between candidates—which did occur—took place at the local, not national, level. Under this structure, the president was chosen by

---

[10] For this point about India, see Jack Snyder, *supra* note 6, at 294. As the resource for this finding, Snyder draws on DENNIS AUSTIN, DEMOCRACY AND VIOLENCE IN INDIA AND SRI LANKA (Council on Foreign Rel. Press 1995).

[11] *See generally* DANIEL POSNER, INSTITUTIONS AND ETHNIC POLITICS IN AFRICA (Cambridge Univ. Press 2005).

the central committee of the ruling party; voters then had the option only of voting for or against this candidate in the general election. As a result, there was no need for parties and leaders to compete for voting support with respect to the presidency. There was, however, substantial competition within individual constituencies for seats in the parliament. Indeed, on average more than four candidates ran for each seat during the era in which the law permitted only one-party competition (indeed, this contrasted with only slightly more than two candidates running per district, on average, when the law permitted multi-party competition). These individual election districts tended to be homogenous by language, but heterogeneous by tribe; 80 percent of them were rural. With the meaningful electoral arenas being these local districts, rather than the national level, political competition responded to the rational incentive structure generated by becoming organized around tribal differences, not language ones.

Posner's careful and detailed study qualitatively and quantitatively documents specifically the ways in which politics became organized around linguistic differences during multi-party competition but around tribal differences during one-party campaigning. Most remarkable is not just that the election structure shaped the relevant ethnic differences mobilized, but that these changes took place so rapidly—strong evidence for the force with which political incentives can encourage mobilization of one or another ethnic identity.

I will highlight only a few of the specific differences Posner chronicles. First, candidates viewed the importance of their identities, tribal and linguistic, differently under the two systems. In the one-party system, where competition was based at the local district level, candidates self-selected to ensure that their tribal identity matched that of the district in which they ran. In multi-party competition, where competition was structured through the incentives created by the national focus of elections, candidates were willing to run outside their own tribal constituencies. Thus, in a particularly telling finding, 83 percent of the candidates who shifted districts between the two systems moved from outside their tribal district to inside their tribal district when the election system shifted from multi-party to one-party.[12] Second, politicians made different kinds of ethnic appeals under the two systems: tribal appeals under one-party competition, linguistic appeals under multi-party competition. Third, in multi-party competition (and only then), political elites sought to build civic associations that united multiple tribes, often along provincial or linguistic lines. Finally, voters tended to vote for candidates from their own tribes in one-party elections but for parties whose leaders were from the voters' same language group in multi-party elections.

So is Zambia divided by tribal differences or by linguistic ones? The answer depends, to a considerable extent, on the institutional structures of political competition. Note that the mechanism at work is that voters do use some form of

---

[12] *Id.* at 208.

ethnicity as a proxy for gauging the extent to which those seeking power through elections will protect or enhance the voter's interests. Ethnicity does become a credible commitment device for promises, explicit or implicit, that candidates and parties make with regard to both material and expressive resources. Indeed, the less information voters have and the more risk averse they are—factors likely to be at their height in the initial stages of democratic transition and early elections—the more likely voters are to use ethnicity as a proxy in these ways. Nonetheless, even with this strong, general sense of ethnic affiliation, the design of democratic institutions and processes dramatically conditions which ethnic identities are mobilized in the public sphere.

This striking example from Africa is more extensively documented than most but is hardly aberrational. In India, for example, during the 1920s and 1930s, voting was limited to those able to meet high property-holding requirements; as a result, political competition was organized around issues that divided the property-holding upper-caste elites. In contrast, when the franchise was broadly expanded in the 1950s, the prior political parties shifted to appeals based on Hindu-Muslim identity differences.[13] Similarly, in then Zaire (now the Democratic Republic of Congo), the first competitive elections were confined to seven major cities; in those elections, the dominant cleavages were tribal ones. Three years later, when national elections began for national and provincial representative institutions, political elites began "defining region rather than [tribe] as the political building block" and essential ethnic cleavage.[14] Again, what makes these changes all the more notable is how quickly they emerged when the structure of political competition was changed. On the one hand, this might seem obvious: shift the way the electorate is constituted and the dynamics of political competition—including the nature and extent of the group conflicts that will be mobilized—will change. On the other hand, we do not appreciate this insight deeply enough when it comes to ethnic identities, which are often viewed as far less fluid and less responsive to the incentives created by the design of political competition than is frequently the case.

A particularly powerful example is offered by the American experience with race. A common misconception is that the black-white racial divide in the American South had an essentially fixed, rigid structure from the end of the Civil War (1865), or the end of Reconstruction (1876), until the civil-rights revolution of the 1960s. This divide is thought to be the quintessential example of a deep, primordial identity attachment that fueled an ideology of white supremacy, segregation, and related state-sanctioned racial practices throughout the long era after the formal end of slavery. But the historical experience with racial differences in the American context is more complex, as my own research and that of others

[13] *See* STEVEN I. WILKINSON, VOTES AND VIOLENCE: ELECTORAL COMPETITION AND ETHNIC RIOTS IN INDIA (Cambridge Univ. Press 2004).
[14] CRAWFORD YOUNG & THOMAS TURNER, THE RISE AND DECLINE OF THE ZAIRIAN STATE 150 (Univ. Wisconsin Press 1985).

on this issue demonstrates.[15] Even with respect to a group difference thought to be so deeply entrenched in American culture, the structure of democratic elections profoundly altered the extent to which racial identities were made salient and were mobilized. For more than a generation in the late nineteenth century, roughly from 1867 to 1890, blacks were legally entitled to vote in the American South. Despite how strongly held racial identities might have been in some sense, the extent to which those identities found public expression depended on the incentives that the structures of political competition generated. In the era in which black men were legally entitled to vote, the nature of political coalition formation—and the resulting effect on officeholding and public policy—was dramatically affected, in ways that most Americans today surely do not realize. In North Carolina, for example, a fusion coalition of Republicans and Populists, with black and white political support, controlled the state legislature from 1894–1898.[16] Numerous black officials were elected to local offices such as justice of the peace, alderman, county commissioner, register of deeds, city attorney, and the like. To be sure, interracial coalitions like these, which existed in other parts of the South as well, did not mean that whites and blacks were living in racial harmony. The incentives created by the pursuit of political power, however, had a powerful effect on the kind of coalitions that were mobilized, and on the kind of the payoffs those coalitions had to make to their constituent members—an effect powerful enough to overcome even ethnic differences seemingly as deeply rooted as that of race in the American context.

This era of interracial coalitions ended when, not surprisingly, the institutional structure for elections was intentionally changed and hence when the political incentives for electoral competition were altered. Starting in the 1890s, southern state legislatures enacted a series of changes designed to remove most blacks and many poor whites from political participation: literacy tests, poll taxes, grandfather clauses, felon disfranchisement provisions, increased registration barriers, and so forth.[17] These successful changes in the electoral rules to disfranchise these voters were not merely an expression of a cultural ideology of racial supremacy. They were an intentional effort to change the dynamics of partisan political competition—an effort that was extremely successful. Proponents of these changes sought to ensure their own political dominance by destroying the conditions that fueled the kind of coalitions that had challenged their authority, including the

[15] *See* Richard H. Pildes, *Keeping Legal History Meaningful*, 19 CONST. COMMENT. 645 (2002); Richard H. Pildes, *Democracy, Anti-Democracy, and the Canon*, 17 CONST. COMMENT. 295 (2000) [hereinafter Pildes, *Democracy*]. The leading work which chronicles the differences in Southern politics before and after black men were disfranchised is MORGAN J. KOUSSER, THE SHAPING OF SOUTHERN POLITICS: SUFFRAGE, RESTRICTION, AND THE ESTABLISHMENT OF THE ONE-PARTY SOUTH, 1880–1910 (Yale Univ. Press 1974). The fluidity of racial politics in the American South before the 1890s is the theme of Comer Vann Woodward's classic work. COMER VANN WOODWARD, THE STRANGE CAREER OF JIM CROW (3d rev. ed., Oxford Univ. Press 1974) (1955).

[16] Pildes, *Democracy, supra* note 15, at 313–315.

[17] *See* KOUSSER, *supra* note 15.

kind of interracial coalitions that had controlled state politics in a place like North Carolina. The highly visible cultural expressions of white racial supremacy, such as segregation, did not become legally enacted until black voters had been removed through these legal changes from political participation. Another specific example occurred when Congress in 1867 first enfranchised black residents in the District of Columbia. The political parties paraded "for the first time in living memory" *without* banners "in regard to niggers, miscegenation and similar matters".[18] In other words, changes in the structure of political competition enabled or diminished the full flowering of the most powerful symbols of racial difference.

The American experience with race is particularly telling because once the late 19th century changes in elections in the South were put into place, they remained largely intact until the Voting Rights Act of 1965.[19] As a result, the effects of political structures on the culture of race relations faded into the background. Instead, the cultural expressions of racial difference, such as segregation, remained highly visible and publicly displayed on a day-to-day basis. The history of black-white political cooperation from 1867 to 1890 was largely forgotten.[20] The policies and practices of racial conflict and subordination came be seen as natural expressions of essential, refractory racial differences.

Comparative perspective is also illuminating on the extent to which racial differences are, instead, shaped by the structure of democratic political competition. Like the United States, Cuba was one of the last countries in the world to retain a system of racialized slavery; indeed, Cuba abolished slavery even later than did the United States.[21] Yet despite emerging from a culture of racialized slavery, Cuba after independence did not, as did the American South, create an electoral structure that disfranchised blacks.[22] As a result, blacks were more fully appealed to in politics (and hence in culture) and integrated into the structures of political competition and governance. To be sure, race relations in Cuba had their own complexity in the years after independence. But Cuba did not have a comparable history of a strong system of state-sanctioned racial hierarchy and subordination as had the American South, once the electoral rules in the South had changed

[18] ERIC FONER, RECONSTRUCTION: AMERICA'S UNFINISHED REVOLUTION, 1863–1877, at 272 (Harper & Row 1988).
[19] The Voting Rights Act of 1965, Pub. L. No. 89–110, 79 Stat. 445 (codified as amended at 42 U.S.C. §§ 1971, 1973, 1973bb-1 (2000)) (U.S.).
[20] This is the theme of Vann Woodward's *The Strange Career of Jim Crow*. VANN WOODWARD, *supra* note 15.
[21] For the process by which this happened, see REBECCA J. SCOTT, SLAVE EMANCIPATION IN CUBA: THE TRANSITION TO FREE LABOR, 1860–1899 (Princeton Univ. Press 1985).
[22] For a superb study of these issues, see ALEJANDRO DE LA FUENTE, A NATION FOR ALL: RACE, INEQUALITY, AND POLITICS IN TWENTIETH-CENTURY CUBA (Univ. N.C. Press 2000). For a more focused study during the immediate post-slavery period, see ADA FERRER, INSURGENT CUBA: RACE, NATION, AND REVOLUTION, 1868–1898 (Univ. N.C. Press 1999). For a comparative perspective on the role of black political participation in Cuba and the United States following the end of slavery, see REBECCA J. SCOTT, DEGREES OF FREEDOM: LOUISIANA AND CUBA AFTER SLAVERY (Harvard Univ. Press 2005).

to exclude black political participation. To the extent one mistakenly believes cultural attitudes toward race are likely to be rigid and deterministic in societies emerging from longstanding systems of racialized slavery, comparative perspective, detailed appreciation for the fluidity of American history, and recognition of the way structures of political competition shape cultural attitudes undermine any simplistic notion of essential cultural differences—even with respect to the ethnic divide thought to be most rigid and refractory in American political history.

At the outset, I observed that academic work was considerably ahead of practical politics with regard to how fluid and contingent ethnic differences and identities are capable of being. However, scholarship itself has been less attentive to how much the structures of political competition, as opposed to a more vaguely attributed "cultural construction of identity", is a driving force in mobilizing and encouraging these identity formations. Academic culture over the last generation has seen a diminished interest in the humanities in formal politics and a much greater focus on issues of culture.[23] This is a mistake, if we are to understand ethnic identity formation and mobilization properly. It is also a mistake if we are to think soundly about the design of democratic institutions in the midst of ethnic conflicts.

2. Democratic institutions

I now want to turn from analysis of ethnic identity formation to issues of constitutional and democratic institutional design. At the outset, it is helpful to be precise about the nature of the institutional design problem in societies potentially divided deeply along lines of ethnic difference.

The structural nature of the problem is that potentially vulnerable minority groups need credible institutional design commitments that they will not be exploited in an overly majoritarian democratic system. This need is particularly acute for societies emerging out of conflict and forming democratic regimes for the first time. Lawyers tend to think of bill of rights and constitutional courts as the primary institutional solution to this need, but these are relatively weak institutional solutions. Judicial review operates at best as an ex post check or negative veto on the exercise of political power. It can afford, perhaps, a defensive shield. But judicial review rarely is capable of ensuring a fair distributional allocation of goods or of providing affirmative benefits to minority groups. It also does not respond fully to the expressive demands for recognition that are so often central to ethnic minorities and to the legitimacy and stability of democratic institutions across ethnic groups.

---

[23] As Rogers Brubaker, a leading scholar on these issues, puts this point: "Much social analysis today is informed by what might be called an *overethnicized* conception of history, politics, and social interaction. The ethnic categories deployed by political and cultural entrepreneurs are often uncritically adopted by social analysts." BRUBAKER, *supra* note 5, at 151–152.

Minority groups today typically recognize these limitations on bill of rights-style protections and demand greater ex ante forms of security and recognition devices. They also seek to have credible institutional commitments built directly into the structures of political governance, within either or both the legislative and executive branches. At the same time, the risk is that locking in these commitments through the design of political institutions hazards the two consequences noted earlier: first, the creation of even greater incentives to mobilize politics around these identities and thus to increase their broader cultural salience, and, second, the freezing of institutional structures into a mold that reflects the circumstances at the moment of democratic formation. This process of institutional solidification makes it difficult for these institutions at adapting or to be adapted down the road as ethnic identifications change.

Paradoxically, it is precisely when democratic institutions are most successful at stabilizing and compromising among conflicting groups that this problem becomes most acute. The more that experience under democratic institutions convinces potentially vulnerable minorities that the majorities will not exploit these minorities, the more support there will be for integrationist institutions. The structure of democratic institutions however, tends to be self-perpetuating, as ideological, as well as more self-interestedly political, interests crystallize around existing institutional structures. In particular, those who hold political power have a strong stake in preserving the structures and modes of competition through which they have attained that power.[24]

Given an ethnically divided society that is forming or reforming its democratic institutions, in which a fully integrationist approach is not an option (because of practical political constraints or perhaps because such an approach ought to be rejected for more normative reasons), the question is: which strategies, devices, and institutional structures are the best means for accommodating ethnic conflict? In particular, we want to frame this question in dynamic, not static terms. My aim is to identify techniques of accommodation that nonetheless leave the democratic system with the greatest capacity to respond to shifting conceptions of ethnic identity as that system develops.

I highlight five of these approaches here, given constraints of space. I have chosen these particular ones partly because some are more novel and partly because we have some concrete experience with each:

Multistage democratic processes

One strategy is to design the democratic regime so that it comes into full being only in multiple stages. The moment of state formation, that is, expressly entails

---

[24] One of the consistent findings in political science is how little change there tends to be in the basic structure of electoral systems once established. *See* HANDBOOK OF ELECTORAL SYSTEM CHOICE 57 (Josef Colomer ed., Palgrave Macmillan 2004). Uncertainty about the effects of change appears to play a major role. *Id.* at 6.

a commitment to a sequencing of stages in the way the state's democratic institutions will be structured.

In the initial stage, the institutional structures of democracy can be accommodationist. They can, for example, have strong consociational features. At the moment of state formation, the need to ensure inclusive structures of representation is often at its height, as is the risk aversion of relevant minority groups regarding democracy. However, the constitutional design in these sequenced systems also commits to treating this initial stage as transitional. At a later stage, which is itself built into the original constitutional structure, the structures of democracy expressly become more integrationist. Rather than choosing once and for all between accommodation and integration in dealing with ethnic difference, a constitutional system designed in this way negotiates between the two alternatives: accommodationist at the outset, but integrationist as the evolutionary steady state of the democratic system.

South Africa provides a model of this particular technique, as it does, more generally, for a managed, multistage transition to democracy. As the chapter by Richard Simeon and Christina Murray documents, there were strongly conflicting views among the leading players as to whether a democratic South Africa should adopt a power sharing or a Westminster-style majoritarian system of democratic institutions.[25] Instead of choosing one option or the other at the outset, the compromise underlying the 1993 Interim Constitution required that a power-sharing, consociational structure of accommodation be established for the first five years. The first elected government was designed to be a government of national unity. Any party winning 20 percent of the seats in the National Assembly was entitled to appoint a deputy president; any party with more than 5 percent was entitled to cabinet representation. Thus, former National Party president F. W. De Klerk became a deputy president and Mangosuthu Buthelezi, head of the Inkatha Freedom Party, became part of the cabinet, one of nine minor party politicians to do so. As Simeon and Murray note, this was "pure Lijphart": a consociational structure designed to ensure stability and buy-in from the major ethnic and party groups in South Africa by ensuring recognition of these groups in the formal political governance structures.[26] Acceptance by the leaders of the African National Congress of this interim, consociational executive branch, along with the National Party's acceptance of the right to an elected representative parliament, were "the key elements of agreement in South Africa's democratic transition".[27]

This was consociationalism structured, however, to be limited in time. The Interim Constitution contained a five-year "sunset clause". After that time, the democratically elected national Parliament was given the power to write a new

[25] Richard Simeon & Christina Murray, *Recognition without Empowerment: Minorities in a Democratic South Africa* (in this volume).
[26] *Id.* at 425.
[27] *See* KLUG, *supra* note 9, at 105.

constitution, which could keep or reject this power sharing, consociational structure. Once this period was over, South Africa's Parliament abandoned the power-sharing arrangement and moved to a Westminster style, majoritarian system. Thus, an accommodationist structure enabled the evolution into a more integrationist one. As Simeon and Murray conclude, majority rule has won out over a power-sharing model for South Africa democracy. To date, the South African system is considered relatively successful in the primary task of generating stable democratic institutions in a postconflict society filled with a variety of potential ethnic conflicts.

The current Iraqi Constitution makes use of a similar set of devices.[28] Given the intensity of the current ethnic divides in Iraq, a majoritarian structure for governance would not have been accepted by the non-Shiite minorities. However, as in South Africa, the current Iraqi Constitution creates a staged transition process, in which the first stage is more consociational, though with a sunset clause, while the permanent stage is more majoritarian.[29] Thus, the central executive authority is in the hands of a ministerial council, which is headed by a prime minister. However, the prime minister cannot be appointed until the election of the Presidential Council. During the four-year transitional period, this is a three-person body that then charges the leader of the largest party in the legislature with forming the Council of Ministers, which the legislature must in turn approve in a majority vote. The Presidential Council is elected on a single slate by a two-thirds majority in the legislature.[30] The Constitution does not set seats aside on the Presidential Council on the basis of religion or ethnicity, but the two-thirds vote requirement is designed to encourage coalition building. The current Presidential Council consists of a Kurdish president, a Sunni vice president, and a Shi'a Arab vice president. Decisions of the Presidential Council are legally effective only if unanimous. After the four-year transition, the Presidential Council is to be replaced by a single-person presidency, which can be established by a majority vote of the legislature. Thus, the vision behind this structure is consociational power sharing in the first phase of democracy, but with a built-in shift to a more majoritarian, more integrationist political system. In their chapter on Iraq, John McGarry and Brendan O'Leary (who advised the Kurds) call this and other features of the Iraqi constitution a form of "liberal consociationalism". To be sure, this particular structure in Iraq was generated without substantial Sunni participation, and features of that constitution remain a potent source of divisive group conflict. But consistent with the perspective I am urging, the features I have emphasized can be viewed as reflecting an emerging form of constitutional design that recognizes the practical needs to accommodate ethnic differences at

[28] John McGarry & Brendan O'Leary, *Iraq's Constitution of 2005: Liberal Consociation as Political Prescription* (in this volume).
[29] *See* IRAQ CONST.
[30] *Id*. art. 138.

the moment of state formation, but one that also attempts to devise structures that do not lock those differences into place indefinitely.

Of course, the question is why ethnic minority political elites would agree at the outset to a staged sequence in which the ultimate end state is majoritarian democracy, if they are not willing to accept such a system at the outset. Perhaps they believe the accommodationist phase will give them and their constituents enough time to judge whether they can trust a more majoritarian system; if not, perhaps they will seek to escape, including through violence, the terms of the original deal. Perhaps, in some contexts, the alternative of a delayed transition to a full majoritarian system might be better than the alternative options. (Indeed, De Klerk sought to have the power-sharing provisions of the interim constitution inserted as one of the "core" constitutional principles that would be binding for the drafting of the permanent constitution, although he failed in this effort.)[31] Generally speaking, we have little academic grasp of the time horizons within which political elites function.

There are many ways in which temporal sequencing instruments might be used, with the initial democratic stage tacking to the side of greater inclusiveness and broader formal representation of ethnic differences, while later stages seek to diminish the intensity of these differences in the political arena. For example, proportional representation (PR) systems can be designed with low thresholds at the outset, to address the risk averseness of small minority groups and parties. But instead of taking a static approach to this question, which might lock a 1 percent threshold into place in the constitution indefinitely, the constitution can specify raising that threshold by specific amounts over time. Again, the contexts in which potentially vulnerable minorities might accept such a two-stage process are hard to specify in general terms. Alternatively, in some systems, electoral thresholds are initially set at a high level, to minimize fragmentation, but could be designed in the original constitution to ratchet down in a preset way over time. Institutional designers and political negotiators should at least be aware of these kinds of options, ones that build greater dynamic flexibility into constitutional systems.

Novel voting systems

The conventional choice between voting systems is between proportional representation and districted elections with plurality or majority elections (single-member districting). There are particular risks to both systems in ethnically divided societies. The effect of elections based on single-member districts will

---

[31] James Hamill, *A Disguised Surrender? South Africa's Negotiated Settlement and the Politics of Conflict Resolution*, 14 DIPLOMACY & STATECRAFT 1, 9 (2003). Hamill suggests three specific contextual factors account for De Klerk's willingness to accept a delayed transition to majoritarian government: lack of international support for minority-protecting provisions to benefit whites in the South African context; the ability of the ANC to destabilize South Africa if its demands were not met; and a young generation of NP politicians who viewed the transition to majoritarianism as inevitable. *Id.* at 16–19.

depend heavily on the geographic distribution of the relevant ethnic groups. One risk occurs when an ethnic minority is relatively dispersed, with the consequence that it represents a minority in *all* districts. In single-member districts elections, that minority will be outvoted in all of these districts, if the voting is heavily polarized along ethnic lines. A second risk is that single-member district elections require the creation of individual election districts, which must be revised regularly to keep up with population changes. This introduces the risk of gerrymandering, depending on who is given the power to draw the lines. In Malaysia, for example, election districts were originally designed to be balanced between Malay and Chinese parties. But by 1974, these boundaries had been so heavily gerrymandered by the Malay majority that a vast number of districts were Malay majority, while the Chinese were overwhelmingly packed into a few districts in which most of their votes were therefore wasted.[32]

Even under the best of circumstances, with a non-partisan, independent body assigned this power, the way district lines are mapped will constantly entail a direct confrontation of ethnically-charged issues. Line drawing can affect the distribution of political power; those in charge must decide whether, for example, to create two districts in which a particular ethnic group constitutes 30 percent in each district—in which case, with polarized voting, those groups will always be on the losing side—or one district in which that group constitutes a 60 percent majority. Each time issues of this sort are confronted can be divisive and further polarizing. For example, South Africa reportedly chose to avoid using single-member districts because that would force decisions to be made, and remade, about the racial composition of districts—a process that political leaders believed would be explosive.[33]

Proportional representation systems can avoid some of these problems through nationwide elections. Such systems can ensure the formal representation of less-than-majority groups. For this reason, they are often favored by ethnic minorities in divided societies. If political parties have a strong ethnic cast, the society's ethnic differences will be fully represented in a parliament that "mirrors" those differences. If no party manages a majority, coalitions will have to be made across ethnic lines to have a functioning government. One standard objection to proportional representation in ethnically divided societies is that it assumes political leaders will have an incentive to exercise a kind of "statesmanship" and construct coalitions across ethnic divides. But as a leading critic points out, there are a number of reasons experience offers to question that assumption.[34] Leaders are

[32] Donald L. Horowitz, *Constitutional Design: An Oxymoron?*, *in* Designing Democratic Institutions 253, 265 (Ian Shapiro & Stephen Macedo eds., NYU Press 2000).
[33] This is based on private communications from an ANC leader in the negotiation process over constitutional design in South Africa.
[34] *See* Donald L. Horowitz, *Constitutional Design: Proposals Versus Process, in* The Architecture of Democracy: Constitutional Design, Conflict Management, and Democracy 15, 20–22 (Andrew Reynolds ed., Oxford Univ. Press 2002).

Richard H. Pildes

not necessarily less ethnically divisive than their supporters. Even if leaders are inclined to be, they can face a high price from competitors prepared to punish them. In ethnically bipolar states, where conflicts are often the most intense, proportional representation will give one party complete dominance. Put in other terms, "[c]oalitions that are created after elections merely to form a government of 50 percent plus one of the seats in parliament may prove to be fragile when divisive ethnic issues arise".[35]

However, there is one further limitation inherent in proportional representation as a solution to ethnic conflict, a limitation that is particularly deep, even if insufficiently appreciated. Proportional representation is a top-down solution to ethnic conflict. Indeed, it might exacerbate these conflicts among the mass of voters, even as it seeks to give incentives to political elites to overcome these conflicts. Proportional representation encourages the formation of smaller, more ideologically coherent parties—including ethnically based parties—because any party receives representation in proportion to its votes so long as it surmounts the election threshold (rarely higher than 5 percent). It encourages coalitions and compromises to form after the election, among political leaders, not before, among voters. Proportional representation generates no incentive for voters to vote outside their natural affinity groups, nor does it require voters to take into account the different views and preferences of voters outside the former's natural group. Proportional representation seeks to represent faithfully in the parliament the differences that exist among groups in society; it does not seek to overcome those differences at the level of individual citizens.

A third option is to make greater use of what are called votepooling systems or preference-voting systems. These have different forms and go under different names (single-transferable voting, alternative vote, preference voting, instant runoff voting). The core concept is that voters spread their votes out among more than one candidate. As a rough illustration, the system starts with voters ranking candidates in order of preference, rather than voting for just one candidate. The first choices of voters are then tabulated. If no candidate gets enough votes to be elected, the last place candidate is eliminated, and the votes of all the voters who voted for that last place candidate are now transferred to those voters' second choice candidate. This process continues until one candidate emerges with an outright majority (at least 50 percent plus one vote).

The logic behind these systems is that both candidates and voters are given incentives to campaign and vote beyond their natural affinity groups. Instead of appealing only to their natural base (which in ethnically divided societies with proportional representation might well be their fellow ethnics), candidates realize they can benefit from being the second or third or even later choice of other groups of voters. Thus, these systems encourage candidates to appeal across ethnic

---

[35] Donald L. Horowitz, *Electoral Systems: A Primer for Decision Makers*, 14 J. DEMOCRACY 115, 119 (2003).

lines. The system can also encourage parties to form and announce preelection coalitions, so that their supporters have clear cues about which candidates and parties to rank second, third, and so forth. Similarly, for voters the vote that actually counts might not be their first choice, but their second or later. Voters are thus encouraged to think more broadly than for their favorite candidate. There is an ex ante effect that might moderate ethnic divides among voters. In theory, these votepooling systems thus encourage a bottom-up and top-down mode of political action that encourages surmounting ethnic differences at the same time they recognize the reality of current ethnic divides. These systems also are inherently responsive to changes in ethnic identity over time; voters can choose in each election what their strongest voting identities ought to be.

In the recent constitutional redesigns for South Africa, Bosnia and Herzegovina, and Fiji, proponents urged adoption of alternative voting. Fiji was the first country to adopt this system for nationwide legislative elections for the intended purpose of minimizing ethnic conflict.[36] Since independence, Fiji has had ongoing tension between the indigenous Fijian (52 percent) and Indian (44 percent) communities. Following a military coup in the late 1980s, an agreement on a new constitution was created in 1997. Donald Horowitz, a leading alternative-voting proponent, directly influenced this Constitution and has claimed the election results in the years since as at least a mixed success.[37] In the first election after this system went into effect, two multi-ethnic coalitions emerged; both made arrangements for sharing seats and exchanging preference votes. And, for the first time, a prime minister from the smaller, Indian community was chosen; Indian-led coalition parties also won seats even in districts with only 20 to 30 percent registered Indian voters.[38]

Unfortunately, matters are not so simple regarding this important first experiment. The elected coalition was overthrown a year later by a military coup. More specifically, a careful study of how voters and parties used the alternative-voting system claimed that the alternative-voting system had not worked as its proponents predicted; in fact, on this interpretation, "far more preference votes were transferred *from* moderate parties *to* the more radical parties than vice versa".[39] The reason is that the moderating effects of alternative voting will emerge only if voters rank candidates (or parties, to the extent voting is based on party affiliation) from more to less ethnically extreme. The assumption that voters will do so is critical to the ethnic moderating justification for alternative voting. In many contexts, that assumption, which is prima facie plausible in societies polarized

---

[36] Jon Fraenkel & Bernard Grofman, *Does the Alternative Vote Foster Moderation in Ethnically Divided Societies? The Case of Fiji*, 39 COMP. POL. STUD. 623, 631 (2006).

[37] It should be noted that the circumstances in which alternative voting can be effective in encouraging votepooling require ethnic heterogeneity in the relevant electoral constituencies and multiple political parties. These circumstances did exist in Fiji.

[38] Fraenkel & Grofman, *supra* note 36, at 633–634.

[39] *Id.* at 647.

along ethnic lines, will no doubt be warranted. But that political preferences will have this structure cannot be taken for granted. According to critics of Horowitz, in Fiji, for reasons perhaps having to do with a peculiar feature of the unique alternative-voting system created, the second choice of voters was not the more moderate party of their ethnic group, but a party chosen for purely tactical reasons.[40] This particular instance does not indict the theory of alternative voting, nor undermine the case for votepooling structures of this type. But the Fijian experiment is a cautionary tale that institutional designers must have knowledge of the local context in projecting how any system is likely to work.[41]

Votepooling structures do remain promising as means of ensuring minority representation and influence in divided societies, while building in enough flexibility so that the system will not entrench ethnic identities needlessly nor be unable to adapt should ethnic differences diminish. In the United States, there has been a good deal of success at the local government level with cumulative voting systems, which are systems closely related to alternative voting.[42] In addition, there are other electoral structures that draw on ideas similar to those that underlie votepooling. Nigeria's distributional requirements for the election of its president, in a presidential system of government, can be viewed as an example. As described in John Boye Ejobowah's chapter, Nigeria has long been divided by three major, geographically concentrated groups.[43] After civil war in the late 1960s, Nigeria moved to a presidential system, to promote nation building and political integration through a unified executive. But to promote cross-ethnic political competition, the constitution required that the president obtain both a majority of national votes and 25 percent of the vote in at least two-thirds of all

---

[40] Fiji's system allowed voters to rank order candidates "above" or "below" the line on the ballot. Below the line, voters simply rank ordered candidates. But the (moderate) parties that designed the system feared that Fijian would only give preferences to Fijian candidates, and Indian voters to Indian candidates. Thus, political parties were required pre-election to file preference lists ranking all candidates in each district. Voters were given the option of just voting for a single candidate, which was called voting "above" the line. If they did so, they would automatically be assigned the preference rankings below their express first choice based on the list the party they had voted for had filed. Ninety-two percent of voters voted above the line. Thus, the vote transfer was not the product of individual voter choice, but of the coalitions the parties selected in advance. According to Fraenkel and Grofman's account, the parties formed these coalitions based not on policy, including policy on ethnic issues, but on purely tactical bases—whatever coalition was most likely to defeat the incumbent officeholders. Thus, as soon as they won office, the coalition, lacking any policy coherence, fragmented. *See id.* at 632, 635 & n.13. Horowitz disputes this account. *See infra* note 41.

[41] Horowitz has responded to Fraenkel and Grofman, asserting that the Fiji evidence still supports the claim that alternative voting generally increases moderation. *See* Donald L. Horowitz, *The Alternative Vote and Interethnic Moderation: A Reply to Fraenkel and Grofman*, 121 PUB. CHOICE 507 (2004); Donald L. Horowitz, *Strategy Takes a Holiday: Fraenkel and Grofman on the Alternative Vote*, 39 COMP. POL. STUD. 652 (2006).

[42] *See, e.g.,* Richard H. Pildes & Kristin A. Donoghue, *Cumulative Voting in the United States*, 1995 U. CHI. LEG. F. 241.

[43] John Boye Ejobowah, *Integrationist and Accommodationist Measures in Nigeria's Constitutional Engineering: Successes and Failures* (in this volume).

the states. According to Ejobowah, this votepooling structure for the presidency has required major parties to court and award office to minority politicians.[44]

This distributional requirement for the presidency is similar to America's much criticized electoral college for presidential elections. However, if the electoral college is considered antiquated, it is partly because the previous state and sectional divisions that once seemed so divisive now seem no longer nearly as meaningful. The electoral college, that is, may be a victim of its own success (as well as the success of other factors that have diminished the power of earlier state and sectionally based identities). In Nigeria, it is easy to understand why regionally based distributional requirements would continue to be means of accommodating ethnic divides while minimizing the entrenchment of ethnic identities. As my discussion of federalism will note, geographically based structures of dealing with ethnic conflict can be particularly adaptable because they leave open the possibility that mobility will erode the meaningfulness of these differences over time. Structures like the American electoral college can recognize the need to take account of certain powerful dimensions of difference without entrenching those differences in the way formal consociational structures do. The problem with America's electoral college is not that it lacked a plausible, integrative justification when first created. It is that the Constitution failed to create an effective mechanism by which the electoral college could be modified or abolished over time, if state-based identities became, as they have, far less divisive and meaningful than they were originally. As I noted at the beginning of this chapter, the electoral college is a prime example of how institutions designed to deal with "ethnic differences" can endure long beyond the point at which the differences that originally motivated them have diminished. That is why institutional designers and negotiators must be attentive to this risk at the outset and search for devices and structures that retain as much flexibility as possible, *given* the need at the moment of state formation to accommodate ethnic differences, to some extent, in the design of political institutions.

Integrationist political spheres and accommodationist cultural spheres

Minority groups often seek recognition of their cultural distinctiveness, as well as some assurance of control over the institutions of control reproduction, such as schools, and recognition of their right to use their own language in various contexts, including, perhaps, in interacting with the government. Cultural and recognition interests of these sorts often underlie demands for power-sharing arrangements in the design of political institutions. Ethnic groups fear that their cultural interests will be overridden unless the state's institutions are built to reflect "their" communities. This fear can generate undifferentiated general demands for accommodationist institutions and policies across the board.

[44] *Id.* at 13.

One strategy for addressing these conflicts that does not entrench ethnic identities into the processes of democratic political competition, with all the attendant consequences, is for the constitutional system to differentiate the political and cultural spheres. The constitution can guarantee specific cultural rights, both negative and positive ones, in a way that accommodates these particular concerns; however, doing so need not require the same structures of accommodation in the design of the processes of electoral competition and representation itself. Instead, the formal political institutions of the state can rest on a more integrationist foundation. Indeed, the very fact that constitutional negotiators are willing to recognize an ethnic group's cultural claims, in spheres such as education, might make it easier to find agreement to design electoral processes and political institutions in this more integrationist manner.

The advantage of this kind of differentiation is that the powerful incentives provided by the structures of political competition will encourage a less ethnicized politics, even as the cultural sphere does recognize distinct cultural claims. Systems designed in this way retain a greater capacity to adapt to changing ethnic self-identifications, since the sphere of formal democratic politics is not built on the basis of the ethnic identities salient at state formation. To the extent constitutional designers believe a constitution must be either accommodationist or integrationist across the board, they miss the opportunity for more subtle differentiations of this sort.

Again, the South African Constitution provides an example. As noted above, that Constitution ensured the possibility, after an interim period, that political institutions would not be structured along ethnic lines. The structure of electoral democracy, in the long-term, was integrationist. At the same time, the Constitution has some of the strongest provisions in any constitution for recognizing the language and cultural rights of minority groups. These are not the conventional negative rights of liberal constitutionalism. For example, in a critical provision the Constitution protects the right "to receive education in the official language or language of [one's] choice".[45] It requires the state to take "positive measures to elevate the status and enhance the use" of eleven officially identified languages.[46] The Constitution also establishes the Commission for the Promotion and Protection of the Rights of Cultural, Religious, and Linguistic Communities.[47] Yet though these provisions reflect a high degree of ethnic accommodation in the cultural sphere, none of it spills over into the way the constitution constructs the political sphere.

Professors Simeon and Murray call the overall constitutional system one of "recognition without empowerment". This is an incisive description of the underlying constitutional vision. Where political circumstances make it a feasible

[45] S. Afr. Const. 1996 § 29(2).
[46] *Id.* § 6.
[47] *Id.* § 185–186.

strategy, this differentiation of the political and cultural spheres—rather than an all-or-nothing approach to accommodation—offers another set of tools for democratic institutional designers to build more flexibility into their systems even as they negotiate amongst ethnically divided groups.

Courts as unwinders of ethnic political bargains

As I noted above, once the framework for democratic elections is designed in ways that create incentives for a more ethnically-oriented form of political competition, it becomes extremely difficult to change that framework down the road, even if the initial conditions that motivated and justified it have changed. This reality is a subset of the larger "iron law" of electoral rules, which is that such rules, once in place, are highly resistant to change. Not only do vested personal and political interests arise around such rules, but in order to change those rules citizens must appeal to the very political actors who owe their political fortunes to the rules at issue. What is missing are intermediate institutions staffed by actors who stand at some remove from existing electoral laws and who could be trusted with the power to determine when circumstances have changed in ways that justify modifying electoral laws created to deal with earlier, different circumstances.

To describe such a power is to suggest how disquieting it is. Nonetheless, there is one institution that can be viewed as playing such a role, at times, in at least some systems. That institution is the courts. The problem is the way the passage of time might make earlier laws, including electoral laws, obsolete in whole or in part.[48] If obsolete is too strong a term, perhaps a better phrase is that changes over time have made some of the law's underlying assumptions no longer as accurate as they were initially. Political institutions generally have a difficult time dealing with the problem of obsolete laws, for reasons of inertia, a problem exacerbated— in the context of the laws of democratic competition—by the self-interested personal and partisan considerations noted above.

I can provide a few accounts of judicial systems that might be seen as exercising this kind of "updating" power.[49] In the American context, the Voting Rights Act was designed to deal with the problem of racially discriminatory voting laws.[50] First enacted in 1965, then significantly amended in 1982, the act had been left largely unchanged since then by Congress (until recent 2006 amendments which I will discuss). Coming out of an era of near complete black exclusion

[48] The problem of electoral laws becoming outdated, yet remaining unchanged, is a subset of the larger problem of the difficulty established the democracies have, generally, in modernizing statutory law. For the argument that courts in general have a proper role to play in using interpretation to "update" older statutes, see Donald C. Langevoort, *Statutory Obsolescence and the Judicial Process: The Revisionist Role of the Courts in Federal Banking Regulation*, 85 MICH. L. REV. 672 (1987).

[49] I have written about these examples at greater length elsewhere. *See* Pildes, *supra* note 1, at 83–101.

[50] The Voting Rights Act of 1965, Pub. L. No. 89–110, 79 Stat. 445 (codified as amended at 42 U.S.C. §§ 1971, 1973, 1973bb-1 (2000)) (U.S.).

from political participation in the South, the need to ensure black political participation and representation was, at these earlier legislative moments, undoubtedly compelling. There was a substantial, well-justified concern that white voters would not vote for black candidates; thus, in electorates with white majorities, black candidates could not be elected, even if the rules for casting a ballot were not discriminatory.

A legislative means for ensuring more black representation which emerged was the creation of what have been called "safe" minority election districts—ones intentionally designed to concentrate minority voters into being the majority, so that they can control election outcomes. This constituted a mild element of consociationalism in the American context: the intentional creation of safe, majority-black election districts (with the concomitant effect of making other districts more white). This technique was effective in its immediate aim; it led to the election of many more minority officeholders.[51]

But by the 2000s, nearly twenty-five years after the United States Congress had last revisited the issue, a variety of questions had arisen about whether various circumstances had changed enough to undermine the need for the continuation without any modification at all of these racially-defined election districts—structures that had always been justified as a "second best" approach, one made necessary by the practical difficulty of more directly breaking down racial differences enough so that white voters would vote for black candidates. Despite the time that had passed since the policy had been adopted, and the intervening changes, Congress evinced no inclination to revisit these issues. That is not surprising, given that the issues are divisive and all the sitting members of the House had been elected under this system.

Faced with the absence of any legislative attention to these policies, the Supreme Court, in a series of decisions in the 1990s and 2000s cut back a bit on the scope of the consociationalism embedded in these policies.[52] Employing the Constitution's Equal Protection clause, the Supreme Court acknowledged the legality of some degree of ethnic accommodation policy; the Court endorsed the use of race to design election districts when polarized voting precluded minorities from being elected. At the same time, however, the Court also imposed constitutional limits on the extent to which election districts could be intentionally designed for this purpose. Thus, constitutional boundaries were imposed on the extent of permissible accommodation. Even more interestingly, the Court began to reinterpret the earlier legislation in a way that read more flexibility into it. Where earlier decisions had treated the obligation to draw "safe" minority-controlled election districts as a fairly unyielding one, recent decisions permitted these districts to be unwound

[51] For the relevant data, see Richard H. Pildes, *The Politics of Race*, 108 Harv. L. Rev. 1359 (1995).
[52] *See, e.g., Georgia v. Ashcroft*, 539 U.S. 461 (2003); *Holder v. Hall*, 512 U.S. 74 (1994); *Shaw v. Reno*, 509 U.S. 630 (1993). *See generally* Richard H. Pildes, *The Decline of Legally Mandated Minority Representation*, 68 Ohio St. L.J. (forthcoming).

a bit in the service of recognizing or fostering a greater capacity for the interethnic politics today. These decisions could be viewed as reflecting a judicial recognition that the conditions that warranted more "accommodationist" policies when the United States was emerging from an era of racial exclusion ought to be modified forty years after the law was first passed and twenty-five years since Congress last revisited it.

A similar view might be thought to animate a decision by the Constitutional Court of Bosnia and Herzegovina, a court that the Dayton Peace Agreement had created for the two entities forged out of the breakup of the former Yugoslavia, the Republika Srpska (where most Serbs live) and the Federation of Bosnia-Herzegovina (where most Croats and Bosniaks live).[53] The original agreement appeared to leave the legal power to define their respective "constituent peoples" to each of these entities, which had done so in ethnically exclusive ways. Nonetheless, the court rejected this strong form of consociationalism and held that even though these entities were created to accommodate profound ethnic differences, they did not have the power to constitute themselves in ethnically exclusive terms.[54] This judicial decision is even more striking than the American ones, for not only were the ethnic issues involved more explosive, but far less time had passed between the original political deal, which recognized a need for ethnic accommodation, and the Court's willingness to unwind at least one element of that deal.

To be sure, there are serious normative and pragmatic concerns with courts playing the role of institutional agents for transitioning away, even modestly, from ethnic accommodation in the design of democratic institutions. Normatively, the legitimacy of courts in partially undoing political agreements reflected in legislation is problematic, although perhaps less so the longer the interval between the original agreement and the court's action. Pragmatically, to the extent judicial interventions of these sorts rest, in part, on the view that circumstances have changed enough to justify moves toward a more integrationist political sphere, they require exquisitely charged judgments. Should a court be wrong about the extent of change, its decision could fuel ethnic conflicts.

At the same time, there is at least one less-obvious potential advantage to judicial action. When political institutions address issues at the intersection of ethnic conflict and the design of democratic institutions, it might be that placing these issues in the political arena tends to be more divisive and polarizing than when courts take similar steps. Judicial processes are often less rhetorically charged;

[53] The Dayton Peace Accords on Bosnia (1995), *available at* <http://www.state.gov/www/regions/eur/bosnia/bosagree.html>.
[54] Case No. U–05/98, Request for Evaluation of the Constitutionality of Certain Provisions of the Constitution of Republika Srpska and the Constitution of the Federation of Bosnia and Herzegovina, Partial Decision pt. 3, ¶ 61 (July 1, 2000). *See generally* Anna Morawiec Mansfield, *Ethnic but Equal: The Quest for a New Democratic Order in Bosnia and Herzegovina*, 103 COLUM. L. REV. 2052 (2003).

moreover, court decisions have less visibility. In addition, while the losing side might blame the judges, that can be less inflammatory than blaming "the people". The main justification for judicial unwinding of the sort described here must be in similarly pragmatic terms, namely, the absence of other institutions likely to take responsibility for this role. My aim here is not to defend the legitimacy of courts doing so, but to point out that courts in several systems can be understood to have taken on precisely such a role.

Federalism and territorially-based devolution

Federalism or territorial devolution can take many forms, but, increasingly, it is becoming one of among the most important structural and constitutional mechanisms for dealing with ethnically divided societies. Writing in 1984, Daniel J. Elazar observed that the "federalist revolution is one of the hidden revolutions of our times, despite the fact that few have paid attention to it".[55] What was true then has become only more so, since. Federalism increasingly serves as a proxy for enabling minorities to experience some degree of autonomy, security, and recognition. Indeed, while federalism historically arose when once-autonomous units decided to join together, federalism in recent years has also been used to disaggregate previously centralized regimes—a novel use suggesting the modern appeal of the federal approach. A proper synthesis of experience with federalism would require at least a chapter of its own. For reasons of space, I will limit myself here to four brief points.

First, from the perspective of the dynamic approach advocated here, federalism is particularly attractive as compared with the more overtly consociational features conventionally, and frequently, used in divided societies. This may be so whether or not the federal units as initially constituted are homogenous or more intermixed with respect to the country's salient ethnic dimensions. As a form of power sharing or power dividing, federalism has the virtue of not formally designing state institutions on the basis of ethnic identities as such. This is in strong contrast to consociational arrangements, such as those in Lebanon's National Pact from 1943 to the civil war of the mid-1970s, which required that the president be a Maronite, the prime minister a Sunni, the speaker of the House a Shiite, the vice-president a Greek Orthodox, and so on.[56]

Most importantly, not only is federalism only a proxy for ethnic group identity, but it is a particularly malleable proxy. Federalism might ensure vulnerable minorities some degree of autonomy and protection at the outset of state formation. However, if ethnic identities diminish over time as a source of conflict, individuals will move between units (as long as free movement is guaranteed) in a way that makes territory and identity correspond less and less directly. Movement

[55] Daniel J. Elazar, *The Role of Federalism in Political Integration, in* FEDERALISM AND POLITICAL INTEGRATION 13, 28 (Daniel J. Elazar ed., Univ. Press Am. 1984).
[56] The Ta'if Accord, 1989, art. II(6) (Leb.).

and changing demographics provide a built-in mechanism that enables a democratic system to be responsive to diminished ethnic conflict over time. As Carl J. Friedrich, a leading modern theorist of federalism, noted, "[t]he study of social structure in relation to federalism has, therefore, helped us to understand better the dynamic nature of federal orders, to look upon a federal system as subject to continual change, rather than a static design fixed forever in an immutable distribution of factors".[57] Indeed, there are nations originally designed as formally federal in structure that are considered "non-federal" today because, despite these federal structures, the relevant political actors (political leaders, parties, interest groups, voters and the like) view politics overwhelmingly in national terms; Austria, Germany, and the United States are the three countries typically classified as formal federations with non-federal societies.[58] It is true that federal systems will entrench geographically-based distinctions long after they have become less meaningful than they were initially, as has been true in the United States. But that is better than entrenching ethnic identities themselves, which are likely to be far more divisive.

Second, to the extent actual political power is devolved from the center to the federal units, there may be at least two particular benefits with respect to defusing potential ethnic conflicts. One is that pressure is taken off competition over the control of institutions and policies at the national level. Federalism can be a form of gag rule, in which competing parties agree not to contest certain divisive issues at the national level. By removing those issues from the national level, the stability and acceptance of national institutions can be enhanced. To the extent that divisive issues are resolved through competition at the unit level instead, those resolutions are more segmented and confined. In addition, enhanced competition in units differently constituted than the national political arena can have other benefits, as will be noted in a moment.

Third, there is a longstanding debate about whether, from various perspectives, it is better in various contexts that the units in a federal structure be ethnically homogenous or intermixed. As a practical matter, the options are often sharply constrained, including by whether the relevant ethnic groups are geographically concentrated or not. But leaving the broader issue to the side, it is important to recognize that federalism can contribute to democratic legitimacy and stability in divided societies regardless of whether the units are ethnically homogenous or not. If the units are homogenous, competition for power at that level often will bring out conflicts *within* the particular ethnic group along lines other than ethnicity (or the dimension of ethnicity that divides the society more generally). This can help diminish the more profound and potentially more explosive conflicts at the center. As Horowitz puts it, where ethnic groups are geographically concentrated, devolution can diminish ethnic conflict not because it provides group autonomy,

---

[57] CARL J. FRIEDRICH, TRENDS OF FEDERALISM IN THEORY AND PRACTICE 54 (Praeger 1968).
[58] *See, e.g.,* Jan Erk, *Austria: A Federation without Federalism*, 34 PUBLIUS 1, 2 (2004).

but because once power is devolved, the very idea of "the group" can become more difficult to maintain.[59] Homogenous units, differently constituted in comparison with the nationwide ethnic configuration, also can provide opportunities for distributional goods, such as jobs, that minorities might fear will not be available to them in a unitary state. Heterogeneous units, of course, can generate incentives for interethnic coalitions and accommodations that may not exist at the center.

To be sure, federal structures that address ethnic conflicts may take various forms. The extent to which mobility over time, in particular, is a realistic prospect can vary with the social foundation of the federal units as well as the nature of their formal powers. Federalism can be based on linguistic divisions, for example, as in Canada, Belgium, and India. To the extent the linguistic basis is merely de facto and not further entrenched in any additional policies of the federal units, systems of this sort might retain a meaningful capacity for movement between the units, particularly for the second generation. But if the federal units have the additional power to try to lock-in a dominant language through de jure requirements—by insisting that education only be in a particular language or through other "official-language" policies—then the effective capacity of residents to move between units might be expected to be diminished. We do not have enough comparative data on actual mobility within different federal systems to know how effective mobility varies among differently structured federal regimes.

Fourth and finally, American scholars frequently underappreciate the contribution federalism can make to managing ethnic conflict. Federalism's tainted history in the United States, linked to slavery and racial segregation, makes it difficult to recognize the extent to which federalism has been an essential institutional means elsewhere for bringing about political integration, stability, and accommodation between diverse groups, including in ethnically divided societies. Modern federal systems, however, are more likely to ensure that national institutions, including courts, are given the power to ensure that fundamental rights are protected at all levels. There are no general acontextual rules for how best to structure federal arrangements in all contexts—how many units to create, with what powers, composed in what ways—and careful examination of which forms have worked best in which contexts cannot be undertaken here. But federalism offers particularly promising opportunities for institutionalizing the dynamic approach urged here to designing democratic institutions and in ways that accommodate, without needlessly entrenching, ethnic divides.

3. A dynamic perspective on institutional design

Designing democratic institutions to address ethnic conflicts has become the most pressing problem in modern constitutional design. Several reasons account

---

[59] DONALD H. HOROWITZ, ETHNIC GROUPS IN CONFLICT 627 (Univ. Cal. Press 1985).

for this fact. In the third wave of democracy that has emerged since 1989, democracy has been viewed as the appropriate institutional solution even for societies previously wracked by violent, internal group conflicts. With forced population relocation no longer widely considered legitimate, the aspiration has been to deploy democratic institutions to stabilize heterogeneous societies, including post-conflict ones. In addition, the Cold War fueled a state-strengthening dynamic, with the United States and the Soviet Union building up centralized authorities, particularly through military aid. With the end of the Cold War and the softening of central authority, latent ethnic differences are more easily mobilized and given expression. Even more established democracies have seen the rise of ethnic identities and political claims, whether in the United Kingdom, Spain, Latin America, or, with increased demands for group recognition of African-Americans, Hispanics, and others, in the United States.

Thus far, much academic analysis and practical institutional design have taken too static an approach to these issues. Ethnic identities can be fluid, with the incentives that the structure of political competition creates being a particularly powerful force for mobilizing those identities along one dimension or another. There is (or can be, in many contexts) a dynamic relationship between the design of democratic institutions and the ethnic identities expressed. To the extent that democratic institutions being designed today must accommodate ethnic differences for practical reasons, institutional designers must avoid thinking only in terms of the structure of those differences at the immediate moment. The aim should be to accommodate those differences, while building in as much flexibility as possible to enable democratic institutions to be responsive to changes in ethnic identifications over time. In this chapter, I have analyzed some of the most promising means of doing so.

PART III
CASE-STUDIES

7

Indonesia's quasi-federalist approach: Accommodation amid strong integrationist tendencies

*Jacques Bertrand**

1. Introduction

Over the past decade, Indonesia's institutions have been gradually transformed in response to ethnic tensions. After the fall of President Suharto's authoritarian regime in 1998, which had endured for more than thirty years, the Constitution was amended and new laws were passed to democratize Indonesia's political system. As part of this democratization, steps were taken to increase the flexibility of the political system in the face of pressure in favor of decentralization, devolution of power, and accommodation of demands from ethnonationalist groups in East Timor, Aceh, and Papua.[1]

These changes have occurred against the backdrop of a long history that emphasized strong, integrationist strategies. Indonesian nationalism, underpinning the creation of the Indonesian state, was premised on building a single nation from the diverse peoples of the former Dutch East Indies. The design of the state was grounded in a strong republican integrationism, which gave way, over time, to assimilationist tendencies.[2] For the most part, this integrationist

* Associate Professor, Department of Political Science, University of Toronto. Research for this project was funded by the Social Sciences and Humanities Research Council of Canada and the United States Institute of Peace. Email: jacques.bertrand@utoronto.ca

[1] In this chapter, absent an explicit distinction, "Papua" refers to the current provinces of Papua and West Irian Jaya. Being the western part of the island of New Guinea (the eastern part belongs to the sovereign nation of Papua New Guinea), this area was known as West New Guinea when it was a Dutch colony. After its cession to Indonesian rule in 1962, the Indonesian government called it "West Irian", until formal integration in 1969, when it named the new province "Irian Jaya". With the implementation of the Special Autonomy Law of 2001, it was renamed "Papua". In 2003, it was split into two provinces, with the central and eastern parts remaining "Papua", while the western portion was designated as "West Irian Jaya".

[2] For a clarification of republican integrationism, see John McGarry, Brendan O'Leary & Richard Simeon, *Integration or Accommodation? The Enduring Debate in Conflict Regulation* (in this volume).

strategy worked. Of the diverse constellation of peoples across the archipelago, only a handful have ever mobilized along ethnic lines, which attests to the success of the revolutionary struggle in creating a unifying bond and, subsequently, a system of rewards that benefited ambitious elites from various regions. Where resistance occurred, it was treated as a threat to national unity and harshly repressed.

The Constitution of 1945—drafted hastily to declare independence, in the wake of the retreating Japanese occupation forces and in anticipation of the returning Dutch—embodied the concept of a single nation and gave little recognition to ethnic diversity.[3] This Constitution was inspired by organicist theories that espoused strongly centralized, integrative mechanisms tying together state and society.[4] This integralist state became the basis of Indonesia's authoritarian state when the Constitution of 1945 was readopted in the late 1950s; it was retained after the military takeover of 1965, which launched the so-called New Order regime of Suharto.[5] When that regime crumbled in 1998, the 1945 Constitution was again retained, although it was amended, and legislation adopted to introduce ethnic accommodation and democratic principles. Despite the state's considerable history as a centralized state, the legislation on Aceh and Papua has gone to some lengths to accommodate ethnic demands.

In both Aceh and Papua, ethnonationalist movements have sought independence from the Indonesian state since the 1970s; however, they were denied recognition and systematically repressed, all in accordance with the logic of the Indonesian integrationist state. These movements resurfaced when the New Order regime collapsed. The Free Aceh Movement resumed a military insurgency, which had been its main strategy since its creation in the mid-1970s. At the same time, however, a strong civilian movement arose to demand greater autonomy for Aceh. Papua's armed Free Papua Movement also has remained active but has ceded the spotlight to a large and vocal civilian movement, since the latter has garnered vast support among the Papuan population. The Indonesian government did not abandon its repression of these groups, but it came around, nonetheless, to enacting successive pieces of legislation that, to some extent, accommodate the demands of the Acehnese and Papuans. The latest legislation concerning Aceh, Law no. 11, 2006 on Acehnese government, emerged from the Helsinki memorandum of understanding signed between the Indonesian government and the Free Aceh Movement on August 15, 2005;[6] it constitutes the first

---

[3] Undang-Undang Dasar Republik Indonesia 1945 [The Constitution of the Republic of Indonesia of 1945] (Original Version) [hereinafter Indon, Const. (Original)] pmbl., arts. 1, 18 (there is no explicit recognition of ethnic groups, article 18 does distinguish among regions, but regions do not necessarily coincide with the territorial homeland of ethnic groups).

[4] *See infra* text accompanying notes 36–38.

[5] David Bourchier, *Totalitarianism and The "National Personality": Recent Controversy About the Philosophical Basis of the Indonesian State, in* Imagining Indonesia: Cultural Politics and Political Culture 174 (Barbara Martin-Schiller & James William Schiller eds., Ohio Univ. Ctr. for Int'l Stud. Press 1997).

[6] Undang-Undang Republik Indonesia Nomor 11 Tahun 2006 Tentang Pemerintahan Aceh [Law No. 11, 2006 of the Republic of Indonesia on Aceh Government] [hereinafter *Law on Aceh Government*].

peace agreement ever reached between the two parties. With regard to Papua, Special Autonomy Law no. 21, 2001 has been in place since January 2002.[7]

What should we expect from these rapid and significant changes? The litera-ture on accommodation and integration is divided concerning the conditions leading to stability.[8] In this chapter, I make the claim that the move away from a highly integrationist strategy to an accommodative one has contributed signifi-cantly to a reduction of conflict in Papua and Aceh. In both instances, conflict had been fueled in the past by highly integrationist strategies that were precur-sors to repression. Integrationist strategies generally were successful in the rest of Indonesia, but in the provinces of Aceh and Papua, where they included the adoption of repressive policies meant to preserve the integrationist whole, they proved counterproductive. By changing course to accommodate demands for autonomy, making special provisions for these regions, the Indonesian state has reduced group mobilization, military or otherwise. As I will explain, this flexibil-ity promises more stability than the previous, more oppressive approach.

Nevertheless, there are some reasons to reserve judgment regarding the general amelioration. The implementation of the Aceh peace accord has gone smoothly enough. In contrast with past initiatives that failed to ease tensions and resolve the conflict,[9] partly because of inadequate follow-up and partly because of lacu-nae in their drafting, the Aceh accord is a specific and strongly worded agree-ment that has allowed the disbanding of the Free Aceh Movement's combatants and its transformation of the organization into a political, rather than military, organization. For Papua, the Special Autonomy Law of 2001 has been less effect-ive. It was implemented over the objections of many Papuan leaders who made demands for a stronger degree of accommodation and greater redress of histor-ical grievances.[10] In addition, there have been many complaints that the Special Autonomy Law has not been properly implemented, and that it has been under-mined by the subsequent adoption of seemingly contradictory laws.[11] In 2005,

[7] Undang-Undang Republik Indonesia Nomor 21 Tahun 2001 Tentang Otonomi Khusus Bagi Provinsi Papua [Law No. 21, 2001 of the Republic of Indonesia on Special Autonomy for the Province of Papua] [hereinafter *Law on Special Autonomy for Papua*].

[8] McGarry, O'Leary & Simeon, *supra* note 2.

[9] Among various laws that were intended to reduce tensions and resolve the conflict with Aceh, but were never properly implemented or were rejected for their ineffectual response to popular demands, the most important was Undang-Undang Republik Indonesia nomor 18, tahun 2001 tentang Otonomi Khusus bagi provinsi Daerah Istimewa Aceh Sebagai Provinsi Nanggroe Aceh Darussalam [Law no. 18, 2001 of the Republic of Indonesia on Special Autonomy for the Province of the Special Region of Aceh as the Province of Nanggroe Aceh Darussalam]. There was a law that had sought to invoke Islamic law to counter the Free Aceh Movement's demands. *See* Undang Undang Republik Indonesia nomor 44 tahun 1999 tentang penyelenggaraan keistimewaan propinsi Daerah Istimewa Aceh [Law no. 44, 1999 of the Republic of Indonesia on the implemen-tation of the "special" status of the Special Region of Aceh].

[10] See *Indonesia Flashpoints: Papua*, BBC News, June 28, 2004, *available at* <http://news.bbc.co.uk/2/hi/asia-pacific/3815909.stm> (last visited July 19, 2007), for Papuan demands for a legit-imate referendum on independence and redress of Indonesia's past centralization of wealth taken from Papuan natural resources.

[11] For example, in 2003 President Megawati issued a decree to revive the law dividing Papua into three separate provinces, which would contradict the spirit of extending autonomy to all of Papua,

for example, more than 10,000 people joined leaders of the Dewan Adat Papua (the Papuan Customary Assembly) for an official ceremony that purported to "return" the Special Autonomy Law of 2001 to the central government.[12]

Perhaps most importantly, the Special Autonomy Law of Papua lacks precision in comparison with the Aceh law. For instance, although the Special Autonomy law creates a new assembly to represent Papua customary groups (the Majelis Rakyat Papua, or Papuan People's Assembly), its role is not clearly differentiated from that of the legislature. While the law on Aceh has whole sections that provide oversight on security forces, there are no such sections in the Special Autonomy Law for Papua. Finally, on fiscal matters, the Aceh law sets forth, in reference to various levels of government, the categories of expenditure, mechanisms of allocation, and the means for calculating percentages, whereas the Special Autonomy Law for Papua only specifies percentages of allocations without sufficient precision as to which portions of the fiscal pie will be allocated to which sector.

The spirit of the Indonesian Constitution and many of its institutions continue to support an integrationist approach. As the following section shows, the history of integrationism in Indonesia has created powerful behavioral norms that pull the Indonesian political elite persistently in the direction of supporting strong measures to preserve national unity rather than accommodating diversity. These tendencies have not disappeared and may render some of the recent institutional accommodation meaningless, if various weaknesses are exploited.

2. From integration to accommodation in Indonesia: Decentralization and "special" autonomy

Theorists on ethnic conflict and institutional design fall into two camps— supporters of accommodation and those who favor integration. As McGarry, O'Leary, and Simeon explain, integration favors a single identity that is

especially since the decree made no specification as to the applicability of autonomy to the three provinces. *See* Undang Undang Republik Indonesia nomor 45 tahun 1999 tentang pembentukan propinsi Irian Jaya Tengah, Propinsi Irian Jaya Barat, Kabupaten Paniai, Kabupaten Mimika, Kabupaten Puncak Jaya, dan Kota Sorong [Law no. 45, 1999 of the Republic of Indonesia on the Formation of the Province of Central Irian Jaya, the Province of West Irian Jaya, the Regency of Paniai, the Regency of Mimika, the Regency of Puncak Jaya, and the city of Sorong]. *See also* Instruksi Presiden Republic Indonesia nomor 1 tahun 2003 tentang percepatan pelaskanaan Undang-undang Republik Indonesia nomor 45 tahun 1999 tentang pembentukan propinsi Irian Jaya Tengah, Propinsi Irian Jaya Barat, Kabupaten Paniai, Kabupaten Mimika, Kabupaten Puncak Jaya, dan Kota Sorong [Presidential Decree no. 1, 2003 on the acceleration of implementation of Law no. 45, 1999 of the Republic of Indonesia on the Formation of the Province of Central Irian Jaya, the Province of West Irian Jaya, the Regency of Paniai, the Regency of Mimika, the Regency of Puncak Jaya, and the City of Sorong].

[12] *UU Otsus Papua dikembalikan* [*The law on Special Autonomy for Papua returned*], SUARA PEMBARUAN (Indon.), Aug. 12, 2005, *available at* <http://www.suarapembaruan.com/News/2005/08/12/Utama/ut01.htm> (last visited Aug. 14, 2007). While lacking any legal status, the Dewan Adat Papua enjoyed broad support, as evidenced by large turnouts during the various congresses that it organized in 2000.

coterminous with the state; accommodation, on the other hand, leads to flexible legal arrangements that recognize and empower ethnic diversity in a variety of ways.[13] According to integrationists, stability is fostered by using institutional strategies to relegate collective cultural diversities to the private realm while, at the same time, recognizing equal rights and citizenship for all individuals in the state. The accommodationists reply that such strategies are more likely to produce instability because group differences, although not fixed or primordial, neverthe-less remain relatively inflexible in many circumstances. They suggest, instead, various strategies to foster accommodation, including multiculturalism, consoci-ation, or pluralist federation.

Mixed strategies are a common feature of polities and, in the case of Indonesia, a most promising one. As I will show, given the structure of ethnic politics in Indonesia, many accommodationist strategies, such as consociation, are inappro-priate. Federation would be particularly relevant, given the territorial concentra-tion of most ethnic groups in the country. What has been adopted, however, is a quasi-federal form of decentralization, designed to introduce flexibility without threatening the integrationist core. Born of a strong Indonesian nationalist move-ment, the Indonesian republic was conceived as a unitary state much concerned with resisting disintegrative tendencies. Faced with several challenges to the uni-tary state in the first decade after independence, the government reinforced its integrative measures. Nominal concessions were made to extend recognition or representation to ethnic groups; however, in practice, these had little effect, since other actions were taken to strengthen the power of the central state.

Only recently have significant measures been taken to decentralize and devolve power to regional units that coincide, in some instances, with ethnic groups. The provinces of Central and East Java, for example, correspond to a substantial portion of the territory occupied by Javanese. The province of West Java is mainly occupied by the Sundanese and that of West Sumatra, by the Minangkabau. The new province of Gorontalo was created to give more power to the Muslim Gorontalese, whose area had been included previously in the Christian Minahasan-dominated province of North Sulawesi. While there is no formal recognition of the ethnic character of regional units, the new decentral-ization laws have had the effect of giving more power to ethnic groups. Thus, the Indonesian state has moved from a strong unitarist approach toward a quasi-federal posture; meanwhile, it has resisted any tendency toward a pluralist fed-eration, except in the cases of Aceh and Papua. This asymmetrical organization is probably the most stabilizing feature of the Indonesian polity, preserving its successful integrationism for most of its territory and introducing accommoda-tion where integration would fail. The arrangement falls short of federacy, which would likely be even more stabilizing in this particular case.

Indonesia is one of the most diverse countries in the world. As the fourth most populous country, with the world's largest Muslim population, it has more than

---

[13] McGarry, O'Leary & Simeon, *supra* note 2.

fifty ethnic groups scattered across an archipelago where more than 450 languages have been identified.[14] While no group clearly dominates, the most powerful is the Javanese, constituting some 60 percent of the population. Other major groups include the Sundanese, Minangkabau, Acehnese, Papuans, Balinese, and Bugis-Makassarese.[15] It was largely the Indonesian experience that inspired Benedict Anderson to theorize about the constructed nature of nationalism, particularly in the "last wave" of nationalism that swept across the developing world. In his view, the emergence of nationalism was related intrinsically to the emergence of a shared experience of colonialism by elites from different groups, as well as a common vernacular language that reinforced this common experience.[16]

Prior to Dutch colonialism, there had been no empire, state, or large political community from which an "Indonesian" core could be derived. As the colonial power constructed an Indonesian nation that unified the various ethnic groups within the Dutch East Indies, Indonesian nationalism grew out of the emerging consciousness of an elite that shared a common experience under colonial rule.[17] The Dutch educated people from various areas of the archipelago to serve in its colonial bureaucracy. Shared experiences and common points of reference as the result of service in the colonial administration strengthened the affinity among them; at the same time, they supported the spread and development of the Malay lingua franca.

Malay provided a common language for commerce and communication that created a bond among elites from around the archipelago. Although Islam was also a fairly common cultural characteristic, it was not sufficient to provide the basis for a truly unifying nationalism as there were areas of Indonesia with significantly large Christian communities, which enthusiastically adhered to a nationalist movement based on a common language. The adoption in 1921 of Malay, renamed Indonesian, as the official language of the movement gave it a cultural dimension that distinguished the new Indonesian elites from the colonial rulers and created a stronger basis for a common bond.[18] Language was more effective

---

[14] The National Language Institute issued a linguistic map of Indonesia in 1972, which counted 418 different languages across the archipelago. There is some debate about the extent to which some of these languages are dialects of others, and many languages had not yet been counted in Irian Jaya, but the number is a fair estimate. *See, e.g.,* P.W.J. Nababan, *Language in Education: The Case of Indonesia,* 37 INT'L REV. EDUC. 115 (1991).

[15] LEO SURYADINATA, EVI NURVIDYA ARIFIN & ARIS ANANTA, INDONESIA'S POPULATION: ETHNICITY AND RELIGION IN A CHANGING POLITICAL LANDSCAPE (Inst. of S.E. Asian Stud., Indonesia's Population Series No. 1, 2003).

[16] *See* BENEDICT ANDERSON, IMAGINED COMMUNITIES: REFLECTIONS ON THE ORIGIN AND SPREAD OF NATIONALISM 116–134 (Verso 1983).

[17] *Id.* Anderson's argument about the development of a nationalist consciousness arising out of shared colonial experience and a common language is the most convincing explanation of the strong bond that Indonesian nationalism forged among the diverse peoples of the archipelago. *See also* GEORGE McTURNAN KAHIN, NATIONALISM AND REVOLUTION IN INDONESIA (Cornell Univ. Press 1955) (detailing events leading to the creation of a nationalist coalition that spearheaded the revolution and the creation of the Indonesian state).

[18] ANDERSON, *supra* note 16, at 132–133.

than Islam in this regard, in large measure, because such religious identification would have deterred Christians from joining the movement. As a leader in the movement, Soekarno, who would be the first president of Indonesia, was very much aware of the need to underplay the role of Islam in order to gain support for a new state from Christian areas of the archipelago, where he had spent a significant amount of time.[19]

Before long, Soekarno gained ascendancy as the leader of the nationalist movement, which was organized primarily by the Indonesian Nationalist Party. He was particularly skilful at uniting diverse elements within the movement, including Islamists and communists, who struggled together against colonial rule but whose visions of an independent state were based on competing and quite disparate ideologies.[20] The Japanese conquest and occupation of Indonesia during the Second World War[21] gave support to the nationalists and, unintentionally, prepared them for self-government. Recognizing the popularity of Soekarno and other nationalist leaders, the Japanese recruited them to a Central Advisory Board, promising them self-government in exchange for their collaboration with the Japanese war effort. In addition, by training an Indonesian militia to help Japanese troops protect Indonesian territory from an Allied invasion, the Japanese laid the basis for the formation of the Indonesian army, which would fight the returning Dutch administration after the Japanese defeat in 1945.[22] As a result, former leaders of the Nationalist Party, with Soekarno at their helm, were well placed to broker an agreement among various elements in the movement when, in that same year, it came time to declare independence and to adopt a constitution.

The 1945 Constitution, drafted in haste in the dying days of the Japanese occupation, laid the basis for the current state of Indonesia. In the vacuum being created by the Japanese departure and in anticipation of the arrival of Allied troops, there was a sense of urgency around declaring independence and forming a new government to forestall the resumption of Dutch colonial administration. An Independence Preparatory Committee formed, led by Soekarno and dominated by nationalist leaders; it appointed a commission from among its members to draft a constitution.[23] Supomo, its main architect, advocated the adoption of integralism or organicism, "a theory in which the state was committed not to individual

---

[19] *See* B.J. BOLAND, THE STRUGGLE OF ISLAM IN MODERN INDONESIA 27–35 (Verhandelingen Van Het Koninklijk Instituut Voor Taal-, Land- En Volkenkunde No. 59 [Essays of The Royal Institute for the Study of Language, Country and People No. 59] Nijhoff 1971); on the role of language, see Jacques Bertrand, *Language Policy and the Promotion of National Identity in Indonesia*, *in* FIGHTING WORDS: LANGUAGE POLICY AND ETHNIC RELATIONS IN ASIA 263 (Michael Edward Brown & Sumit Ganguly eds., MIT Press 2003).
[20] KAHIN, *supra* note 17, at 90–133.
[21] The Japanese occupation of Indonesia during the Second World War lasted from 1942 to 1945.
[22] KAHIN, *supra* note 17, at 106–110.
[23] *Id.* at 134–138.

rights or particular classes but to society conceived as an organic whole".[24] This principle, much influenced by totalitarian ideas and the examples of Japanese imperialism and the Third Reich, guided the writing of the Constitution. With a few notable exceptions, such as article 28, which guarantees the freedom of association and expression, the Constitution rejected individual protections as well as checks on the executive.[25] It created the basis for a strong presidency and conceived the institutional framework of the state as an organic whole with strong powers to control all sectors of society.

The original Constitution of 1945 stated that Indonesia was a unitary state and a republic.[26] Ultimate power was vested in the People's Consultative Assembly (Majelis Permusyawaratan Rakyat, or MPR), which was composed of members of the People's Representative Assembly (Dewan Perwakilan Rakyat, or DPR), as well as representatives from regions and functional groups (representing defined economic and social categories, such as farmers and veterans). Having functional groups represented in the MPR, the highest organ of the state, gave that body some claim to social inclusiveness.[27] The president, who was selected by the MPR, was vested with executive power and was accountable to the legislature, in turn, only with regard to declaring war or negotiating treaties with other states.[28] Bills adopted by the legislature would become law only upon approval by the president, who had ultimate veto power.[29] The president could issue regulations to replace laws in exceptional circumstances, subject to subsequent legislative approval.[30] The power to declare states of emergency belonged solely to the president.[31]

With regard to administrative and political divisions, the Constitution stated that they should follow the logic of administrative hierarchy (*susunan pemerintahan*), keeping in mind both the principles of deliberation (*musyawarah*) in the governmental system as well as well as respect for the "hereditary rights of special territories". The Constitution also forbade the designation of any subdivisions as "states" within the unitary state of Indonesia.[32] It made no mention of any special representation for particular regions or ethnic groups. The principle of the unitary state was clearly enshrined as superior to any accommodation of Indonesia's ethnically diverse communities.

[24] Bourchier, *supra* note 5, at 161.
[25] *Id.* at 161–162.
[26] INDON. CONST. (ORIGINAL) pmbl.
[27] *Id.* arts. 1, 2, 4.
[28] *Id.*
[29] *Id.* art. 20.
[30] *Id.* art. 22.
[31] *Id.* art. 12.
[32] *Id.* art. 18; *id.* §5, ch. VI (section 5, titled Elucidation of the Constitution, contains annotations explicating the various articles and thus more clearly defining the parameters of the laws in question. In this case it is only the annotations to article 18, not the article itself, that forbid the establishment of regions "with the character of 'states'" within the jurisdiction of Indonesia. But the annotations are nonetheless binding).

The revolution of 1945–1949 reinforced the nationalist credo of unity. When the Dutch returned in 1945, they faced the Republic of Indonesia, which had declared independence but did not yet control all of the former territory of the Dutch East Indies.[33] As the Dutch regained control over large parts of the archipelago, they set about creating states, which corresponded to large ethnic groups, such as Pasundan in West Java for the Sundanese, in order to undermine the nationalist appeal of the Indonesian republic. In addition to armed struggle, the Dutch and the republic engaged in negotiations under United Nations supervision and reached several agreements regarding Indonesian independence, including one that provided for the creation of a federation—the United States of Indonesia—in which the constituent units were the Dutch-created states, with the Republic of Indonesia as the largest unit of the federation.[34] When the Dutch finally departed a few months later, Indonesia gained its independence, and the Republic of the United States of Indonesia was inaugurated, in December 1949. However, this federation lasted only nine months before a provisional constitution was adopted that replaced it with a single, unitary republic. Most of the Dutch-created states subscribed to this model.

The enduring conception of a unitary state derives from the revolutionary period. Federalism—rejected at that time, given its association with Dutch tactics—continued to be viewed, over the years, as divisive and dangerous.[35] The republican ideal and the unitary state, on the other hand, were regarded, henceforth, as the most suitable institutional expression of the unity of the Indonesian nation, and so have been retained to this day.

A second effect of the revolution was the organizational consolidation of the nationalist forces. When the Dutch withdrew, the government of the republic, led by the Nationalist Party with Soekarno at its helm, was uncontested as the leadership of the new unified Indonesia. Although recognizing the need to compromise and form coalitions with other parties, the Nationalist Party and Soekarno nevertheless had gained ascendancy.[36] The speed with which Dutch-created states disbanded and joined the republic confirmed and solidified this strength. In addition, the armed forces enjoyed strong support among the population for their role as a revolutionary power, giving them the aura of legitimate defenders

---

[33] *See generally* A. ARTHUR SCHILLER, THE FORMATION OF FEDERAL INDONESIA, 1945–1949 (W. van Hoeve 1955). The brief resistance from the RMS movement (Republic of South Moluccas movement) was quickly defeated by the Indonesian Armed Forces in 1950. The movement was largely seen as gaining its strongest support from former soldiers of the Dutch colonial army, rather than from a broad-based movement among Ambonese and other Moluccans, most of whom supported the republic.

[34] U.N. Sec. Council, U.N. Comm'n for Indon., *Appendices to the Special Report to the Security Council on the Round Table Conference,* at 22, U.N. Doc. S/1417/Add.1 (Nov. 14, 1949).

[35] Hans Antlöv, *Federations-of-Intent in Indonesia, 1945–49, in* CRAFTING INDONESIAN DEMOCRACY: INTERNATIONAL CONFERENCE TOWARD STRUCTURAL REFORMS FOR DEMOCRATIZATION IN INDONESIA: PROBLEMS AND PROSPECTS 263 (R. William Liddle ed., Penerbat Mizan 2001); KAHIN, *supra* note 17, at 464; JOHN DAVID LEGGE, SUKARNO: A POLITICAL BIOGRAPHY 223, 238–239 (2d ed., Allen & Unwin 1985).

[36] KAHIN, *supra* note 17, at 154–155; LEGGE, *supra* note 35, at 209–212.

of the state. This would be seen, subsequently, to justify their role in politics and their control of the polity under the New Order.[37]

For the most part, regional or ethnic tensions during the 1950s paled in comparison with the integrative strength created by the strong nationalist movement and the revolution. Integration strategies were more a reflection of support for a unifying nationalism than an attempt to counter the influence of groups seeking to institutionalize differences. In this sense, the unifying power of a constructed nationalism, as described by Anderson,[38] was clearly evidenced in Indonesia, and it made integrative strategies not only appropriate but desirable. This helps to explain why, for the most part, later ethnonationalist mobilization would be the exception rather than the rule.

Ethnonationalism and resistance to the unitary state came later, when the drive toward republican integration was increasingly accompanied by repression and assimilation. The Constitution of 1945 was readopted in 1959, when Soekarno abandoned liberal democracy in favor of what was called Guided Democracy, essentially an authoritarian form of government that paid lip service to deliberation and consensus among political parties and representatives of functional groups.[39] During the 1950s, successive governments faced a series of economic and political crises that led to instability and unrest. A constituent assembly, formed in the aftermath of the 1955 elections, failed to agree on what should be the basis of the state. In particular, there were significant divergences between the nationalists favoring Pancasila—"five principles" developed by Soekarno as a state ideology—as the basis of the state and the Islamists seeking to create an Islamic state. The most important principle of Pancasila was "belief in (one) God", which was meant to acknowledge the importance of religion in Indonesia without adopting Islam as a state religion. On the basis of its first principle, Pancasila became a nationalist credo against the Islamic alternative.[40]

In the late 1950s, the government also faced regional crises in Sulawesi and Sumatra, where disgruntled regional elites contested the increasing centralization of power in Jakarta.[41] Faced with these successive crises, in 1959 Soekarno

---

[37] Harold A. Crouch, The Army and Politics in Indonesia 24–42 (Rev. ed., Cornell Univ. Press 1988); Robert Edward Elson, Suharto: A Political Biography 148–149 (Cambridge Univ. Press 2001); David Jenkins, Suharto and His Generals: Indonesian Military Politics, 1975–1983, at 1–5 (Cornell Mod. Indon. Project, S.E. Asia Program, Cornell Univ. 1984).

[38] Anderson, *supra* note 16.

[39] On Guided Democracy, see Herbert Feith, The Decline of Constitutional Democracy in Indonesia 541–542, 591–595 (Cornell Univ. Press 1962).

[40] Indon. Const. (Original) pmbl. Originally set forth in a speech, the Pancasila (five principles) was integrated into the 1945 Constitution. Other principles include: "justice and humanity, the unity of Indonesia, democracy guided by the inner wisdom of deliberations amongst representatives and the realization of social justice for all of the people of Indonesia." Except for its first principle, deemed to be a basis for the state, the other principles were devoid of political and legal ramifications. Pancasila was a symbolic statement of a nationalist state ideology.

[41] Cornelis van Dijk, Rebellion under the Banner of Islam: The Darul Islam in Indonesia (Verhandelingen Van Het Koninklijk Instituut Voor Taal-, Land- En Volkenkunde

decreed a return to the Constitution of 1945 and to the Pancasila he had established years earlier. With the restoration of strong presidential power entailed by this decree, he steered the country in an authoritarian direction.

The creation of the New Order regime in 1965 assured the authoritarian future of the Indonesian state. General Suharto, who effectively had assumed power in 1965 before being officially selected as president in 1966, reaffirmed the Constitution of 1945 and the principles of Pancasila.[42] By eliminating the Communist Party, which had acquired increasing influence in the early 1960s, the armed forces gained ultimate supremacy.[43] The Constitution of 1945 allowed the regime to consolidate the power of the president and the armed forces, while appearing to follow constitutional formulas.[44] The Constitution's basic framework had allocated strong powers to the president and made that office accountable only to the MPR. According to the Constitution, the exact nature of representation in the MPR was to be determined by law, which meant that the number of representatives of the various parties, regions, and functional groups and the means by which they would be selected, could be altered by ordinary legislation.[45] It was thus relatively easy for Suharto to manipulate legislation in such a way as to ensure that members of the armed forces were strongly represented, and that the membership of both the regional and functional groups could be influenced by the president as well. Through legislative and extrainstitutional means, the president could also control membership in the legislature. As a result, the executive attained maximum power while still operating in accordance with the Constitution of 1945.

The autocratic and integrationist spirit of the Constitution and its unitary principles guided the regime's responses to regional challenges. The Regional Law of 1974 established the framework for regional representation,[46] clearly placing the provinces and regencies, or municipalities, under the authority of the central government. Governors (provincial heads) and *bupatis* (regency heads) had powers that devolved from the central government. They were unelected officials, selected by regional and provincial assemblies, with the approval of the Ministry of the Interior and the president; they were dually responsible for representing their constituencies and for being the local executive representing the central government. All revenues, except for minor taxes, were collected by the central government before budget allocations were redistributed to provinces and regencies.

No. 94 [Essays of The Royal Institute for the Study of Language, Country and People No. 94], Nijhoff 1981); BARBARA S. HARVEY, PERMESTA: HALF A REBELLION (Cornell Mod. Indon. Project, S.E. Asia Program, Cornell Univ. 1977).

[42] ELSON, *supra* note 37, at 143–144.
[43] The Communist Party was banned by the regime and in subsequent months many Communist members were eliminated in a genocide that was encouraged by the armed forces.
[44] ELSON, *supra* note 37, at 159–165, 86–90; JENKINS, *supra* note 37, at 37–48.
[45] INDON. CONST. (Original) art. 2(1).
[46] Undang Undang No. 5, Tahun 1974 Tentang Pokok-Pokok Pemerintahan Di Daerah [Law No. 5, 1974 on the Basic Principles of Administration in the Regions] (Indon.).

Only relatively small portions of the total revenue collected were returned for discretionary allocation by lower levels of government. The central government reserved the largest part to disburse through various development programs and presidential initiatives.

As a result, the New Order regime created a full-blown infrastructure that strengthened the integralist and unitary nature of the state. Within this framework, there was no room for regional differences or the accommodation of ethnic groups. With the Village Law of 1979, the government went so far as to attempt a full homogenization of village government and administration across the archipelago, despite significant variations in village governance.[47] The educational system was standardized, as well, and a top-down curriculum adopted, thereby creating an exclusive narrative of the country's history meant to inculcate a sense of single Indonesian nation. Local languages could be used only in the first few years of primary school in selected regions; Indonesian was the only language for all subsequent levels of education.[48] Cultural differences were acknowledged only with respect to artifacts that could be displayed in museums, in colorful dress for weddings, or as a way to promote tourism; such differences were not permitted to seep into the realm of politics, government, and administration.[49]

It can come as no surprise that the New Order regime adopted a heavy-handed approach when it integrated Papua and East Timor into the republic. In negotiations with the Dutch in the late 1940s, Soekarno had abandoned the republic's claim to West New Guinea but not without making forceful arguments for its inclusion within Indonesia. Despite a colonial administration and history that were largely separate from that of the rest of the Dutch East Indies, West New Guinea was seen by Soekarno as belonging within an independent Indonesia and therefore launched a successful "West Irian" campaign, which included plans to invade West New Guinea if a negotiated settlement were not found.[50] Negotiations with the United Nations and the Dutch eventually led to the cession of West New Guinea—renamed West Irian—to Indonesia in 1962, and to the Act of Free Choice in 1969,[51] which was a plebiscite for the people of the

---

[47] Undang-Undang Nomor 5 Tahun 1979 Tentang Pemerintahan Desa [Law No. 5, 1979 on Village Government] (Indon.).

[48] Bertrand, *supra* note 19.

[49] *See* JOHN PEMBERTON, ON THE SUBJECT OF "JAVA" (Cornell Univ. Press 1994).

[50] KAHIN, *supra* note 17, at 444–445; LEGGE, *supra* note 35, at 226, 247–250.

[51] G.A. Res. 1752, GAOR, 17th Sess., Supp. No. 17, at 70, U.N.Doc. A/5217 (1962). Although the act was signed by Indonesia and the Netherlands in 1962, the UN secretary-general only appointed a representative to observe the proceedings in 1969. In June, eight local consultative assemblies were called in West Irian, and these voted in support of retaining ties with Indonesia. *See* Gregory H. Fox, *The Right to Political Participation in International Law*, 17 YALE J. INT'L L. 539, 575–576 (1992). During the "Act of Free Choice" plebiscite of 1969, the Papuan population chose Indonesian rule and rejected independence. *See* Agreement between the Republic of Indonesia and the Kingdom of the Netherlands Concerning West New Guinea (West Irian), Indon.-Neth., Aug. 15, 1962, 437 U.N.T.S. 273, arts. XVII–XVIII, *available at* <http://www.freewestpapua.org/docs/nya.htm> (also known as the New York Agreement). The referendum was governed by the New York

territory to choose, under UN supervision, whether or not they wanted to fully integrate Indonesia. The people of West Irian voted to join Indonesia, thus making the integration official and legitimate according to the UN. The Act of Free Choice was widely disputed because of its procedures, by means of which representatives were pressured into choosing integration to Indonesia.[52]

After its integration, West Irian, renamed Irian Jaya, was restructured to conform to Indonesia's political and administrative structures. It was designated a province, and its territory was subdivided into regencies, districts, and villages in accordance with the Regional Law of 1974. There were no modifications made to account for the socioeconomic, political, and cultural differences that distinguished the new territory from other provinces. A provincial military command structure was also created, emulating the internal security structure across the archipelago.[53]

The application of such homogenizing structures fit comfortably with the unitary view of the state—that is to say, with the strong Indonesian nationalist principle underlying the regime, as well as its integralist orientation. For the Indonesian government, the state represented the successful struggle of all the peoples of the archipelago against Dutch colonial rule and, therefore, by extension, the Papuans of what was now Irian Jaya were simply latecomers to this Indonesian family.[54] Once integrated, they would acquire a sense of loyalty to the Indonesian nation and create linkages with other groups that shared their colonial experience.

Papuans, however, saw these policies as repressive and uncompromising.[55] They had never participated in the rise of Indonesian nationalism, in its articulation as a unifying ideology, or in the revolution that had created the sense of common belonging for other peoples of the archipelago. Instead, the Papuan elites had developed an alternative Papuan nationalism, nurtured and developed by the Dutch for two decades after the creation of the Indonesian state. Furthermore, the process by which West Irian had been integrated by Indonesia was felt by Papuans to be coercive, despite the fact that it was carried out under UN auspices. In effect, the Indonesian government selected Papuan representatives favorable to the Indonesian regime to participate in the Act of Free Choice

---

Agreement of 1962 between the United States (on behalf of the Indonesian government) and the Netherlands to transfer sovereignty of Western New Guinea.

[52] CARMEL BUDIARDJO & LIEM SOEI LIONG, WEST PAPUA: THE OBLITERATION OF A PEOPLE (3d rev. ed., TAPOL: The Indon. Hum. Rts. Campaign 1988). Results of the Act of Free Choice were widely rejected among community leaders, nongovernmental organizations, and Papuan nationalist leaders, including at least one of those who had been one of the "representatives" chosen to cast their vote (confidential interviews, Jayapura, August 2001).

[53] Law no. 5, 1974 was applied to all provinces when it was implemented in 1974, after West New Guinea's integration into Indonesia.

[54] ELSON, *supra* note 37, at 178–179.

[55] *See generally* JACQUES BERTRAND, NATIONALISM AND ETHNIC CONFLICT IN INDONESIA 144–153 (Cambridge Univ. Press 2004).

process. This selection was coupled with an intense campaign of intimidation by the Indonesian armed forces to obtain full support for integration. As a result, Papuans have resisted the Indonesian state ever since. The Free Papua Movement, a loosely structured and weak organization, on occasion has used violence against the symbols of the Indonesian state; at the same time, various forms of civilian protest have emerged, such as displaying the Morning Star flag as a symbol of independence.

The response of the government was to adopt assimilationist policies to strengthen integrationist institutions in Papua. More so than in other regions, it imposed stringent restrictions on cultural expression through the educational system or other public forums. Indonesian was decreed the sole language of education, and a national curriculum, with almost no local content, was imposed on Papuans; even local songs were banned in some instances.[56] Political expression, such as the raising of the Morning Star flag, was strongly repressed, as was the revival of calls for the integration of West Irian or for alternative political representation.[57]

In contrast, ethnonationalist mobilization in Aceh did not arise from a lack of participation in the emergence of Indonesian nationalism or from a separate colonial experience. Indeed, the Acehnese joined the republic early on and rejected attempts by the Dutch to create a separate Acehnese state. However, they had developed a relatively strong political identity as an ethnic and religious group and had resisted Dutch colonialism through a sustained war (1873–1880 and 1883–1904), whereas the rest of the archipelago had succumbed quite easily to Holland's superior strength. Furthermore, close adherence to Islam was a feature of Acehnese culture that reinforced the strength of their community. Nevertheless, they were strong supporters of the Indonesian revolution.[58]

The Acehnese mobilization arose in reaction to a series of misguided integrationist, assimilationist, and repressive state policies that caused this basically strong community to turn away from the common Indonesian core. Initially, the Acehnese sided with the Islamist version of Indonesian nationalism, which was defeated by Soekarno's vision of Pancasila and secular nationalism. Participation by Acehnese elites in an Islamic rebellion in the 1950s was met with repression and integration with the North Sumatra province. This triggered, in turn, a regional

---

[56] *See generally* BUDIARDJO & LIONG, *supra* note 52. Widely held perceptions of cultural genocide and of the Indonesian government's assimilationist orientation, were confirmed by local organizations (confidential interviews, Aug. 2001).

[57] GABRIEL DEFERT, L'INDONÉSIE ET LA NOUVELLE-GUINÉE-OCCIDENTALE: MAINTIEN DES FRONTIÈRES COLONIALES OU RESPECT DES IDENTITÉS COMMUNAUTAIRES, RECHERCHES ASIATIQUES 369–370 (Editions L'Harmattan 1996); Amnesty International, *Indonesia: Continuing Human Rights Violations in Irian Jaya* 8–10 (Amnesty Int'l Publ'ns 1991).

[58] *See generally* ANTHONY REID, THE BLOOD OF THE PEOPLE: REVOLUTION AND THE END OF TRADITIONAL RULE IN NORTHERN SUMATRA (Oxford Univ. Press 1979); Eric Eugene Morris, Islam and Politics in Aceh: A Study of Center-Periphery Relations in Indonesia 19–53 (Aug. 1983) (unpublished Ph.D. dissertation, Cornell University) (On file with author and with Cornell University).

resistance to the Indonesian state.[59] Next, even though Aceh was restored to the status of a province in 1959, a Free Aceh Movement was created in the mid-1970s in response to other centralizing policies. During the 1970s, when oil and gas resources were discovered in Aceh, from which few benefits accrued locally, a new Acehnese elite, less Islamist and more regionalist, became disillusioned with the centralization of political and economic power.[60] Initially, there was relatively little support for the movement in the 1970s, when it was swiftly crushed by the Indonesian armed forces. Its reappearance in the late 1980s likewise enjoyed minimal popular support until the armed forces designated the whole province a military zone and sweeping operations throughout the 1990s led to human rights abuses and the intense repression of civilians in order to "weed out" Free Aceh Movement supporters.[61] It was this intransigence on the part of the Indonesian state, the failure to redistribute benefits of oil and gas exploitation, as well as the intense repression of the Acehnese population that fueled an ethnonationalist movement. Thus, Indonesian state policies of assimilation and repression ruptured the previously strong attachment of Acehnese to a unifying Indonesian nation.[62]

In both Aceh and Papua, there was renewed ethnonationalist resistance after the downfall of Suharto in 1998. For the most part, this mobilization did not seek to alter the strong unitary orientation of the state or to change the status of the groups in question within the republic. The unifying force of the Indonesian nation, as well as the state's integrationist strategies, had been successful in that regard. It was only in a few instances that groups sought to renegotiate their terms of inclusion in the Indonesian polity, most dramatically in the cases of certain Acehnese and Papuans who sought independence. Mobilization occurred at this critical juncture because the people involved were anxious about the future orientation of the state under a democratic regime and saw opportunities as the repressive apparatus was shaken by the sudden downfall of the authoritarian regime.[63] As a result, the Free Aceh Movement reemerged in force, this time with strong popular support, and it superseded a parallel civilian movement that had organized in favor of a referendum on independence. In Papua, the remobilization was largely civilian but gained widespread support as a large Papuan People's Congress, organized locally without legal status, strongly endorsed demands for independence.

Against this backdrop, the institutional changes after 1998 have been near-revolutionary. The Constitution of 1945 was amended to recognize regional differences and enshrine principles of autonomy. New laws created autonomous

[59] Morris, *supra* note 58, at 115–243, 260–268.
[60] Tim Kell, The Roots of Acehnese Rebellion, 1989–1992 (Cornell Mod. Indon. Project, S.E. Asia Program, Cornell Univ. 1995).
[61] *Id.* Geoffrey Robinson, *Rawan Is as Rawan Does: The Origins of Disorder in New Order Aceh*, 66 Indonesia 127 (1998).
[62] Bertrand, *supra* note 55, at 161–172.
[63] *Id.*

regions, and decentralization extended fiscal authority to these autonomous entities. Special autonomy laws were passed to accommodate the demands of Aceh and Papua, while East Timor was allowed to hold a referendum on independence and to secede from Indonesia. These measures constituted a radical turn of events over a period of less than a decade, thereby reversing the firm, centralizing tendencies of the Indonesian state during the previous fifty years.

The Constitution of 1945 was preserved but amended to include several provisions that allow for regional differences and autonomy. Regional units (provinces and regencies) are now accorded wide-ranging autonomy in all spheres except those that, by law, were specified as within the jurisdiction of the central government.[64] It also includes sections recognizing the need to respect the "diversity of regions" and creating "regional authorities that are special and distinct".[65]

These constitutional changes were implemented alongside legislation that significantly altered the architecture of state-region relations. Laws no. 22 and no. 25, 1999 established new frameworks for regional autonomy and fiscal decentralization and were designed, principally, to give autonomy to regencies.[66] These were subsequently replaced, respectively, by Laws no. 32 and no. 33, 2004, which were much more specific and gave autonomy to provinces as well as regencies. Autonomous regions obtained powers in all jurisdictions except foreign policy, defense, security, justice, monetary and fiscal policy, as well as religion.[67] Law no. 33, 2004 and subsequent government regulations provided for the significant devolution of fiscal resources to the provinces and districts, as well as for the sharing of revenues from the development of natural resources.[68]

In addition, regions are now represented in a separate legislative chamber, the Regional Representative Council (Dewan Perwakilan Daerah, or DPD). Previously, the regions were represented solely in the People's Consultative Assembly, allotted a number of designated seats alongside the functional groups and members of the People's Representative Assembly (Dewan Perwakilan Rakyat, or DPR). The new chamber, the DPD, is a feature of the amended

---

[64] Undang-Undang Dasar Republik Indonesia 1945 [The Constitution of the Republic of Indonesia of 1945] (Amended Version) [hereinafter Indon. Const. (Amended)] arts. 18, 18A–B (these articles provide that all unspecified powers, aside from those powers explicitly arrogated to federal authority by the Constitution or ordinary legislation, are subject to local or regional autonomy). The Constitution has been heavily amended four times, but for the purposes of this chapter I am distinguishing only between the most recent version, called the Amended Version, and the original text of 1945, or Original Version).

[65] Indon. Const. (Amended) arts. 18, 18A–B. The levels of administration in Indonesia include: central level, provinces, regencies, districts/municipalities, and villages.

[66] For an overview of the 1999 laws, see Bertrand, *supra* note 55, at 201–202.

[67] Undang-Undang Republik Indonesia Nomor 32 Tahun 2004 Tentang Pemerintahan Daerah [Law No. 32, 2004 of the Republic of Indonesia on Regional Government], arts. 1–3, 10–18. Articles 10 to 18 explain the divisions of powers in greater detail, as well as responsibilities of various levels of government.

[68] Undang-Undang Republik Indonesia Nomor 33 Tahun 2004 Tentang Perimbangan Keuangan Antara Pemeritah Pusat Dan Pemerintahan Daerah [Law No. 33, 2004 of the Republic of Indonesia on Fiscal Balance between the Central Government and Regional Administrations].

Constitution and also is considered, primarily, a consultative body.[69] Each province is allotted the same number of representatives, even though the sizes of their populations vary significantly.[70] The DPD has powers to propose legislation to the DPR, as well as to participate in the discussion of bills and to oversee and evaluate the implementation of laws on issues relating specifically to regions, or to region-center relations, such as regional autonomy, the management of natural resources, the redrawing of regional boundaries, and the financial balance between central and regional governments, as well as taxation, education, and religion as these relate to the provinces.[71]

In just a few years, Indonesia has shifted from integrationist strategies that did not allow for regional representation to strategies that now permit more flexibility. The administrative and fiscal decentralization vis-à-vis provinces and regencies does not amount to a federalization of Indonesia but, certainly, it introduces elements that have created a quasi-federal system. The underlying principle of this reorganization, however, has retained the unitary state at its core; moreover, the autonomous units that it recognizes do not coincide with ethnic groups.[72]

At the same time, special autonomy proposals or laws have aimed at accommodating the more forceful demands of the East Timorese, Acehnese, and Papuan ethnonationalists and clearly introduced accommodationist strategies along plural federalist lines. Initially, by enacting local autonomy laws applied to the whole country, the administration of President Bacharuddin Jusuf Habibie (1998–1999) had sought to address some of the grievances in these regions; however, as mobilization escalated in all three areas, alternative solutions were sought. For East Timor, Habibie offered a referendum that eventually led to the territory's secession.[73] For Aceh, several laws were passed. Initially, the Habibie government offered Islamic law but, again, to no avail as violent conflict continued to deepen. Subsequently, a special autonomy law was adopted, designed to devolve more powers to the provincial level and allow more fiscal resources to be retained locally.[74] Again, in the face of continued conflict, the law was not implemented and, instead, a military emergency administration was formed.[75] Only later, in 2006, in the wake of the devastating effects of the December 2005 tsunami and signs that the Free Aceh Movement was losing strength, did the two parties reach a peace agreement that led to new legislation on the administration of

[69] INDON. CONST. (Amended) arts. 22C–D.
[70] *Id.* art. 22C(2).
[71] *Id.* arts. 22D(1)–(3).
[72] In recent years, some new provinces and regencies have been created to coincide more closely with the territories of particular ethnic groups, but this is a relatively recent phenomenon and by no means a general trend.
[73] BERTRAND, *supra* note 55, at 142–143.
[74] *Id.* at 178, 182.
[75] *See* International Crisis Group, *Aceh: How Not to Win Hearts and Minds* (Asia Briefing Paper No. 27, July 23, 2003), *available at* <http://www.crisisgroup.org/home/index.cfm?id=1778&l=1>; and *Aceh: Why the Military Option Still Won't Work* (Asia Briefing Paper No. 26, May 9, 2003), *available at* <http://www.crisisgroup.org/home/index.cfm?id=1777&l=1>.

Aceh, meant to implement the Helsinki accord of February 2006.[76] In the case of Papua, a special autonomy law was passed in 2001, which is currently in effect.

In a little over three years, the Indonesian government has proceeded to amend the Constitution, passing a set of laws that dramatically shifts the balance of power between the central government and regions. The Constitution now recognizes the importance of regions and their diverse character, and it empowers them, in principle, by providing a new institution to represent regions in the central government while, at the same time, giving autonomy to lower levels of administration.

3. Special autonomy: An ambiguous reconciliation for Papuans

Against a backdrop of the significant changes in the relations between the central government and its regions, the 2001 Special Autonomy Law for Papua appears to be a genuine effort to accommodate Papuan demands. It may be interpreted as one of many signs that the Indonesian government has taken a turn toward accommodationist rather than integrationist strategies with regard to ethnic conflict. The law provides for many new areas of local authority, substantial fiscal resources, much greater control over the region's natural resources, and creates new institutions to recognize the specific traditions and customs of Papuans.

At the same time, there are two circumstances that mitigate somewhat the nature of the autonomy gained by the Papuans. First, when we take a closer look at the constitutional amendments and the Special Autonomy Law, it is not entirely clear that Papuans have an irreversible and secure authority to manage their own affairs. Although the Special Autonomy Law provides broad new areas of administrative and political authority, it does not constitute a federacy between Papua and Indonesia in the sense of constitutionally guaranteed divisions of power between the federated unit and the unitary state. Furthermore, the Indonesian state continues to be unitary, and the Constitution still preserves powers for the central government that can override those of the autonomous Papuan government.[77] Second, the language of the law remains vague and imprecise. In the context of a country with weak judiciary institutions, such vagueness can be exploited to render the law meaningless. Third, in its implementation of the law and subsequent actions toward the province, the central government continues to invoke its history as a strong, central state that places the unity of the Indonesian nation above regional differences.

The Special Autonomy Law for Papua provided, on paper, a large number of new powers for Papuans. It granted autonomy at the provincial level,

---

[76] *See Aceh: A New Chance for Peace* (International Crisis Group, Aug. 15, 2005), *available at* <http://www.crisisgroup.org/home/index.cfm?id=3615&l=1>.

[77] *Law on Special Autonomy for Papua*, art. 4.

whereby the Papuan government obtained jurisdiction over all matters except foreign policy, defense, monetary and fiscal policy, religion, and justice.[78] The Papuan People's Representative Assembly (Dewan Perwakilan Rakyat Papua, or DPRP)—representing all of the people in Papua—was created as the main legislative body. On the other hand, a new assembly, the Papuan People's Assembly (Majelis Rakyat Papua, or MRP) was created, specifically, to represent indigenous Papuan groups and included local customary groups, as well as religious and women's groups. It was given the mandate of promoting and protecting the rights and customs of Papuan people and endowed with the powers of consultation and assent regarding both candidates for the position of governor and decisions and regulations relating to the basic rights of Papuans.[79] Finally, the law provided for the creation of a truth and reconciliation commission to investigate the process of Papua's integration into Indonesia, with the objective of reconciling the Papuan people to the Indonesian state and preserving its unity.[80]

In fiscal matters, the law provided substantial new revenues for the province. The most important source of revenue was derived from the exploitation of natural resources, particularly mining. Papua is to receive 80 percent of the proceeds from mining, forestry, and fisheries, and 70 percent from oil and gas exploitation. In addition, a greater proportion of tax revenues were to accrue to the province.[81] Overall, the Special Autonomy Law afforded an unprecedented accommodation of Papuan demands. It acknowledged the need to revisit the process of integration with Indonesia, accorded broad powers, wide-ranging autonomy, and significant fiscal resources to the Papuan government, and created the MRP in order to represent indigenous Papuans.

Nevertheless, there were no guarantees that the special autonomy status could not be altered or undermined, at some point, by the Indonesian state. A review of the division of powers under the Special Autonomy Law, read in tandem with the amended Constitution, reveals several provisions that have precisely that potential.

First, there are ambiguities in the law. Most importantly, the roles of the DPRP and the MRP are not clearly distinguished, although the former represents all of the people living in Papua, including the significant number of migrants from other regions, whereas the latter represents only the indigenous Papuans and local groups. However, the MRP is granted rights of consultation and approval on issues related solely to native rights, and only in relation to special regulations implementing the Special Autonomy Law, which means that it might prove a relatively powerless body.[82]

---

[78] *Id.* arts. 4(1)–(2).
[79] *Id.* arts. 19–21.
[80] *Id.* art. 46.
[81] *Id.* art. 34.
[82] *Id.* arts. 6–7, 19–20, 22.

The governor, as head of the Papuan administration, is also in an ambiguous position. On the one hand, he is an elected representative, with executive powers and the right to submit bills to the DPRP. However, he also represents the central government and, therefore, must "socialize the national policies and facilitate the enforcement of statutory regulations in the Papua Province", as well as uphold and protect the integrity of the unitary republic.[83] This dual role potentially undermines the Papuan government's ability to serve as a true representative of Papuan interests and gives the central government leverage to pressure the governor into responding positively to its policies. This is especially the case since the president has the power to remove the governor from office.

Security forces are not subject to the authority of the Papuan government. The Papuan police remain formally under the authority of the national police with no provincial oversight and only a minor consultative role for the governor in the nomination of Papua's police chief.[84] More importantly, there are no provisions in the law for consultation with any of the executive or legislative branches of the Papuan government regarding the operations of the Indonesian military in Papua. As a result, the military can invoke national security to override, at will, the Papuan government's authority, as happened in Aceh after the special autonomy law of 2001 was suspended and martial law declared in May 2003.

In addition, several articles in the law, as well as several clauses in its preamble, stress the integrity of the unitary state of the Republic of Indonesia. Taken together, these provisions provide various limitations as well as active obligations to preserve and enforce this integrity.[85] The limitations could be interpreted as simply an assumption that no actions should be taken that violate the integrity of the state. However, the legal situation has broad implications, since proposals to hold referenda, or even consultations on possible secession, could be construed as violating the law, which was clearly designed to prevent such political actions. The original draft, as proposed by a special committee of Papuans that included the governor, had a clause that would have allowed for a referendum on independence if the Special Autonomy Law was deemed to have failed to reach its objectives.[86] However, this possibility was rejected and the language of the law seems to prevent any official discussion or consultation on such a possibility.

Second, there are certain clauses in the Constitution that make it possible to render the Special Autonomy Law ineffective. First and foremost, because the Special Autonomy Law was promulgated by Parliament, it may as easily be amended or revoked by Parliament. Although the Constitution enshrines principles of considerable autonomy and respect for the diversity of regions these

---

[83] *Id.* arts. 14–15.

[84] *Id.* art. 48.

[85] *Id.* pmbl(a)&(d), arts. 1(a), 2(1), 10(1)(a), 12(f), 14(b), 15(g), 23(1)(a), 46(2)(a) & 53(2).

[86] Draft Law on Special Autonomy for Papua, delivered to Indonesia's President and Parliament by the Governor of Papua Province, J.P. Salossa, on Apr. 16, 2001 (unpublished document, on file with author 2001).

statements are vague and do not guarantee any specific rights or powers for regions.[87] The Special Autonomy Law does specify mechanisms by which the DPRP or the MRP can propose amendments to the national Parliament, but there is no constitutional or legal obligation on the part of the national Parliament to consult the Papuan bodies if it decides to amend or revoke the law.[88]

In addition, constitutional amendments since 1998 have not removed the president's emergency powers; indeed, the president's ability to undermine special autonomy concessions, if a crisis arises, has probably strengthened. Under these new provisions, the president can suspend the Special Autonomy Law, as was done in Aceh in 2003, when President Megawati Sukarnoputi declared a military emergency. The armed forces are free to pursue unconstrained operations in the province in order to preserve national security.[89] With direct presidential elections and strengthened decree powers, in the words of Blair A. King,[90] "Indonesia will have one of the most powerful democratically-elected presidencies in the world".[91]

Beyond the constitutional and legal provisions that cast doubt on the long-term viability of Papua's autonomy, the Indonesian government's implementation of the law and its actions toward Papua suggest that past practices have not entirely faded away. As soon as the Special Autonomy Law was passed, the government revived Law no. 45, 1999 on the division of Papua into three provinces,[92] which had been part of the Habibie government's strategy to undermine the secessionist movement. The law had been introduced but placed on hold after meeting with strong local resistance. President Megawati, however, decided to revive it; she issued Decree no. 1, 2003, reaffirming the division of the province.[93] When renewed protests emerged, particularly over the institution of a Central Irian Jaya province, the creation of the latter was postponed indefinitely. However, the province of West Irian Jaya was created, and it remained uncertain whether the

[87] INDON. CONST. (Amended) art. 18(5). Although the law states that regional administrations will exercise the broadest possible autonomy, it is vague as the matters under their control are not specified. Instead, these must be specified by law and, therefore, can be revoked by parliament.

[88] *Id.*

[89] *Id.* art. 12 (providing that the President may declare a state of emergency, whose conditions and consequences are to be regulated by law).

[90] Senior program manager for Asia, National Democratic Institute for International Affairs, Washington, DC.

[91] Blair King, Empowering the Presidency: Interests and Perceptions in Indonesia's Constitutional Reforms, 1999–2002, at 54 (2004) (unpublished Ph.D. thesis, Ohio State University, 2004) (on file with author).

[92] *See* RICHARD CHAUVEL, CONSTRUCTING PAPUAN NATIONALISM: HISTORY, ETHNICITY, AND ADAPTATION 76–77 (East-West Ctr. Wash. 2005).

[93] Instruksi Presiden Republic Indonesia nomor 1 tahun 2003 tentang percepatan pelaskanaan Undang-undang Republik Indonesia nomor 45 tahun 1999 tentang pembentukan propinsi Irian Jaya Tengah, Propinsi Irian Jaya Barat, Kabupaten Paniai, Kabupaten Mimika, Kabupaten Puncak Jaya, dan Kota Sorong [Presidential Decree no. 1, 2003 on the acceleration of implementation of Law no. 45, 1999 of the Republic of Indonesia on the formation of the province of Central Irian Jaya, the province of West Irian Jaya, the regency of Paniai, the regency of Mimika, the regency of Puncak Jaya, and the city of Sorong].

Special Autonomy Law would extend to this new province, thereby creating an entirely new arena of legal ambiguities and potential conflicts concerning ultimate authority.

Regulations designed to implement the Special Autonomy Law were delayed. As of October 2006, only one regulation has been passed, whereas it has been estimated that at least twenty-four would be required to specify in adequate detail the implementation of the law. One of the reasons for the delay was the ambiguity in the division of roles between the MRP and DPRP.[94]

The formation of the MRP also suffered many delays. Despite being officially implemented since January 2002, the MRP was formed only after numerous criticisms from local groups, who accused the government of deliberately delaying its creation in order to undermine the province's emergent autonomy. On August 12, 2005, more than 10,000 people protested against the failure to implement the province's Special Autonomy Law and, specifically, the failure to create the MRP. This protest was directed, simultaneously, against the formation of the province of West Irian Jaya.

In addition, security forces increased their presence in the region, despite complaints from local groups. The total number of troops grew between 2004 and 2006, although plans to create a new strategic reserve command were shelved after protests that this would significantly augment the number of troops in the area.[95] Nevertheless, operations along the border have continued, and access to these areas has been restricted. Internal security matters have increasingly been transferred to the local police but some units, particularly Brimob—(Brigade Mobil [Mobile Brigade], a special police force in charge of riot control)—have overstepped their powers on occasion. In March 2006, for example, after clashes between students and Brimob troops in Abepura, in which three policemen were killed, some Brimob troops stormed student dormitories in the days following, attacked civilians, and fired shots in the air, with a stray bullet killing a young woman.[96]

4. The Law on Aceh: All but federacy

Law no. 11, 2006 concerning Aceh constitutes a substantially superior autonomy arrangement than has been provided Papua. It is much more developed and precise in its content and is much more consistent in its specification of relative

---

[94] *Pemda, Dprp, Dan Mrp Saling Menyalahkan [The regional government, DPRP, and MRP blame each other]*, SINAR HARAPAN (Indon.), Oct. 4, 2006, *available at* <http://www.suarapembaruan.com/News/2006/10/04/Nasional/nas02.htm>.

[95] *See* International Crisis Group, *Papua: Answers to Frequently Asked Questions* 10 (Asia Briefing Paper No. 53, Sept. 5, 2006), *available at* <http://www.crisisgroup.org/home/index.cfm?id=4364&l=1>.

[96] *Id.* at 10.

competences. It accords significant powers at the provincial level and requires, as well, substantial consultation and oversight authority vis-à-vis central government decisions affecting the region.

This text is a vast improvement over the 2001 Special Autonomy Law of Aceh.[97] Even at a superficial level, it is quite clear that the new law pertaining to Aceh is superior. The 2001 Special Autonomy Law of Aceh has 34 articles; the Special Autonomy Law for Papua (2001) has 79 articles, while the Law on Aceh Government of 2006 has 210. The latter includes much more detailed elaboration of the rights and obligations of the governor and the Aceh legislature, the local electoral process, determinants of fiscal revenues, and control over the exploitation of natural resources. It also includes articles on such issues as human rights, security forces, and the obligations of the Aceh government to provide services in the social and health sectors. Clearly, the latest version covers a much broader range of issues and is more specific in its details than its previous incarnation.

Because adoption of the 2001 Special Autonomy Law for Aceh failed to prevent a continued escalation of the armed conflict, its provisions were never put fully into effect. During the previous two years, the civilian Acehnese movement for self-determination had been increasingly sidelined as the military struggle intensified. The law had been an initiative of the local governor and a group of moderate Acehnese who saw a potential compromise in special autonomy status. However, as soon as the law took effect on January 1, 2002, it was immediately rejected by the Free Aceh Movement, which continued to demand a better agreement in negotiations. Fighting continued, which prevented several provisions of the law from being fully implemented and the autonomous government from gaining the powers and revenues accorded to it by law.

The original autonomy law of 2001 was vague, incomplete, and imprecise concerning the specific powers and jurisdictions granted to the provincial government. Although the governor and regency heads were to be elected, mechanisms for their removal were not clear. The central government retained substantial powers of appointment and oversight in security matters and the judiciary; there was no provision for provincial oversight or consultation on matters pertaining to the operations of the Indonesian military in the province. The Aceh police remained a branch of the Indonesian National Police, with only a minor consultative role for the governor on the appointment of police chief. The provincial government was accorded a weak consultative role with respect to the appointment of judges.[98]

In fiscal matters, the law provided—for a period of eight years—for an 80 percent share of tax revenues from forestry, mining, and fisheries to accrue to

---

[97] *See* Undang-Undang Republik Indonesia nomor 18, tahun 2001 tentang Otonomi Khusus bagi provinsi Daerah Istimewa Aceh Sebagai Provinsi Nanggroe Aceh Darussalam [Law no. 18, 2001 of the Republic of Indonesia on Special Autonomy for the Province of the Special Region of Aceh as the Province of Nanggroe Aceh Darussalam].

[98] *Id.* arts. 3, 9, 14, 15, 20, 21, 22 & 24.

the provincial government, with 55 percent of the revenues from oil and 40 percent from gas going to the province. At the end of eight years, these latter allocations were to be reduced to 35 percent for oil and 20 percent for gas.[99] Although this represented a substantial increase over previous revenues, it fell to the central government to calculate the amounts, collect the taxes, and distribute the provincial share, which was, of course, controversial because of the potential for manipulating revenue amounts. In most respects, the first Special Autonomy Law shared the same weaknesses as that for Papua and never produced the expected results of increasing political stability.

The Law on Aceh Government, which was passed in July 2006, is much more extensive in all respects, more specific in substance, more detailed in language, and has a much greater chance of success than Papua's Special Autonomy Law. Resulting from peace negotiations with the Free Aceh Movement, it was developed in sufficient detail to respond to the movement's major demands. It has greater popular acceptance not only because it is endorsed by the Free Aceh Movement, but also because it accords substantive powers to the region that are specified in great detail. In several articles, it elaborates extensively on the powers, duties, rights, and obligations of various aspects of the executive, legislative, and judiciary bodies in Aceh, as well as the election process for the governor and regency heads.[100]

In terms of jurisdictions, the Aceh government is granted authority over all sectors except those reserved to the central government, such as foreign relations, defense, national security, monetary and fiscal policy, and justice.[101] The same arrangement obtains in the 2001 Special Autonomy Law for Papua. The exception is religion, which falls under central government jurisdiction in Papua as in the rest of the country but is under provincial jurisdiction in the case of Aceh.

The Law on Aceh extends Islamic law to the region, giving the Aceh provincial government the responsibility for its implementation and enforcement. The central government, however, does retain the power to appoint judges to the Islamic court, which is established in parallel to the secular court system and applies to specific areas of Islamic law. The head of the court is appointed by the Supreme Court of Indonesia; other judges are appointed by the president on recommendation of the Supreme Court.

Executive and legislative powers and obligations are much more clearly specified in the Aceh law. There are articles that spell out in detail the governor's authority and tasks, such as enforcing Islamic law, raising standards of living, or enhancing democratic life.[102] These articles even specify forbidden practices,

[99] *Id.* art. 4.
[100] Undang Undang Republik Indonesia nomor 11 tahun 2006 tentang Pemerintahan Aceh [Law no.11, 2006 of the Republic of Indonesia on Aceh Government], arts. 6–64.
[101] *Id.* art. 6.
[102] *Id.* arts. 36–39.

such as corruption and nepotism, on which previous laws were silent, for all that their proscription seems obvious. In a country where the judiciary is sometimes subjected to political interference, such explicitness gives greater impetus to possible future actions, such as, for example, removing a corrupt governor or holding him accountable. The mechanism for removal of a governor is also much more complex than in the prior autonomy laws, thereby placing a clear constraint on presidential arbitrariness and giving a strong oversight role to the local legislature. Responsibilities are also spelled out for the legislature, with extensive powers of oversight that give it much greater clout than the previous law had provided.[103]

In fiscal matters, the Law on Aceh Government provides for even greater sharing of resources than had the previous Special Autonomy Law. Aceh receives 80 percent of the equalization payments relating to a specified subset of tax revenues on forestry, mining, fisheries, and the oil and gas sector.[104] As an independent government, it also is accorded additional revenues from the exploitation of natural resources, including 70 percent of oil and gas revenues from the state's share of income from these resources (over and above the tax revenue specified above) and 80 percent of revenues from all other resources in the province.[105] This is a much greater proportion than the previous law had granted, and the law is much more specific as to the derivation of these revenues. The accounting process is relatively complex and, in the past, was easily obscured. The adoption of more rigorous specifications means that revenue allocations are classified according to well-defined categories. Furthermore, the Aceh government is charged with calculating the relative allocations among different levels of government and remitting the central government's share, thereby reversing the previous assignment of responsibilities in this area. Although the percentages are specified by statute, this reflects an important increase in the trust reposed in the provincial government as well as heightened transparency of the central government's operations. There had been a widespread sense in the past that the latter, due to corruption, had been retaining more than its share of total revenues. Finally, the Aceh government gains the authority to administer all natural resource exploitation; this is an unprecedented delegation of powers over revenues.

The new law also confers on the province several additional powers or rights that were completely absent in the original Special Autonomy Law. For example, local political parties in Aceh now have the right to organize, thereby creating an exception to the countrywide legal requirement that all political parties have a national outlook.[106] This provision, which was one of the most sensitive points in the Helsinki peace negotiations, allows the Free Aceh Movement to reconfigure

---

[103] *Id.* arts. 20, 22.

[104] Equalization payments are allocations of tax and other state revenues to various levels of government (central, provincial, regency) calculated according to set percentages.

[105] *Law on Aceh Government,* art. 150.

[106] *Id.* art. 65.

itself as a political party in order to run for gubernatorial and regency elections, as well as local legislative elections. In fact, candidates in the December 2006 elections for governor and regency heads ran under the banner of the Free Aceh Movement, even though it had not constituted itself formally as a political party by that point.

Also under the new law, the province gained more oversight powers with regard to the security organizations operating in Aceh.[107] The governor and the Aceh legislature must be consulted and their approval obtained in the appointment of the Aceh chief of police. They also must be consulted before military troops may be stationed in Aceh for defensive purposes. Restrictions are imposed on the deployment of the so-called special forces, which were those most involved in military operations in the past. Furthermore, the law spells out specific requirements for the military to respect human rights and local customs.[108] These provisions are significant, since no regional government has ever obtained any legislative power to restrict the armed forces. Additionally, there are provisions for a truth and reconciliation commission to investigate past abuses by the armed forces. This is a very significant concession to the Acehnese considering the level of violence and suspected human rights abuses over the last fifteen years, and the armed forces' previous resistance to any form of accountability.

Finally, the law clearly specifies its role relative to other legislation. It supersedes all other legislation pertaining to Aceh, including the 2001 Special Autonomy Law of Aceh. As a result, this provision forestalls some of the ambiguities and contradictions that significantly weaken—for instance—the Special Autonomy Law for Papua.[109]

Overall, the Law on Aceh Government is a vast improvement on the earlier 2001 Special Autonomy Law of Aceh, in spite of some remaining weaknesses. Certainly, the central government can still override the Aceh government in some respects. The emergency powers of the president are fully in effect, since they remain firmly entrenched in the Constitution. The Law on Aceh Government may also be modified or revoked by the Indonesian Parliament. However, because the law also specifies that any legislation from the Indonesian Parliament pertaining to Aceh should be reviewed and receive approval by the Aceh parliament, attempts to modify or revoke the Aceh Government law in the national Parliament could be contested in courts. In sum, it constitutes a much more detailed, complete, and substantive autonomy package, with many restrictions explicitly imposed on central power. Although short of federacy, Aceh has achieved a very considerable institutionalization of its autonomy.

[107] On the Province of Aceh's police power, see *id*. art. 99; on its military forces, see *id*. art. 162.
[108] *Id*.
[109] *Id*. art. 206.

5. Conclusion

The example of Indonesia shows that integrationist strategies can create a strong basis for stability and democracy in multiethnic states, but they may also lead to violent conflict applied inflexibly. When integrationist strategies are relaxed to the point where, in effect, they emulate federalist arrangements, they can contribute significantly to reducing potential tensions. At times, however, the most effective way to proceed is to adopt mixed strategies, implementing strong accommodationist measures to reduce conflict with specific groups while pursuing a more general integrationist approach. This mixed approach requires that accommodationist compromises be fully credible, that is to say, they be institutionalized with clear, precise, and detailed legislation, particularly where a state historically has pursued integrationist strategies through force and assimilation. A weak accommodationist response, such as the government of Indonesia attempted in the early years after democratization, may be perceived as manipulative and deceptive.

Integrationist strategies worked in Indonesia, originally, because they were first implemented in response to a strong, unifying nationalist movement that created a coherent political project in which the various ethnic groups in the archipelago could participate. A common language, the shared experience of Dutch colonial rule, and, to some extent, Islam united ethnic groups so that, as a result, they rejected federalist proposals by the Dutch. From the beginning, the federal alternative was seen as a deliberate manipulation to divide Indonesians. Although the Dutch did create some ethnically based states that subsequently joined the United States of Indonesia, the federation itself was disbanded shortly after the colonial power departed. It was only after the departure of the Dutch that subsequent regionalist movements contested the perceived excessive centralization of power; however, such movements were more intent on reforming the Indonesian state than in rejecting its integrationist premises.

After a return to democratic rule, the movement toward a quasi-federalist set of institutions, in fact, has strengthened this integrationist core. The authoritarian regime had energetically pursued the integrationist approach, using repression and assimilation when threats to national unity were perceived, as in Aceh and Papua. Furthermore, fiscal and administrative centralization and homogenization were pushed to the point where the regions had lost control over their fiscal or natural resources and where they did not have the discretion to choose policies reflective of the very significant differences across the archipelago. Since 1998, the adoption of legislation that accorded substantial autonomy to provinces and regencies, combined with related constitutional amendments, has rebalanced the distribution of power. The creation of a legislative chamber to represent the regions has further increased regional power. By introducing greater flexibility and allowing for diverse policies tailored to regional needs, tensions between the regions and the center have eased. It has created a quasifederal system that preserves the integrationist approach of the Indonesian state.

Although these steps have ameliorated matters, the possibility of conflict between center and periphery remains. Were Indonesia to adopt a constitutional amendment situating Aceh or Papua in a more formal federacy arrangement, this would reduce greatly the possibility of the Indonesian president or the national Parliament exerting their power to undermine accommodationist legislation. This option seems remote, however, given the strong, enduring tendency of the Indonesian state to view itself as the guardian of national unity. In the case of Papua, a more realistic objective might be to emulate the Law on Aceh Government as a model for the state's dealings with Papua.

As the preceding pages have shown, recalibration of the relations between the central and provincial governments has reduced considerably the tension and violence within Indonesia. However, as we have also seen, there are many factors that can undercut the effectiveness of the special autonomy laws, especially as they pertain to Papua. It will be of great interest to all concerned to see if the powers-that-be in Indonesia are able to keep their balance even as they try to sustain the equilibrium so recently achieved.

8

Integrationist and accommodationist measures in Nigeria's constitutional engineering: Successes and failures

*John Boye Ejobowah**

Integration and accommodation have emerged as the two most prominent approaches to constitutional engineering in divided societies. The first seeks a homogeneous public sphere and a differentiated nonpublic domain, drawing its theoretical matrix from conventional liberalism animated by the ideas of John Rawls and Brian Barry.[1] The latter envisages a differentiated public sphere consistent with the identity cleavages in the nonpublic sphere and is driven by theories ranging from liberal multiculturalism to consociationalism. The institutional repertoires of these two approaches function accordingly. Institutions of integration work to create a national community that has a single identity in which its members have uniform rights. On the other hand, institutions of accommodation generate and sustain a political community in which multiple identities coexist and in which rights are allotted to these multiple identities as societies see fit. It is not certain if the institutions of these two competing approaches overlap, are mutually exclusive, or could be blended to achieve desired outcomes. This chapter attempts to clarify these uncertainties through examining constitutional engineering in Nigeria.

There are good reasons for dwelling on Nigeria. First, the country designed its arrangements in the mid-1970s when the international environment, according to the then-prevailing norms, frowned on public discussion of issues relating to identities. Second, the design was original, not adapted from elsewhere or drawn from any theoretical text. This constitutional invention received so much international acclaim that Donald Horowitz drew on it to formulate his theory of liberal

* Assistant Professor; Chair, Department of Global Studies, Faculty of Arts, Wilfrid Laurier University. Email: jejobowah@wlu.ca

[1] *See* John Rawls, *Justice as Fairness: Political not Metaphysical*, 14 PHIL. & PUB. AFF. 223 (1985); JOHN RAWLS, POLITICAL LIBERALISM (Colum. Univ. Press 1993); BRIAN BARRY, CULTURE AND EQUALITY: AN EGALITARIAN CRITIQUE OF MULTICULTURALISM (Harvard Univ. Press 2001) (especially ch. 4).

integration and even recommended it for postapartheid South Africa.[2] Third, in spite of its constitutional engineering, the country has experienced intense conflict up to the present and is ranked seventeenth in the 2007 global index of failed states by the Fund for Peace and Foreign Policy.[3] In light of this state of affairs, the chapter to follow will show that integrationist and accommodationist institutional repertoires can be combined in a variety of ways, and that this combination can accomplish some of the goals of both approaches while failing in others. The failures, the chapter argues, come from the integrationist component; however, the solution would not require doing away with this component. Instead, it has to be complemented with more accommodationist repertoires.

1. The background

Nigeria is by no means Africa's largest country. With a total land area of 356,664 square miles (924,000 square kilometers) and a coastline that stretches 530 miles (853 kilometers), the country ranks tenth in size on the African continent and thirty-second in the world after Tanzania.[4] However, Nigeria is easily Africa's most populous country. A national census conducted in 2006 put the total national population at 140 million, making the country the ninth most populous in the world after China, India, the United States, Indonesia, Brazil, Pakistan, Bangladesh, and Russia.[5] The 2006 census figure, though widely disputed, represents a 157 percent increase over the 1991 census figure of 88.9 million.[6] This huge and rapidly increasing population comprises an estimated 350 diverse ethnolinguistic groups that occupy discrete territorial spaces. Three of these groups account for about 60 percent of the total national population but none is large enough to claim a majority.[7] These three are: the Igbo, who are mainly Christians and are in the southeast; the Hausa-Fulani, who are predominantly Muslims and are found in the north; and the Yoruba, half of whom are Christians and the other half Muslims, who occupy the southwest. The others

---

[2] *See* DONALD HOROWITZ, A DEMOCRATIC SOUTH AFRICA?: CONSTITUTIONAL ENGINEERING IN A DIVIDED SOCIETY (Univ. Cal. Press 1992).

[3] *The Failed States Index 2007*, 161 FOREIGN POL'Y 57 (2007).

[4] Daniel Bach, *Inching Towards a Country Without a State: Prebendalism, Violence and State Betrayal in Nigeria, in* BIG AFRICAN STATES: ANGOLA, DRC, ETHIOPIA, NIGERIA, SOUTH AFRICA, SUDAN 43 (Christopher Clapham & Jeffrey Herbst eds., Witwatersrand Univ. Press 2006); AFR. DEV. BANK, HUMAN DEVELOPMENT INDICATORS 27 (2007), *available at* <http://www.afdb.org/pls/portal/docs/PAGE/ADB_ADMIN_PG/DOCUMENTS/STATISTICS/SEL07_HUMAN_0.PDF>.

[5] Martins Oloja, *Nigeria's Population Now 140 million*, NIG. GUARDIAN, Dec. 30, 2006, *available at* <http://www.guardiannewsngr.com/news/article01/301206>.

[6] Nat'l Population Comm'n Nigeria, Nigeria Population Facts and Figures, *available at* <http://www.population.gov.ng/factsandfigures.htm> (last visited Aug. 24, 2007); *id.*

[7] Richard L. Sklar, *Unity or Regionalism: The Nationalities Question, in* CRAFTING THE NEW NIGERIA: CONFRONTING THE CHALLENGES 39 (Robert I. Rotberg ed., Lynne Rienner 2004).

are minorities that range in size from millions of people to thousands and are located at the geographic margins of the aforementioned majority groups. The three majority groups have dominated their respective areas and have sought to dominate the entire country. Competition for national dominance has generated tensions and conflict that once led to civil war in 1967–70 and which continues to threaten political breakup.

Economically, Nigeria is reliant on primary products. About 60 percent of the population is engaged in small-scale farming, which accounts for 24 percent of the gross national product (GDP).[8] Primary produce such as cocoa, groundnut, and rubber were the main source of external earnings until 1972 when they were displaced by oil, located in the Niger delta region. Commercial production of oil began in 1959, but revenue was marginal, only £65,000 during the 1958–59 fiscal year and only 5 percent of the total national earnings in 1965.[9] After the price hike by the Organization of Petroleum Exporting Countries (OPEC) in 1973, the product rose in importance to account for 40 percent of annual GDP and 82 percent of public sector income.[10] International oil market volatility causes revenue to fluctuate widely; nevertheless, the product has consistently accounted for over 90 percent of Nigeria's export earnings since 1974.[11] The contribution of oil to total export revenue was 96 percent in 1980, 97 percent in 1985, 96 percent in 1991, 98 percent in 1993, and 99.6 percent in 2000.[12] With these figures, Nigeria is among the top three most-oil-dependent countries in the world.[13] The entire revenue went into a centrally consolidated account, which was named—in the Independence Constitution of 1960—the Distributive Pool Account.[14] The 1979 constitution renamed the account the Federation Account.[15]

Constitutionally, there are no fixed criteria for sharing the funds in the Federation Account. The 1979 constitution declared that any moneys in the account should be shared among the federal, state, and local governments "on

[8] WORLD BANK, WORLD DEVELOPMENT REPORT 2007: DEVELOPMENT AND THE NEXT GENERATION 295 (2006).

[9] SAM EGITE OYOVBAIRE, FEDERALISM IN NIGERIA: A STUDY IN THE DEVELOPMENT OF THE NIGERIAN STATE 51 (Palgrave McMillan 1985); Chibuike Ugochukwu Uche & Ogbonnaya C. Uche, *Oil and the Politics of Revenue Allocation in Nigeria* 18 (Afr. Stud. Ctr., Working Paper No. 54, 2004). During the colonial period, Nigeria used the West African pound as its legal tender. In 1962, the currency was substituted by the Nigerian pound and, in 1973, the naira was introduced

[10] John Udeh, *Petroleum Revenue Management: The Nigerian Perspective* 2 (Paper Presented at World Bank Workshop on Petroleum Revenue Mgmt., October 23–24, 2003); Ehtisham Ahmad & Raju Singh, *Political Economy of Oil-Revenue Sharing in a Developing Country: Illustrations from Nigeria* (Int'l Monetary Fund, Working Paper No. 3/16, 2003).

[11] Brian Pinto, *Nigeria During and after the Oil Boom: A Policy Comparison with Indonesia*, 1 WORLD BANK ECON. REV. 419, 421 (1987); Energy Info. Admin., OPEC Revenues: Country Details, *available at* <http://www.eia.doe.gov/cabs/orevcoun.html> (last visited Aug. 24, 2007).

[12] For statistical listing of the yearly earnings of crude oil beginning from 1970, see ORG. PETROLEUM EXPORTING COUNTRIES, ANNUAL STATISTICAL BULLETIN 15 (2005).

[13] See Michael Ross, Nigeria's Oil Sector and the Poor (Paper Prepared for U.K. Dep't for Int'l Dev., "Nigeria: Drivers of Change" Program, 2003).

[14] NIG. CONST. 1960, sched. II, § 135.

[15] NIG. CONST. 1979, § 149(1).

such terms and in such manner as may be prescribed by the national assembly".[16] Similarly, the 1999 Constitution, currently in force, requires the president to propose a revenue-sharing plan to the National Assembly after seeking the advice of the Revenue Mobilization Allocation and Fiscal Commission. But there is the condition that the principles of "population, [the] equality of states, internal revenue generation, land mass, terrain as well as population density must be reflected".[17] During the 1980s and 1990s, revenue was shared vertically by allocating 1 percent to the oil-producing states, between 48 and 55 percent to the center, 24 to 30.5 percent to the states, and 10 to 20 percent to the local governments. The states' share was, in turn, shared horizontally by allocating 40 percent on the principle of equality which was taken to mean sameness, and another 30 to 40 percent on the principle of population size. The remaining 20 percent was allocated on principles of social development internal revenue generation efforts, and terrain.[18] From 2002 to present, the share returned to the oil-producing states has been 13 percent, in accordance with the requirements of the 1999 Constitution, while the states and local government, in combination, receive less than 50 percent.[19] The automatic countrywide redistribution of oil revenue has generated resentment and unrest in the Niger delta that threatens to cause the disintegration of the country.

Threats to Nigeria's corporate existence date back to the country's creation in 1914, when the British amalgamated their northern and southern protectorates into a single polity. Political unification was resisted by the Muslim elites of the north, who preferred that the region remain a separate entity. However, the British persuaded them to accept unification with the promise that the region would be administered separately; that the hierarchical Islamic rule, centered at Sokoto in the northwest and Borno in the northeast, would be supported; and that northern Islamic societies would be protected from missionary activities and Western influences. These promises were faithfully kept. Nonetheless, during the immediate post-World War II period, northern elites considered political unification a regrettable act because the south, which had been open to and had benefited from Western education, made unilateral demands for the country's independence. Expressions of regrets about 1914 unification, along with threats and counterthreats of political secession, caused the British to express doubts about the future political survival of what was then their dependency.

To prevent Nigeria's political disintegration, British political rulers and the country's regional leaders negotiated a compromise in 1954. The compromise

---

[16] *Id.* § 149(2).

[17] Nig. Const. 1999, § 160(2).

[18] Rotimi T. Suberu, Federalism and Ethnic Conflict in Nigeria 54, 59, & 65 (U.S. Inst. Peace 2001).

[19] Udeh, *supra* note 10, at 8; Alifa Daniel, *Federal Government Gets More in New Revenue Formula, Raises New Derivation Board*, Nig. Guardian, Jan. 25, 2005; John-Abba Ogbodo, *Governor's Forum Demand Review of Revenue Sharing Formula*, Nig. Guardian, Jun. 21, 2007; Suberu, *supra* note 18, at 54 & 59.

took the form of a triregional federation.[20] Consequently, the 1960 Independence Constitution institutionalized a political federation of three regions whose internal boundaries appeared to be blind to ethnic difference.[21] Furthermore, the constitution granted a great deal of autonomy to the regions (including rights to resources), conferred few governmental activities on the center, required that the boundaries of the regions not be altered without the consent of the regional governments, and also provided for regional constitutions.[22] Finally the constitution provided for a parliamentary system of government that often resulted in coalition government, a sort of power sharing among rivals.[23] The overall goal was to minimize contact among regional and ethnic leaders so that political fights would be avoided.[24] Fiscal devolution worked to the advantage of the northern and western regions, which were endowed with agricultural resources, but to the disadvantage of the eastern region, which was not so well endowed and had to rely, partly, on federal bailouts.[25]

The constitutional arrangement turned out to be poor one for four reasons. First, the three regions were closely associated with the majority groups whose elites were the main, if not exclusive, controllers of power. This caused minorities, which were tucked away at the margins of the regional maps, to be apprehensive of their political future and to demand recognition in separate states. Second, the party system was ethnically regionalized, with the consequence that political competition was reduced to a violence-prone, three-player ethnic game in which each tried to eliminate its rivals. Third, one of the regions, the northern region, was more than double the combined size of the eastern and western regions and used its size and population (55 percent of the total) to control the federation.

---

[20] The British worried that ethnic difference would be heightened if political institutions were designed around groups, and that such arrangement could empower groups to secede: *see* GREAT BRITAIN, NIGERIA: REPORT OF THE COMMISSION TO ENQUIRE INTO FEARS OF MINORITIES AND MEANS OF ALLAYING THEM 88 (Her Majesty's Stationery Office 1958). For a discussion of Nigeria as a political compromise, see Richard Sklar, *Foundations of Federal Government in Nigeria, in* NIGERIA'S STRUGGLE FOR DEMOCRACY AND GOOD GOVERNANCE: A FESTSCHRIFT FOR OYELEYE OYEDIRAN 3–17 (Adigun A.B. Agbaje, Larry Diamond & Ebere Onwudiwe eds., Ibadan Univ. Press 2004).

[21] NIG. CONST. 1960, sched. II, § 3.

[22] *Id.* sched. I § (5), sched. II §§ 3–5 & 134, scheds. III, IV, & V.

[23] *Id.* sched. II §§ 33–36 & 62.

[24] Oliver Lyttelton, the British colonial secretary from 1951–1954, noted that "the diverse elements in Nigeria…left to themselves…would clearly fall apart in a few months.…It was clear that Nigeria, if it was to become a nation, must have a federation, with as few subjects reserved for the Central Government as would preserve national unity." OLIVER LYTTELTON CHANDOS, 1ST VISCOUNT, MEMOIRS: AN UNEXPECTED VIEW FROM THE SUMMIT 409 (Bodley Head 1962). For a discussion of the constitutional reduction of the importance of the center, see Peter Ekeh, *Obasanjo and the Burden of Civilianization*, 27 ISSUE: J. OPINION 73 (1999).

[25] For example, the federal government provided the eastern region with a grant of £500,000 during the 1954–55 fiscal year and £250,000 during the 1955–56 fiscal year. It was expected that these amounts would cushion the region while the latter looked for ways of raising revenue. See Memorandum by the Action Group Delegation, *Commentary on Sir Louis Chick's Report on Financial Effects of Proposed New Constitutional Arrangements, in* RECORD OF THE PROCEEDINGS OF THE RESUMED CONFERENCE ON THE NIGERIA CONSTITUTION 200, NC/B12 (1954).

Fourth, the Westminster system encouraged the formation of a coalition government between the dominant parties of the eastern and northern regions. But the coalition partners aimed at eliminating the dominant party of the western region as a way of enhancing their strength in the federation. They actually did so by dividing the western region in two in 1963 and jailing its key political actors.[26]

Ethnic fragmentation was accelerated by the adoption of an affirmative action policy. In early 1962, the northern political elites, constituting the senior coalition partners, used their control of the federal government to introduce a quota system that would ensure balanced representation in the officer corps of the Nigerian army, which at the time was dominated by easterners (mainly Igbo).[27] In January 1966, there was a coup led by junior officers of Igbo origin. The coup violently terminated the elected government of Tafawa Balewa, but failed to dislodge senior military officers who rallied to defend the government of Balewa. Power passed into the hands of senior military officers. Coincidentally the most senior officer was of Igbo origin. The new Igbo military leader, General Aguiyi Ironsi, passed the Constitution Suspension and Modification Decree 34 of 1966, which declared Nigeria a unitary state and abolished the regions.[28] This was interpreted by northerners as an attempt to replace the quota system with the merit principle, thus ensuring the dominance of Igbos, who were considered educationally more advanced and who had migrated to other parts of the country for economic reasons. The presence of Igbo immigrants in various parts of the country reinforced the belief that the abandonment of the quota system for the merit principle was a strategy for ensuring Igbo political dominance. The reaction was the Igbo pogrom (mass killing of Igbos resident in northern Nigeria), a northern officers' coup against the Igbo officer-led military government, and the enactment of the Constitution (Suspension and Modification) Decree 1967, returning the country back to a federal system.[29]

These events resulted in the 1967 declaration of the secession of the Eastern Region as the Republic of Biafra. This declaration occurred at a time when oil, located within the eastern region, was emerging as a principal source of revenue.[30] In an attempt to defeat secession, the military government, led by the northern officers, separated ethnic minorities of the eastern region into two new states so that they would assume the primary role of resisting the Biafran secession.[31] The government also met some northern minorities' aspirations for political

---

[26] Claude Ake, *The Nigerian State: Antinomies of a Periphery Formation, in* POLITICAL ECONOMY OF NIGERIA 26 (Claude Ake ed., Longman 1985); BEN O. NWABUEZE, A CONSTITUTIONAL HISTORY OF NIGERIA (C. Hurst 1982).

[27] For the details, see BILLY J. DUDLEY, INSTABILITY AND POLITICAL ORDER: POLITICS AND CRISIS IN NIGERIA (Ibadan Univ. Press 1973).

[28] *See* NWABUEZE, *supra* note 26, at 221.

[29] *Id.* at 221.   [30] Ake, *supra* note 26.

[31] JOHN BOYE EJOBOWAH, COMPETING CLAIMS TO RECOGNITION IN THE NIGERIAN PUBLIC SPHERE: A LIBERAL ARGUMENT ABOUT JUSTICE IN PLURAL SOCIETIES 102 (Lexington Books 2001).

separation as a way of countering Igbo charges about northern domination of the country. The result was a federation of twelve states and the submission of Biafra in 1970.

2. Constitutional engineering through the combination of integrationist and accommodationist devices

Biafran secession and the civil war of 1967–70 were clear indications that ethnicity is an important political variable in Nigerian politics and that it could not be disregarded in the design of the country's political institutions. In 1975, Nigeria's military rulers assembled local political experts to come up with a constitutional architecture for curbing ethnic domination and preventing the future political disintegration of the country. The result was the Constitution of the Second Republic—that is, the 1979 constitution.[32] Its essential features include:

1) The fragmentation of all types of groups into 301 local governments and nineteen states, dispersing power to these subnational arenas and entrenching these local governments in the Constitution. This was done with a view to protecting them against abolition by overbearing state governments.[33]

2) The promotion of nation building and political integration through the abandonment of the Westminster system for a presidential system of government, which makes for a unifying executive who is elevated over groups.[34] The prospects for such unification were not left to chance. An integrationist electoral device was ingeniously employed requiring that the president, in order to be elected, must obtain a simple majority of national votes plus a "geographic spread", which required 25 percent of the vote in at least two-thirds of all the states.[35] The assumption was that ethnic elites would be induced to cross deep divides, take a moderate stand on issues, form preelection political alliances with ethnic enemies, and share power upfront. The candidate most successful in doing all this would be victorious at the polls.[36]

3) The furtherance of political accommodation through the use of a consociation device requiring that appointments and recruitment into public positions at the federal, state, and local levels reflect the "federal character", or diversity, of the population within the territorial jurisdiction of each level of government.[37] One of the political parties—the National Party of Nigeria—that emerged

---

[32] NIG. CONST. 1979, § 14 (3) & (4), & sched. I, pt I.
[33] *Id.* §§ 3 (1)–(5).
[34] *Id.* §§ 124(4) & 125(a) & (b).
[35] NIG. CONST. 1979, § 125.
[36] For an extended discussion of this assumption, see EJOBOWAH, *supra* note 31.
[37] *See* NIG. CONST. 1979, §§ 14(3) & (4).

and won elections during the Second Republic applied this requirement to itself by allocating limited key federal positions among members drawn from the country's various geocultural zones. This zoning principle, as it was called, was a way of ensuring balanced ethnoregional representation in the highest positions of government.[38]

4) The enhancement of political integration through federal control and ownership of oil resources. This was achieved through the use of revenue derived from oil to sustain the component units of the federation through a redistributive program.[39]

5) The dissociation of political parties from ethnicity and religion. To achieve this, various requirements were spelled out: that the parties' names and emblems not have such ethnic connotations, that their headquarters should be in the national capital, that their activities should not be confined to a specific part of the country, and that their executive bodies be drawn from a minimum of two-thirds of the states.[40]

6) Finally, the further affirmation of political accommodation through the adoption of legal pluralism that would allow any state to institute the Shari'a penal code, to be applied in personal matters and to consenting Muslims only.[41] To administer the penal code, which operated under an overarching modern law, such states were constitutionally permitted to establish Islamic courts, including a Shari'a Court of Appeal supervised by the Federal Court of Appeal and the Supreme Court.

The foregoing devices are consistent with the contemporary recommendations of liberal integrationists, liberal multiculturalists, and experts of constitutional design for divided societies. Indeed, Donald Horowitz declared the design a "real constitution" and advised that "if one is looking for...democracy in a divided society, the place to look is Nigeria".[42] But the 1979 constitution collapsed in December 1983, following a military coup that sacked the civilian government of Alhaji Shehu Shagari. The imperfections of the 1979 constitution have been singled out by Omo Omoruyi as a probable reason for the Shagari regime's breakdown. In his view, the political parties of the Second Republic—in spite of the constitution's strictures—were reincarnations of ethnoregional parties of the First Republic; additionally, the constitutional requirement for electoral victory (the 25 percent geographic-spread vote) was so difficult to fulfill that parties had

[38] For a critical discussion of the federal character principle, *see* Anthony H.M. Kirk-Greene, *Ethnic Engineering and the Federal Character of Nigeria*, 6 ETHNICS & RACIAL STUD. 457 (1983).

[39] NIG. CONST. 1979, § 149(2); NIGERIAN PANEL ON CREATION OF STATES, FEDERAL MILITARY GOVERNMENT VIEWS ON THE REPORT OF THE PANEL ON CREATION OF STATES 13 (Federal Ministry Info. Printing Div. 1976).

[40] NIG. CONST. 1979, §§ 202–203.

[41] *Id.* §§ 240, 242–244.

[42] HOROWITZ, *supra* note 2, at 136–137.

to resort to fraud.[43] There is also a further, weighty argument that holds that resource centralization and the resultant patronage made for the collapse of the Second Republic.[44] These arguments will be developed further below.[45]

Officially, the successor military regime did not inquire into the collapse of the Second Republic. Nevertheless, a government commission—the Political Bureau—was established in 1986 to conduct a national debate on the political future of the country. The Political Bureau recommended a slight revision of the 1979 constitutional design with the creation of a minimum of two states and a maximum of six to separate groups in conflict and to accommodate minorities more adequately.[46] The Political Bureau's report was expected to lead to a new constitution for a Third Republic, but the result of a presidential election held in 1993 was annulled by the military government, thereby aborting the transition to civilian rule. The annulment of the election result, which would have demo-cratically transferred power from the north (which still dominated the military) to the south for the first time in the country's political history, hardened ethnic divisions, provoked violence, and gave rise to an exodus of ethnic groups from the major southern cities.[47] According to Peter Lewis, there were ethnic fissures and resentment within the military, as well, "raising the spectre of wider civil conflict and state collapse".[48] The military regime of General Sanni Abacha convened a constitutional conference in 1994–95 to head off the prospect of state collapse.

The 1994–95 constitutional conference produced the draft constitution of 1995. The draft constitution was modified by the regime of General Abacha and became the draft Constitution of the Federal Republic of Nigeria 1995 (with Amendment).[49] Based on the country's experiences, the constitution made substantive innovations to the 1979 Constitution. The innovations, which were all of an accommodationist nature, included:

1) Division of the country into six geopolitical zones for the purpose of rotat-ing key political offices including the presidency. The zones were as follows: the Yoruba-speaking southwest; the Igbo-speaking southeast; the ethnically diverse, oil-rich minority south-south (comprising six states in the Niger delta and its adjacent wetlands); the Hausa-speaking and emirate heartland of the northwest; the ethnically diverse but emirate-dominated north-central area;

---

[43] *See* Omo Omoruyi, *Federal Character and the Party System in the Second Republic, in* FEDERAL CHARACTER AND FEDERALISM IN NIGERIA 214–215 (Peter Ekeh & Eghosa Osaghae eds., Heinemann 1989).

[44] *See* Shehu Othman, *Classes, Crises and Coup: The Demise of Shagari's Regime,* 83 AFR. AFF. 441 (1984).

[45] The arguments are developed from § 4 onwards.

[46] NIGERIA REPORT OF THE POLITICAL BUREAU 179–180 (Fed. Ministry Info. 1987).

[47] For a detailed discussion of the failed transition and the attendant conflict, see Peter M. Lewis, *Endgame in Nigeria? The Politics of Failed Democratic Transition,* 93 AFR. AFF. 323 (1994).

[48] *Id.* at 327.

[49] DRAFT NIG. CONST. 1995 (with Amendment); FEDERAL REPUBLIC OF NIGERIA, 1 & 2 REPORT OF THE CONSTITUTIONAL CONFERENCE CONTAINING THE DRAFT CONSTITUTION (Nat'l Assem. Press 1995).

and the predominantly Kanuri-speaking but also partly emirate and nonemirate northeast.[50]

2) A single five-year-term presidency. The intended effect was that the office would rotate at the end of five years, and the incumbency factor, which caused so much electoral fraud, would cease to be relevant.[51]

3) An end to a winner-take-all system. This would be achieved through the requirement that political parties with no less than 10 percent of seats in the National Assembly should be represented in the federal executive cabinet in proportion to their number of seats.[52]

4) The application of all these accommodationist devices to state and local levels of government.[53]

5) The stipulation that the rotation principle will remain for a period of thirty years commencing from the date the constitution came into force. The idea was that, during the thirty-year period, each zone would have produced the presidency once, and the country would make the transition from a mere geographic expression to a nation.[54]

6) The requirement that states from which oil is derived must receive at least 13 percent of the oil revenues. This 13 percent derivation principle was an increase from what was 1 percent derivation.[55]

The above innovations, made at a time when Nigeria was on the brink of disintegration, did not come into force. General Abacha passed away in 1998, and, in the aftermath of his death, the draft constitution was not promulgated. The Constitutional Debate Coordinating Committee, set up by the successor regime under General Abdulsalami to review the 1995 draft constitution for the Fourth Republic, rejected these innovations. The committee, whose members had little expert knowledge of politics in multiethnic societies, rejected the 1995 constitution on grounds that "it was a product of disputed legitimacy", and that "Nigerians raised compelling reservations about it".[56] The 1979 constitution was revived and adopted as the 1999 Constitution with minor adjustments that included acceptance of an increased derivation share of revenue to 13 percent.[57] The reason given for the readoption of the 1979 constitution was that it "had been tried and tested and, therefore, provides a better point of departure in the quest for constitutionalism in Nigeria".[58]

[50] Draft Nig. Const. 1995 (with Amendment), §§ 229(1)–(4).
[51] *Id.* §§ 138, 140.　　　[52] *Id.* §§ 148(7)–(8).
[53] *Id.* §§ 149(4), 184(1) & 229(2).　　　[54] *Id.* § 229(1).
[55] *Id.* § 160; Federal Republic of Nigeria, *supra* note 49, vol. 2 at 142.
[56] Alex Ekwueme, *What Nigerians Lost by Abacha's Untimely Death*, Nig. Guardian, May 29, 2005, *reprinted at* <http://www.dawodu.com/ekwueme1.htm>.
[57] Nig. Const. 1999, §162.
[58] Ekwueme, *supra* note 56.

3. Accomplishments of the Nigerian design

What, then, are the strengths of the 1979 Nigerian constitutional design, as revived in 1999 Constitution?

One of the accomplishments of the original document, and now recovered, is the accommodation of both majority and minority groups in several states and local governments, thereby making it possible for groups that otherwise would be locked out of national power to have their own internal governments. The state governments were progressively raised from 19 in 1976 to 21 in 1987, 30 in 1991 and 36 in 1996. The local governments were also increased from 301 in 1976 to 589 in 1991 and to 774 in 1996, and then given legal protection through listing in the 1999 Constitution.[59] The criterion for drawing the boundaries of the subnational units was geographical, ostensibly, but the boundaries followed ethnic and subethnic group territories very closely, with the result that each of the three major groups was divided into several states. Simultaneously, minority groups that were large enough to have their own homogenous states were given institutional recognition, while smaller ones or those that were numerically unviable were grouped with others in heterogeneous states. Thus, Nigeria adopted what Ivo Duchacek called polyethnic federalism, that is, a federation whose internal boundaries coincide with ethnicity.[60]

Critics argue that such proliferation makes a mockery of federalism since the states and local governments are economically unviable. Critics also maintain that this multiplicity of entities undermines the federal principle because of the problem of representing all the states in national institutions.[61] These objections may well be correct, but the institutional proliferation has made it possible for groups to be accommodated fairly, thus creating a sense of reasonableness or legitimacy. It also has given rise to the informal zoning of important national offices vis-à-vis the six geocultural zones, even though the 1999 Constitution had not provided for it. Furthermore, given the existence of several states, nearly equal in size, and all the local governments, the political capacity to threaten secession has been reduced. For example, threats to secede by Yoruba leaders in the aftermath of the annulment of the 1993 presidential election proved to be empty, since the fragmentation of the Yorubas into several states made it impossible for them to unite.[62]

Nigerian constitutional engineering has also achieved the remarkable goal of quarantining some conflicts within a local area, thereby preventing them from

---

[59] NIG. CONST. 1999, § 3 & sched. I, pt. I.

[60] *See* IVO D. DUCHACEK, COMPARATIVE FEDERALISM: THE TERRITORIAL DIMENSION OF POLITICS (Holt, Rinehart & Winston 1970). For an extended discussion of Nigeria as a polyethnic federation, see Sklar, *supra* note 20.

[61] Bach, *supra* note 4, at 60; Rotimi T. Suberu, *Reinventing the Architecture of Nigerian Federalism*, 12 BROWN J. WORLD AFF. 139 (2005).

[62] Brennan Kraxberger, *The Geography of Regime Survival: Abacha's Nigeria*, 103 AFR. AFF. 413 (2004).

engulfing the entire country. Formal territorial dispersal of powers has produced, at the local level, a complete set of legislative, executive, and judicial institutions that serve as focal points of political contestation, thereby providing a buffer for the center. In Anambra, Oyo, and Ekiti states, violent struggles for power by armed factions during the period from 2003 to 2007 remained localized and less threatening, unlike the era of the triregional federation of the 1960s, when such struggles would have been nationally destabilizing.

Simultaneously, institutional devolution has made it possible for compartmentalized conflicts to peter out. For example, on the country's return to civil rule in 1999, twelve northern states expanded the jurisdictional scope of the Shari'a penal code to cover criminal cases in apparent violation of the country's Constitution.[63] In one particular state, Kaduna, this triggered deadly riots that claimed over 2,000 lives in the year 2000.[64] Yet, Nigeria's multistate structure isolated and quarantined the sectarian violence, a compartmentalization that was reinforced by the prudence of the country's national leaders in keeping silent regarding the Shari'a controversy, which they regarded as local to the affected states. Furthermore, in the affected Muslim states, the operation of constitutionally provided appellate Shari'a courts helped to check the excesses of the Shari'a penal system.

The case of Amina Lawal is an example that has received a great deal of international attention.[65] In March 2002, a lower Shari'a court sitting in Bakori, Katsina State, sentenced her to death by stoning for having a child outside wedlock. This sentence was reversed in September 2003 by the Katsina State Shari'a Court of Appeal. If this court had not reversed it, the case would have gone up to the Federal Court of Appeal, where it would probably have been struck down. The use of devolved formal structures and institutions to respond to challenges and curtail outrageous punishments, as in Amina's case, has caused the states that practice Shari'a to back off from the most stringent aspects of that penal code. There is the further factor of severe economic circumstances, which has forced women to undermine Shari'a law that prohibits them from commuting on motorbikes with knees exposed and their hands clutching an unrelated male driver. The absence of alternative modes of travel has forced Shari'a law into a retreat.[66] Instead of a strict Shari'a penal system, the result is a mild version that emphasizes social justice and almsgiving.[67] The evidence seems quite conclusive:

---

[63] Agaju Madugba, *The Nigerian Constitution and Sharia Law*, EQUAL JUSTICE 25 (2000) (a quarterly publication of Human Rights Monitor); Abdul Raufu Mustapha, *Ethnicity and the Politics of Democratization in Nigeria*, in ETHNICITY AND DEMOCRACY IN AFRICA 257, 268–271 (Bruce Berman, Dickson Eyoh & Will Kymlicka eds., James Curey 2004).

[64] Suberu, *supra* note 61.

[65] *See* Human Rights Watch, *"Political Shari'a?" Human Rights and Islamic Law in Northern Nigeria*, 16 HUM. RTS. WATCH 35 (2004).

[66] Edward Harris, *In Nigeria's North, A Compromise between Islamic Law, Secular Culture*, WASH. POST, Apr. 15, 2007, *available at* <http://www.washingtonpost.com/wp-dyn/content/article/2007/04/14/AR2007041401279.html>.

[67] *Id.*

the multistate federal system has compartmentalized damaging sectarian conflict, and legal pluralism resulting in constitutionally devolved legal structures has defused much conflict.

Furthermore, Nigerian constitutional innovation has allowed for the political representation of the country's ethnic minority groups. The electoral device of vote pooling has worked to raise the political profile of ethnic minorities, so much so that the parties' presidential candidates cannot meet the conditions for victory without courting these minority politicians. These politicians and their followers shape the outcome of national elections by giving greater leverage to any party with which they align. This elevated profile, together with the accommodative character of federal policy regarding appointment and promotion, has ensured minority appointments to important national offices. To illustrate, the elected regime of President Olusegun Obasanjo had Abubakar Atiku as vice president. Atiku was Fulani from the northeastern end of the minority's middle belt, not the core north that controls national political power. At various times during the tenure of the regime, the most important ministerial portfolios, such as works, internal affairs, police affairs, and power and steel, went to southern minority elites. The current regime of Umaru Yar'Adua also has a minority member from the oil-rich Bayelsa State as vice president. While one cannot yet speak of "minority power" in Nigeria the way Donald Smiley wrote about "French power" in Canada since the Trudeau era, Nigerian minority elites are emerging as players in the country's power politics.[68]

Finally, the rules governing the formation of parties and the votepooling electoral system have worked to maintain the country on a secular path, avoiding the sort of tragedy that befell Algeria when the religious parties emerged to contest and win the country's elections in 1991. The design not only has prevented the emergence of political parties related to religion or identity but also has forced politicians to abandon religious extremism. General Muhammad Buhari, a former military ruler, was known to have put his weight behind the adoption of full-blown Shari'a law, described earlier. However, after becoming the presidential candidate for the main opposition All Nigerian Peoples Party, during the national elections of 2003, he kept silent regarding Shari'a in order to win political support in the predominantly Christian south.[69] Another example was Umaru Yar'Adua, a vocal supporter of Shari'a legal system, who was governor of Katsina State in 2002 when Amina Lawal was sentenced to death by stoning. In December 2006, Yar'Adua was anointed the presidential candidate of the ruling Peoples Democratic Party (PDP) for the presidential election of April 2007. Soon after his selection, he began to make frantic efforts to convince the Christian community, human rights groups, and the international community that he was

[68] *See* DONALD SMILEY, THE FEDERAL CONDITION IN CANADA 39 (McGraw-Hill Ryerson 1987).
[69] Senan Murray, *Water Wars in Arid North Nigeria*, BBC NEWS, Apr. 18, 2007, *available at* <http://news.bbc.co.uk/2/hi/africa/6569057.stm> (last visited Aug. 25, 2007).

"a changed politician".[70] The incentive, amounting to a compulsion, for politicians to be secular and moderate is one cardinal virtue of the Nigerian constitutional invention. That incentive has saved the country from the possibility of becoming a theocracy and, consequently, from political perdition.

4. Inadequacies of the Nigerian design

If constitutional engineering has accomplished much, it has also demonstrated certain inadequacies that have set the country back.

One inadequacy is the violation of universal citizenship rights through the operation of the "federal character" principle (which requires recognition of the ethnic diversity of the federation). In the state and local governments, there is discrimination against nonindigenes (internal immigrants) in terms of political appointments and provision of public services and goods. At the federal level, the application of this principle in the civil service and national institutions has sacrificed merit to place of origin. Human Rights Watch has detailed extensive government discrimination against nonindigenes, and several studies have also analyzed the discrimination.[71] Elsewhere, the federal character principle was defended as a strategy for ensuring equal group access to political and economic resources; moreover, the argument was made that the violation of rights on account of federal character could be addressed by using residency as the basis for defining state and local government membership.[72] Membership in terms of residence in a relevant unit should serve as the criterion. From a liberal standpoint, residence translates into attachment to community and language competence, both of which, in turn, allow migrants to enjoy political and social rights wherever they live.

Another fundamental inadequacy of the design is its failure to accomplish, satisfactorily, the stated objective of reducing political domination by majority group elites. The creation of states was expected to be a political leveler, but this potential has not been fully realized, as the cultural ties and sentiments rendering the three major groups internally cohesive continue to endure. The old regional blocs—the north, east, and west—dominated by these groups, and the majority/minority differentials within them, have continued to persist in people's

[70] *Amina Lawal Haunts Yar'Adua*, Daily Times of Nigeria, Dec. 30–31, 2006, *reprinted at* <http://www.wluml.org/english/newsfulltxt.shtml?cmd%5B157%5D=x-157-548395>.

[71] *See* Human Rights Watch, *They Don't Own this Place: Government Discrimination Against Non-Indigenes of Nigeria*, 18 Hum. Rts. Watch (2006). For critical discussion of rights violations on account of the federal character principle, see Eghosa Osaghae, *Interstate Relations in Nigeria*, 24 Publius 83 (1994); Daniel Bach, *Indigeneity, Ethnicity and Federalism, in* Transition without End: Nigerian Politics and Civil Society under Babangida 333 (Larry Diamond, Anthony Kirk-Greene & Oyeleye Oyediran eds., Lynne Rienner 1997); Olufemi Taiwo, *Of Citizens and Citizenship, in* Constitutionalism and Society in Africa 55 (Okon Akiba ed., Ashgate 2004).

[72] *See* Ejobowah, *supra* note 31, at 148–150.

consciousness. Consequently, political competition essentially remains a three-player ethnic game in which minorities participate to tip the balance.

One reason for this continued dominance is the distribution of the states among groups and the effect of this distribution on the electoral system. The integrative electoral system was supposed to induce the formation of cross-ethnic alliances but, in fact, favors politicians whose ethnic groups have several states they can count on as virtual vote banks. Politicians from the majority groups can count on five, six, or even nine states for automatic political support, which provides the foundation for meeting the constitutional requirement for victory in presidential elections. On the other hand, politicians from minority groups that occupy a single state, or share one with other groups, have their guaranteed support confined to that state or a fraction thereof. For these politicians, meeting the conditions for victory requires that they stretch themselves to cover a greater part of the country, building more political bridges than are required of their more advantaged counterparts. Yet, in a divided society, where ethnic categories are the primary lens for viewing politics, ethnic minority politicians are hardly accepted outside their home base. This structural impediment has compelled minority elites to play the role of clients to majority elites, a role in which they deliver their states to a majority group presidential candidate in return for visible and rewarding public appointments.

The evidence is damning: with few exceptions, presidential elections held between 1979 and 2003 did not see the emergence of an ethnic minority politician as a presidential candidate. The exceptions were the quixotic Reverend Chris Okotie in 2003 and Alhaji Ibrahim Waziri in 1979.[73] Tired of playing second fiddle, politicians from the oil-producing south-south geoethnic zone met in 2004 to form the South-South People's Assembly for the explicit purpose of producing a president of Nigeria in 2007. They threatened to seek political confederation and take full control of their resources should their mission fail.[74] The mission failed.

Another reason for the majority groups' continued dominance is the flagrant violation of the unstated rules of the electoral system. The political actors have a tendency to meddle in the operation of the electoral system, preventing it from operating as it should. In the original conception of the electoral system, it was assumed that politicians would have ethnic followers, and that these politicians would be induced, necessarily, to reach out to rivals with a view to hammering out preelection bargains. The operation of the votepooling electoral system depended

---

[73] Reverend Chris Okotie was an Urhobo, a minority group in the Niger Delta. During the 2003 presidential elections, he obtained 119,547 (30 percent) of the total votes cast. Most of these were from his church followers. *See* African Elections Data Base, *available at* <http://africanelections.tripod.com/ng.html> (last visited Aug. 25, 2007). Waziri was a Kanuri, a minority group in the northeast. His party, the Great Nigerian Peoples Party, had difficulty maintaining offices outside Borno State, his home state. By 1983, the party had effectively ceased to exist outside home state and, in the elections of that year, the party lost Gongola. *See* Omoruyi, *supra* note 43.

[74] Southern Forum, *The Communique*, NIG. VANGUARD, Dec. 21, 2005; *South-South Peoples Assembly Clarifies on Presidency*, AKWA IBOM STATE NEWS, Oct. 20, 2006.

on the presumed presence of these sorts of politicians—not those without ethnic followers. This was a cardinal but unstated condition. Yet the Nigerian political elites violate this important condition by choosing presidential candidates who have no home support, causing the electoral system to malfunction and generate conflict.

For example, in the party primaries that led to the 1999 presidential election, Alex Ekwueme, from the Igbo-speaking southeast, contested the PDP's presidential ticket.[75] Few thought that he would lose: he was well educated; had served as vice president to Alhaji Shehu Shagari during the Second Republic of 1979–83; had led the formation of the Group of 34 Eminent Nigerians (also known as G34), that was transformed into the party; had the five Igbo-speaking states as guaranteed vote banks he could deliver to the party during elections; and opinion polls conducted by newspapers had him as the front runner.[76] Above all, the northern caucus within the party had conceded the presidential ticket to the south as a way of addressing charges of a northern monopoly of power. Yet he lost the PDP's primary election to Olusegun Obasanjo, whom the northern elite sponsored as their agent even though they had conceded the presidency to the south.

Obasanjo had a good track record. He had served as military ruler from 1977–79 and respected northern interests during his rule. And, when he voluntarily relinquished power in 1979, he faithfully returned it back to the north. Other than this record of trustworthiness, he was not a member of the PDP, was not privy to its formation, and had no knowledge of its history since he was in jail from 1995 to 1998. More importantly, Obasanjo did not have the political following of Yorubas that he would need for alliance formation. Instead, the latter rallied behind the Chief Olu Falae, the presidential candidate of the Alliance for Democracy, which was a reincarnation of the Yoruba parties of the First and Second Republics.

Thus, Obasanjo was a solitary politician, not even in the position to deliver the votes of his own home state, Ogun, let alone of all the six Yoruba states. Technically, the votepooling electoral system ought not to have generated him as a presidential candidate. Yet the northern caucus of the party anointed him on the reasoning that he would defend northern interests the way he did in the past. This was a blatant violation of the unstated rules of the electoral system. The violation caused an uproar among Igbo supporters of Alex Ekwueme, and they interpreted the latter's loss to mean a continuation of the civil war against Igbos.[77] Within a year, the secessionist Movement for the Actualization of the Sovereign State of Biafra (MASSOB) was born. In the five years that followed,

---

[75] Francis C. Enemuo, *Elite Solidarity, Communal Support, and the 1999 Presidential Election*, 27 Issue: J. Opinion 3 (1999).

[76] The Group of 34 Eminent Nigerians was organized in 1998 to resist attempts by military ruler General Abacha to succeed himself as a civilian president. After Abacha's death, the group metamorphosed into the People's Democratic Party. See Peter Lewis, *Nigeria, From Despair to Expectation*, 98 Current Hist. 223 (1999).

[77] Enemuo, *supra* note 75.

the political history of eastern Nigeria would be that of lawlessness and blood, as MASSOB carved the territory east of the Niger River into several Biafran provinces, hoisted a Biafran flag, established a radio station called the Voice of Biafra, operated Biafran headquarters from Okwe in Imo State, introduced and circulated its own currency, collected revenues and taxes, and adopted a national anthem and established other symbols of sovereignty.[78]

5. Political patronage, godfathers, and lawlessness

Oil is not only of great importance to the Nigerian economy it also gives the country a global presence. In world ranking for 2006, Nigeria was the twelfth largest producer of the commodity and the eighth largest net exporter—with only Saudi Arabia, Russia, Norway, Iran, the United Arab Emirates, Venezuela, and Kuwait as greater net exporters.[79] Nigeria's brand of oil is called the "Bonny Light Sweet" crude because it has less sulfur and low viscosity. It refines easily at lower temperatures compared with highly viscous oil that requires high temperatures and catalysts to process.[80] For this reason, it is preferred by several countries including the United States and India. The country's proven reserves are estimated at thirty-four billion barrels.[81] At the current production rate of 1.7–2.4 million barrels per day, the reserve will last for another four decades.[82] In addition, proven natural-gas reserves were estimated at 184.6 trillion cubic feet (for 2006), making Nigeria the seventh largest source of natural gas in the world.[83] The country has begun to liquefy and export this product with the prospect of further raising the contribution of petroleum to the economy.[84]

Given these facts, it is reasonable to assume that, in the next decades, Nigeria's reliance on oil exports will grow rather than decrease. It is unfortunate, then, that a major difficulty in Nigerian constitutional design arises out of the use of oil as an integrative device.

[78] Ise-Oluwa Ige, *MASSOB Leaders turn Down FG's Prerogative of Mercy, says They are Ready for Trial*, NIG. VANGUARD, Feb. 14, 2007; Unu Habib, *The MASSOB Insurgency*, NIG. VANGUARD, Jun. 17, 2005; Agaju Madugba, *MASSOB Threatens to Disrupt 2003 Polls*, THISDAY, Nov. 16, 2004, *available at* <http://www.thisdayonline.com/archive/2001/12/16/20011216news01.html> (last visited Aug. 26, 2007); Gbenga Osinaike, *Biafra Dollar*, SUNDAY PUNCH, Jun. 5, 2005; Lawrence Njok, Chuks Collins, Gbenga Akinfenwa & Uzoma Nzeagwu, *MASSOB Protest Grounds S'East*, NIG. GUARDIAN, Dec. 6, 2005.
[79] Energy Information Administration (EIA), Top World Oil Producers, *available at* <http://www.eia.doe.gov/emeu/cabs/topworldtables3_4.html> (last visited Aug. 26, 2007).
[80] Ron Singer, *Nigeria Slippery Politics*, 61 BULLETIN OF THE ATOMIC SCIENTISTS 3 (2005); Felix Ayadi, *Oil Price Fluctuations and the Nigerian Economy*, 29 OPEC REV. 199, 205 (2005).
[81] Energy Info. Admin, *supra* note 11, at 19.
[82] Ross, *supra* note 13, at 3.
[83] Energy Info. Admin., World Crude Oil and Natural Gas Reserves, Jan. 1, 2006, *available at* <http://www.eia.doe.gov/pub/international/iea2005/table81.xls> (last visited Aug. 26, 2007).
[84] Nig. Nat'l Petroleum Corp. (NNPC), Gas Investment Opportunities, *available at* <http://www.nnpcgroup.com/nigeriagas.htm> (last visited Aug. 27, 2007).

Dependence ought not to be an economic problem if the revenue derived is well utilized. The actual problem, which is political, begins with the restricted location of the oil. The commodity is found in the Niger delta and the adjoining wetlands that are home to various ethnic minority groups, the most numerous being the Ijaw, believed to be the fourth largest ethnic group in the country. Currently, there are no fewer than 606 operational oil fields in this region, 355 of which are onshore, accounting for 60 percent of Nigeria's petroleum output. The remaining 251 are in the wetlands and offshore, accounting for 40 percent of output.[85] Nigerian constitutional engineers have used oil as an integrative device by centralizing it under the control of the federal government and statutorily sharing its benefits vertically, between the federal and lower-tier governments, and horizontally, among the states and local governments, using distributive principles such as interunit equality and population. At the same time, some attempts to take into account the interests of the oil-producing states have been made through the allocation of 13 percent of oil revenue and the establishment of a centrally controlled Niger Delta Development Commission to respond to the regions' developmental needs.[86] This use of oil as an integrative device ostensibly frees the national government from charges of ethnoregional bias while simultaneously providing a source of funding for the integrative and accommodative arrangements. The importance of the oil revenue for the multiethnic federal arrangement can be measured by the fact that it accounts for about 80 percent of the annual income of the federal, state, and local governments.[87]

However, resource centralization, as an integrationist device, has proved to be a source of conflict throughout the country and, more so, in the Niger delta region for a number of reasons. First, resource redistribution, even though well intentioned, turned out to be a way of shifting a disproportionate cost of Nigeria's multiethnic federal arrangement onto the ethnic minority, oil-bearing communities. Directly or indirectly, these communities, through the resources in their lands, bear financial responsibility for the integrative and accommodative arrangements that were designed to keep the country intact.

Second, the redistribution program confers great economic importance on executive offices such as the presidency, the governorships of the states, and local chairmanships, all of which ethnic entrepreneurs have sought to control by efficient if illegitimate means. The struggle for the presidency is particularly intense because of the importance of the office. The presidency has direct access to the central bank through constitutional provisions that require its occupant to prepare a revenue-sharing formula, to release funds to each state and local government, and to draw up the annual budget of the federation.[88] In addition, the presidency

---

[85] *See* Nig. Nat'l Petroleum Corp. (NNPC), Development of Nigeria's Oil Industry, *available at* <http://www.nnpcgroup.com/development.htm> (last visited Aug. 26, 2007).

[86] NIG. CONST. 1999, § 162; Niger Delta Development Commission (Establishment Etc.) Act No. 6 (2000).

[87] SUBERU, *supra* note 18, at 48.   [88] NIG. CONST. 1999, §§ 80–82 & 162.

dominates the oil industry through the Ministry of Petroleum, which allocates oil blocks and licenses. Nigerian politicians, fractured by ethnicity and region, vie fiercely for control of this office and its spoils, a struggle that sometimes spirals so out of control as to threaten stability. Those unable to pursue the presidency compete for state governorships or local government chairmanships, and because these offices are limited there is considerable demand for the creation of new state and local governments. On the eve of the collapse of the Second Republic, thirty-two requests for more states were processed by the National Assembly. In 1986, seventeen requests were submitted to a government commission established by the military regime of Ibrahim Babangida. There were yet more demands: thirty-five during the constitutional conference of 1994–95, and twenty-three during the failed national political reform conference of 2005.[89] Some of these demands were driven by legitimate concerns regarding the political marginalization of certain groups, but most were aimed at having a share of the oil wealth.

Third, competition for power and resources has spawned several patronage networks that permeate the public domain. In Nigeria, elites compete for power not in a random or isolated manner but within a traditional ethnic-based power structure. It is a structure in which ethnic entrepreneurs maintain dominant positions in their communities by patronizing an array of clients, who, in turn, play the role of patrons by maintaining their own local clients in a network whose tentacles reach into every town, village, and residential area. Ethnic support is mobilized from the bottom up, and, in return, patronage flows from the top down. This local ethnic compact among elites is deployed by politicians as they compete for power and resources at all tiers of government. Once in office, politicians utilize public resources to service and expand these networks, a practice that is somewhat akin to what Houchang E. Chehabi and Juan Linz have described as neopatrimonialism.[90] Neither cabinet positions nor the creation of states nor crude oil is spared. Regarding cabinet positions, the constitutional provision that requires the equitable distribution of public appointments is used as a cover for multiplying ministerial positions in order to expand the patron-client networks across ethnic lines. In 1978, on the eve of the adoption of these constitutional mechanisms, there were a total of twenty federal ministerial portfolios. By comparison, there were twenty-five federal ministers in 1979, thirty-five in 1983, and forty in 2007.[91]

[89] NIGERIA REPORT, *supra* note 46, at 169; FEDERAL REPUBLIC OF NIGERIA, *supra* note 49, vol. 2 at 192.
[90] *See* Houchang Esfandiar Chebabi & Juan José Linz, *A Theory of Sultanism 1: A Type of Nondemocratic Rule, in* SULTANISTIC REGIMES 3 (Houchang E. Chebabi & Juan Linz eds., John Hopkins Univ. Press 1998); Houchang E. Chebabi & Juan J. Linz, *A Theory of Sultanism 2: Genesis and Demise of Sultanistic Regimes, in* SULTANISTIC REGIMES, *supra* note 90, at 26.
[91] Partly derived from ABDUL RAUFU MUSTAPHA, ETHNIC STRUCTURE, INEQUALITY AND GOVERNANCE OF THE PUBLIC SECTOR IN NIGERIA 18 (U.N. Res. Inst. Soc. Res., Democracy Governance & Hum. Rts. Programme Paper No. 4, Nov. 2006).

Regarding the ongoing creation of new states and local governments, discussed earlier, the multiplication of entities was done, ostensibly, in the "national interest", to "redress inequity", to "guarantee justice and fair play", and to "give minorities a voice in local and national affairs".[92] Nonetheless, some of this also was done in return for regime support. Brennan Kraxberger has made an empirical study of the creation of Ekiti State in 1996. He noted that General Sani Abacha, who ruled as military head of state from 1993 to 1998, used state creation to make political inroads into Yoruba land, where the organized Yoruba leadership under Egbe Afenifere had mounted opposition to his regime. According to Kraxberger, Abacha formed a network with Ekiti political elites, which had been lobbying vainly for a state since 1980. In exchange for Abacha's promise to create Ekiti State, the local leaders spurned the Egbe Afenifere–led campaign to isolate Abacha's regime.[93] After the state was created, the local leaders organized a rally at the Ado-Ekiti soccer stadium, "where representatives of all communities supported Abacha's bid to transform himself into a civilian head of state".[94]

On crude oil, Nigerian leaders went for the kill, offering political clients licenses to sell the commodity in the international market. From the early 1990s, when the military ruled, senior military officials and politicians began to head illegal oil rackets, not all that different from what William Reno has termed the "shadow state".[95] By 2005, racketeering was well entrenched and costing Nigeria 15.2 percent of its annual oil production, a loss that Tony Blair's Commission for Africa has estimated at $4.4 billion dollars per annum.[96]

What emerges, then, is the spectacle of patron-client networks pervading all strata of government and many aspects of the economy and society. Those at the helms of these pyramidally structured networks become, as it were, godfathers or political strongmen. These strongmen install protégés in office and dispose of them as the need arises. Some of these strongmen preside over vast patronage networks that crisscross ethnic lines so well that these elites could be seen as godfather-led multiethnic coalitions. The coalition blunts deep ethnic divisions among actors, giving the impression that the constitutional engineering goal of building panethnic elites, a sort of community of the whole whose interests transcend ethnicity, has been realized.[97] This is false for two reasons.

---

[92] FEDERAL REPUBLIC OF NIGERIA, 2 REPORT OF THE CONSTITUTIONAL CONFERENCE, *supra* note 49, at 55.
[93] Kraxberger, *supra* note 62.
[94] *Id.* at 429.
[95] William Reno, *Clandestine Economies, Violence and States in Africa*, 53 J. INT'L. AFF. 434 (2000).
[96] *See* Salisu Na'inna Dambatta, *Tackling Vandalism in Nigeria's Oil Industry*, NIG. VANGUARD, Oct. 13, 2003, for full report from the Blair Commission for Africa; *see also* COMM'N FOR AFR., OUR COMMON INTEREST: REPORT OF THE COMMISSION FOR AFRICA (2005), *available at* <http://www.commissionforafrica.org/english/report/thereport/english/11-03-05_cr_report.pdf>.
[97] *See* Richard Sklar, Ebere Onwudiwe & Darren Kew, *Nigeria: Completing Obasanjo's Legacy*, 17 J. DEMOCRACY 100, 105 (2006).

First, the godfather-led patronage network has nothing to do with nation building or idealistic goals of political stability. It is simply a system in which self-seeking elites of different ethnic hues are united in their rapacious aims. This predatory point of unity also sets the elites in head-on collision, a collision that leads to mutual assassinations, actual and attempted, in much the same way outlaws might eliminate each other over the loot. In almost every state of the Nigerian federation, there have been high-profile political assassinations without a single prosecution of the killers. In August 2006, the country's Senate, apparently helpless, passed a motion condemning "the spate of assassinations in the country" and summoning the Inspector General of Police to explain "the apparent inability of the Security Agencies to conclusively apprehend and prosecute the perpetrators".[98]

Second, the godfather-led multiethnic coalition is the quintessential manifestation of how the use of oil as an integrative device must fail. A coalition of this sort permits strongmen to convert the country into fiefdoms. It is prone to intense conflicts that spill over into the streets when protégés fight to establish independence from their godfathers or when rivals struggle to undermine each other. In states such as Anambra and Oyo, attempts by protégés to free themselves from their godfathers have made for an all-out war. In the case of Anambra State, the then governor Chris Ngige was abducted and removed from office in 2003 for reneging on an agreement to turn over the state's monthly share of federal revenue to his godfather who was himself a protégé of the president.[99] On another occasion, the governor was bombed and driven out of his residence by the same strongman. At some point, Ngige adopted a nomadic lifestyle, moving from place to place in order to elude capture. Eventually, he was removed by legal means in 2006.[100] Still, peace remained elusive. A similar situation emerged in Oyo State in the Yoruba southwest, where Rashidi Ladoja, upon being sworn in as the legitimate governor in 2003, refused to hand over the state's monthly security allocation to his seventy-eight-year-old political strongman.[101] In January 2006, the strongman removed the governor from office and replaced him with another protégé, using illicit violence and manipulation of the federally controlled police force. The governor was reinstated by the courts in December 2006, but there

---

[98] Senate of the Federal Republic of Nigeria, Order Paper 36–37 (5th Nat'l Assem. Fourth Session No. 18, Aug. 22, 2006).

[99] Olawale Olayele, *Anambra: Ngige and the Growing List of Casualties*, Thisday, Nov. 16, 2004.

[100] Ise Oluwa Ige, *Why Andy Uba Had to Go, by Supreme Court*, Nig. Vanguard, July 14, 2007; Chief Audu Ogbeh's Letter to President Olusegun Obasanjo Re: Anambra and Related Matters, Dec. 6, 2004; President Olusegun Obasanjo's Reply to Ogbeh's Letter, Dec. 12, 2004, *available at* <http://www.waado.org/nigerdelta/Politics/PDP_crisis/ogbeh_obasanjo.html> (last visited Aug. 26, 2007).

[101] Emmanuel Okodolo, *Ladoja: A Final Showdown*, Daily Independent, May 18, 2007; Ola Ajayi, *Gunfire in Ibadan as Ladoja, Adedibu Supporters Clash*, Nig. Vanguard, Dec. 23, 2005; Eddy Odivwri, *Oyo PDP: Between the Hammer and the Anvil*, Thisday, Nov. 16, 2004.

continued to be violent confrontations between armed fighters of both sides.[102] In February 2007, the military was deployed into the streets of Ibadan, the state capital, to "prevent total breakdown of law and order".[103]

These two cases are typical and should inspire the legitimate fear that Nigeria could suffer the fate of Sierra Leone or Liberia, where the states simply collapsed. In these two countries, state failure was triggered by the violent struggle for power by rival strongmen. In Nigeria, conflicts between strongmen and protégés have been common at the subnational arena; moreover, at the national level, such struggles are not unheard of. During his second tenure as elected president, Obasanjo used the power of the presidency to build an extensive patron-client network that could have made him a newly emergent godfather, thereby marginalizing the rivals who were standing in his way. In pursuing this, he came into direct confrontation with Abubakar Atiku, his deputy but also an established godfather in his own right, who, by all accounts, was in control of the ruling party. The power struggle between these two leaders in Abuja seemed to suggest that Nigeria could collapse.

Collapse is not likely, however, given the capacity of the country's godfathers and protégés to make compromises when their brinkmanship threatens to let national power drain into the streets. This is an attribute of the Nigerian elites that has served to keep the country intact and derives, chiefly, from the bitter experiences of the Biafran civil war of 1967–70. From the war, they have learned that their collective interests, if not necessarily the public good, would be best served if the country does not fall apart. Thus, the elites seem to back off when their political struggles verge on breaking up the country. Though the ability to compromise during critical junctures has been displayed since the 1990s, it is rarely driven by altruism or public interest. The elites' private motivations remain self-interest and the pursuit of power and wealth, similar to John Stuart Mill's moral action of saving a drowning person in order to fulfill his motive to inflict more pain on her.[104]

6. Constitutional rescue

What should be done, given the failure of the integrationist electoral system to free national power from the control of a few powerful ethnic groups? What can

---

[102] Bolade Omonijo, Ola Ajayi, Dayo Johnson, and Umory Henry, *Ladoja Sacked*, NIG. VANGUARD, Jan. 13, 2006; Bolaji Omoniyi, *What Ladoja Must Do Now*, NIG. VANGUARD, Dec. 9, 2006.

[103] Akin Durodola, Tope Abiola, Rotimi Omole, and Banjo Alabi, *Soldiers Drafted to Ibadan*, NIG. TRIBUNE, Feb. 6, 2007, *available at* <http://www.tribune.com.ng/06022007/news/news1.html>.

[104] *See*, for a discussion of the relationship between intention and morality, JOHN STUART MILL, UTILITARIANISM, ON LIBERTY, CONSIDERATIONS ON REPRESENTATIVE GOVERNMENT 12 (Harry B. Acton ed., Dent 1972).

be done, given the problems of patronage and the intense conflicts arising from the use of oil as an integrationist device? Should these devices be abandoned?

The answers to these questions may be found in the several proposals for constitutional change that have been made since 1995. The relevant proposals are, first, a consociational single-term rotational presidency among the six geoethnic zones, as contained in the rejected 1995 draft constitution, and, second, the partial devolution of rights to natural resources from the center to the constituent states.[105] These proposals have normative weight and can easily be reconciled with liberal democratic principles. The strongest normative feature is that rotation meets the liberal principle of equality, since it creates equitable conditions for majority and minority elites to compete, equally, for the highest office of the land. Resource devolution also satisfies the principle of self-determination, because it creates the conditions whereby groups, internally separated by their own politics, can generate their revenue needed to run their affairs and to operate their institutions. I need not elaborate on these normative arguments for rescuing Nigeria's constitutional arrangements. Instead, I will consider the factors that have militated against the adoption of these prescriptions.

First, a rotational presidency reconcilable with liberal principles finds its most formidable roadblock in the emirate sectors of the north. The emirate sectors are primarily Muslim domains traditionally ruled by emirs who owe allegiance to their suzerain, the Sultan of Sokoto (supreme head of all Muslims). In these sectors, there is the fear that formalizing the six geoethnic zones and rotating the presidency among the zones would amplify the emirate–nonemirate fissure that exists in the north, decisively free nonemirate areas from emirate authority, and completely undermine the system through which emirs retain control over much of the north. For this reason, the power establishment from the emirate north is averse to formal zoning and rotation of the presidency. The most they can agree to is rotation between the north and south.

Second, any resource devolution that is consistent with the principle of self-determination is resisted by the ethnic minority states of the middle belt, which make up the north-central zone. In this zone, there is sufficient opposition to devolution that it has the potential to diminish the ability of the central government to check the excesses of local power brokers. The elites of these northern minority states prefer the current system of centralized oil revenue because it renders the states and local governments dependent on the center and enables the latter to act as a check against the hegemony of the emirates. The current system, which structurally constrains the autonomy of local rulers, is regarded as a defense mechanism against emirate power.

However, the chief obstacle to devolution is the relatively small area in which oil is to be found, primarily in the ethnic minority states of the Niger delta. Of the existing thirty-six states, only nine produce oil, and of these three are marginal

---

[105] DRAFT NIG. CONST. 1995 (with Amendment), *supra* note 49.

producers.[106] This asymmetry makes it difficult for the remaining twenty-seven, which are in the majority, to commit to devolution. Devolution, if it occurs, has the prospect of driving these have-not states into immediate financial crisis and possible political collapse. Even partial devolution, which entails granting a 50 percent derivation, could compromise the economic sustenance and political stability of the have-not states. Indeed, such devolution could prompt the have-not states to seek financing from the wealthier states, possibly resulting in the latter emerging as creditors to the former. Consequently, ethnic majority states would be big debtors to the ethnic minority oil states with the potential of the latter's elites becoming the main controllers of national power. On account of this anticipated consequence, majority group elites have been impervious to pressure for resource devolution.

These combined factors have worked to prevent Nigerian ethnic elites from mobilizing for constitutional rescue. Contrary to commonly expressed views, the lack of a national consensus regarding the above prescriptions has little to do with the purportedly lengthy procedure of persuading the bicameral National Assembly and the unicameral legislatures of the thirty-six states to assent to constitutional amendments.[107] The obstacle is political, rather than procedural, and has to be settled through negotiations. Constitutional negotiations have long been part of Nigeria's political odyssey. The last successfully concluded negotiation, which occurred in 1994–95, during the military regime of General Sani Abacha, was driven by fears of political disintegration. However, the threatening conditions that enabled the 1994–95 negotiations are present now, more than ever before. Evidence is seen in the global roster of failed states in which Nigeria rose from the fifty-fifth ranking in 2005, to twenty-second in 2006, and to seventeenth in 2007.[108] Since 2003, it has consistently appeared on the World Bank's listings of fragile states.[109] In 1994–95, when conditions were less threatening, the Nigerian ethnic elites were able to negotiate innovative consociational devices to complement the constitutional design of 1979.[110] If the conditions of the mid-1990s could prompt ethnic elites to agree on those elaborate accommodationist devices, as complements to the design that was already in place, then present-day conditions are more threatening and, therefore, perhaps even more inviting to the elites to pursue a nationwide constitutional rescue.[111]

---

[106] Calculated by the author from the monthly allocation of revenue to states. *See* Fed. Ministry of Finance, Distribution of Revenue Allocation to the State Governments, *available at* <http://www.fmf.gov.ng/portal/detail.php?link=faac> (last visited Aug. 26, 2007) (Nig.).

[107] *See* Suberu, *supra* note 61, at 151.

[108] *The Failed States Index 2007, supra* note 3; *The Failed States Index 2006*, 149 FOREIGN POL'Y 59 (2005); Anonymous, *The Failed States Index 2006*, 154 FOREIGN POL'Y 53 (2006).

[109] World Bank, *Which Countries are LICUS?, available at* <http://www.worldbank.org/ieg/licus/licus06_map.html> (last visited Aug. 26, 2007).

[110] Lewis, *supra* note 47.

[111] For a discussion of the possibility of Nigeria's political collapse, see Bach, *supra* note 4, at 63.

7. Conclusion

Whereas the contemporary literature on constitutional design for ethnically divided societies often presents integration and accommodation as competing strategies, Nigeria's experiment in constitutional engineering shows that these strategies are not mutually exclusive. The Nigerian design proves that accommodationist and integrationist institutional repertoires can be feasibly combined in a variety of ways that were, perhaps, not previously imagined. Such a combination, as the evidence suggests, has enabled territorially concentrated groups to have their own self-governing units and preserved the country by fragmenting groups and undermining their coherence. Further, this combination raised the profile of minorities by making them key political players, minimized large-scale conflict by devolving legislative, executive, and judicial institutions that respond to local peculiarities and challenges, and made for the emergence of unifying national leaders who respect but elevate themselves above factions. Only a wise constitutional design could realize, simultaneously, the virtues of accommodation and integration as did the Nigerian design.

However, the situation in Nigeria also shows that where integrationist and accommodationist repertoires are combined, the integrationist components can prove problematic. In the specific case of Nigeria, the difficulties include a destructive patronage system and the failure to free the presidency from the control of the most powerful groups. Where patronage networks are extensive, as the information indicates, formal rules and institutions are captured by those at the head of the patronage networks, while political competition is transformed into violent struggles among these leaders. These violence-prone struggles, little different from aristocratic struggles for territory and power during feudal times, may not lead to Nigeria's political collapse as occurred in Liberia and Sierra Leone, but they could keep the country perpetually fragile. The solution, then, is not to abandon the integrationist components but to complement them with more accommodationist measures that involve a rotational presidency and partial devolution of resources. Because these proposals have normative weight, the impediments that stand in their way serve as warnings that constitutional engineering devices are the products of political negotiations not abstract models available to be picked over and applied mechanically.

9

The limits of constitutionalism in the Muslim world: History and identity in Islamic law

*Anver M. Emon**

1. Introduction

In the fields of constitutional law and human rights, protection from discrimination on religious grounds is a significant concern. Constitutions around the world protect religious liberty and conscience, as do various human rights documents. However, sometimes these same constitutions have limiting phrases that also raise human rights concerns. For example, constitutions in the Muslim world, while protecting religious freedom and conscience, also state that no law can violate Shari'a principles. If one defines Shari'a to include the historical tradition that discriminated on religious grounds,[1] a conflict arises between upholding Shari'a and protecting religious freedom. While the rights provisions

* Assistant Professor, Faculty of Law, University of Toronto. This paper was written, in part, during my stay in the beautiful atmosphere of the Schloss Leopoldskron in Salzburg, Austria, where I presented my initial ideas at the Salzburg Seminar. I want to thank (ret.) Justice Richard Goldstone for giving me an opportunity to present my work at the seminar. The paper received substantive feedback when I presented it at the Ethnicity and Democratic Governance Spoke 2 Conference (Univ. Toronto, Nov. 3–4, 2006), Yale Law School's Middle East Legal Studies Seminar (Athens, Greece, Jan. 18–21, 2007), and a seminar at the University of Texas at Austin (Feb. 26, 2007), hosted by Dr. Denise Spellberg. I am grateful to my colleagues and interlocutors at all these events, and especially want to thank Joseph Carens, Sujit Choudhry, Norman Dorsen, Owen Fiss, Robert Gibbs, Wael Hallaq, Will Kymlicka, Chibli Mallat, and Denise Spellberg for their insights, critiques, and feedback. All translations from Arabic sources are by the author, who takes responsibility for any errors that remain.

[1] For varying studies of the historical Islamic legal treatment of non-Muslims, see generally 'ABD AL-KARIM ZAYDAN, AHKAM AL-DHIMMIYYIN WA AL-MUSTA'MININ (Mu'assasat al-Risala 2d ed. 1988); Yohanan Friedman, *Classification of Unbelievers in Sunni Muslim Law and Tradition*, 22 JERUSALEM STUD. IN ARABIC & ISLAM 163 (1998); Clifford Edmund Bosworth, *The Concept of Dhimma in Early Islam, in* 1 CHRISTIAN AND JEWS IN THE OTTOMAN EMPIRE: THE FUNCTIONING OF A PLURAL SOCIETY 37 (Bernard Lewis & Benjamin Braude eds., Holmes & Meier Publishers 1982); Muhammad Hamidullah, *Status of Non-Muslims in Islam*, 45 MAJALLAT AL-AZHAR 6 (1973).

reflect an integrationist approach to religious diversity, the constitutional incorporation of Shariʿa accommodates the dominant religious group to the point of undermining, both in theory and often in practice, the integrationist effort to protect vulnerable minorities. To resort to theories of accommodation or integration, by themselves, in order to resolve tensions in pluralist societies, arguably does not adequately address the roots of the tension or offer constructive modes of resolution.

This tension arises, in large measure, because of how Shariʿa is sometimes defined, namely, in terms of premodern rules of law.[2] One might wonder, perhaps, why the historical tradition of Islamic law should matter in the twenty-first century. Why not leave it in the past? In the wake of postcolonial nationalist movements in regions such as the Muslim world, some have argued that a "time paradox" has arisen, which makes the past substantively relevant for the construction of modern national identity.[3] In the case of Muslim nations, that might mean incorporating premodern Shariʿa rules explicitly into the legal framework, in part, as a symbol of national identity. Such societies, arising out of the ashes of colonialism, seek nationalist definitions that distinguish them from their former colonial masters, establish an authentic identity, and, at the same time, facilitate their participation in a global market and in diplomatic engagement with former colonial powers. The need to be authentic—distinct from prior masters—and, simultaneously, to be participants in a global environment creates a tension in how a relatively new state can distinguish itself without, at the same time, isolating itself from the global stage.[4]

In looking to the past for a sense of identity, Muslim states certainly had options to draw on from the Islamic intellectual tradition. Perhaps Sufism, with its mystical tradition, could be a source of national identity.[5] Similarly, the Islamic philosophical tradition raised considerable questions about religion, politics, and identity that could have been harnessed for creating a sense of the political self. But such substantive modes most likely lack a determinacy that might give comfort to one seeking a source of identity.

If determinacy in tradition is important for defining and anchoring identity, then the rules of Islamic law (*fiqh*) can provide an easy and efficient option for Muslim states. The determinacy of these rules provides an anchor or reference

---

[2] See Anver M. Emon, *Conceiving Islamic Law in a Pluralist Society: History, Politics and Multicultural Jurisprudence*, 2006 SING. J. LEGAL STUD. 331 (2006), for a historical discussion of the political provenance of this particular conception of Shariʿa.

[3] Anne McClintock, *Family Feuds: Gender, Nationalism and the Family*, 44 FEMINIST REV. 61 (1993).

[4] See ROXANNE EUBEN, ENEMY IN THE MIRROR: ISLAMIC FUNDAMENTALISM AND THE LIMITS OF MODERN RATIONALISM: A WORK OF COMPARATIVE POLITICAL THEORY (Princeton Univ. Press 1999), on the way Islamic fundamentalism anchors disputes on political identity.

[5] Historians have noted how Sufi movements have provided an impetus for independence drives against colonial occupation. *See, e.g.,* ITZHAK WEISMANN, TASTE OF MODERNITY: SUFISM, SALAFIYYA, AND ARABISM IN LATE OTTOMAN DAMASCUS (Brill 2001).

point for creating a thick sense of identity against the perceived anemia of the liberal, atomistic individual.[6] Muslim states have often incorporated Islamic law into their legal systems, in part, to offer a fixed source for their legal systems and, thereby, for their national identity.[7] For the purposes of this chapter, then, Shariʿa as political symbol involves the use of historical rules to give substantive content to the political identity of the nation at both the domestic and international level.[8]

What this suggests is that, when analyzing protections of religious minorities in the constitutions of Muslim countries, one cannot ignore the fact that constitutional reference to Islamic law has a political dimension that can impede attempts to reform the law's tenets in accordance with human rights values. Consequently, when new constitutions in the region are heralded as steps forward in democracy, as was the case with the Afghan and Iraqi constitutions, a question necessarily arises about the extent to which religious minorities are sufficiently protected if Islamic law is also part of the constitutional legal order.[9]

Does this mean that Islamic law should not find a place in such constitutions? To suggest as much would be to limit, artificially, the democratic process of drafting constitutions. Rather, constitutions are only first steps in creating a constitutional legal order. They must be only so strong that they do not fail at the outset. By themselves, they can embody only as much meaning as the underlying culture permits. Where the fundamental cultural context is defined in a historical Shariʿa-based language, more than a constitution will be required to ensure a constitutional culture that will respect religious freedom. The scope of constitutional argument likely will be limited by the constraining power of the prevailing normative framework for institutions of law and government. The challenge, therefore, is to recognize that immediate constitutional reform must

---

[6] EUBEN, *supra* note 4, writes about the communitarian logic underlying Islamic fundamentalism. Her important work is significant for understanding the role of tradition and its perceived continuity with the present as a basis for identity construction.

[7] In fact, the nineteenth-century Muslim reformer Muhammad Abduh argued that a nation's laws respond to its prevailing contexts, and he suggests, therefore, that the meaningfulness of law depends on whether it reflects the circumstances, mores, and identity of its people. Muhammad Abduh, *Ikhtilaf al-Qawanin bi Ikhtilaf Ahwal al-Umam, in* AL-AʿMAL AL-KAMILA LIʾL-IMAM MUHAMMAD ABUDUH: AL-KITABAT AL-SIYASIYYA 309–315 (al-Muʾassasa al-ʿArabiyya 1972).

[8] This is especially true in light of the fact that most Muslim countries do not use Islamic law throughout their legal systems but only in piecemeal fashion in areas like family law and, less often, in criminal law. *See* Wael B. Hallaq, *Can the Shariʿa be Restored?, in* ISLAMIC LAW AND THE CHALLENGES OF MODERNITY 21 (Yvonne Yazbeck Haddad & Barbara Freyer Stowasser eds., Altamira Press 2005).

[9] This question was most prominently portrayed in 2006 when an Afghan man, Abdul Rahman, was tried in an Afghan court for abandoning the Islamic faith. M. Cherif Bassiouni, *Leaving Islam is not a Capital Crime*, CHI. TRIB., Apr. 2, 2006, at C9; Margaret Wente, *Death to the Apostate*, GLOBE AND MAIL, Mar. 28, 2006, at A19; Wesal Zaman & Henry Chu, *Afghan Case Dropped but not Closed*, L.A. TIMES, Mar. 27, 2006, at A14. *But cf.* IRAQ CONST. art. 2, § 1 (which provides that no law shall violate the established tenets of Islamic law, the principles of democracy, or the basic freedoms protected under the Constitution), arts. 39–41 (defining and guaranteeing protection of freedoms of thought, conscience, belief, and worship).

be accompanied by long-term efforts to understand those normative frameworks and to offer acceptable alternatives. This chapter is an initial attempt at offering a model for understanding, holistically, the doctrine and history of Shari'a and its role in modern state legal systems. The model offered incorporates historical and hermeneutic models of meaning and understanding, which I call a historicist jurisprudence of Islamic law. By no means is this the first effort at such an approach to Islam.[10] Nor is it alone in challenging the ways in which modern Muslim states use Shari'a to justify discriminating against religious minorities.[11] But its contribution, one hopes, will be in bridging the premodern and the modern contexts of Shari'a by relying on theoretical approaches to legal hermeneutics and by doing so in light of competing frameworks of governance, legislation, adjudication, and legal analysis.

2. Historicist jurisprudence: Manifesting the transcendent through law

The idea of a historicist jurisprudence of Islamic law embraces the claim that the doctrinal rules emerged from extralegal value systems manifest in history, which gave the rules meaning. By using a historicist lens to understand both the transcendent values and how they were manifested in the rules that expressed them, one can determine the extent to which the rules are products of a contextually based jurisprudential vision, and whether that vision resonates similarly in contemporary constitutional states immersed in the international system. If the normative values and context of the present substantially differ from those of the past (which I assume they do), then the continued authority and meaningfulness of the premodern rules may be questioned in light of the dissonances in meaningfulness they create in contemporary constitutional governments. I explicitly assume this historical shift in light of the move from an imperial Islamic past to

---

[10] See Fazlur Rahman, Islamic Methodology in History (Islamic Res. Inst. 1984); Albrecht Noth, The Early Arabic Historical Tradition: A Source-Critical Study (Michael Bonner trans., Darwin Press 2d ed. 1994); Tarif Khalidi, Arabic Historical Thought in the Classical Period (Cambridge Univ. Press 1994); Ebrahim Moosa, Ghazali and the Poetics of Imagination (UNC Press 2005), for a variety of historicist and hermeneutic approaches to Islamic studies.

[11] See Zaydan, *supra* note 1, for an analysis of the historical rules of Shari'a as well as critiques of how Muslim states use Shari'a to discriminate against non-Muslims; *see also* Abdullahi Ahmed An-Na'im, Toward an Islamic Reformation: Civil Liberties Human Rights, and International Law (Syracuse Univ. Press 1990); Ahmad Dallal, *Yemeni Debates on the Status of Non-Muslims in Islamic Law,* 7 Islam & Christian-Muslim Rel. 181 (1996); Fazlur Rahman, *Non-Muslim Minorities in an Islamic State,* 7 J. Inst. Muslim Minority Aff. 13 (1986); Ghazi Salahuddin Atabani, *Islamic Shari'ah and the Status of Non-Muslims, in* Religion, Law and Society: A Christian-Muslim Discussion 63 (Tarek Mitri ed., WCC Publ'n 1995); Ismail R. Al-Faruqi, *The Rights of non-Muslims under Islam: Social and Cultural Aspects, in* Muslim Communities in Non-Muslim States 43 (Islamic Council Eur. 1980).

an international system of states, institutions, and multilateral relations, all of which offer alternative normative systems of limits and boundaries that hinder the imperial mode.[12] I will offer some examples to illustrate how the modern context has changed in ways significant for historicist jurisprudence of Islamic law. However, this study is not the place for an in-depth analysis of the normative frameworks of modern Muslim states.

This is not to suggest that a historicist jurisprudence assumes the constitutional state is inherently normative. Rather, the historical reality is that Muslims live in state systems, that such states are often organized constitutionally, and that the states interact amid international norms and treaties, and it is this situation that contributes to my assumption of change and the existence of a different normative framework of governance, community, and identity.[13] A historicist jurisprudence is concerned with how these facts compel reflection on the meaningfulness of premodern Islamic norms in a context of changed political institutions and modes of identity.

Islamic law at the doctrinal level is considerably diverse. Early Muslim jurists debated the significance of this diversity and what it meant for notions of legal authority, the objectivity of law, and the space for creativity in juristic interpretation.[14] However, the way Islamic law is conceptualized today in the popular press and in political discourse as rigid and unchanging often prevents significant modification of the tradition without engendering conflict at various levels of society.[15] This contemporary depiction of Islamic law also impedes efforts to rethink Shari'a as a rule-of-law system that can be meaningful within constitutional

---

[12] The same international system brings into question the new American imperialism, in which "democracy" is promoted as the new universal value to be disseminated throughout the world, potentially, even by means of coercive military engagement.

[13] For enlightening philosophical accounts of how fundamental values or conceptions of identity can and do change over time, see ALASDAIR C. MacINTYRE, WHOSE JUSTICE? WHICH RATIONALITY? (Univ. Notre Dame Press 1989); CHARLES TAYLOR, SOURCES OF THE SELF: THE MAKING OF THE MODERN IDENTITY (Harvard Univ. Press 1992).

[14] In early Islamic legal theory treatises, jurists asked whether every jurist is correct (*hal kullu al-mujtahid musib*). This question incited a significant debate about the nature of authority and objectivity in the law, and whether the jurist's role is, formalistically, to discover or find the law or, instead, to function as an active participant in the construction of Islamic rules of law: 2 ABU BAKR AL-JASSAS, AL-FUSUL FI AL-USUL 400–440 (Dar al-Kutub al-'Ilmiyya 2000); 4 SAYF AL-DIN AL-AMIDI, AL-IHKAM FI USUL AL-AHKAM 178–197 (2d ed. al-Maktab al-Islami 1981); KHALED ABOU EL FADL, SPEAKING IN GOD'S NAME: ISLAMIC LAW, AUTHORITY AND WOMEN 147–150 (Oneworld Publ'n 2001).

[15] The conflict between Muslim states and the international community is evident when Muslim countries adopt reservations and conditions favoring deference to an ambiguous and seemingly ahistorical Shari'a when ratifying various human rights treaties. *See, e.g.,* ANN ELIZABETH MAYER, ISLAM AND HUMAN RIGHTS: TRADITION AND POLITICS (2d ed. Westview Press 1995); Ann Elizabeth Mayer, *Internationalizing the Conversation on Women's Rights: Arab Countries Face the CEDAW Committee, in* ISLAMIC LAW AND THE CHALLENGES OF MODERNITY, *supra* note 8, at 133. But a conflict between the state and domestic Islamist parties can also arise, thereby complicating a government's reformist agenda, as in the history of Morocco's family-law reform. Ilhem Rachidi, *After Struggle, New Equality for Moroccan Women,* CHRISTIAN SCI. MONITOR, Oct. 24, 2003, at 9.

societies that espouse liberal commitments.[16] Consequently, when constitutions refer to Shariʿa as a source of law, the "Shariʿa" that is often invoked is a premodern tradition of law contained in treatises centuries old.[17] These doctrinal sources contain rules regarding religious practice and social order at both the public and private levels. But these rules are not transparently derived from fundamental scriptural sources such as the Qurʾan and the traditions of the Prophet. Rather, premodern Muslim jurists imaginatively read and interpreted them in order to reach a rule of law.[18]

Given the role jurists played in interpreting Islamic law, rules such as those concerning the treatment of religious minorities necessarily reflect the historically conditioned values of those jurists. Those values operate as "background factors", or, in the words of Charles Taylor and Jürgen Habermas, respectively, "moral frameworks" or "lifeworlds" that influenced how premodern jurists interpreted texts and manifested fundamental values in rules of law that were expressed in the shared, technical, and ultimately coercive language of the law. This is not to say that the rules of law espoused in legal texts differed from region to region, or from author to author, due to idiosyncratic shifts in value. Certainly, one notices, for example, that Shafiʿi rules of law articulated in legal texts generally were similar across regions of the premodern Muslim world. Rather, I suggest that while the continuity of the rules may reflect a need for determinacy in law, akin to the common law doctrine of *stare decisis*, the specific precedents themselves arose out of a process of interpretation in light of normative background values about social and political ordering. By taking a critical historicist perspective, one can come to understand how and why certain values became manifest in rules of law, while also questioning the efficacy and substantive justice of those rules in a contemporary state where background norms and rule-of-law institutions have considerably changed.

The idea that the law reflects underlying normative frameworks that influence legal interpretations is not new to the field of legal theory and hermeneutics. This chapter in no way attempts to survey the field of hermeneutic philosophy. Rather,

---

[16] Emon, *supra* note 2; EUBEN, *supra* note 4.

[17] In his commentary on the 1949 Egyptian Civil Code, ʿAbd al-Razzaq al-Sanhuri wrote that the Shariʿa can be a source of law if the code or custom gives no guidance for a particular matter. He defines Shariʿa as the rules of law in books of *fiqh*, or, in other words, the premodern rules of law. He is careful, though, to articulate two caveats in utilizing the Shariʿa. First, no particular school of law should be preferred over the others; and, second, any derived rule from the *fiqh* cannot violate any general principle established in the Civil Code. 1 ʿABD AL-RAZZAQ AL-SANHURI, AL-WASIT FI SHARH AL-QANUN AL-MADANI AL-JADID 44–50 (Dar al-Nahda al-ʿArabiyya no date).

[18] The concept of juristic interpretation is captured by the Arabic term *ijtihad*. Considerable scholarly work has been devoted to understanding this term, while reformist literature has argued for the need to engage in a new *ijtihad*. For studies of this term and its place in Islamic legal theory, see Wael Hallaq, *Was the Gate of Ijtihad Closed?*, 16 INT'L J. MIDDLE E. STUD. 3 (1984); Joseph Schacht et al., *Idjtihad*, *in* 3 ENCYCLOPAEDIA OF ISLAM 1026 (P.J. Bearman et al. eds., 2d ed. Brill 1960–2005); Shaista Ali-Karamali & Fiona Dunne, *The Ijtihad Controversy*, 9 ARAB L.Q. 238 (1994).

certain theorists offer insights that can help explain the way in which a historicist jurisprudence assesses the law while remaining sensitive to the needs (theoretical and otherwise) of a rule-of-law system. A historicist jurisprudence can aid in understanding the law, provide a mechanism for critique, and suggest alternative orderings or distributions that may not be visible from within prevailing paradigms of Shari'a.

For instance, in his theory of "communicative action", Jürgen Habermas asserts that individuals share normative meaning through a language medium that expresses values and commitments that are not idiosyncratic but, rather, are understood as *separate and distinct* from people. For Habermas, one's relationship to reality through language "contains a reference to something independent of us and thus, in this sense, *transcendent*".[19] Communication is possible because fundamental norms are rendered objective, determinate, and shared within a community; in other words, because of these public norms, meaning can be accessed by and communicated among individuals. One may make a normative claim that is certainly subject to critique. However, what makes the claim potentially meaningful is the fact that a community shares and commits to values that are understood as transcendent but that are manifested in the world of experience.[20]

For Habermas, these shared norms help constitute a lifeworld that allows context-transcending values to find expression in the phenomenal world of daily existence. According to Habermas, "communicative acts are located within the horizon of shared, unproblematic beliefs; at the same time, they are nourished by these resources of the *always already familiar*. The constant upset of disappointment and contradiction, contingency and critique in everyday life crashes against a sprawling, deeply felt, and unshakable rock of background assumptions, loyalties, and skills".[21]

Charles Taylor also relies on a concept of background ideals that inform the way we construct meaning in community through language. One's background values constitute, in Taylor's terms, a "moral framework" from which we see and understand the world around us. According to Taylor, "to think, feel, judge within such a framework is to function with the sense that some action, or mode of life, or mode of feeling is incomparably higher than the others which are more readily available to us...".[22] Furthermore, these frameworks are essential to our existence. In fact, Taylor argues that:

doing without frameworks is utterly impossible for us; otherwise put, that the horizons within which we live our lives and which make sense of them have to include these strong qualitative discriminations. Moreover, this is not meant just as a contingently true psychological fact about human beings, which could perhaps turn out one

[19] JÜRGEN HABERMAS, BETWEEN FACTS AND NORMS: CONTRIBUTIONS TO A DISCOURSE THEORY OF LAW AND DEMOCRACY 14 (MIT Press 1998) (emphasis added).
[20] *Id.* at 18.
[21] *Id.* at 22.
[22] TAYLOR, *supra* note 13, at 20.

day not to hold for some exceptional individual or new type, some superman of disengaged objectification. Rather the claim is that living within such strongly qualified horizons is constitutive of human agency, that stepping outside these limits would be tantamount to stepping outside what we would recognize as integral, that is, undamaged human personhood.[23]

For the purposes of this study, what links Habermas and Taylor is how they understand meaning as arising from shared, transcendent values made manifest as people live their lives together. The way those transcendent values manifest themselves in any given moment reflects the context of that moment and, thereby, opens the door to a historicist concern with context and change amid commitments to enduring values.

In the case of Muslim states that adopt Islamic law, I want to suggest that the meaning and significance of Shari'a-based rules, if subjected to a historicist critique, will illustrate how the meaningfulness of these rules is built upon certain normative frameworks (to modify Taylor's phrase) that manifest transcendent values in a historical moment in the form of laws. But that early historical context—I explicitly assume and shall show, in part—is different from the present. Until that difference is acknowledged, the resort to constitutional reform, or theories of accommodation/integration, will most likely fail to resolve the challenges facing non-Muslims in expressly Muslim states.

3. Muslim state constitutions and protections for religious minorities

Muslim majority countries often incorporate Islam or Islamic law into their constitutions while including express provisions concerning religious freedom and the treatment of religious minorities. Thus, these constitutions seem to display a tension between the definition and application of Islamic law, on the one hand, and how respect for Islamic law may conflict with provisions protecting religious minorities, on the other. The discussion below summarizes some trends in the constitutions of Muslim states and illustrates how the constitutions establish this tension between Shari'a, constitutionalism, and religious freedom without providing a solution.

Muslim countries may specify in their constitutions that Islam is the state religion,[24] although that is not always the case.[25] Some countries specifically establish that the government is secular, keeping religion and state law distinct.[26]

---

[23] *Id.* at 27.

[24] See for example BAHR. CONST. art. 2; MAURITANIA CONST. art. 5; MALAY. CONST. art. 3; MOROCCO CONST. art. 6; SAUDI ARABIA BASIC LAW OF GOV'T, 1993 art. 1; YEMEN CONST. art. 2; TUNIS. CONST. art. 1.

[25] See for example ALB. CONST. art. 10.

[26] See for example ETH. CONST. art. 11; AZER. CONST. art. 7.

Aside from designating a state religion, some Muslim nations also assert that Islam is either "a source" or "the source" of law in the country, thereby bringing into sharp focus the constitutional significance of violating a precept of Shari'a law. [27]

To protect the interests of religious minorities, Muslim state constitutions may include nondiscrimination clauses to protect individuals from religious discrimination. For instance, the Bahrain Constitution reads that "[p]eople are equal in human dignity, and citizens shall be equal in public rights and duties before the law, without discrimination as to race, origin, language, religion, or belief".[28] Eritrea's Constitution provides that "[a]ll persons are equal before the law. No person may be discriminated against on account of race, ethnic origin, language, colour, sex, religion, disability, political belief or opinion, or social or economic status or any other factor...."[29] Generally, the equality clauses are listed among the earliest provisions of "basic rights" and occur without limitation or restriction.

Additionally, Muslim countries may include rights provisions that protect one's religious freedom. Egypt's Constitution states that "[t]he State shall guarantee the freedom of belief and the freedom of practice of religious rites".[30] Indonesia's Constitution provides that "[t]he State guarantees all persons the freedom of worship, each according to his/her own religion or belief".[31] Other countries adopting this unrestrictive approach include Bosnia and Herzegovina, Eritrea, Malaysia, Mali, and Morocco.[32]

---

[27] See for instance BAHR. CONST. art. 2; EGYPT CONST. art. 2; KUWAIT CONST. art. 2; OMAN CONST. art. 2; QATAR CONST. art. 1; SYRIA CONST. art. 3. For a sustained review of constitutions in the Arab world, see NATHAN J. BROWN, CONSTITUTIONS IN A NON-CONSTITUTIONAL WORLD: ARAB BASIC LAWS AND THE PROSPECTS FOR ACCOUNTABLE GOVERNMENT (SUNY Press 2001).

[28] BAHR. CONST. art. 18.

[29] ERI. CONST. art. 14.

[30] EGYPT CONST. art. 46.

[31] INDON. CONST. art. 29(2).

[32] See for example BOSN. & HERZ. CONST. 1995 art. 2, para. 3; ERI. CONST. art. 19; MALAY. CONST. art. 11; MALI CONST. art. 4; Morocco CONST. art. 6. However, the substantive protection these provisions provide religious minorities is subject to further speculation. For instance, although the Malaysian Constitution's article 11 grants all people the right to profess and practice their religion, the recent case involving Lina Joy suggests that the courts may abdicate their protective role. Lina Joy was born a Muslim woman and subsequently converted to Christianity. She sought to have her identity card changed from defining her as a Muslim Malay to Christian Malay. She appealed her case to the highest federal court in Malaysia, which stated that it had no jurisdiction to decide her case and that all matters involving Islamic law should be referred to the Shari'a court. In doing so, the federal court has seemingly undermined the real protection article 11 can provide. *See, e.g.,* Baradan Kuppusamy, *Political Solution Demanded in Malaysia to Halt Concerns of Creeping Islamism,* S. CHINA MORNING POST, Jun. 1, 2007, at 8. See "Article 11: The Federal Constitution: Protection for All", for an example of Malaysian civil society groups advocating for greater article 11 protection, *available at* <http://www.article11.org/> (last visited July 30, 2007). Article 26 of the Eritrean Constitution allows for limits on the rights enumerated in the Constitution on the grounds of national security, public safety, economic well-being of the country, or the public morals and public order of the nation: ERI. CONST. art. 26.

But some Muslim countries also provide qualifying remarks concerning the scope of one's religious freedom. Bahrain's Constitution reads that "[f]reedom of conscience is absolute. The State shall guarantee the inviolability of places of worship and the freedom to perform religious rites and to hold religious processions and meetings *in accordance with the customs observed in the country*".[33] Kuwait's Constitution reads that "[f]reedom of belief is absolute. The State protects the freedom of practicing religion *in accordance with established customs, provided that it does not conflict with public policy or morals*".[34] Both examples illustrate how a statement of absolute freedom is coupled with ambiguous limiting language about "customs", "public policy", and "morals".

4. Illustrating the tension at work: Saudi Arabia and Egypt

The constitutions of Muslim countries provide rights protection for religious minorities, although some have limiting clauses that are not uncommon in constitutions and human rights instruments around the world.[35] However, a constitution is but one step in creating a constitutional culture for a state emerging from sectarian violence, regional feuds, and postcolonial struggles for independence in an international environment. In the gaps between constitutional texts, legislated statutes, and judicial cases are a multitude of moments when social, cultural, and ideological factors may affect legal outcomes. These underlying extralegal factors provide content to a constitutional culture and language that can limit the scope of judicial and legislative activity.[36] And the outcomes, when all is taken into account, may result in de jure discrimination against minorities, despite constitutional protections to the contrary.

For example, Saudi Arabia has no constitution but, rather, various "basic laws". According to the Basic Law of Government, Saudi Arabia "protects human rights in accordance with the Islamic Shari'ah".[37] The scope of human rights protection

---

[33] BAHR. CONST. art. 22 (emphasis added).

[34] KUWAIT CONST. art. 35 (emphasis added).

[35] The Canadian Charter of Rights and Freedoms protects the freedom of conscience and belief, subject to section 1 restrictions "as can be demonstrably justified in a free and democratic society": Canadian Charter of Rights and Freedoms, part I of the Constitution Act, 1982, being Sched. B to the Canada Act 1982, ch. 11 (U.K.), § 1. Likewise, the European Convention on Human Rights (ECHR), art. 9, both protects the freedom of conscience while also acknowledging that it may be restricted by law as necessary "in a democratic society in the interests of public safety, for the protection of public order, health or morals, or the protection of the rights and freedoms of others". European Convention on Human Rights, art. 9.

[36] The idea that the extralegal cultural context may influence and delimit judicial analysis is the subject of considerable scholarly attention. See for example BRUCE A. ACKERMAN, WE THE PEOPLE (Harvard Univ. Press 1991); Reva B. Siegel, *Text in Context: Gender and the Constitution from a Social Movement Perspective*, 150 U. PA. L. REV. 297 (2001).

[37] SAUDI ARABIA BASIC LAW OF GOV'T, 1993 art. 26. For an unofficial English translation of this provision, see the International Constitutional Law website on Saudi Arabia, *available at* <http://www.servat.unibe.ch/law/icl/sa00000_.html> (last visited July 28, 2007).

of individual equality, liberty, and freedom will depend significantly on how one understands the scope and content of Shariʻa. In Saudi Arabia, premodern Shariʻa rules (in other words, *fiqh*) govern the majority of cases involving tort, property, and contract.[38] The history of Saudi Arabia's incorporation of Sunni Islam and Shari'a, in particular the Wahhabist strain, as part of its national ethos has been addressed in numerous studies in recent years. Historians have shown that the early resort to Islam, as a defining feature of the Saudi state, was instrumental in forming a political identity that transcended regional and tribal networks.[39] The institution of law, as an ordering and coercive feature of the government, imparts an Islamic content that has facilitated the development of a distinctive Islamic society. Notably, in Sunni Islamic law, there are four doctrinal schools (*madhahib*; singular: *madhhab*) concerning the specific details of law. The doctrinal schools are equally orthodox but often differ from each other on similar points of law. In Saudi Arabia, the Hanbali school generally provides the rules of Islamic legal decision.[40]

The tension embedded in article 26 between Shariʻa rules and rights to equality, for instance, is illustrated by rules governing the measure of wrongful-death damages in Saudi Arabia.[41] According to the Indian consulate in Jeddah, Saudi Arabia, the families of Indian expatriates working in the kingdom can claim wrongful-death compensation pursuant to a schedule of fixed amounts. However, the amounts vary depending on the victim's religious convictions and gender. If the victim is a Muslim male, his family can claim SR100,000. However, if the victim is a Christian or Jewish male, the family can claim only half that amount, namely, SR50,000. Further, if the victim belongs to another faith group, such as Hindu, Sikh, or Jain, his family can claim only approximately SR6,667. The family of a female victim can claim half the amount allowed for her male coreligionist.[42]

It seems that Saudi Arabia patterns its wrongful-death compensatory regime on early Hanbali rules of tort liability. For example, premodern Muslim jurists held that the *diyya,* or wrongful-death compensation, for a free Muslim male is one hundred camels.[43] However, if the victim is a Jew or Christian male, his family

---

[38] Frank E. Vogel, Islamic Law and Legal System: Studies of Saudi Arabia 175, 291 (Brill 2000).

[39] Madawi al-Rasheed, A History of Saudi Arabia (Cambridge Univ. Press 2002); Khaled Abou El Fadl, The Great Theft: Wrestling Islam from the Extremists (Harper 2007); Ibrahim Karawan, *Monarchs, Mullas and Marshalls: Islamic Regimes?* 524 Annals Am. Acad. Pol. & Soc. Sci. 103 (1992); Joseph A. Kechichian, *The Role of the Ulama in the Politics of an Islamic State: The Case of Saudi Arabia*, 18 Int'l J. Middle E. Stud. 53 (1986).

[40] *Id.* at 10.

[41] Saudi Arabia Basic Law of Gov't, 1993 art. 26.

[42] *See* Consulate General of India, Jeddah: Basic Legal Information for Indian Workers in the Kingdom of Saudi Arabia—Death Compensation of Deceased Indians, *available at* <http://www.cgijeddah.com/cgijed/publication/basiceng/complete.htm#dcomp> (last visited Aug. 20, 2007).

[43] Abu Hamid al-Ghazali, al-Wasit fi al-Madhhab 4:64 (Dar al-Kutub al-ʻIlmiyya 2001); Abu Ishaq al-Shirazi, al-Muhadhdhab fi Fiqh al-Imam al-Shafiʻi 3:210 (Dar al-Kutub al-ʻIlmiyya 1995).

can only claim a percentage of that amount. The Shafi'is held that the family is entitled to one-third of what a free Muslim male's family would receive.[44] But the Malikis and Hanbalis granted them one-half of what a Muslim's family could obtain.[45] Furthermore, Sunni and Shi'ite jurists held that if the victim is a Magian (*majus*) his family receives even less, namely, one-fifteenth of what a free Muslim male is worth.[46] More importantly, one-fifteenth of SR100,000 is approximately SR6,667—a figure precisely corresponding to the wrongful-death compensation offered by Saudi Arabia for Hindus, Sikhs, or Jains.

Egypt has often been criticized for abuses in connection with its Coptic Christian citizens.[47] According to the Egyptian Constitution, Islam is the official state religion, and Shari'a is the principle source of law in the country.[48] Article 46 provides in unqualified language that the state guarantees freedom of

[44] MUHAMMAD B. IDRIS AL-SHAFI'I, KITAB AL-UMM 3:113 (Dar al-Fikr 1990); AL-MAWARDI, AL-HAWI AL-KABIR 12:308 (Dar al-Kutub al-'Ilmiyya 1994); AL-GHAZALI, *supra* note 43, at 4:64–67; MUHYI AL-DIN AL-NAWAWI, RAWDAT AL-TALIBIN WA 'UMDAT AL-MUFTIN 9:258 (al-Maktab al-Islami 1991); SHIHAB AL-DIN AL-RAMLI, NIHAYAT AL-MUHTAJ ILA SHARH AL-MINHAJ 7:320 (Dar Ihya' al-Turath al-'Arabi 1992); AL-SHIRAZI, *supra* note 43, at 3:213.

[45] MALIK B. ANAS, AL-MUWATTA' 2:434–435 (Dar al-Gharb al-Islami 1997), related that 'Umar II decided that the *diyya* for a killed Jew or Christian is half the *diyya* for a free Muslim male. See also IBN RUSHD AL-JADD, AL-MUQADDIMAT AL-MUMAHHIDAT 3:295 (Dar al-Gharb al-Islami 1988); IBN RUSHD AL-HAFID, BIDAYAT AL-MUJTAHID WA NIHAYAT AL-MUQTASID 2:604–605 (Dar al-Kutub al-'Ilmiyya 1997); SHIHAB AL-DIN AL-QARAFI, AL-DHAKHIRA 12:356 (Dar al-Gharb al-Islamiyya 1994); IBN QUDAMA, AL-MUGHNI 7:793–794 (Dar Ihya' al-Turath al-'Arabi no date), who said that Ahmad b. Hanbal held the amount was one-third, but then changed his position to half; ABU 'ABD ALLAH B. MUFLIH, AL-FURU' 6:16 (Dar al-Kutub al-'Ilmiyya 1997), also indicated some would provide the Muslim *diyya* for *dhimmis* if the latter were killed intentionally. However, Maliki and Hanbali jurists held that in personal injury cases (*jirahat*), the *diyya* for the injury is whatever a free Muslim male would get. MALIK B. ANAS, AL-MUWATTA' 2:434–435; SAHNUN B. SA'ID, AL-MUDAWWANA AL-KUBRA 6:395 (Dar Sadir no date); IBN QUDAMA, AL-MUGHNI 7:795; MANSUR B. YUNIS AL-BAHUTI, KASHSHAF AL-QINA' 'AN MATN AL-IQNA' 6:23–24 (Dar al-Kutub al-'Ilmiyya 1997).

[46] AL-SHAFI'I, *supra* note 44, at 3:113; AL-GHAZALI, *supra* note 43, at 4:67; AL-MAWARDI, *supra* note 44, at 12:311; AL-NAWAWI, *supra* note 44, at 9:258, who said that the *majus* get *thultha 'ushr* of the *diyya* for a free Muslim male; AL-RAMLI, *supra* note 44, at 7:320; AL-SHIRAZI, *supra* note 43, at 3:213; MALIK B. ANAS, *supra* note 45, at 2:435; SAHNUN, *supra* note 45, at 6:395; IBN RUSHD AL-JADD, *supra* note 45, at 3:296; AL-QARAFI, *supra* note 45, at 12:357; IBN QUDAMA, *supra* note 45, at 7:796; AL-BAHUTI, *supra* note 45, at 6:24. Notably, Ibn Qudama related a minority opinion held by al-Nakha'i and others who equated the *diyya* for the *majus* and free Muslims because both are free and inviolable human beings (*adami hurr ma'sum*). IBN QUDAMA, *supra* note 45, at 7:796. The Ja'farite AL-MUHAQQIQ AL-HILLI, SHARA'I' AL-ISLAM FI MASA'IL AL-HALAL WA AL-HARAM 2:489 (Markaz al-Rasul al-A'zam 10th ed. 1998), related three views, namely that Jews, Christians, and Magians are valued at 800 *dirhams,* or all enjoy the same *diyya* as Muslims, or that Christians and Jews are entitled to four thousand *dirhams*. According to the Ja'farite AL-HURR AL-'AMILI, WASA'IL AL-SHI'A ILA TAHSIL MASA'IL AL-SHARI'A 19:141–142 (Dar Ihya' al-Turath al-'Arabi no date), the *diyya* of a free Muslim male is roughly 10,000 *dirhams*, while the *diyya* of a *dhimmi* Jew or Christian is 4,000 *dirhams*, and the *diyya* of the *majus* is 800 *dirhams*, roughly 40 percent and 8 percent respectively of the *diyya* for a free Muslim male.

[47] For studies on the situation and treatment of Egypt's Coptic Christians, see Randall P. Henderson, *The Egyptian Coptic Christians: The Conflict between identity and Equality,* 16 ISLAM & CHRISTIAN MUSLIM REL. 155 (2005); HUM. RTS. WATCH, WORLD REPORT, 2006, at 439 (2006).

[48] EGYPT CONST. art. 2.

belief and religious practice.[49] Nevertheless, article 41 states that one's freedoms might be curtailed in the interest of public security.[50] By themselves, these provisions set up a similar framework of tensions found in constitutional documents around the world. But the implications of the Egyptian system are problematic, chiefly because of the prevailing conceptions of Islam and Islamic law that also inform the nation's constitutional culture. For instance, according to its 2006 International Religious Freedom Report, the U.S. State Department reported that Egypt partially applies a nineteenth-century Ottoman decree that requires non-Muslims to seek government approval before building or repairing places of worship:

> The contemporary interpretation of the 1856 Ottoman Hamayouni decree, partially still in force, requires non-Muslims to obtain a presidential decree to build new churches and synagogues. In addition, Ministry of Interior regulations, issued in 1934 under the Al-Ezabi decree, specify a set of ten conditions that the Government must consider before a presidential decree for construction of a new non-Muslim place of worship can be issued. The conditions include the requirement that the distance between a church and a mosque not be less than one hundred meters and that the approval of the neighboring Muslim community be obtained.[51]

The report noted some advances in 2005 but indicated that, fundamentally, the regime of licensing and registration continues:

> In December [2005] the president decreed that permits for church repair and rebuilding, previously requiring his approval, could be granted by provincial governors. The purpose of this was to reduce delay. The central government continued to control the granting of permits for construction of new churches. Despite the 2005 decree, as well as a previous presidential decree in 1999 to facilitate approvals, many churches continued to encounter difficulty in obtaining permits.[52]

The tension between the Egyptian government and its Coptic citizens is not a recent phenomenon. Nor is the government's preoccupation with religious groups limited to its Coptic minority. The report also indicates that permits are required before one can build a mosque, that the government pays imams' salaries, and it monitors their sermons.[53] This raises larger questions of religious freedom in Egypt across all religious divides. However, the focus on Coptic Christians is of interest because of the parallels between Egyptian government practice and

[49] *Id.* art. 46.
[50] *Id.* art. 41.
[51] U.S. Dep't of State, Egypt: International Religious Freedom Report 2006, *available at* <http://www.state.gov/g/drl/rls/irf/2006/71420.htm> (last visited Aug. 30, 2007). *See also* Saad Eddin Ibrahim, *Christians Oppressed*, Wall Street J., Nov. 18, 2005, at A16. For a study of nineteenth-century Ottoman reforms to enhance religious equality, such as the Hatti-Humayun and others, see Roderic H. Davison, *Turkish Attitudes Concerning Christian-Muslim Equality in the 19th Century*, 59 Am. Hist. Rev. 844 (1954).
[52] U.S. Dep't of State, *supra* note 51.
[53] *Id.*

premodern Islamic law. While a more extensive history of Islam in Egypt might illuminate further the subtleties of the current regime's attitude toward its Coptic citizens, my own study suggests that the ongoing commitment to the Humayun decree, despite the 2005 reforms on the licensing procedure, illustrates a challenge facing the government about the current meaningfulness of the premodern Islamic tradition in light of Egypt's constitutional and international commitments to religious freedom.[54]

The Egyptian requirement that Coptic Christians apply for government permission to build new churches or repair old ones correlates with premodern Islamic rules that limited non-Muslims from freely building and repairing places of worship in Islamic lands. Non-Muslims, residing peacefully in the Islamic polity, were required to pay a poll tax (*jizya*) to maintain their faith and receive state protection. In the legal tradition, they were called *dhimmis,* since they were granted a contract of protection (*'aqd al-dhimma*) that guaranteed their safety on payment of the poll tax. Under the contract, as will be explained below, their freedom to build or refurbish their religious places of worship was limited.[55]

5. Understanding historical Shari'a

The Shari'a tradition was developed by jurists who generally developed legal doctrine in a decentralized fashion outside the ambit of government control. Their contribution to defining Shari'a reflected one level of selectivity amid a diversity of possibilities. Each doctrinal school of Islamic law could account for majority

---

[54] For instance, Egypt is a signatory to various international human rights instruments that protect religious freedom, such as the International Covenant on Economic, Social and Cultural Rights (ratified on Jan. 14, 1982); the International Covenant on Civil and Political Rights (ratified on Jan. 14, 1982); and Convention on the Elimination of All Forms of Discrimination against Women (CEDAW) (ratified on Sept. 18, 1981). Notably, Egypt and other Muslim countries will often ratify such treaties with reservations that limit their commitment to the treaties' terms in the event they contradict the principles and tenets of Islamic law. For a discussion on this practice among Muslim state signatories to international instruments, see ELIZABETH ANN MAYER, ISLAM AND HUMAN RIGHTS: TRADITION AND POLITICS (Westview Press 1995); Mayer, *supra* note 15, at 133. But what "Shari'a" means in any given reservation is not entirely clear. In the case of CEDAW provisions, reservations in favor of Shari'a may even undermine the effect of the treaty, despite being ratified. Notably, article 19 of the Vienna Convention on the Law of Treaties 1969 holds that reservations that defeat the purpose of a treaty are impermissible, and thereby may offer some limits on the scope of reservations. On the relationship between the Vienna Convention and reservations to CEDAW, see Belinda Clark, *The Vienna Convention Reservations Regime and the Convention on Discrimination Against Women*, 85 AM. J. INT'L L. 281 (1991). The fact that Egypt is a state within an international system, defines itself as bound by Shari'a, and yet participates in multilateral treaty negotiations concerning rights, trade, diplomatic relations, and crimes against humanity contributes to a context of governance (domestic and international) that arguably ushers in a normative framework of governance, community, and identity that is distinct from those operating in the pre modern Muslim world.

[55] See *infra* §§ 5.1–5.3 for discussion on the premodern Islamic legal restrictions on this issue.

and minority opinions, as well as outlier views.[56] This determinacy amid diversity suggests that a process of interpretive selection gave rise to moderately determinate doctrine, which provided, in turn, sufficient notice about one's legal duties and entitlements. Further, these selected legal rulings were subjected to the impact of colonialism and the rise of the modern state with its centralized configuration of lawmaking. By adopting certain Islamic rules of law in centralized state legislative schemes, most likely what occurred was that the initial normative context of the doctrine was forgotten or ignored while the rules themselves remained. Premodern rules were then inserted into the modern state system without accounting for whether those rules remain meaningful, or how the changed normative frameworks might compel different legal manifestations. Arguably, the early normative framework was premised on a universalist Islamic message made manifest through imperial conquest.

5.1 A Qur'anic basis manifested in historical Shari'a?

The Islamic legal treatment of non-Muslims apparently builds on a normative framework of discrimination constructed with reference to the Qur'an, which then branches out into legal doctrine. The discriminatory rules of Shari'a, as will be suggested, were not an inevitable interpretive result of texts such as the Qur'an and the prophetic traditions, or *hadith*. Instead, they may have reflected an extra-textual universalist Islamic ethos made manifest by the early Islamic conquests and reified in law with the aid of a historical-juridical imagination that rendered the law the fulfillment of the community's spiritual and worldly ethos. This universalism is built, in part, on a dichotomy between "us" and "them". Hence, unsurprisingly, the Shari'a rules regarding non-Muslims utilize a superiority/inferiority dichotomy to order society and govern social relations.[57]

One particular Qur'anic verse will provide a starting point for identifying the way religious discrimination became a justified legal value, and how it was selected among alternatives. Specifically, Qur'an 9:29 states:

> Fight those who do not believe in God or the final day, do not prohibit what God and
> His prophet have prohibited, do not believe in the religion of truth, from among those

---

[56] For surveys and theoretical studies on Islamic legal history and theory, see WAEL B. HALLAQ, A HISTORY OF ISLAMIC LEGAL THEORIES: AN INTRODUCTION TO SUNNI USUL AL-FIQH (Cambridge Univ. Press 1999); WAEL HALLAQ, ORIGINS AND EVOLUTION OF ISLAMIC LAW (Cambridge Univ. Press 2005); ABOU EL FADL, *supra* note 14; MOHAMMAD HASHIM KAMALI, PRINCIPLES OF ISLAMIC JURISPRUDENCE (Islamic Texts Soc'y 2005).

[57] This type of universalist narrative is not unique to the Islamic context. As Hendrik Spruyt has illustrated, the Holy Roman Empire was premised on a similar universalist Christian narrative that was subsequently checked by the historical tension between the king and papal authorities, with perhaps the most dramatic moment of resolution being King Henry IV's penitent visit to Canossa to seek forgiveness from Pope Gregory VII during the Investiture Controversy. HENDRIK SPRUYT, THE SOVEREIGN STATE AND ITS COMPETITORS (Princeton Univ. Press 1996).

who are given revelatory books, until they pay the poll tax (*jizya*) from their hands in a state of submission (*saghirun*).[58]

This verse raises three main issues for discussion: who are the people identified in the verse for this special treatment, what is the poll tax, and what does it mean to be in a state of submission? For the purposes of this chapter, the last issue is of immediate relevance.

There are competing views of what "state of submission" means. Some Muslim jurists suggested that by paying the poll tax, non-Muslims residing in Muslim lands (*dhimmis*) effectively acknowledged their humiliated, submissive, and subservient social position as compared with Muslims.[59] Jurists used the law to make clear that submissiveness in social relations, such as when a non-Muslim pays his poll tax: he must stand before the magistrate, who sits when collecting the tax. The standing/sitting distinction conveys to the non-Muslim that he is in a submissive position, given that the magistrate does not rise to greet him.[60] Jurists also stated that non-Muslims must walk on the sides and edges of a pathway, while the honor of walking in the middle of the roadway is reserved for Muslim passersby, both physically and symbolically marginalizing the "religious other".[61] These and other rules illustrate how a universalist Islamic ethos becomes manifest in the law through the use of a superiority/inferiority dichotomy for ordering social relations.

Not all Muslim jurists read the verse as condoning the ethic of subservience and humiliation. Some argued that the verse simply means that the non-Muslim obeys the rule of law. In other words, to remain a full member of society, the

---

[58] Qur'an, 9:29.

[59] See for example Muqatil, Tafsir Muqatil b. Sulayman 2:166–167 (Dar Ihya' al-Turath al-'Arabi 2002) (by giving the *jizya*, the *dhimmis* are made lowly (*madhallun*)); al-Nisaburi, al-Wasit 2:489 (Dar al-Kutub al-'Ilmiyya 1994) (payment of *jizya* renders *dhimmis* lowly and vanquished (*dhalilun muqahharun*)); Muhammad b. Jarir al-Tabari, Tafsir al-Tabari 4:98–99 (Mu'assasat al-Risala 1994). Mahmoud M. Ayoub, *The Islamic Context of Muslim-Christian Relations, in* Conversion and Continuity: Indigenous Christian Communities in Islamic Lands, Eight to Eighteenth Centuries 461 (Pontifical Inst. Mediaeval Stud. 1990); Ziauddin Ahmad, *The Concept of Jizya in Early Islam*, 14 Islamic Stud. 293 (1975); Bosworth, *supra* note 1; Mawil Izzi Dien, The Theory and the Practice of Market Law in Pre-modern Islam: A Study of Kitab Nisab al-Ihtisab 51–52 (E.J.W. Gibb Memorial Trust 1997); Wadi Zaidan Haddad, *Ahl al-Dhimma in an Islamic State: The Teaching of Abu al-Hasan al-Mawardi's al-Ahkam al-Sultaniyya*, 7 Islam & Christian Muslim Rel. 169 (1996).

[60] Al-Mawardi, al-Nukat wa al-'Uyun 2:351–352 (Dar al-Kutub al-'Ilmiyya no date); Fakhr al-Din al-Razi, al-Tafsir al-Kabir 6:25 (3d ed. Dar Ihya' al-Turath al-'Arabi 1999); Abu 'Ali al-Tabarsi, Majma' al-Bayan fi Tafsir al-Qur'an 3:44–45 (Manshurat Dar Maktabat al-Hayah no date); Abu Ja'far al-Tusi, al-Tibyan fi Tafsir al-Qur'an 5:203 (Dar Ihya' al-Turath al-'Arabi no date); Jalal al-Din al-Suyuti, al-Durr al-Manthur 3:411 (Dar al-Kutub al-'Ilmiyya 2000); al-Tabari, *supra* note 59, at 4:98–99.

[61] For premodern treaties addressing this rule, see al-Ghazali, *supra* note 43 at 4:207; al-Nawawi, *supra* note 44, at 10:325; al-Shirazi, *supra* note 43, at 3:313; Badr al-Din al-'Ayni, al-Binaya Sharh al-Hidaya 7:259 (Dar al-Kutub al-'Ilmiyya 2000); Zayn al-Din Ibn Nujaym, Sharh al-Bahr al-Ra'iq 5:192 (Dar al-Kutub al-'Ilmiyya 1997); al-Qarafi, *supra* note 45, at 3:459.

non-Muslim must abide by the Shari'a.[62] This interpretation of the verse, debatably, does not rely on norms of discriminatory subservience but, instead, endorses a conception of political society in which Muslim and non-Muslim alike undertake obligations to uphold the law of the land.

A third position on the notion of submission is that the verse foreshadows legal rules that give non-Muslims incentives to convert to Islam. For instance, Fakhr al-Din al-Razi (died in 1209) held that requiring a poll tax is not intended to facilitate the mutual coexistence of Muslims and non-Muslims, thereby, preserving the continuation of non-Islamic traditions. Rather, it creates, instrumentally, a situation of peace during which the non-Muslim can experience the glory of Islam (*mahasin al-Islam*) and convert.[63]

These three opinions about one such verse suggest that Qur'anic meaning is neither determinate nor transparently accessible from the words on the page. Its meaning is the product of a gradual process of exegetical construction in light of competing views about, inter alia, the political aims sought by and through the law. While Muslim theologians argued about whether the Qur'an itself can be contextualized or must be read as the eternal speech of God,[64] the juristic and exegetical derivation of meanings from the Qur'an is subject to historical shifts in normative frameworks, given the jurists' subjective engagement with the text. This one verse by itself says little until interpreted and applied in a coercive rule-of-law system. By adopting a universalist norm and reading it into the Qur'anic verse using the superiority/inferiority dichotomy, jurists fashioned additional rules that manifested the norm through the law.

5.2 The case of wrongful-death damages

As noted in the Saudi Arabian example above, a troubling aspect of Shari'a rules of law is how the measure of damages in wrongful-death suits depends, in part, on one's religious belief and gender. To understand the underlying normative context that gave meaning to this tort liability scheme requires an investigation

---

[62] Dallal, *supra* note 11, at 189. For this position, see also Haddad, *supra* note 59, at 172–173. As an example see AL-MAWARDI, *supra* note 44, at 2:351–352; RASHID RIDA, TAFSIR AL-MANAR 10:266 (Dar al-Kutub al-'Ilmiyya 1999); AL-SHAFI'I, *supra* note 44, at 4:186.

[63] AL-RAZI, *supra* note 60, at 6:27. *See also* Jane Dammen McAuliffe, *Fakhr al-Din al-Razi on Ayat al-Jizya and Ayat al-Sayf*, CONVERSION AND CONTINUITY, *supra* note 59, at 103.

[64] Premodern Muslims debated whether the Qur'an is the eternal word of God, or whether God revealed the text in history as events unfolded. In the words of Muslim theologians, the debate was whether the Qur'an was created (*makhluq*) by God in time or, rather, was eternal and thereby uncreated (*ghayr makhluq*). For general accounts of this debate, see WILLIAM MONTGOMERY WATT, THE FORMATIVE PERIOD OF ISLAMIC THOUGHT (Oneworld Publ'n 1998); HARRY AUSTRYN WOLFSON, THE PHILOSOPHY OF THE KALAM (Harvard Univ. Press 1976). This theological debate about the Qur'an itself, however, does not adversely affect the critical historicist approach involved in (re) narrating Shari'a rules of law, since the Qur'an itself has relatively few *legal* verses. Nevertheless, to the extent one wants to challenge the notion that Qur'anic verses have legal effect, one will need to grapple with the historicist construction of the Qur'an itself. This issue is the subject of future research but is beyond the scope of this chapter.

into the liability rules for *qisas*, or retribution (also known as *lex talionis*), in cases of negligent homicide. The central question concerns how and why legal liability differs depending on the victim's religious commitments.

Jurists of the Sunni Shafi'i, Hanbali, and Maliki schools, as well as the Shi'ite Ja'farite school held that if a Muslim kills an unbeliever (*kafir*), the Muslim is not executed. However, if an unbeliever kills a Muslim, the former is executed.[65] Maliki jurists held that Muslim perpetrators are executed only if they killed their victims while lying in wait (*qatl al-ghila*).[66] Shi'ite Ja'farite jurists would sentence a Muslim to execution if he was a serial murderer of non-Muslims; however, execution was contingent on the victim's family compensating the Muslim perpetrator's family for the difference in wrongful-death compensation (*diyya*) between the non-Muslim and the Muslim.[67] In other words, if the compensatory liability for a Muslim male's wrongful death is one hundred camels, and for a Christian or Jewish male victim it is fifty camels, then the family of the non-Muslim victim must pay the Muslim serial killer's family fifty camels before the killer can be lawfully executed.

The discriminatory application of the death penalty rule is further illustrated by cases where the perpetrator or victim is an apostate from Islam. If a Muslim kills an apostate from Islam, the killer suffers no liability; but if the apostate kills a Muslim the apostate will be executed.[68] Given the superiority/inferiority framework, this result is perhaps not surprising. A Muslim will be considered superior to an apostate from Islam, and, as a result, will be given preferential treatment under the law. But what if a non-Muslim kills an apostate from Islam? Jurists fell into three camps over the legal consequences:

1. The non-Muslim is executed given his general liability under *qisas*;

2. The non-Muslim is not executed because the apostate enjoys no legal protection;

3. The non-Muslim is executed pursuant to the discretion of the ruler (*siyasa*), although his estate is not burdened with compensatory liability since the apostate is not protected under the law.[69]

---

[65] AL-SHAFI'I, *supra* note 44, at 3:40, who would subject the Muslim killer to prison and *ta'zir* punishment; AL-GHAZALI, *supra* note 43, at 4:36–37; AL-MAWARDI, *supra* note 44, at 12:10; AL-NAWAWI, *supra* note 44, at 9:150; AL-SHIRAZI, *supra* note 43, at 3:171; IBN QUDAMA, *supra* note 45, at 7:652; AL-MUHAQQIQ AL-HILLI, *supra* note 46, at 2:452–453, who also held that the Muslim murderer can be sentenced to discretionary punishment (*ta'zir*) and monetary compensation (*diyya*); AL-HURR AL-'AMILI, *supra* note 46, at 19:127.

[66] In other words, one might argue that lying in wait is an aggravating circumstance that affects sentencing.

[67] MALIK B. ANAS, *supra* note 45, at 2:434–435; IBN RUSHD AL-HAFID, *supra* note 45, at 2:582; AL-MUHAQQIQ AL-HILLI, *supra* note 46, at 2:452–453; AL-HURR AL-'AMILI, *supra* note 46, at 19:79–80. For others reporting the Maliki position, see AL-'AYNI, *supra* note 61, at 13:79.

[68] AL-GHAZALI, *supra* note 43, at 4:36–37; AL-BAHUTI, *supra* note 45, at 5:614; AL-MUHAQQIQ AL-HILLI, *supra* note 46, at 2:455.

[69] AL-GHAZALI, *supra* note 43, at 4:36–37. *See also* AL-SHIRAZI, *supra* note 43, at 3:172. THE Ja'farite AL-MUHAQQIQ AL-HILLI, *supra* note 46, at 2:455, would execute the *dhimmi* because

The non-Muslim does not always enjoy superior protection over the Muslim apostate. This diversity in valuation is further emphasized in a case where an apostate from Islam kills a non-Muslim protected in the Islamic polity. Muslim jurists divided generally into two camps concerning the apostate's liability:

1. The apostate is executed;
2. The apostate is not executed, since his prior adherence to Islam gives him a sanctity that transcends his apostasy and protects him against liability for killing a non-Muslim.[70]

The different treatment of non-Muslims illustrates a tension between competing conceptions of equality and entitlement within Islamic law. An apostate who abandons Islam, and thereby becomes a non-Muslim, may still enjoy the benefit of an Islamic identity over and against someone born a non-Muslim.

Muslim jurists defended the discriminatory application of *qisas* liability by reference to a *hadith* in which the Prophet said "[a] believer is not killed for an unbeliever". Importantly, the full tradition states that "[a] believer is not killed for an unbeliever or one without a covenant during his residency".[71] Jurists who constructed discriminatory rules of liability would rely on the first half of the *hadith* but not the whole tradition. Furthermore, they argued that the rules discriminating against non-Muslims reflected the fact that Muslims were of a higher class than their non-Muslim co-residents. For instance, the Shafi'i jurist al-Mawardi argued that as a matter of law someone from a lower class (*al-adna*) can be executed to vindicate the interests of someone from a higher class (*al-a'la*); but the opposite cannot occur.[72] He justified this legal distinction in religious and eschatological terms by citing Qur'an 59:20, which states that "[t]he companions of the hellfire are not equivalent to the companions of heaven".[73] From this he concluded that just as

the apostate still enjoys, as against the *dhimmi,* the protection that arose with his prior Islamic commitments.

[70] Al-Ghazali, *supra* note 43, at 4:36–37; al-Shirazi, *supra* note 43, at 3:172.

[71] Al-Mawardi, *supra* note 44, at 12:10; al-Bahuti, *supra* note 45, at 5:616; Ibn Nujaym, *supra* note 61, at 9:19, who has a variant of this same tradition. For similar traditions and others with common themes, see the discussion in Ibn al-Jawzi, al-Tahqiq fi Ahadith al-Khilaf 2:307–309 (Dar al-Kutub al-'Ilmiyya no date).

[72] Al-Mawardi, *supra* note 44, at 12:11; al-Nawawi, *supra* note 44, at 9:150, stated that freedom, Islamic faith, and paternity provide exceptions to liability for execution. Where the two parties are of equal status, *qisas* liability applies; otherwise, the person of lower status (*al-mafdul*) is executed for the higher status victim (*al-fadil*), but not the opposite. Al-Shirazi, *supra* note 43, at 3:171, referring to a Qur'anic verse requiring execution of the free for the free, slave for the slave. and women for women, held that if one is executed for killing someone of an equal social standing, then certainly he should be executed for killing someone who is superior to him (*afdal minhu*). The Maliki Ibn Rushd al-Hafid, *supra* note 45, at 2:582, said that there is no dispute that the slave is executed for murdering a free male, just as the one of lower status is executed for killing the higher status (*al-anqad bi al-a'la*). See also al-Qarafi, *supra* note 45, at 12:332; al-Bahuti, *supra* note 45, at 5:617.

[73] Al-Mawardi, *supra* note 44, at 12:11–12. The Hanbali al-Bahuti also relies on the notion of equivalence to justify the differential treatment in sentences for murder. Al-Bahuti, *supra* note 45, at 5:616.

the Qur'an denies any equivalence between these groups in eschatological terms, the law should deny any equivalence between them in legal terms.[74] Furthermore, using the logical axiom of *a minore ad maius*, al-Mawardi held that just as a Muslim bears no liability for falsely accusing a resident non-Muslim of illicit sexual relations, how can he be liable for killing one, which is a much more serious offense?[75]

This is not to suggest all Muslim schools of law held to this discriminatory application of capital punishment. As explained below, Hanafi jurists rejected such discriminatory legal applications. Anticipating a Hanafi critique, the Shafi'i al-Mawardi narrated an incident involving the important premodern Hanafi jurist Abu Yusuf (died in 797). According to the story, Abu Yusuf sentenced a Muslim to death for killing a non-Muslim, which is consistent with Hanafi doctrine. However, he subsequently received a disconcerting poem criticizing him for doing so. The poem read as follows:

O killer of Muslims on behalf of *kafirs*
You commit an outrage, for the just are not the same as the oppressor
O those of Baghdad and its vicinity, jurists and poets
Abu Yusuf [commits] an outrage on the faith when he kills Muslims for *kafirs*
Make demands, cry for your faith, and be patient, for reward belongs to the patient.[76]

Troubled by the thought of a public outcry, Abu Yusuf informed the 'Abbasid caliph Harun al-Rashid (ruled from 786–809) about his predicament. Al-Rashid advised him to use a technical legal loophole to avoid the execution sentence and, thereby, avoid any social discord (*fitna*). Specifically, Abu Yusuf learned that the victim's family could not prove that they paid their poll tax and, therefore, could be denied the full protection of and entitlements under Shari'a. As a result, Abu Yusuf did not execute the Muslim and, instead, held him liable for wrongful-death damages. Al-Mawardi, however, glossed the entire story by suggesting that, since the original decision led to public dissatisfaction (known as *fitna*), it was right and good to avoid that decision generally.[77]

Nonetheless, Hanafi jurists justified executing a Muslim for killing a non-Muslim[78] by referring to a tradition in which the Prophet did so, saying, "I am the most ardent to uphold his security".[79] The Hanafi jurist Badr al-Din al-'Ayni

---

[74] The Maliki AL-QARAFI, *supra* note 45, at 12:356–357, relied on a similar argument to justify different compensatory payments (*diyya*) for wrongful death, depending on the victim's religious commitments.

[75] AL-MAWARDI, *supra* note 44, at 12:13–14. For a discussion of this mode of reasoning in Islamic legal theory, see WAEL HALLAQ, A HISTORY OF ISLAMIC LEGAL THEORIES 96–99 (Cambridge Univ. Press 1997).

[76] AL-MAWARDI, *supra* note 44, at 12:15–16.   [77] *Id.*

[78] MUHAMMAD B. AL-HASAN AL-SHAYBANI, KITAB AL-ASL 4:488 (Wizara al-Ma'arif li'l-Hukuma al-'Aliyya al-Hindiyya 1973), required that the murder be intentional (*'amd*); AL-'AYNI, *supra* note 61, at 13:79; AL-MARGHINANI, AL-HIDAYA: SHARH BIDAYAT AL-MUBTADI' 2:446 (Dar al-Arqam no date).

[79] AL-'AYNI, *supra* note 61, at 13:79; IBN NUJAYM, *supra* note 61, at 9:19; ABU BAKR AL-KASANI, BADA'I' AL-SANA'I' FI TARTIB AL-SHARA'I' 10:258 (Dar al-Kutub al-'Ilmiyya 1997). Notably, AL-MAWARDI, *supra* note 44, at 12:10, held this tradition to be weak.

(died in 1451) explained that other schools discriminate against non-Muslims because they assume an inherent inequality between Muslims and non-Muslims. Shafi'i jurists, he said, consider disbelief (*kufr*) to be a material characteristic that raises ambiguity (*shubha*) about the quality of a non-Muslim's dignity in comparison with a Muslim's.[80]

But for Hanafi jurists, Muslims and non-Muslims are equally inviolable.[81] One's inviolability, or *'isma,* depends on whether one has the capacity (*qudra*) to satisfy his or her legal obligations (*taklif*).[82] In other words, inviolability is not contingent on faith commitments but, instead, on one's ability to abide by the law. Once the non-Muslim agrees to be subjected to the laws of a Muslim polity, he becomes inviolable as a matter of law. Certainly, non-Muslims outside Muslim lands do not enjoy the same legal protections as non-Muslims within the polity. This distinction has to do with territoriality, residence, and social contract. Disbelief (*kufr*) by itself, though, does not irrevocably undermine the inviolability of a non-Muslim who lives peacefully in an Islamic polity.[83] The Hanafis were certainly aware of the tradition of the Prophet's rejecting the execution of a Muslim for killing a non-Muslim. But they read it as a general rule from which those with a contract of protection (such as *dhu 'ahd*) were exempted.[84]

The discriminatory approach to capital punishment for homicide was also used when computing compensation for wrongful death (*diyya*). As noted above, many Sunni schools of law provided a schedule of compensatory liability for wrongful death that discriminated on religious grounds. However, the Hanafis opposed this discriminatory approach and demanded equal compensation across the board. They argued that the compensation for a Muslim and a non-Muslim victim is the same since both are equally inviolable and, therefore, enjoy the same protections under the law.[85] Religious commitment, in other words, was not a relevant factor in determining the scope of one's legal entitlements.[86] Rather, what mattered for the Hanafis was whether or not non-Muslims enjoyed a contract of protection, thus bringing them within the polity on an equal footing with Muslims.

[80] AL-'AYNI, *supra* note 61, at 13:79.

[81] IBN NUJAYM, *supra* note 61, at 9:20; AL-KASANI, *supra* note 79, at 10:246, who required the victim to be inviolable (*ma'sum al-damm*); ABU AL-FATH AL-SAMARQANDI, TARIQAT AL-KHILAF BAYNA AL-ASLAF 522–525 (Dar al-Kutub al-'Ilmiyya 1992).

[82] AL-'AYNI, *supra* note 61, at 13:80; IBN NUJAYM, *supra* note 61, at 9:20; AL-MARGHINANI, *supra* note 78, at 2:446. As such, Hanafi jurists like al-Kasani imposed no *qisas* liability for killing a *harbi* or apostate since they are not *ma'sum*. AL-KASANI, *supra* note 79, at 10:246.

[83] AL-'AYNI, *supra* note 61, at 13:80. Disbelief becomes relevant if the unbeliever threatens the Muslim polity. But since those enjoying a contract of protection (*'aqd al-dhimma*) agree to lawfully reside in Muslim lands, they are entitled to legal protection of their lives and property. AL-'AYNI, *supra* note 61 at 13:81; IBN NUJAYM, *supra* note 61, at 9:20; AL-KASANI, *supra* note 79, at 10:248, 257–258.

[84] AL-KASANI, *supra* note 79, at 10:259; AL-MARGHINANI, *supra* note 78, at 2:464.

[85] AL-'AYNI, *supra* note 61, at 13:171; IBN NUJAYM, *supra* note 61, at 9:75; AL-KASANI, *supra* note 79, at 10:305; AL-MARGHINANI, *supra* note 78, at 2:464; ABU 'ABD ALLAH AL-MARWAZI, IKHTILAF AL-FUQAHA' 429–431 (Maktabat Adwa' al-Salaf 2000).

[86] AL-KASANI, *supra* note 79, at 10:310.

To justify their position, the Hanafis looked to Qur'an 4:92, which addresses the case of a Muslim who has killed another: "and if he [the victim] is from a people with whom you have a treaty (*mithaq*), his people are entitled to a *diyya musallama/muslima,* and [the killer] must free a believing slave". The reference to *diyya* is not entirely clear. Linguistically, it can refer to an agreed-upon amount (known as *diyya musallama*), or it can refer to the *diyya* appropriate for a Muslim (known as *diyya muslima*). Between these two possible readings, Hanafi jurists adopted the latter and held that Muslims and non-Muslims are entitled to the same *diyya* for wrongful death.[87] As additional support for the Hanafi position, Ibn Nujaym referred to the view of the fourth caliph, 'Ali b. Abi Talib (died in 661), who held that since resident non-Muslims are obligated in the same way as Muslims, they also enjoy the same entitlement to damages for personal injury.[88]

The foregoing discussion illustrates how Muslim jurists contended with one another to determine the rules of tort liability amid religious differences in the Muslim polity. The different views indicate that no single position was accepted as inevitable or true, but rather that jurists ruled in light of competing presumptions about identity and community filtering into their determination of the law. Certainly, this doctrinal analysis illustrates the diversity of Shari'a positions on this issue. However, this legal diversity did not come about in a vacuum. Probably, it reflects an historical context in which norms of identity were made manifest through law at a time of conquest, expansion, and a developing ethos of Islamic universalism.

Reconstructing a full historical context and normative framework is no easy task; certainly, it is beyond the scope of this chapter, which is intended merely to introduce how a historicist jurisprudence of Islamic law might allow for a nuanced engagement with both the historical tradition and the contemporary climate of Muslim states. Even within this limited scope, however, we can still discern some trace of the contextual factors that contributed to the doctrine on tort liability. The jurist and philosopher Ibn Rushd (Averroës, died in 1198) relates how the early Muslim historian al-Zuhri[89] recounted that, during the era of the Prophet and his first four successors, non-Muslims would receive the same compensation as Muslims. Furthermore, he noted that, during the caliphate of Mu'awiya (ruled from 661–680) and thereafter, half the *diyya* was paid by the public treasury (*bayt al-mal*). However, the later Umayyad caliph 'Umar II b. 'Abd al-'Aziz (ruled from 717–720) terminated the payments from the public treasury to the families of non-Muslims.[90] This reduction came at a time when the Umayyad dynasty was

---

[87] *Id.* at 10:310–311.

[88] IBN NUJAYM, *supra* note 61, at 9:75.

[89] For a biography and analysis of al-Zuhri's historical contributions, see ABD AL-AZIZ DURI, THE RISE OF HISTORICAL WRITING AMONG THE ARABS (Lawrence I. Conrad trans., Princeton Univ. Press 1983).

[90] Ibn Rushd relates a countertradition in which al-Zuhri states that 'Umar b. 'Abd al-'Aziz did not reduce the *dhimmi*'s *diyya* entitlement. IBN RUSHD AL-HAFID, *supra* note 45, at 2:604. For the purposes of this analysis, however, the fact that 'Umar may have altered the entitlements for

experiencing financial insecurity as its expansionist policies suffered military set-
backs. Furthermore, the caliphate had developed an Islamization policy to deter
the influence of the Byzantines on the Christians residing in Islamic lands.[91]
From Ibn Rushd's text, one may surmise that the doctrine regarding wrongful-
death compensation may reflect political and economic policies that only became
normative over time.

A further study of the public treasury in the eighth century may shed additional light on both the nature of 'Umar II's decision and how it influenced the
legal discourses on *diyya* that arose thereafter. Nevertheless, this review of Islamic
legal doctrine and history concerning non-Muslims and tort liability suffices to
show that jurists did more than report on the Qur'an or prophetic traditions;
rather, their readings were informed, additionally, by reference to competing and
contextualized values regarding identity, inclusion, and exclusion in the Muslim
polity. Certainly, each school of law had its authoritative sources to support its
respective positions on wrongful-death liability. Those positions, however, arose
in a context of shifting political and military developments in early Islamic
history.

5.3 Restrictions on building and repairing religious places of worship

As noted above, Egypt imposes limits on the extent to which non-Muslims can
build or repair religious places of worship; these limits are parallel to, if not caus-
ally derived from, early Islamic rules limiting non-Muslims' freedom to construct/
repair religious buildings. With these limitations, Egypt effectively conceals the
early diversity of rules and thus impedes a critical analysis of the early history of
Islam that gave those rules meaning. Moreover, with its actions, the Egyptian
regime also obscures whether and to what degree the modern Egyptian national
identity suffers from a certain dissonance when these premodern rules concerning
non-Muslims inform a modern constitutional state that otherwise accedes to the
language of rights and religious freedom.[92]

Under premodern Islamic law, generally, non-Muslims could not build new
places of worship in regions where the land was initially cultivated and urbanized
by Muslims themselves (known as *amsar al-islam*). Churches that existed prior
to Muslim conquest and development could remain, according to some jurists,
although others argued for their destruction.[93]

---

dhimmis is significant as it alerts one to the need for further investigation of how the norms and
rules of discrimination may have arisen from a contingent historical development.

[91] Khalid Yahya Blankinship, The End of the Jihad State: The Reign of Hishām Ibn
'Abd al-Malik and the Collapse of the Umayyads 93 (SUNY Press 1994).

[92] For Egypt's international human rights commitments, see *infra* note 51.

[93] Al-Ghazali, *supra* note 43, at 4:207; al-Mawardi, *supra* note 44, at 14:320–321; al-Muzani,
Mukhtasar al-Muzani, in al-Shafi'i, *supra* note 44, at 5:385; al-Nawawi, *supra* note 44, at 10:323;

The difficult legal questions concerned lands that fell under Muslim sovereignty but that already had urban and rural areas in which non-Muslims resided. Whether *dhimmis* could lawfully build or repair places of worship depended on the type of land they occupied, often described in terms of the method by which Muslims had become sovereign (such as by conquest or treaty) or else in terms of land-tax liability.

For example, if Muslims acquired sovereignty by force and conquest, the *dhimmis* living in the region could not erect new religious buildings. Jurists disagreed about whether old ones might remain and whether dilapidated ones could be repaired.[94] Al-Nawawi, for instance, held that if Muslims destroyed the non-Muslims' religious buildings during the conquest, the buildings may not be rebuilt. Also, any religious buildings that remained after the conquest should be removed.[95] The Hanafi jurist Badr al-Din al-ʿAyni illustrated a tension within his legal school. He said that, according to the Hanafis, non-Muslims would be required to convert their existing religious structures into residences, but they need not be razed.[96] However, al-ʿAyni also suggested that dilapidated religious buildings could be refurbished. However, they could not be relocated since that would be akin to building anew; nor could they be refurbished to be bigger than they were previously.[97]

If Muslims and non-Muslims peacefully negotiate a treaty to transfer sovereignty, land-tax liability will be a decisive factor in granting non-Muslims the right to repair and build religious buildings. There are three scenarios jurists discussed, each with different consequences:

1. If Muslims are sovereign over the land and assume land-tax liability (*kharaj*), the non-Muslims can retain the remaining religious buildings but cannot build new ones.[98]

AL-ʿAYNI, *supra* note 61, at 7:255–256; IBN NUJAYM, *supra* note 61, at 5:190; AL-QARAFI, *supra* note 45, at 3:458; IBN QUDAMA, *supra* note 45, at 8:526–527; AL-BAHUTI, *supra* note 45, at 3:151; AL-MUHAQQIQ AL-HILLI, *supra* note 46, at 1:262.

[94] IBN NUJAYM, *supra* note 61, at 5:190; AL-MAWARDI, *supra* note 44, at 14:320–321. IBN NUJAYM, *supra* note 61, at 5:191 held that existing buildings can be repaired but cannot be expanded or transferred. For this same position, see IBN QUDAMA, *supra* note 45, at 8:527–528.

[95] AL-NAWAWI, *supra* note 44, at 10:323. The Maliki al-Hattab likewise indicated the juristic disagreement about whether to allow old religious buildings to remain intact in areas conquered by Muslim forces. AL-HATTAB AL-RAʿINI, MAWAHIB AL-JALIL LI SHARH MUKHTASAR AL-KHALIL 4:599 (Dar al-Kutub al-ʿIlmiyya 1995). The Hanafi jurist al-ʿAyni indicated that al-Shafiʿi, Ahmad b. Hanbal, and Maliki jurists required remaining buildings to be destroyed. AL-ʿAYNI, *supra* note 61, at 7:255–256. See also the Maliki AL-QARAFI, *supra* note 45 at 3:458; the Hanbali IBN QUDAMA, *supra* note 45 at 8:526–527.

[96] AL-ʿAYNI, *supra* note 61, at 7:255–256.

[97] *Id.* at 7:256.

[98] AL-MAWARDI, *supra* note 44, at 14:320–321; AL-ʿAYNI, *supra* note 61, at 7:255–256. The Hanbali Ibn Qudama held that in cases where Muslims retain sovereignty of the land and the *dhimmis* only pay the *jizya*, one must look to the terms of the treaty to determine whether the *dhimmis* have the liberty to erect new religious buildings. IBN QUDAMA, *supra* note 45, at 8:526–527. For this Hanbali opinion see also AL-BAHUTI, *supra* note 45, at 3:151.

2. If Muslims assume sovereignty over the land but the non-Muslims collectively assume land-tax liability, the existing religious buildings can remain; some jurists held that the non-Muslims can negotiate for the liberty to build new religious buildings.[99]

3. If the non-Muslims administer the land but collectively pay the land tax to Muslim sovereigns, they can retain old religious buildings and build new ones.[100]

Hanafi jurists generally did not make distinctions based on tax liability but, rather, on the demographics of each region. They held that non-Muslims could not build new religious buildings in the towns that Muslims built and cultivated (*amsar*). But they had more liberty to build and repair their religious structures in villages where they were demographically dominant.[101] However, the Hanafi al-Marghinani related that some Hanafi jurists prohibited the non-Muslims from erecting religious buildings regardless of demographic analysis, since Muslims could potentially reside in all areas.[102] The Hanafi Ibn Nujaym held that erecting religious buildings was prohibited in both towns and villages in Arab lands, specifically, since the Prophet had indicated there cannot be two faiths in the Arab peninsula.[103]

The legal limits established by these three models illustrate how Muslim jurists manifested a particular, normative vision of Islamic identity amid pluralism and difference. To focus simply on whether non-Muslims could or could not build or refurbish places of worship misses the larger picture of how the legal question was affected by a normative context embedded in an early history of conquest, the nascent development of Islam as a basis for identity, and the effect demographics can have on the budding ethos of an Islamic polity.

Muslim jurists provided a justification for their limits on constructing churches and synagogues that illustrates how they were interested in preserving the Islamic ethos of Muslim controlled lands. Badr al-Din al-'Ayni relates how the caliph 'Umar b. al-Khattab (ruled from 634 to 644) stated that the Prophet forbade erecting religious buildings in Islamic lands.[104] Al-'Ayni held that allowing Jews

[99] AL-NAWAWI, *supra* note 44, at 10:323; IBN NUJAYM, *supra* note 61, at 5:190. The Maliki al-Qarafi held that if the *dhimmis* are responsible for the land tax, they can keep their churches. But if they include in the treaty a condition allowing them to build new religious buildings, the condition is void except in land where no Muslims reside. However, in such regions, *dhimmis* can erect new religious buildings without having to specify their right to do so in any treaty. AL-QARAFI, *supra* note 45, at 3:458.
[100] AL-MAWARDI, *supra* note 44, at 14:320–321; AL-GHAZALI, *supra* note 43, at 4:207; AL-NAWAWI, *supra* note 44, at 10:323; IBN QUDAMA, *supra* note 45, at 8:526–527; AL-BAHUTI, *supra* note 45, at 3:151.
[101] AL-'AYNI, *supra* note 61, at 7:257. See also AL-MARGHINANI, *supra* note 78, at 1:455. See also the Maliki AL-HATTAB, *supra* note 95, at 4:600.
[102] AL-MARGHINANI, *supra* note 78, at 1:455.
[103] IBN NUJAYM, *supra* note 61, at 5:190. *See also id.* at 1:455.
[104] AL-'AYNI, *supra* note 61, at 7:255.

and Christians to construct religious buildings freely would alter the character of Islamic lands.[105] The Shafi'i jurist al-Mawardi also argued that allowing non-Muslims to erect religious buildings in Muslim lands (*amsar al-Islam*) would undermine the dominance of Islam by perpetuating disbelief in the land under Islamic control. Erecting such buildings, he said, is a sin (*ma'siyya*), since those who congregate there perpetuate disbelief (*kufr*). In Islamic lands, he argued, only Islam should be visible (*zahir*).[106]

The concern that Islam should remain visibly dominant may have reflected an early political preoccupation with the development of a nascent Islamic polity contending with the Byzantine and Sassanian empires to its north, as well as with the existing religious diversity in the Arabian Peninsula. In fact, one well-known tradition of the Prophet, already noted, explicitly rejects the possibility that there could be two faiths in the Arabian Peninsula. Based on this tradition, or perhaps on the political ethos it manifested, 'Umar b. al-Khattab (ruled from 634–644) ushered in a policy of expelling non-Muslims from the Arabian Peninsula, which resulted in the Arab-Christian Banu Najran tribe's departure from the region.[107] Certainly, if non-Muslims cannot reside in Arab lands, they could not build religious buildings. But some Muslim jurists went further by prohibiting non-Muslims from building religious buildings in both Arab and non-Arab lands.

The late Muhammad Hamidullah argued that this prophetic prohibition was not directed against religious minorities out of intolerance. Rather, the idea that the peninsula should be reserved for Muslims referred to the Prophet's political aim to secure a safe and secure region for Muslims. In other words, the *hadith* should not be interpreted as an indication of the Prophet's lack of tolerance for religious pluralism but, instead, as a statement of political unity, identity, and cohesion for a nascent community still struggling to survive.[108] While a historical positivist might attempt a reconstruction of the "original" intent of the Prophet, the fact remains that the tradition was read within the context of an emergent political community engaging in conquest and expansion, presumably based on the principle of a universalist Islamic message. As later jurists occupied new geographic spaces, they used the law to order those spaces according to that same universalist Islamic ethos. However, in the era of the nation state, ideological or religious universalism is thwarted by geopolitical borders and commitments to the international system. This geo-political limit, I have suggested, reflects a fundamental historical shift that becomes especially noticeable when premodern Islamic rules regarding non-Muslims are infused into the state system.

[105] *Id.*
[106] AL-MAWARDI, *supra* note 44, at 14:321.
[107] Hugh Goddard, *Christian-Muslim Relations: A Look Backwards and a Look Forwards*, 11 ISLAM & CHRISTIAN MUSLIM REL. 195, 196 (2000).
[108] Hamidullah, *supra* note 1, at 10.

This analysis illustrates that Muslim jurists did not provide a blanket prohibition against non-Muslims from practicing or exhibiting their faith. Nor did they
allow without restriction the expression of non-Muslim religious identity. Rather,
it seems that various interests were balanced that had to do with issues of demographics, sovereignty, tax liability, and the development of an Islamic political
ethos. The balance between competing values led to a particular construction
of legal rules that reflected a time when religion per se was not a distinguishable
category of analysis, separate from other aspects of identity. In other words, in a
nascent Islamic polity, where the conceptual language of identity (political and
otherwise) was Islamic in form and content, everything was expressed in Islamic
terms. However, if everything was expressed in Islamic terms, then nothing was
distinctively Islamic in a religious sense. To be Muslim or non-Muslim in an
Islamic territory was to be more than a member of a faith community; it was an
index of identity, political and otherwise.

However, with the rise of the international system of nation states, with its
boundaries, governance structures, multilateralism, and rights commitments
comes competing modes of identity, whether as state citizen, constitutional subject, and individual rights holder. Before one can begin to use accommodation
or integration models to reform the rules of premodern Shariʿa, one must first
rethink how Shariʿa values can be implemented in light of a normative framework in which the past becomes relevant for defining the present and sketching
the future amid changed modes of political organization and governance. To take
a contemporary state's definition of Shariʿa at face value ignores how the adoption
of one Islamic doctrinal school—to the exclusion of others—can impede efforts
to uncover the underlying values that gave the legal issues significance in the first
place and in a prior time. To uncover the underlying values of a legal issue can
help us explain why premodern jurists reached different and at times conflicting
legal rules, and allow us to contextualize those rules as we develop modern rule
of law systems in pluralist nation states. The significance of a historicist jurisprudence of Shariʿa is that it attempts to understand Shariʿa as a legal system with
jurisprudential integrity, but never fully divorced from its historical context—
political, economic, social, or otherwise.

6. Conclusion

The above examples from Saudi Arabia and Egypt and the discussion of Islamic
legal doctrines, which parallel (if they do not contribute to) the *de jure* discrimination against non-Muslims, illustrate a complex process of state coercion in
the twenty-first century. This is the state of affairs that comes about when premodern legal rules are extracted from a prior context that gave them a certain
meaning at one time, and are then inserted piecemeal into a state context to give

Islamic content to a present-day new nation. The character and definition of this "Islamic" content, though, relies on its assumed objectivity, determinacy, and even its inevitability as God's law.[109] Yet, as was suggested above, the legal rules were the product of a juristic process that used the authority of Shari'a-based language to prioritize some readings over others. The Qur'anic verse requiring non-Muslims to pay the *jizya* in a state of submission could have been interpreted in multiple ways, but it was given the normative power of humiliation and subservience that then may have informed other areas of law. Similarly, the legal liability for negligent homicide need not necessarily discriminate on the grounds of religion. But when Saudi Arabia adopts the Hanbali tradition as the basis for its rule-of-law system, it uses its coercive power to prioritize one view and silence the others. It precludes, thereby, a historical-juridical analysis of the underlying values manifested in tort rules of liability, as well as an analysis of whether those rules remain meaningful for the purposes of governance.[110]

The resort to a historicist jurisprudence of Islamic law illustrates why relying on theories of accommodation and integration alone to theorize governance models is insufficient. To accommodate or integrate another's value system within a governance structure assumes that a certain determinacy and objectivity (or essential constancy) can be attributed to that value system. But to assume such determinacy in the case of Shari'a ignores how its historical doctrine was a contingent manifestation of norms about, inter alia, identity, order, and meaning. Whether one looks to premodern rules limiting church repair or awarding tort damages, the rules were the product of juristic deliberation at a particular time and space. But the context in which those deliberations occurred has materially changed, thus contributing to the logical or social dissonance that arises when the same rules are applied in settings marked by profound institutional, political, and social alterations. The dissonance that results is, perhaps, what has prompted the Islamic legal scholar Wael Hallaq to state that modern Islamization programs suffer from an "irredeemable state of denial".[111] Certainly, Hallaq is right if he means that the uncritical adoption of premodern rules of Shari'a within constitutional state systems will create incoherence in meaning and identity for those living in states that adopt Islamic values, embrace human rights, and participate in an international system that is premised on borders of geography and identity.[112]

[109] For an analysis of how contemporary debates on Islamic law suffer from an overdeterminism of the doctrine, see Emon, *supra* note 2, at 331–335.

[110] It may have been this very phenomenon that al-Sanhuri attempted to avoid when describing how resort to Islamic law under the Egyptian Civil Code should not prioritize one Islamic legal school over another, and should not violate the general principles of the civil code. See discussion in *supra note 17*.

[111] Hallaq, *supra* note 8, at 22.

[112] This dissonance is evident in the ongoing utilization of universalist paradigms by Muslim organizations promoting an Islamic value system. For instance, in 1990 the Organization of the Islamic Conference issued the Cairo Declaration on Human Rights in Islam as an Islamic version

Historicist jurisprudence reveals that the dissonance witnessed in Muslim nation states cannot be resolved if the premodern Shari'a rules are considered— either as a matter of explicit faith or as an assumption of theories of governance— objective, determinate, and unassailable. Rather, a historicist jurisprudence of Islamic law must uncover the multiplicity of values that once existed within the Shari'a tradition, and show how the reality of the international system requires a reframing or a remanifesting of Shari'a in a contemporary Muslim state.

of the Universal Declaration of Human Rights. In the first paragraph of the Preamble, the Cairo Declaration reads:

> Reaffirming the civilizing and historical role of the Islamic Ummah which Allah made as the best community and which gave humanity a universal and well-balanced civilization, in which harmony is established between this life and the hereafter, knowledge is combined with faith, and to fulfill the expectations from this community to guide all humanity which is confused because of different and conflicting beliefs and ideologies and to provide solutions for all chronic problems of this materialistic civilization.

Cairo Declaration on Human Rights in Islam, Aug. 5, 1990, U.N. Doc. A/CONF.157/PC/62/ Add.18 (1993), *available at* <http://www1.umn.edu/humanrts/instree/cairodeclaration.html> (last visited Aug. 30, 2007). The reference to Islam as a universal civilization and the role of a Muslim Ummah to guide a confused humanity certainly suggests that the universalist paradigm of Islam has not been discarded.

10

A tale of three constitutions: Ethnicity and politics in Fiji

Yash Ghai* and Jill Cottrell**

The experience of Fiji provides valuable insights into the debates regarding the dynamics of politics and the appropriate ways of structuring the state in multiethnic societies. Fiji's multiethnic origins lie in colonialism, which, globally, has not only been the greatest creator of multiethnic political entities but has also fashioned policies and institutions tailored to such societies. In contemporary studies of multiethnic states, too little attention is paid to colonial origins and policies. The constitutional framework for the organization of the state and state power in Fiji, since independence, has been of greater critical importance than economic or social frameworks because of ethnic fragmentation and the dominance of the public sphere. Our view—not universally shared in Fiji—is that the country would have done better to pursue its destiny through integrative policies. However, given Fiji's colonial history, which bred distrust and discord between the two major communities as a matter of policy and a syndrome of perceived vulnerability on the part of indigenous Fijians, integration would have required considerable sensitivity and sympathy, qualities that have been in short supply.

The focus of our chapter is Fiji's constitutions. Constitutions can play a particularly important role in multiethnic societies, making up for a deficit of common social bonds and solidarity. Relations between communities are often negotiated as part of constitution making in such societies, where there is a greater need to define the boundary between the public and private spheres; constitutions seek to establish rather than reflect the nation's identity and values. This is not to say that constitutions are generally effective in such settings. Indeed, our conclusion is

* Constitutional Advisory Support Unit, United Nations Development Programme, Nepal, recently retired from Sir Y. K. Pao Chair of Public Law, University of Hong Kong. Email: ypghai@hku.hk

** Constitutional Advisory Support Unit, United Nations Development Programme, Nepal, recently retired from Faculty of Law, University of Hong Kong. Email: cottrell@hku.hk

that, over the years, the artifacts of the successive constitutions in Fiji have borne less and less relationship to the reality and structures of society and have tended, in fact, to produce tension and conflict.

Since independence in 1970, Fiji has had three constitutions. The independence constitution, which lasted until a coup nineteen years later, hovered uneasily between integration and consociation.[1] The coup makers then imposed their own constitution in 1990, proclaiming the unambiguous paramountcy of indigenous Fijian interests and institutions.[2] As a result of international pressure and the contradictions contained in that constitution, it was replaced by the 1997 Constitution, which, in essence, was negotiated between the leaders of the indigenous Fijians and the Indo-Fijians; its aim was to strengthen the multiracial foundations of Fiji. This Constitution was challenged in two coups. It survived the first in 2000, thanks to a decision by the Court of Appeal that it must be reinstated.[3] The fate of the second coup in December 2006 and the fortunes of the Constitution are still uncertain at the time of writing; the coup maker's justification was that he wanted to protect the spirit of the Constitution.[4]

In what follows, we will examine these constitutions in order to uncover their underlying assumptions, aspirations, and dynamics, and to offer some reflections on the Fijian experience as it relates to the theme of this symposium.

1. Background

Fiji became a British colony in 1874, when its principal chiefs signed the Deed of Cession giving their islands to the British Crown in the hope of securing, in their own words, "civilisation and Christianity".[5] For several years before the handover to the British, Europeans and Australians were settling in Fiji, and some trade in sandalwood and sea cucumber was underway. The settlers were appropriating land, and some Fijian chiefs had run up debts they could not easily repay. On one view, at least, insecurity threatened. Britain, which viewed Fiji with interest, seemed capable of restoring order and financial stability. Thus the fortunes of Fijians were taken out of their hands. However, in contrast to the practice in

---

[1] FIJI CONST. 1970, *available at* <http://www.itc.gov.fj/lawnet/fiji_act/cap1.pdf>.
[2] FIJI CONST. 1990, *available at* <http://www.unhcr.org/cgi-bin/texis/vtx/rsd/rsddocview.html?tbl=RSDLEGAL&id=3ae6b57d8> (last visited Jul. 24, 2007).
[3] *Chandrika Prasad v. Republic of the Fiji Islands* [2001] 2 L.R.C. 743. See text accompanying *infra* note 80.
[4] See text accompanying *infra* notes 82–84.
[5] THE DEED OF CESSION OF FIJI TO GREAT BRITAIN, Oct. 10, 1874, *available at* <http://www.vanuatu.usp.ac.fj/library/Paclaw/Fiji/DEED%20OF%20CESSION%20%20FIJI.htm>. A facsimile of the Deed can be found at <http://www.vanuatu.usp.ac.fj/library/Online/Texts/Pacific_archive/Fiji/DeedOfCession.pdf> (last visited June 4, 2007).

other British colonies with outside settlement,[6] the colonial authorities adopted relatively benign policies toward the indigenous people. By maintaining their traditional political, social, and economic structures, the British sought to protect them from the kind of exploitation that other indigenous peoples had experienced. At the same time, however, Britain was anxious to develop the resources of the colony so that it could become self-sufficient and meet the costs of administration. For this purpose, it invited external investment, principally by a sugar company from Australia, and secured cheap indentured labor from India, thus sowing the seeds of a market economy, albeit one carefully administered, and laying the basis for an ethnically divided society.

The dual policies of both protecting indigenous Fijians[7] through the preservation of their traditional system and promoting economic development by importing capital, management, and labor posed a profound contradiction. The traditional system was incompatible with a market economy, although it could not be isolated from it entirely. To develop sugar plantations, land was required. But land was owned collectively by indigenous clans and held under rules that did not allow easy alienation.[8] In any case, alienation would have deeply disrupted traditional political and social orders, for which land—as with any feudalistic arrangement—was central.

To this conflict between tradition and modernity was added the conflict of interests among the three major racial communities, itself fueled by colonial policies. Land was provided to the sugar industry on terms that were conducive neither to sound economic development nor to harmonious relations among the communities. For the most part, the communities lived physically separate from each other and continued to do so when the formerly indentured laborers began to lease land for cane farming from Fijian owners or to move into the towns. The separation of these communities and the isolation of the indigenous people from the market meant that relations among them were largely determined by administrative policies—and this underscored the importance of the political. As a consequence, colonial history is to be understood largely in terms of the administrative regulation of racial claims and relations.[9]

---

[6] *E.g.,* countries such as Kenya, or South Africa, not to mention Australia, where indigenous populations were marginalized and discriminated against, if not, as with Tasmanian aborigines, exterminated.

[7] We use the term "Fijians" to refer to the indigenous peoples of the islands. Under the 1997 Constitution the official name of the state is now the "Fiji Islands".

[8] It suffices for our purposes to note that the British view (that the land was held communally with the superior rights of chiefs) prevailed, with far-reaching consequences both for the indigenous communities, internally, and for their relations with others. *See* Peter France, *The Founding of an Orthodoxy: Sir Arthur Gordon and the Doctrine of the Fijian Way of Life,* 77 J. POLYNESIAN SOC'Y 6 (1968); PETER FRANCE, THE CHARTER OF THE LAND: CUSTOM AND COLONISATION IN FIJI (Oxford Univ. Press 1969).

[9] *See generally* BRIJ V. LAL, BROKEN WAVES: A HISTORY OF THE FIJI ISLANDS IN THE TWENTIETH CENTURY (Univ. Hawaii Press 1992).

The effect of these policies was to treat each community as a corporate entity and, thus, to obscure the differences internal to each. This was most serious with respect to the Fijians; the effect of Britain's rule was not so much to preserve traditional customs and institutions as to transform them. Ideas of chieftaincy, land tenure, and relations among different local communities were altered significantly for the convenience of administration.[10] Differences in the nature of authority and organization among various local communities were ignored and a homogeneity (crystallized in rules and regulations) was imposed, drawing inspiration from the practices in eastern Fiji. On the whole, the western parts of the islands tended to be less hierarchical than those to the east. Yet the eastern structures of chieftaincy, for example, with their accompanying ideology, became the dominant mode through which Britain recognized and dealt with Fijians.[11] Consequently, the status of the chief and the ideology built around the office was consolidated, becoming increasingly rigid. The chiefs were then in a position to mobilize traditional symbols, real and invented, to maintain their authority, with an emphasis on the cohesion of the community, both to preserve culture and to prevail over competitors for the scarce resources from other communities.

Nor was the Indian community entirely homogenous. There were distinctions based on region of origin, language, religion, and occupation. And the absurdity and the unfairness of grouping all the other communities (some partly European, the Chinese, Polynesians, and Melanesians) as "Others" (later as "General") need little comment. Some subgroups within the community of "Others", including the Chinese and later other Pacific islanders, were subordinated to Others, their identity scarcely acknowledged.

The politics of Fiji have been closely tied to its constitutions. The origins of the contemporary social, political, and economic organization of Fiji lie in the policies pursued by the colonial power when it acquired control over the country. As already noted, the centerpiece of these policies was the preservation of traditional institutions, particularly, chieftaincy, land usage, and customary practices, which served both moral objectives (protection of the vulnerable) and administrative

---

[10] For example, according to R. Gerald Ward, claims of the emotional attachment to land (and its centrality to Fijian social structure) have been much overdone. As people moved freely and frequently from settlement to settlement, clans were split, new associations formed, and fresh acquisitions of land took place. Nor has evidence been found of the rule sanctified by the British that land was traditionally inalienable. *See* R. Gerald Ward, *Land, Law and Customs: Diverging Realities in Fiji, in* LAND, CUSTOM AND PRACTICE IN THE SOUTH PACIFIC 198 (R. Gerald Ward & Elizabeth Kingdom eds., Cambridge Univ. Press 1995).

[11] There is considerable literature on the role of chiefs and associated traditional systems. The ideology surrounding them has been a critical factor in the designing and justifying of constitutions and coups. However, it has long been recognized that this system of chieftaincy has been a major cause of the economic discrimination against and backwardness of the indigenous community and of the country's political problems. *See, e.g.,* IAL, *supra* note 9; ROBERT E. NORTON, RACE AND POLITICS IN FIJI (Univ. Queensland 1977); STEPHANIE LAWSON, THE FAILURE OF DEMOCRATIC POLITICS IN FIJI (Clarendon Press 1991); TIMOTHY MACNAUGHT, THE FIJI COLONIAL EXPERIENCE (Austl. Nat'l Univ. Press 1982); FRANCE, *supra* note 8.

convenience (indirect rule). Economic development was based on foreign capital, principally Australian and largely invested in the sugar industry, and indentured labor recruited from India. The various communities of colonial Fiji—Fijians, "Europeans", Indians, Chinese, and the "part-Europeans"—were segregated by race, which determined their entitlements, political rights, and economic situations, and there was no sense of a common political community or identity. It could not even be said, to use John S. Furnivall's phrasing, that the various races met only in the marketplace,[12] while the market itself was highly regulated by means of legal rules ascribing different roles in, and differential access to, the market, with indigenous Fijians embedded more in customary practices than market transactions. Prior to independence in 1970, many of these policies were based on administrative practice, although there were some laws that protected indigenous institutions, land, and customary practices.

2. The 1970 constitution

The first constitution in this story is the 1970 independence constitution, which contained the various compromises necessary to make independence acceptable to Fijians. Britain was anxious to shed her colonies, but independence was contested because, of the two major communities in Fiji, the Indo-Fijians wanted independence whereas the Fijians wanted to maintain British sovereignty, under which they believed Fiji had prospered and would continue to be protected. The Fijians feared that independence would usher in a period of Indo-Fijian dominance. By the 1960s, Indians outnumbered Fijians (240,960 to 202,176).[13] There were small numbers of other settler communities: 6,590 designated as European; 9,687 "part Europeans"; and 17,314 "others", a category that included Chinese and other Pacific islanders, including Rotumans, whose island, Rotuma, some 288 miles (about 465 kilometers) to the north, was administered as part of Fiji.[14] These communities could be counted on to provide political support to indigenous Fijians. It was on this assumption that the systems of elections and government then in effect were incorporated into the independence constitution.

The independence constitution, for the most part, adopted the colonial framework, which had set up a system similar to that in most colonies, with a governor, and an appointed executive council and partially elected legislative council.

[12] John Sydenham Furnivall, Colonial Policy and Practice: A Comparative Study of Burma and Netherlands India 311 (Cambridge Univ. Press 1948): "The foreign elements live in the towns, the natives in rural areas; commerce and industry are in foreign hands and the natives are mainly occupied in agriculture; foreign capital employs native labor or imported coolies. The various people meet only in the market, as competitors or as opponents, as buyers and sellers."
[13] Population of Fiji By Ethnicity (Fiji Islands Bureau of Statistics, June 2007), *available at* <http://www.statsfiji.gov.fj/Key%20Stats/Population/2.2%20pop%20by%20ethnicity.pdf>.
[14] *Id.*

Under the old system, there were four Europeans, four Fijians, and four Indians elected to the latter council by the communities to which they belonged.[15] The constitution was basically a codification of the system of segregation, and thus it devoted considerable space to the status of the racial communities and their differing relationships to the state.[16] A portion was also devoted to the constitution-alization of the social, political, and economic systems of indigenous Fijians.[17] The constitution effectively ensured their political dominance and control of the state.

The constitution of 1970 provided for separate representation of the principal communities in the House of Representatives. However, to meet the Indo-Fijian insistence on a non-racial electoral system, a minority of the seats were racially allocated but voted for by electors of all races; this was to be a first step toward a fully non-racial system. Out of a total membership of fifty-two, twenty-seven seats were distributed for ethnic voting (twelve each for Fijians and Indo-Fijians and three for Others) and twenty-five were allocated for voting on a common roll (ten each for Fijians and Indo-Fijians, and five for Others).[18] The upper house of Parliament, the Senate, established principally to safeguard Fijian interests, had twenty-two members, of whom eight were nominees of the Great Council of Chiefs (GCC),[19] seven were appointed by the prime minister, six by the leader of the opposition, and one by the Council of Rotuma.

These consociational elements were not reflected in the composition of the executive, modeled on the Westminster parliamentary system of majoritarianism and "winner takes all". The allocation of seats in the House of Representatives was such that, with a little support from their traditional allies—Europeans, part Europeans, and Pacific Islanders—Fijians would dominate the executive.

The 1970 constitution also contained various other provisions to protect the interests of Fijians, by insulating the legal framework for that protection from normal processes of amendment.[20] Their land holdings (comprising about 83 percent of all land in the country) were protected against alienation to non-Fijians. Traditional social and political structures (operating at the clan, provincial, and national levels and culminating in the GCC) were retained and woven

---

[15] THE FIJI (CONSTITUTIONAL) ORDER IN COUNCIL 1963, § 30, *available at* <http://www.vanuatu.usp.ac.fj/library/Online/Texts/Pacific_archive/Fiji/1.%20Fiji%20(Consolidated)%20Order%20in%20 Council,%201963.pdf> (last visited July 22, 2007).

[16] *See, e.g.,* FIJI CONST. of 1970 §§ 38 (Constituency Boundaries Commission) and 39 (Constituencies).

[17] *See* FIJI CONST. of 1970 § 45 (providing that Great Council of Chiefs appoints eight members of Senate); FIJI CONST. of 1970 § 68 (protecting various laws, especially relating to the system of Fijian administration and land, from normal amendment processes).

[18] FIJI CONST. of 1970 § 32.

[19] The Great Council of Chiefs (GCC), although a colonial invention, is still in existence and often referred to by its Fijian name, *Bose Levu Vakaturaga.*

[20] *See* FIJI CONST. of 1970 § 68, and the laws listed therein, namely the Fijian Affairs Act, Fijian Development Fund Act, Native Lands Act, Native Land Trust Act, Rotuma Act, Rotuma Lands Act, Agricultural Landlord and Tenant Act, Banaban Land Act, and Banaban Settlement Act.

into the apparatus of the state. The Fijian administration, as it was called, consisted of the Great Council of Chiefs, with largely advisory functions, and the Fijian Affairs Board, composed of senior bureaucrats, and the Fijian members of the legislature. This administration was endowed with the power to review legislative bills before their introduction for their effect on Fijians and to make regulations for Fijian social and economic life. Provincial and district councils were established exclusively for Fijians, in which a key role was reserved for the chiefs. Fijian courts were established to administer customary laws and regulations pertaining to Fijians (although the 1990 constitution did not make provision for these). Appropriate laws and the Fijian Native Land Trust Board were established to deal with customary land, particularly with regard to leases to non-Fijians (mainly, Indo-Fijian cane farmers). All these institutions and laws were the responsibility of the Ministry of Fijian Affairs.

Finally, the constitution introduced the Senate, in which Fijians dominated and which had veto powers over certain legislation. A bill of rights protected all citizens; however, individual rights were qualified by the collective rights of Fijians and were characterized by numerous restrictions and rules for their suspension—clearly, it failed to establish a culture of rights. The constitution, thus, not only paved the way for Fijian political hegemony. It also reinforced the "traditional" Fijian political and social system, maintaining both the dominance of senior chiefs and the distinctions between them and the commoners. In other words, the system the British had partly inherited and partly invented was constitutionally consolidated a hundred years later.

The 1970 settlement thus embodied a mix of the democratic and the oligarchic; liberalism and ethnic separatism; equality of all and paramountcy of Fijians; a market economy and restrictions on land and labor; a unitary state and significant autonomy for one community only; and freedom of religion and the close relationship of one religion, Christianity, to the state. The whole system depended on maintaining the separation of races or, more accurately, on keeping Indo-Fijians outside the alliance of others.

However, in one regard at least, the constitution could be considered deliberately transitional, since it contemplated the review—by an independent commission—of its most critical provision, dealing with the electoral system.[21] Already the 1970 constitution marked an advance on the colonial electoral system when it instituted cross-voting or national seats. These seats, allocated to different races while the voting for them was based on a common roll, were established in order to begin moving the country toward non-racial or interracial politics, the assumption being that candidates would have an incentive to appeal to voters of other races. Moreover, the final settlement of the electoral system was postponed until

---

[21] The section in question was FIJI CONST. of 1970 § 32, and the 1970 constitution provided for a report by a commission to be laid before Parliament before this could be amended. *See* FIJI CONST. of 1970 § 67(4).

the report of the independent commission was received and adopted, following the next general elections. This was a concession to the Indo-Fijians. In 1975, a royal commission consisting of three members, all of them British, was appointed to evaluate the electoral system.[22] It recommended a partial move away from ethnic representation, removing all ethnic restrictions on national seats and, at the same time, introducing an element of proportionality (through the single transferable vote), in an otherwise first-past-the-post system.[23] Although the original understanding[24] had been that the proposals of the royal commission would be final, Ratu Mara and his party had no interest in a further move in the direction of non-racial voting and simply shelved the report, not even giving Parliament an opportunity to debate it. And although the Indo-Fijian National Federation Party (NFP) accused the government of breach of faith, it has also been suggested that the NFP cynically thought that retaining the existing system would be in the interests of the Indo-Fijians because they had declined in numbers to perhaps fewer than the indigenous Fijians.[25]

Notwithstanding the provision for national seats, the logic of the political system was dictated by communal interests. Political parties were racially organized to compete for the communal seats, with one dominant party for each community. The need to contest national seats compelled each of the major parties to extend its appeal beyond the community it principally represented. For the most part this was not successful—each party was content to field only a few candidates of other races. National seats were decided principally by communal votes, so that, for example, Fijian candidates sponsored by the predominantly Indo-Fijian NFP were successful on account of Indo-Fijian votes, and so on. This was possible because of the relative concentrations of Indo-Fijians and Fijians in different parts of the country. Consequently, national seats won by candidates who relied on the votes of the other sponsoring community had little support in their own, while those who relied on votes from their own community had little support in the others. In this way cross-voting seats became an extension of communal seats.

In the years immediately following independence, the Alliance Party was a partial exception to this trend. It attracted a much greater percentage of Indo-Fijian votes, especially for the cross-voting seats (more than 20 percent), than the NFP did of the Fijian votes (barely 5 percent). But the Alliance Party had to maintain its support among Fijians if it was to remain a serious political contender, particularly with militant Fijian parties outbidding it for their support. The logic of the system compelled the Alliance Party to champion Fijian interests

---

[22] Fiji Parliamentary Paper No. 24/1975 (report of what is known as the Street Commission, chaired by British academic lawyer Sir Harry Street).

[23] For views on the various electoral systems, see *id.*

[24] *But see* KAMISESE MARA, THE PACIFIC WAY: A MEMOIR 126 (Univ. Hawaii Press 1997) (in which the former prime minister denies that this was the understanding).

[25] LAL, *supra* note 9, at 224.

ever more exclusively. Its increasing disregard of Indo-Fijian interests led gradually to the erosion of Indo-Fijian support; by 1977, it had lost most of this support, and the parties settled back to their old racial constituencies.

Election results were unpredictable since small swings in voting patterns could result in substantial changes in the number of seats won. Consequently, election periods were tense, fraught with great intercommunal bitterness. The "first-past-the-post" (or winner-takes-all) election rules put a premium on the two-party system, which introduced extreme rigidity into the political system by discouraging factions and coalitions. Since members of Parliament (MPs) represented only the voters of their own community, they had no opportunity, much less incentive, to acquaint themselves with the interests and problems of other communities. These factors merely aggravated ethnic tensions and bitterness.

The racial organization of the political parties reinforced another aspect of the system's inner logic—Fijian dominance of the executive. Consistent with the Westminster system, the constitution did not provide any formal mechanism for power sharing; at most, it allowed for what may be called sequential power sharing in normal situations, where the major parties could alternate in government. However, in the Fiji context that possibility was remote. Although Fijians and Indo-Fijians had an equal number of seats, the balance was held by the "general" electors (that is to say, those who occupied the racial category "general") who had historically sided with Fijians. Consequently the Alliance Party, with the support of the general electors, was able to form a government after each general election with such regularity that Alliance rule appeared the natural condition for Fiji.

Thus, assumptions about how the constitution would ensure the political dominance of the Fijians proved correct. Every government after independence was formed by the Alliance Party, with Ratu Mara as prime minister, until 1977, when the constitution came under some stress because the main Indian party won the elections. The NFP was the largest party in the House of Representatives with precisely half the seats. However, this novel turn of affairs proved temporary because the party failed to act promptly in forming a government, thereby enabling the governor-general to withdraw the invitation he had extended and, following his natural inclination, ask Ratu Mara to do so instead, pending a second election. This new election was won by the dominant Fijian party, the Alliance, and Fijian rule continued for another ten years.

The coherence of the constitution, with its inherent pro-Fijian bias, found itself under strain even as the fundamental policy assumptions for the protection of Fijians seemed progressively shakier. The contradictions of the constitution—torn between the market and insulation from the market, between universal franchise and racial hegemony—had surfaced in the early 1980s. However, in 1987 the Fijians came to realize that the 1970 constitution could no longer be counted on to guarantee them political control.

For the 1987 election the dominant Indo-Fijian party, the NFP, formed a coalition with the new Fiji Labour Party (FLP). The latter had emerged in the mid-1980s as a party based not on ethnicity but, rather more, on class interests. It was headed by a Fijian retired civil servant, Dr. Timothy Bavadra, who led the coalition into the 1987 election. The party's secretary was an Indo-Fijian.

Within the Fijian community the new alignment reflected the emergent distinction between the traditionalists, who were happy to uphold communal traditions and the role of chiefs in politics, and those who saw the communal lifestyle as holding back the development of the Fijian community and saw no place for chieftaincy in modern politics. It also reflected the gap between Fijians of the western division—who were more modern, less bound to clan and chief, and felt marginalized by the dominant east—and the rest. The Alliance Party countered by entering into its own coalition agreement with the general electors.

The FLP-NFP coalition won the April 1987 elections by 28 to 24, although voting was still largely along ethnic lines.[26] Bavadra was invited to form government, which consisted of seven Fijian (Home Affairs, Primary Industry, Lands and Minerals, Labor and Immigration, Education, Youth and Sports, Rural Development and Rehabilitation) and seven Indo-Fijian cabinet ministers—these were to hold the portfolios that had gone, typically, to Indo-Fijians in past Alliance governments. One month later Lieutenant-Colonel Sitiveni Rabuka led a military takeover.

The roots of the crisis that led in 1987 to the overthrow of an elected government and the repudiation of the constitution lie deep within the colonial system. Major societal changes, coming about through education, the economy, physical and social mobility, urbanization, and integration into the world economy, undermined many of the assumptions of the 1970 constitution. None of the racial communities remained—if they ever were—monolithic or unified by common interests. None could be isolated from the mainstream of the economy or state administration. Common interests had developed that cut across racial divides. Economic incentives and efficiency could not be maintained in the face of the conflicting interaction of ancient rules and market economy. Thus, the traditional system came under great stress. Yet the maintenance of that system was critical to the logic of the political settlement embedded in the 1970 constitution. In the end, the steady undermining of the assumptions underlying that settlement greatly reduced its ability to handle Fiji's intricate problems and racial relations.

Another factor, insufficiently considered throughout the postcoup period, was the rise of a faction of educated commoners, who had ambitions for high public office and sought the use of state resources for their own advancement. Indeed this factor was obscured by the constant reiteration of Rabuka, a commoner, that he had staged the coup to preserve the Fijian traditional system and maintain the authority of the chiefs (he accorded great deference, but little obedience, to his

[26] For an account of the election, see Brij Lal, *Before the Storm: An Analysis of the Fiji General Election of 1987*, 12 PAC. STUD. 71 (1988).

own high chief, Sir Penaia Ganilau, then governor-general). In many important respects, the 1987 coup marks the beginnings of a shift in power from the chiefs to the commoners, although this is certainly not evident from the constitution with which Rabuka replaced the independence constitution. What was needed, of course, was a new dispensation, broadly fair and acceptable to all the communities, to restore stability, revive the economy, and produce a modicum of national consensus. However, the coup makers and their supporters still thought in terms of adjusting, rather than transcending, racial claims and entitlements. The constitution-making process became a surrogate for pursuing racial strife, resulting in the militarily imposed constitution of 1990.

3. The 1990 constitution

Space does not allow for a detailed examination of the 1990 constitution, which functioned as a bridge between the 1970 and 1997 constitutions—a reaction to the former, it triggered a crisis that gave rise to a search for new values that find expression in the latter. Unlike the independence constitution, which was a negotiated document, the 1990 constitution was basically imposed on the people and in the face of the unanimous opposition of one major community, the Indo-Fijians, along with considerable opposition from others. The new constitution rejected multiracialism in favor of Fijian dominance and attempted to close constitutional loopholes that might have frustrated the goal of ensuring Fijian supremacy for all time. It reinforced the segregation of races and the political subordination of Indo-Fijians. Finally, it aimed at the enhanced dominance of purely Fijian institutions over the state. In what follows we summarize some of the features of this constitution.

The new constitution retained the parliamentary system of government and a bicameral legislature, though with significant changes meant to guarantee Fijian dominance. No cross-voting seats were provided for, so all representation became communal. In the seventy-member House of Representatives, thirty-seven seats were reserved for Fijians; this meant that they would not need to make alliances with any other community in order to form a government.[27] Other Pacific islanders, who previously had appeared in the electoral roll of Fijians, were reclassified as so-called "general" electors. The registration of all Fijian voters was now tied to the traditional rules of descent for each subordinate communal group within Fijian society; final decisions were left to the Native Land Commission (which also affected land rights).[28] This led to some separation of traditional groups within the Fijian community, a tendency that was further reinforced by making the provinces the basis for Fijian constituencies. In the allocation of seats,

---

[27] FIJI CONST. of 1990 § 41.
[28] *Id.* at § 49(6).

there was also discrimination against urban Fijians,[29] who were assumed to be less strongly bound by communal ties than rural people.

The Senate consisted of twenty-four members nominated by the GCC, one by the Rotuman Council, and nine members nominated by the president of Fiji to represent other communities (without any requirement for consultations).[30] The president himself was to be appointed by the GCC and would presumably be a Fijian, although this was not specified in the text as a qualification.[31] This overrepresentation of Fijians, when they also had an absolute majority in the other house, belied the justification for the second chamber.

In addition, the 1990 constitution enhanced the entrenchment of legislation protecting Fijian land and other interests. And the protection given to these specific acts was now extended to any bill "which affects land, customs or customary rights".[32] Amendments required the support of not less than eighteen of the twenty-four Senate members appointed by the GCC. The 1990 constitution also changed the rule whereby minerals belonged to the state. Now minerals were vested in the owners of the land where they were found—potentially, a major shift of resources from the state to the one community that owned most of the land.[33]

Provision was made to guarantee a Fijian administration: only a Fijian could be prime minister. Because the president had to appoint to this office a person who commanded the support of a majority in the House, the implicit assumption was that there would always be a clear Fijian majority bloc. This constitution gave even more power to the executive than the 1970 text had, since the moderating role of the leader of the opposition (a post traditionally held by an Indo-Fijian) was much diminished,[34] and the prime minister was given a direct and decisive say in appointments to various offices.[35] The chairman and one other member of the three-member Police Service Commission had to be Fijian[36]—an arrangement clearly designed to establish dominance over the police, in which institution there had previously been racial parity. Further, the legislature and the executive were given unlimited powers to establish programs and policies for "promoting and safeguarding the economic, social, educational, cultural, traditional and other interests of the Fijian and Rotuman people".[37]

---

[29] *See id.* at § 48(2)(b).

[30] *Id.* at §§ 54 and 55.

[31] *Id.* at § 31.

[32] *Id.* at § 78.

[33] Law could vest minerals in the state, but even then there was a presumption that royalties ultimately benefited customary land owners. *Id.* at § 9(7).

[34] *E.g.*, this officer was no longer to be consulted on various appointments such as to the Constituency Boundaries Commission. *Id.* at § 47.

[35] *E.g.*, members of the Public Service Commission. *Id.* at § 126(1).

[36] *Id.* at § 128.

[37] *Id.* at § 21.

The 1990 constitution enhanced the role of indigenous institutions. It gave special status to Fijian customary law, which also increased the separation of Fijians from the other communities. In its proceedings, Parliament had to take into account the application of this customary law and had to have a "particular regard to the customs, traditions, usages, values and aspirations of the Fijian people".[38] Native Fijian courts had to be revived. The interpretation of native customs, traditions, and usages (including land rights) and the determination as to the existence, extent, or application of customary laws were to be made by the Native Lands Commission. Customary laws were freed from the application of the right to equality.[39]

While native institutions intruded upon the constitutional scheme, the 1990 constitution was not allowed to impose its discipline over them. For example, the acts of the GCC were excluded from the purview of the ombudsman, an office established by the 1970 Constitution. Not accountable to any institution or process, the GCC was now effectively above the law.[40] It was also placed beyond criticism, as Parliament was authorized to curb freedom of expression in order to protect "the reputation, dignity and esteem of institutions and values of the Fijian people, in particular the Bose Levu Vakaturaga [Great Council of Chiefs] and the traditional Fijian system and titles or reputation, dignity and esteem of other races in Fiji, in particular their traditional systems".[41] The ombudsman was also prevented from reviewing the actions of the Native Land Commission, the Native Fisheries Commission, and the Native Lands Trust Board.[42] Similarly, many of these decisions, especially those made by the Native Lands Commission,[43] were removed from the jurisdiction of the courts.

On the one hand, the indigenous institutions had been largely freed of constitutional supervision; on the other, however, many of the native institutions had been so recomposed and manipulated they could no longer be regarded as indigenous but, rather, as instruments of those Fijians who controlled the state. This is evident in the way in which the leaders of the coup changed the membership of the GCC to exclude the supporters of the democratically elected government they overthrew, thereby increasing their own power to nominate members. Another consequence was that the close control of the state by the native institutions prevented other races from influencing the state's policies and undermined the capacity or willingness of the state to promote interethnic bargaining and accommodation.

Predictably, the weakening of institutions of accountability facilitated corruption and impropriety in public life and produced an inefficient government. This

---

[38] *Id.* at § 100(2).
[39] *Id.* at § 16(3)(d).
[40] *Id.* at § 135(2)(v).
[41] *Id.* at § 13(2)(d).
[42] *Id.* at §§ 135(2)(vi), (vii), and (viii).
[43] *Id.* at § 100(4).

state of affairs led to a major crisis of confidence in the future of Fiji and to the emigration of a substantial number of talented citizens. The situation that emerged was perceived as a principal cause of the stagnation of the economy, retarding the social and economic advancement of all the communities; was much criticized abroad; and, finally, secured Fiji's expulsion from the Commonwealth.

Most importantly, the new constitution reinforced internal divisions among Fijians. Once Indo-Fijians were sidelined, there was little to maintain the political unity of Fijians. The passing of power to commoners undermined the chiefly class, which had sedulously cultivated both the ideology of traditionalism and a sort of unity under eastern hegemony. Given the resultant multiplicity of parties among Fijians, no one party could form a government without the support of an Indian party. Needing that support, Rabuka agreed to a speedy review of the constitution, in accordance with a provision for a review at the end of seven years.[44]

4. The 1997 constitution

The failures of the 1970 and 1990 constitutions prompted the search for a new basis for the state and for intercommunity relations, with an emphasis on the need for national harmony and respect for the rights of all communities. The 1997 constitution was constructed through a process, insisted upon by the Indo-Fijians, that distinguished it from any previous practice in Fiji. A three-person commission—consisting of the chairman (Sir Paul Reeves, a former Anglican archbishop and governor-general of New Zealand, and by whose name the commission came to be known) and one Fijian (Tomasi Vakatora) and one Indo-Fijian (Brij Lal)—reviewed the 1990 constitution. It made recommendations for "promoting racial harmony and national unity and the economic and social advancement of all communities and bearing in mind internationally recognized principles and standards of individual and group rights" as required by its terms of reference.[45]

The third constitution of our narrative was the product of the recommendations of the Reeves commission as amended and approved by a parliamentary select committee.[46] In what follows, we outline the approach of the commission and discuss the fate of two issues that were central to its work and subsequent negotiations—the electoral system and power-sharing arrangements.

[44] *Id.* at § 161.
[45] Terms of Reference of the Fiji Constitution Review Commission, issued by the President of the Republic of Fiji, Mar. 15, 1995.
[46] THE FIJI ISLANDS: TOWARDS A UNITED FUTURE, REPORT OF THE FIJI CONSTITUTION REVIEW, Fiji Parliamentary Paper No. 34/1996 [hereinafter THE REEVES REPORT]. A detailed analysis of the process of constitution making by the present authors will be published in a forthcoming publication of the United States Institute of Peace.

4.1 The approach of the commission

The main concern of the commission was to encourage and facilitate the forma-tion of multiethnic governments, asserting that "progress towards the sharing of executive power among all ethnic communities is the only solution to Fiji's con-stitutional problems".[47] The key to this goal was the electoral system. However, the establishment of multiethnic government would also involve removal or adjustment of the four principal problems that the commission had identified: communal representation, the ethnic base of political parties, majority govern-ment, and the paramountcy principle.

The commission dealt with the principle of Fijian paramountcy by highlight-ing its role in the protection of the rights and interests of Fijians rather than in the domination of other communities. It made a series of recommendations under this principle: to give the GCC constitutional status; to retain the constitutional entrenchment of laws protecting Fijian interests; to transfer the veto from the Senate to the GCC; and to elect the president, who would be a Fijian, at a joint meeting of the two chambers on the nomination of the GCC.

On power sharing, the commission rejected proposals for a requirement either that the prime minister should appoint a specified number of ministers from the different communities or for the constitution to entitle every political party that secured at least 20 percent of the parliamentary seats to a proportionate share in the cabinet.[48] These suggestions would not, in its view, have fundamentally altered the nature of politics, parties, or modes of representation or reduce the salience of the ethnic factor.[49] Nor was there any guarantee that a multiethnic government in these conditions would provide a sufficient degree of goodwill and trust for fair and effective government. Instead, electoral and other incentives were needed for parties to cooperate, merge, and broaden their appeal for support.[50]

The commission believed that the overriding goals of multiethnic govern-ment, racial harmony, and national unity could not be achieved until the elect-oral system moved away from communal seats ("reserved" seats) to non-racial seats ("open" seats). It proposed a House of Representatives of seventy members divided into forty-five open seats (without ethnically based restrictions on can-didates or voters) and twenty-five reserved seats (twelve for indigenous Fijians and Pacific Islanders, ten for Indo-Fijians, one for Rotumans and two for general voters), thus reversing the proportion between the two types of seats in the 1970 constitution. Otherwise, the demands of the racial community would dominate, and "parties would have little inducement to become multiethnic in their mem-bership and policies".[51]

---

[47] *Id.* at para. 2.69.
[48] *Id.* at 18.
[49] *Id.* at para. 9.87.
[50] *Id.* at paras. 2.76, 9.96.
[51] *Id.* at para. 9.155.

The commission proposed removing any criteria from the membership of the Senate. Each province would return two senators, without any racial restriction on candidates or voters (in addition to limited representation, by way of presidential nomination, for small communities that did not make it to the lower house). This proposal built on the "distinctive identity" of provinces. "... [M]embers of all communities share a sense of belonging to the provinces with which they have their closest links."[52] This would enhance identities within provinces and integrate provinces with the nation, especially as political parties would play a key role in elections.[53]

In order to facilitate racial integration, the commission opted for the alternative-voting (AV) system[54] for both the House of Representatives and the Senate,[55] rejecting the first-past-the-post system (as undemocratic) and the proportional system (as encouraging voting by ethnicity). The main attraction of alternative voting was the incentive it provided for moderation and cooperation across ethnic lines. As the winning candidate must secure at least 50 percent of the votes plus one, which few candidates or parties would be able to muster from their own community, each party would have an incentive to enter into arrangements with another party to trade their second-place preferences. In due course, this type of cooperation would lead to multiethnic or non-ethnic parties, and facilitate national unity and a broader national agenda.

The commission made several other recommendations not just to ease ethnic tensions but to provide for the strong protection of human rights and to ensure social justice, especially by means of affirmative action for the genuinely disadvantaged and rules requiring that the composition of national institutions, such as the civil service and judiciary, reflect the national makeup. The commission also sought to reinforce what it hoped would be a less confrontational style in Parliament by providing for a committee system to carry out much of the work of government scrutiny. The commission was anxious that all its proposals be seen as part of a coherent and interdependent scheme. For example, the reconceptualization of the Senate would complement and reinforce changes in the composition of and voting for the House of Representatives. The rules proposed for the election of the president were intended to bring the issue before the more inclusive chamber and to afford the executive greater legitimacy (notwithstanding that only an indigenous Fijian qualified for office).

---

[52] *Id.* at para. 9.177.
[53] *Id.* at para. 9.179.
[54] Under alternative voting (sometimes known as majority-preference, or instant-runoff, voting), voters rank the candidates in order of preference. If no candidate receives a majority of votes on the first count, then the candidate with the smallest number of votes is eliminated, and his/her first-choice votes are transferred to the second-choice candidate on each of those ballots. This process of elimination and reallocation continues until one candidate has netted a majority of the votes and is the winner.
[55] The Reeves Report, *supra* note 46, at ch. 10.

4.2 Modifications by the Joint Parliamentary Select Committee

While not without some internal inconsistencies, the commission's proposals displayed a clear logic in their approach to achieving gradual change to a fundamentally different system as well as in the confrontation with the difficulties surrounding the sacred cow of Fijian interests in land, customs, and chieftaincy. The decisions of the bipartisan Parliamentary Select Committee set up to review the Reeves commission recommendations, whose members had probably not fully absorbed the closely reasoned justifications of the commission, introduced serious contradictions.

Many politicians were not happy with the commission's emphasis on national identity at the expense of communal affiliations and institutions. A great number of them had become accustomed to and were comfortable with racially oriented electorates and politics. Others, who had not looked approvingly on the commission's interest in comparative constitutions and experiences, emphasized the uniqueness of Fiji's circumstances. President Ratu Mara cautioned that, with all the talk about multiracial harmony, it was important to "recognise the existence of our different races, cultures and customs. Only so can we fully respond to the challenge of achieving this harmony we all desire, and which will be the richer for being structured in an honest, realistic and disciplined way".[56] Rabuka reminded the select committee of the diversity of ethnic groups, cultures, and faiths in Fiji, which give "identity, solace and confidence to our citizens as individuals and distinct groups".[57] If the select committee proved unable to work out an agreement on a particular issue they would turned it over to Prime Minister Rabuka and Leader of the Opposition Jai Ram Reddy, who had achieved a remarkable working relationship.

The main amendments of the select committee pertained to the system of government. The committee reversed the proportion between open and reserved seats. Out of a House of seventy-one members, only twenty-five seats would be open; the balance would be divided among indigenous Fijians, with twenty-three, Indo-Fijians with nineteen, general electors, with three, and Rotumans, with one (representing slight overrepresentation of indigenous Fijians and the general voters). This change would reduce the incentives to form multiethnic parties or mergers, since both Fijians and Indo-Fijians, if each was fully united,

---

[56] Report of the Joint Parliamentary Select Committee on the Report of the Fiji Constitution Review Commission [hereinafter Select Committee Report], Parl. Paper No. 17, Annex II (2) (1997).

[57] *See* Select Committee report, Annex IV(4). He went on to say, "Coercing what cannot be understood or what is not desired at times results in disenchantments and resistance. We are not embarked upon some experimental academic exercise and we cannot be determined upon social engineering in a haste and with concepts and values that could arouse uncertainty, anxiety and suspicion."

could expect to win elections or be in a position to enter the cabinet. Although the alternative-voting system was accepted, its significance from a non-racial perspective was diminished not only by reducing the number of open seats but also by specifying that those seats be contested in single-member constituencies, thus restricting the extent of ethnic heterogeneity.

The proposal for an elected Senate was rejected. This eliminated the prospect of further elections on an open-seat basis and thus foreclosed opportunities for cooperation among parties of different ethnic communities. Moreover, the identity of nominees proposed for membership on the GCC retained a distinct ethnic element, as did the veto vested in certain members, ethnically defined. The appointment of the president by the GCC, rather than by the more representative Parliament, likewise continued to evince a strong ethnic element.

Rejecting opportunities to move toward a more multiracial or non-racial ordering of the legislative system, and perhaps realizing that this would reduce the prospect of power sharing through the electoral process, the select committee opted for a mandatory coalition government. But here, too, its approach differed from that of the commission.[58] It decided that any party that obtained at least 10 percent of the seats in the House of Representatives would be entitled to a proportionate number of ministerial positions. The commission had complained, previously, that in the submissions by political parties on coalition national government, few had given any details or appeared to have thought through how such a design would work. It seems that in agreeing on a system against which the commission had set its face, the politicians paid even less attention to its implications.[59] For example, the commission had recommended that the maximum number of ministers should be fifteen; this was to prevent the appointment of a larger cabinet as a means of discouraging scrutiny of the government's conduct or averting votes of no confidence. The committee ignored this limit, even though in coalitions the tendency may be to increase the number to please coalition partners.

We now turn briefly to the consequences of the 1997 constitution, by examining the operation of its critical provisions with regard to elections, power sharing, and the Fijian administration, as it is called, which refers to a set of laws and

[58] One member of the Select Committee, from the Fiji Labour Party, has explained why the commission approach was rejected. His party, committed to nonracial distinctions, could not accept the notion of multiethnic government, while multiparty government, which the Select Committee adopted, was more congenial: Krishna Datt, Speech at the University of the South Pacific Conference on Democracy and Good Governance (Sept. 30, 2003). The explanation is puzzling, since the vehicle for representation in the cabinet in the commission proposal was parties, not ethnic groups as such.

[59] No doubt in the rush of events, the select committee (or the drafter) did not have time to iron out internal inconsistencies. A glaring one is the inconsistency of section 99 on the compulsory multiparty cabinet with the Compact: *see* Select Committee report, *supra* note 56, at § 6(g) (referring to coalitions only of the willing).

institutions designed both to protect the interests of Fijians and to grant them autonomy in customary matters as well as in local government.

4.3 The operation of the Constitution: The electoral system

The electoral system was envisaged by the Reeves commission as a way of encouraging moderation by offering incentives to parties, on one side, to cooperate across the racial divide with moderate parties on the other, by trading preferences—that is, having their supporters agree to put the other party to the agreement in second place on their ballots. In fact, we find a picture of increasing polarization. In 1999, the more "radically Indian" Fiji Labour Party won outright,[60] while, in 2001, the Soqosoqo Duavata ni Lewenivanua (SDL, or United Fiji Party) of Prime Minister Laisenia Qarase was able to form a government with a conservative Fijian party ally. In 2006, the SDL gained an absolute majority, winning every Fijian communal seat while the FLP won every Indian communal seat. In all elections, the parties with the greatest cross-cultural claims have been left out in the cold. In 1999, these were the two parties that tried to work together in the spirit of the Reeves commission, much as they had done in the Joint Parliamentary Select Committee—Rabuka's Soqosoqo ni Vakavulewa ni Taukei (SVT) and the Indo-Fijian NFP. In 2006, the NFP ran forty-five candidates, none of whom came anywhere near to winning, while none of the fifty candidates of a new multiracial party (National Alliance Party of Fiji, or NAPF) won a seat.[61] To a limited extent, this is a result of the alternative-voting system, which tends to exaggerate differences even more than the winner-takes-all system. The other smaller parties simply have not obtained sufficient votes. The NFP obtained only 6.35 percent of first preferences in 2006, which would have entitled it to four seats on a strictly proportional basis. The NAPF would have won two seats on that basis. In other words, moderation is apparently not appealing to the voters at present.

Since the 1999 election, Jon Fraenkel and Bernard Grofman have been engaged in a controversy with Donald Horowitz as to whether the Fiji electoral experiment has been a failure from the standpoint of encouraging moderation.[62] Fraenkel points out that while the Reeves commission assumed that "[o]nly moderate

[60] It is a bit misleading to characterize the FLP as radical Indian, though they may be so viewed by many Fijians. But for purposes of analyzing the 1999 election, especially, it tends to be regarded as such because the NFP was behaving moderately by virtue of its alliance with the SVT.

[61] For detailed election results see the website of the Election Commission of Fiji at <http://www.elections.gov.fj/results2006.html>.

[62] *See, e.g.,* Jon Fraenkel & Bernard Grofman, *A Neo-Downsian Model of the Alternative Vote as a Mechanism for Mitigating Ethnic Conflict in Plural Societies*, 121 Pub. Choice 487 (2004); Jon Fraenkel & Bernard Grofman, *Does the Alternative Vote Foster Moderation in Ethnically Divided Societies?: The Case of Fiji*, 39 Comp. Pol. Stud. 663 (2006); Donald L. Horowitz, *The Alternative Vote and Interethnic Moderation: A Reply to Fraenkel and Grofman*, 121 Pub. Choice 507 (2004) [hereinafter Horowitz, *The Alternative Vote*]; Donald L. Horowitz, *Strategy Takes a Holiday: Fraenkel and Grofman on the Alternative Vote*, 39 Comp. Pol. Stud. 652 (2006) [hereinafter Horowitz, *Strategy Takes a Holiday*].

parties with conciliatory policies will agree to trade preferences", in fact, all the parties did so, and most voters left the ranking to their parties, as the ballot permitted them to do.[63] Furthermore, one would expect a Fijian voter or party either to give first preference to an extreme Fijian party, followed by a more moderate one, or the other way round, followed by a progression through a more moderate Indian party with the more extreme Indian party at the bottom. Instead, there were instances of very different rankings. In certain open constituencies, some parties had the following pattern of preferences: "radical" Fijian party, "radical" Indian party, "moderate" Fijian party, "moderate" Indian party. In twelve open constituencies, the order of preference among FLP's electors was as follows: "radical" Indian (FLP), "moderate" Fijian, "radical" Fijian, "moderate" Indian. Fraenkel and Grofman attribute counterintuitive patterns like these to the overwhelming emphasis placed by the FLP and its allies on excluding the SVT and NPF. There was even one Fijian party—Veitokani ni Lewenivanua Vakarisito (VLV, or Christian Democrat Alliance) whose policy objective was to make the country a Christian state—that entered into agreements with the FLP for precisely those reasons—and in six constituencies assisted the FLP to win.[64]

Elsewhere Fraenkel has written:

> ... party preference transfers were not, to any significant degree, associated with political deals on ethnically divisive issues. More important motives included negative ranking of parties that posed the greatest electoral threat, elevation higher up the rankings of no-hope candidates or independents who were likely to pose little political threat inside Parliament, personality-specific deals and efforts to make arrangements in the hope of securing political office.[65]

In this emphasis on the desire to exclude the other coalition we see a pattern not uncommon in developing countries, where politics is so often concerned with obtaining power, as an end in its own right, rather than with what is to be done with power once acquired (other than feathering one's own nest).

It seems that in 1999 the Labour Party understood this system and made it work to its advantage to a far greater extent than other parties. In the 1999 election, the result for one half of the contested seats involved counting second or other preferences. Of the thirty-six seats at stake, the result in twenty-one was the same in terms of individuals elected as if the first-past-the-post system had been in operation, but in fifteen instances the result was different, and the Labour Party was the winner in most of these.

[63] ELECTION WATCH II: A CITIZENS' REVIEW OF THE FIJI ISLANDS GENERAL ELECTIONS 2001 89 (Arlene Griffen ed., Citizens' Constitutional Forum 2001).

[64] Horowitz has replied to the analysis of Fraenkel and Grofman, arguing that the evidence from Fiji still supports the thesis that alternate voting generally offers an incentive to moderation. *See* Horowitz, *The Alternative Vote*, and Horowitz, *Strategy Takes a Holiday, supra* note 62. Arguably, the 2006 election offers some evidence against this view.

[65] Jon Fraenkel, *Electoral Engineering and the Politicisation of Ethnic Friction in Fiji, in* CAN DEMOCRACY BE DESIGNED? 200, 248 (Sunil Bastian & Robin Luckham eds., Zed Press 2003).

In 2001, only twenty-eight seats were decided on preferences, and, of these, only ten were won by a party other than the one that had obtained a majority of first preferences. But, of these, nine were won by the SDL by virtue of a transfer of votes, usually from a more "moderate" party. So the SDL, too, seems to have learned to play the electoral game.

In 2006, all but eleven seats were decided on first ballot (of these, nine were in open seats). In other words, in communal constituencies the alternative-voting system has become largely irrelevant, and was relevant in only a minority of open seats. The FLP and the NFP had an agreement for trading preferences, though not a watertight one. The NFP's preferences led to the SDL's winning in a few instances, and to the FLP's winning in a few others; the same is true of the NAPF's preferences. All the open seats were won by one or the other party (SDL, thirteen; FLP, twelve). The results in the open seats broke down along lines that approximated the ethnic makeup of the electorate: more Fijian constituencies voted for SDL, and more Indo-Fijian constituencies for FLP; and, at either end of this racial spectrum, candidates also mirrored the local position.

Fraenkel also suggests that the results in 1999 are not explained by the decision to have fewer open seats than those proposed by the Reeves commission. Indeed, he suggests that more open seats would have led to an even greater swing to Labour in 1999—and to the SDL in 2001.[66] He also suggests that more ethnically heterogeneous constituencies would have had a similar effect.

Preferential voting is an appealing idea. But it is not surprising that the alternative-voting system has been received skeptically by many in the Fiji Islands.[67] The system, being so strongly majoritarian, makes it very difficult for a new party (like the NAPF) or a party trying to recover from a serious decline (like the NFP) to enter Parliament. Fiji politics actually do involve some issues of policy—unlike many developing countries. But there is no evidence, so far, that benefiting from a moderate party's support has had any moderating influence on party politics. The SDL would fear losing the 80 percent of Fijian voter support that it enjoys were it to move in that direction. Actually, having the support of a moderate member in Parliament is likely to have more impact; but, unless and until the FLP and SDL splinter, the existing system may prevent any other mono- or multiethnic party obtaining a toehold in the government. Indeed, the power-sharing executive may have a more significant impact on the two main parties.

4.4 Power sharing

Any party that receives 10 percent of the seats in Parliament is entitled to seats in the cabinet, although it is not required to accept them. In 1999, the SVT had

[66] Jon Fraenkel, *Redistricting Via Coups and Constituencies: The Construction of Ethnically-Mixed Constituencies in Fiji 1970–2001*, 28 J. Pac. Stud. 23 (2005).
[67] *See, e.g.,* Election Watch II: A Citizens' Review of the Fiji Islands General Elections 2001 (Arlene Griffen ed., Citizen's Constitutional Forum 2002).

the necessary number of seats, but when the then prime minister, Mahendra Chaudhry, whose FLP had the largest number of parliamentary seats, offered SVT seats in the cabinet, the party responded with a number of conditions, which the prime minister interpreted as a rejection. The Supreme Court held that these conditions were such that the prime minister was not bound to accept them.[68] Thus, although the courts endorsed Chaudhry's position, he did seem to construe the SVT response as a rejection with almost indecent haste, and this was not in accordance with the Compact—the non-justiciable part of the Constitution that calls on parties to try to resolve disagreements through good faith negotiation.

After the 2001 election, the shoe was on the other foot. Qarase invited the FLP to join the cabinet—it was the only other party that met the constitutional criterion—but did so in the most unwelcoming terms:

> Our policies and your policies on a number of key issues of vital concern to the long-term stability of our country are diametrically opposed. Given this, I genuinely do not think there is sufficient basis for a workable partnership with your party in my Cabinet. [69]

When Chaudhry replied, accepting the invitation but indicating that he thought the policies should be negotiated, the prime minister tried to treat this as a rejection, and the dispute again came before the courts. This time the Court decided that Qarase was obliged to offer seats and that Chaudhry's letter, in this instance, did not amount to a rejection. The Supreme Court observed that the development of conventions, governing this sort of situation, would call for "a degree of give and take and good faith on all sides".[70]

The issue went back to the courts over the number of cabinet members that the FLP was entitled to. The Supreme Court held that if the prime minister wanted to give cabinet posts to other parties in his coalition these had to come from the share that was rightly that of his party.[71] After months of wrangling, Chaudhry decided not to occupy any ministries.

The power-sharing rules could produce, potentially, a very odd situation where one party does not win the election outright. For example, suppose one party obtains 35 percent of the seats and is able to form an alliance (either before or after the election) with several small parties, none of which has the eight seats that would constitute 10 percent but which, among them all, would have 20 percent. Each of these is likely to demand at least one seat in cabinet. Another party has perhaps 30 percent of the parliamentary seats and is thus entitled under the Constitution to 30 percent of the seats in cabinet. In that scenario, only 15 percent

[68] *President of Fiji Islands v. Kubuabola* [1999] F.J.S.C. 8, Misc. Case No. 1 of 1999 (Sept. 3, 1999).
[69] *Qarase v. Chaudhry* [2003] F.J.S.C. 1, CBV0004.2002S (July 18, 2003). The correspondence between the party leaders is appended to the decision.
[70] *Id.*
[71] In re the President's Reference, *Qarase v. Chaudhry* [2004] F.J.S.C. 1, Misc. 001.2003 (July 9, 2004).

of the members remain in opposition, and the party that won may end up with fewer seats in cabinet than the one that came in second.

The first multiparty cabinet was inaugurated after the 2006 elections. The government consisted of twelve SDL cabinet ministers, plus two Fijian senators and one independent (all essentially SDL supporters), and nine FLP ministers, and twelve ministers of state (none FLP). Twelve ministers and nine ministers of state were Fijian, and eight ministers and one minister of state were Indo-Fijians. The result was hardly proportionate to the party makeup in the House or to its ethnic composition (thirty-seven Fijians, thirty Indo-Fijians, one Rotuman, and three "Others"). Chaudhry remained outside the cabinet, although the two parties' leaders agreed to form a joint party committee to lay down ground rules for the operation of the multiparty cabinet.[72]

Ethnic diversity and party diversity in the cabinet are not necessarily the same thing. In 1999, Chaudhry's cabinet had a majority of Fijian members, including his deputy prime minister. While for most of 2001–2006 there were no Indo-Fijian cabinet members,[73] there were two "Others".[74] In 2006, one SDL minister was an Indo-Fijian, and two FLP Ministers were Fijian. Fraenkel has suggested that multiethnic innovations may come from within the major parties rather than as a result of constitutional engineering.[75] If so, these may nevertheless take some time. In 1999, six FLP MPs were Fijians, in 2006 only four, while there are two Indo-Fijian SDL MPs. Although each party put forward candidates in the "opposite" communal seats (FLP having fifteen candidates in Fijian communal seats, and the SDL occupying all but one of the Indo-Fijian seats), the number of votes received were derisory, and one assumes that the motive is to give some electoral experience to candidates rather than any expectation of winning.

The 1997 Constitution provides for another sharing arrangement. The leader of the opposition appoints eight members of the Senate (as compared with the nine appointed by the prime minister)—a provision carried over, essentially, from the non-power-sharing model in the 1970 constitution. The current Constitution requires that the leader of the opposition's nominees must be from the parties entitled to sit in the cabinet.[76] In other words, the notion that some Senate members would represent a non-government view is completely lost. This was clearly

[72] Fiji Gov't Press Release, Prime Minister and FLP leader make further progress (Oct. 18, 2006), *available at* <http://www.fiji.gov.fj/publish/page_7649.shtml>.

[73] There was one on the ticket of the SDL, but he had to resign due to allegations of financial impropriety.

[74] This assigning of ethnicity is distasteful and may be a bit haphazard; we base the ethnicity on names and photos on the Parliament website if there is any uncertainty. *See* <http://www.parliament.gov.fj/mp/hr.aspx>.

[75] Jon Fraenkel, The Perils of Majoritarianism in Fiji: The 2006 Polls in Perspective, (unpublished manuscript, *available at* <http://www.usp.ac.fj/fileadmin/files/Institutes/piasdg/governance_papers/The_Perils_of_Majoritarianism_in_Fiji__the_2006_elections_in_Perspective.pdf>).

[76] Fiji Const. § 64(2).

a matter of drafting oversight and has led to litigation.[77] The Supreme Court found itself compelled to decide along these lines, though there was a dissenting judgment from Sir Arnold Amet from Papua New Guinea who tried to make the provision work in a way that realized his view of the objective, namely, broadening the membership of the Senate.

A power-sharing government seemed to offer a glimmer of hope for consociational approaches after the formation of a SDL-FLP government, following the 2006 election. This was especially the case, as the FLP team was led not by the difficult Chaudhry but by the widely respected teacher, trade unionist, and labor minister Krishna Dutt, who favored conciliation and wanted to make power sharing work (and, in fact, had tried to ensure that parliamentary committees worked in that spirit). However, once again, the government was overthrown by the military, in December 2006.[78]

4.5 Fijian administration

The system of Fijian administration, entrenched in the 1970 constitution, was strengthened in the 1990 constitution, with a commitment to the reintroduction of Fijian customary courts. The Reeves commission had reservations about this but felt unable to recommend repeal or radical modification. It did recommend the constitutional recognition of the GCC and giving it the power to veto changes to protective Fijian legislation as well as to nominate (but not appoint) the president. This was done in order to open up opportunities for the reform of the Senate and to make it less racially oriented. The commission also sought to deemphasize the link between Fijians and provinces by making the provinces multiracial electorates for the Senate. None of these recommendations were accepted (apart from the constitutionalization of the GCC).

Conceived by colonial authorities as a means of indirect rule, Fijian administration was used for maintaining the authority of the chiefs and the cohesion of the community. The GCC acquired great political authority (even though its legal powers were not significantly increased), and provincial administration became a device to develop Fijian consensus, particularly on matters connected with relations to Indo-Fijians. It became increasingly a system that, from a communal base, affected and shaped the policies of the state, representing a reversal of the original purpose; it came to dominate the state, rather than being an adjunct to it. At the same time, Fijian administration has proved discriminatory and exclusionary. Indeed, the GCC has been mobilized by those Fijian politicians wanting indigenous political supremacy and used in attempts to legitimatize all the coups that are widely perceived as anti-Indo-Fijian. The Fijian administration has prevented

---

[77] In re the Constitution, Reference by HE the President [2002] F.J.S.C. 1, Misc. 001.2001S (Mar. 15 2002).
[78] See *infra* text in § 5.

the full integration of the indigenous people into the modern economy—itself a primary reason for the coups. Thus, it has retarded fair and amicable interracial relations and a more integrated political system. In the end, the use of the GCC to justify coups greatly politicized it, and ultimately it lost legitimacy.

5. Coups and overthrow of the constitution

The tale of the 1997 constitution would not be complete without some mention of the two coups aimed at its overthrow. The first coup, executed by a businessman cum adventurer, George Speight, took place on May 19, 2000, about a year after the first government under the new Constitution assumed office. Brij Lal has said that Prime Minister Chaudhry had antagonized many people with his abrasive and confrontational style, but far more significant was the opposition orchestrated by defeated politicians, some of whose colleagues were in the government. According to Lal, "Speight was the front man for an assortment of institutions and individuals aggrieved by the People's Coalition government: defeated politicians seeking revenge, those who had amassed enormous wealth during the Rabuka years in the 1980s, the unemployed and the unemployable, the human casualties of globalization".[79] The military government to which Speight handed over power, in return for amnesty, abrogated the Constitution and declared its intention to install a new constitution entrenching Fijian supremacy. However, its efforts were thwarted by a Supreme Court decision that, quite rightly in our view, declared the coup unconstitutional and decreed the restoration of the 1997 constitution.[80]

The second coup occurred on December 5, 2006, five years after the Constitution had been fully restored and was led by the commander of the Fiji Military Forces at the time, Frank Bainimarama. He insisted he had intervened to protect the Constitution and its spirit against the policies of the Prime Minister Qarase, who was intending to pass controversial legislation that would benefit Fijians at the expense of others and grant amnesty to the perpetrators of the Speight coup—all of which would "divide the nation and will have very serious consequences to our future generations".[81] He declared his firm commitment to the Constitution; the military force "not only adheres to the rule of law and the Constitution but more importantly believes in the adherence to the spirit of law and the Constitution".[82] Accordingly, the Constitution would remain in force

---

[79] Brij V. Lal, *Constitutional Engineering in Post-Conflict Fiji*, *in* THE ARCHITECTURE OF DEMOCRACY: CONSTITUTIONAL DESIGN, CONFLICT MANAGEMENT, AND DEMOCRACY 267 (Andrew Reynolds ed., Oxford Univ. Press 2002).

[80] *Chandrika Prasad v. Republic of the Fiji Islands* [2001] 2 L.R.C. 743.

[81] Fiji Gov't Press Release, *Commander RFMF—Public Declaration of Military Takeover*, 2 (Dec. 5, 2006), *available at* <http://www.fiji.gov.fj/publish/page_8092.shtml>.

[82] *Id.* at 3.

except for those parts "necessitated under the doctrine of necessity",[83] and elections under the Constitution would be held in due course.[84] And that is where things rest.

6. Conclusion

Neither the alternative-voting electoral system nor power sharing has eased Fiji's ethnic competition and tensions. This resulted from the seemingly cynical manipulation of the systems by some key political parties. They were more concerned, for partisan reasons, with defeating parties whose policies were closer to their own than parties firmly opposed to them. Those espousing extremist racial positions garnered more votes from their community. As a result, alternative voting did not produce coalitions of moderates; instead, the moderates were wholly marginalized. As matters stand, coalition governments are unlikely to work, at least to the extent that they might bring together the extremists from the two major communities.[85] In this respect, Fiji's experience is not so different from that of other consociational states (as seen, for example, in the 2007 elections in Northern Ireland, which were won by the extremist parties of the Catholics and Protestants).

The complicated and confusing rules governing the formation and operation of coalitions enabled parties to involve the courts in their disputes, not so much to secure a place in the cabinet as to frustrate government administration.[86] Fraenkel comments that "[i]nstead of fostering compromise, the power sharing provisions in the constitution had become the principal focus of inter-ethnic antagonism, serving to sustain and entrench the polarisation of 1999–2000".[87] Fraenkel notes, as well, another problem, namely, that the consociation-oriented power-sharing arrangements were at odds with and under threat from the majoritarian electoral system.[88] With their varying versions of consociation, neither the 1990 nor the 1997 constitutions were able to promote ethnic understanding and amity.

The political order of Fiji has always been organized on a basis of treating the communities as corporate entities. Many important rights depend on membership in a community. For Fijians, certain powers are exercised on an

---

[83] *Id.* at 6.

[84] *Id.* at 7–8.

[85] As mentioned earlier, the only power-sharing government to come into being was sworn in only a few months before the most recent coup; so far, it seems to have been working without tearing itself apart.

[86] There were serious structural faults with the power-sharing system. *See* Jon Fraenkel, *Power Sharing in Fiji and New Caledonia* (presented at Australian National University conference "Globalisation, Governance and the Pacific Islands," Oct. 25–27, 2005), *available at* <http://www.usp.com.fj/fileadmin/files/Institutes/piasdg/governance_papers/fraenkel_power_sharing.pdf>.

[87] *Id.* at 16.

[88] *Id.* at 24.

exclusive communal foundation, which assumes some form of group autonomy. Representation in the legislature has always been secured primarily or exclusively through communal electorates. At times, the view that the composition of the cabinet and the public services should reflect ethnic diversity has prevailed and was given constitutional force in 1997. Successive constitutions have provided for communal vetoes on important legislation. So what insight does the Fiji experience give into the dynamics of consociation?

It should be noted that the purportedly consociational arrangements in Fiji were not the result of consociation (that is, of free association). They were a colonial imposition. In this respect, Fiji's consociation is not so different from some other countries, which is or was the result of external pressure (for example, Cyprus, Bosnia-Herzegovina, and Northern Ireland—and, in the last two, it is the constant intervention of external factors which sustains the governance system). The arrangements in Fiji were sustained, after the British left, by a constitutional compromise between Fijians and Indo-Fijians brokered or, more accurately imposed, by the British. More to the point, these arrangements were sustained by the self-interest of the Fijian elite, which acceded to power at independence and became their principal beneficiaries.

The consociational measures were not devised to resolve a conflict; rather, the British imposed them as part of its divide-and-rule policy. The colonial pioneers of these arrangements wished to preserve the traditional Fijian hierarchy because of their own preference for indirect rule. It is not surprising, therefore, that what they preserved was not traditional but invented to suit administrative convenience. Far from trying to promote harmony between the races, the colonial authorities and settlers repeatedly criticized the Indo-Fijians and persuaded Fijians that their interests were under threat from the ambitions of former. As a result, it is possible to see the consequences of consociation-type arrangements in a society that did not start with ethnic conflicts and could have been organized in a different manner.

We have already referred to the consequences of these arrangements. From early times, they led to the separation of races and, along with it, racial suspicions and animosity. Everyone seems to have fallen into the habit of viewing issues through the racial prism rather than, say, the national interest. Classifying people by racial categories produced false stereotypes that then became hard to overcome. Differences *within* racial groups were obscured or disregarded for purposes of hegemony (thus, effectively, reducing diversity), while differences *between* them were exaggerated (thus, making diversity more problematic than it need be). Meanwhile, the constitutions have focused on the larger community, to the disadvantage of smaller minorities.

The constitutions have been based on the assumptions (*a*) that there are distinct communities separated by their race (thus privileging this identity over all else); (*b*) that these communities are homogenous, sharing common interests (thus ignoring the many divisions within each of the communities); and (*c*) that their interests are antagonistic (thus subverting the aspirations of the many people of all communities who yearn for integration and common identity). The rules for access to state power have given some reality to the ideology implicit in the foregoing. Rules for elections and the formation of governments have helped those politicians who have set themselves up as the so-called protectors of ethnic and communal interests against the ostensible designs or conspiracies of other communities. Politicians have become comfortable with racial politics, having had little opportunity and even less incentive to learn of the problems facing other communities. So strong has this become the political tradition that even constitutional devices to promote accommodation and integration have been turned to adversarial uses.

Given the trappings of consociation, community representation, vetoes, proportionality, and communal autonomy, it is easy to overlook the tendency toward the hegemony of a community—or that there has been a massive degrading of human rights. Citizenship rights are downgraded in favor of group rights, with an emphasis of community and custom prevailing over the rights of the individual. The consciousness of human rights is dulled, leading to a ready acquiescence in the violation of the rights of members of other communities.

Thus, the acceptance of rights has become conditional and selective, as in the manipulation of indigenous rights by a faction of Fijians. Until about the mid-1990s Fijians showed no interest in the international movement of indigenous rights and, as far as we can tell, did not participate in any of the meetings of the international working committee on indigenous rights—and scrupulously ignored the underlying principle of group-rights treaties, namely, that the rights of others must not be violated in pursuit of group advancement. Social justice has become a matter of ethnic negotiation, not the elimination of disadvantage wherever poverty or discrimination strikes.[89]

It is, of course, difficult to tell how Fiji would have fared under a different kind of dispensation, one emphasizing a non-racial approach and providing incentives for cooperation across racial boundaries. It would be naïve to assume that relations among communities would have been better or more harmonious. However, it is not our purpose to speculate on this, or to suggest arrangements that might have been more favorable and acceptable.

We end with some comments on the dichotomy between integration and consociation. Fiji's experience shows that it not always easy to analyze constitutions and politics in terms of integration versus consociation. We have tried to show that consociation is a problematic concept. Fiji's constitutions display some of the features of consociation, such the division of society into ethnic fragments and the conferral of corporate status on communities, requiring that important kinds

---

[89] It is worth noting that the 2000 coup took place on the same day and in the same place as the introduction of the Social Justice Bill, aimed at ensuring benefits to the most disadvantaged of all communities, amid Fijian fears that their previous, exclusive entitlements were under threat. Concerning issues around affirmative action, see Jill Cottrell & Yash Ghai, *Constitutionalising Affirmative Action in the Fiji Islands*, 11 INT'L J. HUM. RTS. 227 (2007).

of individual rights be exercised through membership of a community. But these constitutions have fallen well short of the consociational elements of power sharing and symmetrical self-government as well as proportionality. Fiji's politics and constitutions may be seen as characteristic of "plural societies", which acknowledge but do not celebrate diversity and which are based on the hegemony and control of one community over another. Any rights non-Fijians can enjoy must come from their submission to Fijian paramountcy. Sometimes, in more generous moments, the relationship is defined as that of hosts and guests—but guests without rights, dependent on the goodwill of the hosts.

This Fijian hegemony is based, not on any civilizing mission or moral or intellectual superiority, but purely on difference and on being indigenous. In fact, Fijian claims to hegemony have varied over time—first, based on their vulnerability, then, on the terms of the surrender of their sovereignty to the British in the nineteenth century, and, more recently, on international norms regarding the rights of indigenous people.[90] Thus, there is consistency of purpose with flexibility of rationalization.

Of particular interest has been the way in which constitutions have made Fijian traditions, institutions, resources, and symbols the source of authority and legitimacy and central to the political and administrative system. In 1970, all this apparatus was massively constitutionalized; the 1990 constitution increased its scope and depth; and the 1997 Constitution, inspired by the wish to move away from racialism, could only tentatively step back from it. While the tendency in the 1997 Constitution is toward change, it is caught uneasily between consociation and the political integration of different communities.

The self-proclaimed mission of the 2006 coup maker is to resolve this ambiguity in favor of integration. In a recent statement[91] by the new government, which calls itself the interim government, it announced plans for the review of the 1997 Constitution with the goal of "rid[ding] the Constitution of provisions that facilitate and exacerbate the politics of race [in] such areas as the registration of voters and the election of representatives to the House of Representatives through separate racial electoral rolls". The government claims to advocate the abolition of voting in "terms of racial classifications", so that "each voter should vote for a candidate of his/her choice in a common roll, with each vote having equal value". If this is achieved, the pendulum will have swung to the opposite extreme from past preoccupations with race. And Fiji's fortunes may then tell us something more about the relative merits of consociation and integration.

---

[90] *See* U.N. High Comm'r For Hum. Rts., Draft United Nations Declaration on the Rights of Indigenous Peoples, *available at* <http://www.unhchr.ch/huridocda/huridoca.nsf/(Symbol)/E.CN.4.SUB.2.RES.1994.45.en> (approved by the Human Rights Council in 2006 but not yet adopted by the General Assembly).

[91] Fiji Ministry of Information, Moving in the Right Direction (Apr. 2007), *available at* <http://www.fiji.gov.fj/uploads/Roadmap_2007.pdf> (last visited June 4, 2007).

11

Rival nationalisms in a plurinational state: Spain, Catalonia, and the Basque Country

*Michael Keating**

1. Accommodating national diversity

Two principal mechanisms for constitutional accommodation of national and ethnic diversity are recognized in the literature: territorial autonomy and consociational power sharing at the center. Territorial autonomy is often seen as appropriate where the groups in question are spatially concentrated without significant internal minorities (as in Scotland), while consociationalism is seen as preferable where groups contend for control of the same territory (as in Northern Ireland).

Both approaches have been criticized for assuming that we can identify the groups concerned, that these have a stable existence, and that their boundaries are known. This is quite apart from the normative criticism of accommodative policies, namely, that they force politics into an ethnic or national mode and inhibit the expression of other social cleavages, including those associated with progressive politics, a question not addressed in this chapter. The first objection, the ontological one, about who the groups are and how we know, is a major problem for the application of accommodative politics in practice. We can recognize an ideal type of multinational state, in which there are constituent nations, with their own territorial boundaries and traditions (Great Britain might be close to this, if not the United Kingdom). We can also recognize an ideal type of multiethnic state, in which politics is organized along ethnic lines, with stable and recognized social (nonterritorial) boundaries. More problematic, although more common, is what I have elsewhere called the plurinational state.[1] This is a state in

---

* Professor of Political and Social Science, European University Institute; Professor of Politics, University of Aberdeen. Email: keating@eui.eu

[1] MICHAEL KEATING, PLURINATIONAL DEMOCRACY: STATELESS NATIONS IN A POST-SOVEREIGNTY ERA (Oxford Univ. Press 2001).

which there exist not just competing nations, nor even just competing definitions of the boundaries of those nations, but competing conceptions of the meaning of nationality itself. For some people, at some times, nationality may be little more than a cultural reference. For others, it carries political connotations, varying from a demand for local autonomy to the insistence that each nation must have its own state. For some, the principle of the nation is unitary, so that only one nation can exist on a given territory or in the consciousness of a given individual. For others, the concept is plural, so that nations can exist within nations. This allows for some creative semantics, as we have seen in the recent decision of the Canadian Parliament to recognize Quebec as a nation within the nation of Canada,[2] or the tortuous definitions in some of the new statutes of autonomy in Spain. In some contexts, there are furious battles over the definition of these terms and their legal implications. In others, such as Great Britain, there is more semantic freedom, so that Scotland and Wales are known as nations, as is Great Britain as a whole.

Moreover, nations are not static; they can be created. I do not subscribe to the idea that nations can be created *ex nihilo* by political entrepreneurs. Most people, most of the time, are satisfied with their existing national identity and do not change it for short-term opportunistic reasons. Yet, if nations have been created in the past, they can be created in the present and in the future, given the right sociological and political conditions. This is not just a semantic argument. If nationality is interpreted in a political mode as carrying the implication of a right to self-government of some sort, then the multinational state can resolve the issue through federalism, and the multiethnic state through consociationalism. The plurinational state, however, will be driven in the direction of more complex and asymmetrical arrangements.

Spain is an example of such a plurinational state (as is Canada). In most of the territory, there is only one identity, that of Spain as a whole; other territories have dual identities, while others only identify with one of the minority nations. This makes for a fundamental asymmetry, since, however much Catalans and Basques (and some outside observers) try to frame the majority as "Castilian", there is no such national identity,[3] just as there is not an English-Canadian identity that excludes Quebec but includes all the rest. These identities are not fixed but have been reforged over time, notably in the late nineteenth century, under the impact of modernization, the end of Empire, and globalization; and then again, one hundred years later, in response to new domestic and international challenges.

[2] Resolution Respecting the Recognition that the Québécois Form a Nation within a United Canada, H.C. 87, 39th Parl. (2006).
[3] Juan Linz, *Early State-Building and Late Peripheral Nationalism Against the State: The Case of Spain, in* BUILDING STATES AND NATIONS 32 (Shmuel Noah Eisenstadt & Stein Rokkan eds., Sage 1973).

2. Political traditions in Spain

Spain is one of the oldest states in Europe, but one whose territorial and national configuration has never been resolved completely. Like other European states, it was formed as a conglomeration of territories in medieval and early modern times, with its components retaining many of their indigenous institutions. Until 1714, it consisted of three kingdoms, Castile, Aragon, and Navarre, each with its own privileges, assemblies, and judicial authorities. Aragon was itself a confederation of Aragon, Catalonia, Valencia, and the Balearic Islands, and even within Catalonia there were federal elements. The Basque provinces of Vizcaya, Guipuzcoa, and Alava within the kingdom of Castile retained traditional privileges or *fueros*, which included the right to raise their own taxes, no compulsory military service, and a tariff regime giving them free trade with the rest of the world while maintaining customs posts with the rest of Spain. These privileges were abolished only in the nineteenth century and, even then, some remained, notably the fiscal system or *concierto económico*.

Nationalist rhetoric on both sides has often obscured the complex history of accommodation of these territories to Spain. For centuries, it was the Basques who were more integrated into the Spanish state on an individual and social level, due to their incorporation into the kingdom of Castile.[4] Basques served in the royal and imperial administration, the armed forces (especially the navy),[5] and in the modern era were prominent in the banking sector in Madrid. Catalans, who had their own state tradition and, before 1714, their own autonomous state linked with Castile, were less prominent at the center and in the Empire. This is worth emphasizing, given the more separatist tradition of Basque nationalism from the end of the nineteenth century.

Since the nineteenth century, Spain has been the site of competing national projects, none of which managed to secure total victory, and it ended the twentieth century as a complex plurinational state. The nationalities question has been a preoccupation for Spanish constitution makers, who have veered between dogmatism and pragmatism, according to changing regimes. We can recognize several distinct constitutional traditions in Spain, although individuals and parties may mix and match them in their own ways.[6] There is a conservative, centralist tradition that regards Spain as a unitary nation and refuses to countenance any internal differentiation. This attitude culminated in the Franco regime

---

[4] Juan Pablo Fusi Aizpurúa, Identiades Proscritas: El No Nacionalismo en las Sociedades Nacionalistas (Seix Barral 2006).

[5] A recent novel recounts the exploits of the medieval counts of Vizcaya as lords of Castile, in a rather obvious reference to current political issues. Antonio Villanueva Edo, Señores de Vizcaya, Caballeros de Castilla (Roca 2006).

[6] Javier Tusell, España, una Angustia Nacional (Espasa Calpe 1999); Juan Pablo Fusi Aizpurúa, España: La Evolución de la Identidad Nacional (Temas de Hoy 2000).

(1939–75), whose ideology was suffused with traditionalist Spanish nationalism derived from imperialism and the reactionary side of Catholicism. The present conservative Popular Party (Partido Popular [PP]) is a democratic movement and has discarded the dictatorial aspects of Francoism, but remains the vehicle for an uncompromising defense of Spanish unity and the idea that there can only be one nation on the territory of the state. On the liberal and left side of Spanish politics, there is a Jacobin tradition of unity and centralization derived from French doctrines, which regards peripheral nationalism as reactionary and divisive. In this view, sovereignty resides in the unified Spanish people as encapsulated in democratic constitutions, notably those of 1812 and of 1978. This strand of opinion is influential in one section of the Socialist Party (Partido Socialista Obrero Español [PSOE]). There is a federal tradition, which never prospered after the failure of the federal First Republic in the 1870s, but which has retained some influence within the Socialist Party, especially in Catalonia.

In Catalonia and the Basque Country there are various nationalist traditions, some of which are exclusive, believing that sovereignty belongs only with their respective nations, while others are more accommodating and sustain visions of shared and mixed sovereignty. Justifications for nationalist demands are based on a mixture of historic rights claims and appeals to the present will of the populations concerned, the balance varying according to time and place. What is striking is that none of these has a vision for Spain as a complex, plurinational, and asymmetrical polity, and that no vision is shared across the whole state. Only recently have intellectuals and politicians sought a new formula to reconcile them in the "plurinational state", an idea that hitherto has been more philosophical than constitutional, but which has informed some recent developments in constitutional reform.

3. Catalonia

Catalan nationalism emerged in the late nineteenth century, led by a modernizing bourgeoisie frustrated with the archaic Spanish state, especially following defeat by the United States in the war of 1898. It built on a distinct language and identity and rediscovered history of pactism and accommodation of Catalonia before 1714 as a trading nation within a multinational polity. This is not, of course, the only version of Catalan history available, and the stereotype of moderation and compromise is supplemented by that of violence and revolution. The two are summed up in the twin attributes of *seny* (common sense and moderation) and *rauxa* (rage and extremism).[7]

---

[7] SALVADOR GINER ET AL., LA CULTURA CATALANA: EL SAGRAT I EL PROFÀ 62 (Edicions 1996).

Catalonia was host to a large-scale immigration from the rest of Spain in the early twentieth century and, again, after the 1960s. In the first phase immigrants tended to come from Aragon or the *països catalans* (the other Catalan-speaking regions of Valencia and the Balearic Islands), with historic connections under the old crown of Aragon. The later immigration was predominantly from southern Spain, especially Andalucia. In both cases, Catalan nationalists preached an inclusive nationalism, in which the incomers could become Catalan, notably, by learning the language (not a difficult task given its common base with Castilian Spanish).

Catalan nationalism has a weak separatist tradition, and there exists a recurrent theme of helping to modernize the Spanish state—"catalanizing" Spain. So Catalan nationalists have not hesitated to support governments in Madrid, usually in exchange for concessions for Catalonia and have not excluded participating in Spanish coalition governments, although in practice this has not come to pass since the transition to democracy. In the 1980s, there was even a failed bid to establish a Spanish liberal party with its base in Catalonia's moderate nationalist party.

Early conservative Catalan nationalism had a fatal ambiguity. It wanted home rule for Catalonia, but, at the same time, it needed the protected Spanish market for its goods, which were not competitive on an international level, as well as the help of the Spanish state in repressing its own revolutionary proletariat. Its collapse in the 1930s paved the way for a left-wing nationalism, which led to the devolved government established under the Second Republic. This nationalism was more separatist in orientation but not unambiguously so. On the fall of the monarchy in 1932, Francesc Macia, leader of the Esquerra Republicana de Catalunya, proclaimed a Catalan state in the context of a (nonexistent) Iberian confederation, which would also include Portugal.[8] Catalan nationalism is still divided into these two camps. On the conservative and moderate side is Convergència i Unió, an alliance of a Liberal party (Convergència) and a Christian Democrat one (Unió), which is in favor of strong Catalan autonomy within an asymmetrical Spanish confederation. On the left is the historic Esquerra Republicana de Catalunya (ERC), now in favor of independence but only in the long term, as part of a Europe of the Peoples.

Catalanism, as a general sentiment, goes well beyond the nationalist parties to include part of the socialist movement in the form of the Partit dels Socialistes de Catalunya (PSC; affiliated to the Spanish PSOE). Iniciativa per Catalunya (IC), formed from postcommunists, Greens, and left nationalists, also takes a pro-Catalan but not explicitly nationalist line. Both of these parties need to appeal both to Catalan workers and to incomers from the rest of Spain and so form a bridge between the communities. In 2006, José Montilla, who was born in

---

[8] *See* SANTIAGO VARELA, EL PROBLEMA REGIONAL EN LA SEGUNDA REPÚBLICA ESPAÑOLA (Unión Editorial 1976).

Andalucia and came to Catalonia as a teenager and who at the time was serving as a minister in the central government, was the successful Socialist candidate for president of the Catalan autonomous government. Swathes of civil society, while not seeing themselves as explicitly nationalist, also believe in self-government and the preservation and development of a distinct Catalan culture. This avoids a sharp division between nationalists and non-nationalists and facilitates a consensus on immediate measures for devolution and matters such as language policy.

Antinationalism has been represented only in sectors of the Popular Party, which has not flourished in Catalonia. Recently, however, an explicitly antinationalist party known as the Ciutadans/Ciudadanos (CiU) has emerged and gained representation in the Catalan Parliament in the elections of 2006 by taking votes from the PP. There have also been movements of intellectuals, opposed to the extension of the Catalan language, which have included some left-wing elements.

Catalonia is not a divided society, with a sharp ethnic and political cleavage between communities. Certainly, there is a distinction between native Catalans and newcomers, with the former much more likely to be nationalists. On the other hand, there is a high degree of assimilation, especially in the second generation. In the latest survey, 12 percent of the population consider themselves only Spanish; 9 percent more Spanish than Catalan; 40 percent equally Spanish and Catalan; 25 percent more Catalan than Spanish, and 12 percent only Catalan.[9] This suggests a high incidence of dual identity and a lack of polarization. There is a linguistic division, but all Catalan speakers command Castilian, and the children of Castilian-speaking families and even many adults do acquire Catalan.

The Popular Party and some social movements have sought to exploit the division between Catalans and incomers, but the latter are overwhelmingly working class and few would consider voting for the PP; instead, they provide an important part of the support base for the Socialists, who are committed to integration. Working-class immigrants, for their part, are keen for their children to learn Catalan as a means for social promotion. Despite the efforts of some organized groups and sections of the media, then, the language question has failed to trigger mass social mobilization. Support for independence usually runs at about 17 percent, although in the 2005 survey it was only 11.6 percent,[10] perhaps because of the prospect of increased autonomy under a new statute. Intriguingly, however, regular surveys by the Institut de Ciènces Polítiques i Socials show around 35 percent in favor of the concept of an independent Catalonia, twice the level of those reporting in the same survey as favoring independence against other options. It appears that in Catalonia, as in Quebec, independence is a flexible concept, covering a range of options, rather than a constitutional rupture.

[9] INSTITUT DE CIÈNCIES POLÍTIQUES I SOCIALS (ICPS), SONDEIG D'OPINIÓ CATALUNYA 2005 (2005).

[10] OBSERVATORIO POLÍTICO AUTONÓMICO (OPA), SONDEO DE OPINION 2005 (ICPS 2006).

Catalan nationalism has a strong European vocation. This is part of the early legacy, when Europe represented modernization and release from the backward grip of Madrid. Since the transition to democracy, it has represented the hope of a third way between autonomy and independence. Catalan nationalists and intellectuals have consistently stressed what some of us have called postsovereignty,[11] in which sovereignty is shared and divided among levels of government. The gradual development of European integration has allowed them to sustain an ambiguity about their eventual goals, arguing that these must evolve in parallel with the European project itself.

4. The Basque Country

Basque identity is very old, but Basque nationalism is a product of the late nineteenth century, when the province of Vizcaya first experienced rapid industrialization, social change, and immigration from other parts of Spain. Its founder, Sabino Arana, expounded the most exclusive form of ethnic nationalism, insisting on the ethnic purity of the real Basques. Members of the Basque Nationalist Party (Partido Nacionalista Vasco [PNV]), at that time, had to demonstrate four Basque surnames (indicating four Basque grandparents).[12] Language was an important badge of identity, but Arana, who had learned Basque as an adult, once declared that if the immigrants were to learn Basque then the true Basques would have to find another language to distinguish themselves.[13] He invented a history in which the traditional privileges of the Basque provinces (initially just Vizcaya) represented independent statehood, with only a nominal common allegiance to the person of the king of Castile/Spain as lord of Vizcaya.[14] Arana, who had learned about nationalism during a stay in Barcelona, despised Catalan nationalism, which he regarded as weak, and he insisted that the whole of the rest of Spain was a single nation. While not opposed to industrialization as such, Arana was strongly against its socially modernizing and secularizing effects, which he saw as a threat to the conservative traditions of Basque society.[15]

This uncompromising nationalism drew on various traditions, including Carlism (a movement in favor of a rival branch of the royal family bearing some

---

[11] Neil MacCormick, Questioning Sovereignty: Law, State, and Nation in the European Commonwealth (Oxford Univ. Press 1999); Keating, *supra* note 1.

[12] Santiago de Pablo & Ludger Mees, El Péndulo Patriótico: Historia del Partido Nacionalista Vasco 1895–2005 (Crítica 2005).

[13] Sabino Arana, *Errores Catalanistas,* Bizkaitarra, Apr. 22, 1894, *reprinted in* Documentos Para la Historia del Nacionalismo Vasco: De los Fueros a Nuestros Días 35 (Santiago de Pablo, José Luís de la Granja & Ludger Mees eds., Ariel 1998).

[14] Manuel Montero, Historia del País Vasco: De los Origenes a Nuestros Días (Txertoa 1995).

[15] De Pablo & Mees, *supra* note 12.

similarities to Jacobitism in the British Isles), Catholic traditionalism, and insu-
larity. It was soon moderated by the influx of a sector of the Basque bourgeoisie
in the early twentieth century and, indeed, Arana himself seems to have changed
his views shortly before his early death. During the 1920s and 1930s, the Basque
Nationalist Party, despite some splits and reunions, extended itself as a broad
social movement through Basque society so that during the Second Republic
(1932–1939), it was hegemonic. Over time, a moderate and pragmatic sector
developed, and the PNV became an early supporter of European integration
and a member of the Christian Democratic International. The ethnic exclusiveness was downplayed, and now everyone who lives in the Basque Country and
wishes to be Basque, along with the Basque diaspora, is recognized as a member
of the nation.

The Aranist strain does survive, however, and, from time to time, some nationalists come up with exclusive definitions of Basqueness or talk of the immigrants
as another people. The PNV has always been profoundly ambivalent about the
issue of independence, insisting on the right of self-determination but interpreting it in different ways. The matter is complicated by the dispute over the physical extent of the Basque Country. In addition to the three provinces within the
existing Autonomous Community, nationalists claim Navarre (which is partially
Basque linguistically) and three provinces in France (Labour, Soule, and Basse
Navarre). In recent years, many nationalists have adopted a postsovereignist discourse, but there is not the same continuum of opinions that exists in Catalonia.
The PNV has long stressed the historic rights of the Basque Country and its constituent territories. Shorn of the Aranist fiction of the primitive independence,
these rights have been reframed as a form of limited and shared sovereignty lend-
ing themselves well to the new world of complex government and European integration.[16] A breakaway group from the PNV, Eusko Alkartasuna (EA) is a social
democratic party with a somewhat stronger line on nationalism and, in recent
years, has been allied with the PNV.

The moderate Basque nationalist parties are strong supporters of European
integration but this does not strike as strong a chord among their electors as is
the case in Catalonia. It is not that Basques are anti-European, since there is a
strong European consensus across Spain, but surveys show them identifying less
strongly with Europe than do Catalans.[17]

Since the 1960s, the PNV has faced a rival in the form of the violent group ETA
(Euskadi Ta Askatasuna, or the Basque Homeland and Liberty) and its allied
party, which has undergone a variety of name changes to avoid proscription, being

---

[16] Xabier Ezeizabarrena, La Ciaboga Infinita: Una Visión Política y Jurídica del
Conflicto Vasco (Política 2005); Pedro Ibarra Güell, Nacionalismo: Razón y Pasión
(Ariel 2005).
[17] José Luis Sangrador García, Identidades, Actitudes y Estereotipos en la España
de las Autonomías, Opiniones y Actitudes No. 10 (Centro de Investigaciones Sociológicas
1996).

most recently known as Batasuna. Around this group is an amorphous network of social movements known as MNLV (Movimiento Nacional de Liberación Vasco, or the Basque national liberation movement), which provides sustenance for the radicals without being directly implicated in violence. The decision of ETA to continue its violence after the transition to democracy split nationalism and weakened its force, although sections of the radicals have periodically come over to the democratic camp. The ETA/Batasuna is a group of uncompromising supporters of Basque independence and opponents of the European Union who do not propound a doctrine of ethnic exclusiveness, insisting that anyone can become a Basque nationalist.

Non-nationalism is represented by the Socialist Party, which appeals to working-class incomers as well as Basque workers and is divided between those who accept Basque distinctiveness and those who take a strongly Spanish stance. To the left, Ezker Batua is the Basque equivalent of the postcommunist Spanish Izquierda Unida. It is not nationalist but has supported the PNV's proposals for self-determination in an effort to find a solution to the conflict. The PP is stronger than in Catalonia. It is resolutely antinationalist and Spanish in orientation and draws on the support of the Spanish-leaning middle classes. As in Catalonia, immigrants, being largely working class, are not drawn to the PP.

There is a division in Basque society between nationalists and non-nationalists, and between Spanish and Basque identifiers, which is stronger than in Catalonia. Survey figures for 2003 show that just 2.8 percent consider themselves only Spanish; 5.6 percent more Spanish than Basque; 32 percent equally Spanish and Basque; 22 percent more Basque than Spanish; and 32 percent only Basque.[18] This indicates a much higher number of strong nationalist identifiers than in Catalonia (and one that has grown over recent years), although just over half the population have a dual identity of one sort or another. It would, moreover, be misleading to identify the Basque Country as an ethnically divided society, since the division runs through the community of native Basques as well as between them and the incomers. As Juan Pablo Fusi has recently reminded us, a strong Spanish identification is historically part of Basque tradition—in fact, in some versions, they are presented as the original and best Spaniards.[19] There is considerable assimilation of immigrants, especially in the second generation, where assimilation is at least as high as in Catalonia and perhaps higher.[20] On the other hand, nationalist voting is correlated with birth and origin to the extent that immigrants are less likely to join the nationalist community. The instrumental logic of the violence of ETA, apart from destabilizing the Spanish state, is to force a division between "true" Basques, defined not by birth or descent but according

[18] Observatorio Político Autonómico (OPA), *supra* note 10.
[19] Fusi Aizpurúa, *supra* note 4.
[20] Felix Moral, Identidad Regional y Nacionalismo en el Estado de las Autonomías, Opiniones y Actitudes No. 18 (Centro de Investigaciones Sociológicas 1998).

to whether they support the campaign, and the others. In this way, an ethnic border is created and defined where previously it was hazy and porous.

Support for independence in the Basque Country is around 30 percent, twice the level found in Catalonia, although about 60 percent of the population support other forms of autonomy short of independence (fewer than 1 percent favor the abolition of autonomy).[21]

5. Accommodating nationalism

For over one hundred years, one of the pressing problems of the Spanish politics has been to resolve the relationship of Catalonia and the Basque Country to the state, and that of internal relations within the two territories. The Spanish term *convivencia* translates loosely as "coexistence" but has a stronger meaning, encompassing harmony and cooperation, and has been a recurrent theme. The first comprehensive effort was under the Second Republic (1932–39), which provided for the *estado integral*, a semifederal arrangement inspired, in part, by Weimar Germany.[22] Regions were allowed to accede to autonomy after a complex process including a referendum.[23] The first statute to be approved was for Catalonia, whose restored historic self-government, the Generalitat, governed until the fall of the republic except for an interlude in 1934–36 when it was suspended by a right-wing government in Madrid.[24]

The Basque problem was more difficult because of Spanish suspicions of Basque separatism and the close links of the PNV with the Catholic Church— some republicans worried about the prospect of a "Vatican Gibraltar".[25] A Basque statute was approved only on the eve of the Civil War and applied until the fall of Bilbao to Francoist forces in 1937. The third historic nationality, Galicia, voted for an autonomy statute at the same time before falling immediately to the insurgents. As a result, the statute was never applied.

Other statutes, including one for Andalucia, were stillborn. The Generalitat lasted longer and, with Barcelona cut off from Madrid, functioned almost as an independent state. With the victory of Franco, all self-governing institutions were abolished, the Basque and Catalan languages proscribed, and the elected leaders hunted down and, when found, executed. It was this experience that forged an alliance between peripheral nationalism and democratic forces in the rest of Spain, although nationalist history has tended to obliterate the memories of the

---

[21] Observatorio Político Autonómico (OPA), *supra* note 10.
[22] Juan Antonio Lacamba, *Las Autonomies en la Segunda República*, 45 Documentación Social 105 (1981).
[23] Constitución de la República Española 1931, art. 12 (Spain).
[24] Eduardo Moreno & Francisco Martí, Catalunya para Españoles (Dopesa 1979).
[25] José Luis de la Granja Sáinz, *Autonomías Regionales y Fuerzas Políticas en las Cortes Constituyentes de 1931*, 40 Sistema 79 (1981).

substantial numbers of the Basque and Catalan elites who collaborated with the Franco regime.

Restoring self-government in Catalonia and the Basque Country was an imperative of the democratic regime during the transition of the 1970s, and the 1978 Constitution (Constitución Española) makes elaborate provision for this. It attempts to reconcile a number of distinct principles and create a new form of state largely on the lines of the Second Republic. In order to reconcile Spanish unity with the recognition of diversity, there is a clause asserting the unity of the Spanish nation while recognizing the "nationalities and regions" of which it is composed.[26] Although nationalities are a clear reference to Catalonia, the Basque Country, and Galicia, this is not spelled out in order to leave the category open. The term ("nationalities") seems to be presented in contradistinction to the "nation" of Spain, but it is open to the peripheral nations to see the terms as equivalent if they choose.

Autonomy is open to any region of Spain under two tracks. The slow track requires an initiative from the provincial councils and two-thirds of the municipalities representing half the population.[27] Along with senators and members of Parliament for the region, they can then propose a statute of autonomy, to be approved by the Spanish Parliament (Cortes). There is a list of powers they can

---

[26] SPAIN CONST. art. 2:

La Constitución se fundamenta en la indisoluble unidad de la Nación española, patria común e indivisible de todos los españoles, y reconoce y garantiza el derecho a la autonomía de las nacionalidades y regiones que la integran y la solidaridad entre todas ellas. [The Constitution is based on the indissoluble unity of the Spanish Nation, the common and indivisible homeland of all Spaniards; it recognizes and guarantees the right to self-government of the nationalities and regions of which it is composed and the solidarity among them all.]

[27] *Id.* art. 143:

1. En el ejercicio del derecho a la autonomía reconocido en el artículo 2 de la Constitución, las provincias limítrofes con características históricas, culturales y económicas comunes, los territorios insulares y las provincias con entidad regional histórica podrán acceder a su autogobierno y constituirse en Comunidades Autónomas con arreglo a lo previsto en este Título y en los respectivos Estatutos. [In the exercise of the right to self-government recognized in section 2 of the Constitution, bordering provinces with common historic, cultural and economic characteristics, insular territories and provinces with a historic regional status may accede to self-government and form Self-governing Communities (Comunidades Autónomas) in conformity with the provisions contained in this Part and in the respective Statutes.]

2. La iniciativa del proceso autonómico corresponde a todas las Diputaciones interesadas o al órgano interinsular correspondiente y a las dos terceras partes de los municipios cuya población represente, al menos, la mayoría del censo electoral de cada provincia o isla. Estos requisitos deberán ser cumplidos en el plazo de seis meses desde el primer acuerdo adoptado al respecto por alguna de las Corporaciones locales interesadas. [The right to initiate the process towards self-government lies with all the Provincial Councils concerned or with the corresponding inter-island body and with two-thirds of the municipalities whose population represents at least the majority of the electorate of each province or island. These requirements must be met within six months from the initial agreement reached to this aim by any of the local Corporations concerned.]

3. La iniciativa, en caso de no prosperar, solamente podrá reiterarse pasados cinco años. [If this initiative is not successful, it may be repeated only after five years have elapsed.]

obtain immediately, but after five years they can gain more powers. The fast track allows regions to gain the full powers immediately but requires a more complex process.[28] This involves all the provinces, three-quarters of the municipalities in

---

[28] *Id.* art. 151:

1. No será preciso dejar transcurrir el plazo de cinco años, a que se refiere el apartado 2 del artículo 148, cuando la iniciativa del proceso autonómico sea acordada dentro del plazo del artículo 143(2), además de por las Diputaciones o los órganos interinsulares correspondientes, por las tres cuartas partes de los municipios de cada una de las provincias afectadas que representen, al menos, la mayoría del censo electoral de cada una de ellas y dicha iniciativa sea ratificada mediante referéndum por el voto afirmativo de la mayoría absoluta de los electores de cada provincia en los términos que establezca una ley orgánica. [It shall not be necessary to wait for the five-year period referred to in section 148, subsection 2, to elapse when the initiative for the autonomy process is agreed upon within the time limit specified in section 143, subsection 2, not only by the corresponding Provincial Councils or inter-island bodies but also by three-quarters of the municipalities of each province concerned, representing at least the majority of the electorate of each one, and said initiative is ratified in a referendum by the overall majority of electors in each province, under the terms to be laid down by an organic act.]

2. En el supuesto previsto en el apartado anterior, el procedimiento para la elaboración del Estatuto será el siguiente: [In the case referred to in the foregoing paragraph, procedure for drafting the Statute of Autonomy shall be as follows:]

   1. El Gobierno convocará a todos los Diputados y Senadores elegidos en las circunscripciones comprendidas en el ámbito territorial que pretenda acceder al autogobierno, para que se constituyan en Asamblea, a los solos efectos de elaborar el correspondiente proyecto de Estatuto de autonomía, mediante el acuerdo de la mayoría absoluta de sus miembros. [The Government shall convene all Members of Congress and Senators elected in the constituencies of the territory seeking self-government, in order that they may set themselves up as an Assembly for the sole purpose of drawing up a Statute of Autonomy, to be adopted by the overall majority of its members.]

   2. Aprobado el proyecto de Estatuto por la Asamblea de Parlamentarios, se remitirá a la Comisión Constitucional del Congreso, la cual, dentro del plazo de dos meses, lo examinará con el concurso y asistencia de una delegación de la Asamblea proponente para determinar de común acuerdo su formulación definitiva. [Once the draft Statute has been passed by the Parliamentarians' Assembly, it is to be sent to the Constitutional Committee of the Congress which shall examine it within two months with the cooperation and assistance of a delegation from the Assembly which has proposed it, in order to decide by common agreement upon its final form.]

   3. Si se alcanzare dicho acuerdo, el texto resultante será sometido a referéndum del cuerpo electoral de las provincias comprendidas en el ámbito territorial del proyectado Estatuto. [If such agreement is reached, the resulting text shall be submitted in a referendum to the electorate in the provinces within the territory to be covered by the proposed Statute.]

   4. Si el proyecto de Estatuto es aprobado en cada provincia por la mayoría de los votos válidamente emitidos, será elevado a las Cortes Generales. Los plenos de ambas Cámaras decidirán sobre el texto mediante un voto de ratificación. Aprobado el Estatuto, el Rey lo sancionará y lo promulgará como ley. [If the draft statute is approved in each province by the majority of validly cast votes, it shall be referred to the Parliament. Both Chambers, in plenary assembly, shall decide upon the text by means of a vote of ratification. Once the statute has been approved, the King shall sanction it and shall promulgate it as law.]

   5. De no alcanzarse el acuerdo a que se refiere el apartado 2 de este número, el proyecto de Estatuto será tramitado como proyecto de ley ante las Cortes Generales. El texto aprobado por éstas será sometido a referéndum del cuerpo electoral de las provincias comprendidas en el ámbito territorial del proyectado Estatuto. En caso de ser aprobado por la mayoría de los votos válidamente emitidos en cada provincia, procederá su promulgación en los términos del párrafo anterior. [If the agreement referred to in paragraph ii) of this subsection is not reached, the legislative process for the draft Statute in the Cortes Generales

each province, and approval by referendum, with an absolute majority of registered electors in each province. The only region to achieve this was Andalucia.[29] However, under the Second Transitional Disposition of the Constitution, those who had voted for autonomy statutes in the past were allowed to proceed directly to the enhanced powers.[30] This recognizes the legitimacy of the Second Republic and, again, implicitly privileges the three historic nationalities, which were the only ones to vote for the autonomy statutes under it. All three historic nations did produce autonomy statutes, which were approved by referendum. More surprisingly, the autonomy process then spread, under article 143, throughout Spain.[31]

Spanish constitutional doctrine insists that the 1978 Constitution is the source of all law and the basis for all political institutions. This conflicts with assertions in Catalonia and the Basque Country of the right of self-determination, as well as with Basque insistence on their *fueros* or historic rights, as original and pre-constitutional. Again, a compromise was adopted in the form of First Additional Disposition, which states that the Constitution protects and respects the historic

> shall be the same as that for a bill. The text passed by the latter shall be submitted to a referendum of the electorate of the provinces within the territory to be covered by the draft Statute. In the event that it is approved by the majority of validly cast votes in each province, it shall be promulgated as provided in the foregoing paragraph.]
> 3. En los casos de los párrafos 4. y 5. del apartado anterior, la no aprobación del proyecto de Estatuto por una o varias provincias no impedirá la constitución entre las restantes de la Comunidad Autónoma proyectada, en la forma que establezca la ley orgánica prevista en el apartado 1 de este artículo. [In the cases described in paragraphs iv) and v) of the foregoing subsection, failure by one or several of the provinces to ratify the draft Statute shall not prevent constitution of the remaining provinces into a Self-governing Community in the manner to be provided for by the organic act contemplated in subsection 1 of this section.]
> (unofficial translation from Presidency of the Spanish Government, *available at* <http://www.lamoncloa.es/NR/rdonlyres/C511DC05–40C5–4739-8AB6-FA3CEE3B4F28/0/Constitucion_EN.pdf> (last visited Aug. 22, 2007), except for § 151(2)(4) from International Constitutional Law, *available at* <http://www.servat.unibe.ch/law/icl/sp00000_.html> (last visited Aug. 22, 2007)).

[29] Strictly speaking, they missed fulfilling the criterion since one province, while approving the statute massively, did not deliver an absolute majority of electors. The Cortes let them proceed anyway.

[30] Spain Const., Disposiciones Transitorias [Transitional Provisions], § 2:

> Los territorios que en el pasado hubiesen plebiscitado afirmativamente proyectos de Estatuto de autonomía y cuenten, al tiempo de promulgarse esta Constitución, con regímenes provisionales de autonomía podrán proceder inmediatamente en la forma que se prevé en el apartado 2 del artículo 148, cuando así lo acordaren, por mayoría absoluta, sus órganos preautonómicos colegiados superiores, comunicándolo al Gobierno. El proyecto de Estatuto será elaborado de acuerdo con lo establecido en el artículo 151, número 2, a convocatoria del órgano colegiado preautonómico. [The territories which in the past have, by plebiscite, approved draft Statutes of Autonomy, and which, at the time of the promulgation of this Constitution, have provisional regimes of autonomy, may proceed immediately in the manner provided in Article 148(2), when agreement thereon is reached by an absolute majority of their pre-autonomous higher collegiate organs, and the Government is duly informed. The draft statutes shall be drawn up in accordance with the provisions of Article 151(2) when so requested by the pre-autonomous collegiate organ.]
> (unofficial translation from International Constitutional Law, *available at* <http://www.servat.unibe.ch/law/icl/sp00000_.html> (last visited Aug. 22, 2007)).

[31] *Id.* art. 143.

rights of the foral territories and allows the autonomous communities to update them.[32] Again, there is little detail about what exactly this refers to, or what the relationship of these historic rights is to the other provisions of the Constitution. Catalan nationalists were able to accept these ambiguities and support the 1978 Constitution. The PNV, along with radical Basque nationalists, refused to accept any suggestion that their historic rights were subordinate to the Constitution and recommended abstention in the referendum. While this did pass in the Basque Country, it failed to gain an absolute majority of electors, allowing the nationalists to claim that Basques had not accepted the Constitution, which thus had the effect of casting possible doubt on its legitimacy. This did not, however, stop the nationalists from using the constitutional provisions to set up their own autonomous government. The Statute of Autonomy of the Basque Country makes extensive reference to the historic rights and, more crucially, incorporates the *concierto económico*,[33] allowing the Basque Country to control nearly all taxes, passing on a negotiated quota to Madrid for common services.[34]

The ambiguities in the Constitution has allowed for two different readings. For Catalans and Basques, it recognizes a distinction between regions and nationalities; it lays down two routes to autonomy; it allows for strong asymmetries; it recognizes historic rights; and it allows regions to negotiate and renegotiate their autonomy statutes with the state. For the Spanish center, however, it affirms the unity of the Spanish nation and does not give any juridical status to "nationalities"; all autonomous communities can achieve the same status over time; there are no formal asymmetries, apart from the Basque *concierto económico;* historic rights are subordinated the Constitution; and all autonomy statutes are creatures of the Constitution, requiring approval by the Cortes.

As the autonomy process spread in the early 1980s, the Spanish parties agreed on a pact to limit it.[35] The 1981 Ley Orgánica de Armonización del Proceso

---

[32] *Id.* Disposiciones Adicionales [Additional Provisions], § 1:

La Constitución ampara y respeta los derechos históricos de los territorios forales. La actualización general de dicho régimen foral se llevará a cabo, en su caso, en el marco de la Constitución y de los Estatutos de Autonomía. [The Constitution protects and respects the historic rights of the territories with traditional charts (fueros). The general updating of historic rights shall be carried out, where appropriate, within the framework of the Constitution and of the Statutes of Autonomy.]

(unofficial translation from the website of Presidency of the Spanish Government).

[33] Estatuto de Autonomía del País Vasco [Statute of Autonomy of the Basque Country], art. 41.1:

Las relaciones de orden tributario entre el Estado y el País Vasco vendrán reguladas mediante el sistema foral tradicional de Concierto Económico o Convenios. [Tax relations between the State and the Basque Country shall be regulated by the traditional system of the Economic Agreement or Conventions.]

(unofficial translation from Proposal for Coexistence in the Basque Country, *available at* <http://www.nuevoestatutodeeuskadi.net/docs/state_of_autonomy.pdf> (last visited Aug. 22, 2007)).

[34] *Id.* art. 9. To be precise, it is the three provinces (or historic territories) that raise the taxes in accordance with old foral principle. They then agree to fund the needs of the Basque government.

[35] Eliseo Aja et al., El Sistema Jurídico de las Comunidades Autónomas 183 (Tecnos 1985).

Autonómico (LOAPA) sought to homogenize the statutes of autonomy by reducing the power of the strongest and boosting that of the weakest. Its key provisions were struck down by the Constitutional Court, which argued that while the Constitution guaranteed equal rights for all Spaniards, this did not mean that all autonomous communities should have the same powers. Provisions for the Spanish Parliament to overrule the laws of autonomous communities were also rejected.[36] The Spanish parties then agreed on a series of enhancements to the article 143 regions, to bring them up to the level of the others. This strategy, known as *café para todos* (coffee all round), was intended to reaffirm the unity of the state by diluting the special status of the 151 regions and reaffirming the role of the center. In response to this, Catalans and Basques determined to reestablish their distinctiveness or *hecho diferencial* and to give it constitutional recognition. The four more powerful regions (Basque Country, Catalonia, Galicia, and Andalucia) retained their ability to call early elections, but this was not extended to the others.

The division of powers between the two levels of government is regulated by the Constitutional Court under a variety of provisions. A complaint of unconstitutionality can be brought against a state or a regional law by either level of government, the parliament of an autonomous community, fifty members of the Spanish Parliament, fifty senators, or the Spanish ombudsman (*defensor del pueblo*).[37] There are incentives to encourage governments to resolve their differences by negotiation, notably a provision to delay a court ruling for up to nine months if the parties have declared their willingness to negotiate.[38] During the 1980s, a series of cases in the Constitutional Court, mainly stemming from Catalonia and the Basque Country, served to define the limits of autonomous power. These peaked in 1985, with one hundred and thirty-five cases brought to the Court. Thereafter, the number settled down to the low twenties each year, before rising to sixty-two in 2002, although, after 1990, the Basque government refused to refer cases in protest against a negative decision.[39] The fall in the number of cases also reflected the growth of case law, the improvement in the drafting of laws, and the increasing tendency to resolve issues by negotiation among the political parties.

Territorial devolution has not been matched by formal consociational devices at the center or even by formal mechanisms for involving the autonomous communities in national policy making. In particular, proposals to convert the Senate into a chamber of territorial representation have not progressed. Yet there have been weaker and less formal consociational mechanisms through the political

---

[36] S.T.C. 76/1983, Aug. 5, 1983, *available at* <http://www.boe.es/g/es/bases_datos_tc/doc.php?coleccion=tc&id=SENTENCIA-1983–0076>.

[37] Spain Const. art. 162.1(a).

[38] Eliseo Aja, El Estado Autonómico: Federalismo y Hechos Diferenciales (Ariel 2006).

[39] *Id.*

parties. Indeed, since the mid-1980s, the main mechanisms for reconciling peripheral autonomy with state integration and assuring intergroup relations within the minority nations have been party-political rather than legal and constitutional. State-level pacts governing the transfer of powers to autonomous communities have occurred at intervals, notably in 1981 on LOAPA,[40] but more recently, these pacts have been struck with the territorial parties.

There are two forms of party alliance in governing at center and periphery: the formal coalition, which is rare in Spain; and a minority government's receiving external support from another party. CiU, in office in Catalonia between 1980 and 2004, has played a traditional Catalan game in Spanish politics, consciously contributing to the governability of Spain. When the Socialists under Felipe González returned as a minority in 1993, CiU agreed to a pact of external support. Between 1996 and 2000, they had a similar pact with the minority PP government of José María Aznar. After the PP gained an absolute majority in 2000, CiU was reduced to a minority in Catalonia and was obliged to vote for the reinvestiture of Aznar in return for similar PP support in Catalonia. In 2004, Socialist governments came to office in Spain and in Catalonia without absolute majorities. A coalition of the Socialists, the ERC, and IC was formed in Catalonia, while in Madrid both Catalan nationalist parties acquiesced in the investiture of Socialist prime minister José Luís Rodríguez Zapatero. This complex game of reciprocal dependence greatly stabilized relations between the two levels and has meant that, for most of the time since 1993, CiU has been a key player in central politics.

Basque politics has shown weaker signs of this practice. Within the Basque Country, a compact (providing external support for a minority government) and then a full coalition of the PNV and Socialists between 1987 and 1998 served to integrate nationalists and non-nationalists, natives and incomers. All the democratic parties (nationalists, socialists, conservatives, and centrists) signed an agreement in 1988, the Pact of Ajuria Enea, condemning terrorism and isolating ETA and Batasuna.[41] In 1998, in conjunction with an ETA ceasefire, the PNV broke this strategy in favor of a nationalist front consisting of a PNV/EA government supported externally by Batasuna. The Pact of Estella (or Lizarra in Basque) linked the PNV, EA, HB (Herri Batasuna, the then name for Batasuna), two nationalist trade unions and the postcommunists.[42] The agreement started with a long preamble about the Northern Ireland peace process, an analogy recurring regularly over the years.[43] This was intended to bring extreme nationalists into the process but alienated non-nationalists. The Basque elections of 1998

---

[40] *See supra* text accompanying notes 34–36.
[41] De Pablo & Mees, *supra* note 12.
[42] *Id.*
[43] Michael Keating, *Northern Ireland and the Basque Country, in* Northern Ireland and the Divided World 181 (John McGarry ed., Oxford Univ. Press 2001).

saw a sharp increase in votes for the Herri Batasuna. The peace process did not, however, thrive, and the ceasefire was broken in January 2000, leaving the PNV isolated. As the Socialists and PP formed an antinationalist front and made a serious bid for power at the elections of 2001, the PNV emerged strengthened. The lesson seemed to be that neither a nationalist nor an antinationalist front appeals to the median Basque voter. Although Basque nationalists have not sought the role in the governability of Spain relished by their Catalan counterparts, they did make a pact with the PP in 1996. Although theoretically applying for the whole legislature, the pact was dead within a year as a result of the polarization within the Basque Country described above. Since 2001, the Basque Country has been ruled by a coalition of PNV/EA and Izker Batua.

In return for their support in 1996, and again in 2000, the autonomist parties obtained additional powers, including a limited tax-variation power for the communities other than the Basque Country. In 2000, bilateral mechanisms were agreed to regulate relations between the Basque Country and the state, but these were never consolidated and faded away after the pact of Estella. The PP, in a further effort to undermine the distinct status of the historic nationalities, allowed Aragon and the Canaries and to revise their statutes of autonomy so as to describe themselves as nationalities. During the period in which the PP enjoyed an absolute parliamentary majority (2000–2004), there were moves toward recentralization, and a new Spanish nationalist vocabulary was deployed against the periphery.

A weaker but important mechanism for territorial integration is the practice of governments of both statewide parties to include Basque and Catalan ministers. Indeed, when José Montilla was brought back from Madrid to Barcelona to run as the Socialist candidate for the presidency of the Generalitat, the Catalan Socialists (PSC) were able to replace him in the central government with one of their own (Joan Clos, mayor of Barcelona).

6. Renegotiating autonomy

Some twenty years after the statutes of autonomy had been agreed, moves were begun to update and extend them. In Catalonia, this was part of a process that had been launched in the early 2000s, which gained momentum with the change of government to the Socialist/ERC/IC coalition and the almost simultaneous arrival of the Spanish Socialist government of José Luís Rodriguez Zapatero, who declared himself open to a revision of the system on the basis of a plurinational state. This, indeed, provided a cue for the revision of autonomy statutes across Spain. In the Basque Country, constitutional revision, while caught up in the search for peace and the prospect of another ETA ceasefire, finally was announced in 2006.

The Catalan process was based on consensus, with all the parties except the PP eventually agreeing to the proposal sent to the Spanish Parliament in 2006 despite displays of brinkmanship on the way. Then the consensus broke down in an unexpected way, one that displays the typical crosscutting cleavages of Catalan politics. The Spanish central government objected to certain clauses and proceeded to do a deal with CiU over the head of the Catalan coalition. The Catalan Socialists had to accept this, provoking protests from ERC. Eventually ERC broke the consensus, refused to accept the new statute with its compromises, and, under pressure from their militants, even campaigned for a "no" vote in the referendum. This was of little avail, and the statute was accepted easily with a 70 percent "yes" vote. Thus, the key to the negotiation of a new Catalan statute was the cooperation of nationalist and non-nationalist parties, not in an overarching consensus but in the process of political competition among coalitions most of which contained both nationalist and non-nationalist elements.

The most controversial items in the negotiations concerned finance, judicial affairs, language, and a range of symbolic issues. Catalan nationalists have often demanded a system of fiscal autonomy similar to that of the Basque Country. Since they do not have a historic basis for this, Catalan nationalists must found their claim as merely a current demand. In this case, they have difficulty explaining why such a system should be given to them and not the other autonomous communities. Their other demand has been to limit the amount paid by Catalonia (a wealthy region) to support poorer autonomous communities. The initial proposals coming from Catalonia provided for a Catalan treasury to gather all the moneys due to Catalonia and make transparent the transfers to other regions. The final agreed-upon text is less clear, providing for a Catalan treasury but closely linked to the Spanish one. There is a provision that fiscal equalization should be capped such that it does not alter the ranking of Catalonia in the list of autonomous communities by per capita income.[44]

A similar arrangement was made in response to the demand for a separate judiciary. The final text provides for a distinct Catalan pillar within the Spanish judiciary, with most appeals ending in Catalonia, except where rulings are needed on the overall interpretation of Spanish law. There is provision for an input into the nomination of judges, but the system remains part of the Spanish judicial hierarchy (unlike, for example, the system in Scotland).[45] There is also recognition of Catalan civil law, rather stronger than in the old statute, with the provision that it applies to all Catalan citizens, except naturalized Spanish citizens who choose to opt out of it. The old statute had declared that Catalan was Catalonia's own language and that both Catalan and Castilian were official. Citizens had the right to use either and had the duty to know Castilian (as Spanish citizens). The new

---

[44] Statute of Autonomy of Catalonia, art. 206.5.
[45] *Id.* art. 95.

text extends the duty to know to Catalan, but only for Catalan citizens, defined as Spanish citizens with their official residence in Catalonia.[46]

The greatest contention, however, was reserved for the symbolic issue of whether Catalonia can call itself a nation. The old text follows the Constitution in describing Catalonia as a nationality. With the support of all parties except the PP, the new draft changed this to "nation". This was not acceptable to the Spanish parties, which insisted on taking it out, provoking the breach with the ERC. With the support of CiU, a tortuous form of wording was agreed, which reads:

> The Parliament of Catalonia, recognizing the sentiments and will of the citizenry of Catalonia, has by a substantial majority defined Catalonia as a nation. The Spanish Constitution, in its second article, recognizes the national reality of Catalonia as a nationality.[47]

There was also a controversy over the issue of historic rights, raised by CiU in order to outflank ERC, after the latter had staked its nationalist credentials on the "nation" issue. The result was another vague clause:

> The self-government of Catalonia is also based on the historic rights of the Catalan people, its age-old institutions and the Catalan juridical tradition, which the present statute incorporates and updates according to the second transitional disposition and other precepts of the Constitution, from which stem the recognition of a singular position for the Generalitat in relation to civil law, language, culture, the projection of these in the educational system, and the organization of the institutions of the Generalitat itself.[48]

Several features stand out about the process and outcome of the negotiation of a new Catalan statute. One is the brinkmanship displayed as the political parties threatened to close down the whole process but nevertheless, arrived at a compromise. The ERC, whose militants were unused to the politics of compromise and negotiation, was forced by pressures from below to campaign against the statute in the referendum, once the leaders had threatened to walk out over the nation clause. Another feature is bilateralism, as Catalonia sought a special deal with the Spanish state. The Constitution does allow regions to launch reforms of their autonomy statutes and negotiate them with the center, but the Catalan statute now contains provisions with implications for Spain as a whole, negotiated bilaterally with the center. This is true, notably in connection with the new fiscal system, which guarantees Catalonia's ranking among the Spanish regions. Bilateral institutions include a general commission between Catalonia and Spain, and the Fiscal and Judicial Councils. Were these to be extended to all seventeen autonomous communities, it would transform the state in a radical manner. All of these provisions are intended to push Catalan autonomy as far as possible, while remaining within the limits of the existing Constitution. The underlying

---

[46] *Id.* art. 33.
[47] *Id.* pmbl (unofficial translation).
[48] *Id.* art. 5 (unofficial translation).

philosophy is one of constitutional reinterpretation rather than rupture. The clause about historic rights, vague as it is, forms a central part of this strategy, serving a similar purpose to the Quebec "distinct society" clause in the Meech Lake and Charlottetown accords.[49]

At the time of writing, there have been no cross-party negotiations on a revised Basque statute of autonomy, and politics is still polarized. There was, however, one proposal coming from the Basque government itself, the Ibarretxe Plan, launched by the president of the Basque government, Juan José Ibarretxe.[50] The Ibarretxe Plan, as it was presented both to the Basque regional parliament and to the Spanish Cortes, claims the right of self-determination for the Basque Country, starting with the three provinces of the Autonomous Basque Community of Euskadi but with provision for Navarre and the three Basque provinces in French territory to come in by their own decision.[51] The plan provides for a Basque community "freely associated" with the "Spanish state", with the possibility of further change in the future according to the principle of self-determination.[52] Basque citizenship, based on Spanish citizenship rules, would be open to all residents of the Basque Country and to people of Basque ancestry outside, with a provision that nobody would be subject to discrimination on the basis of identification or non-identification with the Basque nation. The community would be bilingual with equal respect for Spanish and Basque. It would have its own court system, and a special section of the Spanish Constitutional Court would deal with interpretations of the bilateral relations between the governments of Spain and the Basque Country. A bilateral commission would deal with other matters of contention. The King of Spain would remain as head of state.[53]

[49] 1987 CONSTITUTIONAL ACCORD (Can.), sched. Constitution Amendment, 1987, § 1 (unofficial text of the Meech Lake Accord, with proposed amendments including an addition to the Canadian Constitution that "the recognition that Quebec constitutes within Canada a distinct society"); CONSENSUS REPORT ON THE CONSTITUTION (Can.), pt. I, § A(1) Canada Clause (1992) (final text of the Charlottetown Accord, with proposed additions to the Canadian Constitution of the following: "Quebec constitutes within Canada a distinct society, which includes a French-speaking majority, a unique culture and a civil law tradition" and that "[t]he role of the legislature and Government of Quebec to preserve and promote the distinct society of Quebec is affirmed"); for a discussion on Canada, see Sujit Choudhry, *Does the World Need More Canada? The Politics of the Canadian Model in Constitutional Politics and Political Theory* (in this volume).

[50] Michael Keating & Zoe Bray, *Renegotiating Sovereignty: Basque Nationalism and the Rise and Fall of the Ibarretxe Plan*, 5 ETHNOPOLITICS 347 (2006).

[51] Political Statute of the Community of the Basque Country, *available at* <http://www.nuevoestatutodeeuskadi.net/docs/dictamencomision20122004_eng.pdf> (2004) (unofficial English version)[hereinafter Ibarretxe Plan]; *see generally id.*

[52] The expression, Estado Libre Asociado (free associated state), is that used in Spanish for the Commonwealth of Puerto Rico. RUTH LAPIDOTH, AUTONOMY: FLEXIBLE SOLUTIONS TO ETHNIC CONFLICTS (US Inst. for Peace 1997).

[53] This seems a striking concession for nationalists to make, but the PNV has never been republican in principle. The foral tradition recognizes the monarch as a contractually bound overlord. It may also be easier to cater to complexity and plurality in monarchies than in republics, with their equal citizenship.

The plan allocates administrative powers and responsibilities in a rather confusing manner (as does the Spanish Constitution). Powers reserved to the central Spanish state authority are listed as Spanish nationality; defense and the armed forces; arms and explosives; currency; customs and tariffs; merchant marine and air navigation; and international relations, without prejudice to the Basque Country's ability to project itself abroad in areas where it has constitutional responsibility.[54] The Spanish state would be able to pass framework laws in criminal law; commercial law; civil law, except for foral law and family law; intellectual and industrial property; and weights and measures.[55] The Spanish national police force would enforce Spanish state laws.

All matters not so reserved are deemed to belong to the Basque Country, although the Ibarretxe Plan also lists a series of exclusive Basque competences covering domestic policy fields.[56] Shared areas of responsibility include social security (at the insistence of the PNV's coalition partners EB, who wanted a continued link with statewide insurance), state enterprises, and property rights. The *concierto económico* would continue as the basis for funding. There is a provision for "direct" Basque representation in the institutions of the EU, although it is not clear exactly how this would work.[57] In the critical matter of the Council of Ministers, the Basques would participate in the Spanish delegation, with the policy line presumably decided in bilateral negotiation.

This project, as presented, certainly amounts to a third way proposal stopping short of secession and retaining the Spanish state framework for a number of crucial issues.[58] It bears a strong resemblance to the Quebec project of sovereignty/association and its 1995 equivalent of sovereignty with partnership. Like the Northern Ireland agreement, it allows for differential interpretation by nationalists and unionists, and for individuals to express different identities according to their preferences, so overcoming the fundamental division between the two groups. The allocation of areas of responsibility, while it may not be entirely clear, is presented as a basis for negotiation rather than as a final settlement. Yet the ambivalence in parts of the plan means that it can be used either as a basis for convergence on new understandings of community, boundaries, sovereignty and autonomy, or as a stage on which to rehearse traditional and conflicting understandings.

The tactical positions of the parties, as the plan made its way through the Basque and Spanish parliaments, reflected these differences. Arguing that the plan is unconstitutional and so should not be a subject for discussion, the PP and its local branch, the PPE, sought to stop the Basque parliament's debating it at all.

---

[54] For the Spanish state's powers with regard to its relations with Basque Country, see Ibarretxe Plan, art. 45(1).

[55] *Id.* art. 45 (2).

[56] For a series of exclusive public policies of the Basque Country, see generally *id.* Heading IV The Exercise of Authority in the Community of the Basque Country, ch. 4.

[57] *Id.* art. 65(2).

[58] Although in customary Basque nationalist manner, it refuses to speak about Spain and insists on the term "Spanish state".

When it was approved, nonetheless, by the Basque parliament and transferred to Madrid, the PP sought to prevent a debate taking place there. The Socialist Party was less rigid, raising no objection to the plan being debated in the Basque Country or in Madrid. Prime Minister Zapatero, however, made it clear that he regarded the plan as unconstitutional, threatening that it would be blocked if necessary by the Constitutional Court.

Batasuna's tactical position was crucial, since the votes of its six representatives in the Basque parliament could determine whether the plan was accepted there or not. In the event, Batasuna cast three votes in favor and three against, allowing its acceptance in a move the party explained thus: "Three votes for the plan signified a 'yes' to self-determination, to a popular consultation and to an agreement, while the three votes against the Plan signified a 'no' to a re-introduction of the autonomous statute, to a Plan which does not resolve conflict and to another fraud."[59] By letting the plan go through, Batasuna could avoid accusations of thwarting an initiative designed to allow a popular referendum. By expressing its disapproval, it could maintain its claim to be the only "real" Basque party in not totally buying into the political project of the other, more compromised Basque nationalist parties.

7. The issues at stake

What is remarkable about the debate on the Catalan statute and the Ibarretxe Plan is how little political energy was expended on the distribution of powers, the precise design of institutions, or relations with the central state. The main substantive debate concerned Catalonia's demands for more fiscal powers, while the balance of the debate concentrated on a series of highly symbolic and ideologically charged elements, as well as on competing interpretations of both the existing Constitution and proposed changes.

In the Catalan case, there was a serious dispute over the attempt in the preamble to define Catalonia as a nation, thereby marking an advance over those of the other autonomous communities that had been able to redefine themselves as nationalities. In Catalan eyes, the others' use of the term rendered it banal. The term "nation" also implied an equality of status with the Spanish nation and suggested a right of self-determination, even though this was not spelled out. The final compromise was, as we have noted, a convoluted form of words that all sides could accept.[60] The Ibarretxe Plan steered away from this argument, avoiding the terminology of "nation" and preferring to speak of the Basque people and their inherent rights.

[59] Keating & Bray, *supra* note 50.
[60] The wording in the subsequent statute for Andalucia was even more convoluted, speaking of a "national reality".

The issue of sovereignty has never been resolved in a consensual manner, as it does seem to be possible for a polity to survive without an agreed meaning for it.[61] The Ibarretxe Plan addressed this head-on, asserting the sovereignty of the Basque people, a proposition rejected outright by the Spanish parties, for whom all power stems from the Constitution of 1978 representing a unitary Spanish people. Indeed, this was the basis on which the parties deemed the Ibarretxe Plan not to be a basis even for negotiation. The Catalans, on the other hand, chose not to make an issue of this, although the nationalist parties and a section of the Socialists are convinced of the validity of doctrines of divided and shared sovereignty under which Catalonia has its own inherent and preconstitutional rights.

Historic rights are an essential part of Basque nationalist discourse and did feature in the Ibarretxe Plan. Yet greater emphasis, on this occasion, was placed on the criterion of present will, with self-determination seen as, above all, a democratic right. Historic rights, in modern times, have not been central to Catalan nationalist discourse, which has emphasized themes of modernity and democracy. In the recent debates, however, they were deployed by CiU to try and outflank ERC and its partners in the coalition government. For the Catalans, historic rights are not based simply on their medieval status or the institutions lost in 1714 and hardly at all on foral principles. They are based on a living principle and include the Autonomy Statute of 1932 as an act of self-determination accepted by the Spanish state.

Both Catalonia and the Basque Country have sought a bilateral relationship with Spain as a means of securing their status and differentiating themselves from the non-historic regions. The Ibarretxe Plan takes this very far, giving almost equality of status to the two sides, something that was clearly unacceptable to the Spanish parties. The Catalan statute introduces elements of bilateralism, but these are not as strong as the nationalist parties would have preferred.

A recurring theme of Catalan and Basque nationalism over the years has been the European Union and the opportunities it offers for stateless nations to bypass their respective states and to constitute themselves as actors in a broader arena. Other European federal and devolved states have provisions allowing constituent governments to participate in meetings of the EU Council of Ministers, either by right (as in Germany[62] or Belgium) or by invitation (in the United Kingdom).[63]

[61] This has long been the case in Scotland. The famous case *MacCormick v. Lord Advocate,* [1953] S.C. 396, produced the pronouncement by Lord Cooper that the English doctrine of parliamentary sovereignty does not apply in Scotland. However, this made no practical difference. In the late 1980s, the Labour Party signed the *Claim of Right for Scotland* in 1988 stating that sovereignty belonged to the people of Scotland but subsequently passed the Scotland Act stating that Westminster parliamentary sovereignty was absolute. Scotland Act, 1998, c. 46.

[62] For Germany's provisions allowing constituent governments to participate in meetings of the European Union Council of Ministers, see GRUNDGGESETZ (GG) arts. 23, 50–51 (F.R.G.).

[63] Although the UK government is responsible for EU negotiations, the Joint Ministerial Committee on the European Union provides a forum for the executives of devolved administrations to participate in policy development on EU issues. *See generally Concordat on Co-ordination of European Union Policies, in* CABINET OFFICE, MEMORANDUM OF UNDERSTANDING AND

Extending such a provision to Spain has been a consistent demand of the autonomous communities since the Treaty of European Union (Maastricht Treaty) of 1992.[64] Recently, the Zapatero government also has conceded the request. Catalan and Basque nationalists, however, have treated this demand with some reserve since it would involve a multilateral arrangement in which all the autonomous communities would have to come to an agreement under the Spanish government leadership.[65] Instead, they have pressed for bilateral arrangements. Although a weak form of this was conceded by the Aznar government to the Basques as part of their pact in 1996, nothing came of it. As already noted, the Ibarretxe Plan speaks of direct Basque participation in European affairs but does not elaborate on what this would mean. Earlier versions of the plan, however, were much more ambitious, referring to the proposal by French politician Alain Lamassoure for regions to become "partners of the Union" and claiming that this would provide a framework for their freely associated state. This was another piece of conceptual stretching, since the Lamassoure idea was actually about administrative decentralization and was further weakened in its application. It was not about high-level political partnership.

Catalan and Basque nationalists (along with others in Europe) had placed considerable hope in the Convention on the Future of Europe and the draft constitutional treaty that was to come out of it. In the course of the convention, however, the regional interest was marginalized in favor of consolidating the relationship between the EU and the member states.[66] The parties of stateless nations and national minorities, represented in the European Free Alliance, came up with some ideas, such as that of "internal enlargement", whereby parts of member states could become independent members in their own right, but this proposal failed to progress. The result was that the draft constitutional treaty received a lukewarm reception in Catalonia and the Basque Country. ERC and EA campaigned against it in the Spanish referendum of 2004, while PNV and CiU gave only qualified support. Although the referendum in support of the draft constitution was successful throughout Spain, support in Catalonia and the Basque Country was lower than elsewhere, thus breaking the historic link between peripheral nationalism and European integration. This ensured that Europe did not

---

SUPPLEMENTARY AGREEMENTS: BETWEEN THE UNITED KINGDOM GOVERNMENT, SCOTTISH MINISTERS AND THE CABINET OF THE NATIONAL ASSEMBLY FOR WALES, 1999, Cm. 4444; OFFICE OF THE DEPUTY PRIME MINISTER, MEMORANDUM OF UNDERSTANDING AND SUPPLEMENTARY AGREEMENTS: BETWEEN THE UNITED KINGDOM GOVERNMENT, SCOTTISH MINISTERS AND THE CABINET OF THE NATIONAL ASSEMBLY FOR WALES AND THE NORTHERN IRELAND EXECUTIVE COMMITTEE, 2001, Cm. 5420.

[64] Treaty of European Union (Maastricht Treaty), Feb. 7, 1992, 1992 O.J (C 191) 1, 321 I.L.M. 247.

[65] DE PABLO & MEES, *supra* note 12.

[66] CHARLIE JEFFERY ET AL., THE LOCAL AND REGIONAL DIMENSION IN THE EUROPEAN CONSTITUTIONAL PROCESS (European Union Committee of the Regions 2004).

figure substantially in the debate on the reform of the autonomy statutes, and the question reverted to the previous Spanish state framework.

8. Conclusion

In thirty years, Spain has learned a lot about accommodating its constituent nationalities. The 1978 Constitution has proven flexible enough to yield different readings on both symbolic and substantive matters and to provide for a gradual evolution toward a more decentralized and asymmetrical system. There is certainly a tendency among the regions to imitate whichever one has gained the most symbolic recognition and substantive autonomy, in a process that Luís Moreno has labeled "ethno-territorial concurrence".[67] Some fear that this will empty the state of its prerogatives over time and call for a limitation of the process and a uniformization of the statutes of autonomy. Miguel Herrero de Miñon, on the other hand, sees the very effort to impose a uniform system as the cause of instability, since it encourages competitive region building.[68] Instead, he advocates a clearer recognition of the specificity of the historic territories, which would have a distinct relation with the center. This arrangement would more closely resemble the evolution of the United Kingdom than it would the constitutional reform efforts in Canada.

Another perspective is to argue that there is no fixed end point of evolution, thus allowing the different nationalities the scope to dream of realizing their different aspirations. One possibility emerging is that of a plurinational state, in which the different nationalities will not only realize their own identities but will do so in different ways, emphasizing various symbolic and substantive questions that vary from one case to another. Some may be deeply integrated into the idea of a Spanish nation; others committed to a different and more pluralist Spain (as in Catalonia). Yet others may see Spain as a partner in the way the member states of the European Union see each other. This gradual evolution is favored by most Catalan nationalists and draws on the possibilities of reinterpreting the constitution as an alternative to rupture with it.[69] Basque nationalism tends, rather, to rupture but, increasingly, as a prelude to renegotiating a partnership. Again, there is a parallel with Quebec, where the Parti Québécois has held out for sovereignty followed by partnership, while the more nationalist wing of the Liberal Party has favored pushing for more powers within the Constitution. The Spanish experience is also rather positive on the internal cohesion of Catalonia and the Basque Country. Ethnic tensions exist but have been handled reasonably well under a

---

[67] Luís Moreno, La Federalización de España: Poder Político y Territorio (Siglo Veintiuno 1997).

[68] Miguel Herrero de Miñon, Derechos Históricos y Constitución (Taurus 1998).

[69] Stephen Tierney, Constitutional Law and National Pluralism (Oxford Univ. Press 2004).

formula allowing all to be members of the national community, while nationalist discourse has tended to be inclusive. Moderation on the independence issue also helps, here, since it permits people living in Catalonia and the Basque Country to maintain an attachment to Spain and does not force them to choose between rival national identities.

Yet there is a less optimistic scenario. The European framework, in which these different visions were embedded, has weakened since the failure of the draft constitution. The bilateralism of the Catalans has fostered resentment elsewhere, creating difficulties for the central government. The Basque insistence on a bilateral foundation to their whole arrangement with Spain is rejected elsewhere. The Constitution has worked for as long as there were possibilities of extending autonomy gradually. Further extensions, however, including a move to overt federalism could mean reopening the Constitution and bringing additional items onto the agenda. Should the Basque question be peacefully resolved, the Spanish Constitution will have met its ultimate test. At the time of writing, however, the various parties are still very distant.

12

Iraq's constitution of 2005: Liberal consociation as political prescription

John McGarry* and Brendan O'Leary**

1. Introduction

When it comes to managing national and religious diversity, democracies have two broad choices—integration or accommodation.

Integrationist states seek to construct a single overarching public identity. Integrationists believe conflict results from group-based partisanship and recommend a state that is impartial, meritocratic, and that promotes equal citizenship through a bill of individual rights. They frown on ethnic political parties or civic associations and praise parties that stand for non-ethnic or cross-ethnic agendas, such as the Republican and Democratic parties in the U.S., or Labour and the Conservatives in the U.K. They reject proportional electoral systems, which facilitate segmental appeals, and support those that discourage the mobilization of cultural differences and require winners to achieve majority or plurality broad-based support. Integrationists back executive systems that favor candidates who rise above religious, linguistic, and ethnic factions. They favor a unitary centralized state, or a federation that is constructed on non-ethnic criteria, and they frown on any form of autonomy, territorial or non-territorial, that is based on groups.[1] Integration is the preferred approach of most democratic states and international organizations. It is associated with dominant communities within states,

* Professor of Political Studies; Canada Research Chair in Nationalism and Democracy, Queen's University; Kingston, Ontario. McGarry would like to thank the Carnegie Corporation of New York and Social Science and Humanities Research Council of Canada for research funding. Email: john.mcgarry@queensu.ca

** Lauder Professor of Political Science, director of the Penn Program in Ethnic Conflict, University of Pennsylvania. O'Leary would like to thank the Lauder endowment and the Social Science and Humanities Research Council of Canada for aiding his research. Email: boleary@sas.upenn.edu

[1] For examples of integrationist thinking, see BRIAN BARRY, CULTURE AND INEQUALITY (Polity Press 2000); PAUL BRASS, ETHNICITY AND NATIONALISM: THEORY AND COMPARISON (Sage 1991); ROGERS BRUBAKER, ETHNICITY WITHOUT GROUPS (Harvard Univ. Press 2006); SEYMOUR MARTIN LIPSET, POLITICAL MAN: THE SOCIAL BASES OF POLITICS (Expanded ed. Heinemann 1983); Philip G. Roeder, *Soviet Federalism and Ethnic Mobilization*, 43 WORLD POL. 196 (1991).

as well as with small, dispersed minorities, such as immigrant communities, or "middlemen" minorities—as petit bourgeois communities whose members are neither present in security institutions, nor protected by trade unions, are known to sociologists.

Accommodationist democratic states recognize dual or multiple public identities through consociation.[2] Consociation accommodates groups: (*a*) by involving all sizable communities in executive institutions provided they wish to participate; (*b*) by promoting proportionality throughout the public sector, not just in the executive and legislature but also in the bureaucracy, including the army and the police; (*c*) through autonomy of either the territorial or non-territorial variety; and (*d*) through minority vetoes, at least in those domains the minority communities consider important. While integrationists mostly believe that identities are malleable, transformable, soft, or fluid, consociationalists think that—in certain contexts—they may be resilient, durable, and hard.[3] From the latter's perspective, political prudence and morality require considering the special interests, needs, and fears of groups so that they regard the state as fit for them. Accommodating groups through consociation is less popular with states than integration, but it is more popular among minorities, particularly sizable and territorially clustered minorities.[4]

These are the democratic institutional choices facing divided polities everywhere, from Bosnia-Herzegovina to Lebanon, from Northern Ireland to Sri Lanka and Sudan. Additionally, integration and accommodation are the dominant and

[2] Consociational theory is most closely associated with the work of Arend Lijphart. *See, e.g.*, AREND LIJPHART, THE POLITICS OF ACCOMMODATION: PLURALISM AND DEMOCRACY IN THE NETHERLANDS (Univ. Cal. Press 1968); AREND LIJPHART, DEMOCRACY IN PLURAL SOCIETIES: A COMPARATIVE EXPLORATION (Yale Univ. Press 1977); Arend Lijphart, *Self-Determination versus Pre-Determination of Ethnic Minorities in Power-Sharing Systems, in* THE RIGHTS OF MINORITY CULTURES 275 (Will Kymlicka ed., Oxford Univ. Press 1995) [hereinafter Lijphart, *Self-Determination*]; Arend Lijphart, *The Wave of Power-Sharing Democracy, in* THE ARCHITECTURE OF DEMOCRACY: CONSTITUTIONAL DESIGN, CONFLICT MANAGEMENT AND DEMOCRACY 37 (Andrew Reynolds ed., Oxford Univ. Press 2002). For other instances of consociational thinking, see ERIC NORDLINGER, CONFLICT REGULATION IN DIVIDED SOCIETIES (Occasional Papers in Int'l Aff., Ctr. for Int'l Aff., Harvard Univ. 1972); Brendan O'Leary, *Debating Consociational Politics: Normative and Explanatory Arguments, in* FROM POWER-SHARING TO DEMOCRACY: POST-CONFLICT INSTITUTIONS IN ETHNICALLY DIVIDED SOCIETIES 3 (Sid J. R. Noel ed., McGill-Queen's Univ. Press 2005); JOHN McGARRY & BRENDAN O'LEARY, THE NORTHERN IRELAND CONFLICT: CONSOCIATIONAL ENGAGEMENTS (Oxford Univ. Press 2004); KENNETH DOUGLAS McRAE, CONSOCIATIONAL DEMOCRACY IN SEGMENTED SOCIETIES (McClelland & Stewart 1974).

[3] For an example of the former view, see DAVID MILLER, MARKET, STATE AND COMMUNITY: THE FOUNDATIONS OF MARKET SOCIALISM 237 (Oxford Univ. Press 1989). For an example of the latter view, see John McGarry, *Political Settlements in Northern Ireland and South Africa*, 46 POL. STUD. 853 (1998).

[4] Here, we treat accommodation and consociation as synonyms, but this decision is slightly misleading. Elsewhere we have divided accommodation strategies into four categories: (*a*) territorial pluralism (meaningful territorial self-government for communities as well as power sharing in the federal or union government); (*b*) consociation (executive power sharing, self-government, proportionality and minority vetoes); (*c*) centripetalism (votepooling electoral systems, power-sharing coalition based on moderates, decentralization); and (*d*) credible multiculturalism (proportionality and self-government). *See* John McGarry, Brendan O'Leary & Richard Simeon, *Integration or Accommodation? The Enduring Debate in Conflict Regulation* (in this volume).

broad prescriptions offered for addressing the conflict in Iraq, even when this specific vocabulary is not employed. Those who favor integration for Iraq stress the commonalities Iraqis share and argue for "nation building". They call for a strong, centralized, and ethnically impartial Iraqi state, which they see as necessary for multiple reasons: to end the current insurgency (or, properly, insurgencies); combat crime; hold the country together; promote a civic national identity against ethnocentric and sectarian elites; defend the state against its neighbors; prevent Iraq from becoming a haven for the export of international *jihadism*; and allow the U.S.-led coalition to withdraw its troops.

Integrationists see Iraq's current problems as based on sectarianism and ethnocentrism, usually of recent origin, rather than rooted in established or age-old hatreds. The sources of discord are often seen to stem from the invasion of 2003, though it is recognized that they were exacerbated by Saddam's privileging of sectarian and tribal loyalties. The U.S.-led coalition, from this perspective, came to Iraq with a superficial "tribal" and atavistic reading of the country—one that downplayed the cross-cutting ties that bound Iraqis together.[5] The coalition thus provided an advantage to sectarian and ethnocentric leaders, who exploited these interpretations, and the descent into civil war began. In the integrationist account, these leaders negotiated a sectarian, decentralized, and unfair Constitution in 2005 that has further polarized matters.[6] The integrationists insist that if the decentralizing provisions in this Constitution, particularly its provisions on natural resources, are not radically changed, they will break Iraq apart, plunge the region into war, and provide a boon to international terrorism.[7] "Rather than being the glue that binds the country together", warns a report of the International Crisis Group—a Brussels-based non-governmental organization—the Constitution "has become both the prescription and the blueprint for its dissolution".[8]

[5] For examples of this view, see Yahia Said, *Federal Choices Needed,* Al-Ahram Weekly, Mar. 2–8, 2006, *available at* <http://weekly.ahram.org.eg/2006/784/sc6.htm> (last visited May 28, 2007); Tulin Daloglu, *End Sectarian Violence,* Wash. Times, Apr. 17, 2006, at A17; Int'l Crisis Group, *The Next Iraqi War? Sectarianism and Civil Conflict* (Middle East Report No. 52, Feb. 27, 2006), *available at* <http://www.crisisgroup.org/library/documents/middle_east___north_africa/iraq_iran_gulf/52_the_next_iraqi_war_sectarianism_and_civil_conflict.pdf>.

[6] According to Yahia Said, "international actors have not been innocent bystanders. They have contributed to sectarianism in many ways, including by subscribing to a 'realist' narrative that argues that Iraq is an artificial state; that the groups comprising it were only held together by tyranny, and that disintegration is a byproduct of liberation from authoritarianism. This narrative, which is antithetical to nation-building, has been embraced by sectarian politicians in Iraq and has found its reflection in post-invasion policies, including the dissolution of the army and the new constitution." Said, *supra* note 5. *See also* Daloglu, *supra* note 5 (accusing the United States of enforcing an "ethnic and sectarian calculus onto the infrastructure of the Iraqi Governing Council"); and Int'l Crisis Group, *supra* note 5, at i and 23 (arguing that the U.S.-led coalition prized "communal identities over national-political platforms").

[7] *See, e.g.,* Kanan Makiya, *Present at the Disintegration,* N.Y. Times, Dec. 11, 2005, at 13, §4 (Constitution must be "overhauled"); Int'l Crisis Group, *supra* note 5, at 11 (calling for Constitution to be "totally revised").

[8] Int'l Crisis Group, *supra* note 5, at 11.

Broad integrationist sentiment is dominant among Iraq's small, centrist secular parties and is popular among Sunni Arabs, at least among those who have given up on a return to the status quo ante. It is the preferred public position of all the surrounding Arab states and of Turkey, where it is associated with the founding philosophy of the Turkish state. Integration, in this sense, is arguably the most popular prescription in the West, among supporters of the 2003 invasion, in the Bush administration and elsewhere, as well as among the invasion's critics, in the Democratic Party in the U.S., and among a broad swathe of European political opinion.[9] Nonetheless, many integrationists apparently see themselves as losing the battle to the forces of sectarian and ethnic division.[10]

The second approach, which is consociational, focuses on the accommodation of Iraq's different communities. It is labeled by its integrationist critics as "primordialist", "tribalist", "atavistic", "sectarian", "ethnocentric", and "partitionist", but by its supporters as "realist" or "pluralist".[11] The consociational approach tacitly underlay the decision by the Coalition Provisional Authority (CPA) to appoint the broad-based Interim Governing Council (IGC) in the summer of 2003, and was more prominent in the 2005 Constitution, which confirmed autonomy for the region of Kurdistan and offered other protections to Iraq's diverse communities.[12] The consociational approach has also informed proposals both to partition Iraq into three states—for its Kurdish, Shi'a Arab, and Sunni Arab communities respectively—and, more recently, to decentralize the government of Iraq along these same ethnic lines. Prescriptions of this sort have been put forward by, among others, U.S. senator Joseph Biden, Leslie Gelb (the former chair of the Council of Foreign Relations),[13] Peter Galbraith (former U.S. ambassador to Croatia),[14] and Michael O'Hanlon (of the Brookings Institution).[15]

[9] The latest integrationist blueprint, emblematic of the conventional wisdom, is the bipartisan report of the U.S. Iraq Study Group: JAMES A. BAKER III & LEE H. HAMILTON, THE IRAQ STUDY GROUP REPORT: THE WAY FORWARD—A NEW APPROACH (Vintage Books 2006). For a critique of the report, see Brendan O'Leary, *Iraq's Future 101: The Failings of the Baker-Hamilton Report,* 6 STRATEGIC INSIGHTS, Mar. 2007, *available at* <http://www.ccc.nps.navy.mil/si/2007/Mar/o%27learyMar07.pdf> (last visited May 28, 2007).

[10] This is the message conveyed generally by Daloglu, *supra* note 5, and the Int'l Crisis Group, *supra* note 5. *See also* Toby Dodge, *State Collapse and the Rise of Identity Politics, in* IRAQ: PREVENTING A NEW GENERATION OF CONFLICT 23 (Markus E. Bouillon, David M. Malone & Ben Rowswell eds., Lynne Rienner 2007).

[11] For examples of the consociational approach applied to Iraq, see generally THE FUTURE OF KURDISTAN IN IRAQ (Brendan O'Leary, John McGarry & Khaled Salih eds., Univ. of Pennsylvania Press 2005), particularly at 47–142.

[12] IRAQ CONST. art. 113 (guaranteeing autonomy for Kurdistan); IRAQ CONST. arts. 116–117 (defining the powers of an autonomous region); IRAQ CONST. arts. 118–119, 121 (defining protections for smaller communities).

[13] Leslie Gelb, *The Three State Solution,* N.Y. TIMES, Nov. 25, 2003, at A27 (late edition). *See also* Joseph Biden & Leslie Gelb, *Unity through Autonomy in Iraq,* N.Y. TIMES, May 1, 2006, at A19 (late edition).

[14] PETER W. GALBRAITH, THE END OF IRAQ: HOW AMERICAN INCOMPETENCE CREATED A WAR WITHOUT END (Simon & Schuster 2006).

[15] Michael E. O'Hanlon, *Voluntary Ethnic Re-location in Iraq,* L.A.TIMES, Aug. 27, 2006, *available at* <http://www.mafhoum.com/press9/285S23.htm>.

These contrasting prescriptions for regulating Iraq's conflict have produced a vigorous debate. Integrationists accuse consociationalists of exaggerating the monolithic nature of Iraq's communal and ethnic groups and of downplaying an Iraqi identity coterminous with the state.[16] In giving power to the very ethnic and sectarian politicians responsible for the conflict and by reifying identities that are fluid and contingent, consociationalists are said to have made matters worse. Group-based thinking in Iraq, it is argued, "is a static caricature that does great damage to a complex, historically grounded, reality"[17] or betrays a "sublime artificiality" and ignorance of the historical record.[18] By contrast, consociationalists see the current civil war, and recent election and referendum results, as evidence that Iraq is deeply divided, with a divided past.[19] They believe that these divisions cannot be overcome easily in the near future, and that there is a need, therefore, for accommodation, extensive territorial autonomy, or partition. Consociationalists criticize integrationists for ignoring the reality of divisions on the ground and for exaggerating the basis for unity. They think that integrationist prescriptions will produce the very disasters that integrationists seek to avoid.

In this chapter, we argue that the integrationist prescriptions have deep flaws, and that Iraq's integrationists, ironically enough, exaggerate the monolithic nature of consociational approaches. While some consociationalists are guilty of the errors the integrationists describe, not all are. The main division in consociational approaches is between those who favor a "corporate consociation" and those who favor a "liberal consociation",[20] or, differently put, between those who prefer "predetermination" and those who prefer "self-determination".[21] A corporate or predetermined consociation accommodates groups according to ascriptive criteria, such as ethnicity or religion, on the assumption that group identities are fixed and that groups are both internally homogeneous and externally bounded.[22] This thinking indeed privileges such identities at the expense of those group identities that are not accommodated, and/or at the expense of intragroup or transgroup identities. Politicians associated with these unprivileged categories find it more difficult to thrive.[23] A liberal or self-determined consociation, by

[16] *See* Dodge, *supra* note 10, at 25; Int'l Crisis Group, *supra* note 5; *see also* Reidar Visser, *Iraq's Partition Fantasy*, Open Democracy, May 19, 2006, *available at* <http://www.opendemocracy.net/conflict-iraq/partition_3565.jsp> (last visited June 1, 2007).
[17] *See* Dodge, *supra* note 10, at 25.
[18] *See* Visser, *supra* note 16.
[19] Brendan O'Leary, *Power-Sharing, Pluralist Federation, and Federacy, in* THE FUTURE OF KURDISTAN IN IRAQ, *supra* note 11, at 47; GALBRAITH, *supra* note 14; Biden & Gelb, *supra* note 13, at A19.
[20] O'Leary, *supra* note 2, at 15–16.
[21] *See* Lijphart, *Self-Determination, supra* note 2.
[22] For an integrationist criticism of this approach, see BRUBAKER, *supra* note 1.
[23] Lebanon is an example of a corporate consociation. It currently allocates three of its most important political offices—the presidency, premiership, and speaker of the legislature—to a Christian, Sunni Muslim, and Shi'a Muslim, respectively. This creates a hierarchy among the three communities, as the offices to which they are entitled are not equal in stature, but it also creates a hierarchy between the three communities and communities that are not accommodated, such as

contrast, rewards whatever salient political identities emerge in democratic elections, whether these are based on ethnic or religious groups, or on subgroup or transgroup identities. Liberal consociations also take care to ensure that the rights of individuals as well as groups are protected. While academic consociationalists are invariably exponents of liberal consociation,[24] integrationists and other critics of consociation almost always identify consociation with its corporate form.

Important parts of Iraq's new Constitution are consistent with liberal consociational principles, and we shall argue that if Iraq is to have a future as a democratic and united state, the 2005 Constitution will need to be defended and, particularly where it is incomplete or vague, developed in a liberal consociational direction.

2. Iraq's constitution: Self-rule and shared rule

Iraq's new Constitution creates a federation. Federations incorporate elements of self-rule in the sense that their component units enjoy a certain degree of autonomy vis-à-vis the federal government even as they share in the control of that government.

Self-rule rests on the resolution of two important questions, namely, what is the nature of the *self*, or community, to be given self-rule, and how much *rule* should this community enjoy? In answering the first question, integrationists favor partly autonomous provinces founded on administrative or territorial principles, not on ethnic or religious principles. In Iraq, several integrationists have argued for a federation based on the existing eighteen governorates.[25] The governorate boundaries are preferred because they are purely administrative entities, rather than the focus of historic or ethnic loyalties, and, indeed, this had been the rationale for establishing and redrawing them—even under Saddam. It is believed that internal boundaries based on governorates would be more consistent with Iraqi nation building because they would stress citizenship over ethnicity or communalism and because they would politically fragment communal and ethnic groups spread across different provinces, giving rise to intragroup divisions and cross-cutting loyalties. Integrationists also argue that it is virtually impossible to create ethnically homogeneous federal units in Iraq, and that an ethnically based federalism would inevitably condemn local ethnic or non-ethnic

Lebanon's Druze, or the various cross-cutting communities (environmentalists, socialists, feminists) who prefer to stress a programmatic politics rather than one based on religion.

[24] *See* Lijphart, *Self-Determination*, *supra* note 2; O'Leary, *supra* note 2; and McGarry & O'Leary, *supra* note 2.

[25] Makiya, *supra* note 7; Adeed Dawisha & Karen Dawisha, *How to Build a Democratic Iraq*, 82 Foreign Aff. 36 (2003); Dawn Brancati, *Is Federalism a Panacea for Post-Saddam Iraq?*, 25 Wash. Q. 14 (2004); Andreas Wimmer, *Democracy and Ethno-Religious Conflict in Iraq*, 45 Survival 124 (2003).

minorities to discrimination and second-class citizenship and thus would be a source of injustice as well as instability.[26]

Iraq's recently enacted Constitution deviates from the model of eighteen governorates by recognizing Kurdistan, which comprises three governorates at present as well as fragments of others, as an established federal region. Integrationists have generally come to accept this as an immovable fact, though hardly enthusiastically.[27] They continue, however, to object to two other parts of the Constitution, which also break with the model of administrative federation: the provision that allows Kirkuk to join Kurdistan, should a majority of its population decide to do so in a plebiscite to be held by December 2007;[28] and the provision that allows all governorates, except Baghdad, to amalgamate to form "regions, following a referendum in each governorate".[29] The concern is that these provisions will promote an ethnic or communal federation, with associated dangers of ethnocentrism/sectarianism and dissolution.[30]

For corporate consociationalists, the internal boundaries of Iraq's federation should be organized ascriptively. There should be a tripartite federation of Kurds, Sunni Arabs, and Shi'a Arabs. This approach has been advocated by U.S. Senator Joseph Biden and Leslie Gelb.[31] A similar arrangement, they point out, was tried by the United States in Bosnia-Herzegovina under the Dayton Accords, when separate units of self-government were established for Bosniaks, Croats, and Serbs, respectively.[32] The result was a decade of relative peace and, now that memories of civil war are fading, Bosnians are beginning to rebuild their federal government.[33]

Both approaches have flaws. The main problem with adopting an integrationist (administrative) federation in Iraq is that it would prevent communities that want to enjoy collective self-government from doing so. Such an approach would not promote unity or peace and is undemocratic. Kurdistan's authorities and parties would never have accepted a federation based on the eighteen governorates, since this would not have recognized Kurdistan. Given the attachment of Kurds to Kirkuk and to other disputed territories, any attempt to prevent their union

[26] *See* Wimmer, *supra* note 25, at 123: "federalization may heighten, rather than reduce the risks of gross human rights violations, especially for members of ethnic minorities living under the rule of the majority government in a federal unit." *See also* Imad Salamey & Frederic Pearson, *The Crisis of Federalism and Electoral Strategies in Iraq*, 6 INT'L STUD. PERSP. 190 (2005).
[27] *See* Makiya, *supra* note 7; Int'l Crisis Group, *supra* note 5, at ii.
[28] IRAQ CONST. art. 140.
[29] *Id.* art. 119.
[30] BAKER & HAMILTON, *supra* note 9 (arguing that the referendum on Kirkuk be postponed); for comments, see O'Leary, *supra* note 9.
[31] Biden & Gelb, *supra* note 13, at A19.
[32] Technically, the Dayton Accords divided Bosnia-Herzegovina into two federal units, the Federation of Bosnia-Herzegovina and Republika Srpska, respectively. However, the former is divided into Croat and Bosniak-controlled cantons. The Dayton Peace Accords on Bosnia (1995), *available at* <http://www.state.gov/www/regions/eur/bosnia/bosagree.html>.
[33] Biden & Gelb, *supra* note 13, at A19.

with Kurdistan, after an affirmative plebiscite, or to prevent such a plebiscite from being held, would likely provoke more violence, rather than peace. The difficulty with the corporate consociational approach, on the other hand, is that it requires ascriptive communities to adopt collective self-government in advance of clear evidence that all of the relevant communities seek it. It is not yet unambiguously clear that Iraq is divided into three parts, like Caesar's Gaul, or Bosnia-Herzegovina. While there is "near unanimity" among Kurdish political leaders and much of the populace on a Kurdish identity and, accordingly, on the need for Kurdish collective autonomy, the same cannot be said with respect to Shi'a and, in particular, Sunni Arabs.[34] There are divisions among the Shi'a—between those with primarily a Shi'a identity, particularly supporters of the Supreme Iraqi Islamic Council (SIIC), previously known as the Supreme Council for the Islamic Revolution in Iraq (SCIRI),[35] and those who claim to have more of an Iraqi identity, predominantly, the Sadrists and *Da'wa*. Among the Shi'a, there is a minority that is more centralist than decentralist; there are, in addition, well-known divisions on the question of a Shi'a super-region in the south.[36] It may be that Sunni Arabs will come to embrace the notion of collective self-government, but they have not done so yet, as their support for the eighteen-governorate model suggests.

Given these facts, a liberal consociational approach—one that leaves it to local democratic constituencies to decide if they want to amalgamate into federal regions or not—seems both prudent and democratic. This is the approach of the 2005 Constitution.[37] The Kirkuk governorate, after normalization (the restoration of its expelled people, the rectification of boundaries, and incentives paid to settlers to return to their places of origin), can choose to join Kurdistan if its valid electorate wants to do so.[38] Governorates in other parts of the country—with the exception of Baghdad, which may not aggregate with any other governorate—are permitted to unite, forming regions, if there is democratic support in each governorate.

[34] *See* Phebe Marr, *Iraq's Identity Crisis, in* IRAQ: PREVENTING A NEW GENERATION OF CONFLICT 41, 45–49 (Markus E. Bouillon, David M. Malone & Ben Rowswell eds., Lynne Rienner 2007).

[35] The name change occurred in May 2007, and was explained by the party as reflecting the successful revolutionary overthrow of the Ba'athist regime. It may have also reflected a wish on the part of its leadership to distance the party from its formation in, and past sponsorship by, Ayatollah Khomeni's Iran.

[36] Integrationists often point to intragroup divisions in order to criticize consociationalism, and, in Iraq, they point to internal divisions among both Kurds and Shi'a Arabs. However, while the Kurds clearly have internal party-based divisions, these exist alongside a consensus on collective self-government. The Kurdish perspective is that internal divisions can be managed within a self-governing Kurdistan. There is not yet a similar consensus on collective self-government among Shi'a Arabs.

[37] As a constitutional adviser to the Kurdistan Regional Government in the making of Iraq's Constitution, and, therefore, as someone privileged to see both public and private texts, O'Leary attributes the emergence of this approach to a memorandum written by the UN specialist South African professor Nicholas Haysom, which resembled some of the features of the Spanish Constitution.

[38] IRAQ CONST. art. 140.

Two democratic thresholds are proposed before aggregation: a measure to trigger a referendum within the respective governorates, and a referendum.[39] (Federal enabling legislation has subsequently been passed.) It is, therefore, possible under the Constitution for much of Biden and Gelb's tripartite solution to be implemented, if there is support for it, though it is not mandatory.[40] The one exception is Baghdad, which may form a region of its own but may not be part of any other region. It is also possible for Shi'a-dominated governorates that do not accept SIIC/SCIRI's vision to retain their original status, and, indeed for any governorate that may be, or may become, dominated by secularists, to avoid inclusion in what they might fear will be a *Shari'a*-ruled Shi'astan or Sunnistan.

There is another reason why the Constitution's provisions on self-rule may be more conducive to stability apart from the fact that they are more consistent with democratic preferences. Federations that have only two or three regions are less stable than those with many.[41] Two-region federations especially are prone to collapse, as the experience of Czechoslovakia, pre-1971 Pakistan, and, more recently, Serbia and Montenegro suggests, because there are few opportunities for shifting alliances and the two units tend to be pitted against each other on every issue. But three-unit federations are also fragile, since opportunities for shifting coalitions are still limited, notwithstanding the instance of Bosnia-Herzegovina's survival, which we judge to be an outcome of the will of the international community, specifically, the European Union and the U.S. It is, therefore, an advantage of Iraq's Constitution that it allows for the possibility of multiple federal units, without mandating it.

The second important question on self-rule concerns its extent, that is, how decentralized should Iraq's federation be? Integrationists' chief criticism of the new Constitution is that, as Donald Horowitz writes, it has established "probably the weakest federation in the world".[42] They insist that only a centralized government with a strong "capacity" can perform vital nation-building tasks; hold the country's fissiparous regions together; defeat the insurgency; fend off avaricious neighbors, particularly Iran; and protect minorities throughout the state.[43] They argue that this is not only desirable but politically popular. Reidar Visser describes the situation in Iraq as involving a "dualism" of weak regional identities combined with a "quite robust Iraqi nationalism".[44] Toby Dodge maintains that

---

[39] The Iraqi Constitution provides for a referendum if there is "a request by one-third of the council members of each governorate intending to form a region" or "a request by one-tenth of the voters in each of the governorates intending to form a region". *Id.* art. 119.

[40] For the tripartite solution, see Biden & Gelb, *supra* note 13, at A19.

[41] RONALD L. WATTS, COMPARING FEDERAL SYSTEMS 113–114 (McGill-Queen's Univ. Press 1999).

[42] Donald Horowitz, *The Sunni Moment*, WALL ST. J., Dec. 14, 2005, at A20.

[43] *See* Dodge, *supra* note 10, at 35.

[44] Visser, *supra* note 16, He claims that Iraqi nationalism remains "flourishing" and that "even today, in a climate of growing sectarian terrorism calculated to obliterate the idea of coexistence, many Iraqis stubbornly refuse to reveal their ethno-religious identity when interrogated by western journalists. Many simply say they are Iraqis." There are, of course, good reasons why Iraqis may refuse to reveal their identities to foreigners and other Iraqis.

there is a "widespread wish for a strong unitary state centered on Baghdad" and claims that a collective appreciation of the state's administrative capacity would contribute to a "collective sense of identity that can rival or even replace sub-state, centrifugal political mobilization".[45]

Those who argue that the Iraq federation is weak (that is, decentralized) usually point to the Constitution's provisions on natural resources; they argue, correctly, that Baghdad's control over the country's natural resources is a *sine qua non* for centralization. The Constitution makes clear that natural resources are not an exclusive competence of the federal government.[46] Article 111, which states that "oil and gas are owned by all the people of Iraq", is deliberately not a subclause of the preceding article 110, which specifies precisely the exclusive competences of the federal government.[47] Article 111 should also be read in conjunction with article 115, which states that all powers that are not exclusively federal competences belong to the regions (and governorates not organized into a region), and that where competences are shared and there is a clash, then the regional laws prevail.[48] Article 111 should be read, too, in conjunction with article 121, which establishes that the regions have a general power of nullification outside the domain of exclusive federal competences.[49]

Article 112, the second important constitutional article dealing with oil and gas, states that the "federal government, with the producing governorates and regional governments shall undertake the *management* of oil and gas extracted from *present fields*", and that "the federal government, with the producing regional and governorate governments, shall *together* formulate the necessary strategic policies to develop the oil and gas wealth in a way that achieves the highest benefit to the Iraqi people".[50] Article 112 is also subject to articles 115 and 121, which authorize regional legal supremacy.[51] Together, these clauses make it plain that the federal government's constitutional role in control of oil and gas is prescribed and delimited in a number of ways; it is managerial, shared with the regions and governorates; subordinate to the regions and governorates in the event of clashes; and confined to current fields.[52] Nothing in these provisions, however, prevents

---

[45] *See* Dodge, *supra* note 10, at 29.

[46] For a more detailed construction and defense of the constitution's clauses on natural resources, see Brendan O'Leary, *Federalizing Natural Resources, in* IRAQ: PREVENTING A NEW GENERATION OF CONFLICT 189 (Markus E. Bouillon, David M. Malone & Ben Rowswell eds., Lynne Rienner 2007).

[47] IRAQ CONST. art. 110–111.

[48] *Id.* arts. 111 & 115.

[49] *Id.* arts. 111 & 121.

[50] *Id.* art. 112 (emphasis added).

[51] *Id.* arts. 115 & 121.

[52] Some supporters of a centralized Iraq, in which Baghdad would control natural resources, argue with breathtaking early revisionism that the Constitution actually mandates their preferred world. This appears to be the curious position of the oil minister, Hussain al-Shahristani, appointed in 2006, who claimed on assuming office that the federal government's (alleged) control over exploration extended to all oil fields in the country, including those that are not yet in production: Steve Negus, *Iraq Faces Clash with Kurds Over Oil Deals*, FIN. TIMES (U.K.), May 23–24, 2006, *available*

the Iraqi federal government—in concert with its regions—from agreeing on cooperative arrangements that resemble those proposed in some versions of the draft federal oil bill.

From the integrationist perspective, the Constitution's treatment of oil and natural gas is not just decentralist but partisan, allegedly privileging Shi'a and Kurdish regions while collectively punishing Sunni Arabs for the sins of the Ba'athists. It is said to underlie Sunni Arab grievances and to have fueled the insurgency. Kanan Makiya has described the Constitution as a "punitive" document that penalizes Sunnis "for living in regions without oil".[53] The Constitution suggests, according to him, that the "state owes the Sunnis of the resource-poor western provinces less than it does the Shiites and Kurds".[54] Yahia Said, another centralist, writes that the Constitution means that "Baghdad and the non-oil-producing regions will be at the mercy of the oil-producing ones".[55] The International Crisis Group has warned that if Shi'a Arabs construct a nine-province Shi'a region, as permitted by the Constitution, it would "leave the Sunni Arab community landlocked and without oil".[56] Many who believe this conventional wisdom see control over natural resources at the heart of the struggle for Kirkuk. Why else, the argument goes, does Kurdistan want to incorporate Kirkuk, if not for the fact that it sits atop of some of the world's largest oilfields?[57] When integrationists talk about the need for the Constitution to be revised, it is most often the provisions regarding natural resources that are singled out. Typical of such criticism is the International Crisis Group's call for a "total revision of key articles concerning the nature of federalism and the distribution of proceeds from oil sales".[58] This organization argues further that revenues from natural resources must be "centrally controlled".[59] Other defenders of centralism in Iraq advocate placing natural resources under central control because they believe that this is the way it is arranged in all federations.[60]

---

at <http://www.ft.com/cms/s/3d56aa60-ea7c-11da-9566–0000779e2340.html>. The Turkish government has taken a similar line, seeking through its official spokesmen to play down the extent to which Iraq's Constitution gives any control over oil to Iraq's regions: *Turkey Wary of Iraqi-Kurd Plans to Export Oil,* DEUTSCHE PRESSE-AGENTUR (F.R.G.), June 27, 2007, *available at* <http://www.pukonline.com/eng/modules.php?name=News&file=article&sid=1182>. This position is vigorously contested by the Kurdistan Regional Government. Telephone interview by Brendan O'Leary with Khaled Salih, official spokesman, Kurdistan Regional Government, (May 30, 2007).

[53] Makiya, *supra* note 7.
[54] *Id.*
[55] Said, *supra* note 5.
[56] Int'l Crisis Group, *supra* note 5, at ii.
[57] For example, Joost Hilterman of the International Crisis Group alleges that "the Kurds are using the historic opportunity of rolling back Arab domination to sue for independence through the acquisition of Kirkuk and its oil wealth". Joost R. Hiltermann, *Kirkuk and the Kurds: A Difficult Choice Ahead,* ASSYRIAN INT'L NEWS AGENCY, May 22, 2007, *available at* <http://www.aina.org/news/200705229921.htm>. However, he has no stated sources for this view; it is mere surmise—though widely shared among critics of the Kurds.
[58] Int'l Crisis Group, *supra* note 5, at ii.
[59] *Id.*
[60] Dawisha & Dawisha, *supra* note 25, at 38.

Those who take a corporate consociational view take a contrary position, arguing for decentralization. Thus, Gelb and Biden extol the virtues of the Dayton Accords,[61] which provided for a very decentralized federation in Bosnia-Herzegovina, and even allowed "Muslims, Croats and Serbs to retain separate armies".[62] This is seen as the most effective way to prevent sectarian violence and, paradoxically, to maintain a united Iraq. Decentralization, in Biden and Gelb's view, is consistent with a fair sharing of revenues, though the details on how to achieve this are not spelled out.

There are problems with both positions, but particularly with the first. It is odd that a centralized Iraq is marketed by some integrationists, including those in the U.S. administration, as important for regional stability, given that the last centralized Iraq launched aggressive wars against two of its neighbors, Iran and Kuwait, and attacked Israel with missiles while funding the families of Palestinian suicide bombers. Moreover, there is also considerable evidence that important constituencies in Iraq oppose centralization and have, as well, a weak or non-existent Iraqi identity. Dodge's contention that there is "widespread" support for a Baghdad-centered unitary state arguably misrepresents Iraq's "complex reality" far more than the claim that it is based on three major communities.

Support for decentralization is strongest among the Kurds. Not only did they suffer terribly from the last strong state in Baghdad, but they have enjoyed unprecedented stability and prosperity in their autonomous zone since 1991. In two elections in 2005, almost all Kurds and the other residents of Kurdistan gave their support to parties that called for the preservation or possible expansion of Kurdish self-government.[63] In the October 2005 referendum on the Constitution, which by the integrationists' own admission provided for extensive decentralization, the three Kurdish-dominated provinces voted overwhelmingly in favor (Dahuk, 99.13 percent; Sulaimaniya, 98.96 percent; Irbil, 99.36 percent).[64] To the extent that the Kurdish community is divided on the issue of decentralization, the fault line is between a younger generation that wants independence and an older one that also prefers independence but believes it more prudent to try to operate within an Iraqi federation. This is why balanced integrationists like Makiya generally preface their remarks regarding the need for a centralized Iraq, with "except for Kurdistan".[65] Such qualifications are missing from Dodge's account. Kurdish support for decentralization means that centralization cannot happen, at least

---

[61] The Dayton Peace Accords on Bosnia, *supra* note 32.

[62] Biden & Gelb, *supra* note 13, at A19. Bosnia-Herzegovina now has a single army, with ethnically homogeneous units.

[63] Independent Electoral Commission of Iraq, *available at* <http://www.ieciraq.org/English/Frameset_english.htm>.

[64] *Iraqi Voters Back New Constitution*, BBC News, Oct. 25, 2005, *available at* <http://news.bbc.co.uk/2/hi/middle_east/4374822.stm#map> (last visited June 29, 2007).

[65] Reidar Visser also acknowledges that the Kurdish desire for autonomy is more widespread than elsewhere but argues that there are intra-Kurdish divisions on the question. *See* Visser, *supra* note 16.

not within the constitutional order. This is because the Kurds possess an effective veto over any constitutional change that is against their perceived interests.[66]

The evidence suggests that most Shi'a also oppose a strong centralized state. Many in this community, like the Kurds, have bad memories of Iraq's last unitary state, and their worst nightmare is a strong Baghdad-centered state once again falling under Sunni Arab or Ba'athist control. If there is such widespread support for centralization, as Dodge and Visser maintain, why did the ten Shi'a-dominated governorates, including Baghdad, support Iraq's Constitution in the recent referendum, with levels of support averaging more than 90 percent, and why was the Constitution supported by 79 percent of Iraqis overall?[67]

Another important problem with the integrationist position on centralization is that it assumes that centralization will involve an impartial central government—promoting what Dodge describes as a "shared vision of the future".[68] However, there is important comparative experience to suggest that this is not the only form a centralized Iraq might take, or even the most likely one. When Eastern Europe democratized in the 1990s, the dominant pattern was for the leading community in each state to seek to "nationalize" the state in its own image and to exclude others.[69] This pattern resulted in ethnically based discrimination; policies of coercive assimilation; the abolition of previously existing arrangements for self-government; and, in some cases, including Bosnia-Herzegovina and Kosovo, ethnic cleansing. There followed what Rogers Brubaker has described, following Lord Curzon, as an "un-mixing of peoples", that is, the migration of several million people from minority groups seeking more hospitable havens in other states; a considerable number of civil wars;[70] and the de facto secession of several regions.[71]

In Iraq, support for the impartial and secular vision championed by integrationists is concentrated in the centrist parties, including that led by Ayad Allawi.

---

[66] IRAQ CONST. art. 126(4) states that it may not be amended "if such amendments take away from the powers of the regions" except with the approval of the concerned region's legislature and its people voting in a referendum. IRAQ CONST. art. 142, which suspends art. 126 for the transitional period, states that constitutional change requires the support of a majority of voters and must not be rejected by two-thirds of the voters in three or more governorates. As the Kurds make up the overwhelming majority of voters in three governorates, this translates into a Kurdish veto.

[67] One integrationist response from a leading Iraqi integrationist is that Iraqi voters did not read the Constitution and, therefore, did not know what they were voting for (response from Rend Rahim al-Francke, President, Iraq Foundation, to question by John McGarry at "Advancing Rights in the New Iraq" conference, in Ottawa, Canada, Mar. 2, 2006). In our view, Iraqis may not have read the text but they broadly knew what they were doing when they followed the guidance of their political leaders as to how to cast their ballots.

[68] *See* Dodge, *supra* note 10, at 35.

[69] *See generally* JACK SNYDER, FROM VOTING TO VIOLENCE: DEMOCRATIZATION AND NATIONALIST CONFLICT (W.W. Norton 2000); ROGERS BRUBAKER, NATIONALISM REFRAMED (Cambridge Univ. Press 1995).

[70] *E.g.*, in Croatia, Bosnia, Macedonia, Moldova, Georgia, Russia, and Azerbaijan.

[71] *E.g.*, Trans-Dniestria; Abkhazia; South Ossetia; Nagorno-Karabakh; and, before its forced reincorporation into Russia, Chechnya.

However, these parties are overwhelmingly Arab in composition and support. They are also, at the moment, politically marginalized. Centrist parties won less than 10 percent of the vote in the elections of December 2005. They have, in historian Phebe Marr's words, "too little support to play much of a role in the political dynamics of the future".[72] The most enthusiastic and numerous supporters of a centralized Iraq are not the liberal centrists, but the parties rooted in Iraq's Sunni Arab community. However, their support for centralization is mostly ethnocentric in nature and based on nostalgia for the Iraq that Sunni Arabs controlled since its creation. It also appears related to the belief among Sunni Arabs—widespread, until recently—that they represent a majority of Iraq's population, as high as 60 percent in some estimates.[73] Even Sunni Arabs' calls for a government based on technocracy and for a "professional" army are not as impartial and civic as they might seem, since Sunni Arabs dominated both the technocratic and army officer class under Saddam.

What of the Shi'a centralizers associated with Muqtada al-Sadr and the *Da'wa* party? Much of their support for centralization reflects the thinking likely to be present in a majority group under conditions of democratization—as seen in Eastern Europe. Some Shi'a centralizers aspire to control a centralized Iraq and use it to promulgate Shi'a religious values—values that Sunni Arabs, Kurds, and secularists would find difficult to live with, to put it mildly.[74] It is hardly an exaggeration, then, to argue that there is no guarantee that a centralized Iraq would evolve in the benign, neutral way envisaged or implied in integrationist accounts, even if there were widespread support for it, which we doubt for the reasons just given.

Given the dangers of a centralized Iraq, and the opposition it would engender, we should be wary of calls to place natural resources under the control and ownership of Iraq's federal government.[75] But are the current constitutional provisions governing natural resources unfair, as critics maintain? According to the Constitution, revenues from current fields are "to be distributed in a fair manner in proportion to the population distribution in all parts of the country, specifying an allotment for a specified period for the damaged regions which were unjustly deprived of them by the former regime, and the regions that were damaged afterwards in a way that ensures balanced development in different areas of the country, and this shall be regulated by a law".[76] There is, therefore, a constitutional obligation to ensure the just allocation of revenues from current fields,

---

[72] *See* Marr, *supra* note 34, at 51.

[73] Int'l Crisis Group, *supra* note 5, at 32. It may be hoped that this myth has been shattered by recent election results, which should eventually force a Sunni Arab rethink on the merits of centralization.

[74] *See also* Marr, *supra* note 34, at 48.

[75] Dawisha & Dawisha, *supra* note 25, at 38. In spite of Adeed and Karen Dawisha's argument, it is not the case that natural resources in federations are always under the control of federal authorities, as the examples of Canada and the U.S. show.

[76] IRAQ CONST. art. 112.1.

as well as an obligation to redress past misallocations, in a time-limited fashion and in a way that is consistent with a "balanced" development strategy. Also, as this constitutional provision makes clear, the territorial status of the Kirkuk governorate has been decoupled from the oil revenues that flow from its oilfields. As Kirkuk's oil comes from currently exploited fields, its revenues are to be redistributed across the state regardless of whether Kirkuk joins Kurdistan or not. This fact needs to be clearly understood: it is a major constitutional compromise.

Revenue from current fields, it is reasonable to project, will constitute the lion's share of oil revenues for some time to come: 100 percent in 2007, 90 percent in 2017, and 80 percent in 2027. The gradualism of these arrangements will enable appropriate development strategies, for both future resource-rich and resource-poor regions, wherever these will be. Well-run governorates and regions will plan according to their respective anticipated futures, tailoring their cloths appropriately—economic diversification planning should start now. There will also be opportunities for exploration *throughout* Iraq, because all three major communities predominate in some territory where there are good prospects of new fields. Allah in his infinite generosity has blessed Anbar as well as Basra and Kirkuk.[77] Baghdad, which should become a region unto itself, also straddles some good prospects. Indeed, the conventional wisdom that Sunni Arab regions have only sand but no oil or gas is incorrect, though it is difficult to explore for oil and gas during an insurgency. Finally, the Constitution does not prevent the regions—those that will control revenue from future fields—from agreeing to share revenues from these fields with the rest of Iraq on a per capita basis. That is not merely a hypothetical statement: such provisions for sharing are already part of the draft federal oil law that has been agreed to by Kurdistan, though it has reservations about proposed licensing arrangements. Taken together, these arrangements for oil and gas are fair; the integrationist critique is simply based on factual errors about the Constitution. Moreover, the provisions on natural resources are in line with a constitutional order that will help prevent the type of overcentralized rentier oil state, which led Iraq to disaster.

The corporate consociational or three-regions approach, associated with Biden and Gelb and others, has the virtue of being much closer to existing political opinion in Iraq; after all, the referendum and election results suggest that there is widespread support for decentralization, not centralization.[78] However, while integrationists, who believe there is a strong Iraqi identity, seek to impose a one-size-fits-all centralized system on the whole country, these corporate consociationalists appear to want a one-size-fits-all decentralized model. This mode of thinking cannot currently accommodate Sunni Arabs, who embrace a vision of Arab or Iraqi nationalism, or those Shi'a Arabs who reject regionalism. This

---

[77] *See, e.g.*, James Glanz, *Iraqi Sunni Lands Show New Oil and Gas Promise*, N.Y. Times, Feb. 19, 2007, at A1 (with "Iraqi Sunni" referring to Arabs). This is an article that brings U.S. readers up to date on what has been well known by the informed for a long time.

[78] Biden & Gelb, *supra* note 13, at A19.

criticism of the corporate approach is suggested by Horowitz's argument that the Constitution represents a "Kurdish agenda to which Shiites signed on",[79] that is, its provisions for decentralization reflect primarily Kurdish preferences. Indeed, it would be unfair if all of Iraq was decentralized to the extent sought by the Kurds for Kurdistan, just as it would be unfair if all of the U.K. was decentralized to the extent sought by the Scots for Scotland, or Canada's federal government was weakened throughout the country just because the Québécois sought a weak federal presence in Quebec.

However, Iraq's Constitution actually eschews both the one-size-fits-all preference of the integrationists and the inclination of the three-regions advocates, in favor of a bespoke, flexible, or voluntarily asymmetrical federation tailored to whatever (legitimate) preferences exist, or come to exist, among Iraq's democratic constituencies. In this respect, the Constitution takes a liberal consociational approach that is focused on democratic preferences rather than on predetermined ethnic or communal categories. At least four parts of the Constitution are relevant here.

First, while the Constitution allows governorates to become regions, which have more authority and power, it does not require them to do so. Nor is changing from a governorate into a region simply a decision to be made by the governorate's politicians, who arguably might have a vested interest in assuming more powers; for such a change to occur, article 119 requires a local referendum and leaves open the possibility of other hurdles to be decided later by Iraq's federal legislature.[80] Second, article 121 gives regional authorities the right to alter how federal legislation is applied within that region, if this legislation is outside the exclusive authority of the federal government.[81] This also means, conversely, that a region is free to accept federal legislation in areas of shared jurisdiction. Third, article 126 provides that any region, with the consent of its legislative assembly and the majority of its citizens in a referendum, may surrender some or all of its powers to the federal authorities by constitutional amendment.[82] Finally, while article 115 of the Constitution gives legal supremacy to regional (and governorate) governments in disputes with the federal government over shared powers, a governorate or region could decide to accept a federal intrusion rather than to dispute it.[83]

---

[79] Horowitz, *supra* note 42, at A20.
[80] IRAQ CONST. art. 119.
[81] *Id.* art. 121.
[82] *Id.* art. 126.
[83] *Id.* art 115. It may appear unthinkable that politicians would ever surrender jurisdictional responsibilities or miss the opportunity to acquire more, but there is evidence to the contrary from comparative experience. In Canada, only Quebec has opted to take up its own pension plan, and all other Canadian provinces have been happy with the federal plan. *See* An Act Respecting the Québec Pension Plan, R.S.Q. 1965 (1st sess.), c. 24, §10. There are many other examples, under Canada's practice of asymmetrical federalism, of Quebec being the only province to exercise a degree of autonomy that is available to all provinces.

There are, thus, several channels in the Constitution that permit any part of Iraq to defer to the government in Baghdad if it chooses. Governorates can retain their status as governorates rather than become regions; regions or governorates can accept federal legislation in areas of shared jurisdiction; and both can consent to the transfer of some of their constitutional powers to the federal government. Thus, governorates that are dominated by Shi'a Arab and Kurdish regionalists can have what they want, while those Shi'a Arab–or Sunni Arab–dominated governorates that want to be governed from Baghdad may also have their preferences met. Should all of Arab Iraq decide to be ruled centrally from Baghdad, that is quite possible under the constitutional order.[84] What is ruled out is the imposition of a centralized Iraq on a community that rejects it (the dirigiste, integrationist preference popular among Sunni Arabs cannot be imposed on the Kurds)[85] or the imposition of a weakened relationship with Baghdad on a community that rejects this (this option, as implied by the three-regions approach, cannot be imposed on Sunni Arabs). Moreover, the Constitution allows decisions regarding both decentralization and centralization to be taken now or later. Sunni Arab-dominated Iraq can choose centralization now and opt for more autonomy later, should it find that centralization means unacceptable intrusions from Shi'a-controlled security services or a Shi'a-Kurdish–dominated army. Such flexible asymmetry is desirable, and particularly so in contexts, as in Sunni Arab and Shi'a Arab parts of Iraq where, arguably, there has not been enough experience of democratic politics to test long-run preferences, and when it is not certain how a decentralized or centralized Iraq will evolve.[86]

One common and important integrationist objection to decentralization that allows regions to be dominated by particular communal or ethnic communities, is that such arrangements will contribute to the abuse of regional minorities. The liberal consociational response is twofold: first, minorities would also exist under the integrationists' preferred institutional arrangements, whether in a federation with internal boundaries organized on administrative or territorial principles, or in a unitary state. There is no compelling comparative evidence, particularly from Iraq or the surrounding region, that minorities are better protected in territorial federations or unitary states. Second, the abuse of regional minorities can and should be prevented through the promotion of liberal consociational principles

[84] This is one reason why Laith Kubba supports the Constitution. He believes it provides for a centralized Arab Iraq linked to a decentralized federacy of Kurdistan: Interview with Laith Kubba, Personal Advisor to former Prime Minister Ibrahim al-Ja'afari, at the "Iraq: Preventing another Generation of Conflict" conference, in Ottawa, Canada (May 11–12, 2006).

[85] Our point, here, is that each of Iraq's communities has the right to choose how it should be governed, but not the right to choose how others should be governed. The current preference of many Sunni Arabs is for all of Iraq, including Kurdistan and the Shi'a South, to be ruled from Baghdad. This is an illegitimate preference, as it would entail imposing centralization on communities that do not want it.

[86] Integrationists should like flexible arrangements for asymmetrical decentralization, as it seems suited to their view that identities, and associated political aspirations, are fluid.

at the regional level, and through the promotion of regional and federal bills of rights.

Iraq's Constitution offers some protection to regional minorities, but it is incomplete. The Constitution provides for a wide-ranging Bill of Rights with possible statewide effect, which, among other points, outlaws discrimination on the basis of ethnicity or religion.[87] Small minorities that are unlikely to be able to control governorates or regions, such as the Turkmen, Assyrians, and Armenians, have the right to educate their children in their mother tongue in "governmental educational institutions".[88] The Turkmen and Syriac languages are also given official status in the "administrative units in which they constitute density of population".[89] The Constitution, under the chapter heading "Local Administrations", guarantees "the administrative, political, cultural, and educational rights of the various nationalities, such as Turkomen, Chaldeans, Assyrians and all other constituents".[90]

These constitutional protections for local minorities are poorly or vaguely worded and should be detailed and strengthened, at least in the enabling legislation, if not in the Constitution itself, or in the constitutions of the relevant regions. As we shall see the likely weakness of the Supreme Court has implications for the likely strength of the federal bill of rights. Indeed, it will be particularly crucial, given the extensive provisions for decentralization in Iraq's Constitution, that local minorities are protected, not just in Iraq's Constitution but, most emphatically, within the regional constitutions. The promotion of the rights of regional minorities is an area where outsiders can help. Encouragement and incentives should be given to the governments of regions and governorates to incorporate generous provisions for their minorities, including Turkmen and Arabs in Kirkuk, and Kurds in Mosul, and numerous communities in Baghdad. Such protections should provide guarantees of local self-government where minorities are territorially concentrated, local-level power sharing in mixed areas, and institutions that provide for cultural autonomy, including school boards that are controlled by linguistic minorities.

3. Iraq's constitution and federal shared rule

The main debate concerning Iraq's political institutions has focused on the question of centralization versus decentralization. Neither integrationists nor those who prefer a corporate consociational approach have given as much attention to the institutional arrangements *within* the federal level of government. Yet a

---

[87] IRAQ CONST. art. 14.
[88] *Id.* art. 4.
[89] *Id.*
[90] *Id.* art. 125.

federation involves shared rule as well as self-rule, and how Iraq's different communities and regions share power within institutions at the federal level will determine, arguably, whether loyalty to the federation can be developed and if the state will survive intact.

When integrationists consider federal institutions, they usually insist that the federal government be "strong", possess "capacity", and be able to act "decisively". Makiya criticizes not just the Constitution's division of powers between the federal government and the regions, but also the separation of powers at the federal level between the president, prime minister, and legislature, which he sees as contributing to conflict and indecisiveness.[91] Others call for a "technocratic" government, that is, one that is professional, and isolated from sectarian passions and corruption. Before the Constitution's adoption, some suggested the need for a strong executive presidency on the American model, which would be capable of both stabilizing and unifying the state.[92] Other integrationists have criticized the proportional electoral system used in Iraq's federal elections for facilitating ethnic and communal fragmentation.[93] When considered along with their views on centralization, Iraq's integrationists appear to endorse a majoritarian federation—one that Alfred Stepan calls "demos-enabling", albeit one that is impartial among its different constituencies, that is, a federation that both concentrates power at, and within, the federal level of government.[94]

Corporate consociationalists, by contrast, favor federal institutions that share power proportionately among ascriptive, or predetermined, communities. This is the model implicit in Biden and Gelb's belief that Iraq has much to learn from the Dayton Accords.[95] The Dayton Accords not only divided Bosnia-Herzegovina into autonomous units, dominated by Bosniaks, Croats, and Serbs, respectively, but also created corporate consociational institutions within Bosnia-Herzegovina's federal government. The latter government is presided over by a rotating presidency based on one Bosniak and one Croat from the Federation of Bosnia-Herzegovina and one Serb from Republika Srpska.[96] The indirectly elected upper chamber of the federal legislature comprises five Bosniaks and five Croats from the Federation of Bosnia-Herzegovina and five Serbs from the National Assembly of Republika Srpska.

Again there are limits to both approaches. Because Iraq's current political leadership is overwhelmingly based on communal or ethnic groups, there is a danger that strong majoritarian institutions of the sort recommended by integrationists would exclude minorities, such as the Kurds, Sunni Arabs, and other smaller

---

[91] Makiya, *supra* note 7.

[92] Brancati, *supra* note 25, at 18.

[93] *See* Salamey & Pearson, *supra* note 26.

[94] For an explanation of "demos-enabling" federations, see Al C. Stepan, *Federalism and Democracy: Beyond the U.S. Model*, 10(4) J. DEMOCRACY 19 (1999).

[95] The Dayton Peace Accords on Bosnia, *supra* note 32; Biden & Gelb, *supra* note 13, at A19.

[96] BOSN. & HERZ. CONST. 1995, art. V.

minorities. Any attempt to prevent ethnically based majoritarianism by privileging "centrist" politicians—through elaborate electoral distributive requirements—would be unacceptable to the currently dominant political leadership and would, therefore, encounter a serious implementation problem. Also, it would not be as ethnically neutral as integrationists tend to assume, because very few Kurds, in particular, support either centrist or Iraq-wide parties.

Corporate consociational arrangements would be unfair and unstable in Iraq as well, but for different reasons. They would be unfair because they privilege certain ascriptive identities and exclude those who hold other group identities or no group identity. Thus, in the case of Bosnia-Herzegovina, citizens who were not Bosniak, Croat, or Serb—or who did not want to define themselves ethnically—were barred from the highest offices of the state. The original institutions also turned into second-class citizens the Serbs who lived in the Federation of Bosnia-Herzegovina, and the Bosniaks and Croats who lived in Republika Srpska, as they could not become members of the rotating presidency or win seats in its upper chamber.[97] Corporate consociational institutions are unstable, not just because they cause resentment among the excluded but because they are not flexible enough to accommodate demographic shifts even among the included.

This latter problem was particularly obvious in Lebanon, the experience of which is often cited to counsel against consociation in Iraq. Lebanon had corporate consociational features in its legislature, which, after 1943, awarded seats to Christians on a 6:5 ratio, regardless of their actual share of the population. By convention, the president is also a Christian. As it became increasingly clear that Christians were a declining minority, these privileged arrangements contributed to resentment among non-Christians, the Shi'a in particular, and also the Druze. The Ta'if Accord of 1989,[98] which accompanied the end of the Lebanese civil war, dealt with this problem rather unsatisfactorily; it failed to remove these corporate features from Lebanon's consociation, and simply reduced the Christians share to a still-inflated 50 percent, while downgrading the powers of the presidency.[99]

---

[97] These arrangements also work at cross-purposes with the international community's expressed aim of encouraging Bosnia-Herzegovina's ethnically cleansed to return home. *See also* text accompanying note 23.

[98] The Ta'if Accord, 1989, pt. II, § A(4) & pt. II, § B (Leb.).

[99] *See* Brendan O'Leary, *Foreword* to MICHAEL KERR, IMPOSING POWER-SHARING: CONFLICT AND COEXISTENCE IN NORTHERN IRELAND AND LEBANON *passim* (Irish Acad. Press 2006). Although critics of consociation everywhere cite the example of Lebanon to buttress their arguments, it is not at all clear that the Lebanese precedent supports their interpretation. Consociation maintained peace in Lebanon for most of the period between 1943 and the outbreak of civil war in 1975, and it is instructive that the Ta'if Accord went back to (modified) consociational arrangements. The weaknesses of Lebanon's consociation had something to do with its corporate features, but the civil war was largely a result of the destabilizing influence of the Israeli-Palestinian conflict, which produced a significant influx of Palestinian refugees, rather than consociation. Lebanon's current problems (as of June 2007) appear related to the same cause; arguably, what Lebanon needs is liberal consociation rather than no consociation.

Liberal consociation avoids the problems of both integration and corporate consociation. It circumvents the danger of majoritarian exclusion associated with integration by ensuring that federal institutions are more broadly based than what is required by majoritarian rules. It is based on elites who possess democratic mandates, rather than on centrists who lack them. Liberal consociation avoids, as well, the dangers of corporatism by accommodating leaders who are based on democratically mobilized parties, rather than ascriptive (ethnic or religious) communities. It avoids privileging certain "group" identities while remaining responsive to demographic shifts that register electorally. Liberal consociationalists value consensus and stability over decisiveness in divided societies because they believe that decisiveness without consensus can lead to disaster.

The provisions of Iraq's Constitution relating to shared rule have a liberal consociational flavor. Its federal executive is a hybrid presidential-parliamentary executive, although most executive authority is held by the Council of Ministers, headed by a prime minister. During the transitional period, there is a three-person Presidential Council, with a president and two vice presidents, elected by a two-thirds majority in the Council of Representatives.[100] This weighted majority has the effect of making it likely that the Presidential Council will be broadly representative, though it does not require that any member of the Presidential Council come from a particular ethnic or religious group. The Presidential Council then charges the nominee of the largest party in the Council of Representatives with forming the Council of Ministers, which must be approved by majority vote.[101] Although this rule suggests a majoritarian cabinet,[102] the fact that the prime minister cannot be appointed until the Presidential Council is elected means that any party or parties with more than one-third of the votes in the Council of Representatives have leverage in the negotiations that lead to cabinet composition. The clout of smaller parties is also helped by the fact that certain types of legislation require weighted majorities. Hence, if a government is to pursue successfully its entire legislative agenda, it will have to be more broadly representative than the majoritarian rule that applies to the cabinet's composition would suggest.

Other features of Iraq's political system point in the same direction. Its proportional representation–party list electoral system makes it unlikely that there can be a one-party government, or that a majority in the legislature (Council of Representatives) can be artificially constructed from a plurality in the electorate, as happens in countries with plurality electoral systems, including the United States, Canada, and the U.K., or with double-ballot majoritarian systems such

---

[100] IRAQ CONST. art. 138.

[101] *Id.* art. 76.

[102] The majoritarian decision-making rule for cabinet composition does not represent the triumph of integrationist principles of nonpartisanship. Rather, it reflects the preference of the Shi'a majority for an executive that it could control.

as those in operation in France.[103] Proportional representation is criticized by integrationists in Iraq for promoting national fragmentation.[104] However, insofar as it provides for the fair democratic expression of whatever constituencies exist in a state, it may be considered more conducive to fairness, stability, and democratic inclusiveness.[105] Ironically, proportional representation is far more likely to facilitate the election of non-sectarian (secular) political parties in Iraq's current circumstances than the rival plurality or majoritarian electoral systems associated with integration. It is also more likely to promote intraethnic or intrareligious group divisions through party fragmentation, another integrationist goal.

The likelihood that the federal government will want to enjoy reasonable relations with the regions, given the number of shared jurisdictional responsibilities and the fact that there is regional paramountcy in cases of dispute, also creates incentives for an executive that is responsive to different regional constituencies. The effect of these various institutional provisions is apparent already. The Presidential Council is currently made up of a Kurdish president, and Sunni and Shi'a Arab vice presidents. The prime minister is a Shi'a Arab, while his two deputies are Kurdish and Sunni Arab. The cabinet roughly reflects the country's diversity.[106] A "decisive" majoritarian executive of the sort advocated by some integrationists would not as easily permit this sharing of the spoils, and in our view would be more divisive than decisive.

Indeed, if Iraq's executive arrangements are problematic, it may be because they are insufficiently consociational. They do not, after all, offer guarantees of inclusiveness, as many consociational systems do, including those in Belgium, Bosnia-Herzegovina, and Northern Ireland.[107] Iraq's Constitution allows for the possibility of a federal cabinet drawn entirely from its Arab majority, or even its

---

[103] The electoral system is not a part of the Iraqi Constitution, but the Constitution stipulates that any election should provide for the "representation of all components of the Iraqi people", which suggests a proportional representation system, as does the provision mandating that at least one in four Iraqi assembly members must be women—which obliges a proportional representation system because single-gender districts or constituencies would violate the constitutional mandate for equality between the sexes. IRAQ CONST. art. 49. Any electoral system that is not based on proportional representation, such as the single-member plurality or alternative-vote systems that are favored by integrationists, would have the effect of under-representing minorities, particularly small minorities, and could be subject to court challenges.

[104] Salamey & Pearson, *supra* note 26.

[105] *See* O'Leary, *supra* note 19.

[106] The cabinet's thirty-six members include nineteen Shi'a Arabs, eight Sunni Arabs, eight Kurds, and one Christian.

[107] BELG. CONST. art. 99 (guaranteeing that there be as many French-speaking members as Dutch-speaking members in the Council of Ministers, with the possible exception of the prime minister); BOSN. & HERZ. CONST. 1995, art. V.1(a) (providing that the presidency be comprised of one Croat and one Bosniak, each elected from the territory of the Federation of Bosnia-Herzegovina, and one Serb, elected from the territory of Republika Srpska); Northern Ireland Act, 1998, §§16–18 (Guaranteeing ministerial representation to members of all significant parties in the legislature that wish to avail of the opportunity to join the cabinet, and guaranteeing that the first and deputy first ministerships be shared between representatives of the nationalist and unionist communities).

Shi'a majority.[108] This possibility is arguably more likely after the four-year transitional period, when the Presidential Council is to be replaced by a single-person presidency, which can be established by a simple majority vote in the assembly if two-thirds support is not available.[109] This means both that the presidency will no longer be able roughly to mirror Iraq's diversity, as it will consist of one person rather than three, and that the legislative threshold necessary to start executive formation will be lowered.[110] These arrangements are consistent with a recent argument in the academic literature that while special antimajoritarian devices may be called for during transitional periods, they are both unnecessary and undesirable afterward.[111] But one cannot know in advance when Iraq will have made the transition to a stable polity, and, at this point, four years to stability seems like a very optimistic projection. Extending the existing arrangements would, in our view, be a wise amendment to the Constitution.

There are other executive models that Iraqis might have considered, or might still consider. One of these, as just suggested, is to retain the three-person Presidential Council, as well as the two-thirds rule required for its establishment, beyond the transitional period. This would be a relatively easy change. More radically, and less likely, Iraqis could opt for a more powerful, and possibly larger, executive Presidency Council, which would replace the current hybrid presidential-parliamentary executive, and, instead, draw its membership from the different *regions* of the country. This was the model that operated in Yugoslavia under Tito, and it was the attempt by Serbia to take over Yugoslavia's collective presidency (the Federal Council) that helped to foment the country's breakup. It was not the existence of a collective presidency per se that broke Yugoslavia apart, as an integrationist might argue, but the fact that it became unrepresentative of Yugoslavia's diversity. Switzerland, the world's longest-running federation to have avoided civil conflict and war since its formation, also has a representative (seven-person) presidential council.

Another option would be a fully inclusive parliamentary executive that is automatically drawn from the legislature by a mechanical rule, such as d'Hondt.[112] Under this model, all significant parties in the legislature would be entitled to a proportional share of seats in the cabinet. One advantage of d'Hondt, in addition to guaranteeing an inclusive executive, is that it would have avoided

---

[108] IRAQ CONST. art. 76.

[109] *Id.* art. 70.

[110] The two deputy premierships also disappear after the transitional period.

[111] Donald Rothchild, *Reassuring Weaker Parties after Civil Wars: The Benefits and Costs of Executive Power-Sharing Systems in Africa*, 4 ETHNOPOL. 247 (2005); IAN O'FLYNN & DAVID RUSSELL, POWER-SHARING: NEW CHALLENGES FOR DIVIDED SOCIETIES (Pluto Press 2005).

[112] Invented in 1878 by Belgian mathematician and lawyer Victor d'Hondt, the d'Hondt method is a highest-averages formula for allocating seats in party-list proportional representation. *See* Brendan O'Leary, Bernard Grofman & Jorgen Elklit, *Divisor Methods for Sequential Portfolio Allocation in Multi-Party Executive Bodies: Evidence from Northern Ireland and Denmark*, 49 AM. J. POL. SCI. 198. (2005).

the political squabbling over executive formation that led, in early 2006, to a three-month delay in the establishment of Iraq's government. D'Hondt would also create obstacles to a dominant party's monopolizing a number of strategic portfolios. This is because it ensures that medium-sized parties will be able to pick particular cabinet portfolios irrespective of the preferences of the largest party.[113] This feature would help to deal with Sunni Arab concerns about both the key Interior and Defense ministries falling into the hands of the United Iraqi Alliance.[114] Neither Iraq's current arrangements for appointing its federal executive nor the changes suggested here privilege particular identity groups. These arrangements are open, in principle, to ministers from any such groups and those identified with no group, and are more likely in practice—in contemporary Iraq—to reward secular parties than the majoritarian alternatives promoted by integrationists. The existing provisions are therefore not subject to some of the most serious and common charges that are leveled against consociational arrangements.

Another complementary way to protect Iraq's minorities would be to ensure the proper design of two important federal institutions that are named in the Constitution but not yet established: the Federation Council and the Supreme Court.[115] Both institutions typically perform in federations what Al Stepan has described as a "demos-constraining" function, that is, they prevent the state's federal demos, or dominant community, from riding roughshod over its various demoi.[116]

A Federation Council, or federal second chamber, performs just such a function because it is based typically on regional rather than popular representation, and because it has antimajoritarian decision-making rules, at least for some purposes. One way for Iraq to proceed would be to allow the Federation Council to be appointed by the regional (or governorate) governments or even, as in Germany, to consist of members of those governments. This would both give the regions a stake in the center and help make the Federation Council the locus for negotiations among the regional governments and between the regional governments and the center. There is no other mechanism for intergovernmental relations in the current Constitution and, if the Federation Council does not perform this role, some other institution will have to do so. The Federation Council, in addition to possessing a role in passing legislation and constitutional amendments, could be given some voice in appointments to federal institutions, including the Supreme Court.

---

[113] *Id.*

[114] The d'Hondt method would have to be supplemented by a rule that prevents opportunistic party fragmentation aimed at seizing key portfolios.

[115] The Federation Council is referred to in IRAQ CONST. art. 62, whereas the Supreme Court is referred to in arts. 92–94.

[116] Stepan, *supra* note 94.

The Supreme Court is given three functions that may make it a pivotal institution for protecting Iraq's diverse communities and individuals.[117] First, it is tasked with "interpreting the provisions of the constitution", including its various minority-protection provisions. Second, it will umpire disputes between the government of the federal demos and those of the regional demoi. Third, it is responsible for "overseeing the constitutionality of laws and regulations",[118] that is, it will decide if legislation of the federal and regional legislatures complies with the Constitution's rights-protection clauses. The rules governing the court's operations and rules of appointment have yet to be decided, though the rules will require legislation with the support of two-thirds of the representatives in Iraq's National Assembly. It is exceptionally unlikely that Kurdistan will allow the Supreme Court to have strong powers or permit an integrationist approach to its composition.

The best liberal consociational approach to Supreme Court appointments is to ensure that they are regionally (not ethnically) representative, and that the appointment power is spread across the state's constituencies. One way to proceed here would be to adopt one Canadian practice while rejecting another. The practice to emulate is that part of Canada's Supreme Court Act stipulating that three of its nine Supreme Court justices come from Quebec.[119] In Iraq, it would make sense for one quarter of Iraq's top court to come from Kurdistan and the rest to come, proportionately, from other regions, with perhaps one fifth coming from the four Sunni Arab-dominated or plurality governorates. (After the unification of Kirkuk and the disputed territories with the existing and officially recognized Kurdistan Region, the total population of the region is likely to comprise at least one fifth of Iraq's population, especially as the region is at present the favored internal destination of displaced people.) The practice to avoid is Canada's unusual tradition of concentrating the appointment power in the hands of the federal government, which is tantamount to allowing one side to a conflict to pick the referee. The alternative is to give the Federation Council input into Supreme Court appointments or, failing that, the regional governments directly.

4. Conclusion

What lessons can be derived from Iraq's experience for other seriously divided polities, such as Sri Lanka or Sudan, that have yet to undergo a transition from autocracy to democracy or from war to peace? First, and obviously, transitions

[117] IRAQ CONST. art. 93; it is our view, shared by Peter Galbraith (GALBRAITH, *supra* note 14), that, because the federal Bill of Rights is not specified as an exclusive competence of the federal Supreme Court, legal supremacy over the Bill of Rights belongs to any established region. Consequently, it is to regional constitutions that we must look—where regions are established—for the best protections of minorities.
[118] IRAQ CONST. art. 90.
[119] Supreme Court Act, R.S.C., ch. S-19, § 6 (1985).

are extremely difficult and may fail as a result of civil war, spoilers, and external interventions. Second, Iraq's recent politics suggest that it is very unlikely that victims of state policies of ethnocentrism, discrimination, ethnic expulsion, and genocide will accept the integrationist model championed by well-meaning liberals. Large, territorially concentrated minorities like the Kurds are much more likely to prefer independence to any form of integrationist inclusion in a state that has abused them. Their situation is roughly analogous to those of Sri Lanka's Tamils, Cyprus's Turkish-Cypriots, and Sudan's southern (Black, Christian, and animist) communities.

Third, dominant, or formerly dominant, communities, like Iraq's Sunni Arabs, are much more likely to embrace an integrated and centralized state. However, this is not generally because they have been converted to the values of civic impartiality but, rather, because of their nostalgia for how such a state promoted their community's interests in the past, and their hope that it will do so again in the future.[120] Formerly dominated communities normally—and accurately—interpret the support of dominant groups for integration in the same way, which, of course, steels their resolve to resist it. It is usually only small or dispersed minorities, like Iraq's Turkmen or Assyrians, who are likely to champion the idea of an integrated and impartial state, because their numbers or territorial concentration make it difficult for them to aspire to accommodation strategies, and because the alternative to impartial integration is the one-sided ethnocentric variety.

Fourth, the way forward in such situations, if state reconstruction rather than destruction is the priority, usually lies in splitting the difference between the options of secession and integration. Settling for their respective second preferences will point community decision makers toward consociational and federal arrangements, provided they have abandoned the goal of domination. We have argued in this chapter that progress in Iraq requires the maintenance—and extension—of the principles of liberal consociation already present in Iraq's federation: executive power sharing, proportionality throughout the public sector, community self-government, and veto rights over constitutional amendments. So long as one community cannot impose its will on the others, the foregoing principles are the only ones likely to win all-around support, though this realization may take time. This is as likely to be as true for Sri Lanka, Sudan, and Cyprus, as it is for Iraq.

Fifth, constitutions, even fair ones, like Iraq's 2005 Constitution, cannot guarantee peace. In fact, Iraq's Constitution coexists with multiple insurgencies that threaten to tear the country apart. Peace requires not just a balanced constitutional order but a disposition on the part of all sizable communities to accept

---

[120] Formerly dominated communities in severely divided polities may embrace integration for ethnocentric purposes if they come to see themselves as potentially dominant. This is how we understand Moqtada al-Sadr's support for a centralized Iraq.

compromise. For this to happen, all sides must perceive that there is, as William Zartman has put it, a "hurting stalemate".[121] The key problem within Iraq is that important elements within the Sunni Arab community remain wedded to a vision of the past in which it was hegemonic. Ironically, calls from Western governments and academics for an integrated, centralized Iraq, one that has no chance of winning significant support among Kurds and Shia Arabs, who represent approximately 80 percent of Iraq's population, sustain such wishful thinking and stand in the way of an inclusive, effective, and stable settlement.

[121] I. William Zartman, *The Timing of Peace Initiatives: Hurting Stalemates and Ripe Moments*, 1 GLOBAL REV. ETHNOPOL. 8 (2001).

13

Consociation and its critics:
Northern Ireland after the Belfast Agreement

John McGarry* and Brendan O'Leary**

1. Introduction

Divided polities everywhere are faced with the two broad democratic choices outlined in this volume. They may choose integration, which involves the construction of a single public identity through the promotion of individual rights; social mixing in schools, residential neighborhoods, and workplaces; and political institutions that favor political appeals across ethnic communities.[1] Integration comes in different varieties, depending on whether it is informed by republicanism, liberalism, or socialism.

Alternatively, they may choose accommodation, that is, the acceptance of dual or multiple public identities. Accommodation includes four distinct strategies, some of which can be combined, namely: *centripetalism*, which involves the construction of a power-sharing coalition among moderates from different ethnic communities; *consociation,* which enlists all sizable communities in executive institutions, promotes proportionality throughout public administration, grants communities autonomy in their own affairs, and, in rigid consociations, builds minority vetoes into the constitution or lawmaking; *credible multiculturalism,* with proportional representation of groups in common institutions and self-government in their own cultural affairs; and *territorial pluralism,* where distinct communities enjoy territorial self-government and power sharing in a federal or union government.[2]

* Professor of Political Studies; Canada Research Chair in Nationalism and Democracy, Queens University. McGarry would like to thank the Carnegie Corporation of New York and Social Science and Humanities Research Council of Canada for research funding. Email: mcgarryj@post.queensu.ca

** Lauder Professor of Political Science; director of the Penn Program in Ethnic Conflict, University of Pennsylvania. O'Leary would like to thank the Lauder endowment and the Social Sciences and Research Council of Canada for aiding his research. Email: boleary@sas.upenn.edu

[1] For examples of integrationist thinking, see BRIAN BARRY, CULTURE AND EQUALITY: AN EGALITARIAN CRITIQUE OF MULTICULTURALISM (Polity Press 2000); PAUL BRASS, ETHNICITY AND NATIONALISM: THEORY AND COMPARISON (Sage 1991).

[2] The main varieties of integration and accommodation are explained at greater length in John McGarry, Brendan O'Leary & Richard Simeon, *Integration or Accommodation? The Enduring Debate in Conflict Regulation* (in this volume).

Integrationists and accommodationists have rival views of the social roots of conflict. Integrationists insist that identities are malleable, fluid, soft, or transformable, whereas consociationalists think that—in certain contexts—they may be inflexible, resilient, durable, and hard. From the accommodationist perspective, political prudence and morality requires considering the special interests, needs, and fears of groups so that they regard the state as fit for them. On the other hand, integration is the preferred approach of most democratic states and international organizations. It is favored by dominant communities within states, and by small, dispersed minorities that cannot aspire to a state of their own. Integration is, arguably, the dominant approach among academics who study ethnic and religious conflict. Accommodating groups through consociation and its related strategies is less popular with most states than integration, and, arguably, less popular in the academy, though it is often the preference of minorities, particularly sizable minorities.

The debate between the advocates of these two rival choices has played a central role in political and academic discourse in Northern Ireland. However, academic debate in Northern Ireland has also focused importantly on the respective merits and demerits of two forms of accommodation, namely, consociationalism and centripetalism. Indeed this latter controversy dominates the academic literature to "such an extent that it can rarely be avoided by students of Northern Irish politics".[3] The importance of these debates is intricately connected to the fact that, since 10 April, 1998, Northern Ireland has had a squarely consociational agreement (the Belfast Agreement).[4] Defenses and criticisms of the agreement are usually seen through either consociationalist or integrationist and centripetalist lenses, respectively, though we—as participants in the debate—would also emphasize the agreement's territorial pluralist dimensions.[5]

We have identified at least three varieties of integrationist critics of the agreement, who may be irritated mightily in being classed with the others as sharing the same normative orientation.

Republicans (Irish civic nationalists)

Republican "rejectionists" include Republican Sinn Féin, the 32 County Sovereignty Movement, and their respective military wings, the Continuity and Real IRAs. Republicans include a number of academics and intellectuals.[6]

---

[3] Aaron Edwards, *Interpreting the Conflict in Northern Ireland*, 6 ETHNOPOLITICS 139 (2007).

[4] Agreement Reached in the Multi-party Negotiations, Ir.-N. Ir.-Brit., Apr. 10, 1998, Cm. 3883, *available at* <http://www.nio.gov.uk/agreement.pdf> [hereinafter Belfast Agreement]. For more details on the consensus that the agreement is squarely consociational, see John McGarry & Brendan O'Leary, *Power-Shared after Deaths of Thousands*, in NORTHERN IRELAND PROBLEM, CONSOCIATIONAL SOLUTION?: MCGARRY-O'LEARY AND THEIR CRITICS (forthcoming 2008).

[5] JOHN MCGARRY & BRENDAN O'LEARY, THE NORTHERN IRELAND CONFLICT: CONSOCIATIONAL ENGAGEMENTS 272–279 (Oxford Univ. Press 2004).

[6] Exponents and critics can be found in THE REPUBLICAN IDEAL: CURRENT PERSPECTIVES (Norman Porter ed., Blackstaff Press 1998).

Republican rejectionists argue that unionists have a soft political identity, maintained by the presence of the British state in Ireland. They regard the agreement as profoundly counterproductive; it entrenches British rule in Ireland and supports the view that Ireland is divided between two sectarian communities. Rejecting the agreement is seen as the way forward, followed by the withdrawal of the British state from Northern Ireland, and the incorporation of all of its citizens into a thirty-two-county Irish republic. Some republican rejectionists support the use of force to achieve their ends.

Civic unionists (British civic nationalists)

"Unionist rejectionists", including those in the United Kingdom Unionist Party (UKUP) and the short-lived Northern Ireland Unionist Party (NIUP), maintain that most of Northern Ireland's Catholics would be happy to be citizens of the United Kingdom, provided their individual rights and culture were protected. In some accounts, so long as it was clear that a united Ireland was not a realistic alternative then Catholics would reconcile themselves to the Union.[7] Integration with Great Britain is regarded as the correct political goal, rather than the new institutions in the agreement that encourage Catholics to look to Dublin—and allegedly threaten the British civil liberties of all Northern Ireland's citizens. Strong unionist integrationists reject substantive devolution of any sort, with or without power sharing. Any territorial self-government should be minimalist, on the model of London or in Wales.

Postnational transformers

A third perspective, popular with the academic left and represented in small parties from outside the ethnonational blocs, including the Alliance, Democratic Left, the Labour Party, and the Northern Ireland Women's Coalition, emphasizes the need for Northern Ireland's "society" to be transformed from the bottom up. "Transformers" typically blame regional divisions on social segregation, economic inequality, and ethnocentric appeals by elites in both communities. They argue that the elite-negotiated agreement has focused politics on divisive constitutional questions, which has obscured crosscutting issues, such as those based on class. Transformers call for policies to promote social integration,[8] increased public spending to tackle the "material basis" of sectarian identities,[9] and for support to be given to (progressive) civil society organizations prepared

[7] Dennis Kennedy, *Dash for Agreement: Temporary Accommodation or Lasting Settlement?*, 22 FORDHAM INT'L L.J. 1440 (1999).
[8] PETER SHIRLOW & BRENDAN MURTAGH, BELFAST: SEGREGATION, VIOLENCE AND THE CITY (Pluto Press 2006).
[9] Rupert Taylor, *A Consociational Path to Peace in Northern Ireland and South Africa?*, in NEW PERSPECTIVES ON THE NORTHERN IRELAND CONFLICT 171 (Adrian Guelke ed., Aldershot 1994).

to challenge sectarian elites.[10] Among transformers, we include the exponents of emancipation, such as emancipation from existing conflicting identities.[11]

The expression "centripetalism" was coined by Andrew Reynolds and Benjamin Reilly to characterize the outlook of the American political scientist Donald L. Horowitz, who favors shaping and reshaping political institutions so that they converge on those with moderate preferences, whence centripetalism.[12] Horowitz has applied his ideas to Northern Ireland,[13] where they have attracted admiration from some local academics.[14] Horowitz and his local endorsers argue that Northern Ireland's political institutions should be redesigned to encourage power sharing among moderates from each community. They dislike party-list proportional representation and the single transferable vote system of proportional representation in six-member districts, which are said to damage the prospects for interethnic cooperation because the relatively low quota required for winning seats makes it too easy for hardline parties and their candidates to be successful.[15] They advocate the "alternative vote", which involves preferential voting—like the single transferable vote—but requires each winning candidate to win majority support in single-member districts. They believe the alternative vote can encourage politicians to "vote pool" to build an inter or transethnic majority. The alternative vote, it is argued, can provide the underpinnings for a coalition of moderates, which is thought to be more stable than the inclusive coalition proposed by consociationalists.

Consociational theory is most closely associated with the work of the distinguished Dutch and American political scientist, Arend Lijphart.[16] It was first applied to Northern Ireland by Lijphart himself, in the *British Journal of Political Science*.[17] But, as he has often observed, practice does not require theory.

---

[10] Rupert Taylor, *Consociation or Social Transformation?*, in NORTHERN IRELAND AND THE DIVIDED WORLD: POST-AGREEMENT NORTHERN IRELAND IN COMPARATIVE PERSPECTIVE 37, 47 (John McGarry ed., Oxford Univ. Press 2001).
[11] JOSEPH RUANE & JENNIFER TODD, THE DYNAMICS OF CONFLICT IN NORTHERN IRELAND: POWER, CONFLICT AND EMANCIPATION ch. 11 (Cambridge Univ. Press 1996).
[12] BEN REILLY & ANDREW REYNOLDS, ELECTORAL SYSTEMS AND CONFLICT IN DIVIDED SOCIETIES (Nat'l Acad. Press 1999).
[13] Donald L. Horowitz, *Explaining the Northern Ireland Agreement: The Sources of an Unlikely Constitutional Consensus*, 32 BRIT. J. POL. SCI. 193 (2002); Donald Horowitz, *The Agreement: Clear, Consociational and Risky*, in NORTHERN IRELAND AND THE DIVIDED WORLD, *supra* note 10, at 89 [hereinafter Horowitz, *The Agreement*].
[14] Rick Wilford & Robin Wilson, *From the Belfast Agreement to Stable Power-sharing*, 13–14 (paper presented at the PSA Territorial Pol. Conference, Queen's Univ., Belfast, Jan. 2006); Ian O'Flynn, *The Problem of Recognising Individual and National Identities: A Liberal Critique of the Belfast Agreement*, 6 CRITICAL REV. INT'L SOC. & POL. PHIL. 129 (2003).
[15] Horowitz, *The Agreement, supra* note 13, at 99.
[16] *See, e.g.,* AREND LIJPHART, THE POLITICS OF ACCOMMODATION: PLURALISM AND DEMOCRACY IN THE NETHERLANDS (Univ. Cal. Press 1968); AREND LIJPHART, DEMOCRACY IN PLURAL SOCIETIES: A COMPARATIVE EXPLORATION (Yale Univ. Press 1977)
[17] Arend Lijphart, *Review Article: The Northern Ireland Problem: Cases, Theories, and Solutions*, 5 BRIT. J. POL. SCI. 83 (1975).

Consociational principles were already evident in the ill-fated Sunningdale Agreement of 1973–74. They were tacitly at work in the British and Irish governments' approach to Northern Ireland between 1972 and 1975, and particularly since 1985. They were present in the negotiations led by the Ulster Unionist Party (UUP) and Social Democratic and Labour Party (SDLP) that produced Strand One of the Belfast Agreement, and present in the subsequent negotiations between the Democratic Unionist Party (DUP) and Sinn Féin that led to a resumption of power sharing in May of 2007. Consociation has its supporters among academics who specialize on Northern Ireland, including those who work in law, political philosophy, and comparative politics.[18] Consociational theory has helped us craft our joint and individual writings.[19]

Below we use the Belfast Agreement to reflect on consociational theory. The first section engages critically but constructively with consociational theory and shows how Northern Ireland's experience can contribute to consociation's "progressive research program", to use Imre Lakatos's expression.[20] Then we evaluate the debate between consociationalists and their integrationist and centripetalist critics with respect to the fundamental criteria of stability, democracy, and fairness. We argue that critics of consociation can learn from Northern Ireland's experience, though this may reflect the triumph of hope over experience on our part. We maintain that consociational theory provides the most sensible basis for understanding and prescribing for Northern Ireland and many other—though not all—sites of ethnonational and communal conflict.

2. Consociational theory and Northern Ireland's Belfast Agreement

The simple achievement of the Belfast Agreement invalidates one important criticism of consociation: that it is unachievable in deeply divided societies and apt only for societies with moderate divisions.[21] But the Northern Irish experience also highlights some weaknesses in classical consociational theory.

---

[18] Colin Harvey, *Human rights and the Good Friday Agreement*, FORTNIGHT, July/Aug. 2003; Colin Harvey, *Implement the Agreement*, FORTNIGHT, Feb. 2005; Shane O'Neill, *Mutual Recognition and the Accommodation of National Diversity: Constitutional Justice in Northern Ireland*, *in* MULTINATIONAL DEMOCRACIES 222 (Alain Gagnon & James Tully eds., Cambridge Univ. Press 2001); Stefan Wolff, *Introduction: From Sunningdale to Belfast, 1973–98*, *in* PEACE AT LAST? THE IMPACT OF THE GOOD FRIDAY AGREEMENT ON NORTHERN IRELAND 1 (Jörg Neuheiser & Stefan Wolff eds., Berghahn 2002); MICHAEL KERR, IMPOSING POWER-SHARING: CONFLICT AND COEXISTENCE IN NORTHERN IRELAND AND LEBANON (Irish Acad. Press 2005).

[19] See our writings on Irish politics, listed at McGARRY & O'LEARY, *supra* note 5, at 404.

[20] IMRE LAKATOS, THE METHODOLOGY OF SCIENTIFIC RESEARCH PROGRAMMES (Cambridge Univ. Press 1978).

[21] DONALD L. HOROWITZ, ETHNIC GROUPS IN CONFLICT 572–573 (Univ. Cal. Press 1985).

2.1 The neglected treatment of self-determination disputes

Traditional consociational theory developed from a concern with religious and class divisions in a number of European countries—the Netherlands, Belgium, Austria, and Switzerland.[22] It neglected self-determination disputes that involve ethnonational communities in contested homelands. The emphasis in traditional consociational theory is on *who* should exercise power at the level of the central government. However, self-determination disputes are often about the legitimacy of the central government itself—about *how much* power should be exercised by the central government (autonomy disputes), and about whether there should be one or more central governments (independence disputes). Though autonomy is an important value in consociational arrangements, the emphasis is often on corporate autonomy rather than the territorial autonomy insisted upon as a minimum desideratum by most self-determination movements. Consociational theory, at least in its early modern forms, like other theories of conflict regulation, particularly integrationist theories, provided institutional prescriptions that assumed the integrity of a state's territory.[23] It was "internalist". Yet self-determination disputes may involve national communities bisected or multisected by state borders. Here the partitioned fractions of the nation may seek links, including political institutional links, with their conationals across state borders.

That he was overlooking the specificities of self-determination disputes was evident in Lijphart's otherwise masterly analysis of the Northern Ireland conflict.[24] With his background in the Catholic and Protestant divisions of the Netherlands, Lijphart initially underappreciated the fact that Northern Ireland's conflict was based squarely on rival national movements. He saw the two groups in conflict as "Catholics" and "Protestants", and the primary cleavage as "religious", even though he was fully aware that the groups gave virtually all of their support to "nationalist" and "unionist" parties, respectively. He argued that the key difficulty was the absence of support for power sharing among Protestants, first, because they were capable of exercising hegemonic power alone, and, second, because they were predisposed to Westminster majoritarian practices rather than continental power-sharing norms.[25]

This analysis was accurate but limited. Northern Ireland's Catholics, as Irish nationalists, were opposed to mere internal power sharing within the United Kingdom. Radical Irish nationalists (republicans) wanted a complete withdrawal of the British state from Ireland, whereas moderate nationalists wanted the consociation to be internationalized, in other words, for the power-sharing

---

[22] LIJPHART, DEMOCRACY IN PLURAL SOCIETIES, *supra* note 16, at 143–145.

[23] Much of Lijphart's focus has been on consociational arrangements at the level of the state as a whole.

[24] Lijphart, *supra* note 17; LIJPHART, DEMOCRACY IN PLURAL SOCIETIES, *supra* note 16, at 134–141.

[25] Lijphart, *supra* note 17, at 100.

arrangements to have an all-Ireland dimension and a role for the Irish government. Even if unionists had solidly supported a consociation in the 1970s, it would have been insufficient for Irish nationalists. Indeed, a key reason why unionists opposed consociation was because they were British nationalists, profoundly concerned about Irish nationalists' insistence on links with Ireland. They also had no incentive to share power for most of the period after 1972, since the default option was direct rule from Great Britain, their preferred nation-state.

These facts explain why no consociational settlement was reached in Northern Ireland before 1998. An early attempt at a consociational agreement in 1974 collapsed after just five months because it was attacked by both Irish republican and British unionist hardliners. The former thought that it did not go far enough toward establishing Irish self-determination. The latter feared that it undermined the Union with Great Britain and portended a united Ireland. Subsequent initiatives between 1974 and 1998 failed, again, because they could not achieve agreement on both sides or on either side. Any feasible agreement had to deal squarely with the disputes that had flowed from the inequitable legacies of the partition of Ireland in 1920, which had occurred without any formal respect for Irish self-determination.

Three parts of the 1998 Belfast Agreement are relevant here, and all depart from traditional consociational accords.

The North-South Ministerial Council and the British-Irish governmental conference

The moderate nationalists in the Social Democratic and Labour Party (the SDLP) signed because the agreement provides for a number of political institutions that joined both parts of Ireland and maintains an oversight role for the republic's government. Without such an Irish dimension there would have been no agreement. The most important all-island institution is the North-South Ministerial Council (NSMC), a body nominated by Ireland's government and the new Northern Ireland premiers.[26] It meets in plenary at least twice a year, and in smaller groups to discuss specific sectors (such as agriculture or education) on a regular and frequent basis. In addition, the agreement provides for cross-border or all-island "implementation" bodies. Six in number, they cooperate regarding inland waterways, food safety, trade and business development, special EU programs, the Irish language and Ulster Scots, and aquaculture and marine matters. A further six functional areas of cooperation were established including some aspects of transport, agriculture, education, health, the environment, and tourism. The British-Irish intergovernmental conference (B-IGC), the successor to the Intergovernmental Conference established under the Anglo-Irish Agreement of 1985,[27] guarantees Ireland's government access to policy formulation on

[26] Belfast Agreement, strand two.
[27] *Id.* strand three, British-Irish Intergovernmental Conference.

all matters not or not yet devolved to the Northern Ireland Assembly or to the NSMC. In the event of the collapse of the Belfast Agreement, this institution resumes the more encompassing role its predecessor had under the Anglo-Irish Agreement. Meanwhile, it promotes bilateral cooperation between the Irish and British governments on all matters of mutual interest within their respective jurisdictions.

Recognition of Irish self-determination

Irish republicans would not have approved the agreement had the U.K. government not recognized, in a treaty, the right of the people of Ireland, meaning the whole island, to exercise their right to self-determination, albeit conjointly and severally as "North" and "South", to bring about a united Ireland if that was their wish.[28] The referendums and the British-Irish Agreement (the treaty incorporating the Belfast Agreement)[29] make the partition of Ireland—and its continuation—and the agreement and its institutions dependent upon the expressed will of the people of Ireland. The consociation established by the agreement is the first that has been endorsed in referendums that required concurrent consent in jurisdictions in different states.

Recognition of the principle of consent and the British-Irish Council

Unionists, who were ambivalent about the agreement, were persuaded to ratify it because it entrenched the principle of consent. That is, Northern Ireland cannot constitutionally become part of a unified Ireland unless a majority in Northern Ireland agrees in a referendum.[30] Ireland's Constitution was changed, after a referendum in both jurisdictions, to reflect this principle. Unionists also secured a new east-west institution, the British-Irish Council (BIC), to reflect their link with Great Britain.[31]

In addition to these three distinct sets of institutions and rules for institutional change, other key provisions in the Belfast Agreement, or those which flowed from it, mark it as a settlement between national communities. Ministers in the power-sharing executive have to take a "Pledge of Office", not an "Oath of Allegiance".[32] This cements the binationalism at the heart of the agreement: nationalist ministers do not have to swear an oath of allegiance to the Crown—or the Union. As a result of the agreement and the implementation of the recommendations of the Independent Commission on Policing (the Patten Commission) established under the agreement, the name of the police has been changed from

[28] Belfast Agreement, Constitutional Issues, paras. 1(ii) & 2.
[29] Agreement between the Government of the United Kingdom of Great Britain and Northern Ireland and the Government of Ireland, Ir.-N. Ir.-Brit., Apr. 10, 1998, Cm. 4292 (available in Belfast Agreement under Annex) [hereinafter British-Irish Agreement].
[30] Belfast Agreement, Constitutional Issues, para. 1(i).
[31] *Id.* strand three, British-Irish Council.
[32] *Id.* annex A, Pledge of Office.

the still-partisan Royal Ulster Constabulary (RUC) to the more neutral Police Service of Northern Ireland.[33] The RUC's emblem, which had shown a crown on top of a harp, and which to nationalists symbolized the subjugation of Ireland to Britain, has been replaced by a new, impartial badge: a Saint Patrick's cross surrounded by six symbols—a harp, crown, shamrock, laurel leaf, torch, and scales of justice. Patten also recommended that the display of the Union flag and the portrait of the Queen in police stations should be eliminated.

To render consociational governance operational, the agreement also required that members elected to the Northern Ireland Assembly designate themselves, not as Catholics and Protestants, but as "nationalists, unionists, and others".[34] Until the St. Andrews Agreement of October 2006,[35] the copremiers, who head the executive, had to be nominated with the support of a majority of both nationalists and unionists, as well as a majority in the Assembly as a whole. Similarly, the designation rules provide legislative vetoes to both the nationalist and unionist communities. Key legislation requires either "parallel consent", that is, a concurrent majority of both nationalists and unionists as well as a majority in the Assembly, or a "weighted majority", that is, 40 percent of both nationalists and unionists as well as 60 percent in the Assembly overall.[36]

The basic consociational framework in the agreement has similarities with some of the arrangements that historically have been practiced in countries such as the Netherlands, once divided between Catholics and Protestants, and in Lebanon, divided among ethnoconfessional blocs, and, more recently, the arrangements in the interim constitution of racially and ethnically divided South Africa. The additional features in the agreement recognize that Northern Ireland, unlike these other societies, has been divided nationally, in other words, divided between two national communities who want to be ruled by their respective nation-states. In short, a purely internal consociational arrangement would have been inadequate. It would have addressed the minority's desire to resist majority rule but would have done nothing to satisfy its nationalist aspirations for a united Ireland, or for institutional links across Ireland, or to remedy its complaint that the very existence of Northern Ireland as part of the U.K. is an injustice. The two governments sensibly agreed that justice and stability required institutional arrangements that go beyond the boundaries of the United Kingdom to include the republic of Ireland.

---

[33] *See* A New Beginning: Policing in Northern Ireland—The Report of the Independent Commission for Policing for Northern Ireland (1999), *available at* <http://www.nio.gov.uk/a_new_beginning_in_policing_in_northern_ireland.pdf>.

[34] Belfast Agreement, strand one, para. 6.

[35] *See, generally,* Agreement at St. Andrews, Ir.-Brit., Oct. 13, 2006, *available at* <http://www.nio.gov.uk/st_andrews_agreement.pdf>; Northern Ireland (St. Andrews Agreement) Act, 2006, c. 53 (implementing the St. Andrews Agreement); Northern Ireland (St. Andrews Agreement) Act, 2007, c. 4 (modifying the Northern Ireland (St. Andrews Agreement) Act, 2006).

[36] Belfast Agreement, strand one, paras. 5(d)(i) & (ii).

The instability that affected Northern Ireland's political institutions, post-Belfast Agreement, between 1999 and 2007, reflected the continuing legacies of the rival self-determination claims. Many unionists' lack of enthusiasm for the agreement reflects their view that it moves too far in a nationalist direction. They fear the agreement is not a "settlement", or a long-term or permanent arrangement, but a "process" aimed at hollowing out the Union and achieving Irish unification. Steps by nationalists to strengthen the north-south bodies, and to strip British symbols from police stations and court houses, are correctly interpreted in this light, as was the reluctance of armed republicans to relinquish their weaponry before the summer of 2005 and, similarly, the speeches by the Irish prime minister and leader of Sinn Féin, which envisaged a united Ireland in their lifetimes.[37]

On the nationalist side, the perceived difficulty was the unwillingness of unionists to work with the political institutions, including the power-sharing executive and the north-south bodies. They also feared that the British government was not implementing the agreement's self-determination provisions in a forthright manner. The U.K. government's initial response to the Patten report's recommendations was minimalist, retaining much more power for the British state than had been recommended by Chris Patten or advocated by nationalists. The U.K. secretary of state Peter Mandelson responded to UUP leader David Trimble's difficulties with his party and the unionist public, by unilaterally suspending the Assembly, which was subsequently to be repeated on three occasions. This was in breach of the international treaty that had been signed with Ireland and the previously agreed-upon view that the people of Ireland (in both jurisdictions) should determine their own future.[38] These events help explain the IRA's reluctance to decommission its weaponry before 2005, which, in turn, worsened the position of unionist moderates. Decommissioning occurred, in part, because, by 2003, the British government had agreed to address republicans' concerns regarding self-determination by repealing its suspension power and by supporting the devolution of justice and policing as soon as there was agreement among the local parties.[39]

Consociational theory has no intrinsic or normative objection to the accommodation of stateless nations. Its past neglect of minority nationalities flows from its genesis in reflections on a number of small Western European democracies that were divided religiously, culturally, and socioeconomically but that were not strongly divided nationally. Consociationalists firmly think that politically

---

[37] For Prime Minister Bertie Ahern's comments, see *Ahern: Irish Unity in My Lifetime,* BBC News, Nov. 22, 2006, *available at* <http://news.bbc.co.uk/1/hi/events/northern_ireland/latest_news/219653.stm> (last visited Aug. 27, 2007). For Gerry Adams's comments, see *Sinn Fein Likely to Cherry-pick at Peace Agreement, Adams Indicates,* Irish Times, Apr. 20, 1998.

[38] British-Irish Agreement, art. 1(ii).

[39] *See* Joint Declaration by the British and Irish Governments, May 2003, paras. 9 & 20, *available at* <http://www.nio.gov.uk/joint_declaration_between_the_british_and_irish_governments.pdf> [hereinafter Joint Declaration].

salient groups should be treated fairly. Self-government, shared government, and cross-border confederal or federal arrangements are consistent with what is needed in plurinational places, once we have clarified what justice mandates. The same cannot be said about integrationist theory, which is intrinsically opposed to the accommodation of groups qua groups, particularly those based on national divisions.

2.2 The neglected role of external actors in the promotion and operation of consociations

Early consociational theory was internalist. It tended to downplay outside factors, both in explaining how consociational settlements emerge and when seeking to engineer their creation. Of the much-debated nine factors, initially listed by Lijphart as conducive to a consociational settlement, only one is exogenous.[40] According to Lijphart, if a state's warring factions perceive a common external threat, this will increase the prospects of internal solidarity and accommodation. Lijphart's recognition flowed from the history of a number of small European democracies (Belgium, the Netherlands, Switzerland, and Austria) threatened by larger neighbors, but he did not consider that outside forces, in fact, could facilitate consociation through benign, rather than malign, intervention—for example, by mediation or by inducing or encouraging warring or potentially warring parties to reach agreement.

Benign external interventions facilitated Northern Ireland's Belfast Agreement. The most important exogenous influence, outside the region if not the state, was the U.K. government. After a brief fling with the idea of integrating Northern Ireland with Great Britain in the late 1970s, London moved toward a more evenhanded approach, though inconsistently.[41] In December 1985, the U.K. government abandoned unalloyed direct rule, and the republic of Ireland was given a limited role in policy making in Northern Ireland and comprehensive consultative rights, with the promise that the new intergovernmental conference would decline in salience if an agreement on a devolved government could be reached between nationalists and unionists.[42] The U.K.'s default policy had shifted toward London-Dublin cooperation. Unionists feared this shift would be irreversible and would deepen.

The U.K. had several reasons of its own for signing the Anglo-Irish Agreement; nonetheless, pressure from the United States was also an important factor. From the early 1980s, leading U.S. politicians, prompted by the Irish government

---

[40] *See* LIJPHART, DEMOCRACY IN PLURAL SOCIETIES, *supra* note 16, at 53–105.
[41] *See* McGARRY & O'LEARY, *supra* note 5, at 194–235.
[42] Agreement between the Government of United Kingdom of Great Britain and Northern Ireland and the Government of the Republic of Ireland, Nov. 15, 1985, Cmnd. 9690, art. 2(b) [hereinafter Anglo-Irish Agreement]. *See* Brendan O'Leary, *The Anglo-Irish Agreement: Statecraft or Folly?*, 10 W. EUR. POL. 5 (1987).

and Irish Americans, encouraged Great Britain to cooperate more closely with Ireland. President Ronald Reagan, whom Margaret Thatcher respected, put his personal clout behind this message. Consequently, American pressure prepared the groundwork for 1998 even before President Bill Clinton was elected in 1992. There was no immediate movement to consociation by means of the coercive inducements of the Anglo-Irish Agreement, because unionists thought, at first, that they could destroy that agreement through protest. But the agreement proved durable. Unionists hoped it could be incrementally reversed while the Conservatives were in power in London, especially during the 1992–97 Parliament when the Major government depended on unionist support in the House of Commons. The Ulster Unionist Party (UUP) began to negotiate seriously with nationalists only after Labour's landslide victory in May 1997 and the signal by the new prime minister Tony Blair that he was committed to achieving a settlement within his first year of office.[43]

The United States and Irish Americans played a constructive role in the promotion of the Anglo-Irish Agreement[44] and an even more significant role in the making of the 1998 Belfast Agreement. Influenced by Irish American lobbies and by the end of the Cold War, which freed U.S. presidents from traditional constraints about interfering in the U.K.'s internal affairs, the U.S. gave unprecedented attention to Northern Ireland in the 1990s. President Clinton took office in 1992 and approved an indirect collective envoy, the Morrison delegation, which visited Ireland and met with all parties during the early stages of the peace process.[45] Clinton put his senior advisers to work on the subject, including the national security adviser Anthony Lake, and visited the region three times in five years, becoming the first U.S. president to go there. Northern Ireland's political leaders had open access to the White House. Clinton persuaded former Senate majority leader George Mitchell to chair, first, an economic initiative, then a crucial commission to arbitrate disputes between the U.K. and Irish governments over the decommissioning of paramilitary weapons and the timing of negotiations and lastly to preside over the final negotiations that led to the Belfast Agreement.[46]

On several occasions, President Clinton intervened personally and productively in the political negotiations. American diplomatic involvement increased the confidence of Irish republicans about the merits of negotiations, and it shored up the positions of the Irish government in its negotiations with Great Britain

[43] Brendan O'Leary, *The Belfast Agreement and the Labour Government: How to Handle and Mishandle History's Hand, in* THE BLAIR EFFECT: THE BLAIR GOVERNMENT 1997–2001, at 448 (Anthony Seldon ed., Little, Brown & Co. 2001).

[44] PAUL ARTHUR, SPECIAL RELATIONSHIPS: BRITAIN, IRELAND AND THE NORTHERN IRELAND PROBLEM (Blackstaff Press 2000).

[45] CONOR O'CLERY, THE GREENING OF THE WHITE HOUSE: THE INSIDE STORY OF HOW AMERICA TRIED TO BRING PEACE TO IRELAND (Gill & Macmillan 1996).

[46] GEORGE C. MITCHELL, MAKING PEACE (Univ. Cal. Press 2000).

and of the constitutional nationalists led by John Hume of the SDLP.[47] Clinton's decision to issue a visa to Sinn Féin leader Gerry Adams in 1994 is credited with pulling in hard-line Irish republicans behind a peaceful strategy. Adams claimed it brought forward the IRA ceasefire, which occurred in August 1994, by one year. The ceasefire was a prerequisite for the possibility of comprehensive and inclusive negotiations. While the Clinton administration's role in coaxing republicans into negotiating has been acknowledged, it is less often noted that it managed this task without alienating unionists. Unionists were given unprecedented access to the White House and the administration was careful to appear impartial throughout. The UUP leader David Trimble acknowledged that reassurances from Clinton helped convince him to sign the agreement.[48]

Benign exogenous action has facilitated power-sharing settlements elsewhere, not just in Northern Ireland. The United States, the United Nations, NATO, and the European Union, using their good offices, sanctions, incentives, and military powers, have played pivotal roles in promoting (or establishing) power-sharing institutions in Bosnia and Herzegovina, Macedonia, Iraq, and Afghanistan. Indeed, it is difficult to imagine settlements in any of these countries without outside intervention.

Early consociational theory also neglected the possibilities of positive roles for outsiders both in the implementation and in the active operation of power-sharing settlements. An international commission, headed by the Canadian General John de Chastelain, oversaw the decommissioning of paramilitary weapons and disarmament. Witnesses to IRA acts of decommissioning included the former Finnish president Marti Ahtisaari and Cyril Ramaphosa of the African National Congress. Proposals regarding the details of police reform were handed to an independent commission, with representation from the United States and Canada, as well as Great Britain and Ireland. Overseeing the implementation of policing reforms has been the responsibility of an American, Tom Constantine, and a Canadian, Al Hutchinson. Amid continuing difficulties in achieving full implementation of the agreement, the two governments established in January 2004 an Independent Monitoring Commission (IMC) in which there was international representation.[49] It was tasked with putting paramilitary activity under surveillance and formulating sanctions against political parties associated with offending organizations. The four-person body consisted of two members nominated by the U.K. government (one from Northern Ireland); a member nominated by the Irish government; and a fourth nominated by the American administration. While the IMC was conceived outside of the agreement, by 2006–7, it

[47] Roger MacGinty, *American Influence on the Northern Ireland Peace Process,* 14 J. CONFLICT STUD. 31, 34 (1997).
[48] Based on personal communication from Professor Andrew Wilson, who interviewed Trimble on this matter. See Andrew Wilson, *From Beltway to Belfast: The Clinton Administration, Sinn Féin, and the Northern Ireland Peace Process,* 1 NEW HIBERNIA REV. 23 (1997).
[49] Northern Ireland (Monitoring Commission etc.) Act, 2003, c. 25.

played an important role in persuading unionist leaders and their supporters that the IRA was wholly intent on avoiding paramilitary and criminal activities. Its reports enabled the DUP to enter, for the first time, into serious negotiations with Sinn Féin on power-sharing and, ultimately, to reach agreement in March 2007. The European Court of Human Rights already performs a role in the protection of human rights in Northern Ireland. A Canadian judge, Justice Peter Cory, has been involved in uncovering evidence of collusion between the security forces and protestant paramilitaries.

This extensive external involvement mirrors developments in other recent power-sharing agreements. There is external representation in several of the institutions established in Bosnia and Herzegovina, including the Supreme Court and central bank, as well as in Kosovo; both arrangements are presided over by external high representatives and have included external agents in providing security. Outsiders have retrained the police and army in Bosnia and Herzegovina, Kosovo, and Iraq, with varying degrees of success. In addition, outsiders have funded economic reconstruction and the integration of former paramilitaries into postconflict occupations. The failed UN plan for Cyprus envisaged a central tie-breaking role for outsiders in that island's Supreme Court. In short, the implementation and the operation of consociational settlements should no longer be considered the internal preserve of sovereign independent states. There is an emergent repertoire of international interventionist techniques and norms, and the application of these in Northern Ireland is perhaps the exemplar.

Outsiders can play positive roles and can tip the balance in favor of negotiated or induced agreements.[50] This does not mean that externally induced settlements are necessarily better. Settlements reached primarily under exogenous pressure may have shallow endogenous foundations. Intervention, even if well-meaning, may not always produce positive results. Secretary of State Mandelson moved the U.K. government away from the binational and bigovernmental approach that had helped to secure the Belfast Agreement. His mishandling of policing reform and suspension of the political institutions in 2000 backfired, as we have argued.[51] His personal style engendered acrimony all around and led some nationalists to nickname him Pinocchio for reasons beyond the physical resemblance.[52] Under Mandelson's successors, London got back on track. It promoted confidence-building measures to encourage republicans to decommission and accept the police, while telling unionists that a failure to respond to republican's "acts of completion" by sharing power would result in increased Anglo-Irish cooperation. This strategy facilitated the successful resumption of power sharing in May of 2007.

---

[50] See also KERR, *supra* note 18.

[51] *See* McGARRY & O'LEARY, *supra* note 5, at 371–403.

[52] *See* John McCormick, A Directory of Murals, Album 23, No. 762, *available at* <http://cain. ulst.ac.uk/mccormick/album23.htm> (last visited on Aug. 27, 2007).

2.3 The neglected treatment of security issues

Consociational theory has traditionally had a narrow focus on the design of and need for agreement on *political* institutions, such as legislatures, executives, and electoral systems. Little attention has been paid to a number of crucial sectors in violently divided places, such as the design of the police and security forces; the handling of paramilitary offenders; demilitarization of both state and paramilitary forces; the integration of former paramilitaries; transitional justice processes (such as truth commissions); the return of exiles and the management of refugees; new mechanisms to protect human rights; economic reconstruction; and provisions for monitoring ceasefires. This theoretical blind spot is important, because a failure to resolve issues in these sectors may prevent a viable peace process. This omission in early consociational theory, like the two that have already been discussed, is connected with its genesis in the small European democracies, which were not nationally divided or the object of benign external intervention but, at the same time, were not cases of recent and protracted violent division.

The rival parties in Northern Ireland disagreed strongly on security issues, and more strongly on these issues than on the design of the political institutions. For Irish republicans, a fully legitimate police service and British army demilitarization were "red line" questions. For Ulster unionists, it was equally important that the IRA completely abandon its armed struggle, decommission its arsenal, and that Sinn Féin endorse the police. There was no resolution of these issues at the time of the Belfast Agreement. The provisions on decommissioning merely stated that the parties that informally represented paramilitary organizations in the negotiations were to "use any influence they may have, to achieve the decommissioning of all paramilitary arms within two years following endorsement in referendums North and South of the agreement and in the context of the implementation of the overall settlement", by May 2000.[53] The parties to the negotiations agreed to hand the issue of policing over to an independent commission.[54] There was a general commitment to demilitarization on the part of the British government, including a return to "normal" arrangements, such as the scaling down of British troop numbers and fortifications. But these changes, while they were to take place "as early as possible", were linked to the nature of the security threat. There was, unlike the measures on decommissioning, no timetable.[55]

This failure to resolve the security issues destabilized the consociational institutions. Unionist politicians were divided between those who insisted that Sinn Féin be excluded from government until the IRA decommissioned and others who insisted that the IRA decommission shortly after Sinn Féin was permitted

---

[53] Belfast Agreement, Decommissioning, para. 3.
[54] *Id.* Policing and Justice, para. 4.
[55] *Id.* Security, paras. 1–4.

to take up its executive positions. A classic outbidding scenario occurred between the two main unionist parties and within the UUP. This led the UUP leader Trimble into first resisting the establishment of the institutions until December 1999, nineteen months after the agreement, and then issuing an ultimatum that he would collapse the institutions unless the IRA decommissioned. Trimble's position was weakened by the report of the Patten Commission, which presaged important changes to policing that were opposed by unionists. It was in this context, in May 2000, that Secretary of State Mandelson suspended the institutions and failed to fulfill the U.K. government's commitments. For its part, Sinn Féin failed to assume its responsibilities under the agreement to secure IRA decommissioning. Its recalcitrance was partly a consequence of the fact that the agreement did not state when decommissioning had to begin and had proposed its completion in the context of the implementation of other parts of the agreement. These included British army demilitarization, radical policing and justice reform, respect for the provisions on self-determination, and a commitment by unionists to the political institutions.

From 2000 to 2007, and especially since 2003, the core security issues were dealt with. More robust policing reform was delivered through an amended Police Act (Northern Ireland) 2000[56] and by the Police (Northern Ireland) Act 2003.[57] In the Joint Declaration of 2003, the British government promised to support the devolution of policing and justice powers, providing this was agreed to by local parties. It detailed steps toward "normalization of security arrangements", in other words, demilitarization—over a *defined* time frame between then and April 2005—and promised to repeal the Northern Ireland Act 2000 (the "Suspension" Act).[58] These "acts of completion" by the government were to be implemented in the context of similar acts by paramilitaries, including decommissioning and an end to violent and criminal activity, by Sinn Féin's acceptance of the police, and by taking its positions on the Policing Board.[59] IRA decommissioning followed in July 2005, and Sinn Féin's acceptance of the police in January 2007. In October 2006, and again in March 2007, the IMC reported that the IRA had "abandoned" terrorism and violence and was "firmly committed to the political path",[60] paving the way for the resumption of power sharing.

Security concerns are important in all polities that have endured violent conflict, and where there has been no military victory by one side. In post-2003 Iraq, it was vital for the Kurds that control over the security forces be formally regionalized, and that restraints be placed on the Iraqi army's ability to operate

[56] Police (Northern Ireland) Act, 2000, c. 32.
[57] Police (Northern Ireland) Act, 2003, c. 6. *See also* McGARRY & O'LEARY, *supra* note 5, at 395–399.
[58] Northern Ireland Act, 2000, c. 1.
[59] *See* Joint Declaration, particularly paras. 12–24.
[60] Fourteenth Report of the Independent Monitoring Commission, Mar. 12, 2007, *available at* <http://www.independentmonitoringcommission.org/documents/uploads/14th_IMC_Report.pdf>.

internally. It was important to Bougainville's 2001 peace agreement that it could establish its own police, provide for the withdrawal of Papua New Guinea's army and its police riot squads from the island, and limit their future deployments. In Mindanao, provisions were made in its 1996 agreement to integrate Muslim (MNLF) paramilitaries into the Philippines army. This foreshadowed a more representative army, as well as offering employment to former paramilitaries who might otherwise have reverted to violence.

It is better if agreement can be reached on security-related concerns to coincide with a political settlement. Horowitz suggests we should avoid maximalism, but that is not always a good thing if it means leaving important security issues to the medium or long term.[61] As Northern Ireland shows, simultaneous agreement on security and political questions may not be possible, but it also shows the value of reciprocal confidence building, with concessions from one party clearly linked to concessions by the other, accompanied, ideally, with a clear timetable for delivery. Neither side should lose face. Trust should be promoted, and each should have incentives to deliver its side of the bargain.

Our analysis suggests that instability cannot always be blamed on consociational institutions per se. Had the security issues been better managed from the start, it was not inevitable that the institutions would have been unstable, and the belated resolution of these issues in Northern Ireland have arguably put its political institutions on a more stable footing than hitherto.

3. The debate between consociationalists and their integrationist and centripetalist critics

Vigorous debate is waged between supporters of the agreement and its critics. As we have argued, this debate is invariably waged through consociationalist or integrationist and centripetalist lenses, respectively. The debate focuses on whether the agreement contributes positively to three fundamental sets of values: stability, fairness, and democracy. We address these values in order, in each case providing the position of the critics of consociation and following it with the consociational response.

3.1 Stability

Integrationist and centripetalist critics of the Belfast Agreement argue that it has not, and cannot, provide stability. Some of them talk of a flawed or even a "failed" peace process.[62] They allude to continued and even increased violence since the

---

[61] *See* Horowitz, *The Agreement, supra* note 13, at 90–91, 103–105.
[62] GARY K. PEATLING, THE FAILURE OF THE NORTHERN IRELAND PEACE PROCESS (Irish Acad. Press 2004).

agreement was signed,[63] arguing that there has been "no peace dividend",[64] or they claim (as late as 2006) that a "sustainable peace is not in sight".[65] The critics point to political instability; to the fact that it took a year and a half for power-sharing institutions to be established; and that between 1998 and 2007 these institutions have been more often suspended than operational. There is a pronounced emphasis on what Anthony Oberschall and Rendall Palmer call the "failure of moderate politics" and Henry Patterson calls the "victory of the extremes", in other words, the rise of Sinn Féin and the DUP since the agreement as the leading parties in the nationalist and unionist blocs, respectively, at the expense of the more moderate SDLP and UUP—combined with the marginalization of small moderate and formally cross-ethnic and cross-confessional parties.[66] The agreement's critics all agreed that this political polarization represented a significant obstacle to the resumption of power sharing, or even to the achievement of the prerequisites for power sharing, including IRA decommissioning and Sinn Féin's acceptance of the police.[67] When these prerequisites were met, and when there was agreement on the resumption of power sharing, the critics shifted from arguing that power sharing could not be achieved to claiming "it cannot work" and "would inevitably fail".[68]

We have already shown that much of this instability can be explained by security-related controversies rather than by the agreement's institutions. We have explained elsewhere that some instability flowed from flawed institutional rules, primarily those relating to the first and deputy first ministers, but that the relevant rules were "centripetalist" rather than consociational.[69] Moreover, in our view, it is no longer debatable whether post-agreement Northern Ireland has been much more stable than pre-agreement Northern Ireland. We believe that this change is overwhelmingly because of the Belfast Agreement, and the onus is on its critics to demonstrate otherwise. We will also argue that had any of the main integrationist or centripetalist alternatives to the agreement been implemented, they would have had seriously destabilizing effects and would have cost hundreds of lives.

---

[63] Robin Wilson, *Making the Agreement Stick: Prospects for Peace in Northern Ireland,* 17 RENEWAL 20 (1999); Robin Wilson & Rick Wilford, *Northern Ireland: A Route to Stability,* DEMOCRATIC DIALOGUE, Aug. 2003, at 9.

[64] Robin Wilson and Rick Wilford think it is the only example of consociation around. Wilson & Wilford, *supra* note 63, at 9–10.

[65] Rupert Taylor, *The Belfast Agreement and the Politics of Consociationalism: A Critique,* 77 POL. Q. 218 (2006).

[66] Anthony Oberschall & L. Rendall Palmer, *The Failure of Moderate Politics, in* POWER-SHARING: INSTITUTIONAL AND SOCIAL REFORM IN DIVIDED SOCIETIES 77 (Ian O'Flynn, David Russell & Donald Horowitz eds., Pluto Press 2005); Henry Patterson, *What Victory of the Extremes Means for All of Us,* IRISH INDEPENDENT, May 7, 2005.

[67] *See, e.g.,* Taylor, *supra* note 65, at 220; O'Flynn, *supra* note 14, at 142; Patterson, *supra* note 66.

[68] The quotes are respectively from Kevin Myers, *This Latest Northern Deferral is Part of the Dance of Deception,* IRISH INDEPENDENT, Mar. 27, 2007, and Republican Sinn Féin, *No New Era Yet,* THE BLANKET, Mar. 27, 2007.

[69] John McGarry & Brendan O'Leary, *Stabilising Northern Ireland's Agreement,* 75 POL. Q. 213, 220 (2004).

The Belfast Agreement has been unambiguously associated with a highly significant reduction in political violence. Lethal political violence dropped from 509 killed in the nine years before the agreement (1989–97) to 134 in the nine years after (1998–2006), a decline of three-quarters.[70] While 105 members of the security forces were killed in the earlier period, only two were killed after the agreement, both in 1998. Not one member of the security services has been killed in political violence since 1998. One of the most dangerous places in the world to be a police officer during the 1970s and 1980s is now, arguably, one of the safest. The war between the IRA and the British state is over. A significant proportion of those killed since 1998, 29 of 134, died in a single atrocity—the Omagh bombing of August 1998, planted by those we may fairly call republican integrationist extremists who opposed the agreement. The raw death tolls do not differentiate intracommunity from intercommunity violence; yet only the latter is a fair measurement of ethnonational conflict.[71] Internecine loyalist paramilitary violence has been very noticeable since 1998 and is arguably a temporary side effect of peace, because loyalists and republicans were not fighting. However, this is not distinguished in the data. Since January 2003, there have been no deaths from intercommunity violence. If data is taken from a longer time frame, namely, the twelve years before and after the peace process began in 1994, then the decline in violence is even more noteworthy: 909 people were killed between 1983 and 1994, but only 179 since 1994, a decline of over four-fifths. In 2006, a United Nations report indicated that Belfast was the world's second safest city for crime, with its crime levels lower than those in the developed countries covered in the report. The report, strangely, did not cover violent crime, but even on this criterion, Northern Ireland is safer than Scotland, or England and Wales.[72]

There has also been a "peace dividend". The reduction in violence has been followed by record high employment levels in 2006, and property price increases that were the highest in the United Kingdom in 2005.[73] A US newspaper recently reported that Belfast's city center was "a showcase of prosperity".[74]

[70] Police Service of Northern Ireland, Security Statistics, *available at* <http://www.psni.police. uk/index/statistics_branch/pg_security_stats.htm> (last visited Aug. 27, 2007).

[71] We show elsewhere that of all conflict-related deaths between the beginning of 1998 and March of 2007 in which the identity of the perpetrators is widely known, 66.1 percent were a result of violence within each of the two communities, rather than violence between them. *See* McGarry & O'Leary, *supra* note 4.

[72] *Crime Rate in the North "World's Lowest", says UN*, Sunday Times, Sept. 18, 2005. *See also* Northern Ireland Tourist Board, Fact-Finder Japanese Market, *available at* <http://www.nitb. com/article.aspx?ArticleID=1271> (last visited Aug. 27, 2007).

[73] Press Release, University of Ulster, Northern Ireland is the UK's Regional Hotspot for House Prices Rises, Nov. 30, 2005, *available at* <http://news.ulster.ac.uk/releases/2005/1952.html> (last visited Aug. 27, 2007).

[74] Jeffrey Stinson, *Peace (Finally) at Hand in Northern Ireland?*, USA Today, Mar. 19, 2007, *available at* <http://www.usatoday.com/news/world/2007-03-19-cover-northern-ireland_N.htm>.

There is little prospect of a significant resurgence of political violence. The IRA, responsible for 49 percent of all deaths between 1966 and 2001,[75] has destroyed its arsenal and "disbanded its operational structures". Defections to dissident republican paramilitary organizations have been minimal. The recent resumption of power sharing has been followed by a statement from the Ulster Volunteer Force (UVF) that it had "deactivated" its service units and placed "all ordnance beyond reach".[76] The agreement has resulted in demilitarization by the British Army, its return to barracks and to a normal peacetime garrison;[77] and in the construction of a new police service, more widely accepted than before. This is collective evidence of a palpably successful peace process, rather than the flawed or failed one described by the agreement's critics, and, for many, it constitutes sufficient ground for heralding the agreement as a success.

The thesis of political polarization appears more plausible than the thesis of continuing or increasing violence. Both the DUP and Sinn Féin have increased support relative to the UUP and SDLP in the twenty-first century and have done so by attracting the supporters of these latter parties rather than by mobilizing previously abstentionist voters.[78] But a movement of support from moderate party A to radical party B is evidence of polarization only if the differences between the parties remain constant or deepen during the period in question, or if there is evidence of radicalization in voter sentiment. However, careful inspection of the data shows no polarization, rather, precisely the opposite—a narrowing of differences between the moderate and radical parties and a convergence between nationalist and unionist voters in accepting the core aspects of the agreement. This evidence was demonstrated by the ease of the recent decision by the DUP and Sinn Féin to share power and the overwhelming support given to parties committed to power sharing in the election of March 2007.

The policy differences between Sinn Féin and the SDLP narrowed considerably during the peace process. Sinn Féin abandoned, at least tacitly, virtually all of the positions that distinguished it from the SDLP: its support for violence; the demand that the British state withdraw from Ireland or indicate its intent to withdraw; opposition to taking seats in a Northern Ireland Assembly or government; opposition to the "consent" principle, which legitimized Northern Ireland; opposition to the decommissioning of IRA weapons; and opposition to the PSNI.

[75] Calculated from DAVID MCKITTRICK ET AL., LOST LIVES: THE STORIES OF THE MEN, WOMEN AND CHILDREN WHO DIED AS A RESULT OF THE NORTHERN IRELAND TROUBLES, tbl. 2 (Mainstream Publ'g 1999).

[76] David McKittrick, *UVF "Deactivates" and Agrees to Put Weapons "Beyond Reach"*, THE INDEPENDENT, May 4, 2007. Note, however, that the UVF did not "decommission" its weapons under the aegis of the Independent International Commission on Decommissioning (the IICD).

[77] See David McKittrick, *Northern Ireland: The Longest Tour of Duty is Over*, THE INDEPENDENT, Aug. 4, 2007, *available at* <http://news.independent.co.uk/uk/ulster/article2819591.ece>.

[78] Paul Mitchell, Brendan O'Leary & Geoffrey Evans, *Northern Ireland: Flanking Extremists Bite the Moderates and Emerge in Their Clothes*, 54 PARLIAMENTARY AFF. 725 (2001).

From being "violently opposed to consociation" in the 1980s,[79] by 2006, Sinn Féin was prepared to nominate the leader of the DUP as first minister. By 2007, one of its arch critics argued that it was "rapidly becoming indistinguishable from the SDLP".[80]

The differences between the DUP and the UUP have never been as stark as those between Sinn Féin and the SDLP, so it has been relatively easy for members to cross from one party to the other. While the UUP accepted the agreement and the DUP opposed it, the latter talked of renegotiating it, rather than wrecking it. Both unionist parties were devolutionist and participated in the executive. The major issues between the two unionist parties between 2001 and 2006 revolved not around power sharing or the agreement's other institutions, which were accepted in principle, but over Sinn Féin's fitness for office and its relations with the IRA. By 2007, both parties supported inclusive power sharing, and, during the March 2007 elections, unionist and nationalist intrabloc disagreement was so minimal that the newspapers complained the election was a "humdrum" affair,[81] and that the election lacked "oomph" because the "extremes have moved to the centre ground, leaving it a very crowded place for the old moderates, the SDLP and the Ulster Unionists".[82]

Survey data between 1998 and 2003 indicate the resilience of rival ethnonational identities but also show attitudinal convergence between nationalists and unionists on many of the main points of the agreement. Among Sinn Féin partisans, the period 1998–2003 saw support for the "consent" principle—that Northern Ireland should remain in the U.K. as long as a majority of Northern Ireland's citizens supported this—increase from 55 percent to 66 percent. By 2003, two out of three republican voters supported what had previously been an anathema. Likewise, support for decommissioning among Sinn Féin supporters increased from 63 percent to 85 percent. Among DUP adherents, support for the agreement's north-south institutions increased from 17 to 35 percent while opposition to these bodies declined from 58 percent to 33 percent. Remarkably, support for the establishment of the Northern Ireland Assembly increased among partisans of both parties, from 57 to 70 percent in the case of DUP supporters, and from 76 to 94 percent in the case of Sinn Féin supporters. Support for "required" power sharing reached very high levels among partisans of both "extremes", climbing from 32 to 65 percent among DUP supporters and from 84 to 96 percent among Sinn Féin partisans. A mere 15 percent of DUP supporters were opposed to power sharing.[83]

---

[79] Brendan O'Leary, *The Limits to Coercive Consociationalism in Northern Ireland*, 37 Pol. Stud. 452 (1989).

[80] The critic was Ruairí O'Brádaigh, the president of Republican Sinn Féin. Gerry Moriarty, *Six RSF Candidates to Stand in Assembly Election*, Irish Times, Feb. 14, 2007, *available at* <http://www.ireland.com/newspaper/ireland/2007/0214/1170364437290.html>.

[81] *Fire has Gone Out of Election*, Irish News, Feb. 27, 2007.

[82] *Tough Talk is Losing its Edge as Ulster's Election Trail Goes Cold*, The Times, Mar. 1, 2007.

[83] All data from Paul Mitchell, Geoffrey Evans & Brendan O'Leary, *Extremist Outbidding in Ethnic Party Systems Is Not Inevitable: Tribune Parties in Northern Ireland* (Pol. Sci. & Pol. Econ.

This data surfaced in the midst of divergent perceptions about the overall agreement and about who had benefited from it. DUP partisans increasingly believed that nationalists were the main beneficiaries of the agreement (up from 65 to 90 percent) and were more likely to believe this than members of the UUP (54 to 76 percent). Support for the agreement overall dropped among DUP supporters from 36 to 23 percent and among UUP supporters from 89 to 68 percent.[84]

The evidence from the policy positions of the parties, combined with this data, cannot be squared with the simplistic polarization thesis advanced by integrationists and centripetalists. The radical parties discovered the limits of electoral growth while maintaining ultraextreme positions and moved to capture available voters. They sought, successfully, in a period of intense negotiations, to market themselves as the most effective representatives of their bloc. They acted, in effect, as tribunes for their communities. This "ethnic tribune" politics, which helped fend off party fragmentation and outflanking threats from new, more radical parties, obscured for some observers the underlying trend toward moderate positions. Key voters are prepared to support political compromise but want to be represented in negotiations by their most effective bloc representatives. This evidence suggests that consociational power sharing can work, though it will not be without difficulty.

Integrationists, and particularly centripetalists, believed that pacts like the one achieved between the DUP and Sinn Féin in March 2007 would not be made, so its achievement casts a significant shadow over the merits of their analysis. But they also suggest that such pacts will not flourish. From their perspective, the DUP–Sinn Féin pact should experience even more serious difficulties than its predecessor, the executive which held office intermittently between December 1999 and October 2002. Although one should not underestimate the difficulties facing a power-sharing executive fronted by Sinn Féin and the DUP, the new executive, nonetheless, has clear advantages that its predecessor lacked. The institutions are supported by *all* parties in the Assembly as of July 2007, representing 93.3 percent of voters. The sole party that contested the election on a clear antiagreement platform, the integrationist United Kingdom Unionist Party, received a derisory 1.5 percent of the vote, and lost its only seat. The DUP and Sinn Féin remain strongly united behind power sharing, and there is little evidence of imminent party fragmentation and intrabloc outbidding of the sort that destabilized power sharing in 1974 or the period 1999–2003. The DUP cooperated closely with Sinn Féin in agreeing to a program of government, and even in allocating ministerial portfolios, prior to running d'Hondt. It participated enthusiastically in the first North-South Ministerial Council meeting since power sharing resumed. The

Group (PSPE), Working Paper No. 6, 2006), *available at* <http://www.lse.ac.uk/collections/government/PSPE/pdf/PSPE_WP6_06.pdf>.

[84] Bernadette C. Hayes, Ian McAllister & Lizanne Dowds, *The Erosion of Consent: Protestant Disillusionment with the 1998 Northern Ireland Agreement*, 15 J. ELECTIONS, PUB. OPINION & PARTIES 147 (2005).

DUP, in short, appears more committed to power sharing in 2007 than Trimble's UUP did between 1999 and 2002, which is difficult to square with the centripetalist analysis. Of course, the issues which caused instability between 1999 and 2007, such as decommissioning, demilitarization, police reform, and Sinn Féin's acceptance of the police, have now been largely settled. The devolution of policing and justice, an important demand of Sinn Féin's, has yet to take place, but there are no other obvious time bombs on the immediate horizon, and the desire to achieve agreement on the devolution of policing and justice should help to prevent Sinn Féin from unnecessarily antagonizing unionists.

In any case, as we have often insisted, if the DUP–Sinn Féin pact does not survive, the agreement has a default option, one made clear in the lead-up to the resumption of power sharing: increased cooperation between the London and Dublin governments through the British-Irish Intergovernmental Conference, possibly combined with increased responsibilities for larger, more efficient local governments, particularly those prepared to accept power sharing. The British and Irish governments will, if necessary, underline the existence of this default to keep the executive's parties, and particularly the DUP, the newest convert to consociation, focused on cooperation.

Northern Ireland is, therefore, as a critic of the agreement has acknowledged, "at its most stable . . . in a generation".[85] But would it be even more stable if, counterfactually, any of the critics' alternatives had been implemented? Centripetalists suggest that a minimum winning coalition of moderates would be more stable than a grand consociational coalition that includes radicals. This appears plausible, but Northern Ireland's experience suggests the reasoning is faulty. Excluded radicals can destabilize power-sharing institutions. They may accuse moderates from their bloc of treachery, which might prevent the latter from making the compromises necessary for successful power sharing. Excluded radicals may engage in violence, creating a polarized atmosphere that pressurizes moderates and, again, makes compromise difficult. This is exactly what happened during Northern Ireland's previous experiment with a power-sharing coalition of moderates: the Sunningdale experiment of 1973–74.[86] The coalition was attacked by radicals on both sides. It found it difficult to reach substantive internal agreement, amid mounting violence, and collapsed after less than five months in office. This experience was one of the reasons why even the moderates of the SDLP insisted on an inclusive coalition, which included Sinn Féin.[87] The SDLP's refusal to consider a centripetal coalition meant this option was not available.

[85] Pete Shirlow, *Why It's Going to Take Two to Tango*, Belfast Telegraph, Mar. 14, 2007, *available at* <http://www.belfasttelegraph.co.uk/news/opinion/article2356125.ece> (last visited Aug. 28, 2007).

[86] Wolff, *supra* note 18; Stefan Wolff, *Context and Content: Sunningdale and Belfast Compared*, *in* Aspects of the Belfast Agreement 11 (Rick Wilford ed., Oxford Univ. Press 2001).

[87] Joanne McEvoy, *The Institutional Design of Executive Formation in Northern Ireland*, 16 Reg'l & Fed. Stud. 447, 454 (2006).

Properly structured consociational executives can create incentives for radicals to moderate, something that Horowitz wrongly sees as an exclusive attribute of moderate coalitions. The agreement links inclusion in office to a pledge that involves a commitment to constitutional politics, thus ruling out certain unacceptable types of "honest" radicals. The d'Hondt rule for executive composition does not just permit inclusion of any party that achieves a certain threshold of electoral support; it links each party's share of ministerial portfolios *and* its pick of ministerial portfolios to its share of seats in the legislature, a strong incentive to win more votes. Also, there are incentives for parties to win a majority of their (nationalist or unionist) bloc's representation, as this ensures entitlement to one of the copremierships. The sole way radical parties can expand their support, barring the mobilization of new voters, is at the expense of more moderate parties, so this creates an incentive to moderate. Sinn Féin has been faced with another incentive to moderate, the possibility of legislative seats and executive office in the Irish republic. These incentives, we believe, helped facilitate compromises on Sinn Féin's part and (albeit later on) the DUP's. Contrary to Horowitz's own views on Sinn Féin, its behavior is a textbook example of one of his key assumptions—if they have to, parties will moderate in order to win office.[88]

The Belfast Agreement shows that consociational institutions can be designed to mitigate the problems of having radical rivals in government. The d'Hondt process reduces the transaction costs of bargaining over portfolios and, as a consequence, promotes stability through being patently fair. No program of government has to be negotiated in advance between the parties entitled to government. The design creates strong incentives for parties to take up their entitlements to ministries, because if they do not then the portfolios go either to their ethnonational rivals or to rivals in their own bloc. Parties can use this argument to persuade reluctant supporters that they should go into the executive. The d'Hondt allocation procedure requires no vote of confidence by the Assembly, either for individual ministers or for the executive committee as a whole. These incentives produced positive results in the immediate postagreement period: the DUP, while engaging in ritualized protest, took its seats on the executive between 1999 and 2002 and fought the 2001 Westminster general election and the 2003 Assembly election not on a pledge to scrap the agreement but to renegotiate it. In short, the Assembly differed in a positive fashion from the Sunningdale power-sharing experiment of 1973–74, which sought to maintain traditional U.K. notions of collective cabinet responsibility. The DUP's readiness to sit in an executive with Sinn Féin, however reluctantly, prepared its supporters for its eventual full acceptance of power sharing in 2007. The DUP's acceptance of power sharing was also facilitated by the provision in the St. Andrews Agreement that effectively

[88] Donald L. Horowitz, *Making Moderation Pay: The Comparative Politics of Ethnic Conflict Management, in* CONFLICT AND PEACEMAKING IN MULTIETHNIC SOCIETIES 451–475 (Joseph P. Montville ed., Lexington 1989).

extended d'Hondt to the election of the first and deputy first minister, with the necessary proviso that both the first minister and deputy first minister could not come from the same designation.[89] This allowed the DUP and Sinn Féin in March 2007 to nominate not just ministers but also copremiers, without explicitly endorsing the nominees of the other parties; this allowed power sharing where trust was lacking.

The alternative vote is a deservedly lost cause as a prescription for Northern Ireland. It would never be endorsed by hard-line parties entering a constitutional settlement if they believed it would likely undermine their electoral support. Since the agreement was made possible by the inclusion in negotiations of radical parties associated with paramilitary organizations, such as Sinn Féin, the Ulster Democratic Party (UDP), and Progressive Unionist Party (PUP), it would have been perverse for their leaders to agree to an electoral system that minimized their future prospects. The leaders of political parties, particularly radical parties, are more likely to settle on a proportional electoral system than on one that requires them to transform themselves into transethnic or non-ethnic parties or coalitions. The adoption of the alternative vote is particularly unlikely when the elites involved in negotiations owe their positions to a prior, proportional electoral system, as in Northern Ireland. Horowitz's electoral prescriptions may have greater likelihood of acceptance at the formation of a competitive party system, but not thereafter. Once party pluralism has occurred, there will be few agents with incentives to endorse his electoral prescription. If a third party or outside power does so, it would be a severe provocation to the less moderate parties and, therefore, likely would reignite ethnonational tensions. Exclusion, after all, is a cause of conflict.

The alternative vote's purportedly moderating effects, per Horowitz, may materialize in multiethnic political systems with no actual or potentially dominant group in given districts, but this situation does not obtain in Northern Ireland. Its conflict is binational, and most of its constituencies, however drawn, have clear unionist or nationalist majorities. In these circumstances, a majoritarian electoral system like the alternative vote will result in most constituencies returning representatives from the locally dominant group, not in the election of political moderates who transcend ethnic groups. Even where the demographic conditions exist for the alternative vote to have some prospects of yielding moderate winners, its assumption—that the electorate will endorse politicians with cross-ethnic appeals just because only these politicians can win elections—may not be warranted.[90] Centripetal power sharing, in short, is dependent on an already existing degree of moderation—the charge, ironically, that centripetalists level at consociationalists. Where divisions are deep (or where constituencies have

[89] Agreement at St. Andrews, *supra* note 35, annex A, § 9.
[90] *See* Sumantra Bose's account of the presidential election in Republika Srpska in 2000, which was based on alternate voting. SUMANTRA BOSE, BOSNIA AFTER DAYTON: NATIONALIST PARTITION AND INTERNATIONAL INTERVENTION 233 (Oxford Univ. Press 2002).

a dominant group), ethnic leaders will continue to make ethnocentric appeals, and voters may continue to vote ethnically, or else may simply abstain. Indeed, the imperative of leaders staying in the count under the alternative vote, such as getting as large a first or second preference vote as possible, may dictate continuing ethnocentrism.

The single transferable vote, by contrast, worked to induce moderation within Northern Ireland's political parties. It had already helped to moderate the policy stance of Sinn Féin. After that party's first phase of electoral participation in elections in Northern Ireland in the 1980s and in the Irish republic in the latter half of the 1980s, the party discovered it was in a ghetto. Its candidates piled up large numbers of first-preference ballot papers and then sat unelected as a range of other parties' candidates passed them to achieve quotas on the basis of lower-order preferences. They received very few lower-order preferences from SDLP voters. However, once the party moderated its position, promoted the IRA's ceasefires, and became the champion of a peace process and a negotiated settlement, it found that its first-preference vote, its transfers from SDLP voters, and its seats won all increased. The use of the single transferable vote, as well as the lowering of the electoral threshold permitted by increasing the seats in each constituency from five to six, also allowed for the inclusion of the loyalist Progressive Unionist Party (PUP), something which helped to maintain loyalist ceasefires.

Both republican and unionist integrationists have a fundamental problem. Neither of their projects has the remotest prospect of winning cross-community support, let alone of delivering stability. For over a century, historic Ulster, and the Northern Ireland that was carved from it, has been divided electorally into two rival ethnonational blocs. The divisions became particularly intense during the thirty years preceding the Belfast Agreement. While nationalist and unionist parties won an average of 82 percent of the vote during the five regionwide elections held between 1973 and 1975, they received an average of 91 percent in the five campaigns held between 1996 and 1999. Within the nationalist bloc, moreover, the republican share of the vote has been increasing. In its first five election campaigns (1982–87) Sinn Féin won an average of 37.3 percent of the nationalist vote. In the five campaigns between 1996 and 1999 its average increased to 41 percent. And then, more dramatically, since the 2001 Westminster elections, it has become the majority party in votes within the nationalist bloc.[91] Patterns within the unionist bloc are more complex, because both major unionist parties were equally intransigent for most of the period between 1971 and 1998. There is evidence, however, that the UUP's apparent willingness to compromise with republicans after 1998 cost it electoral support to the advantage of the DUP.[92]

But there has been no swing voting between the two ethnonational blocs over the last three decades, and any change in their respective shares of the poll has

[91] Mitchell, O'Leary & Evans, *supra* note 78.
[92] *Id.*

been caused by different birth, death, emigration, and electoral participation rates. The rising nationalist share of the vote, from 24.1 percent in the 1973 election to the Northern Ireland Assembly, to an average of 32.5 percent in seven regionwide elections between 1982 and 1989, and 39.8 percent in five elections between 1996 and 1999, had nothing to do with the conversion of unionists. It was the result of Sinn Féin's participation in electoral politics since 1982, a higher electoral participation rate by Catholics, and an increase in the Catholic share of the population.[93] Nor is there any evidence of support increasing for parties outside of the two ethnonational blocs, which could be construed as voters in transition from one bloc to the other. Indeed the self-styled "nonethnic", "non-sectarian", "middle ground" has been squeezed in recent decades. The largest of the middle-ground parties, the Alliance Party, averaged 8.4 percent of the vote in its first five regionwide election campaigns (1973–75), but just 6 percent in the five election campaigns between 1996 and 1999. During the three regional elections that took place between 1996 and 2003, the vote share of parties outside the ethnonational blocs averaged around 8 percent. These data are powerful evidence of national polarization and deeply held identifications, realities that will not be easily transformed by changes in the electoral system.

The two major communities have distinct national identities, not merely ethnic heritages. Neither unionists nor nationalists want to be subsumed within the other's nation-state, even if they are guaranteed equal citizenship. Even moderate nationalists insist, at a bare minimum, on internal power sharing and external institutional links between Northern Ireland and Ireland. Nationalists, and particularly republicans, also insist on a constitutional route to a united Ireland, as a necessary *quid pro quo* for recognizing the consent principle. Even moderate unionists, prepared to tolerate cross-border institutions to accommodate nationalists, insist on retaining strong political links with Great Britain, now and in the future.

While partisan nationalist and unionist versions of integration are both unfair and unrealistic, post-nationalists and social transformationists are merely unrealistic with regard to any feasible medium-term future. As the elections results just discussed indicate, there is little support for parties that support a post-national or overarching identity. Transformers' optimism in the face of this electoral data usually stems from the belief that the voting record reflects elite machinations and perverse incentives and is not representative of a considerable consensus that allegedly exists outside conventional politics. But, if so, they are obliged to explain why, in free and open elections, only nationalists and unionist elites win significant numbers of votes, while elites that stress overarching identities or cross-cutting issues, such as class or civic values, receive small levels of support.

[93] Brendan O'Leary, *More Green, Fewer Orange,* FORTNIGHT, Feb. 1990; BRENDAN O'LEARY & JOHN MCGARRY, THE POLITICS OF ANTAGONISM: UNDERSTANDING NORTHERN IRELAND 192 (Athlone 1993).

Turnout in Northern Ireland elections is both higher than in the United Kingdom, as a whole, and higher than anywhere else in Great Britain. The simple fact is that the position of the main political parties on constitutional issues broadly reflects the public preferences reported in survey data.[94]

The political preferences of Northern Ireland's "civil society", in other words, its numerous civic associations, do not differ noticeably from those of its political parties. The most popular civil-society organizations in Northern Ireland, the Orange Order and Gaelic Athletic Association, are solidly unionist and nationalist, respectively. True, several smaller, peace and conflict-resolution organizations reach across the national divide and seek to promote a transcendent identity, but just as many—if not more, according to the academic who has most closely studied them—are nationalist or unionist groups that want an honorable binational compromise.[95] These realities explain why the British and Irish governments eventually converged on accepting versions of proposals first articulated by the SDLP: accommodating the two ethnonational blocs in power-sharing institutions with trans-state dimensions. Such a settlement was not possible during most of the past thirty years. It became so only when republican and unionist political agents stepped back, however haltingly, from their respective integrationist absolutisms. Ironically, the only prospect for social transformation, or for a genuine democratic deliberation that contributes to transformation, is within the context of a mutually acceptable settlement among the two communities and their democratic representatives. Successful consociation can be biodegradable, as the Dutch example suggests.

3.2 Fairness

Integrationists, and some of Horowitz's supporters, maintain that the Belfast Agreement's consociational institutions are "unfair" because they privilege certain group identities.[96] The institutions discriminate, allegedly, against individuals who do not possess group identities, against those whose attachment to a group is less than others, those who are attached to underprivileged groups, and even—because privileges are "fixed"—against individuals from currently privileged groups who decide in the future to withdraw from them.[97] This criticism of

---

[94] For data on the turnout rate in Northern Ireland, see McGarry & O'Leary, *supra* note 5, at 309, n. 47. Survey data ranging from the 1960s to the 1990s and analyses are consistent in showing ethnic polarization—although they generally underreported extremist preferences at the ballot box. *See, e.g.,* E. Moxon-Browne, *National Identity in Northern Ireland, in* Social Attitudes in Northern Ireland: The First Report 23 (Peter Stringer & Gillian Robinson eds., Blackstaff 1991); Karen Trew, *National Identity, in* Social Attitudes in Northern Ireland: The Fifth Report 140 (Richard Breen, Lizanne Dowds & Paula Devine eds., Appletree 1996).

[95] Feargal Cochrane, *Unsung Heroes? The Role of Peace and Conflict Resolution Organizations in the Northern Ireland Conflict, in* Northern Ireland and the Divided World, *supra* note 10, at 137, 153.

[96] Taylor, *supra* note 65, at 219.

[97] For a general critique of consociation's basic unfairness, see Brass, *supra* note 1, at 342.

the agreement is particularly popular with the Alliance Party. Along with some academics, the party complains that the agreement and consociation are overly focused on the contending communities, taking insufficient account of the fact that not all the members of these communities are equally attached to them, and not everyone is in such communities.[98] Some critics even associate consociation with the indisputably and profoundly unjust system of apartheid, with one arguing that consociation entails "separate, but not necessarily equal", treatment.[99]

The criticism that consociation privileges certain identities is not groundless. Many consociations have privileged particular identities over others: they have been "corporate" rather than "liberal" in form.[100] Some have had corporate electoral rolls, which oblige citizens to vote only within their own ethnic community for their own ethnic parties. To vote for the community councils in newly independent Cyprus, citizens had to opt for registration on separate Greek Cypriot or Turkish Cypriot rolls. Lebanon's electoral law has specified that successful candidates from certain constituencies must come from particular communities. Several consociations specify that particular officeholders must be from one ethnic community or another. Lebanon's executive arrangements, which allocate the presidency, premiership, and speakership to a Christian, Sunni Muslim, and Shi'a Muslim, respectively, discriminate against groups such as the Druze, against socialists and environmentalists, or individuals with no group attachment. They even discriminate within the "privileged" categories, as the three offices are not equal. Corporate consociations create institutional obstacles to the dissolution of the protected identities, which is not to say that they would necessarily wither in the absence of such institutions.

But let us be clear about the Belfast Agreement. It does not, contrary to the assertion of a recent article in *Foreign Affairs*, "set aside seats for Catholics and Protestants", or for unionists and nationalists, for that matter.[101] Citizens vote on a common roll; they vote for any candidates or parties they prefer; they can vote across blocs; and they can express first- or lower-order voting preferences outside their blocs. So the election of members of the legislative assembly (MLAs) does not privilege particular identities. Ministers become ministers by an allocation algorithm that is "difference-blind": it operates according to the proportion of seats won by parties in the Assembly, not their national identity. However, certain parts of the agreement do privilege unionism and nationalism over other forms of identity. MLAs are required to designate themselves as "unionists",

---

[98] *See* Ian O'Flynn, *Democratic Values and Power-sharing, in* POWER-SHARING: NEW CHALLENGES FOR DIVIDED SOCIETIES 17–18, 23 (Ian O'Flynn & David Russell ed., Pluto 2005); Donald L. Horowitz, *Foreword* to POWER-SHARING, *supra* note 98, at viii.

[99] Paul Dixon, *Why the Good Friday Agreement in Northern Ireland is not Consociational*, 76 POL. Q. 357, 358–359 (2005).

[100] *See* John McGarry & Brendan O'Leary, *Iraq's Constitution of 2005: Liberal Consociation as Political Prescription* (in this volume).

[101] Adeed I. Dawisha & Karen Dawisha, *How to Build a Democratic Iraq*, 82 FOREIGN AFF. 36, 45 (2003).

"nationalists", or "others". Before 2007, the election of the first minister and deputy first minister required concurrent nationalist and unionist majorities as well as a majority of MLAs. Additionally, the passage of important ("key") laws requires either such a concurrent majority or, if that is unavailable, a weighted majority, namely, the support of 60 percent in the Assembly, including at least 40 percent of both registered nationalists and unionists. While Northern Ireland's voters have shown no signs of adopting new (non-unionist and non-nationalist) identities for over a century, it is, nonetheless, true that such rules arguably create disincentives for them to change their behavior. There is an incentive for voters to choose nationalists or unionists, as members from these groups will, *ceteris paribus*, count for more than "others" or be more pivotal. The rules have the effect of predetermining, in advance of election results, that nationalists and unionists are to be better protected than "others". The "others", if they were to become a majority, would be pivotal in the passage of all normal legislation, but any key decision requiring cross-community support would still turn on the choices made by nationalists and unionists.

Corporate mechanisms, however, are not intrinsic to consociational design. Most modern consociationalists eschew these devices and prefer liberal rules that protect equally whatever groups emerge in free elections. Since we are liberal consociationalists, we think it would be desirable to see changes in the agreement's rules and institutions that removed as many corporate principles as possible, though we believe any such changes should occur within the rules governing the agreement. In 2004, we argued that the d'Hondt formula should be used for the nomination of the first minister and the deputy first minister. This would mean that the first and second largest parties would nominate the first minister and the deputy—thus they could come from any party, not just a unionist or nationalist party. We also argued that the rule governing the nomination of the premiers should be that the two premiers could not be both unionist or both nationalist, though one could be drawn from the ranks of the "others", should they increase in size.[102] Changes similar to these were introduced by the St. Andrews Agreement in October 2006.[103] One criticism of the agreement, after these changes, is that they maintain designations, including "others".[104] As the cardinal principle we are seeking to guard is that no sizable democratic community should be excluded from a fair share of executive power, we have no difficulty with an alternative arrangement consistent with this principle that dispenses with group designation. It would be possible to secure these goals by mandating that a collective or rotating presidency be drawn from the ranks of all sizable parties in the Assembly, and that there be a weighted majority rule that prevents one group from exercising dominance in both the executive and the legislature.

[102] McGarry & O'Leary, *supra* note 69, at 222–223.
[103] Agreement at St. Andrews, *supra* note 35.
[104] Taylor, *supra* note 65, at 220.

Simplifying and changing the current rules used for the passage of "key" measures to a simple weighted majority of at least 60 percent of MLAs has merit. This threshold would presently be sufficient to protect both unionists and nationalists, without privileging their votes over those of "others". Nationalists consistently have over 40 percent of the popular vote in recent elections, and the Catholic share of the population, which normally votes nationalist, is increasing. In most Assembly elections, these electoral and demographic facts will translate into nationalists winning over 40 percent of the seats (or 44 out of 108). In the 1998 and 2003 elections, nationalists fell just short of this mark, winning only 42 seats, although they received 44 in 2007 and may exceed this in future. Even if they failed to pass this threshold in the future, nationalists could only be outvoted on key measures if opposed by everyone else, including those currently designated as "others". Since these "others" stand on platforms of formal impartiality between unionism and nationalism, this is an unlikely scenario. Effectively, then, a 60 percent weighted majority rule will protect nationalists, now and later. Nationalists, and nationalists and others, by contrast, fall short of 60 percent, so they could not coerce all unionists in the foreseeable future. But, under such a rule change rejectionists would be unlikely to command 40 percent support in Northern Ireland—and the Assembly—as a whole, and, therefore, could not block measures that enjoyed substantial support among nationalists, unionists, and others.[105] That said, we recognize why both nationalists now, and unionists in the future, may wish to avail themselves of the protection created by parallel and weighted consent.

Though we accept the partial merits of a small number of integrationist difficulties with the agreement, we observe that most of these critics fail to note that the agreement generally is liberal rather than corporate—apart from the exceptions just considered. In fact, its institutional rules are more conducive to the emergence of new parties and identities than the majoritarian political systems typically favored by integrationists and centripetalists. The single transferable vote in multimember constituencies allows parties to win seats with much smaller thresholds than are normally required under single-member plurality, or the majoritarian electoral system recommended by Horowitz. Voters are less likely than voters in Westminster elections to regard voting for a new or a small party as a waste of time. Proportional representation and the single transferable vote provide an opportunity, though no guarantee, of both intercommunal and transcommunal transfer of lower-preference votes. These systems are more conducive to extrabloc voting than the plurality rule. Any party, not just nationalist and unionist parties, is entitled to seats in the executive if it meets the quota established by the d'Hondt system. A party is entitled to membership in government

---

[105] We have argued elsewhere that the bill of rights envisaged under the agreement, to be effective, must have the support of a majority of the Assembly, and at least 40 percent of nationalist and unionist MLAs. McGarry & O'Leary, *supra* note 69.

with a much smaller share of seats in the legislature than normally is required in any Westminster system, so new parties have a better chance of promoting their visibility, influencing public policy, and demonstrating to their supporters that voting for them is a meaningful exercise. D'Hondt helps small parties entitled to executive positions by preventing large parties from monopolizing the most important portfolios.[106] We have argued for making the executive even more inclusive and, thus, fairer to non-dominant political parties by extending its size. A larger executive, constituted by the d'Hondt mechanism, might give a seat to the Alliance or other small parties. Alternatively, the executive could be constituted by the Sainte-Laguë mechanism, which is more advantageous for small parties than d'Hondt.[107] It is ironic that integrationists support electoral systems and executive composition rules that make it difficult for small parties to be elected, because in deeply divided societies, the parties that integrationists prefer are often small.

The Belfast Agreement not only stresses equality ("parity of esteem") between nationalists and unionists, rather than the inequality of a real apartheid regime, but it also offers protection to individuals, including those who regard themselves as neither unionist nor nationalist. Each minister is required under the agreement to behave in a non-partisan way and "to serve all the people of Northern Ireland equally, and to act in accordance with the general obligations on government to promote equality and prevent discrimination". The agreement looks forward to the enforcement of the European Convention on Human Rights in Northern Ireland law,[108] which has made it easier for individual citizens to bring cases against authorities. It has established a new Northern Ireland Human Rights Commission;[109] it will lead to a bill of rights for Northern Ireland;[110] and has produced a new statutory Equality Commission.[111] The U.K. government, under the agreement and the 1998 Northern Ireland Act,[112] imposes a statutory obligation on public authorities "to promote equality of opportunity in relation to religion and political opinion; gender; race; disability; age; marital status; dependants; and sexual orientation".[113] Public bodies are required to draw up statutory schemes indicating how they will implement these obligations. While education was not a negotiated part of the agreement, Northern Ireland's current education system is that of a liberal consociation. It allows children to

[106] Brendan O'Leary, Bernard Grofman & Jorgen Elklit, *Divisor Methods for Sequential Portfolio Allocation in Multi-party Executive Bodies: Evidence from Northern Ireland and Denmark*, 49 Am. J. Pol. Sci. 198, 198 (2005).
[107] *See* John McGarry & Brendan O'Leary, Explaining Northern Ireland: Broken Images 373–375 (Blackwell Publ'g 1995).
[108] Belfast Agreement, Rights, Safeguards and Equality of Opportunity, para. 2.
[109] *Id.* Rights, Safeguards and Equality of Opportunity, para. 5.
[110] *Id.* Rights, Safeguards and Equality of Opportunity, para. 4.
[111] *Id.* Rights, Safeguards and Equality of Opportunity, para. 6.
[112] Northern Ireland Act, 1998, c. 47.
[113] Belfast Agreement, Rights, Safeguards and Equality of Opportunity, para. 3.

attend Catholic or state (in effect, Protestant) schools without requiring them to do so and now funds each system equally. Parents may opt to send their children to a third, funded and integrated sector. The likeliest alternatives to these arrangements, including discrimination in favor of the integrated sector, would be coercive. The universities in the region are also formally liberal.

Lastly, the agreement establishes the Civic Forum alongside the elected Assembly.[114] This institution is made up of representatives of organizations outside conventional politics and presents an opportunity for those who do not feel represented by conventional political parties to have their voices heard. It has no counterpart elsewhere in the U.K., including in the newly devolved regimes in Scotland and Wales. Arguably, it overrepresents the unelectable "others".[115]

There are other ways in which integrationist and centripetalist prescriptions are less fair than what is provided for in the agreement. Proportional representation, the single transferable vote, and d'Hondt match popular support with shares of legislative and executive seats. The majoritarian and plurality systems associated with integration and centripetalism, by contrast, give disproportionate shares of legislative and executive seats to majority or plurality groups. Alternate voting favors larger over smaller groups, because the candidates from such groups have to attract fewer votes. More generally, integrationism invariably privileges one *national* community over another.[116] This is most obvious with overtly unionist or republican projects, such as those of the UKUP and republican Sinn Féin. By celebrating only individual rights within their preferred nation-state, and thereby ignoring the minority's existence as a national minority, they both end up privileging the majority, and thereby endangering individual equality.[117]

3.3 Democracy

A third criticism of the Belfast Agreement's consociational institutions is that they lack democratic virtues. Critics argue that the agreement has "weak democratic moorings";[118] that it is in "breach of every basic principle of democracy" and represents a "macabre parody of democracy".[119] Criticisms of the agreement's

---

[114] *Id.* strand one, para. 34.

[115] The Civic Forum was dissolved when the political institutions were suspended in 2002, but there are prospects of resurrection. *See Civic Forum Invite Issued*, UTV Newsroom, May 31, 2007, *available at* <http://www.u.tv/newsroom/indepth.asp?pt=n&id=82600> (last visited Aug. 29, 2007).

[116] As we have argued, consociation can also be charged with privileging the state and hence those groups that dominate or support the state. But this is an oversight in classical consociational theory that works against its general logic.

[117] More generally, see Will Kymlicka, Multicultural Citizenship: A Liberal Theory of Minority Rights (Oxford Univ. Press 1995).

[118] Wilford & Wilson, *supra* note 14, at 26.

[119] Robert McCartney, *Devolution is a Sham*, Observer, Feb. 20, 2000; Robert McCartney, *This is a Situation Hardly Calculated to Produce Either Clarity or Truth*, Belfast Telegraph, Oct. 26, 2006 [hereinafter McCartney, *This is a Situation*].

democratic failings come in three forms, all of which are also standard objections to consociation.

First, there are concerns about democratic accountability. It is said that Northern Ireland's inclusive executive leaves a rather small portion of the Assembly's membership free to serve as an opposition for standard adversarial parliamentary debating in the classic Westminster model.[120] Others have argued that ministerial discretion within the executive has undermined the doctrine of collective responsibility, making it difficult for voters to hold the authorities to account.[121] Second, consociation is said to have reduced voters' choices and undermined competition between parties. The inclusion of all major parties in the executive is said to have limited, or even deprived, voters of their freedom to choose and change the government.[122] One unionist integrationist critic even claims that the agreement "requires" Sinn Féin to be in government,[123] while another critic argues that d'Hondt has resulted in a "permanent coalition" of "four faith-based parties" that "can never be removed".[124] These problems, centripetalists argue, are missing from their preferred institutions, which provide for an opposition to hold government to account and to pose as an alternative government.[125] Third, social transformers decry consociation's alleged focus on (secret) negotiations among—and governance confined to—ethnic elites.[126] Consociationalists are said to distrust the masses, preferring a "passive and demobilised population" and electoral systems that strengthen party leaders over voters.[127] These values are seen as at odds with those of a modern participatory democracy. Modern democracies, transformers argue, empower voters and do not restrict civic responsibility to voting in elections or even membership in political parties; such modern democracies encourage active and ongoing political deliberation through a wide range of voluntary associations and public consultations. Taylor argues from this perspective that the agreement was negotiated behind closed doors by ethnopolitical elites rather than through a "wide-ranging deliberation in the public sphere", and that the "ethnonational group-based understanding of politics" in the agreement has foreclosed the space for a "more deliberative form of democracy around a common citizenship".[128] Some social transformers, including supporters of the Alliance Party, believe one result of the agreement's (ethnic) elitism is a focus on ethnic issues and the screening out of genuinely popular

---

[120] *See* Taylor, *supra* note 65, at 219; Horowitz, *The Agreement, supra* note 13, at 104.

[121] Patrick Roche, *A Stormont Without Policy*, BELFAST TELEGRAPH, Mar. 30, 2000.

[122] McCartney, *This is a Situation, supra* note 119.

[123] Cedric Wilson, *Rejection of the Belfast Agreement is Entirely Compatible with the Unionist Commitment to "Equal Citizenship"*, BELFAST TELEGRAPH, Oct. 28, 2003.

[124] John O'Farrell, *Today, We have Agreed,* NEW STATESMAN, Apr. 2, 2007.

[125] Horowitz, *The Agreement, supra* note 13, at 46. O'Flynn argues that a centripetal coalition would give rise to a particularly vibrant opposition, as the latter would be dominated by radicals. O'Flynn, *supra* note 98, at 26.

[126] Taylor, *supra* note 10, passim.

[127] Dixon, *supra* note 99, at 359.

[128] Taylor, *supra* note 65, at 217 & 221.

cross-cutting issues, such as questions of class and gender.[129] Thus Wilson argues that Northern Ireland's current "democratic deficit" involves neglect of "bread and butter" issues and the underrepresentation of women, issues which he sees as "historically . . . at the heart of the Northern Ireland problem".[130]

The charge that consociation is incompatible with an opposition capable of holding the government to account must be tempered by the fact that the backbenchers from other parties also in government are likely to hold the governmental minister of a different party to account in the Assembly. (Ironically, the same people who criticized Northern Ireland's consociation for having no opposition have lamented the high level of adversarial debate in the Assembly between the members of the governing parties.)[131] Mechanisms for rigorous accountability exist. Ministers face an Assembly Committee in their jurisdiction headed by a representative of another party.[132] This inhibits full-scale party fiefdoms in any functional sector—which cannot be said for the Westminster system. Indeed, two critics of the agreement who closely observed the institutions in action between 1999 and 2002 acknowledged that the committees had performed well in holding ministers to account.[133] In addition, the values of ministerial accountability (control of ministers by the Assembly) and collective responsibility (control of ministers by the executive) have to be weighed, in a deeply divided polity, against the need for minority representatives to have some independent initiative if power-sharing is to be meaningful. "Collective responsibility" and "traditional ministerial responsibility" may be used as tools for promoting majoritarianism within the framework of formal power sharing institutions. Minority ministerial discretion may be considered particularly important where minorities do not enjoy substantial powers of self-government, whether of a territorial or non-territorial sort. What is needed in these circumstances, then, is a balance between the values of ministerial initiative and those of ministerial accountability and collective responsibility.

D'Hondt, in fact, ensures that not every party is in the executive; there are, automatically, some opposition backbenchers. Between 1999 and 2002, five parties and nineteen MLAs were in opposition and, since May 2007, the numbers are three and ten, respectively. Neither is there any requirement that the executive comprise even all the major parties, in spite of the loaded and inaccurate

---

[129] For Alliance's views on this matter, see McEvoy, *supra* note 87, at 459.

[130] Robin Wilson, *Devolved Government Must Address Democratic Reform*, Irish Times, April 19, 2007.

[131] *See, e.g.,* Rick Wilford & Robin Wilson, *A "Bare Knuckle Ride": Northern Ireland, in* The State and the Nations: the First Year of Devolution in the United Kingdom 79 (Robert Hazell ed., Imprint Acad. 2001).

[132] The 1998 Northern Ireland Act prevents the committees from being chaired or deputy-chaired by ministers or junior ministers. The committees are required, where feasible, to be organized in such a way that the chair and deputy chair be from parties other than that of the relevant minister. The Northern Ireland Act, 1998, c. 47, § 19A.

[133] Wilford & Wilson, *supra* note 14, at 7–9.

description of the executive by centripetalists as a "mandatory" coalition.[134] The agreement simply entitles all major parties that qualify under d'Hondt to executive positions, but does not require these parties to take these positions. There is nothing to stop the SDLP and/or the UUP, or any other party, from deciding to go into opposition at any point. Indeed, members of the UUP and SDLP indicated a desire to do exactly that in the wake of the 2003 Assembly elections, and one observer advised them, after the 2007 elections, that it would be in their interests do so.[135] It may be ironic to have the two "radical" parties share power with the "moderates" in opposition, but this would be consistent with the agreement's rules. More generally, the view that consociation and opposition are incompatible is attributable to Horowitz's claim that consociation entails a fully inclusive "grand coalition" in which "everyone is to be included".[136] A consociation, however, merely requires joint government, involving the polity's major communities; it is not true that it requires a grand coalition, understood as all parties and communities being fully represented in the executive.[137] It may either be "complete", in Horowitz's reading of Lijphart's grand coalition; "concurrent", when restricted to parties commanding majority but not total support within their respective segments; or "weak", if at least one of the segmental parties in office commands only a plurality support within its group.[138] Between 1999 and 2002, Northern Ireland operated as a concurrent consociation and now operates, once again, as a concurrent consociation—with more support than before, since all four major parties of nationalism and unionism are committed to the new order.

There is nothing "permanent" about any party's place in the Assembly or in government, and plenty of reasons for parties to compete for voters' support. Under the agreement's rules, any party's share of seats in either institution is dependent on democratic support, and voters are free to withhold that support and to vote for other parties instead. Voters can expel all four incumbent parties from the executive or Assembly, or, more realistically, alter their share of positions. Thus, the executive established under the agreement in May 2007 looks different from that which existed from 1999 to 2002. While between 1999 and 2002, the first minister and deputy first minister positions were held by the UUP and SDLP, respectively, they are now held by the DUP and Sinn Féin. The UUP and SDLP share of ministerial portfolios has declined from six to three, while the DUP's and Sinn Féin's has increased from four to seven. The success of executive incumbents in Northern Ireland's elections since 1998 is, therefore, significantly less than their counterparts in the Westminster and U.S. Congressional systems

[134] For a brief disagreement with this language, see McGarry & O'Leary, *supra* note 5, at 25.
[135] David Adams, *Assembly Needs an Opposition*, The Blanket, Mar. 16, 2007.
[136] Donald L. Horowitz, *Constitutional Design: An Oxymoron?*, in Designing Democratic Institutions 256 (Ian Shapiro & Stephen Macedo eds., NYU Press 2000).
[137] Brendan O'Leary, *Debating Consociational Politics: Normative and Explanatory Arguments*, in From Power-Sharing to Democracy: Post-Conflict Institutions in Ethnically Divided Societies 3, 12–15 (S.J.R. Noel ed., McGill-Queens Univ. Press 2005).
[138] *Id.* at 15–17.

during the same period, where voters are said to have greater flexibility to "throw the rascals out". What the agreement prevents is not an alternation in government but the exclusion from the executive of a party that satisfies the d'Hondt threshold.

If we consider democracy as an institutional arrangement, or regulative ideal for governing a set of institutional arrangements, where members of a community make decisions about their collective affairs as equals, it is not at all clear that consociational democracy is inferior to the integrationist or centripetalist alternatives. Quite the opposite, consociation is more representative. Consociation is based on proportional representation, including versions, such as the single transferable vote, that are not based on party lists. The design of these systems is more likely than plurality or majoritarian electoral systems to produce "authentic" representation, or, in other words, to allow voters to elect the politicians they want. Proportional representation ensures that relatively few votes are wasted, compared with its majoritarian and pluralitarian alternatives, and better meets the fundamental democratic test of equality among citizens. Plurality and majoritarian systems are explicitly designed by their supporters in divided societies to produce "strategic" voting, or to give incentives to voters to select a particular sort of elite (those preferred by the electoral engineers) rather than those that voters would freely choose. On the face of it, this seems profoundly undemocratic. It appears to be based on the premise that the politicians people want, if they are ethnocentric or sectarian, are not the ones they need, and it helps to explain why Horowitz and his supporters often call for outsiders to push locals to adopt centripetal institutions when there is no internal agreement on them.[139]

A more sympathetic interpretation of Horowitz's thinking, including his criticism of consociation as undemocratic (which suggests that he possesses democratic values), is that the justificatory basis of his support for democracy is interest based. In the normative literature on democracy, there have been, traditionally, two types of defenses of democratic institutional arrangements. One is autonomy based, the other interest based.[140] An autonomy justification for democracy locates the central value of democratic governance in an appeal to individual— and collective—autonomy, allowing people to have collective control of the conditions of their existence. On the interest-based account, the central justification for democratic institutions is the protection of certain interests. The usual candidates for the relevant interests that democracy should protect are stability, access to resources and opportunities, education, health care, and public goods.[141] It is not clear, however, as we have demonstrated, that centripetalism fares better than consociationalism on an interest-based defense of democracy, where the interest at stake is stability. In addition, it is not clear that interest-based accounts

---

[139] Horowitz, *supra* note 136, at 277.
[140] *See* Daniel M. Weinstock, *The Real World of (Global) Democracy,* 37 J. Soc. Phil. 6 (2006).
[141] *Id.*

of democracy are adequate. An interest-based account seems to suggest that the only reason to prefer democracy to other forms of government is because it works better—an instrumental argument. It seems to imply that monarchy or aristocracy would be preferable to democracy if Plato was right that philosophers were better at governing. We maintain that *liberal* consociation, importantly represented in the agreement's institutions, has a greater affinity with the autonomy-based justification for democracy. It places value on the agency of the people who are making decisions. It does not attempt to manipulate election results on an output basis; rather, it places importance on input considerations, on the fact that all people's voices are respected and included in some way in the government that is formed, and hence the decisions that it makes. This is what it means to respect the collective agency of the people, and their capacity to have control over the collective conditions of their existence.

Consociationalists do not stop at promoting the equality of citizens within the legislature but extend it to the executive also. An inclusive grand coalition has democratic advantages in this respect over the "exclusive" majoritarian—even the weighted majoritarian—executives favored by centripetalists. Consociation, by bringing together authentic (representative) leaders, is designed to facilitate genuine democratic deliberation. It is much more likely to do this than centripetalist arrangements, which exclude certain voices from the legislature and executive, and far more likely than bottom-up models of social transformation, which face significant practical obstacles and which tacitly suppose that existing voters suffer from false consciousness.

Consociationalists accept that deals between leaders may need to be negotiated in camera to facilitate compromise, but they also understand that, particularly in modern democracies, it helps that the resulting settlements have popular resonance. Thus, it is a strength of Northern Ireland's agreement that it was ratified by referenda in both parts of Ireland. This popular backing is one reason why the agreement has been more resilient than the Sunningdale Agreement. Consociationalists acknowledge that leaders find it easier to govern or make deals where followers are deferential. Some argue that undemocratic consociations are better than the undemocratic alternatives,[142] but this hardly means that consociationalists think that public deference is possible or desirable in modern democracies. The electoral systems favored by consociationalists are in serious tension with public deference, since they are aimed at enhancing turnout and voter choice. Liberal consociationalists also have no objection to the participation of an active civil society, as long as it is genuinely representative, and as long as its role is designed to complement rather than supplant authentically representative and democratically elected political leaders. What distinguishes consociationalists from social transformers is that the latter appear to favor unelected

---

[142] Katharine Adeney, The limitations of Non-consociational Federalism—The Example of Pakistan (paper presented at the Annual Conference of the Pol. Stud. Assoc., U.K., Apr. 2007).

representatives of civil society—and only those that support a transformative agenda—over elected politicians.

As for the argument that consociational politics promotes a superficial ethno-national politics at the expense of more popular questions of class or gender, we submit that there is no evidence, either from public opinion data or from elections, that the latter questions are popular—even if we might wish it otherwise. If they were, then why do people not vote for parties that put such questions at the top of their agenda? Elections in Northern Ireland are free and fair, and turnouts are reasonably high when compared with other democratic jurisdictions. So the lack of support for class or gender-based parties cannot be explained by undemocratic structural impediments or by the presence of a large segment of the electorate that does not vote.[143] The correct empirical conclusion is that class and gender questions have not been in the forefront of politics in Northern Ireland because they have not been in the forefront of voters' minds—though if that changes the new institutions will allow that transformation.

4. Conclusion

There are places and times where integration is the appropriate normative strategy for resolving conflicts. Contemporary Northern Ireland is not one of them. A British or an Irish integration strategy has been available and either been imposed or demanded throughout the last century—orthodox Unionism and Irish nationalism, respectively. These rival programmatic visions have been at the heart of conflict. There is a third prescriptive integration program that is possible on paper, namely, integration into a Northern Irish identity; however, that has the obvious limitation that a sovereign and independent Northern Ireland commands far less support than either British unionism or Irish nationalism. We believe that if the current institutions endure, a common Northern Irish identity may come to be shared by most unionists and nationalists. But that will be the work of at least two decades, and it will be consociation that eases the path to this shared identity.

The Belfast Agreement is a consociational compromise between British unionists and Irish nationalists, an agreement on coexistence supported by their respective states. It is a confederalizing compromise, linking both major governments in Ireland and all the autonomous governments in the Isles, while granting Northern Ireland the capacity to become as independent in policy making as it wishes. This complex consociational and territorially pluralist settlement invalidates the centripetalist proposition that consociations are never made in or never appropriate for deeply divided places. We shall see whether it will show that consociations can be stable over the longer run amid nationally divided peoples. Its

---

[143] McGarry & O'Leary, *supra* note 5, at 309–310.

chances are fair. Meanwhile, integrationist critics of the agreement are free to mobilize and transform the identities that they hold culpable for the conflict. They are equally free to transform the institutions they believe, wrongly, freeze these collective identities. We are skeptical of their chances of success in our life-times, but if they succeed, we would say that consociation enabled them to suc-ceed. It is reasonable to think that, within this century, a majority will emerge within Northern Ireland that favors an all-Ireland state. But if that happens, and if it is matched with sufficient support in independent Ireland, we believe that the reunification of Ireland should take a confederal or federal form, preserve con-sociational arrangements within Northern Ireland, and should keep Northern Ireland linked to Great Britain through the British-Irish Council, if that is what unionists want. The experience of stable consociation within the sovereign frame-work of the U.K., with confederal links to Ireland, will ease any such transition. In short, whatever difficulties lie ahead—and we are sure there will be some—consociation will shape any political accommodation that genuinely recognizes the local major peoples without significantly discriminating against the others.

14

Recognition without empowerment: Minorities in a democratic South Africa

Christina Murray* and Richard Simeon**

The new democratic South Africa, the result of the transition in the early 1990s from the minority-dominated apartheid regime to a democratic "non-racial" and "non-sexist"[1] regime, has proudly proclaimed itself to be a "rainbow" nation,[2] united in its diversity.[3] These words encapsulate the victory of the African National Congress (ANC), for which a non-racial South Africa was a central aspiration. But many observers of the transition have thought that managing diversity would be a fundamental challenge to the new nation. How could reconciliation be achieved between the newly empowered black majority and the white minority, given the legacies of apartheid, minority rule, and the continuing and profound economic and social inequalities between black and white people? How would the now-disempowered (but not disenfranchised) white minority respond to its new status? What relations would develop between the so-called African[4] majority and other historic minorities—white people, the largely Afrikaans-speaking[5] "coloured"

* Professor of Constitutional Law and Human Rights, University of Cape Town. Email: Christina.Murray@uct.ac.za

** Professor of Political Science and Law, University of Toronto; MacKenzie King Visiting Professor, Department of Government, Harvard University. Email: rsimeon@wcfi a.harvard.edu

[1] S. AFR. CONST. 1996, ch. 1, §1.

[2] This was a term coined by Archbishop Desmond Tutu to describe post-1994 South Africa. The phrase was given weight by President Nelson Mandela in his first month of office, when he announced: "Each of us is as intimately attached to the soil of this beautiful country as are the famous jacaranda trees of Pretoria and the mimosa trees of the bushveld—a rainbow nation at peace with itself and the world." *See* KATHRYN A. MANZO, CREATING BOUNDARIES: THE POLITICS OF RACE AND NATION 71 (Lynne Rienner 1996).

[3] S. AFR. CONST. 1996, pmbl.

[4] Note that all the terms are contested. Except where indicated otherwise, this chapter uses the terminology of Statistics South Africa, the government statistical service. These are the terms used by the apartheid government now used to assess the success of measures intended to remedy the effects of apartheid.

[5] Approximately 82.1 percent of the colored population in South Africa speaks Afrikaans. *See* STATISTICS SOUTH AFRICA, THE PEOPLE OF SOUTH AFRICA POPULATION CENSUS 1996, at 12 (1998).

population,[6] and those of Indian descent? Also, would the old linguistic and tribal divisions, so assiduously cultivated by the apartheid regime in a divide-and-rule strategy that included tribal "homelands", or "bantustans", assert themselves once the common enemy was removed? Would Xhosas, Zulus, and others be at each others' throats once the underlying black-white division was eradicated?

These were and, to some extent, remain important questions. What is most noteworthy is that a considerable number of external commentators predicted that some or all of these fault lines would have a profound effect on the new South Africa, and that they would prove exceptionally difficult to manage. Observers debated alternative constitutional and institutional strategies for containing the potential conflicts.

It is now more than a decade since the adoption of the Constitution of 1996, and more than fifteen years since the transition began. Today, many issues related to minorities, in fact, do remain on the South African political agenda, although none of them seems likely to divide the country as had been predicted. There are, indeed, deep divisions within contemporary South Africa, within its governing party, the ANC, and between it and its allies. The most significant division remains that between white and black South Africans though the threat it offers has receded in the years since the 1994 elections. Other sources of conflict relate more to competing economic and class divisions and differing economic strategies than they do to the culturally based dichotomies that were expected to dominate modern politics.

In this chapter, we ask why and how this is so. Specifically, why have levels of hostility among the many racial or ethnic groups composing the South African rainbow nation been relatively low? And how can we explain this largely peaceful transition to democracy? Much of the explanation lies in the nature of the transition, particularly, in its historical context, the timing and length of the process, and the style of leadership in the most significant parties. These factors still have a profound (although perhaps waning) influence on South African politics. Indeed, the degree to which the accommodation reached in the transition will survive the changing modes of political interaction is yet to be seen. However, these matters

---

[6] It is notoriously difficult to offer a definition of "colored" in South Africa. Even the apartheid classification in the Population Registration Act 30 of 1950 relied on relative and intuitive concepts, defining colored people as being *not* European and *not* African or black, but generally accepted as "members of the race known as Cape Coloured". *See* IAN GOLDIN, MAKING RACE: THE POLITICS AND ECONOMICS OF COLOURED IDENTITY IN SOUTH AFRICA xvi (Longman 1987) (noting that no single definition of colored person exists). Similarly, the term "mixed race" is unsatisfactory since it tends toward racial identification based only on parentage. Although miscegenation between white European settlers and indigenous peoples undoubtedly contributed to the emergence of the colored people in South Africa, Peter Carstens refers to Cape Coloreds as "those South Africans of mixed cultural and racial stock whose ancestors include Europeans, Khoi and other indigenous African people, and Asians": Peter Carstens, *Cape Coloureds, in* 9 ENCYCLOPEDIA OF WORLD CULTURES: AFRICA AND THE MIDDLE EAST 58–60 (John Middleton & Amal Rassam eds., GK Hall & Company 1994). The label "mixed race" ignores the fact that today the parentage of colored persons can rarely be attributed to a particular "race" or "races".

are not the focus of this chapter. Here we are concerned primarily with issues of constitutional design. We begin with a brief analysis of the demographic characteristics of modern South Africa and of the historical forces that have shaped these traits. We then turn to the debate about how the many dimensions of difference found in the country should be reflected and represented within the new constitutional order. Should differences be recognized, emphasized, and institutionalized; or should they be blurred, transcended, and crosscut? In the comparative literature on the management of diversity, this remains one of the most contentious questions. It was also vigorously debated both among South Africans themselves and among outside observers. In particular, we focus on the debate, which has dominated the international literature, between the political scientists Arend Lijphart, the prime advocate of the "consociational" model that envisions a South Africa based on distinct, autonomous groupings,[7] and Donald Horowitz, an advocate of a more integrationist model.[8] Each has had important allies and supporters within South Africa.

Next, we explore the answer that South Africans provided in their final Constitution: namely, a strategy we describe as "recognition, without empowerment". This approach is consistent with a broader South African attitude. As Anthony Butler puts it, "Black South Africans combine awareness of the artificiality of tribal division with pride in the diverse history and culture of African peoples".[9] We then fast-forward to the present. What is the status of the diverse minorities in South Africa today, what are the current debates, what are the possibilities for the future? "Identity politics", we conclude, have not disappeared from South Africa, although such politics do not dominate the landscape.[10] This, we argue, is explained by a number of factors: by the views and attitudes of leaders of the liberation struggle, reflecting the long history of non-racial and inclusive politics; by the demographic fact that there is no single ethnic or linguistic majority in South Africa; by the design of South African institutions, which emphasize inclusion rather than institutionalizing difference; and by the overarching

---

[7] Lijphart has written widely on consociationalism and elite accommodation. *See* Arend Lijphart, Democracy in Plural Societies: A Comparative Exploration (Yale Univ. Press 1977); Arend Lijphart, *Constitutional Choices for New Democracies*, 2 J. Democracy 72 (1991); Arend Lijphart, *Prospects for Power-Sharing in the New South Africa, in* Elections '94 South Africa: The Campaigns, Results, and Future Prospects 221 (Andrew Reynolds ed., James Currey 1994); Arend Lijphart, *The Wave of Power-Sharing Democracy, in* The Architecture of Democracy: Constitutional Design, Conflict Management and Democracy 40 (Andrew Reynolds ed., Oxford Univ. Press 2002); Arend Lijphart, *Constitutional Design for Divided Societies*, 15 J. Democracy 96 (2004).

[8] Donald L. Horowitz, A Democratic South Africa? Constitutional Engineering in a Divided Society (Univ. Cal. Press 1991).

[9] Anthony Butler, *The State of the African National Congress, in* State of the Nation: South Africa 37 (Sakhela Buhlungui et al. eds., HSRC Press 2007).

[10] For an excellent assessment of identity politics in contemporary South Africa, see Steven Friedman, *A Voice for Some: South Africa's Ten Years of Democracy, in* Contested Terrain: Electoral Politics in South Africa's First Democratic Decade 3 (Jessica Piombo & Lia Nijzink eds., David Philip 2005).

accommodation between black and white South Africans, in which political power unambiguously flowed to the former, while the latter have largely retained their economic position.

We do not wish to paint too rosy a portrait; ethnic tensions remain present in many forms. Evidence of this includes the continuing (though much-diminished) tension between the two largest African groups, the Xhosa and the Zulus, and the related concerns of smaller groups that they will be marginalized; the worries by white and colored Afrikaans-speakers and speakers of other languages about the survival and status of their language; the claims by representatives of the colored and Indian communities that they are marginalized in modern South Africa; and a resurgence of claims by "traditional authorities" for a greater role.[11] Relations between the black majority and the white minority also remain fundamental. While now conducted in the language of normal political debate, black resentment at continuing white economic privilege, a parliamentary opposition that speaks largely for the white community, and contentious policy debates over issues such as affirmative action remain important aspects of South African politics. Despite these areas of contention (inevitable in any society as diverse as South Africa), this chapter will focus on the by-and-large peaceful transition and consolidation of democracy in South Africa.[12]

1. Mapping diversity in South Africa

By almost any measure, South Africa is a remarkably diverse society. But how these diversities are defined and measured and how they are played out in the political process is itself a contentious issue.

First, the national census, *Statistics South Africa,* classifies the population by racial group.[13] Here the image is of a society dominated by one racial group— "Africans"—who make up 79.4 percent of the total. "Whites", a category that includes both Afrikaans and English speakers and a number of other citizens of "European" descent, make up 9.3 percent. Slightly less numerous is the

[11] For examples of tension between ethnic groups, see text accompanying *infra* note 132; for concerns about the survival of Afrikaans, see the discussion of Afrikaans schools in text accompanying *infra* notes 100–108; For a discussion of "colored" identity in South Africa, see Now That We Are Free: Coloured Communities in a Democratic South Africa (Wilmot James et al. eds., Lynne Rienner 1996). For a discussion of the claims of traditional leaders, see Lungisile Ntsebeza, Democracy Compromised Chiefs and the Politics of Land in South Africa (HSRC Press 2005).

[12] See Friedman, *supra* note 10, at 3; *see also* Tom Lodge, Mandela to Mbeki 174 (David Philip & James Currey 2002).

[13] Statistics South Africa, Mid-year Estimates for South Africa by Population Group and Sex 1 (2005), *available at* <http://www.statssa.gov.za/PublicationsHTML/P03022005/html/P03022005.html>.

"coloured" group at 8.8 percent. People of Indian and Asian descent make up just 2.5 percent of the population.

Midyear Estimates for South Africa by Population Group and Gender (2005)[14]

Population Group	Male		Female		Total	
	number	% of total population	number	% of total population	number	% of total population
African	18,320,400	79.4	18,885,300	79.3	37,205,700	79.4
Colored	2,036,700	8.8	2,112,100	8.9	4,148,800	8.8
Indian/ Asian	565,100	2.4	588,800	2.5	1,153,900	2.5
White	2,148,100	9.3	2,231,700	9.4	4,379,800	9.3
Total	23,070,300	100.0	23,817,900	100.0	46,888,200	100.0

The apartheid regime, of course, institutionalized the dominance of the white minority in all spheres of life. The liberation struggle, as a result, was largely cast in terms of the black majority's search for equality against white resistance.[15] It is important to recall, however, that a small number of members of the white population was also prominent in the fight against apartheid. As we shall see, the central goal in the constitution-making process for the white minority was to ensure a liberal democratic constitution, which would include some important restraints on unlimited majority rule. It was clear, nonetheless, that any plausible version of democratic politics in South Africa would have to reflect the power of the black (or perhaps the African) majority.

There are some important differences in the racial composition of the South African provinces. In three largely rural provinces—Limpopo, Mpumalanga, and North West—Africans make up over 90 percent of the population. In three others—Free State, Eastern Cape, and KwaZulu-Natal—they range from 80 to 90 percent. In Gauteng, the most populous, urbanized, and industrialized province, almost three-quarters of the population is African while others represent just over a quarter of the population. In two provinces—the large Western Cape that includes Cape Town and the huge but sparsely populated and more rural Northern Cape—the colored population constitutes the majority. This is changing in the Western Cape as Africans from the Eastern Cape and other parts of the country migrate into the province.

[14] *Id.*
[15] Following the usage of many of those opposed to apartheid, "black" here refers to everyone who is not white.

Racial Composition of South African Provinces[16]

	Black African	Colored	Indian/Asian	White	Total
Eastern Cape	87.5%	7.4%	0.3%	4.7%	100%
Free State	88.0%	3.1%	0.1%	8.8%	100%
Gauteng	73.8%	3.8%	2.5%	19.9%	100%
KwaZulu-Natal	84.9%	1.5%	8.5%	5.1%	100%
Limpopo	97.3%	0.2%	0.2%	2.4%	100%
Mpumalanga	92.4%	0.7%	0.4%	6.5%	100%
Northern Cape	35.7%	51.6%	0.3%	12.4%	100%
North West	91.5%	1.6%	0.3%	6.6%	100%
Western Cape	26.7%	53.9%	1.0%	18.4%	100%
Total	79.0%	8.9%	2.5%	9.6%	100%

The second dimension of difference in South Africa is reflected in its linguistic diversity, though language is also—in some ways—a surrogate for ethnic identification within the larger "African" group. While Africans constitute a clear national majority, there is no such single-group dominance with respect to language. IsiZulu is the most widely spoken home language (23.8 percent), followed closely by isiXhosa. Afrikaans, spoken both by many whites and much of the colored population, ranks third, followed by English. Other languages—siSwati, Tshivenda, and isiNdebele, as well as others—are the home languages spoken by far fewer people.[17]

Again, language use varies across regions and provinces. In the Eastern Cape, for example, more than 80 percent speak isiXhosa, followed by Afrikaans. In KwaZulu-Natal, more than 80 percent speak isiZulu as their home language. Afrikaans is the majority language in the Western Cape and Northern Cape. In Free State, Limpopo, and North West, minority languages such as Sesotho, Setswana, and Sepedi predominate. In cosmopolitan Gauteng, no single language commands a majority.[18]

These data suggest that there was a rich potential for the emergence of a politics of language, tied closely to ethnic identity, in the new South Africa. This was especially the case in light of the apartheid regime's strategy of highlighting linguistic, ethnic, and tribal differences in order to frustrate African unity. The most

[16] STATISTICS SOUTH AFRICA, ACHIEVING A BETTER LIFE FOR ALL: PROGRESS BETWEEN CENSUS '96 AND CENSUS 2001 16, Table 2.1 (2001), *available at* <http://www.statssa.gov.za/Publications/Report-03-02-16/Report-03-02=16.pdf>.
[17] It should be noted that most South Africans speak at least two and usually three or four languages. Moreover, for all that Afrikaans was in many ways a language identified with the white apartheid government, it is spoken as a second or third language by many Africans.
[18] STATISTICS SOUTH AFRICA, CENSUS 2001 (2001), *available at* <http://www.statssa.gov.za/census01/html/key%20results_filesw/key%20/results.pdf>.

Languages Most Often Spoken at
Home 2001[19]

Language	1996	2001
isiZulu	23.8%	22.9%
isiXhosa	17.6%	17.9%
Afrikaans	13.3%	14.5%
Sepedi	9.4%	9.2%
English	8.2%	8.6%
Setswana	8.2%	8.2%
Sesotho	7.9%	7.7%
Xitsonga	4.4%	4.4%
siSwati	2.7%	2.5%
Tshivenda	2.3%	2.2%
isiNdebele	1.6%	1.5%
other	0.6%	0.5%

dramatic instance of this strategy was the creation of the bantustans, or home
lands, designed to contain designated ethnic groups in ethnically homogeneous
regions, using language to determine ethnicity.

Ten of these homelands were created in South Africa.[20] All were essentially
puppet regimes, despite a number having some nominal independence. Building
on the homeland (or reserve) structure of the past, the National Party government's first move in this regard, after its election in 1948, was the introduction
of the Bantu Authorities Act in 1951.[21] The system was developed further in the
1959 Bantu Self-Government Act,[22] and again in 1970 with the Black Homelands
Citizenship Act,[23] which designated Africans as citizens of their remote and poor
homelands, not of South Africa. Between 1976 and 1981 four of these bantustans
were declared independent and raised their own flags in celebration of the inaug-
uration of their presidents.[24] A major task for the transformed South African
regime was the reintegration of these areas into the country, including their
incorporation into the nine new provinces, which, unlike the bantustans, were
not designed as ethnic enclaves. There was resistance from some bantustan elites;
but a more important consequence proved to be the lasting legacy of corruption and poor administration that has plagued several provincial governments.

---

[19] *Id.*
[20] Another ten in South African-controlled territory of South West Africa (now Namibia).
[21] Bantu Authorities Act 68 of 1951.
[22] Bantu Self-Government Act 46 of 1959.
[23] Black Homelands Citizenship Act 23 of 1970.
[24] The bantustans were independent in name only, remaining heavily influenced by and
dependent on the South African government. None received international recognition. *See* JOHN
DUGARD, INTERNATIONAL LAW: A SOUTH AFRICAN PERSPECTIVE 101–102 (3d ed., Juta 2005).

Building on British colonial practice, the old regime had supported and placed on salary many so-called traditional leaders, relying on ethnic and linguistic identities and hierarchical and elitist attitudes toward authority and government that were—and remain—in sharp contrast to the modern aspirations and design of the new Constitution.[25]

Ethnicity and language are not the only, or the most important, divisions in contemporary South Africa. Class and economic divisions, closely aligned with race historically, have long run through South African life. Trade unions, represented by the Congress of South African Trade Unions (COSATU), and the Communist Party of South Africa (SACP) were important elements of the liberation struggle's coalition, in alliance with the ANC. Not surprisingly, a major element of the apartheid strategy was to protect the privileges of the white working class against black competition. Class, as we shall see, remains important in South Africa. Moreover, while class is still largely determined by race, the emergence of a new black middle class, partly as a result of specific government policies, has introduced an element of class politics into the life of the majority as well.[26] Economic inequality has grown rather than diminished since the end of apartheid.

The colored population centered in the Western Cape and the Northern Cape is another dimension of difference with political consequences. Historically, the old regime accorded some limited recognition and privileges to this community, creating a political separation between the colored community and the majority African population. Today, many members of the colored community feel excluded from the new regime. They argue that the colored minority is not accommodated by either of the dominant political parties in the new South Africa, which may be viewed as having their roots, on the one hand, in the liberation struggle (ANC) or, on the other, in the race politics of apartheid (Democratic Alliance or DA). In neither of these is the colored population at home or at ease.[27] Indeed, empirical evidence from Afrobarometer confirms that the colored community does not feel fully included in the ANC.[28] Politics in the Western Cape province and in the city of

[25] The 1996 Constitution continues to recognize traditional leaders: S. AFR. CONST. 1996, ch. 12. Moreover, their authority has been secured and, perhaps, enhanced over the past ten years. *See* Tom Bennett & Christina Murray, *Traditional Leaders, in* CONSTITUTIONAL LAW OF SOUTH AFRICA, ch. 26 (Stuart Woolman et al. eds., Jutas 2006); NTSEBEZA, *supra* note 11.

[26] *But see* JEREMY SEEKINGS & NICOLI NATTRASS, CLASS, RACE AND INEQUALITY IN SOUTH AFRICA 370–375 (Univ. of KwaZulu-Natal Press 2006) (observing that, despite the fact that policies since the end of apartheid have not been pro-poor, and despite a growing consciousness of class, the emergence of political attitudes that are differentiated along class lines has been very limited).

[27] *See, e.g.,* NOW THAT WE ARE FREE, *supra* note 11; Megan Addis, *Between a Rock and a Hard Place: The Marginalization of Coloured and Indian Interests in South African Politics,* 27 ISSUE: J. OPINION 37 (1999).

[28] Karen E. Feree, *The Micro-Foundations of Ethnic Voting: Evidence from South Africa* (Afrobarometer, Working Paper No. 40, 2004). The official opposition, the Democratic Alliance, made significant electoral gains among colored voters in the 2004 elections. Susan Booysen, *The*

Cape Town are now a closely fought battle, seesawing between the largely African ANC and the DA, which is supported by significant segments of the colored population as well as the traditional white elite.

The much smaller Indian community, based chiefly in the eThekwini (Durban) area of KwaZulu-Natal, provided a disproportionate share of leadership in the liberation struggle. But, for reasons similar to those regarding the colored population, the Indian community also faces marginalization in the new South Africa. Survey data shows that the Indian population does not identify fully with either the majority ANC or the DA.[29]

Finally, gender remains a deep fault line within South African society. In traditional African societies, as elsewhere in the world, patriarchies prevail and women are subordinated despite their enormous contributions to both economic and social life. The 1996 South African Constitution places considerable weight on gender equality and a nonsexist society. However, inequality and the sexual exploitation of women remain a profound problem, not easily addressed by constitutional norms or policy pronouncements. Although there has been much progress in making major South African institutions more representative of the ethnic makeup the country, there has been much less progress in making them more representative in terms of gender. For example, in 1994, at the start of the transition, there were only three black male and two white female judges in South Africa. By 2005, there were 82 Africans, colored, and Indians on the bench (41.4 percent) while 108 judges were white. By contrast, there were twenty-eight women—less than 15 percent.[30]

Democratic Alliance, in ELECTORAL POLITICS IN SOUTH AFRICA 129, 142 (Jessica Piombo & Lia Nijzink eds., Palgrave Macmillan 2005).

[29] For an empirical study, see Feree, *supra* note 28. For theoretical studies, see Herman Giliomee, James Myburgh & Lawrence Schlemmer, *Dominant Party Rule, Opposition Parties and Minorities in South Africa, in* OPPOSITION AND DEMOCRACY IN SOUTH AFRICA 161 (Roger Southall ed., Frank Cass 2001); Addis, *supra* note 27.

[30] The public service presents a similar picture. *See* SOUTH AFRICA PUBLIC SERVICE COMMISSION, STATE OF THE PUBLIC SERVICE REPORT 2005, at 11 (2005). The Department of Public Service and Administration (D.P.S.A.) resolved in 2003 to have thirty percent of its senior management positions filled by women by March, 2005: SOUTH AFRICA DEPARTMENT OF PUBLIC SERVICE & ADMINISTRATION, A STRATEGIC FRAMEWORK FOR GENDER EQUALITY WITHIN THE PUBLIC SERVICE (2006–2015) DPSA CONSULTATION DOCUMENT, at 4, *available at* <http://www.dpsa.gov.za/documents/ee/Strat_frmwrk.pdf> [hereinafter *A Strategic Framework*]. This objective was achieved only a year later in March 2006. The current goal is to have half of senior management positions filled by women by 2009. Geraldine J. Fraser-Moleketi, *Foreword* to *A Strategic Framework*. Women are better represented in the body of DPSA employees. In March 2005, the public service employed 1,073,033 people. Of these, 86.5 per cent were black, while 53.3 per cent were women. *A Strategic Framework*, at 7. *See also* John-Mary Kauzya, *Managing Diversity in the Public Service: One of Africa's Least Tackled Issues* (paper presented to the American Society for Public Administration, March 2002); Katherine Neff & Frederick Uys, *Realizing a Representative Bureaucracy in South Africa: Success or Failure?* (paper presented to the Midwest Political Science Association, Apr. 2005).

2. Designs for a new South Africa

Given these diverse elements, and the divisive and exploitative history that gave rise to them, a fundamental question confronted South Africans as they began the democratic transition. What sort of constitutional order would facilitate reconciliation, mitigate conflict, embrace democracy, human rights, and the rule of law, and so provide South Africans with a framework for governance enabling a new government to meet the immense developmental challenges ahead?

In the late 1980s, as the apartheid government began to experience more pressure both from within and from the international community, it became apparent that a move to democracy was not only possible in South Africa but inevitable. The central question for scholars and policy makers was, therefore, not whether South Africans would or should adopt democratic institutions but, rather, what sort of democratic institutions were most likely to secure stable and legitimate government in South Africa. The common assumption uniting all those involved in the debate was that the design of new South African political institutions would be a key factor affecting the potential for peace and stability. In short, institutions and political engineering mattered. However, beyond this common assumption, policy makers and scholars diverged quite significantly in their convictions regarding which democratic institutions would be best suited for the new order. The ANC was deeply committed to a non-racial system in which ethnicity had no relevance.[31] Scholars such as Philip Mayer,[32] Michael Macdonald,[33] and Roger Southall[34] agreed with the ANC and advocated a Westminster-style majoritarian democracy in South Africa. The National Party, supported by scholars including Lawrence Schlemmer, Hermann Giliomee,[35] David Welsh,[36] Donald Horowitz,[37] and Arend Lijphart[38] advanced arguments for power-sharing models. Even within the majoritarian and power-sharing

[31] *See* TOM LODGE, BLACK POLITICS IN SOUTH AFRICA SINCE 1945, at 82–86 (Ravan Press 1983); Nhlanhla Ndebele, *The African National Congress and the Policy of Non-Racialism: A Study of the Membership Issue*, 29 POLITIKON 133 (2002) (for a discussion of the emergence of non-racialism in the ANC).

[32] *See* Philip Mayer, *Class, Status and Ethnicity as Perceived by Johannesburg Africans, in* CHANGE IN CONTEMPORARY SOUTH AFRICA 153 (Leonard Thompson & Jeffrey Butler eds., Univ. Calif. Press 1975).

[33] *See* Michael Macdonald, *The Siren's Song: the Political Logic of Power-Sharing in South Africa*, 18 J. S. AFR. STUD. 709 (1992).

[34] *See* Roger Southall, *Consociationalism in South Africa: The Buthelezi Commission and Beyond*, 21 J. MOD. AFR. STUD. 77 (1983). *See also* GERHARD MARE, BROTHERS BORN OF WARRIOR BLOOD: POLITICS AND ETHNICITY IN SOUTH AFRICA (Ravan Press 1992).

[35] *See* HERMAN GILIOMEE & LAWRENCE SCHLEMMER, FROM APARTHEID TO NATION BUILDING (Oxford Univ. Press 1989).

[36] *See* FREDERICK VAN ZYL SLABBERT & DAVID WELSH, SOUTH AFRICA'S OPTIONS: STRATEGIES FOR POWER SHARING (David Philip 1979).

[37] *See* HOROWITZ, *supra* note 8, passim.

[38] *See* AREND LIJPHART, POWER-SHARING IN SOUTH AFRICA (Univ. Cal. Berkeley 1985).

camps, a great deal of variation existed as to the specific institutional designs that would create a lasting and democratic peace.

The root of these divergent prescriptions was not a simple disagreement over the benefits of different conflict-regulating mechanisms. Instead, the debate concerning which democratic institutions were best suited to South Africa reflected a more fundamental clash in beliefs about the nature of ethnicity in the country, specifically, and the fluidity and malleability of ethnic identity, more generally.[39] There was great disagreement among scholars about the salience of ethnic identity in South Africa, and there were many different predictions about how ethnic identifications might change with the ending of apartheid. Each of the perspectives on ethnicity in South Africa was intimately connected to a belief about the nature of ethnic identity more broadly, with some scholars holding primordial perceptions of ethnicity and others believing ethnic identity to be a socially constructed and fluid phenomenon. The section to follow will outline the various institutional models advanced by scholars and policy makers for the new democratic South Africa and tie each of these models to their theoretical underpinnings regarding ethnicity.

2.1 The Lijphart-Horowitz debate

Two of the most prominent foreign observers of the developments in South Africa were political scientists Arend Lijphart and Donald Horowitz—both noted students of other divided societies. Lijphart and Horowitz were in agreement that the fundamental divisions within South African society went well beyond the black-white division upon which the liberation struggle was focused.[40] For Lijphart, "it is wrong to characterize the basic problem in terms of a dichotomous black-white conflict. Far from being homogeneous communities, the black and white groups are each deeply divided...".[41] For Horowitz, South Africa "is also characterized by ethnic cleavages within the racial categories".[42]

Both also predicted that once the scourge of apartheid had been removed, these differences would gain greater prominence. Said Horowitz: "There is a potential for intra-African conflicts to supersede Black-White conflicts. ... "[43] As Lijphart put it: "[E]thnic cleavages are currently muted by the feelings of black solidarity in opposition to white minority rule, but they are bound to re-assert themselves in a situation of universal suffrage and free electoral competition".[44]

Lijphart and Horowitz also agreed that, in such a divided society, with an extremely lopsided majority and minority, simple majority rule would not suffice.

---

[39] HOROWITZ, *supra* note 8, at 1.
[40] *See* Macdonald, *supra* note 33, for an excellent survey of these differences.
[41] LIJPHART, *supra* note 38, at 19.
[42] HOROWITZ, *supra* note 8, at 42.
[43] *Id.* at 70.
[44] *Id.* at 20.

It would result either in civil war, or exclusion of the minorities, or both. Lijphart suggested that "majority rule in plural societies spells majority dictatorship and civil strife".[45] Horowitz agreed that the political institutions that emerge in divided societies must "counter conflict and foster inter-group accommodation".[46] Both argued that there must be some form of power sharing.

But here they diverged. For Lijphart the answer was "consociational democracy". Given the racial and ethnic differences and the strength of their associated identities, the proper response would be, first, to institutionalize them by way of substantial autonomy for each group, whether by way of federalism or by other means. Second, consociational democracy would promote accommodation among elites through power sharing at the center, with inclusive cabinets, a proportional electoral system that guarantees that all groups have at least some voice in the legislature, proportionality in the allocation of public positions in the public service, the judiciary, and the military, and mutual vetoes for minorities on issues crucial to them. For Horowitz, as well as for other critics, consociationalism would freeze, entrench, and otherwise perpetuate the very divisions it was meant to accommodate.[47] Moreover, it was suspiciously close to the apartheid policy of "separate development", manifested most egregiously in the bantustans. Horowitz believed that ethnic and racial differences were more fluid, more of a social construct, than Lijphart was prepared to accept. For Horowitz, these differences would remain salient in a new South Africa, to be sure, but the preferred strategy was an integrationist or centripetal design, one that would create strong incentives for political leaders to build coalitions cutting across racial and ethnic groups. Horowitz's preferred option was to rely heavily on the electoral system. His choice was "vote pooling", best achieved through single member districts, using a transferable vote to ensure that each elected member is supported by a majority of constituents.[48]

We focus on the Lijphart-Horowitz debate for two reasons: first, because their views—within the South African context—were called on frequently in support of or in opposition to various alternatives; and, second, because the debate between integrationist and consociational strategies—whether to institutionalize differences, or to blur, crosscut, and transcend them—has become one of the central theoretical and practical questions running through the literature on the accommodation and management of difference in modern societies.[49] However,

---

[45]   Lijphart, *supra* note 38, at 19.

[46]   Horowitz, *supra* note 8, at xiii.

[47]   *See, e.g.*, George Tsebelis, Nested Games: Rational Choice in Comparative Politics (Univ. Cal. Press 1990).

[48]   For a careful review of the electoral system debate—in particular, of the relative merits of single member versus proportional representation models in divided societies, see Andrew Reynolds, *Constitutional Engineering in Southern Africa*, 6 J. Democracy 86 (1995).

[49]   For excellent recent statements of the Horowitz-Lijphart debate, see Donald L. Horowitz, *Constitutional Design: Proposals versus Processes*, *in* The Architecture of Democracy: Constitutional Design, Conflict Management, and Democracy 15 (Andrew Reynolds ed., Oxford Univ. Press 2002); Arend Lijphart, in *The Wave of Power-Sharing Democracy*, The

this ethnic/linguistic pluralist perspective was by no means the only lens through which one could analyze the emerging South Africa. Indeed, Horowitz[50] identifies no fewer than twelve competing sets of images and narratives, themselves overlapping and evolving, and each associated with alternative political goals and constitutional prescriptions.

For example, the ANC's 1955 Freedom Charter embraced an inclusive view, namely, that "South Africa belongs to all who live in it, black and white".[51] Ethnic divisions were real, but they were essentially the creations of apartheid, and once that was abolished then a democracy based on neither race nor ethnicity would be able to emerge. In a free and democratic South Africa, equal rights would be guaranteed for all.

This view contrasted with that of other groups, such as PAC (the Pan Africanist Congress) and AZAPO (the Azanian Peoples Organisation), which propounded a more "Africanist" and majoritarian view. The first task was to abolish colonialism and introduce majority rule. Linguistic and ethnic differences within the African community were again perceived to be socially constructed creations of white domination, with no place in the new South Africa. Simple demographic facts meant that a majority government would be an African government.

The white community itself was divided between the larger and politically more dominant Afrikaner community, and the smaller but, historically, economically more dominant English speakers. They were united in their fear of unfettered majority rule. For some, the preferred option was to create a liberal regime, with strong guarantees of individual rights, a commitment to constitutionalism and the rule of law, and with checks and balances to restrain the majority and to ensure limited government. Others argued for a "two nations" model. At one extreme, this envisioned the creation of an Afrikaner *Volkstaat*, in which an Afrikaner society would coexist with the African nation. But the model that most appealed to those who supported protection for separate identities was consociationalism. This meant each racially or linguistically defined group would have some considerable degree of autonomy and its own sphere of influence, the incorporation of all groups into the executive, mutual vetoes on issues critical to each group, and so on. A truly federal South Africa in which groups had some true political autonomy was an important part of such proposals, both to provide checks and balances and to provide political space for the constituent groups.[52]

ARCHITECTURE OF DEMOCRACY: CONSTITUTIONAL DESIGN, CONFLICT MANAGEMENT, AND DEMOCRACY 37 (Andrew Reynolds ed., Oxford Univ. Press 2002).

[50] HOROWITZ, *supra* note 8, at 3–8. *See also* Robert Mattes, *Democracy Without the People: Political Institutions and Citizenship in the New South Africa* (paper submitted to Harvard Univ. Comm. for Afr. Stud. Occasional Papers Series 2005).

[51] The Freedom Charter (June 26, 1955), *available at* <http://www.anc.org.za/ancdocs/history/charter.html>.

[52] The first developed model of a consociational solution for South Africa was published by the government of the KwaZulu bantustan in 1981. *See* THE BUTHELEZI COMMISSION, 1–2 THE

Other, more radical groups argued that such consociational proposals were little more than "a refurbishing of traditional segregationist ideology by emphasizing 'group plurality' rather than race as a continuing basis for white dominance, and/or were part of a ruling-class strategy for coopting subordinate racial elites within a profoundly conservative, yet 'de-racialised' and 'power-sharing' framework".[53]

All these and many other views contended both within and between the various communities as South Africans began to contemplate the future of a post-apartheid South Africa in the 1980s. Of course, these were not abstract theoretical debates. They took place in a context of escalating violence. While the fundamental conflict was between white and black, some of the worst violence took place within the black community, between the ANC and the Inkatha Freedom Party (IFP), a Zulu nationalist movement[54] represented by Mangosuthu Buthelezi, leader of the KwaZulu bantustan, and his Inkatha movement. Elements of the outgoing regime, interested in division in the African community, contributed to the violence.[55]

3. Constructing "The New South Africa"

The South African transition was a lengthy process.[56] Few believed that it could be achieved peacefully, and, indeed, violence erupted sporadically throughout the process. The transition began with the release of political prisoners, most notably Nelson Mandela, and the unbanning of the ANC and other organizations that opposed apartheid. The negotiators had two fundamental tasks: first, to bring an end to the protracted struggle; second, to develop a constitutional framework for the future democratic governance of South Africa.[57] The changed international

REQUIREMENTS FOR STABILITY AND DEVELOPMENT IN KWAZULU AND NATAL (1981). For a review and critique, see Southall, *supra* note 34.

[53] *See* Southall, *supra* note 34, at 77.

[54] It is debatable whether or not to describe the IFP as a "nationalist" movement. Certainly its rhetoric and its goals of greater autonomy for KwaZulu-Natal point in that direction. But others, including Zulu supporters of the ANC, reject this idea, and its implication that South Africa is a "multinational" country. Nevertheless, Zulus are the only group in South Africa analogous to Canadian Quebecers or Spanish Catalans.

[55] The complicity of certain members of the South African Defence Force was confirmed by a report completed in 1992 but made public only in 2006. For a summary of the Steyn report, see Chiara Carter, *Apartheid Army's Deadly Secrets*, INDEPENDENT ONLINE, Apr. 30, 2006, *available at* <http://www.iol.co.za/index.php?set_id=1&click_id=13&art_id=vn20060430083249898C116766> (last visited May 30, 2007). *See also* Shula Marks, "*The dog that did not bark, or why Natal did not take off*": *Ethnicity and Democracy in South Africa—KwaZulu-Natal, in* ETHNICITY AND DEMOCRACY IN AFRICA 183 (Bruce Berman, Dickson Eyoh & Will Kymlicka eds., Ohio Univ. Press 2004).

[56] Of course, taking the concept in its fullest sense, the transition is not yet complete.

[57] Christina Murray & Richard Simeon, *Parachute or Strait-Jacket: The Legacy of South Africa's Pacted Constitution* (paper presented at Constitution Building in Africa, Post-1989, a workshop of the Global Legal Studies Initiative, Univ. of Wisconsin Law School, Oct. 15–16, 2005).

environment following the end of the Cold War facilitated the process. Each side had considerable bargaining leverage now that the dominant white group realized it could not hold on to power forever, and the majority of Africans realized they could not prevail over white military power. The story of the resulting negotiations has been well told.[58]

For the whites, it was critical to negotiate a settlement while they still held the reins of power and before democratic elections, which would inevitably spell the end of their political domination and of their ability to shape the new constitution. For the blacks, there could be no legitimate constitution until after elections, and its ratification by a democratically elected parliament. As a result, the constitution-making process proceeded in two stages. First, the parties negotiated an interim constitution (IC) in 1993.[59] Then, the first democratic elections were held, in 1994. Following that, the newly elected upper and lower houses, constituted as a constitutional assembly, had two years in which to negotiate a final constitution. In order to maintain some bargaining power in the final negotiations, the outgoing government succeeded in winning agreement on a set of thirty-four "constitutional principles", which were appended to the IC.[60] These were to govern the last negotiations. The new Constitutional Court would have to certify the final constitution as being in full compliance with these principles before it could take effect. In the event, once agreement in the constitutional assembly was reached in 1996, the results of its work were duly submitted to the Constitutional Court. The Court found a few sections at odds with the agreed-upon constitutional principles and some final changes were made to the text before it was formally proclaimed South Africa's new Constitution.[61]

The broad architecture of the Constitution is clear: South Africa is to be "one sovereign democratic state".[62] It is committed to equality, human rights, non-racialism and non-sexism, constitutionalism and the rule of law, and to free competitive elections. In short, it is a model of modern liberal constitutionalism. The Constitution does not assert unlimited majoritarianism, nor does it envisage the kind of binational state that some whites had argued for. It does explicitly

---

[58] *See, e.g.,* THE SMALL MIRACLE: SOUTH AFRICA'S NEGOTIATED SETTLEMENT (Steven Friedman & Doreen Atkinson eds., Ravan Press 1994); ALISTAIR SPARKS, TOMORROW IS ANOTHER COUNTRY (Chicago Univ. Press 1996); THE POST-APARTHEID CONSTITUTIONS: PERSPECTIVES ON SOUTH AFRICA'S BASIC LAW (Penelope Andrews & Stephen Ellmann eds., Witwatersrand Univ. Press 2001); RICHARD SPITZ & MATTHEW CHASKALSON, THE POLITICS OF TRANSITION: A HIDDEN HISTORY OF SOUTH AFRICA'S NEGOTIATED SETTLEMENT (Witwatersrand Univ. Press 2000).

[59] S. AFR. (Interim) CONST. 1993.

[60] *Id.* sched. 4.

[61] Significantly, the Constitutional Court found that provisions relating to the allocation of power to the provinces did not comply with the principles. The principles concerning the devolution of power to provinces had been negotiated, with no little difficulty, before the 1994 election and Inkatha's participation in the 1994 elections was conditional on their inclusion. For a comparison of the interim and final constitutions, see Per Strand, *Finalizing the South African Constitution: The Politics of the Constitutional Assembly*, 28 POLITIKON 47 (2001).

[62] S. AFR. CONST. 1996, ch. 1, § 1.

recognize differences ("united in our diversity"),[63] but it seeks to build a model in which differences can be reflected in cultural and social life yet are not to be entrenched and institutionalized in the political process.

3.1 Elections, legislatures, and executives

Lijphart and others strongly recommend proportional representation in the electoral systems of divided societies. Proportional representation ensures that even small minorities will be guaranteed representation and a voice in legislatures. By promoting a multiparty system, it creates a strong tendency to form inclusive, broadly representative coalition governments, thus avoiding the potential domination of a single group. (The danger, of course, is that in an ethnically mixed society, it may also engender a large number of narrow, ethnically based parties, making stable government hard to achieve.)

South Africa has one of the purest proportional representation systems in the world. The first goal of the system has been achieved. In the first democratic elections of 1994, twenty-seven parties competed, of which seven won seats.[64] The overwhelming majority of votes went to the ANC (252 of 400 seats in the National Assembly), with smaller numbers accruing to the IFP and the largely white and colored National Party (forty-three and eighty-two seats, respectively); the remainder was scattered among four other small parties.[65] In the third general election, in 2004, even more parties competed, of which twelve won at least one seat. But the largest parties achieved even greater control. The ANC held 279 seats with close to 70 percent of the vote; the National Party (NP)[66] had disbanded, and the white opposition was concentrated in the DA; meanwhile, the IFP was left with just twenty-eight seats and 7 percent of the vote. The rest of the parties' percentages were in the single digits.

Thus, proportional representation has indeed facilitated a multiparty system. It has not encouraged coalition government, but this is chiefly because of the continued, overwhelming popular support for the ANC, which is still seen as the party of liberation and as a broad-church, umbrella party, with support across all classes and linguistic groups within the black majority. The ANC needs no coalition partners in order to govern. For the same reason, proportional representation has not fostered the instability and division some had feared.[67]

---

[63] *Id.* pmbl.

[64] Elections results are found at <http://www.electionresources.org/za/1994> and <http://www.electionresources.org/za/2004>.

[65] *See* ELECTIONS '94 SOUTH AFRICA: THE CAMPAIGNS, RESULTS, AND FUTURE PROSPECTS (Andrew Reynolds ed., James Currey 1994); LAUNCHING DEMOCRACY IN SOUTH AFRICA: THE FIRST OPEN ELECTIONS OF APRIL, 1994 (Richard W. Johnson & Lawrence Schlemmer eds., Yale Univ. Press 1996).

[66] Reconstituted as the New National Party (NNP) from 1998 to 2004.

[67] There is a handful of ethnic parties in addition to the IFP. The tiny United Christian Democratic Party has its roots in a form of Tswana nationalism developed in the Bophuthatswana

However, an important element in the compromise that led to the 1993 interim constitution was a provision for power sharing that would be in place only for the first five years of democracy. It required that the first elected government be a government of national unity (GNU). Any party winning 20 percent of the seats in the National Assembly (distributed on a pure list proportional representation system) would be entitled to appoint a deputy president,[68] and any party with more than 5 percent of Assembly seats would be entitled to representation in the cabinet.[69] As a result, former National Party president F. W. de Klerk became deputy president, and Mangosuthu Buthelezi, leader of the IFP, became one of nine minority party politicians in the cabinet. This was pure Lijphart, as it were, designed to ensure stability by including representatives of the major oppositional forces in the new regime.[70] It had been suggested that shared government meant that members of the outgoing apartheid government would bear some responsibility, as well, for the transformation and thus ensure that the ANC was not held wholly responsible for all the problems that would arise in the face of its reforming agenda. This argument made the interim arrangement a slightly less bitter pill for the ANC to swallow.

The GNU was important as a transitional device. However, it did not endure. The National Party soon withdrew, preferring a more Westminster style of opposition,[71] while the other major opposition party in the new South Africa, the IFP, continued to be represented in the cabinet until 2004.[72] Today, with the final remnants of the NP having joined the ANC, the leading opposition party, the Democratic Alliance (DA), fills the traditional role of the opposition. The government in South Africa now follows the Westminster pattern. The difference is that the electoral dominance of the ANC (winning more than two-thirds of the vote in the 2004 elections), together with the fact that elections remain in large measure an "ethnic census", where "voters do not so much register a choice

bantustan. *See* Peris Sean Jones, *From 'Nationhood' to Regionalism to the North West Province: 'Bophuthatswananess' and the Birth of the New South Africa,* 98 AFR. AFF. 509 (1999). There is also a Muslim party with seats in Parliament. However, neither threatens to "ethnicize" politics.

[68] S. AFR. (Interim) CONST. 1993, § 84.

[69] *Id.* § 88.

[70] A very nice analysis of this is found in Jonathan Steele, *South Africa in Transition: Persuading the Old Rulers to Help Build a New Country,* GUARDIAN, Apr. 30, 1994, *available at* <http://www.guardian.co.uk/southafrica/story/0,,1191576,00.html> (last visited May 26, 2007).

[71] The term refers to the British model of parliamentary government, which normally entails a single-party government, responsible to a majority in the House of Commons, and operating by majority rule. Thus the governing party in the Commons faces the "opposition" across the floor.

[72] The last leader of the New National Party, Martinus van Schalkwyk, remains in the cabinet, but now as a member of the ANC. In KwaZulu-Natal ties between the ANC and the IFP have all but ended. The IFP governed the province until 1999; between 1999 and 2004 the ANC and IFP governed in coalition and described themselves as partners. Since 2004, when the ANC won the provincial elections, although formal ties between the parties remain, the relationship between them is not strong. Edward West, *ANC-IFP Ties "In Name Only" Now,* BUSINESS DAY, Oct. 25, 2006.

as an identity",[73] means that alternation in government for the foreseeable future is unlikely. In other settings, the South African system of proportional representation might have resulted in multiparty coalition government. But the enormous popularity of the ANC has forestalled this.[74] In general, then, majority rule has won out over a power-sharing model as the structure of South African democracy.[75] Robert Mattes puts the point most strongly: "What ultimately resulted from six long years of constitution-making was a relatively majoritarian system with few veto players, which enables a majority to do what it wants with little effective opposition."[76]

3.2 Language and cultural rights: Recognizing diversity in the private sphere

Constitutional Principle XI stated that "[t]he diversity of language and culture shall be acknowledged and protected, and conditions for their promotion shall be encouraged".[77] The primary tools for respecting minority rights are to be found in the provisions set forth in the Bill of Rights, which opens with the statement that it is a "cornerstone" of democracy in South Africa.[78] These rights take two forms: first, and most clearly set out, are the rights of individuals; second, are community or cultural rights.[79] The stage is set in chapter 1, "Founding Provisions", which includes provisions on "human dignity", "equality", and "the advancement of human rights and freedoms"; "non-racialism and non-sexism"; and a "common South African citizenship" in which everyone is "equally entitled to [its] rights, privileges and benefits".[80]

---

[73] *See* James L. Gibson, *The Legacy of Apartheid: Racial Differences in the Legitimacy of Democratic Political Institutions and Processes in the New South Africa*, 36 COMP. POL. STUD. 777 (2003), citing HOROWITZ, *supra* note 8, and Robert Mattes, Helen Taylor & Cherrel Africa, *Judgement and Choice in the 1999 South African Election*, 26 POLITIKON 235 (1999). *See also* Friedman, *supra* note 10; Antoinette Handley, Christina Murray & Richard Simeon, *Learning to Win, Learning to Lose* (paper presented at a workshop, "Learning to Lose", Univ. Toronto, Mar. 2006).

[74] Normally, proportional representation systems are associated with multiparty coalition government and Westminster systems with single member electoral systems. The overwhelming support for the ANC gives it the majority to operate the Westminster-style system of government.

[75] *See* James Hamill, *A Disguised Surrender? South Africa's Negotiated Settlement and the Politics of Conflict Resolution*, 14 DIPLOMACY & STATECRAFT 1 (2003) ("What the South African Transition actually produced was a comprehensive victory for a majoritarian political philosophy at the expense of group-based or consociational models. ... ")

[76] Mattes, *supra* note 50, at 12.

[77] S. AFR. (Interim) CONST. 1993, sched. 4.

[78] S. AFR. CONST. 1996, ch. 2.

[79] The Bill of Rights also contains an ambitious set of social and economic rights including the right to "access to adequate housing", S. AFR. CONST. 1996, ch. 2 Bill of Rights, § 26; rights to access to "health care services", "sufficient food and water" and "social security", S. AFR. CONST. 1996, ch. 2 Bill of Rights, § 27; and a right to education, S. AFR. CONST. 1996, ch. 2 Bill of Rights, § 29.

[80] S. AFR. CONST. 1996, pmbl.

The Bill of Rights, then, spells out comprehensive individual rights to equality before the law, along with a prohibition against unfair discrimination on a wide variety of grounds. There are strong guarantees of freedom of speech, expression, and association, as well as the right to a fair trial and other elements of due process in the legal system.[81]

Somewhat less specific are the linguistic, community, and cultural rights. These appear in various sections of the Constitution. Chapter 1 lists eleven official languages, provides for support of small indigenous languages, and states that national and provincial governments must each choose at least two official languages for purposes of government.[82] Section 6 requires the state to take "positive measures to elevate the status and enhance the use of these languages", given their "historically diminished use and status".[83] The employment of official languages by both the national government and the individual provinces is to take into account "usage, practicality, expense, regional circumstances and the balance of the needs and preferences of the population".[84] This section further says all official languages must "enjoy parity of esteem and must be treated equitably".[85] A Pan South African Language Board is to promote the official languages, as well as the indigenous Khoi, Nama, and San languages, sign language, and a wide variety of other languages used by South Africans in their personal and religious lives.[86]

The Bill of Rights extends these provisions by granting everyone "the right to use the language and to participate in the cultural life of their choice".[87] But the status of this language right is not precisely the same as that of most other rights. Section 30 specifies that "no one exercising these rights may do so in a manner inconsistent with any provision of the Bill of Rights".[88]

The key language provision, the result of hard bargaining, is probably that which secures the right "to receive education in the official language or languages of [one's] choice".[89] This clause attempts to straddle the interests of Afrikaners, by expressly permitting "single-medium institutions"[90] (in language clearly referring to Afrikaans-medium schools), and the interests of the ANC, by emphasizing equity and "the need to redress the results of past racially discriminatory laws and practices".[91]

---

[81] *Id.* ch. 2, Bill of Rights.
[82] S. Afr. Const. 1996, ch. 1, § 6.
[83] *Id.* ch. 1, § 6(2).
[84] *Id.* ch. 1, § 6(3).
[85] *Id.* ch. 1, § 6(4).
[86] For a discussion of its work in language promotion and coordination, see <http://www.pansalb.org.za>.
[87] S. Afr. Const. 1996, ch. 2 Bill of Rights, § 30.
[88] *Id.*
[89] S. Afr. Const. 1996, ch. 2, § 29(2).
[90] *Id.*
[91] *Id.* ch. 2, § 29(2)(c).

Section 15, "Freedom of Religion", permits religious observance in public institutions, so long as it is "free and voluntary".[92] Legislation may recognize cultural differences in marriage and family law, but only if such practices are consistent with other constitutional provisions.[93] More broadly, section 31 states that people belonging to specific cultural, religious, or linguistic communities have the right to "enjoy their culture, practice their religion, and maintain related associations and other organs of civil society".[94] Thus, although South Africa is clearly a secular state, it does not embrace that emphatic exclusion of religion from activities linked to the state characteristic of the United States or France. Again, there is the proviso that none of these cultural or religious rights can override other sections of the Bill of Rights.

In an attempt to ensure that the cultural and language rights enshrined in the Constitution are actively protected, the Constitution establishes the Commission for the Promotion and Protection of the Rights of Cultural, Religious and Linguistic Communities.[95] It is one of several of the so-called Institutions Supporting Constitutional Democracy set out in chapter 9 of the Constitution. Its mandate is to "promote respect for the rights of cultural, religious and linguistic communities" and to promote peace, tolerance, and unity among them.[96] The commission's powers are limited to monitoring, investigating, researching, educating, lobbying, advising, and reporting on issues relating to communities. It has no regulatory or enforcement powers. The membership of the Commission is to be broadly representative of the main cultural groups and of the gender composition of South Africa. However, legislation creating the commission (known as CRL) was not passed until 2002, and it did not become operational until two years later.

The government's approach to language rights shows equally little sense of urgency. A law drafted in 2000 would go a long way to strengthening broad enjoyment of language rights. The objectives set forth in the draft are "to give effect to the letter and spirit of section 6 of the Constitution; to promote the equitable use of the official languages of South Africa; to enable all South Africans to use the official languages of their choice as a matter of right within the range of contexts specified in this Act with a view to ensuring equal access to government services and programmes, and to knowledge and information; to provide for a regulatory framework to facilitate the effective implementation of the constitutional obligations concerning multilingualism".[97] Despite receiving cabinet approval, the text has not been introduced into Parliament.

---

[92] *Id.* ch.2, § 15.   [93] *Id.*
[94] *Id.* ch.2, § 31(1)(b).
[95] *Id.* ch. 9, § 185–186.
[96] *Id.* ch. 9, § 185(1)(a).
[97] South African Languages Bill (final draft, May 2000), *available at* <http://www.pmg.org.za/bills/030804salanguagesbill.htm>. Details of the policy are set out in SOUTH AFRICA DEPARTMENT OF ARTS & CULTURE, NATIONAL LANGUAGE POLICY FRAMEWORK (Final Draft, Nov. 13, 2002), *available at* <http://www.info.gov.za/otherdocs/2002/langpolframe.pdf>.

Finally, hidden in the last chapter of the Constitution, in a grab bag of General Provisions, is a section on self-determination.[98] It states: "The right of the South African people as a whole to self-determination, as manifested in this Constitution, does not preclude, within the framework of this right, recognition of the notion of the right of self-determination of any community sharing a common cultural and language heritage, within a territorial entity in the Republic or in any other way, determined by national legislation".[99] This rather Delphic provision was a response to assertions at the time of constitution making that an Afrikaner homeland or *Volkstaat* should not be ruled out completely. Today, most regard the section as meaningless, though its revival is not precluded.

Language and language-use issues in South Africa remain contentious and intertwined with issues of race.[100] Despite the constitutional promise that all eleven official languages will be promoted, English is ever more predominant as the *lingua franca* in most areas of public life.[101] This has provoked, in particular, the Afrikaans speakers, who fear the marginalization of their language and culture.[102] Their concern focuses on the language of education, which was, ironically, the trigger for the sustained resistance in the 1970s and 1980s that spelled the end of apartheid. At that time, the apartheid regime required African schoolchildren to be taught in Afrikaans. Now, traditionally (white) Afrikaans-language institutions are under pressure to accommodate African students' demands for English-language instruction.[103]

The new legal regime is relatively conservative, giving the primary and high schools' governing bodies considerable latitude in determining both language

---

[98] S. Afr. Const. 1996, ch. 14.

[99] *Id.* ch. 14, § 235.

[100] Afrikaans was used as a central element in the 1940s in the National Party project of mobilizing Afrikaners. *See* T. Dunbar Moodie, The Rise of Afrikanerdom: Power, Apartheid and the Afrikaner Civil Religion 235–245 (Univ. Calif. Press 1980).

[101] *See* Kristin Henrard, *Post-Apartheid South Africa's Democratic Transformation Process: Redress of the Past, Reconciliation and "Unity in Diversity"*, 1 Glob. Rev. Ethnopolitics 25–27 (2002); and Neville Alexander, *Language, Class and Power in Post-Apartheid South Africa* 6 (Project for Alternative Education in South Africa, Univ. of Cape Town, paper presented at the Harold Wolpe Memorial Trust open dialogue event, Oct. 27, 2005), *available at* <http://www.wolpetrust.org.za/dialogue2005/CT102005alexander_paper.pdf>.

[102] The language provisions in the Constitution were challenged before the Constitutional Court in the certification process for a number of reasons including the way in which they treat Afrikaans. The interim constitution stipulated that the status of Afrikaans should not be diminished (section 3). It was argued that the 1996 Constitution contravened this provision. However, as the Court remarked, it was not called upon to gauge the 1996 Constitution against the interim constitution but against the constitutional principles. It added, less convincingly, that, in any event, by retaining Afrikaans as an official language, albeit one of eleven, the 1996 Constitution did not downgrade it. Ex parte Chairperson of the Constitutional Assembly: In re Certification of the Constitution of the Republic of SA, 1996 (4) SA 744 (CC); 1996 (10) BCLR 1253 (CC) para. 212.

[103] A 1999 report by the South African Commission on Human Rights demonstrates clearly the use of language by white schools as a device to exclude black pupils. Salim Vally & Yoliswa Dalamba, *Racism, "Racial Integration" and Desegregation in South African Public Schools* (South African Human Rights Commission 1999), *available at* <http://www.sahrc.org.za/final_combined_school_racism_report.PDF> (last visited Jan. 6, 2007).

and admissions policies.[104] However, a handful of high-profile cases before the High Court[105] suggests that the practice at the provincial level is often less accepting of school autonomy, since provincial politicians and bureaucrats are inclined to impose their own interpretation of schoolchildren's language rights. In the Western Cape province, the court concluded that, because an Afrikaans-medium primary school was implementing a properly established language policy, the provincial government could not compel it to accept English-speaking children and offer them instruction in English.[106] But in the Northern Cape, the court upheld an instruction issued by the provincial government requiring three Afrikaans-medium schools to become dual medium (English/Afrikaans).[107] In the latter case, the schools argued that the government's instruction should be set aside because it was based on an ulterior motive and issued in bad faith. To support their claims, they cited a speech in which the provincial official responsible for education had lamented the racial exclusivity of certain schools in the Northern Cape, describing them as "lily-white", and suggesting that their policies were designed to perpetuate racial exclusivity. Again, the question of the schools' formal language policies was key to the outcome; the court held that, because the schools in question had no such policies in place, it was acceptable for the government to determine a policy, provided that policy had a valid basis.[108] In both cases the schools had capitulated, to some extent, to the government's demands by the time the judgment was rendered. Nonetheless, the question remains whether, as popular pressure grows for the education in English for African children, national policies will pursue that objective more aggressively.

The dominance of English in most areas of public life has had at least one important and beneficial consequence for linguistic harmony that is usually overlooked. It has meant that, although there is concern that other languages should not be neglected, there is no divisive struggle for preeminence among the indigenous languages.

---

[104] Universities are governed by a separate regime and have considerable autonomy. Nevertheless, tensions are evident. A leading Afrikaans cultural organization, the Federation of Afrikaans Cultural Associations (FAK), tried to insert a conciliatory note into a recent acrimonious debate (concerning the language of instruction at the historically Afrikaans Stellenbosch University) that reflects the dilemma such universities face when it is argued that the goal should be to accommodate non-Afrikaans-speaking students without eroding the position of Afrikaans as a language of instruction and research. FAK press statement, *available at* <http://www.fak.org.za/artikel_print.php?id=73>. Whether this can be done remains unclear.

[105] The High Court of South Africa, like its predecessor, the Supreme Court, is organized in thirteen geographically defined divisions, as well as circuit courts.

[106] *Governing Body, Mikro Primary School, and Another v. Minister of Education, Western Cape, and Others* 2005 (3) SA 504 (C).

[107] *Seodin Primary School and Others v. MEC of Education, Northern Cape and Others* [2006] 1 All SA 154 (NC).

[108] *Id.* at para. 16. Although the case concerns an order relating to the schools' language policy, the problem that the court appears to accept as needing remedying is the racial composition of the schools.

Taken together, the rights and institutions set out in the Constitution amount to a strong affirmation of South African diversity as well as recognition of the presence of multiple communities. The implementation of these constitutional provisions reflects the disparate nature of the claims for the protection of diversity in South Africa. Battles over the language of education do not result in the state's insisting that one language dominate. The policy is couched in the language of diversity and accommodation with no suggestion of hegemony with respect to any single racial or other sort of group. However, the demand that African children have the opportunity to learn in their respective mother tongues seeks to undo previous disadvantages. In contrast, the claims by Afrikaners to maintain Afrikaans schools are easily perceived as claims to perpetuate long-standing privilege. Nonetheless, Afrikaners, acutely conscious of their minority status, not surprisingly, see the policy as a threat to their own cultural vitality.

Despite the recognition of diversity in personal and private lives, there is in the Constitution no suggestion that the various groups be accorded political power or authority. Several of the rights mentioned are explicitly limited by the other provisions of the Constitution. And all are subject to a limitation based on section 1 of the Canadian Charter of Rights and Freedoms:[109] they may be overridden by a law that is "reasonable and justifiable in an open and democratic society based on human dignity, equality and freedom".[110] This is an integrationist rather than a consociational vision.

3.3 Multilevel governance

The primary constitutional device for empowering minorities (provided they are territorially concentrated) is federalism. It creates the political space for minorities to pursue their own development priorities and to counteract the imposition of majority views. Some form of federal system was, possibly, the chief priority for the white community in negotiating the constitutional settlement. Federalist

---

[109] Section 1 of the Canadian Charter states: "The *Canadian Charter of Rights and Freedoms* guarantees the rights and freedoms set out in it subject only to such reasonable limits prescribed by law as can be demonstrably justified in a free and democratic society." Following this wording closely and its interpretation in the Canadian Supreme Court's decision in *R v. Oakes* [1986] 1 SCR 103 (Can.), section 36 of the South African Constitution states:

(1) The rights in the Bill of Rights may be limited only in terms of law of general application to the extent that the limitation is reasonable and justifiable in an open and democratic society based on human dignity, equality and freedom, taking into account all relevant factors, including—
  (a) the nature of the right;
  (b) the importance of the purpose of the limitation;
  (c) the nature and extent of the limitation;
  (d) the relation between the limitation and its purpose; and
  (e) less restrictive means to achieve the purpose.
(2) Except as provided in subsection (1) or in any other provision of the Constitution, no law may limit any right entrenched in the Bill of Rights.

[110] S. Afr. Const. 1996, ch. 2, Bill of Rights, § 36.

ideas were central to the thirty-four constitutional principles that were negotiated prior to the first democratic elections, and that were to govern the deliberations of the constitutional assembly. With the history of apartheid bantustans in mind, and with an agenda for economic and social development that would require a strong and effective central government, the ANC and its allies were deeply suspicious of federalism.[111] The result in the final Constitution is what might be termed "quasifederalism". The term federalism itself does not appear. As we have noted, South Africa is to be one, sovereign, democratic state.[112]

However, chapter 3 of the Constitution sets out a system of multilevel government, with national, provincial, and local governments constituting "spheres" that are to be "distinctive, interdependent and interrelated".[113] All three spheres are independently elected. Chapter 3, entitled "Co-operative government", requires that all three respect each other's powers and responsibilities and enjoins them to "cooperate with each other in mutual trust and good will".[114] The national government is accorded broad legislative power to legislate on "any matter" except those contained in a short list of "exclusive" provincial powers.[115] In addition to their limited exclusive powers, the provinces also have the power to legislate on matters contained in a long list of concurrent powers, although the center has broad power to override provincial laws. Even in areas exclusive to the provinces, the central government may legislate when necessary to maintain security, economic unity, or national standards or to prevent a province harming others. This central legislative dominance is buttressed by the concentration of revenue-raising power at the center.

Provincial interests are to be given some protection against complete central dominance through the National Council of the Provinces (NCOP). This is the second chamber of Parliament, modeled broadly on the German Bundesrat and designed to represent provincial interests in the central legislature. Its members include ministers of provincial governments. It can initiate or amend legislation. When it considers national legislation directly affecting the provinces ("Section 76 legislation"), each delegation votes as a single bloc on instructions from their provincial legislatures. It requires a supermajority of the National Assembly to overturn its decision. On other matters, NCOP members vote as individuals, and a simple majority of the Assembly can overrule them. Thus the federalist elements of the Constitution clearly envisage provinces as subordinate actors within the multilevel system.

Critically, the provinces were not organized along ethnic lines. Although there was much bargaining over the geographical design of the provincial system, the

---

[111] For a review, see Christina Murray & Richard Simeon, *Multi-Sphere Governance in South Africa: An Interim Assessment*, 31 Publius: J. Federalism, Fall 2001, at 65.

[112] *Id.*

[113] S. Afr. Const. 1996, ch. 3, § 40.

[114] *Id.* ch. 3, § 41(1).

[115] *Id.* ch. 4, § 44(1) read with sched. 5.

final boundaries are close to those developed in the 1980s for the purpose of industrialization and development. As we have seen, several provinces have clear linguistic majorities, but there was no attempt to constitute provinces as linguistically or culturally homogeneous, as the consociational model might suggest.[116] Indeed, in a recently contested case involving adjustment of the border between largely Zulu KwaZulu-Natal and largely Xhosa Eastern Cape, language and ethnicity were not an issue.[117]

Nevertheless, and despite the wording of the Constitution, the existence of provinces provides at least the potential for the political mobilization and empowerment of minorities. This potential has been fulfilled, thus far, in only two provinces—KwaZulu-Natal and the Western Cape.[118] There are several reasons for the lack of provincial assertiveness. First is the overwhelming political dominance of the ANC, both nationally and in most provinces. While local and provincial bodies within the ANC have some autonomy—for example, in creating lists of candidates—the national ANC has the strongest voice. Provincial premiers are chosen not through local processes but are appointed by the center. Provincial premiers and legislatures show little tendency to act autonomously or to see themselves as vigorous promoters of provincial interests in competition with the center or with other provinces. Rather, their statements and strategies appear to follow closely not only national legislation but also the political guidelines emanating from the governing party. More recently, this pattern appears to be changing somewhat, as provincial leaders increasingly seek some autonomy, and provincial branches of the ANC chafe at central control.[119] However, since the disputes about the HIV-Aids programs about five years ago,[120] no province has implemented a policy against the wishes of the national ANC government.

Second, most provinces lack the bureaucratic and fiscal capacity to act autonomously. This is more especially the case with many local governments, jurisdictions that were mandated by the Constitution but finally established only in 2000. The provincial role is less to enact its own legislation than to act as an administrative unit delivering programs mandated in national legislation and funded by the center. In many provinces, even this has proven very difficult to

---

[116] *See* Roddy Fox, *Regional Proposals: Their Constitutional and Geographical Significance, in* THE GEOGRAPHY OF CHANGE IN SOUTH AFRICA (Anthony Lemon ed., John Wiley & Sons Ltd. 1995); Yvonne G. Muthien & Meshack M. Khosa, *The Kingdom, the Volkstaat, and the New South Africa,* 21 J. S. AFR. STUD. 303 (1995).

[117] On the contrary, Xhosa-speaking inhabitants of the Umzimkulu district were pleased to be incorporated into KwaZulu-Natal. For an analysis of the issues involved see the judgment of the Constitutional Court in *Matatiele Municipality v. President of the Republic of South Africa,* 2007 (1) BCLR 47 (CC) (S. Afr.).

[118] As we note below, in KwaZulu-Natal where ethnic mobilization was high before the 1994 elections, ethnic politics seem to be less pronounced now. For a discussion of both cases, see Rod Alence, *South Africa After Apartheid: The First Decade,* 15 J. DEMOCRACY 78, 82–83 (2004).

[119] *See* LODGE, *supra* note 12, ch. 2.

[120] Nico Steytler, *Federal Homogeneity from the Bottom Up: Provincial Shaping of National* HIV/ AIDS *Policy in South Africa,* 33 PUBLIUS: J. FEDERALISM, Winter 2003, at 59.

do.[121] Indeed, some South African commentators suggest that it was a mistake—necessitated by the need for political accommodation—to have established the quasifederal system.[122]

However, two provinces are arenas for ethnically based political contestation. In the largely Zulu KwaZulu-Natal, the Inkatha Freedom Party has been the vehicle for a Zulu nationalist movement closely tied to traditional forms of leadership. It argued strongly for a robust federalism in the constitutional discussions.[123] The party narrowly won office in the first provincial elections,[124] only to lose to the ANC in the third democratic elections in 2004. Indeed, the dramatic decline of the IFP in recent years suggests a diminution rather than an increase in ethnic tensions within the province. Violence between ANC and IFP supporters, once endemic in the province, has now virtually disappeared. On the other hand, in the Western Cape and the metropolis of Cape Town itself, with its large colored population, there has also been a complex political contest with ethnic overtones.[125]

To conclude this section: multilevel governance has provided some, albeit limited, space for minority empowerment. As a system, its primary virtue for South Africa may lie less in its capacity to empower than in its delegation of much responsibility for service delivery to the provincial and local governments, thus leaving the central government freer to concentrate on national priorities. At the same time, delegating certain responsibilities transfers to lower levels conflicts that might become more divisive if played out at the national level. As an instance, one may note how ethnic rivalries, linked to tensions between former homeland politicians and those associated with the new regime, have played out in the province of Limpopo.[126]

4. Conclusion

Complaints that the new majority South African government discriminates against its minorities remain a common part of South African political discourse. These include complaints from white people about policies, such as affirmative action and "Black Economic Empowerment", that are seen as discriminatory. Representatives of the Indian and colored communities raise very similar

[121] The national government has established a central agency to take over provincial administration of social grants.

[122] This is discussed in Murray & Simeon, *supra* note 57. For an overview, see David Pottie, *The First Five Years of Provincial Government, in* ELECTION 1999 SOUTH AFRICA: FROM MANDELA TO MBEKI 16 (Andrew Reynolds ed., David Phillip 1999).

[123] *See* Nico Steytler, *Federal Arrangements as a Peacemaking Device during South Africa's Transition to Democracy,* 31 PUBLIUS: J. FEDERALISM, Fall 2001, at 93.

[124] A win widely believed to have been made possible by the ANC in order to permit the IFP to play a legitimate role in the political system and thus to forestall a more radical revolt.

[125] *See* Pearle Joubert, *We Have Big Race Issues Here,* MAIL & GUARDIAN, Sept. 15, 2006, at 15 (interview with ANC Western Cape chairperson James Ngculu).

[126] LODGE, *supra* note 31, at 39, 45.

concerns and worry that, once marginalized under white rule, they are now no more secure under majority rule. There is also some discussion as to whether the government favors Xhosa interests over others in its appointments.[127]

But what is most striking is not the intensity of these debates but, rather, the lack of intensity. There is no suggestion that the African majority is riven by internal linguistic and ethnic differences. There is no suggestion of systematic exclusion or repression of minorities by the majority. The debates we have noted are no greater than one might expect in any other society as diverse as South Africa.

Thus, the predictions of Horowitz and others that, once apartheid rule was ended, new ethnic conflicts would polarize the country have proven unfounded. In fact, some observers, notably Anthony Butler, suggest that the very reverse has happened.[128] It is true that South Africa remains a society divided along several fault lines. The division between black and white remains the most profound. Steven Friedman argues that this preoccupation often raises trivial issues (such as membership on sports teams) and makes efforts to address profound issues like HIV-AIDS more difficult.[129] As Friedman puts it: "There are issues of race that will continue to divide us...leaders across the spectrum need to rise to the challenge...white leadership needs to stop fueling prejudice and the government needs to realize that defensiveness, denial and insistence on control do more to fuel bigotry than to end it".[130] White minority parties, notably today the DA, are frustrated by their minority status and engage in strident oppositional politics, while the ANC often sees DA criticism as thinly veiled racism. But the basic accommodations made in the transition process have held. Moreover, white economic privilege remains strong and has not been fundamentally threatened by ANC economic policies or by affirmative action and Black Economic Empowerment.[131] Policies to ensure the redistribution of wealth and of land have been restrained.[132] Despite the enormous disparities in population numbers and the past history of domination, the Truth and Reconciliation Commission that was established in the transition pact emphasized reconciliation over retribution,[133] and the new governing majority has followed this approach.

---

[127] "The ANC has performed this function [of controlling racial and ethnic antagonism] with exceptional dedication and success. It has relentlessly promoted non-racialism as an ideology and as a guide to practice. Moreover, it has made ethnicity almost invisible, despite a history of systematic 'balkanization'." Butler, *supra* note 9, at 42.

[128] *Id.* at 38.

[129] Steven Friedman, *How Obsession With Race Stops SA From Meeting Its Challenges*, BUSINESS DAY, Sept. 20, 2006, *available at* <http://www.businessday.co.za/articles/topstories.aspx?ID=BD4A274755>.

[130] *Id.*

[131] *But see* Roger Southall, Does South Africa have a "Racial Bargain"? A Comparative Perspective (an unpublished conference paper April 2006, on file with authors), arguing that the racial bargain, which maintains a balance between black and white, was renegotiated with the introduction of more state interventionist and assertive black empowerment strategies in the late 1990s.

[132] But policies are not absent. For an introduction to the debate, see THE LAND QUESTION IN SOUTH AFRICA: THE CHALLENGE OF TRANSFORMATION AND REDISTRIBUTION (Lungisile Ntsebeza & Ruth Hall eds., Hum. Sci. Res. Council 2007).

[133] Promotion of National Unity and Reconciliation Act 34 of 1995.

At the same time, the predicted reemergence of ethnic-linguistic conflict within the black majority has not occurred. This is not to say that such identities have disappeared. South Africans continue to identify themselves far more in terms of race than they do in class-related categories.[134] Nevertheless, the ANC and its governing partners, the South African Communist Party (SACP) and the Congress of South African Trade Unions (COSATU), are today in deep disagreement. Their differences are far more closely linked to economic and social policy—class, broadly conceived—than they are to ethnic, cultural, or religious issues.[135] It is economic issues and the issues relating to the distribution of services and wealth, rather than language and ethnicity, that dominate South African political debate today.[136]

This raises the question of why the expected dog did not bark. Is it that those who predicted the rise of ethnocultural tensions were simply wrong—that the supposed deeply suppressed ethnic identities never really existed and were, indeed, mostly a creation of apartheid ideologues? Or were they correct in their worries, but the conflict has been largely avoided by the minority protections built into the Constitution—by proportional representation, the initial GNU, broad cultural and linguistic rights, and multilevel government? Or does harmony prevail largely because of the restraint exercised by the majority, rooted in its deep ideological commitment to unity, equality, and an open and plural society? Perhaps the explanation is to be found partly in each of these. Or does the divide between white and black, which continues to dominate all politics in South Africa, put all other actual or potential divisions in the shade? If this is the case, then Horowitz's and Lijphart's predictions may prove right in the long run—that ethnic and linguistic conflict will increase once the fundamental racial divide is closed. But there is little evidence to suggest that this will happen soon.[137]

In comparative terms, India may prove to be an interesting analogue. It, too, came out of its post-colonial transition with a single dominant party, the Congress Party. Like the ANC, the Congress Party had a broad economic and

[134] *See* SEEKINGS & NATTRASS, *supra* note 26, at 369 (also suggesting that a shift is occurring). For instance, in a 2003 survey, the highest number of respondents (over 30 percent) identified class as the biggest division in South Africa today, over both race and party. *Id.* at 370.

[135] The latter differences do sometimes arise. In a recent battle for COSATU leadership, delegates to a convention supported one of two competing candidates based on their ethnic origin. As some delegates are reported to have said, "You can't have two Xhosas leading COSATU" [and] "We, the Sotho provinces, will not allow Vavi [Xhosa] and his like to take over COSATU"; Vakani Mda, *Ethnic spectre looms large again*, WEEKENDER, Sept. 30, 2006, *available at* <http://www.businessday.co.za/Articles/TarkArticle.aspx?ID=2251684>.

[136] This is fueled by data that show that inequality has increased since the transition. Despite notable progress in providing housing, electricity, schools, and clinics to disadvantaged groups, much remains to be done. *See* SEEKINGS & NATTRASS, *supra* note 26 (noting that the South African economy had a relatively high level of redistribution under apartheid and, moreover, that by 1993, old age pensions and grants to children were the same for all races and that the poor did not fare well in the decade after apartheid).

[137] Definitive answers to this question are difficult, not least because of the limited amount of research done on ethnicity in post-1994 South Africa beyond the broad racial question.

social nation-building project that required strong national leadership. Like South Africa, India established a quasifederal regime in which state governments were subordinate to the central government. Since then, however, ethnicity and regionalism have become more prominent in Indian politics.[138] State boundaries have been redrawn to coincide more closely with linguistic divisions, and state governments have asserted their authority vis-à-vis the central government. It is not difficult to imagine a similar scenario in South Africa in the future.

Relative to other transitional countries in Africa, South Africa had two other comparative advantages. First, it had a strong, well-established private sector and higher levels of overall income. Thus, the state was not the only source of incomes and benefits; as a consequence, intergroup competition to control it was not nearly as intense as elsewhere.[139] Second, despite all the perversity of the apartheid era, South Africa did have an established legal system, which was continued into the new democracy.[140]

The larger comparative question is whether, given a divided society, the most effective strategies for managing potential conflicts lie in integrationist models, which aim for universal equality, prohibitions against discrimination, individual rights, representative institutions, and the like; or in consociational strategies, which emphasize maximum autonomy for each constituent group. There can be no general answer to this question. Given a certain level of group identity and mobilization, integrationist strategies are likely to fail. Some variant of autonomy and consociationalism is required. But, when the subnational identities are weak, consociational models may well have the effect of further inventing, exaggerating, and intensifying ethnic identities, thus fueling divisions that might not have been so prominent otherwise.

The ANC strenuously resisted models that emphasized the autonomy of groups, convinced that such approaches would perpetuate division. Even the government of national unity that was to last only five years was reluctantly conceded. Instead, the Constitution seeks to limit and constrain the institutionalization of difference in the public sphere but gives difference generous recognition in the private sphere.[141] Whether this strategy will continue to be effective, and whether it provides useful lessons for other societies remains an open question.

[138] *See* REKHA SEXNA, SITUATING FEDERALISM: MECHANISMS OF INTERGOVERNMENTAL RELATIONS IN CANADA AND INDIA 110–124, 151 (Manohar 2006).

[139] *See* MICHAEL BRATTON & NICOLAS VAN DE WALLE, DEMOCRATIC EXPERIMENTS IN AFRICA REGIME TRANSITION IN COMPARATIVE PERSPECTIVE 237–238 (Cambridge Univ. Press 1996).

[140] *See* Nicholas R. L. Haysom, *Constitution Making and Nation Building, in* FEDERALISM IN A CHANGING WORLD: LEARNING FROM EACH OTHER 224–225 (Raoul Blindenbacher & Arnold Koller eds., McGill-Queen's Univ. Press 2003).

[141] The constitutional provisions on this subject should also be seen in the context of international obligations to respect ethnic and cultural differences. For instance, in protecting the rights of cultural, religious, and linguistic communities, section 31 of the South African Constitution uses language very close to that of article 27 of the International Covenant on Civil and Political Rights.

15

Giving with one hand:
Scottish devolution within a unitary state

*Stephen Tierney**

1. Introduction

> [I]t is hard to see any form of successful accommodation of multiple nations within a single state that does not include federalism.... [1]

This chapter has two points of focus. First, it addresses the devolution settlement for Scotland as a case study in the constitutional implementation of a "plurinational" model of the state. Second, and more broadly, it reflects upon the ever more sophisticated conceptual challenges to particular constitutional orders, and to constitutionalism in general, that are being mounted by substate national societies. Each subject will be examined in the context of the two prevailing public policies used by states to manage national and other forms of diversity. These policies—accommodation and integration—are distinguished by John McGarry, Brendan O'Leary and Richard Simeon in the following way. On the one hand, integrationists aim to ensure the equality of individuals, accepting diversity in the private realm but opposing public recognition of substate group identities; on the other, accommodationists promote "dual and multiple *public* identities", implying "equality with institutional respect for differences" as the best means of managing deep diversity.[2]

Next, in section 1, the idea of accommodation is specifically scrutinized. It is argued that, while an accommodationist discourse can capture many, if not all, of the constitutional outcomes sought by substate national societies, it seems inadequate for the articulation of a second demand, namely, a conceptual reworking

* Reader in law, University of Edinburgh School of Law. I am grateful to Sujit Choudhry and Ailsa Henderson for helpful comments on this paper. Email: s.tierney@ed.ac.uk

¹ Richard Simeon & Daniel-Patrick Conway, *Federalism and the Management of Conflict in Multinational Societies, in* MULTINATIONAL DEMOCRACIES 338, 364 (Alain-G. Gagnon & James Tully eds., Cambridge Univ. Press 2001).

² John McGarry, Brendan O'Leary & Richard Simeon, *Integration or Accommodation? The Enduring Debate in Conflict Regulation*, at 41 (in this volume) (emphasis added).

of the very idea of the plurinational state. When accommodation is formulated in terms of "states managing minorities",[3] it implies a categorical distinction between state national societies and substate national societies, and it is this very distinction that is challenged by the more radical manifestations of contemporary substate nationalism.

Following from this theoretical analysis, section 2 of the chapter will focus on the tension at the heart of the devolution arrangements for Scotland. In terms of the wide areas of devolved competence it contains and the tenor of recognition that this level of autonomy implies, the Scotland Act[4] can be viewed as a genuine attempt to redefine the United Kingdom's constitution in a plurinational direction. In other ways, however, the settlement embodies strong centralizing or integrative tendencies that sustain the categorical distinction between the host state or dominant national society, on the one hand, and the substate national societies, on the other. These assimilationist integrative tendencies (a distinction will be made in section 2 between assimilationist integration and partnership integration) manifest themselves not as self-conscious attempts to undermine cultural differences but, rather, as a network of semi-formal and informal patterns of central control in relations with the devolved institutions. This reflects an enduring unitary-state mentality at work, here, apparent in mechanisms that tend to induce conformity by the devolved institutions with central policy initiatives. This inconsistency between the ostensibly plurinational realignment of the state, represented by the autonomy and recognition elements of the settlement, on the one hand, and the assimilationist integrative tendencies, stemming from the informal centralizing of intergovernmental relations, on the other, is a consequence, at least in part, of political design by the U.K. government and Parliament when framing the Scotland Bill,[5] and in part the result of the constitutional context, whereby devolution was created in an ad hoc manner rather than as one aspect of a more coherent and systematic process of constitutional reform.

With this ambivalence at its core, the new system was made to fit—in many ways incongruously—within an otherwise highly centralized constitutional structure. Of those elements that tend toward integration in an assimilationist sense, section 2 will spotlight mainly the system of informal and quasi-formal intergovernmental relations at the executive level. Observed in passing will be the related lack of structure in interparliamentary relations that results in various tensions, such as overlapping representation (the West Lothian question) and concerns regarding the presence of ministers representing Scottish constituencies who take seats in the central cabinet. Finally, section 2 will also identify other tensions, for example, those possibly latent in the newly planned Supreme Court for

---

[3] *Id.*
[4] Scotland Act, 1998, c. 46 [hereinafter Scotland Act].
[5] Scotland Bill, 1997–1998, Bill [104]; THE SCOTLAND BILL: A GUIDE (Scot. Office 1997).

the United Kingdom, which some feel has the potential to assimilate the distinctive characteristics of the Scottish legal system into the larger English system.

Throughout the chapter one other circumstance will be kept in mind that also helps establish the context for any process toward enhanced autonomy, representation, and recognition for substate national societies within the U.K.—namely, the procrustean bed created by an integrating Europe and its regulatory structures. The expanding powers of the European Union, of course, limit the political capacity and legal competence of member states to act autonomously. However, these EU powers also have the knock-on effect of restricting efforts to reorient the state in a plurinational way, given that many of the devolved powers of substate nations and regions inevitably fall within—and are subject to the normative supremacy of—parallel levels of EU competence.

2. Plurinational constitutionalism: The conceptual challenge

> [E]thnocultural minorities do not go quietly any more; assimilationist nation-building projects tend not merely to be ineffective—they also usually backfire by reinforcing and "nationalizing" minority cultural identities.[6]

The challenge presented by substate nationalism is both unique and profound: unique, in that it calls into question implicit assumptions concerning the demotic composition of the modern state; profound, in terms of the implications it conveys not only for the structure of existing constitutional orders but also for the very conceptual underpinnings of classical accounts of constitutionalism. In light of this, political philosophers in the last decade have led the way—in advance of constitutional theorists—in demonstrating that the traditional schema used to frame debates regarding multiculturalism must be modified when addressing what is distinctive about substate nationalist constitutional claims. In modifying the interpretive schema, as it bears upon nationalist claims, we must consider in a new light the historiographical resources, normative justifications, and substantive aspirations that are specific to these claims in order to see clearly how the multinationalism debate differs in character from traditional multicultural debates.[7] The very structure of the traditional debate concerning the democratic state was based on what we might call a unitary demos thesis—in other words, an assumption that the state embodies a single nation that provides an exclusive societal context for all of its citizens. Within the state, there may be considerable

    [6] Wayne Norman, *Preface*, Negotiating Nationalism: Nation-Building, Federalism, and Secession in the Multinational State xiii (Oxford Univ. Press 2006).
    [7] *See, e.g.,* Will Kymlicka, Multicultural Citizenship (Oxford Univ. Press 1995); Margaret Moore, The Ethics of Nationalism (Oxford Univ. Press 2001); *see generally* Multinational Democracies (Alain-G. Gagnon & James Tully eds., Cambridge Univ. Press 2001).

cultural and ethnic diversity, but these minorities comprise a second-order group, categorically different from that of the national society of the state. One of the advances made by contemporary political philosophers is to have demonstrated how this thesis is rendered deeply problematic by the existence of more than one societal demos within the same polity.[8] It is only very recently that constitutional theorists have begun to work through in detail some of the implications of these theoretical developments for constitutional praxis.[9] From this early work it is apparent that a number of the traditional conceptual devices used by constitutional theorists and practitioners need to be reformulated in light of the radical challenges plurinationalism poses to the very essence of a state's constitutional identity.

Let us begin with the distinction between what may be called, respectively, the plurinational challenge and the multicultural challenge.[10] Treatment of the issue will necessarily be brief. It is certainly the case that these two challenges have features in common, but our purpose, here, is simply to identify one important difference. Debates over multiculturalism in a liberal democracy tend to take place in a context of broad acceptance, even among the cultural minorities themselves, of the unitary demos thesis. People are mostly agreed that there is one national society within the state that establishes a dominant set of cultural practices. The issue at stake, therefore, is how minority groups—which, though culturally diverse are, nonetheless, part of the demotic whole—should have their differences accommodated (that is to say, protected, fostered, and/or promoted) by the state in accordance with principles of justice, while bearing in mind the state's need to cultivate societal cohesion for the national demos as a whole. In other words, the essential issue is the tension of reconciling the politics of difference with the politics of nation building and national consolidation. Deep disputes attend the search for such a balance; nevertheless, there is at least consensus on the existence of a single national society within which these contestations take place.[11]

Substate nationalist arguments for constitutional justice, however, are not about accommodating cultural differences, on the one hand, or facilitating nation building, on the other. Instead they challenge the very conception of the

---

[8] Ferran Requejo, *Democratic Legitimacy and National Pluralism, in* DEMOCRACY AND NATIONAL PLURALISM 157 (Ferran Requejo ed., Routledge 2001); Margaret Moore, *Normative Justifications for Liberal Nationalism: Justice, Democracy and National Identity*, 7 NATIONS & NATIONALISM 1 (2001).

[9] MICHAEL KEATING, PLURINATIONAL DEMOCRACY: STATELESS NATIONS IN A POST-SOVEREIGNTY ERA (Oxford Univ. Press 2001); STEPHEN TIERNEY, CONSTITUTIONAL LAW AND NATIONAL PLURALISM (Oxford Univ. Press 2004).

[10] Sujit Choudhry, *National Minorities and Ethnic Immigrants: Liberalism's Political Sociology*, 10 J. POL. PHIL. 54 (2002).

[11] Deep diversity, of course, characterizes America as a multicultural society, but the commitment to the existence of one American nation remains strong. Richard Posner has argued that this reality was put into sharp focus as Americans, otherwise divided on internal issues of culture, united around their common national identity in response to the attacks of September 11, 2001. Richard A. Posner, *Strong Fibre after All*, ATLANTIC MONTHLY, Jan. 2002, at 22, 22–23.

state as a unitary national site within which only one process of nation building can take place. "Accommodation", when framed as "states managing minorities", cannot capture such a constitutional challenge, given the categorical distinction the idea of accommodation implies between the entity doing the accommodating or managing (the state) and the entity being accommodated or managed (the minority). Precisely because it embodies *the* national society of the state, so the dominant society regards itself as entitled—by the implicit assumption of standard liberal democratic accounts—to make decisions about how far to go in accommodating a cultural minority. It must do this while retaining the right, and indeed the duty, to maintain its own nation-building agenda in the name of societal stability.[12] But it is just this categorical distinction and this assumption of privilege that is questioned by substate nationalists. They contest the idea that the "state" can be neutral with regard to nationality.[13] Instead, the state is shown to be the institutional vehicle for promoting the nation-building agenda of a dominant national society.

The radical claims of substate nationalists are aimed at a conceptual reorientation of the nature of the state. Only by dismissing the possibility of neutrality within existing arrangements can a new conception of the plurinational state be built, based on mutual recognition that the different nations of the state form a partnership of equals. The powerful normative claims to be found in the narratives of substate national societies are rooted, therefore, not in the politics of difference but, rather, in what we might call the politics of similarity. Hence the processes of nation building and consolidation that remain ongoing within substate nations parallel to the equivalent processes at the state level. It will be useful to explore, therefore, how notions of union and equality characterize the self-perception of substate national societies and their conception of relations with other national societies in the host state—in particular the dominant national society of the state. It is in light of these ideas of union and equality that substate national societies call for partnership *with* the dominant society rather than accommodation *by* it.[14]

In presenting a narrative of alternative or multiple nation-building projects within a single state, national societies usually offer alternative historiographies as well; typically, these might concern the origin and nature of the state and its constitution and differ radically from the dominant historical narrative embodied

[12] John McGarry, *Federal Political Systems and the Accommodation of National Minorities*, in THE HANDBOOK OF FEDERAL COUNTRIES 416 (Ann L. Griffiths ed., McGill-Queen's Univ. Press 2002).
[13] Ferran Requejo, *Political Liberalism in Multinational States: The Legitimacy of Plural and Asymmetrical Federalism in* MULTINATIONAL DEMOCRACIES 110, 110–111 (Alain-G. Gagnon & James Tully eds., Cambridge Univ. Press 2001): "Despite the usual liberal defence of a *laissez faire* approach to cultural matters, experience indicates that the state has not been, nor can it be, culturally neutral."
[14] The agenda of sovereignty and partnership advanced by Quebec nationalists at the time of the 1995 referendum on sovereignty is one example. *See* TIERNEY, *supra* note 9, at 293–299.

in the orthodox constitutionalism of the state.[15] This historically-based critique demands a radical reconfiguration of how the state and its vision of sovereignty is imagined.[16] Only through a review of the constitutional historiographies of substate nationalist movements—itself an underdeveloped area of study[17]—can we appreciate how different are the constitutional claims made by these alternate histories when compared with the demands, framed within the discourse of accommodation, that seek a top-down grant of legal rights to facilitate cultural diversity. Indeed, the nationalist constitutional agenda is not driven primarily (or even, in some cases, significantly) by the notion of cultural differences among national societies. The key feature of any claim for the constitutional recognition of national pluralism is the demand to have extensive control of the decision-making processes within the substate national territory and significant influence within the central organs of the state. This degree of control and influence should be understood in terms of autonomy and representation respectively. It seeks the embodiment of these features not only in the constitution's structure but also in the extent to which the constitution recognizes, symbolically, the state's dual or multiple national composition. Indeed, this multiplicity, or plurinationality, must be seen as a feature of the constitution's very identity.[18]

The narratives of union and equality show that arguments for plurinational recognition are arguments for recognition of the similar nature of all national societies within the state and of their equal importance as sites of identity and loyalty for their members. We will now turn, briefly, to each of these narratives—union and equality—as they arise in substate nationalist discourse, with an eye to the evolution of Anglo-Scottish relations within the U.K.

The notion that the substate territory entered the state either as a fully formed or, at least, as an incipient national society is often central to the constitutional claims presented by substate nationalists. Such is true, for example, of debates in Canada, Spain, and the U.K., where the vision of a state shaped by the union of more than one nation remains strong, albeit in different ways, in the national stories of Quebec, Canada's numerous Aboriginal peoples, the Basque Country, Catalonia, and Scotland.[19] This version of the state's evolution has been reinforced in various ways; first, by memories of the cultural and institutional distinctiveness that these territories enjoyed at the time of their inclusion within the

---

[15] EUGÉNIE BROUILLET, LA NÉGATION DE LA NATION: L'IDENTITÉ CULTURELLE QUÉBÉCOISE ET LE FÉDÉRALISME CANADIEN [NEGATION OF THE NATION: QUÉBÉCOIS CULTURAL IDENTITY AND CANADIAN FEDERALISM] (Les Éditions du Septentrion 2005).
[16] Stephen Tierney, *We the Peoples: Balancing Constituent Power and Constitutionalism in Plurinational States, in* THE PARADOX OF CONSTITUTIONALISM: CONSTITUENT POWER AND CONSTITUTIONAL FORM 229 (Martin Loughlin & Neil Walker eds., Oxford Univ. Press 2007).
[17] For a rare example, see DAVID M. THOMAS, WHISTLING PAST THE GRAVEYARD: CONSTITUTIONAL ABEYANCES, QUEBEC AND THE FUTURE OF CANADA (Oxford Univ. Press 1997).
[18] MICHAEL KEATING, NATIONS AGAINST THE STATE: THE NEW POLITICS OF NATIONALISM IN QUEBEC, CATALONIA AND SCOTLAND (Palgrave Macmillan 2001).
[19] KEATING, *supra* note 9.

state. A second factor contributing to this vision of the state's origin lies in the affirmation of the central role played by these territories in the process of state formation; the centrality of these substate national societies to this process, as they understand it, is supplemented, in certain cases, by the conviction that the state's nature as a union of nations was either implicitly or explicitly recognized at these important constitutional moments. And, as a final factor, the state's ongoing evolution is also conditioned by the substate nation's retention of societal distinctiveness in the aftermath of union.

Together, these factors have created a tendency among substate national societies to envision the larger polities to which they belong as, in some sense, "union states".[20] This is a very strong narrative in Scotland, where the idea of union, as articulated in the Acts of Union 1707, is central to constitutional understandings of the historical origins of the state.[21] By this account, the 1707 acts were a kind of protoconstitution in written form, guaranteeing the survival of the distinctive institutions of Scottish public life and, in particular, of a separate legal system. This view of matters has led to an alternative understanding of the nature of the U.K. as a *Rechtstaat,* an outlook that competes with the dominant constitutional story, even on the question of fundamental law.[22] Some important constitutional actors in Scotland continue to accord a higher constitutional status to the Acts of Union than to the legislative competence of the U.K. Parliament, which is otherwise seen as the U.K.'s receptacle of legal sovereignty.[23]

Related to the narrative of union, in the constitutional rhetoric of substate nationalism, is that of equality. "Parity of esteem" was an expression often used in the search for dialogue during the negotiations that led to the Belfast Agreement in Northern Ireland, and, in general, it sums up the constitutional aspirations of many substate nationalist actors in plurinational states. Visions of union and equality were combined in the extraparliamentary campaign in the 1980s and early 90s for constitutional change in Scotland; the effect was to reinvigorate the legalistic "1707" challenge[24] to orthodox notions of sovereignty with the modern dynamics of political self-determination. This campaign involved a broad range

---

[20] Stein Rokkan & Derek Urwin, *Introduction: Centres and Peripheries in Western Europe, in* THE POLITICS OF TERRITORIAL IDENTITY: STUDIES IN EUROPEAN REGIONALISM 11 (Stein Rokkan & Derek Urwin eds., Sage 1982); James Mitchell, *Evolution and Devolution: Citizenship, Institutions, and Public Policy,* 36 PUBLIUS: J. FEDERALISM, Winter 2006, at 153.

[21] Union with Scotland Act, 1706, 6 Ann., c. 11 (Eng.); Union with England Act, 1707, c. 7 (A.S.P.).

[22] Neil MacCormick, *Is There a Constitutional Path to Scottish Independence?,* 53 PARLIAMENTARY AFF. 721, 727 (2000). MacCormick argues in reference to Scotland's position within the U.K.: "There is no doubt that we have a single state, but it is at least possible that we have two interpretations, two conceptions, two understandings, of the constitution of that state."

[23] FACULTY OF ADVOCATES, RESPONSE TO THE CONSULTATION PAPER BY THE SECRETARY OF STATE FOR CONSTITUTIONAL AFFAIRS AND LORD CHANCELLOR: CONSTITUTIONAL REFORM: A SUPREME COURT FOR THE UNITED KINGDOM (Faculty of Advocates 2003).

[24] The legalistic "1707" challenge refers to the argument that the Acts of Union of 1707 constituted fundamental law. *See* Union with Scotland Act and Union with England Act, *supra* note 21; *see* John Robertson, *The Idea of Sovereignty and the Act of Union, in* THE CHALLENGE TO

of political and civic actors and resulted in a declaration that the Scots retained an inherent right to self-government.[25] Such an assumption cannot help but question, implicitly, the idea of a unitary constitutional order purportedly founded on a single source of national constituent power. However, rather than an outright rejection of the union constitution, this process can be seen, in fact, as a reaffirmation of that constitution—the constitution of a union state. This campaign aired the grievance that the union pact, stemming from 1707, had been undermined by subsequent U.K. constitutional practice, in particular, by the constitutional centralization in the 1980s; this process, it was argued, went against the foundation of mutual national respect that was believed to have been embodied in the original union.[26]

These examples highlight the potentially radical nature of the plurinational constitutional challenge. Questions are emerging that bear directly on the normative authority of established patterns of legal supremacy. Such questions create the conditions for a type of *Kompetenz-Kompetenz* dispute that we typically associate with sovereignty struggles between EU member states and the new legal order that they have created.[27] As the constitutional agenda of substate nationalism develops in a number of liberal democracies today, we find that these debates concerning the relationship between union and sovereignty also exist *within* plurinational states. These developments present radical challenges to the internal manifestations of state sovereignty that are similar in conceptual form to the external challenges with which states are more familiar.[28] As substate national societies grow more confident in their developing constitutional competences and in the theoretical underpinnings that are maturing parallel to these changes, it seems we are merely at the beginning of a process that will demand further rethinking of established constitutional orthodoxies. This process is similar to that which normative liberal theory has gone through. With this broader conceptual challenge as context, we now turn to the devolution settlement set out in the Scotland Act, highlighting those elements that go some way toward

WESTMINSTER; SOVEREIGNTY, DEVOLUTION, AND INDEPENDENCE 198 (Harry Thomas Dickinson & Michael Lynch eds., Tuckwell Press 2000).

[25] SCOTTISH CONSTITUTIONAL CONVENTION, SCOTLAND'S CLAIM, SCOTLAND'S RIGHT (1995).

[26] CAMPAIGN FOR SCOTTISH ASSEMBLY, A CLAIM OF RIGHT FOR SCOTLAND, para. 19 (1988). The resilience of this tradition recently resurfaced in the context of plans for a new Supreme Court for the U.K. discussed in section 2, *infra*.

[27] The term *Kompetenz-Kompetenz* (literally "competence concerning competence") originated in Germany in the context of debate as to whether an arbitrator could have the power to rule on his/her own jurisdiction; now it is used more generally to signify the power to allocate decision-making authority. For a discussion of its significance in the EU context, see KAREN J. ALTER, ESTABLISHING THE SUPREMACY OF EUROPEAN LAW: THE MAKING OF AN INTERNATIONAL RULE OF LAW IN EUROPE (Oxford Univ. Press 2001).

[28] States face external challenges both from the expanding normative reach of international law and from new suprastate legal orders, such as, most obviously, the EU. *See* Stephen Tierney, *Reframing Sovereignty: Sub-state National Societies and Contemporary Challenges to the Nation-state*, 54 INT'L & COMP. L.Q. 161 (2005).

meeting the plurinational challenge and those that remain wedded to a unitary state mentality.

3. Devolution for Scotland: Plurinational realignment without federalism?

> When Labour set about changing Britain's constitution in 1997, it did so with the cavalier abandon of a party giddy with popular support. The result was jerry-built. The structures will not weather a constitutional crisis.[29]

In 1998, there was a very strong sense that the devolution settlement in the Scotland Act was a genuine—albeit speedily mounted and somewhat ad hoc—attempt by the U.K. government and Parliament to meet the aspirations of a sub-state national society for meaningful self-government. Although this chapter's focus is only upon Scotland, it should be noted that both the parallel, and more modest, constitutional settlement for Wales,[30] as well as the highly imaginative and constitutionally radical agreement for Northern Ireland contained in the Belfast Agreement,[31] also bear testimony to the decentralizing spirit of the time.

The degree to which a state has dispersed power may be gauged—with reference to a standard institutional grid—along a continuum ranging from strong to weak realignment, with federalism at one end and administrative decentralization at the other. It seems, however, that such traditional, institutionally focused approaches to multilevel government provide only a partial insight into the degree to which a plurinational state's constitution and, as significantly, its constitutional culture are, in fact, aligned to reflect its nature. The realm of institutional models, therefore, is another area that becomes problematic as a result of the plurinational challenge. For example, there is an old distinction between multinational models geared toward aligning the constitution with a plurinational vision and other territorial models that make no distinction between discrete national subunits and other territorial regions that are part of the host state national demos.[32] It is only recently, however, that theorists have begun to engage seriously with the implications of this distinction for constitutional design.[33] One possible approach to this distinction would be to analyze the constituent parts of each model to see where they fall on the scale ranging from federalism to administrative decentralization.

[29] Editorial, *Gordon Brown Must Enter the Devolution Debate*, Observer (London), July 2, 2006.
[30] Government of Wales Act, 1998, c. 38.
[31] Agreement Reached in the Multi-party Negotiations, Ir.-N. Ir.-Brit., Apr. 10, 1998, Cm. 3883, *available at* http://www.nio.gov.uk/agreement.pdf (Belfast Agreement); Northern Ireland Act, 1998, c. 47, § 98.
[32] *See, e.g.*, Kenneth Wheare, Federal Government 49 (4th ed., Oxford Univ. Press 1963).
[33] Ferran Requejo, Multinational Federalism and Value Pluralism (Routledge 2005).

This could be done for various vectors, each of which would represent a way of aligning the constitution in a plurinational direction. We will address three of these vectors in the Scottish context. Two—concerning autonomy and representation—are familiar to traditional types of analysis, while a third, which is more symbolic and concerns recognition, tends to be overlooked in more institutionalist approaches. This exercise will help us not only to assess the extent to which a particular model of constitutional realignment is genuinely plurinational—rather than simply heavily decentralized—but also to examine how a particular set of constitutional arrangements may be strongly plurinational, in certain ways, but weakly so in others.

Such an approach is especially appropriate when seeking to understand the curious model that is Scottish devolution (and devolution in the U.K. more generally). It is widely believed that only federalism offers adequate means to achieve a truly multinational constitution. As a general point, this argument, advanced by Simeon and Conway in the epigraph to this chapter, must be correct; however, it is also the case that other models, such as U.K. devolution or quasi federalism in Spain, while lacking some of the institutional protections federalism provides, nonetheless may provide for a strong plurinational realignment in other ways. Certain elements of the Scottish devolution settlement, such as its very extensive catalogue of devolved powers, its asymmetrical nature, and the explicit and implicit symbolic recognition that this carries, do have a distinctively plurinational flavor. Seen from another perspective, however, the U.K. remains more akin to an institutionally unitary polity that envisages itself as uninational in composition. And, from this angle, it displays integrationist tendencies that are oriented more toward assimilation than partnership. We will now explore this tension as it plays out in the institutional design of Scottish devolution.

3.1 Plurinational elements in the devolution settlement: Autonomy and recognition

The autonomy provisions of the Scotland Act embody a "retaining" model of devolved power, whereby those matters that are reserved to the exclusive competence of Westminster are explicitly articulated within the act, with all other matters devolved.[34] The range of devolved matters is extensive;[35] since there are few explicitly articulated concurrent or shared powers, the Scottish Parliament has, in effect, exclusive competence in these areas, including the power to repeal existing U.K. legislation.[36] Although the act confirms the ongoing power of the U.K. Parliament to legislate in devolved areas,[37] there is now a constitutional

---

[34] Scotland Act, §§ 28–30.
[35] *Id.*, scheds. 4–5.
[36] This competence is of course, in jurisdictional terms, limited to Scotland. *See* Scotland Act, §§ 29(7)(a).
[37] *Id.* at § 28(7).

convention to the effect that the U.K. Parliament will not do so without the consent of the Scottish Parliament.[38]

At the same time, the limitations imposed on the Scottish Parliament are tightly drawn, with strong procedural blocks in the act preventing the passage of ultra vires legislation.[39] Also, in substantive terms, the Scottish Parliament lacks certain notable powers, the most striking of which are tax-varying powers; the only exception to central fiscal control is the power of the Scottish Parliament to vary the basic rate of income tax by 3 pence in the pound.[40] This feature combines with other factors—in particular, central control over intergovernmental relations (discussed below in section 3.2)—to create what we might call soft limitations on the devolved competence. As a consequence, the seemingly strong devolved powers should not be taken at face value since, as a matter of practical reality, the Scottish executive often has little room to maneuver when setting its own policy priorities. Finally, when assessing this devolved autonomy, the policy-setting agenda of the EU is an additional and important consideration. The legislative competence of the Scottish Parliament is constrained by a legal hierarchy within Europe whereby any domestic power that is also an area of EU jurisdiction is subordinate to inconsistent treaty provisions or legislation emanating from Brussels.[41] In practice, this proves to be a particularly restrictive influence, given that many matters devolved to the Scottish Parliament are also matters of European competence.[42]

Turning to the issue of symbolic and related forms of recognition, it may appear that the very language of devolution, in contrast to that of federalism, inherently belies any sense of plurinational recognition. The term "devolution" suggests a top-down grant of power from the center,[43] and, in this respect, federalism, with its clear implication of divided sovereignty, is a much stronger medium through which to articulate, even at the symbolic level, a plurinational approach.[44] In general, this is correct but, again, we should be wary of an overreliance on the traditional rhetoric of decentralization and the concomitant assumption that we can map this taxonomical construction neatly onto models of plurinational realignment. Devolution for Scotland contains elements that, in contrast to the implicitly vertical structure, seem to embody some level of acknowledgment of the state's plurinational nature. These elements are manifested in two ways. The first is implicit in the substantial asymmetry of U.K. devolution, which we see in three respects. First, only territories that can be characterized as substate national

---

[38] *See* Winetrobe, *infra* note 83.
[39] Scotland Act, §§ 31(1)–(2), 32(2)–(3), 33–35.
[40] *Id.* at § 73.
[41] Scotland Act, § 29(2)(d).
[42] Simon Bulmer et al., British Devolution and European Policy Making: Transforming Britain into Multi-Level Governance 3 (Palgrave Macmillan 2002).
[43] Requejo, *supra* note 13, at 110, 114.
[44] Will Kymlicka, Finding Our Way: Rethinking Ethnocultural Relations in Canada 135 (Oxford Univ. Press 1998).

societies have achieved devolution (although the status of Northern Ireland as a substate national society, rather than as a territory containing two substate national societies, is, of course, heavily contested). Second, one substate national society—England—does not have devolved government at all. Third, each of the three models of devolution for Scotland, Wales, and Northern Ireland differ considerably inter se,[45] which reflects the differing historical trajectories of each territory made various by how they entered the state, the nature and resilience of national sentiment in each, and their differing aspirations for a reshaped union in 1998.

The second element—implicitly acknowledging the state's plurinationality—is recognition through the more unequivocal symbolism of multiple nationhoods. This type of recognition is, of course, embodied in the very name United Kingdom, in the design of its flag, and in the common usage of the term "nation" to describe Scotland, Wales, and England. However, it is also to be found in the tenor of the devolution settlement for Scotland. For example, in the white paper that set out the U.K. government's plan for devolution, former Prime Minister Tony Blair declared: "Scotland is a proud and historic nation in the United Kingdom".[46] There are other ways in which the devolution settlement supplements the symbolic recognition of Scottish nationhood, most prominently, in the usage of "Parliament" to name the devolved legislative assembly. The use of this term—hinting at symbolic if not legal parity with Westminster—can be seen as an acknowledgment of Scotland's historical status as an independent country with its own Parliament until 1707. The emblematic significance of this nomenclature is reflected in the asymmetrical language used in framing the U.K.'s other devolved institutions; in contrast, Wales and Northern Ireland have "assemblies", setting a different tone for their relationships with Westminster.

The symbolic recognition of nationhood has been less forthcoming in other plurinational states, even where models of autonomy are federal or quasi federal.[47] To take Canada as an example, attempts to enshrine references to Quebec's distinctiveness in the Constitution have met with failure.[48] However, matters may be changing. Despite strong opposition to the idea of explicitly recognizing Quebec's nationhood, the House of Commons has passed a resolution recognizing that Quebec forms a nation "within a united Canada".[49] Like another decade-old

[45] Compare Scotland Act, Government of Wales Act, *supra* note 30 (although note also the Government of Wales Act 2006, which moves Welsh devolution slightly in the direction of the Scottish model), and Northern Ireland Act, *supra* note 31.
[46] HOUSE OF COMMONS, SCOTLAND'S PARLIAMENT, 1997, Cm. 3658, at v.
[47] As Norman observes, "Perhaps no fundamental feature of the political cultures of multinational democratic states varies more than the ways in which recognition is recognized, so to speak." NORMAN, *supra* note 6, at 157–158.
[48] Most notably in the failed Meech Lake process of 1987: Meech Lake Accord, Draft Constitutional Amendment 1987; and the failed Charlottetown process of 1992: Charlottetown Accord, Draft Legal Text, Oct. 9, 1992.
[49] Resolution Respecting the Recognition that the Québécois Form a Nation within a United Canada, H.C. 87, 39th Parl. (2006).

declaration that recognized Quebec as a "distinct society",[50] this resolution does not have entrenched constitutional status, but it is still highly significant. Second, even though Quebec has used the considerable autonomy that belongs to the provinces to carve out different powers from those used by other provinces and, despite some specific references to Quebec in the Constitution, there has also been considerable resistance to any constitutional grant of asymmetrical powers and to the watering down of the constitutional principle of equality among the provinces.[51]

In Spain, by contrast, the Constitution countenances the development of asymmetrical powers. Both the Basque Country and Catalonia have used this to develop distinctive areas of competence, and, in Catalonia's case, the recently amended Statute of Autonomy extends these.[52] In terms of symbolism, the preamble to the Constitution recognizes Spain's cultural plurality and the right to self-government by the nationalities and regions of which it is composed. However, this is hedged with several qualifications.[53] The new Catalan Statute of Autonomy uses the word "nation" for the first time, but, in doing so, distinguishes Catalan perceptions of itself as a nation from those of the Spanish Constitution, which still conceives of Catalonia as a "nationality" only.[54]

The issue of recognition highlights the limitations of an analysis that uses the classical line running from federalism to devolution as a conclusive guide to the degree of plurinational alignment to be found in a particular constitution. With this model we would understand Quebec, which enjoys the prerogatives that come with a heavily decentralized federal constitution, to have the greatest degree of constitutional recognition, followed by Catalonia, and then Scotland. As we have seen, however, the issue is not so clear-cut. Recognition can also be more important than the mere symbolic act it is often assumed to be. Although, by itself, recognition is not equivalent to substantive constitutional powers, it can be important in terms of the self-confidence of citizens within a substate national society and central to their sense of inclusion within a genuinely plurinational

---

[50] Resolution Respecting the Recognition of Quebec as a Distinct Society, H.C. 273, 35th Parl. (1995).

[51] Stephane Dion, *Le Fédéralisme Fortement Asymètrique: Improbable et Indèsirable* [*Strongly Asymmetric Federalism: Improbable and Undesirable*], *in* Seeking a New Canadian Partnership: Asymmetrical and Confederal Options 133 (F. Leslie Seidle ed., Institute for Research on Public Policy 1994).

[52] Reform of the Statute of Autonomy of Catalonia, Organic Law 6/2006 (Parlament de Catalunya), *available at* <http://www.parlament-cat.net/porteso/estatut/estatut_angles_100506.pdf>.

[53] Spain Const. pmbl. First, the recognition of "nationalities" is tempered by the first phrase in article 2, which states: "The Constitution is based on the indissoluble unity of the Spanish Nation, the common and indivisible homeland of all Spaniards." Second, it is notable that the nationalities are not named, as such; thus, the Constitution does not explicitly juxtapose other national territories with "Spain" in article 2. And third, reference to "nationalities" runs together with a reference to "regions", which suggests a conceptual elision of the two.

[54] Organic Law 6/2006, *supra* note 52.

host state.[55] More significantly, perhaps, it can also have implications at the level of constitutional interpretation. Thus, the difficulty in determining what effect a "distinct society" clause might have when interpreted by an activist Supreme Court made many Canadians wary of its inclusion in the Meech Lake and Charlottetown draft accords.[56]

Finally, the issue of recognition also reminds us of a related problem with adopting an approach to plurinational alignment that is exclusively focused on institutions. Such a perspective may cause us to overlook the pathways of political practice and constitutional convention that exist at the interstices of legal forms and that facilitate informal or semiformal modes of decentralization, representation, and recognition. This blind spot in constitutional analysis is not exclusive to the plurinational context, but it is the case that the informal, symbolic ways in which a constitutional culture can consolidate the plurinational tenor of the state may easily come in under the radar of excessively formal analyses of decentralization.

3.2 Integrationism within the devolution settlement: Intrastate relations

Any notion that Scottish devolution represents a plurinational realignment of the U.K. constitution requires some substantial qualifications. As already noted, Scotland's powers of autonomy are offset by subtle integrationist tendencies in the operation of reserved powers, particularly in the context of taxation. However, in addition to these constraints, there are far more obvious centralizing dynamics at work within the settlement, partly as a result of self-conscious policy decisions by the U.K. Parliament, and partly because devolution occurred in an inchoate way rather than as part of a broader reworking of the constitutional structure of the British state.

The devolution model for Scotland is very lopsided when compared with a federal system. Although containing a great deal of detail concerning the balance between devolved and reserved matters,[57] the Scotland Act is much less explicit with regard to representation at the center—what in federal systems is known as intrastate federalism. There are very few provisions touching upon how intergovernmental and interparliamentary relations should be managed under the devolved arrangements and how these pertain to the creation, structure, and

---

[55] Michael Keating observes in connection with recent debates over further autonomy for Catalonia and the Basque Country: "What is remarkable...is how little political energy was expended on the distribution of powers, the precise design of institutions, or relations with the central state. ... the balance of the debate concentrated on a series of highly symbolic and ideologically charged elements...." Michael Keating, *Rival Nationalisms in a Plurinational State: Spain, Catalonia and the Basque Country*, at 337 (in this volume).

[56] *See supra* note 48.

[57] Scotland Act, § 30, sched. 5.

modus operandi of institutions when coordinating policy for the U.K. as a whole. A formal system of intergovernmentalism is widely seen as a crucial component in any credible decentralized model; not only does such a system protect the subunit's degree of involvement in central decision making but it also helps prevent or, at least, resolve conflicts between different levels of government. All this being the case, substate national societies typically seek certain modes of integration—in other words, formal pathways to representation at the center where they can meet with the dominant national society as partners in a joint multinational enterprise. Sujit Choudhry correctly observes how in a decentralized state not all forms of integration are assimilationist;[58] we need, therefore, to distinguish between what might be called "partnership integration" and "assimilationist integration". The former is to be found in a plurinational federal or confederal model that provides for the equal engagement of the state's national societies; the latter is characterized by the subjection of substate national societies to decisions by the center in the making of which the substate units have only minimally or inadequately participated.

In many ways the latter model characterizes the intergovernmental aspects of the devolution settlement for Scotland, and it seems that this is largely the result of the informal or quasi-formal structures that have accompanied devolution. An important body for relations between Scotland and London is the Joint Ministerial Committee (JMC); this establishes a format for cooperation between the ministers in Whitehall and their counterparts in Edinburgh and the other devolved administrations.[59] Generally, it operates through meetings between officials or in direct relationships between one London department and its devolved equivalent. Its remit is to deal with reserved matters, insofar as they might affect devolved territories, and devolved matters, where they have an impact on the rest of the U.K. Flowing from this arrangement is a series of memoranda of understanding and supplementary agreements known as "concordats".[60] Such a semiformal model is integrative in an assimilationist sense for various reasons. One is the gatekeeper control exercised by the center—a center that, by virtue of the Westminster system, has long had an extremely powerful executive. Since there is no legal requirement to conduct relations with the Scottish executive in any particular way (or indeed at all), the U.K. government can establish the terms for discussions, table the agenda it wants, and offer greater or lesser degrees of cooperation to the devolved administration or to individual departments within it, all based upon political preference.[61] In this way the devolved institutions—in order to gain a role in these discussions—can be persuaded to display greater political compliance.

[58] Sujit Choudhry, *Does the World Need More Canada? The Politics of the Canadian Model in Constitutional Politics and Political Theory* (in this volume).
[59] The JMC was established under the Memorandum of Understanding, 2000, Cm. 4806.
[60] Richard Rawlings, *Concordats of the Constitution*, 116 L.Q. Rev. 257 (2000).
[61] Alan Trench, *Central Government's Responses to Devolution*, in Economic and Social Research Council Devolution Briefing No. 15 (Econ. & Soc. Res. Council 2005).

More importantly, just as there is no legal requirement to enter into negotiations, so there is no obligation on the part of the U.K. government to reach agreement with the devolved institutions on any issue of policy, even where it affects the devolved territory. Intergovernmental cooperation can be, and often is, simply a process of passing on information concerning decisions already taken by the center. Furthermore, such quasi-formal mechanisms as have been established through the JMC have not been utilized systematically, with some departments at U.K. level operating in a significantly more structured way with their Scottish counterparts than others.[62] Another difficulty is that the culture of secrecy that continues to pervade British government, despite freedom of information legislation,[63] has rendered the operation of intergovernmental relations quite opaque.[64]

Several factors have helped matters run smoothly thus far. From 1999 until 2007, the Labour Party was in power in both London and Edinburgh (where it was in coalition with the Liberal Democrats) and, since so much within the existing arrangements depends on political agreement, this was a felicitous coincidence.[65] A second factor in the easy adaptation of administrative processes— and indeed in the lack of transparency that continues to attend them—is the continuation of a unified British civil service from the predevolution system. A strong culture of integrated government survives among civil servants who operate within one employment and promotion system; this is widely regarded as an integrationist factor of considerable practical importance in the operation of devolution.[66]

These centripetal tendencies are underpinned by the taxation system, mentioned above. It was anticipated that the territorial financial arrangements would be a source of conflict in the U.K., as they have been in other decentralized states. But central control over taxation has meant that, in fact, this has not been an issue, certainly not in the sense of provoking competence disputes. Actually, central fiscal power complements control over intergovernmental relations and over the civil service, and this creates a strong gravitational system that tends to draw

[62] CHARLIE JEFFREY, DEVOLUTION: WHAT DIFFERENCE HAS IT MADE?, INTERIM FINDINGS OF THE ESRC DEVOLUTION AND CONSTITUTIONAL CHANGE PROGRAMME (Econ. & Soc. Res. Council 2004).

[63] Freedom of Information Act, 2000, c. 36 (U.K.); Freedom of Information (Scotland) Act, 2002, (A.S.P. 13).

[64] Press releases that have been issued by the JMC have been criticized for their "immense blandness". Robert Hazell et al., *The Constitution: Consolidation and Cautious Advance*, 56 PARLIAMENTARY AFF. 157, 160 (2003). *See also* SELECT COMMITTEE ON THE CONSTITUTION, SECOND REPORT ON DEVOLUTION: INTER-INSTITUTIONAL RELATIONS IN THE UNITED KINGDOM, 2002–03, H.L. 28 (calling for the increased use of formal mechanisms in intergovernmental relations and for greater openness).

[65] Things have now changed since the separatist Scottish National Party now forms a minority government in Scotland following its success in the Scottish parliamentary election on May 3, 2007.

[66] Jonathan Bradbury & Neil McGarvey, *Devolution: Problems, Politics and Prospects*, 56 PARLIAMENTARY AFF. 219, 221 (2003).

Scotland's devolved administration into compliance with the central government's policy objectives.[67]

It should also be noted that there are powerful political as well as institutional pressures encouraging convergence. This is not due simply to the role of the Labour Party in both administrations until May 2007. There are also expectations among citizens and political elites alike that common standards, particularly with respect to public services, will be maintained across the U.K.[68] Thus, there are areas where well-networked policy communities throughout the U.K. look for and expect to find uniformity—higher education is a particular example.[69] This is not uncommon in any decentralized state, plurinational or otherwise, and it speaks to the bonds that unite people. This is yet another instance of how not every integrationist activity is unpopular within substate national societies, given the strong pull among the citizens toward policy integration across a range of areas—when based upon partnership, not assimilation. What seems problematic, however, is the lack of formal mechanisms whereby the nations of the U.K. can debate their different, or indeed their shared, priorities in a systematic and transparent way. The excessively centralized, informal, and secretive devices currently available may well breed dissatisfaction with the process of these deliberations, even when substantive agreement itself is attainable.

One area where convergence with central policy has been a condition of access to decision-making forums is in the U.K.'s policy negotiation with the European Union. Although EU business is reserved to U.K. level, the devolved authorities, inevitably, have demanded a major role in the process by which the U.K. forms its European policy; this is the case simply because so many areas of EU competence are also devolved areas of competence, such as agriculture, structural funds, and the environment. However, with regard to the Scotland Act, where international relations remain a reserved matter,[70] a common front on policy must be accepted by Edinburgh if it wants access to Europe through London.[71] So far things have been managed amicably; the fairly radical contribution presented by the U.K. government in the debate on regions and Europe, at the European convention on the draft Treaty establishing a Constitution for Europe,[72] was largely authored by the Scottish and Welsh governments. However, for devolved institutions, when trying to develop a substate presence in the EU, a possibly more restrictive

---

[67] Trench, *supra* note 61.

[68] MICHAEL KEATING, POLICY MAKING AND POLICY DIVERGENCE IN SCOTLAND AFTER DEVOLUTION, ECONOMIC AND SOCIAL RESEARCH COUNCIL DEVOLUTION BRIEFINGS, BRIEFING No. 21 (Econ. & Soc. Res. Council 2005).

[69] *Id.* Here Keating is referring to the fact that the university system across the UK is highly integrated in terms of research culture, employment structures and student mobility.

[70] Scotland Act, § 30(1), sched. 5(7).

[71] Martin Burch et al., *UK Devolution and the European Union: A Tale of Cooperative Asymmetry?*, 36 PUBLIUS: J. FEDERALISM, Winter 2006, at 75.

[72] Peter Hain, *Europe and the Regions*, Contribution 221 to Convention 526/03 (The European Convention Feb. 3, 2003), *available at* <http://register.consilium.eu.int/pdf/en/03/cv00/cv00526 en03.pdf>.

circumstance is that the EU remains, fundamentally, a state-centered enterprise with little scope open to the regions of Europe to access directly, much less to influence, European decision making.[73]

As for interparliamentary relations between the Scottish Parliament and Westminster there are two notable issues that highlight the potentially unsatisfactory nature of devolution. These concern, first, the coherent division of competences between legislatures and, second, the protection of the prerogatives of a devolved legislature from central encroachment.

The first issue illustrates, clearly, the distinction between a system of legislative devolution and a federal model. The Scotland Act brought with it little change in Scottish representation at Westminster. Scotland, for historical and political reasons, had enjoyed more seats in the House of Commons for most of the twentieth century than a simple per capita distribution across the U.K. would have provided. The Scotland Act set out to correct this anomaly[74]—the reasoning being that with increased autonomy there was no longer any justification for such overrepresentation. A reduction from 72 to 59 members of Parliament (MPs) was effected in time for the 2005 general election.[75]

Nonetheless, an argument persists that Scottish MPs exert too great an influence within the House of Commons. The contention is that since certain matters, which are devolved to the competence of the Scottish Parliament, are dealt with as they pertain to England—and, in certain cases, other parts of the U.K.—by Westminster, it is unfair that MPs who are returned to the House of Commons from Scotland can vote on matters that affect other parts of the United Kingdom but not Scotland.[76] This has been called the West Lothian[77] question, and it has become particularly controversial in situations where the U.K. government has relied upon Scots MPs to pass legislation that does not affect Scotland but would have failed without their support.[78] This is, in reality, an unintended consequence arising from the ad hoc nature of devolution, whereby Scotland achieved autonomy without any similar process for England. The side effect of this somewhat messy arrangement is that it damages the traditional territorial linkage between representatives and voters within a parliamentary democracy. Voters in England

[73] CHARLIE JEFFERY ET AL., THE LOCAL AND REGIONAL DIMENSION IN THE EUROPEAN CONSTITUTIONAL PROCESS (Eur. Union Comm. Regions 2004). Here the advantages of federalism are apparent; for example, in terms of the direct access to EU institutions available to substate territories in Belgium and Germany.

[74] Scotland Act, § 86.

[75] Scottish Parliament (Constituencies) Act, 2004, c. 13.

[76] The same issue arose in Canada at the time of debates over asymmetrical reform for Quebec in the late 1980s and early 1990s. Reg Whitaker, *The Dog That Never Barked: Who Killed Asymmetrical Federalism?, in* THE CHARLOTTETOWN ACCORD, THE REFERENDUM, AND THE FUTURE OF CANADA 107 (Kenneth McRoberts & Patrick Monahan eds., Toronto Univ. Press 1993).

[77] The anomaly was raised in the late 1970s by Tam Dalyell, member of Parliament for West Lothian, Scotland.

[78] Examples include the Health and Social Care (Community Health and Standards) Act, 2003 c. 43; and the Hunting Act, 2004, c. 37.

might feel justifiably aggrieved that their preferences are not being met. This situation does not promote a partnership-integrationist strategy since it also suggests to Scots that the U.K. Parliament is now, increasingly, an English Parliament and that their interests might be better served by gaining more powers for the Scottish Parliament. This state of affairs also increases the likelihood that English voters, resentful of the way in which their priorities are subject to the voting patterns of Scottish MPs, will favor a reduced role for Scotland at Westminster.[79]

Another tension resulting from the West Lothian issue concerns the U.K. executive. It is argued by some that just as it is unfair for MPs from Scotland to vote on English or Welsh matters, for the same reason it is inappropriate for ministers who represent constituencies in Scotland to serve in the U.K. government.[80] According to this argument, ministers should not be formulating policy for England (and, in some cases, Wales) when they are not elected from within these territories and when ministers from England and Wales are restricted as to the policies they can form for Scotland. Once again, however, this debate detracts from any partnership-integrationist strategy. If a convention had emerged that MPs representing Scottish constituencies could not become U.K. government ministers, then Gordon Brown would have been unable to succeed Tony Blair as prime minister, despite enjoying the support of the overwhelming majority of Labour MPs. Such a convention would suggest to Scottish nationalists and others that the U.K. government had become in practice an English government but one that retained competence for many important U.K.-wide matters.

The West Lothian issue, therefore, highlights how Westminster continues to act with the air of a unitary parliament, vastly different from those federal legislatures that are, in effect, negotiating forums for different territorial interests. Nor is there any sign of a significant change in a plurinational direction. The general lack of territoriality is particularly apparent when we consider the House of Lords, which, unlike the second chamber in a number of federal systems, does not function as a "chamber of the regions", reviewing the work of the lower house from a territorial perspective. Certainly, there is an ongoing process of reform of the second chamber but so far this has not led to—nor are there any plans that it should lead to—the conversion of the Lords into a territorial chamber with equal representation or even weighted representation for the three devolved territories.[81]

The second issue, which, according to critics, hints at assimilationist integrationism, has been the centralized coordination of the legislative activity of Westminster and the Scottish Parliament. As mentioned earlier, a convention has developed whereby the U.K. Parliament will not legislate on devolved matters

[79] Patrick Hennessy & Melissa Kite, *68% of English Want Own Parliament*, SUNDAY TELEGRAPH (London), Nov. 26, 2006.
[80] Simon Jenkins, *There is an Easy Answer to the West Lothian Question*, GUARDIAN, Jan. 17, 2007.
[81] House of Lords Act, 1999 c. 34.

without the consent of the Scottish Parliament. Therefore, the Scottish Parliament has instituted the practice of passing resolutions authorizing the Westminster Parliament to legislate on its behalf. These "Sewel resolutions"[82] have been used extensively, largely to ensure U.K.-wide uniformity, to give legislative effect to EU law and other international obligations, and, more controversially, to create time for the Scottish Parliament to pursue other matters. There remains considerable disagreement as to whether this procedure is simply an efficient device in the management of interparliamentary relations, or an instance of Westminster encroaching upon the Scottish Parliament's autonomy.[83]

From interparliamentary relations we turn, now, to the judicial branch. It is notable that, as yet, competence disputes before the courts between the U.K. government and the Scottish Parliament have not surfaced. However, the potential for such disputes is very real and, should they arise, will play out in the context of multiple legal systems within the U.K. As a consequence, different judicial attitudes regarding the boundaries of devolved competence could develop between jurisdictions. In this context, it is particularly noteworthy that the proposed creation of a Supreme Court for the United Kingdom has been criticized, given the potential of such an institution to promote assimilationist integration, thus compromising the independent and distinctive jurisdiction of the Scottish legal system.

At present, the Scottish legal system interacts with two tribunals in London. The Judicial Committee of the Privy Council (JCPC) settles devolution issues arising under the Scotland Act,[84] while the Appellate Committee of the House of Lords hears civil appeals from the Court of Session in Edinburgh (the House of Lords has no jurisdiction to hear appeals in criminal matters from Scotland). The new Supreme Court will assume both of these devolution and civil appellate functions.[85] Currently, when the Appellate Committee convenes, it has the jurisdiction of the territory from which the appeal comes; for example, in an appeal from Scotland, the Committee convenes as a Scottish court. Considerable concern was expressed within the Scottish legal profession and judiciary regarding the extremely speedy way in which proposals for the new Supreme Court were drawn up and, in particular, over the lack of clear thinking about whether such a court, which would convene with one unified jurisdiction, would suit a state with a plurality of legal systems, common law and civilian.[86]

---

[82] Named after Lord Sewel who, speaking for the Government, suggested this process in parliamentary debate on the Scotland Bill. 592 PARL. DEB., H.L. (6th ser.) (1998) 791.

[83] The Scottish National Party has criticized the use of Sewel motions, arguing that the Scottish Parliament should in all cases pass legislation for Scotland. 1 SCOTTISH PARLIAMENT OFFICIAL REPORT (no.11) (June 23, 1999) 694–695 (regarding Deputy Minister of Justice Angus Mackay, M.S.P.); *see also* Barry Winetrobe, *Counter-Devolution? The Sewel Convention on Devolved Legislation at Westminster*, 6 SCOT. L. & PRAC. Q. 286 (2001).

[84] Scotland Act, § 98, sched. 6.

[85] Constitutional Reform Act, 2005, c. 4, § 40, sched. 9.

[86] FACULTY OF ADVOCATES, *supra* note 23.

In addition to its proposed jurisdiction, there is concern over the question of the Court's composition, and, specifically, whether there are appropriate guarantees that a sufficient number of Scots judges will be appointed to hear both appeals from Scotland and devolution issues under the Scotland Act. Others have questioned the degree to which the Court will be independent. On the latter point, there are worries that, since it will be overseen by the U.K. Department for Constitutional Affairs, which is also responsible for the English court system, it may be seen as part of that system. It is thought this might endanger the independence of the Scottish legal system as guaranteed by the Acts of Union. In this broad context, prominent Scottish constitutional actors have declared that the establishment of this Court may be both unconstitutional and unlawful, despite its creation through an act of the U.K. Parliament. The Faculty of Advocates, the body representing the senior branch of the Scottish legal profession, argued that "a Supreme Court which is created must be consistent with the Claim of Right 1689 and the Act of Union 1707. These instruments are fundamental parts of the constitution of the United Kingdom of Great Britain and Northern Ireland, and... any proposal for a Supreme Court which contravened any provision of these instruments would be unlawful".[87]

To some extent, these fears have been allayed by the Constitutional Reform Act in its finally enacted form.[88] However, there remain concerns that the unified court structure could be used as a centralizing device, particularly in the area of human rights law. Despite the fact that human rights is a devolved matter (subject only to the requirement that the devolved institutions not act in a manner contrary to the European Convention on Human Rights),[89] there are already signs, well in advance of the creation of the Supreme Court, that a number of Law Lords assume the interpretation and application of human rights law in both England and Scotland should be identical. Additionally, there is a tendency toward taking the English position as the norm.[90] It seems, therefore, that the existing system provides stronger safeguards against assimilationist integration than the proposed Supreme Court.

As matters stand now, there is a clear separation between the Appellate Committee as a final court of appeal, which, historically, has not always been sufficiently sensitive to the jurisdictional specifics of Scots law, and the JCPC, which has an explicitly demarcated role involving devolution. This distinction

---

[87] *Id.*

[88] Constitutional Reform Act, *supra* note 85, § 41 on jurisdiction, § 27(8) on composition, and § 3(2) on independence.

[89] Scotland Act, § 29(2)(d), § 57(2).

[90] In this context, it also seems that tensions between Scots and non-Scots judges are beginning to develop in respect of the human rights provisions in the Scotland Act. Contrast the English law case before the House of Lords Appellate Committee, Att Gen's Ref. (No.2 of 2001), [2001] 1 W.L.R. 1860, [2003] UKHL 68, with a Privy Council case on a devolution issue under the Scotland Act, where Scots judges formed the majority, H.M.A. v. R. [2004] 1 A.C. 462, (2003) S.C. (PC) 21.

means that constitutional questions arising in the form of devolution issues are dealt with in a context distinct from substantive appeals. One danger in the proposed judicial structure is that the new Supreme Court might be tempted to move beyond the determination of a devolution issue, in a particular case, and address the substance of the case as if it were also an appeal. The Court could also be influenced by what it considers the implications of a devolution issue might be as they pertain to the substantive law in other areas of the U.K.; thus, it might approach certain devolution issues predisposed to achieve uniformity across the U.K. Such an approach, in fact, is hinted at by the *Att Gen's Ref.* (No. 2 of 2001).[91] An alternative to the new Supreme Court would have been to retain the JCPC for devolution issues (or to create a constitutional court for this purpose), while terminating all civil and criminal appeals in the Court of Session in Scotland and Courts of Appeal of England and Northern Ireland. Notably, the Scottish Parliament has the competence to withdraw civil appeals from the jurisdiction of the Supreme Court at any point in the future.[92] If the Supreme Court does indeed show assimilationist tendencies, the reaction of the Faculty of Advocates to date suggests the Scottish legal profession may well lobby for such a development.

4. Concluding remarks

The devolution settlement for Scotland is an example of a decentralized model that remains—in terms of its structure—deeply unstable. The autonomy and symbolic recognition that the settlement delivers are contradicted by mechanisms for intergovernmental relations that are still heavily centralized and exhibit assimilationist integration tendencies. At a deeper level, this paradox speaks of a state that has not fully adapted its unitary mind-set to meet the evolving challenges of resilient national identities. At the same time, the asymmetrical devolution of extensive powers to Scotland and the growing resentment in England regarding the influence of Scottish MPs and government ministers seem to lessen the prospect of devolution leading to a model of partnership integration at the center.

A further difficulty arises in seeking to build a plurinational constitution within any state in Europe today. Thus, while substate national societies increasingly push for direct representation within European institutions, the gatekeeper control exercised by the central state—plus the fact that the EU itself remains such a state-centered enterprise—seems to be increasing the frustration levels of substate actors. This phenomenon is seen not only in Scotland but also elsewhere.[93]

---

[91] [2001] 1 W.L.R. 1860; [2003] UKHL 68. For a critique of this decision, see David Feldman, *None, One or Several? Perspectives on the UK's Constitution(s)*, 64 CAMBRIDGE L.J. 329, 348 (2005).

[92] This is not a reserved matter. Scotland Act, § 30, sched. 5(1)(e).

[93] Keating, *supra* note 55.

Mixed and nested identities remain strong in the U.K., as do commitments to the host state,[94] and these factors make secession by Scotland unlikely, at least in the short term. In addition, the U.K. has been successful, so far, in involving Scotland in its EU policy making through the use of informal channels. However, for as long as only nation-states have a meaningful say in Europe then—particularly as the influence of the EU grows—a further source of instability will be built into the already difficult task of reshaping the constitutional structure and culture of the plurinational state in a unitary constitutional environment.

[94] ALISON PARK ET AL., DEVOLUTION, IDENTITY AND PUBLIC OPINION IN SCOTLAND (Econ. & Soc. Res. Council 2004).

Index

autonomy 38
  asymmetric regimes 3
  fiscal 333
  issues 337–40
  judicial 333
  renegotiating 332–5
  bilateral relationship with Spain 338
  competence, areas of 450
  European Union, as actor in 338–9
  immigration 320
  nation, as 334, 337
  nationalism 319–21
    accommodating 38, 325–32
  nationalist traditions 319
  newcomers to 321
  party alliances 331–2
  political parties 320
  self-government 325–6
  sovereignty, issue of 338
Central Europe
  Canadian constitutional model, interest
    in 153–5
  configuration of states 132
  Kymlicka, work of 157–8
  multinational federations 154–5, 164
    violent collapse of 164
centripetalism
  accommodation policy, as 53–6, 69
  coalitions 77
  coining of term 372
  conciliatory potential of federalism,
    supporting 54
  electoral systems, favoured 54
  integrationist critics of 72
  Nigeria as example of 54–5
  power-sharing coalition, as 369
  vote-pooling, emphasis on 76, 82
citizenship
  civic 6
consociation
  accommodation strategy, as 57–63, 69,
    369
  autonomy, principle of 60
  broken down 72–3
  coalitions 77
  community self-government, principle
    of 60
  competitive politics, fostering 84
  corporate 61–2
  corporate mechanisms 398
  democracy 18–20, 28, 61, 83
    India as 20
    Northern Ireland as 23, 31
  equality of citizens, promotion of 406
  examples 61–3
  external actors, role in promotion and
    operation of 379–82

Fiji, in 292, 313–15
  groups, accommodating 343
  integrationist critics of 72
  internalist theory 379
  Iraq, constitution 31
  liberal 62, 362
  Lijphart, work of 372
  minorities demanding 87
  multiculturalism, differing from 58
  Northern Ireland, in *see* **Northern Ireland**
  power-sharing 58–9
  privileging of communities 80
  proportional electoral systems, emphasis
    on 75–7
  proportional representation, based on 405
  proportionality, principle of 59
  radicals, incentives for moderation by 392
  rigid 60
  self-determination disputes, neglected
    treatment of 374–9
  stateless nations, accommodation of 378
  successful 77
  superficial ethnonational politics,
    promotion of 407
  undemocratic 60–1
    criticism as 405
constitution
  amendment, rules for 167–72
  bill of rights, containing 8
  demos 6
  design 5–7
  divided societies, roles in 7
  multiethnic society, in 287
  pluralist 65
  role of 287
  transplants 157–9
constitutional design
  Canadian model *see* **Canadian
    constitutional model**
  democratic processes, multistage 185–8
  divided societies, for
    bill of rights *see* **bill of rights**
    burden 5
    challenges, response to 9
    choice in 13–14
    comparative politics, debate in 15
    comparative, Lijphart–Horowitz
      debate 13, 15–26
    competing proposals for 22
    demos, constituting 6
    Human Development Report 2004,
      recommendations 7
    human rights, protection of 11
    institutional criteria 19
    international role 39
    political mobilization, response to 12
    regulation 5

recognition of 348
lessons from experience of 366–7
natural resources, control and ownership
of 355–6
official languages 64
power sharing 40
proportional representation–party list
electoral system 362–3
regional minorities
abuse of 358
protection of 359, 365
regions and federal government,
relationship of 363
secession and integration, splitting
difference between 367
sectarianism 344
Supreme Court 366
territorial pluralism 64
three regions approach 356–7
Islamic law
constitutions, in 265–7
constitutions, place in 260
doctrinal diversity 262
historical tradition of 259
historicist jurisprudence 261–5, 285–6
interpretation, role of jurists 263
Muslim states, as option for 259–60
non-Muslims, treatment of 272–4, 284
Shari'a *see* **Shari'a**
state context, inserted into 284–5
wrongful-death compensation 268–9,
274–80
Islamic states *see also* **Muslim states**
constitutions 35

Kosovo
status of 4

language
Canada, question in 109, 150–2
Kurdish, restrictions on 97
meaning in community, construction
of 264
official, disputes over 3
policy, aim of 106
reality, relationship to 264
South Africa, in 414–15, 426–31
Lebanon
civil war 72
consociation 62
corporate consociational arrangements 361
liberals
accommodationism 80–1
American 49
integrationists, as 46–9, 67
multiculturalism of lifestyles, open to 47
political competition, favouring 48

Macedonia
power sharing 40
Malaysia
electoral system 189
minorities
accommodation policies, accepting 135
balance of power 133
Declaration on Rights of 112–13
entitlement 114
ethnic *see* **ethnic minorities**
ethnocultural groups, as 111
historical injustice, appeals to 136
homeland
Africa, Asia, and Middle East, in
121–2, 124
autonomy, seeking 127
indigenous peoples, as 123
irredentist 133–4
kin-state 133
national minority, as 124
old 116–18
postcolonial states, in 123–4
postcommunist Europe, in 127, 131,
134–6
redrawing of state boundaries, effect
of 132–3
security problems 132
self-government, seeking 134
indigenous peoples distinguished 112–13,
117–26
loyalty to state, lacking 135
majorities acting as 134
national
accommodationist approach to 127
accomodationist framework, prospects
for international consensus 140
arms, taking up 128
Asia, in 158
aspirations, support for 138
autonomy of 128
Canada, in 144, 159 *see also* **Canada**
constitutional politics, questions
of 168
ethnic conflicts 129
inconsistent UN treatment 127
indigenous peoples, and 120
indigenous rights 120
international norms as to rights
of 129
larger states, lands incorporated in 117
local majority, forming 130
meaning 116
move away from autonomy 130–1
new minorities, and 119
security threat from 157–8
states, conflicts with 128
support for autonomy for 139